Fodor's 2008

W9-CAV-490

ARIZONA & THE GRAND CANYON

Where to Stay and Eat for All Budgets

Must-See Sights and Local Secrets

Ratings You Can Trust

Fodor's Travel Publications   New York, Toronto, London, Sydney, Auckland
www.fodors.com

FODOR'S ARIZONA & THE GRAND CANYON 2008
Editor: Caroline Trefler

Editorial Production: Tom Holton
Editorial Contributors: Cara LaBrie, Andrew Collins, JoBeth Jamison, Jill Koch, Denise Leto, Mara Levin, Carrie Miner, Mark Sullivan
Maps & Illustrations: Henry Columb and Mark Stroud; David Lindroth, Inc.; Bob Blake and Rebecca Baer, *map editors*
Design: Fabrizio LaRocca, *creative director*; Guido Caroti, Siobhan O'Hare, *art directors*; Tina Malaney, Chie Ushio, Ann McBride, *designers*; Melanie Marin, *senior picture editor*; Moon Sun Kim, *cover designer*
Cover Photo (Vermillion Wilderness, Paria Plateau): Kerrick James
Production/Manufacturing: Steve Slawsky

ISBN 978–1–4000–1810–9

ISSN 1559–6230

SPECIAL SALES
This book is available at special discounts for bulk purchases for sales promotions or premiums. Special editions, including personalized covers, excerpts of existing books, and corporate imprints, can be created in large quantities for special needs. For more information, write to Special Markets/Premium Sales, 1745 Broadway, MD 6-2, New York, New York 10019, or e-mail specialmarkets@randomhouse.com.

AN IMPORTANT TIP & AN INVITATION
Although all prices, opening times, and other details in this book are based on information supplied to us at press time, changes occur all the time in the travel world, and Fodor's cannot accept responsibility for facts that become outdated or for inadvertent errors or omissions. So **always confirm information when it matters,** especially if you're making a detour to visit a specific place. Your experiences—positive and negative—matter to us. If we have missed or misstated something, **please write to us.** We follow up on all suggestions. Contact the Arizona & the Grand Canyon editor at editors@fodors.com or c/o Fodor's at 1745 Broadway, New York, NY 10019.

PRINTED IN THE UNITED STATES OF AMERICA
10 9 8 7 6 5 4 3 2 1

Be a Fodor's Correspondent

Your opinion matters. It matters to us. It matters to your fellow Fodor's travelers, too. And we'd like to hear it. In fact, we need to hear it.

When you share your experiences and opinions, you become an active member of the Fodor's community. That means we'll not only use your feedback to make our books better, but we'll publish your names and comments whenever possible. Throughout our guides, look for "Word of Mouth," excerpts of your unvarnished feedback.

Here's how you can help improve Fodor's for all of us.

Tell us when we're right. We rely on local writers to give you an insider's perspective. But our writers and staff editors—who are the best in the business—depend on you. Your positive feedback is a vote to renew our recommendations for the next edition.

Tell us when we're wrong. We're proud that we update most of our guides every year. But we're not perfect. Things change. Hotels cut services. Museums change hours. Charming cafés lose charm. If our writer didn't quite capture the essence of a place, tell us how you'd do it differently. If any of our descriptions are inaccurate or inadequate, we'll incorporate your changes in the next edition and will correct factual errors at fodors.com immediately.

Tell us what to include. You probably have had fantastic travel experiences that aren't yet in Fodor's. Why not share them with a community of like-minded travelers? Maybe you chanced upon a beach or bistro or B&B that you don't want to keep to yourself. Tell us why we should include it. And share your discoveries and experiences with everyone directly at fodors.com. Your input may lead us to add a new listing or highlight a place we cover with a "Highly Recommended" star or with our highest rating, "Fodor's Choice."

Give us your opinion instantly at our feedback center at www.fodors.com/feedback. You may also e-mail editors@fodors.com with the subject line "Arizona & the Grand Canyon Editor." Or send your nominations, comments, and complaints by mail to Arizona & the Grand Canyon Editor, Fodor's, 1745 Broadway, New York, NY 10019.

You and travelers like you are the heart of the Fodor's community. Make our community richer by sharing your experiences. Be a Fodor's correspondent.

Happy Traveling!

Tim Jarrell, Publisher

CONTENTS

PLANNING YOUR TRIP

Be a Fodor's Correspondent 3
About This Book. 8
What's Where. 9
Quintessential Arizona. 12
If You Like. 14
Great Itineraries. 16
When to Go 18

ARIZONA & THE GRAND CANYON

1 PHOENIX, SCOTTSDALE
  & TEMPE. 19
2 GRAND CANYON
  NATIONAL PARK 117
3 NORTH-CENTRAL
  ARIZONA 167
4 NORTHEAST ARIZONA 217
5 EASTERN ARIZONA. 259
6 TUCSON. 299
7 SOUTHERN ARIZONA 367
8 NORTHWEST ARIZONA &
  SOUTHEAST NEVADA 415
UNDERSTANDING ARIZONA . . 439
ARIZONA ESSENTIALS. 443
  Getting Started. 444
  Booking Your Trip. 446
  Transportation 456
  On The Ground 461
INDEX. 468
ABOUT OUR WRITERS 480

CLOSE UPS

A City Grows in the Desert 32
Top Spas in the Valley
  of the Sun. 70

Baseball's Three Seasons 86
The Lost Dutchman Mine. 108
Tips for Avoiding
  Canyon Crowds. 125
Park Insider: Chuck Wahler 131
Freebies at the Canyon 136
Rafting Basics. 149
Vortex Tour. 187
Red Rock Geology 191
Reservation Rules 224
The Navajo and the Hopi. 242
Tribes & Their Crafts 251
The Writing on the Wall 276
Petrified Forest Flora & Fauna. . . 285
A Campus Tour. 310
Tucson: City in the Foothills 317
The Desert's Fragile Giant 318
Sagauro Flora & Fauna 321
Saguaro Planning. 325
Where the West Is Still Wild. . . . 345
The Legend of Wyatt Earp. 375
No Bullet Shall Pass 392
Snap "Shot" of Tequila. 402
A Short History of Old
  Route 66 422

MAPS

Arizona. 6-7
What to See in Downtown
  Phoenix. 26
What to See in Greater Phoenix. . 29
What to See in Scottsdale. 33
Tempe & Around 36
Where to Eat: Valley
  of the Sun. 40-41
Where to Stay: Valley
  of the Sun. 64-65

Side Trips near Phoenix. 100
Grand Canyon South Rim 124
Grand Canyon Village &
  Rim Trail 132
Grand Canyon North Rim 139
Flagstaff. 174
Sedona. 188
The Verde Valley, Jerome &
  Prescott. 201
Prescott 209
Navajo Nation East 225
Hopi Mesas. 232
Navajo Nation West. 237
Monument Valley. 241
Glen Canyon Dam
  & Lake Powell. 247
The White Mountains. 265
Petrified Forest National Park. . . 286
What to See in Downtown
  Tucson. 306

The University of Arizona 311
Central & East Tucson 314
Catalina Foothills. 315
Northwest Tucson &
  the Westside. 319
Saguaro National Park
  West Unit 323
Saguaro National Park
  East Unit 324
Where to Stay & Eat in
  Tucson. 330-331
Side Trips near
  Tucson map. 359
Southeast Arizona 376
Southwest Arizona. 400
Northwest Arizona. 421
Southeast Nevada 430
Bullhead City & Laughlin. 431

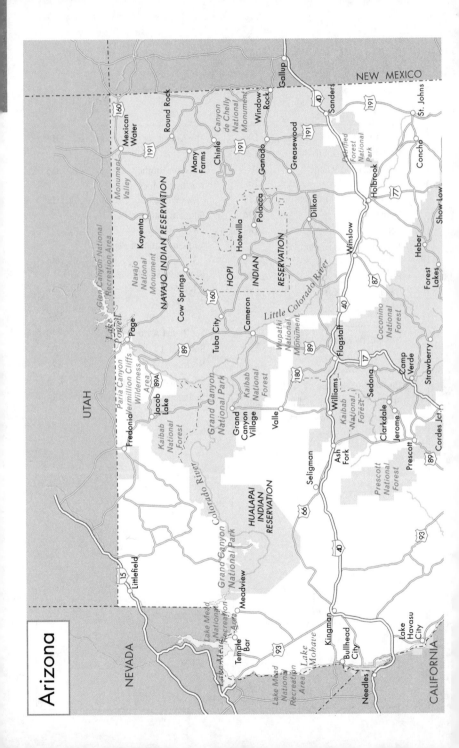

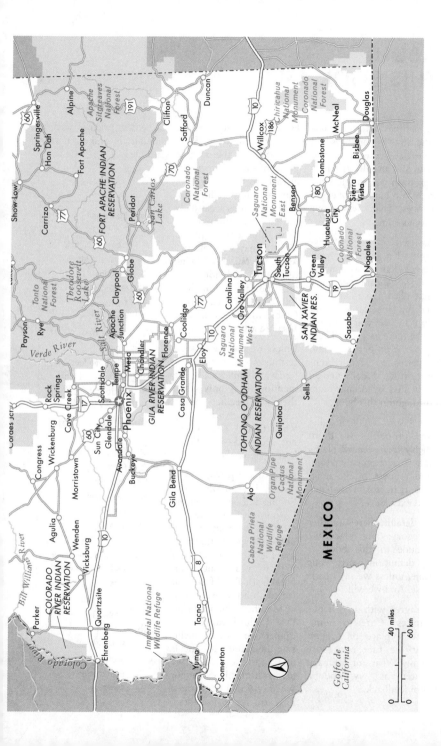

ABOUT
THIS BOOK

Sometimes you find terrific travel experiences and sometimes they just find you. But usually the burden is on you to select the right combination of experiences. That's where our ratings come in.

As travelers we've all discovered a place so wonderful that its worthiness is obvious. And sometimes that place is so experiential that superlatives don't do it justice: you just have to be there to know. These sights, properties, and experiences get our highest rating, **Fodor's Choice**, indicated by orange stars throughout this book.

Black stars highlight sights and properties we deem **Highly Recommended**, places that our writers, editors, and readers praise again and again for consistency and excellence.

By default, there's another category: any place we include in this book is by definition worth your time, unless we say otherwise. And we will.

Disagree with any of our choices? Care to nominate a place or suggest that we rate one more highly? Visit our feedback center at www.fodors.com/feedback.

Hotel and restaurant price categories from ¢ to $$$$ are defined in the opening pages of each chapter. For attractions, we always give standard adult admission fees; reductions are usually available for children, students, and senior citizens. Want to pay with plastic? **AE, D, DC, MC, V** following restaurant and hotel listings indicate if American Express, Discover, Diners Club, MasterCard, and Visa are accepted.

Unless we state otherwise, restaurants are open for lunch and dinner daily. We mention dress only when there's a specific requirement and reservations only when they're essential or not accepted—it's always best to book ahead.

Hotels have private bath, phone, TV, and air-conditioning and operate on the European Plan (aka EP, meaning without meals), unless we specify that they use the Continental Plan (CP, with a Continental breakfast), Breakfast Plan (BP, with a full breakfast), or Modified American Plan (MAP, with breakfast and dinner) or are all-inclusive (including all meals and most activities). We always list facilities but not whether you'll be charged an extra fee to use them,

so when pricing accommodations, find out what's included.

Many Listings
★ Fodor's Choice
★ Highly recommended
⊠ Physical address
✛ Directions
🕮 Mailing address
☎ Telephone
🖷 Fax
⊕ On the Web
✍ E-mail
🕮 Admission fee
☉ Open/closed times
Ⓜ Metro stations
▭ Credit cards

Hotels & Restaurants
🔲 Hotel
🛏 Number of rooms
🛆 Facilities
🍴 Meal plans
✕ Restaurant
🕮 Reservations
↘ Smoking
🕮 BYOB
✕🔲 Hotel with restaurant that warrants a visit

Outdoors
🏌 Golf
🛆 Camping

Other
🕓 Family-friendly
⇨ See also
⊠ Branch address
☞ Take note

WHAT'S WHERE

SCOTTSDALE, TEMPE & THE VALLEY OF THE SUN

Rising where the Sonoran Desert butts up against the Superstition Mountains, the Phoenix metropolitan area, known as the Valley of the Sun, is one of America's fastest growing cities. It includes Scottsdale, Tempe, and some 20 other communities surrounded by a landscape of stunning beauty. There are more than 200 golf courses here and outdoor enthusiasts find the nearby mountains delightful destinations for hiking, birding, and camping. The canal systems provide excellent biking and running trails along their banks. People come from around the world to enjoy the resorts and spas, and with competitive teams in all the major professional sports, there are always opportunities to watch well-paid athletes play ball.

THE GRAND CANYON

The Grand Canyon, one of nature's longest-running works in progress, both exalts and humbles the human spirit. You can view the spectacle from the South Rim, but the North Rim is the rim less traveled. Don't just peer over the edge—take the plunge into the canyon on a mule train, on foot, or on a raft trip.

NORTH-CENTRAL ARIZONA

The laid-back towns of north-central Arizona are as bewitching as the landscape they inhabit. Phoenicians flee the summertime heat of the Valley to cool off in the mountains and explore Prescott and Jerome, with an elevation range of 1,500 feet in its city limits, practically hangs like an oil painting from Cleopatra Hill. Today it's home to artists and craftsmen. The fracturing of the western edge of the Colorado Plateau created the red-rock buttes that loom over Sedona and this landscape has attracted artists and entrepreneurs from all over, as well as New Age followers who believe the area contains some of the Earth's most important vortices of energy. Flagstaff, surrounded by the Coconino National Forest and wrapped around the base of the tallest mountains in the state (the San Francisco Peaks at 12,643 feet), is a vibrant university town of outdoor enthusiasts, artists, and scientists.

NORTHEAST ARIZONA

Most residents of northeastern Arizona are Navajo and Hopi, and although computers are now part of their daily life, traditions endure that predate the conquistadors. Wind and frost have created magical effects in stone, such as the petrified sand dunes in the sunset-hued Antelope Canyon. Monument Valley is the starkly beautiful landscape made popular by Ansel Adams and countless Hollywood Westerns. Along with the

WHAT'S WHERE

	living Navajo and Hopi communities, the White House Ruin in breathtaking Canyon de Chelly and the ruins at Betatakin and Keet Seel in Navajo National Monument are eloquent reminders of how ancient peoples wrested shelter from this fierce land. At Lake Powell, Glen Canyon Dam inverted the equation here: humankind dominated nature, and the lake created is a spectacular meeting of earth and water.
EASTERN ARIZONA	Eastern Arizona is, by turns, verdant or stark and haunting. The White Mountains, northeast of Phoenix, contain the world's largest stand of ponderosa pines, as well as alpine meadows decked with wildflowers and some of the cleanest air you'll ever breathe. If you love the outdoor life, you may fall in love with this place. To the northeast, Homolovi Ruins State Park preserves five Hopi pueblos. The Painted Desert assumes hues from blood red to pink, then back again, as the sun rises, climbs, and sets. And Petrified Forest National Park protects a forest of trees that stood when dinosaurs walked the earth, the pieces of petrified logs looking deceptively like driftwood cast upon an oceanless beach.
TUCSON	The history of Arizona really begins here, where three cultures—Hispanic, Anglo, and Native America—began to become intertwined in the 17th century with the arrival of the Spanish explorers. Colonial Spain and Mexico left a strong imprint on Tucson's art, architecture, and culture—and residents of South 4th Avenue swear the best Mexican food north of the border is served here. Farther out, city slickers enjoy horseback rides at some of the region's many guest ranches, or luxury pampering at local spas.
SOUTHERN ARIZONA	Mountain and desert scenery in southern Arizona is as splendid as anywhere in the state. The 860,000-acre Cabeza Prieta Wildlife Refuge provides a protected habitat for bighorn sheep and other Sonoran Desert wildlife and the Organ Pipe Cactus National Monument is the largest habitat north of the border for organ pipe cacti. Enduring pockets of the Old West in the form of ghost towns are another draw. Once bigger than San Francisco thanks to silver mining in the area, Tombstone centers its fame on a single event: the Gunfight at the OK Corral. Yuma is the "Nile River Valley" of the state. The fertile soil and mild winter climate enable the agricultural industry here to produce 98% of the iceberg lettuce consumed in North America in winter. Kartchner Caverns,

one of the most spectacular wet cave systems in the world, is also in this area.

NORTHWEST ARIZONA & SOUTHEAST NEVADA

From pine-covered peaks to cacti-bedecked deserts, to the Colorado River and three enticing lakes, the under-explored northwest corner of Arizona is worth a closer look. Lake Havasu City offers a bit of Britannia in the form of London Bridge. Old-fashioned Americana reigns around Kingman, a hub on legendary Route 66. Chloride is, as one regular visitor put it, "not as commercial as Oatman," which means you can enjoy the shops and cafés without crowds and traffic. Take a quick jaunt into Nevada for a look at the monumental Hoover Dam and a hand or two of blackjack in a riverside casino at Laughlin.

QUINTESSENTIAL ARIZONA & THE GRAND CA...

Road Trips

Arizona is the place to take a road trip. Get in the car, pick a destination, and go take a look-see. For optimal enjoyment, avoid the Interstate highways and take the state routes instead. Stop at every roadside historic marker (well, OK, you can skip some if you want) and at any place with a sign that reads "pie." Go to Bisbee. Go to Jerome. Go to Oatman. Go to Greer. Travel AZ 260 from Payson to Show Low or historic Route 66 from Ash Fork to Topock; take AZ 60 through the Salt River Canyon, or U.S. Route 191 from Springerville to Clifton; take AZ 88, the Apache Trail, from Apache Junction to Roosevelt Dam. Wherever you go, roll down the windows, turn up the radio, inhale deeply, and enjoy the ride. Regardless of your destination, the wide-open spaces of Arizona entice and amaze anew with every bend in the road.

Chiles Rellenos & Margaritas

You're in Arizona, so join the quest to find the world's most delicious stuffed chiles. Most any restaurant touting Mexican cuisine has chiles rellenos on the menu. The question is: will the chiles be tough and tasteless, a mere vessel for the cheeses and other "secret" ingredients? Or will the chiles come fresh from the fields, tender, succulent, and flavorful? Only taste will tell. The quest for the perfect chile relleno is frequently attended by the search for the world's greatest margarita. There's no guarantee that the two grails will be found in the same restaurant, but it's most efficient to order both.

Arizona is known for its magnificent natural landmarks, its rich history, and its captivating cuisine. Here are some easy ways to get to know the lay of the land and start thinking like an Arizonian.

The Night Sky

Away from the metropolitan areas of Phoenix and Tucson, where the by-products of urban life obscure the firmament, the night sky is clear and unpolluted by lights or smog. In December, in the desert, the Milky Way stretches like a chiffon scarf across the celestial sphere. Lie on your back on the hood of your car at night, allow your eyes time to adjust to the darkness, and you'll see more stars than you could possibly have imagined. For a closer look, you can visit Lowell Observatory on Mars Hill, in Flagstaff, or the Kitt Peak National Observatory in Southwest Arizona (outside of Tucson) and look at celestial objects through large telescopes.

Rodeo

People take rodeo seriously out in Arizona, whether it's a holiday extravaganza like those in Prescott or Payson (which draw top cowboys from around the country), a bull-riding competition at Camp Verde, or a bunch of working cowboys gathered for a team-roping contest in Williams. These days, particularly with the emergence of bull riding as a stand-alone event—and the crowds often cheer as much for the bulls as the cowboys—rodeos are no longer the hayseed and cowpoky events Arizona grandpas might have enjoyed. Rock and roll rodeo has arrived and there is frequently live music as well as roping. So, if you see a flyer posted in a shop window advertising a rodeo, take a walk on the wild side and check out the fine arts of riding and roping. You might be surprised how graceful it all is.

IF YOU LIKE

Hiking

The joke goes, when the Good Lord made the world, he practiced his geologic formations in Arizona. As a result, you can hike in and out, up and down, or just around beautiful and varied landscapes, into canyons, to a mountain summit; or just along a meandering trail through a desert or a forest. Wherever you go, make sure you're well-prepared with water, food, and a good hat.

You could spend the rest of your life hiking the **Grand Canyon** and never cover all the trails. Bright Angel trail is the most famous, but it's tough: with an elevation change of more than 5,000 feet, don't try to hike it to the Colorado River and back in one day. Less strenuous is the 9 mi Rim Trail, a paved, generally horizontal walk. Other outstanding choices are the South Kaibab Trail and the Hermit Trail.

If waterfalls are your thing, check out **Havasu Canyon,** an 8 mi hike that descends 3,000 feet to splashing pools of turquoise water.

The highest of the four peaks that comprise San Francisco Peaks is **Mount Humphreys,** the ultimate goal for hikers seeking the best view in the state. Timing an ascent can be tricky, though, as the snow doesn't melt until mid-July, and by then the summer rains and lightning come almost daily in the afternoon. Go early in the morning and pay attention to the sky.

For some archaeology with your hiking, **Walnut Canyon National Monument** has a paved and stepped trail descending 185 feet into an island of stone where you can explore prehistoric cliff dwellings. There are steps and handrails but the climb out is strenuous.

Water Sports

You don't miss the water until it's not there, but Arizonians do their best to ensure the well doesn't go dry. Dams and canal systems help to fill vast reservoirs, and the resulting rivers and lakes provide all manner of water-sport recreation. You can have it easy, you can have it rough, or you can have it fast.

Easy is a week on a **houseboat** on a lake. Houseboats are available for rent on major lakes along the Colorado River, as well as on Lake Powell, Lake Mead, and Lake Havasu. On smaller lakes motorized boats are prohibited, but kayaks and canoes make for an enjoyable excursion along the pine-covered shorelines. You can even take a rowboat out on Tempe Town Lake.

Rough is a **river raft trip.** There are nearly two-dozen commercial rafting companies offering trips as short as three days or as long as three weeks through the Grand Canyon. Options include motorized rafts or dories rowed by Arizona's version of the California surfer—the Colorado River boatman. The Hualapai Tribe, through the Hualapai River Runners headquartered in Peach Springs, offers one-day river trips. Don't let the short duration fool you: the boatmen take you through several rapids, and thrills abound.

Fast involves a **speed boat** and water skis or Jet Skis. Both are popular on major lakes and along the Colorado River. You can go from dam to dam along the Colorado, and on lakes the size of Powell and Mead you can ski until your legs give out.

Desert

Arizona has a desert for you; actually, it has more than one. The trouble is, any desert is inhospitable to life forms unaccustomed to its harsh realities. People die in the desert here every year, from thirst, exposure, and one inexplicable trait—stupidity. Assuming good sense, you can explore any stretch of desert in April and May and experience a landscape festooned with flowers and blooming cacti.

To experience the desert without running the risk of leaving your bones to bleach in the sun, there are two exceptional alternatives: the **Desert Botanical Garden** in Scottsdale is a showcase of the ecology of the desert with more than 4,000 different species of desert flora sustained on 150 acres. A walk through here is wonderfully soothing.

There's also the **Arizona-Sonora Desert Museum** in Tucson, which isn't really a museum but a zoo and a botanical garden featuring the animals and plants of the Sonoran Desert. If you want to see a diamondback rattlesnake without jumping out of your shoes, this is the place.

And, of course, there are long drives in which you can see the wide expanses from the comfort of your car. Early spring brings the flaming-red blossoms of the ocotillo and the soft yellow-green branches of the palo verde, and the desert will be carpeted with ephemeral flowers of pink, blue, and yellow. Along U.S. Highway 93, south of Wikieup in northwest Arizona, is a good place to see the desert in its most abundant display, but there are countless others, as well.

Native American Culture

John Ford westerns and the enduring myths of the Wild West pale in comparison to the experience of seeing first-hand the Native American cultures that thrive in Arizona. You can stop at a trading post and see native artisans demonstrating their crafts, visit one of Arizona's spectacular Native American museums, or explore a Native American ruin.

Hubbell Trading Post and **Cameron Trading Post** are on Navajo Reservations, while **Keam's Canyon Trading Post** is on the Hopi Reservation. The **Navajo Village Heritage Center** in Page offers an opportunity to understand life on the reservation.

The **Heard Museum,** in Phoenix, houses an impressive array of Native American cultural exhibits. The **Museum of Northern Arizona,** in Flagstaff, has collections related to the natural and cultural history of the Colorado Plateau, an extensive collection of Navajo rugs, and an authentic Hopi kiva (men's ceremonial chamber). The **Colorado River Museum,** in Bullhead City, focuses on the history of the area and includes information and artifacts pertaining to the Mohave Indians. **Chiricahua Regional Museum and Research Center,** in Willcox, focuses on Apache culture.

The **Montezuma Castle National Monument** is one of the best-preserved prehistoric ruins in North America. **Tuzigoot National Monument** is not as well preserved as Montezuma Castle, but more impressive in scope. The **Casa Grande National Monument** is a 35-foot-tall structure built by the Hohokam Indians who lived in the area.

GREAT ITINERARIES

HIGHLIGHTS & HIKES OF ARIZONA

Arizona is full of history, culture, and awe-inspiring natural landmarks. Here are some suggestions for mixing a road trip with some of the state's phenomenal hiking opportunities. Start or end with a few days in Phoenix.

Days 1–2: Wickenburg, Prescott & Sedona

From Phoenix, head northwest to Wickenburg and visit the Desert Caballeros Western Museum. Then proceed to Prescott, "Everyone's Hometown," with its old-fashioned town square, Victorian homes, and pine-covered foothills. In Jerome you'll find a vibrant artist's community. The red rocks of Sedona provide a stunning backdrop to a community famous for its chamber music and art galleries.

In Prescott you can take an extra day to visit the Sharlott Hall Museum and smell the roses in the garden, or hike the popular Thumb Butte Loop Trail. With an extra day in Sedona, a Pink Jeep tour among the towering red rocks is a hoot, and stunning vistas can be seen while hiking along the trails at Red Rock State Park.

Day 3: Flagstaff

In Flagstaff you can visit Lowell Observatory, the Museum of Northern Arizona, and the Arboretum. An evening stroll around the historic downtown district is less than a mile. If hiking and history are your desire, you can take the short drive out of town to Walnut Canyon National Monument with its preserved ancient Native American cliff dwellings. There are two trails to choose from—one easy, one more strenuous—but both are rewarding.

Day 4: The Grand Canyon

A hundred miles north of Flagstaff, the sight of the Grand Canyon's immense beauty has taken many a visitor's breath away. There are hiking and walking options aplenty, for all levels of fitness—if you prefer letting the mules do the trekking for you, book up to 6 months ahead. Whatever you do, though, make sure you catch a sunset or sunrise view of the canyon. A night, or even just dinner at the grand El Tovar Hotel won't disappoint, but again, book early.

Day 5: Navajo National Monument & Monument Valley

The landscape here is incredible, and even if you've seen it in the movies, up-close and personal is an unforgettable experience. There are self-guided driving tours of the area, but a tram tour led by Navajo guides takes you past the sandstone mesas and spires of Monument Valley, where private cars can't go. For those with an equine inclination, a guided horseback tour will probably be the trip of a lifetime.

Days 6–7: Canyon de Chelly

Canyon de Chelly is another of Arizona's unique and fascinating natural wonders. It's smaller than the Grand Canyon, but many say it's just as beautiful—and the archaeological sites and ruins make this a very spiritual sort of place. You can do a self-drive tour, or journey into this magical sandstone landscape on foot, on horseback, or in a guided four-wheel-drive vehicle.

Day 8: The Painted Desert & Petrified Forest

If rocks could talk, those in Petrified Forest National Park and the Painted Desert would tell how eons of wind and

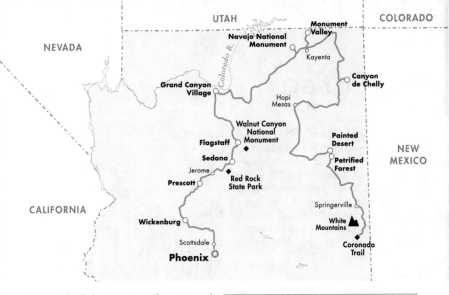

rain polished the remains of a primeval swamp into gem-color hills filled with fossils. While it's true that some visitors are underwhelmed, there's really nothing quite like the Petrified Forest anywhere else in the world.

Days 9–10: Coronado Trail & Scenic Byway

On the scenic Coronado Trail you can find treasure in abundance: aspen and fir trees, lakes stocked with trout, and a variety of wildlife. You'll never hear anybody lament having spent an extra day in the White Mountains, so if you have the time, you probably owe yourself an overnight stay in Greer, either in a fully furnished cabin or in a room at any of the lodges.

TIPS

■ If your budget permits, renting a four-wheel-drive vehicle will allow you to take advantage of side trips to remote areas.

■ Climate extremes, both heat and cold, make Arizona traveling hazardous, so heed the advice of locals. If somebody tells you it's a "little warm" to be poking around in those hills, they're probably correct.

■ Carry plenty of water and if your vehicle should break down, put the hood up and stay with the vehicle.

WHEN TO GO

High season at the resorts of Phoenix and Tucson is winter, when the snowbirds fly south. Expect the best temperatures—and the highest prices—from December through March; the posh desert resorts drop their prices—sometimes by more than half—from June through September. The South Rim of the Grand Canyon is busy year-round, but least busy during the winter months.

Climate

Phoenix averages 300 sunny days and 7 inches of precipitation annually. The high mountains see about 25 inches of rain. The Grand Canyon is usually cool on the rim and about 20°F warmer on the floor. Approximately 6 to 12 inches of snow fall on the North Rim; the South Rim receives half that amount. Temperatures in valley areas like Phoenix and Tucson average about 60°F to 70°F in the daytime in winter and between 100°F and 115°F in summer. Flagstaff and Sedona stay much cooler, dropping into the 30s and 40s Fahrenheit in winter and leveling off at 80°F to 90°F in summer.

Forecasts **Weather Channel** (⊕ www.weather.com).

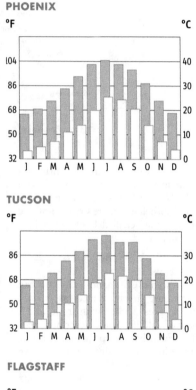

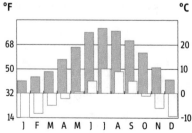

Phoenix, Scottsdale & Tempe

Papago park

WORD OF MOUTH

"If you want a relatively easy trail try Papago Park, and if you want to be up enough to see the sunset, walk up Hole in the Rock, which is a nice red rock itself."

—sphinx41

WELCOME TO PHOENIX, SCOTTSDALE & TEMPE

TOP REASONS TO GO

★ **Resort spas:** With its dozens of outstanding desert spas, Phoenix has massaged and wrapped its way to the top of the relaxation destinations list.

★ **The Heard Museum:** Once considered a "cow town," Phoenix is fast becoming the "now town," and this small but world-renowned museum complex elegantly celebrates Native American people, culture, art, and history.

★ **Shopping & dining:** From Old Town Scottsdale to the Fashion Squares, the Valley of the Sun is a retail mecca, as well as a melting pot of fine and funky dining establishments.

★ **The Great Outdoors:** Sure there's urban sprawl, but Phoenix also has cool and accessible places to get away from it all, like the Desert Botanical Garden, Papago Park, Tempe Town Lake, and the mountain and desert preserves.

★ **Golf:** All year long links lovers can take their pick of top-rated, public and private courses—many with incredibly spectacular views.

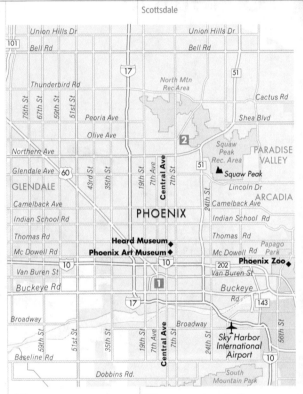

1 Downtown and Central Phoenix. As the site of Arizona's government operations and the state's largest concentration of skyscrapers, used to be strictly business. Nowadays, it's home to some of the Valley's major museums, performance venues and sports arenas, and plenty of high-rise homeowners.

2 Greater Phoenix. Here is an unusual mix of attractions ranging from hip, historic neighborhoods to acres of mountain preserves, to cultural and ethnic centers and corridors of modern commercial enterprise. Hike a couple of peaks, peek at the animals in the Phoenix Zoo, zoom on over to the Phoenix Art and Heard museums, then relax at a luxury mountainside resort—all in one day.

Apache Trail

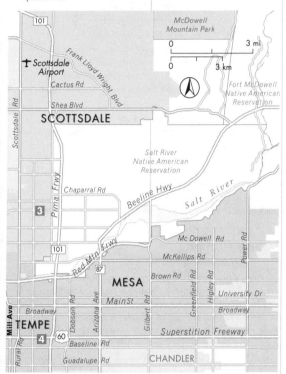

GETTING ORIENTED

It can be useful to think of Phoenix as a flower with petals (other communities) growing in every direction from the bud of Sky Harbor Airport. The East Valley includes Scottsdale, Paradise Valley, Tempe, Mesa, Fountain Hills, and Apache Junction. To the southeast are Chandler, Gilbert, and Ahwatukee. The West Valley includes Glendale, Sun City, and Litchfield Park. Central Avenue, which runs north and south through the heart of downtown Phoenix, is the city's east–west dividing line. Everything east of Central is considered the East Valley and everything west of Central is the West Valley.

3 Scottsdale. Once an upscale Phoenix sibling but now flies solo as a top American destination. A bastion of high-end and specialty shopping, historic sites, elite resorts, restaurants and spas, and more golf than even Tiger can shake a stick at, Scottsdale can easily absorb an entire vacation.

4 Tempe. May be landlocked but it has "lofty" ambitions. The home of Arizona State University and a creative melting pot of residents, Tempe is equal parts party and positively unique, especially along its main artery, Mill Avenue, where commerce and condos are literally skyrocketing.

Fore!

PHOENIX, SCOTTSDALE & TEMPE PLANNER

Planning a Special Day

Dream date Plan a special evening at one of Phoenix's fabulous restaurants or just sit with your sweetie under the stars at the Desert Botanical Garden.

Boy's night out Head downtown for a Diamondback or Phoenix Suns game, followed by a post-game session at Majerle's Sports Bar and Grill. Or haul your clubs to a Scottsdale resort for a game of golf, followed by a hot night at clubs like Axis/Radius.

Girlfriend getaway Take advantage of summer rates at Firesky Resort and Jurlique Spa, then stroll to Scottsdale Fashion Square for fabulous shopping and dining. For ladies who prefer a little more action, plan a trip with Desert Voyages guided raft tours down the Salt River.

Alone time Take an urban-inspired hike up Piestewa Peak and/or a visit to the Biltmore Fashion Park, just a few blocks southeast of the trailhead, where you can get lost in the unique shops, the grassy courtyard, or a latte at the spacious Coffee Plantation.

Making the Most of Your Time

Three to five days is an optimal amount of time to spend in Phoenix if you want to relax, get outside to hike or golf, and see the main sites like the Heard Museum and Scottsdale. Extra time will allow you to make some interesting side trips to nearby places like Tempe, Arcosanti, and Cave Creek and Carefree.

Remember that the Phoenix area is pretty sprawling and you'll probably find yourself driving fairly large distances from one place to another so planning ahead will help you save time and gas. If you're heading to the Heard museum downtown, for instance, you might want to visit the nearby Arizona Science Center and/or the Phoenix Art museum, too. If you're going to Taliesen West, do so before or after spending time in Scottsdale.

Getting Around

Until the city's new light-rail system is up and running (December 2008 at the earliest), Phoenix is best explored by car. Key attractions and activities occur in close-knit clusters, but the clusters are spread out over the Valley, making cabs cost-prohibitive. Rental cars are easy to pick up and return at Sky Harbor Airport; reserve before you go.

If having your own wheels isn't an option, many hotels offer free shuttle service to and from the airport, and to some guest destinations (usually within 5 mi of the hotel).

The Valley Metro bus system is a good alternative to walking from site to site in downtown and central Phoenix, but it gets less appealing in the peak of summer.

Phoenix to Grand Canyon Timing Tip

If you're driving to the Grand Canyon from Phoenix, allow at least two full days, with a minimum drive time of four hours each way. You can always anticipate slow-moving traffic on Interstate 17, but in the afternoon and evening on Friday and Sunday, lengthy standstills are almost guaranteed: something to remember if your plans involve getting back to Sky Harbor airport to catch a flight out.

Local Food & Lodging

With each passing year, Phoenix becomes less of a city born of the Old West and more of a modern metropolis. Large luxury resorts offer comforts and conveniences many never imagined could exist in the middle of a desert—including four-star restaurants with celebrity chefs, golf courses designed by legendary PGA players, European- and Asian-themed spas, and water parks. The good news is that the kind of land required to build such grandiose accommodations no longer exists in central Phoenix, so to compete, older hotels are renovating, adding amenities, and offering competitive rate. Restaurants are experiencing a similar trend. Local menus have gone from meat and potatoes to pan-seared espresso-crusted fillets and Asian sweet-potato compote, and only the strong survive. Yes, you can still visit an authentic dude ranch, and you can certainly find the old hole-in-the-wall hamburger or Mexican food joint—you just have to look a little harder these days.

How's the Weather?

It's a common misconception that Phoenix forever hovers around 100 degrees. That may hold true from May to October, but the winter months have been known to push the mercury down to 35 degrees. The city has also experienced consecutive days of non-stop rain. Such instances are rare, but it's good to be prepared and check weather reports before you pack.

Arizona can get pretty darn hot in the summer, so plan your outdoor activities for the cooler parts of the day and save the air-conditioned stuff for when the sun's at its hottest: the Heard Museum is not only a must-see, it's inside, as is the nearby Phoenix Art Museum.

Festivals to Build a Trip Around

January The FBR Open (formerly the Phoenix Open) is also known as "The Greatest Show on Grass."

PF Chang's Rock & Roll Marathon features live bands every mile of the course and a concert after the race.

February The Heard Museum hosts the spectacular Annual World Hoop Dance Championship, with traditional music and costumes.

March The Heard's Guild Indian Fair & Market has more than 600 Native American artists and artisans showcasing beadwork, katsina dolls, hand-woven rugs, pottery, and traditional food.

The Tempe Music Festival has multiple stages with top acts from a variety of genres.

The Parada del Sol Parade and Rodeo, "The World's Largest Horse Drawn Parade," features cowboys, cowgirls, horses, and floats.

The Scottsdale Arts Festival is jam-packed with arts and crafts, and music.

April The weekend-long Scottsdale Culinary Fest makes mouths water.

The Ostrich Festival in Chandler has music, entertainment, and (of course) ostrich races.

October The Arizona State Fair has something for almost everyone, including arm wrestling and calf roping.

Updated by
JoBeth Jamison

THE VALLEY OF THE SUN, otherwise known as metro Phoenix (i.e., Phoenix and all its suburbs, including Tempe, Scottsdale, etc.), is named for its 325-plus days of sunshine each year. The Valley marks the northern tip of the Sonoran Desert, a prehistoric seabed that reaches from northwestern Mexico with a landscape offering much more than just cacti. Palo verde and mesquite trees, creosote bushes, brittle bush, and agave dot the land, which is accustomed to being scorched by temperatures in excess of 100°F for weeks at a time. Late summer brings precious rain when monsoon storms illuminate the sky with lightning shows and the desert exudes the scent of creosote. Spring sets the Valley blooming, and the giant saguaros are crowned in white flowers for a short time in May—in the evening and cool early mornings—and masses of vibrant wildflowers fill desert crevices and span mountain landscapes.

Although many come to Phoenix for the golf and the weather, the Valley has much to offer by way of shopping, outdoor activities, and nightlife. The best of the latter are in Scottsdale and the East Valley with a variety of hip dance clubs, old-time saloons, and upscale wine bars. Long known as a "cow town," it's rapidly becoming a "now town," and is one of America's fastest-growing major urban centers, with a population of more than 4 million people.

EXPLORING THE VALLEY OF THE SUN

Phoenix has grown around what was once a cluster of independent towns in Maricopa County, but the gaps between communities that were open desert space just a few short years ago have begun to close in and blend the entire Valley into one large, sprawling community. If it were not for the WELCOME signs of various municipalities on roadways, you'd be hard-pressed to tell where one community ends and another begins.

Getting around can be difficult unless you have a car. From Sky Harbor airport, the one-way cab fare to the Four Seasons Resort in North Scottsdale (about 32 mi) can easily cost more than the daily charge for a rental car. Public transit is here in varying degrees and is inexpensive, but services do not connect well within and between communities. A light-rail system connecting Mesa, Tempe, and Phoenix is scheduled to be completed in December 2008, but until then expect delays due to construction along the route (check ⊕*www.valleymetro.org* for traffic restrictions) and around the Phoenix Convention Center expansion project, so allow extra time when traveling to downtown Phoenix.

■TIP➜**First-time visitors are often surprised to discover that some of the area's finest restaurants and shops are tucked into hotels and strip malls.**

DOWNTOWN & CENTRAL PHOENIX

Growth in the Valley over the past two decades has meant the emergence of a "real" downtown in Phoenix, where people hang out: there are new apartments and loft spaces, cultural and sports facilities—including Chase Field (formerly known as Bank One Ballpark and still affectionately referred to as BOB) and the US Airways Center, and large areas for conventions and trade shows. It's retained a mix of past and present, too, and restored homes in Heritage Square, from the original town site, give an idea of how far the city has come since its inception around the turn of the 20th century. Downtown Phoenix is also known as Copper Square.

There are lots of parking options downtown, and they're listed on the free map provided by Downtown Phoenix Partnership, available in many local restaurants (⊕*www.coppersquare.com*). Many downtown sites are served by DASH (Downtown Area Shuttle), a free bus service. You can use DASH to get around or to get back to your car when you're finished.

Numbers in the margin correspond to numbers on the What to See in Downtown & Central Phoenix map.

WHAT TO SEE

❹ Arizona Center. Amid dramatic fountains, sunken gardens, and towering palm trees stands this two-tier, open-air structure: downtown's most attractive shopping venue. The center has about 50 shops and restaurants, open-air vendors, a large sports bar, and a multiplex cinema. ⊠ *Van Buren St. between 3rd and 5th Sts., Downtown Phoenix* ☎ *602/271–4000 or 480/949–4386* ⊕*www.arizonacenter.com.*

★ ☾ **❷ Arizona Science Center.** With more than 300 hands-on exhibits, this is the venue for science-related exploration. You can pilot a simulated airplane flight, travel through the human body, navigate your way through the solar system in the Dorrance Planetarium, and watch a movie in the giant, five-story film theater. ⊠ *600 E. Washington St., Downtown Phoenix* ☎ *602/716–2000* ⊕*www.azscience.org* ▧*Museum $9; combination museum, theater, and planetarium $19* ⊙ *Daily 10–5.*

☾ **❾ Encanto Park.** Urban Encanto (Spanish for "enchanted") Park covers 222 acres at the heart of one of Phoenix's oldest residential neighborhoods. There are many attractions, including picnic areas, a lagoon where you can paddleboat and canoe, a municipal swimming pool, a nature trail, the Kiddieland–Enchanted Island amusement park, fishing in the park's lake, and two public golf courses. ⊠ *15th Ave. and Encanto Blvd., Central Phoenix* ☎ *602/261–8993* ▧*Park free, Enchanted Island rides $1* ⊙ *Park daily 6 AM–midnight; Enchanted Island Wed.–Fri. 10–4, weekends 7–4.*

Arizona
Center 4

Arizona
Mining & Mineral
Museum 8

Arizona
Science
Center 2

Encanto Park 9

Heard
Museum 10

Heritage
Square 1

Museo
Chicano 5

Orpheum
Theatre 7

Phoenix Art
Museum 11

Phoenix
Museum of
History 3

Wells Fargo
Museum 6

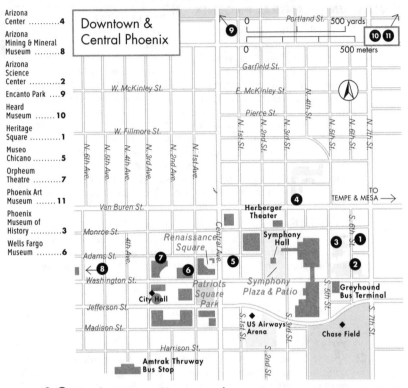

Downtown & Central Phoenix

🖐 **⑩** **Heard Museum.** Pioneer settlers
Fodor'sChoice Dwight and Maie Heard built a
★ Spanish colonial–revival building
on their property to house their collection of Southwestern art. Today
the staggering collection includes
such exhibits as a Navajo hogan,
an Apache wickie-up (a temporary Native American structure,
similar to a lean-to, constructed
from branches, twigs, and leaves,
sometimes covered with hides),
and rooms filled with art, pottery,

jewelry, katsinas, and textiles. The Heard also actively supports and
displays pieces by working Indian artists. A fabulous new long-term
exhibition entitled Home: Native People In the Southwest, opened
in 2005. Annual events include the Guild Indian Fair & Market and
the World Championship Hoop Dance Contest. Children enjoy the
interactive art-making exhibits. ■TIP→**The museum also has an incredible gift shop with authentic, high-quality goods purchased directly from
native artists.** There's a museum satellite branch in Scottsdale that has
rotating exhibits, and another in the West Valley featuring some of

the Heard's permanent collection as well as rotating exhibits. *2301 N. Central Ave., Central Phoenix* *602/252–8848* *www.heard.org* *$10* *Daily 9:30–5* *Heard Museum West: 16126 N. Civic Center Plaza, West Valley Surprise* *623/344–2200* *$5* *Tues–Sat. 9:30–5* *Heard Museum North: 32633 N. Scottsdale Rd., North Scottsdale* *602/488–9817* *suggested $3 donation* *Mon–Sat. 10–5:30.*

❶ Heritage Square. In a parklike setting from 5th to 7th streets between Monroe and Adams streets, this city-owned block contains the only remaining houses from the original Phoenix town site. On the south side of the square, along Adams Street, stand several houses built between 1899 and 1901. The Bouvier Teeter House has a Victorian-style tearoom, and the Thomas House and Baird Machine Shop are now Pizzeria Bianco. The one-story brick Stevens House holds the **Arizona Doll and Toy Museum** (*602 E. Adams St., Downtown Phoenix* *602/253–9337*), which is open Tuesday through Saturday 10 to 4, Sunday noon to 4, closed Mondays and the month of August; admission is $3. **Rosson House,** an 1895 Victorian in the Queen Anne style, is the queen of Heritage Square. Built by a physician who served a brief term as mayor, it's the sole survivor among fewer than two-dozen Victorians erected in Phoenix. It was bought and restored by the city in 1974. *6th and Monroe Sts., Downtown Phoenix* *602/262–5029* *$4* *Wed.–Sat. 10–4, Sun. noon–4.*

NEED A BREAK? The Victorian-style tearoom in the **Bouvier Teeter House** (*622 E. Adams St., Downtown Phoenix* *602/252–4682*), which was built as a private home in 1899, serves authentic teatime fare; there are also heartier sandwiches and salads.

❺ Museo Chicano. Based on and celebrating the culture of Latinos, this unique museum showcases works of artists from the United States and Mexico. Permanent and revolving exhibits include everything from ancient Mayan artifacts to revolutionary works by Frida Kahlo and Diego Rivera, to stirring and colorful pop art that has become a modern signature of Latino style—making this site a premier center for enjoying Latin American art. *147 E. Adams St., Downtown Phoenix* *602/257–5536* *www.museochicano.com* *$2* *Tues.–Sat. 10–4.*

❽ Arizona Mining and Mineral Museum. Arizona's phenomenal wealth and progress has had a lot to do with what lies beneath the actual land, namely the copper, gold, silver, and other earthbound deposits. This museum offers a mother lode of information and features more than 3,000 rocks, minerals, fossils, and mining equipment, including a 43-foot-tall Boras mine head frame and an 1882 baby-gauge steam train locomotive. *1502 West Washington, Downtown Phoenix* *602/255–3795* *http://mines.az.gov/General/museum.html* *$2* *Weekdays 8–5, Sat. 11–4.*

❼ Orpheum Theatre. This Spanish-colonial movie palace has been an architectural focal point of downtown since it was built in 1929. The eclectic ornamental details of the interior have been meticulously restored and the Orpheum is still a venue for live performances, from Broadway shows to ballet to lectures. ⊠*203 W. Adams St., Downtown Phoenix* ☎*602/534–5600* ⊕*http://phoenix.gov/CIVPLAZA/stages.html* ☉*Tours by appointment only.*

🔟 **Phoenix Art Museum.** This museum is one of the most visually appealing pieces of architecture in the Southwest. Basking in natural light, the museum makes great use of its modern, open space by tastefully fitting more than 17,000 works of art from all over the world—including sculptures by Frederic Remington and paintings by Georgia O'Keeffe, Thomas Moran, and Maxfield Parrish—within its soaring concrete walls. The museum hosts more than 20 significant exhibitions annually. Daily one-hour tours are included in the price of admission: the featured exhibition tour at 1 PM; Museum Masterworks at 2 PM (also at 11 AM Saturdays); both tours are repeated on Tuesday at 6 PM. ⊠*1625 N. Central Ave., Central Phoenix* ☎*602/257–1222* ⊕*www.phxart.org* 🖾*$10; free Tues. 3–9 PM* ☉*Wed.–Sat. 10–5, Tues. 10–9.*

❸ **Phoenix Museum of History.** This striking glass-and-steel museum offers exhibits on regional history from the 1860s (when Anglo settlement began) through the 1930s. Interactive exhibits are designed to help visitors appreciate the city's multicultural heritage as well as its tremendous growth. ⊠*105 N. 5th St., Downtown Phoenix* ☎*602/253–2734* ⊕*www.pmoh.org* 🖾*$6* ☉*Tues.–Sat. 10–5.*

❻ **Wells Fargo History Museum.** The museum isn't very big but if the wild west is your thing, there's lots of neat stuff to see, including an authentic 19th-century stagecoach and a replica that you can climb aboard, as well as an interactive telegraph. The artwork of N.C. Wyeth is on display. ⊠*145 West Adams, Downtown Phoenix* ☎*602/378–1852* ⊕*www.wellsfargohistory.com/museums_ph.htm* 🖾*Free* ☉*Mon.–Fri. 9–5.*

GREATER PHOENIX

While suburban towns are popping up all around Phoenix, the city's core neighborhoods just outlying downtown Phoenix, maintain the majority of its history and appeal. There are options aplenty to take you out hiking in the hills, or inside to some of the country's most interesting cultural sites.

WHAT TO SEE

🌵 🔞 **Desert Botanical Garden.** Opened in 1939 to conserve and showcase the
Fodor'sChoice ecology of the desert, these 150 acres contain more than 4,000 differ-
★ ent species of cacti, succulents, trees, and flowers. A stroll along the ½-mi-long Plants and People of the Sonoran Desert trail is a fascinating lesson in environmental adaptations; children enjoy playing the self-guiding game "Desert Detective." Specialized tours are available at an extra cost; check the Web for times and prices. ■**TIP→The Desert Botanical Garden stays open late, to 8 pm year-round, and it's particularly lovely when lighted by the setting sun or by moonlight, so you can plan for a cool**

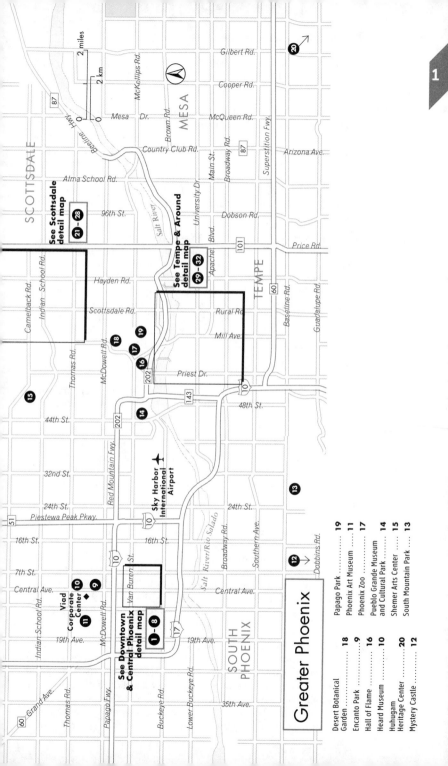

2 miles

2 km

SCOTTSDALE

Bee Line Hwy.

87

Alma School Rd.

96th St.

See Scottsdale
detail map

21 – 28

McKellips Rd.

Mesa   Dr.

MESA

Brown Rd.

Country Club Rd.

Gilbert Rd.

Cooper Rd.

McQueen Rd.

Main St.

Broadway Rd.

87

Arizona Ave.

Superstition Fwy.

20

University Dr.

Dobson Rd.

101

Price Rd.

See Tempe & Around
detail map

29 – 32

Apache   Blvd.

TEMPE

60

Baseline Rd.

Guadalupe Rd.

Hayden Rd.

Scottsdale Rd.

Camelback Rd.

Indian – School Rd.

Thomas Rd.

McDowell Rd.

18

17

16

19

Rural Rd.

Mill Ave.

Priest Dr.

202

Salt River

202

14

143

48th St.

10

15

44th St.

32nd St.

24th St.

Piestewa Peak Pkwy.

51

16th St.

7th St.

Central Ave.

Indian School Rd.

Viad
Corporate
Center

10

9

11

McDowell Rd.

19th Ave.

Grand Ave.

60

Thomas Rd.

Papago Fwy.

Red Mountain Fwy.

Sky Harbor
International
Airport

24th St.

16th St.

Van Buren St.

See Downtown
& Central Phoenix
detail map

1 – 8

10

17

Buckeye Rd.

Lower Buckeye Rd.

35th Ave.

19th Ave.

Central Ave.

Salt River/Rio Salado

Broadway Rd.

Southern Ave.

SOUTH
PHOENIX

Dobbins Rd.

12

13

Greater Phoenix

Desert Botanical
Garden 18
Encanto Park 9
Hall of Flame 16
Heard Museum 10
Huhugam
Heritage Center 20
Mystery Castle 12

Papago Park 19
Phoenix Art Museum 11
Phoenix Zoo 17
Pueblo Grande Museum
and Cultural Park 14
Shemer Arts Center 15
South Mountain Park 13

late visit after a full day of activities. ✉*1201 N. Galvin Pkwy., Papago Salado* ☎*480/941–1225* ⊕*www.dbg.org* 🔊*$10* ☉*Oct.–Apr., daily 8–8; May–Sept., daily 7 AM–8 PM.*

☾ **⑯ Hall of Flame.** Retired firefighters lead tours through more than 100 restored fire engines and tell harrowing tales of the "world's most dangerous profession." The museum has the world's largest collection of firefighting equipment, and children can climb on a 1916 engine, operate alarm systems, and learn fire safety lessons from the pros. Helmets, badges, and other firefighting-related articles dating from as far back as 1725 are on display. ✉*6101 E. Van Buren St., Papago Salado* ☎*602/275–3473* ⊕*www.hallofflame.org* 🔊*$6* ☉*Mon.–Sat. 9–5, Sun. noon–4.*

★ **⑳ Huhugam Heritage Center.** Built to harmonize with the land, the Huhugam Heritage Center mixes cool modern architecture with red earth, and as a whole is an impressive new way of looking at the past. Named for the tribe from which the modern-day Akimel O'odham (Pima) and Pee Posh (Maricopa) tribes descended, the small museum and education center is a celebration and collection of arts, culture, and history of the native people of the Gila River. ✉*4759 N. Maricopa Rd., The Gila River Indian Community, south of Chandler* ☎*520/796–3500* ⊕*www.huhugam.com* 🔊*$5* ☉*Thurs.–Sat. 10–4.*

☾ ★ **⑫ Mystery Castle.** At the foot of South Mountain lies a curious dwelling built from desert rocks by Boyce Gulley, who came to Arizona to cure his tuberculosis. Boyce's daughter Mary Lou has lived here since her father's death in 1945 and leads tours on request. Full of fascinating oddities, the castle has 18 rooms with 13 fireplaces, a downstairs grotto tavern, a roll-away bed with a mining railcar as its frame, and some original pieces of Frank Lloyd Wright–designed furniture. The pump organ belonged to Elsie, the Widow of Tombstone, who buried six husbands under suspicious circumstances. ✉*800 E. Mineral Rd., South Phoenix* ☎*602/268–1581* 🔊*$5* ☉*Oct.–June, Thurs.–Sun. 11–4.*

☾ **⑲ Papago Park.** An amalgam of hilly desert terrain, streams, and lagoons, this park has picnic ramadas, a golf course, a playground, hiking and biking trails, and even largemouth bass and trout fishing. (An urban fishing license is required for anglers age 15 and over.) The hike up to landmark **Hole-in-the-Rock** (a natural observatory used by the native Hohokam to devise a calendar system) is steep and rocky, and a much easier climb up than down. **Governor Hunt's Tomb,** the white pyramid at the top of Ramada 16, commemorates the former Arizona leader and provides a lovely view. ✉*625 N. Galvin Pkwy., Papago Salado* ☎*602/256–3220* 🔊*Free* ☉*Daily 6 AM–11 PM.*

☾ **⑰ Phoenix Zoo.** Four designated trails wind through this 125-acre zoo, replicating such habitats as an African savannah and a tropical rain forest. Meerkats, warthogs, desert bighorn sheep, and the endangered Arabian oryx are among the unusual sights. The Forest of Uco is home to the endangered spectacled bear from South America. Harmony Farm on the Discovery Trail introduces youngsters to small mammals, and a stop at the big red barn provides a chance to groom a horse or milk a cow. The Butterfly Pavilion is enchanting. The 30-minute narrated safari train tour costs $3 and provides a good orientation to the park. ■ TIP→In December the zoo stays open late (6–10 PM) for the popular "Zoolights" exhibit that transforms the area into an enchanted forest of more than 225 million twinkling lights, many in the shape of the zoo's residents. Starry Safari Friday Nights in summer are fun, too. ⊠ *455 N. Galvin Pkwy., Papago Salado* ☎ *602/273–1341* ⊕ *www.phoenixzoo.org* ⊠ *$14* ⊙ *Jan.–May, daily 8–5; June–Sept., weekdays 7–2, weekends 7–4; Oct.–Nov. 6, daily 8–5; Nov. 7–Jan. 6, daily 8–4.*

☾ ⑭ **Pueblo Grande Museum and Cultural Park.** Phoenix's only national land-
Fodor's Choice   mark, this park was once the site of a 500-acre Hohokam village sup-
★   porting about 1,000 people and containing homes, storage rooms, cemeteries, and ball courts. Three exhibition galleries hold displays on the Hohokam culture and archaeological methods. View the 10-minute orientation video before heading out on the ½-mi Ruin Trail past excavated mounds and ruins that give a hint of Hohokam savvy: there's a building whose corner doorway was perfectly placed to watch the summer-solstice sunrise. Children particularly like the hands-on, interactive learning center. Guided tours by appointment only. ⊠ *4619 E. Washington St., Papago Salado* ☎ *602/495–0901* ⊕ *www.pueblogrande.com* ⊠ *$2, free Sun.* ⊙ *Mon.–Sat. 9–4:45, Sun. 1–4:45.*

☾ ★ ⑮ **Shemer Arts Center.** In a former residence near the Phoenician Resort, the Schemer Arts Center features revolving exhibits of current Arizona artists, who have agreed to donate one of their pieces to the center's permanent collection. The collection is largely contemporary and exhibits change every month or so. ⊠ *5005 E. Camelback Rd., Phoenix* ☎ *602/262–4727* ⊕ *www.phoenix.gov/shemer* ⊠ *Free* ⊙ *Mon. and Wed.–Fri. 10–5, Tues. 10–9, Sat. 9–1.*

☾ ★ ⑬ **South Mountain Park.** This desert wonderland, the world's largest city park (almost 17,000 acres), offers a wilderness of mountain-desert trails for hikers, bikers, and horseback riders—and a great place to view sunsets. The Environmental Center has a model of the park as well as displays detailing its history, from the time of the ancient Hohokam people to gold-seekers. Roads climb past picnic ramadas (shaded, open-air shelters) constructed by the Civilian Conservation Corps, winding through desert flora to the trailheads. Look for ancient petroglyphs, try to spot a desert cottontail rabbit or chuckwalla lizard, or simply stroll among the desert vegetation. Maps of all scenic drives as well as of hiking, mountain biking, and horseback trails are available at the Gatehouse Entrance just inside the park boundary. ⊠ *10919 S. Central Ave., South Phoenix* ☎ *602/495–0222* ⊠ *Free* ⊙ *Daily 5:30 AM–10:30 PM; Environmental Education Center: Wed.–Sat. 9–3, Sun. 9–2.*

NEED A BREAK?

If hiking at South Mountain Park has piqued your appetite, or you're looking for some unique picnic fixings, stop at nearby **Carolina's** (⊠ *1202 E. Mohave St., South Phoenix* ☎ *602/252–1503*) for what might be the best flour tortillas you've ever eaten. A burrito is the best way to try 'em out, and you can eat in or get take-out.

A City Grows in the Desert

As the Hohokam (the name comes from the Piman word for "people who have gone before") discovered 2,300 years ago, the miracle of water in the desert can be augmented by human hands. Having migrated from northwestern Mexico, Hohokam cultivated cotton, corn, and beans in tilled, rowed, and irrigated fields for about 1,700 years, establishing more than 300 mi of canals—an engineering miracle when you consider the limited technology available. They constructed a great town upon whose ruins modern Phoenix is built, and then vanished. Drought, long winters, and other causes are suggested for their disappearance.

From the time the Hohokam left until the Civil War, the once fertile Salt River valley lay forgotten, used only by occasional small bands of Pima and Maricopa Indians. Then, in 1865, the U.S. Army established Fort McDowell in the mountains to the east, where the Verde River flows into the Salt River. To feed the men and the horses stationed there, a former Confederate Army officer reopened the Hohokam canals in 1867. Within a year, fields bright with barley and pumpkins earned the area the name Pumpkinville. By 1870 the 300 residents had decided that their new city would arise from the ancient Hohokam ruins, just as the mythical phoenix rose from its own ashes.

Phoenix would rise indeed. Within 20 years, it had become large enough—its population was about 3,000—to wrest the title of territorial capital from Prescott. By 1912, when Arizona was admitted as the 48th state, the area, irrigated by the brand-new Roosevelt Dam and Salt River Project, had a burgeoning cotton industry. Copper and cattle were mined and raised elsewhere but were banked and traded in Phoenix, and the cattle were slaughtered and packed here in the largest stockyards outside of Chicago.

Meanwhile, the climate, so long a crippling liability, became an asset. Desert air was the prescribed therapy for the respiratory ills rampant in the sooty, factory-filled East; Scottsdale began in 1901 as "30-odd tents and a half dozen adobe houses" put up by health-seekers. By 1930 travelers looking for warm-winter recreation as well as rejuvenating aridity filled the elegant San Marcos Hotel and Arizona Biltmore, the first of the many luxury retreats for which the area is now known worldwide. The 1950s brought residential air-conditioning, an invention that made the summers bearable for the growing workforce of the burgeoning technology industry.

The Valley is very much a work still in progress and historians are quick to point out that never in the world's history has a metropolis grown from "nothing" to attain the status of Phoenix in such a short period of time. At the heart of all the bustle, though, is a way of life that keeps its own pace: Phoenix is one of the world's largest small towns—where people dress informally and where the rugged, Old West spirit lives on in many of the Valley's nooks and crannies despite the sprawling growth. And if the summer heat can be overwhelming, at least it has the restorative effect of slowing things down to an enjoyable pace.

5th Avenue ... **27**

Main Street
Arts
District **25**

Marshall Way
Arts
District **26**

Old Town
Scottsdale **24**

Scottsdale
Center for
the Arts **21**

Scottsdale
Historical
Museum **23**

Scottsdale Museum
of Contemporary
Art **22**

Taliesin
West **28**

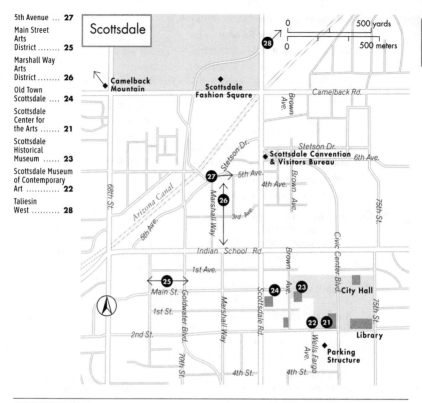

SCOTTSDALE

Nationally known art galleries, souvenir shops, and funky Old Town fill downtown Scottsdale—the third-largest artist community in the United States. Fifth Avenue is known for shopping and Native American jewelry and crafts stores, while Main Street and Marshall Way are home to the international art set with galleries and interior-design shops. Most galleries on Main Street and Marshall Way are open Thursday evenings until 9. Although your tour of downtown can easily be completed on foot, a trolley runs through the area and out to several resorts: Ollie the Trolley service within downtown Scottsdale is free (☎480/970–8130 information). ■TIP→**If you have limited time in the area, spend a half-day in downtown Scottsdale and the rest of the day at Taliesin West.**

Numbers in the margin correspond to numbers on the What to See in Scottsdale map.

WHAT TO SEE

㉗ 5th Avenue. Whether you seek handmade Native American Arts and Crafts, casual clothing, or cacti, you'll find it here—at such landmark shops as Adolfos Espoza, Kactus Jock, and Gilbert Ortega. ⊠*5th Ave. between Civic Center Rd. and Stetson Dr., Downtown Scottsdale* ☎*800/737–0008* ⊕*www.5thavescottsdale.org.*

NEED A BREAK?

The **Sugar Bowl Ice Cream Parlor** (⊠ *4005 N. Scottsdale Rd., Downtown Scottsdale* ☎ *480/946–0051*) transports you back in time to a 1950s malt shop. In business in the same building since 1958, the Sugar Bowl serves great burgers and lots of yummy ice-cream confections. Valley resident Bil Keane, creator of the comic strip "Family Circus," has often used this spot as inspiration for his cartoons, many of which are on display here.

★ ㉕ **Main Street Arts District.** Gallery after gallery display artwork of myriad styles—contemporary, Western realism, Native American, and traditional. Several antiques shops are also here; specialties include porcelains and china, jewelry, and Oriental rugs. ⊠ *Bounded by Main St. and 1st Ave., Scottsdale Rd. and 69th St., Downtown Scottsdale.*

㉖ **Marshall Way Arts District.** Galleries that exhibit predominantly contemporary art line the blocks of Marshall Way north of Indian School Road, and upscale gift and jewelry stores can be found here, too. Farther north on Marshall Way across 3rd Avenue, are more art galleries and creative stores with a Southwestern flair. ⊠ *Marshall Way, from Indian School Rd. to 5th Ave., Downtown Scottsdale.*

㉔ **Old Town Scottsdale.** "The West's Most Western Town," this area has rustic storefronts and wooden sidewalks; it's touristy, but the closest you'll come to experiencing life here as it was 80 years ago. High-quality jewelry, pots, and Mexican imports are sold alongside kitschy souvenirs. ⊠ *Main St. from Scottsdale Rd. to Brown Ave., Downtown Scottsdale.*

㉑ **Scottsdale Center for the Arts.** Galleries within this cultural and entertainment complex rotate exhibits frequently, but they typically emphasize contemporary art and artists. You might be able to catch a comical, interactive performance of the long-running "Late Night Catechism," or an installation of modern dance. The acclaimed Scottsdale Arts Festival is held annually in March. The **Scottsdale Museum of Contemporary Art** is on-site, and there's also a good **Museum Store** for unusual jewelry and stationery, posters, and art books. ⊠ *7380 E. 2nd St., Downtown Scottsdale* ☎ *480/994–2787* ⊕ *www.scottsdalearts.org* ☜ *Free* ☉ *Mon.–Wed., Fri., and Sat. 10–5, Thurs. 10–8, Sun. noon–5; also during performance intermissions.*

㉓ **Scottsdale Historical Museum.** Scottsdale's first schoolhouse, this redbrick building houses a reconstruction of the 1910 schoolroom, as well as photographs, original furniture from the city's founding fathers, and displays of other treasures from Scottsdale's early days. ⊠ *7333 Scottsdale Mall, Downtown Scottsdale* ☎ *480/945–4499* ⊕ *www.scottsdalemuseum.com* ☜ *Free* ☉ *Sept.–June, Wed.–Sat. 10–5, Sun. noon–4.*

22 **Scottsdale Museum of Contemporary Art.** When you step through the immense glass entryway and stroll through the spaces within the five galleries, you realize it's not just the spacious outdoor sculpture garden that makes this a "museum without walls." New installations are planned every few months, with an emphasis on contemporary art, architecture, and design. Free, docent-led tours are conducted on Thursday at 1:30. SMoCA, as it's known locally, is connected with the Scottsdale Center for the Arts. ☒ *7374 E. 2nd St., Downtown Scottsdale* ☎ *480/994–2787* ⊕ *www.scottsdalearts.org* ☜ *$7, free Thurs.* ☉ *Sept.–May, Wed. and Sun. noon–5, Thurs. 10–8, Fri. and Sat. 10–5; June–Aug., Wed. 10–5, Thurs. 10–8, Fri. and Sat. 10–5, Sun. noon–5.*

28 **Taliesin West.** Ten years after visiting Arizona in 1927 to consult on designs for the Biltmore hotel, architect Frank Lloyd Wright chose 600 acres of rugged Sonoran Desert at the foothills of the McDowell Mountains as the site for his permanent winter residence. Today the site is a National Historic Landmark and still an active community of students and architects.

Fodor's Choice
★

> **WORD OF MOUTH**
>
> "Taliesen West is fascinating—not just the main house but the theater and the sculpture garden. One thing you discover in the living room is just how uncomfortable most of the furniture is...!"
> –underhill

Wright and apprentices constructed a desert camp here using organic architecture to integrate the buildings with their natural surroundings. In addition to the living quarters, drafting studio, and small apartments of the Apprentice Court, Taliesin West has two theaters, a music pavilion, and the Sun Trap—sleeping spaces surrounding an open patio and fireplace. Five guided tours are offered, ranging from a one-hour "panorama" tour to a three-hour behind-the-scenes tour, with other tours offered seasonally. In 2005, after a major renovation, Wright's living quarters were opened for the first time to the public. They include a living space and a private bedroom and work space. Times vary, so call ahead; all visitors must be accompanied by a guide. ■ TIP→ **It's a short but very worthwhile side trip from downtown Scottsdale to Taliesin West. Drive 20 minutes north on the 101 Freeway to Frank Lloyd Wright Boulevard. The entrance is at the corner of Frank Lloyd Wright Boulevard and Cactus Road.** ☒ *12621 Frank Lloyd Wright Blvd., North Scottsdale* ☎ *480/860-2700* ⊕ *www.franklloydwright.org* ☜ *$18–$45* ☉ *Sept.– June, daily 8:30–5:30; July and Aug., Thurs.–Mon. 8:30–5:30.*

TEMPE AND AROUND

Tempe is the home of Arizona State University's main campus and a thriving student population. A 20-minute drive from Phoenix, the tree- and brick-lined Mill Avenue is the main drag, lined with student hangouts, bookstores, boutiques, eateries, and a repertory movie house. There are always things to do or see, and plenty of music venues and fun, casual dining spots. This is one part of town where the locals actually hang out, stroll, and sit at the outdoor cafés. The Tempe Festival of the Arts on Mill Avenue is held twice a year (in early December and

Arizona State
University **31**

Mesa Southwest
Museum **32**

Tempe
Center for
the Arts **30**

Tempe Town
Lake **29**

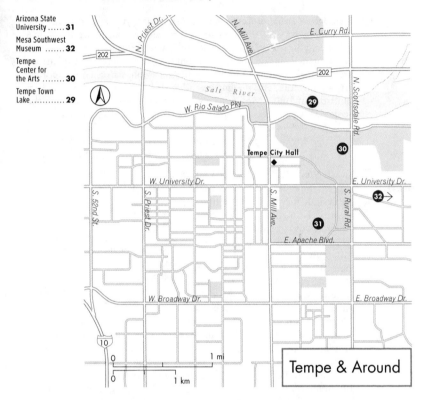

Tempe & Around

March–April); it has all sorts of interesting arts and crafts (⊕*www. tempefestivalofthearts.com*).

The inverted pyramid that is Tempe City Hall, on 5th Street, one block east of Mill Avenue, was constructed by local architects Rolf Osland and Michael Goodwin not just to win design awards (which they have) but also to shield city workers from the desert sun. The pyramid is built mainly of bronzed glass and stainless steel, and the point disappears in a sunken courtyard lushly landscaped with jacaranda, ivy, and flowers, out of which the pyramid widens to the sky: stand underneath and gaze up for a weird fish-eye perspective.

The banks of the Rio Salado in Tempe are the site of a new commercial and entertainment district, and Tempe Town Lake—a 2-mi-long waterway created by inflatable dams in a flood control channel—which is open for boating. There are biking and jogging paths on the perimeter.

Numbers in the text correspond to numbers on the Tempe and Around map.

WHAT TO SEE

③ **Arizona State University.** What began as the Tempe Normal School for Teachers—in 1886, a four-room redbrick building and 20-acre cow pasture—is now the 750-acre campus of ASU, the largest university in the Southwest. The **ASU Visitor Information Center** (✉ *826 E. Apache Blvd., at Rural Rd.* ☎ *480/965–0100*) has maps of a self-guided walking tour (it's a long walk from Mill Avenue, so you might opt for the short version suggested here). You'll wind past public art and innovative architecture—including a music building that bears a strong

resemblance to a wedding cake (designed by Taliesin students to echo Frank Lloyd Wright's Gammage Auditorium) and a law library shaped like an open book—and end up at the 74,000-seat **Sun Devil Stadium** (✉ *ASU Campus, 5th St.* ☎ *866/800–2828*), home to the school's Sun Devils. One of the most outstanding stadiums in the country, it has a spectacular setting. It's literally carved out of a mountain and cradled between the Tempe buttes. While touring the west end of campus, stop into the **Arizona State University Art Museum** (✉ *Mill Ave. and 10th St.* ☎ *480/965–2787* ⊕ *asuartmuseum.asu.edu* ✍ *Free* ☉ *School year: Tues. 10–9, Wed.–Sat. 10–5; summer, Tues. 10–5, Wed.–Sat. 10–5*). It's in the gray-purple stucco Nelson Fine Arts Center, just north of the Gammage Auditorium. For a relatively small museum, it has an extensive collection, including 19th- and 20th-century painting and sculpture by masters such as Winslow Homer, Edward Hopper, Georgia O'Keeffe, and Rockwell Kent. Works by faculty and student artists are also on display, and there's a gift shop. In Matthews Hall, the **Northlight Gallery** (✉ *Matthews Hall, Mill Ave. and 10th St.* ☎ *480/965–6517* ☉ *Mon.–Thurs. 10:30–4:30*) exhibits works by both renowned and emerging photographers. There's no admission charge.

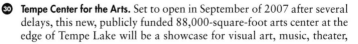

NEED A BREAK?
The outdoor patio of the **Coffee Plantation** (✉ *680 S. Mill Ave.* ☎ *480/829–7878*), a popular café near the ASU campus, is a lively scene—students studying, locals chatting over coffee, and poets and musicians presenting their latest works.

③ **Mesa Southwest Museum.** Kids young and old get a thrill out of the largest collection of dinosaur fossils in the state at this large museum where you can also pan for gold and see changing exhibits from around the world. ✉ *53 N. Macdonald St., Mesa* ☎ *480/644–2230* ⊕ *www.cityofmesa. org/swmuseum* ✍ *$8* ☉ *Tues.–Fri. 10–5, Sat. 11–5, Sun. 1–5.*

③ **Tempe Center for the Arts.** Set to open in September of 2007 after several delays, this new, publicly funded 88,000-square-foot arts center at the edge of Tempe Lake will be a showcase for visual art, music, theater, and dance, featuring local, regional, and international talent. ✉*700 W. Rio Salada Pkwy.* ☎*480/350–5287* 🖷*480/350–5161* ⊕*www. tempe.gov/arts.*

🕙 ㉙ **Tempe Town Lake.** Town Lake is the newest addition to the growth of Tempe and attracts college students and Valley residents of all ages. Little ones enjoy the Splash Playground, and fishermen appreciate the rainbow trout–stocked lake. **Rio Lago Cruises** rents boats and has a selection of short cruise options. ✉*990 W. Rio Salado Pkwy., between Mill and Rural Aves. north of Arizona State University* ☎*480/517–4050 Rio Lago Cruises* ⊕*www.tempe.gov/lake and www.riolagocruise.com.*

WHERE TO EAT

Generations of Arizona schoolchildren have learned the state's four Cs: copper, cattle, cotton, and climate. Today, a good argument could be made for adding a fifth in Phoenix: cuisine. New restaurants have proliferated in the Phoenix metropolitan area due to the Valley's rapid growth and the influence of adventurous chefs who have emigrated here. As a result, an influx of Thai, Peruvian, Vietnamese, and Japanese restaurants has created a culinary scene of sophistication and diversity, and contemporary menus feature touches of the creator's homeland or ethnicity mixed with local recipes and ingredients. Pacific Rim or Latino foods, for instance, are fused with spices native to the Southwest, such as Mexican coriander, fragrant Mexican oregano, *canela* sticks (Mexican cinnamon), and, of course, chiles from mild to explosive. Italian, Spanish, and even French favorites served in Phoenix might have more "bite" than elsewhere.

Many of the best restaurants in the Valley are in resorts, camouflaged behind courtyard walls, or tucked away in shopping malls. Newer, upscale eateries are clustered along Camelback Corridor—a veritable restaurant row, running west to east from Phoenix to Scottsdale—and in Scottsdale itself. Great Mexican food can be found throughout the Valley, but the most authentic spots are in the Hispanic neighborhoods of South Phoenix.

Restaurants change hours, locations, chefs, prices, and menus frequently, so it's best to call ahead to confirm. Show up without a reservation during tourist season, and you may have to head for a fast-food drive-through window to avoid a two-hour wait for a table. All listed restaurants are open for lunch and dinner unless otherwise specified.

WHAT IT COSTS				
¢	$	$$	$$$	$$$$
AT DINNER under $8	$8–$12	$13–$20	$21–$30	over $30

Prices are per person for a main course. The final tab will include sales tax of 8.1% in Phoenix, 7.95% in Scottsdale.

CAMELBACK CORRIDOR, PHOENIX

AMERICAN–CASUAL

¢–$ ✕ **Delux.** Cool tones of blue and gray are accented by a granite-topped bar and a long candle-lit communal table in the center of this small hipster burger joint. Delux serves delicious salads, sandwiches, and burgers made with all-natural Harris Ranch beef (try the Delux Burger, with Maytag blue and Gruyère cheeses and caramelized onions). Crispy fries (regular or sweet potato) arrive in a fun mini–shopping cart. Open every night until 2 AM, this is a great place to grab a late-night bite. ✉3146 E. Camelback Rd., Camelback Corridor ☎602/522–2288 ⌖Reservations not accepted ☰AE, D, DC, MC, V.

ECLECTIC

$$–$$$$ ✕ **Tarbell's.** Cutting-edge cuisine is the star at this sophisticated bistro. The grilled salmon glazed with a molasses-lime sauce and served on a crispy potato cake is a long-standing classic; the focaccia with red onion, Romano cheese, and roasted thyme with hummus is excellent; and imaginative designer pizzas are cooked in a wood-burning oven. Your sweet tooth won't be disappointed by Tarbell's warm, rich, chocolate cake topped with pistachio ice cream. Hardwood floors, copper accents, and a curving cherrywood and maple bar create a sleek, cosmopolitan look, favored by Biltmore golfers. ✉3213 E. Camelback Rd., Camelback Corridor ☎602/955–8100 ⌖Reservations essential ☰AE, D, DC, MC, V ⊗No lunch.

FRENCH

$$–$$$$ ✕ **Bistro 24.** Smart and stylish, with impeccable service, the Ritz's Bistro 24 has a parquet floor, colorful murals, an elegant bar, and an outdoor patio. Take a break from shopping at nearby Biltmore Fashion Park and enjoy the largest Cobb salad in town. For dinner, try classic French steak au poivre with frites, grilled fish, or sushi. Happy hour is every day from 5 to 7 in the bar. Sunday brunch is a local favorite. ✉Ritz-Carlton Hotel, 2401 E. Camelback Rd., Camelback Corridor ☎602/952–2424 ☰AE, D, DC, MC, V.

$$–$$$$ ✕ **Christopher's Fermier Brasserie & Paola's Wine Bar.** Chef Christopher Gross serves simple, delicious French brasserie fare using the freshest ingredients and produce from local farmers. Wine director Paola Gross offers more than 100 wines by the glass and stocks an excellent selection of cigars. Thursday to Saturday from 10 PM to midnight, you'll love the inexpensive "Leftovers from the Kitchen" specials. ✉Biltmore Fashion Park, 2584 E. Camelback Rd., Camelback Corridor ☎602/522–2344 ☰AE, D, DC, MC, V.

GREEK

$–$$$ ✕ **Greekfest.** This informal but elegant restaurant is lovingly decorated with whitewashed walls, hardwood floors, and Greek-imported artifacts. Search the menu's two pages of appetizers for taramosalata (caviar blended with lemon and olive oil) and saganaki (cheese flamed with brandy and extinguished with a squirt of lemon). The moussaka (lamb casserole) is wonderful, and don't forget dessert (try galaktoboureko, warm custard pie baked in phyllo). ✉1940 E. Camel-

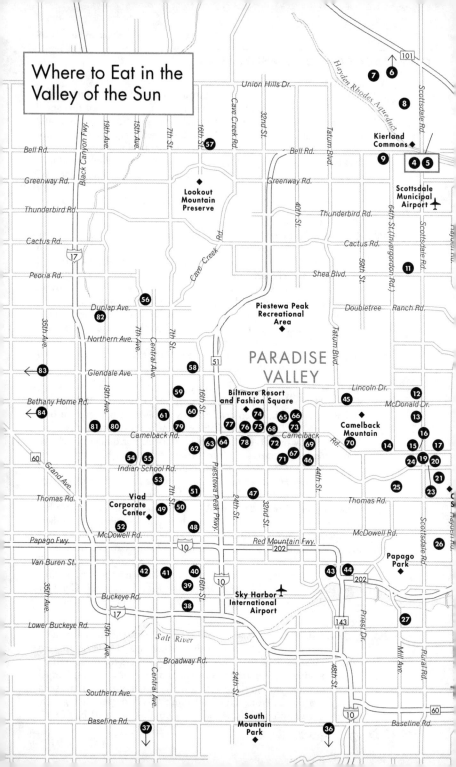

Where to Eat in the Valley of the Sun

Phoenix & Paradise Valley ▼

Avanti **47**
Baby Kay's **64**
Barrio Café **51**
Carolina's **38**
Chelsea's Kitchen **66**
Christo's Ristorante **59**
Convivo Bistro **58**
Coup Des Tartes **62**
Durant's Fine Foods **49**
elements **45**
Fate **39**
FEZ **53**
Fry Bread House **54**
Gourmet House
of Hong Kong **48**
Honey Bear's BBQ **43**
Kai **36**
La Fontanella **46**
La Grande Orange **67**
Lon's at the Hermosa **65**
Los Dos Molinos **37**
MacAlpine's Soda
Fountain **50**
Mediterranean House **60**
Mrs. White's
Golden Rule Café **42**
My Florist Cafe **52**
Pane Bianco **55**
Pizzeria Bianco **41**
Stockyards Restaurant **44**
Tarbell's **68**
Taste of India **57**
Ticoz Resto-Bar **61**
Via Delosantos **56**
Welcome Diner **40**
Zöes Kitchen **63**

Camelback Corridor ▼

Bistro 24 .... **78**
Christopher's
Fermier Brasserie &
Paola's Wine Bar **76**
Daniel's **69**
Delux **75**
Greekfest **77**
Lola Tapas **79**
Postino Wirecafe **71**
Tomaso's **72**
T. Cook's **70**
Vincent on Camelback ... **73**
Zen 32 .... **74**

Scottsdale ▼

Acacia **2**
AZ 88 .... **21**
Bandera **20**
Carlsbad Tavern **22**
Cowboy Ciao **19**
Don & Charlie's **17**
Havana Cafe **9**
La Hacienda **5**
L'Ecole **18**
Kashman's Place **3**
Los Sombreros
Mexican Cantina **13**
Malee's on Main **25**
Marquesa **4**
Mary Elaine's **14**
Michael's at the Citadel **1**
Morton's of Chicago **7**
Nello's **10**
Original Pancake House .. **15**
Pink Taco **24**
Rancho Pinot Grill **12**
Razz's Restaurant & Bar **6**
Roaring Fork **16**
Salt Cellar **26**
Sea Saw **23**
Sushi on Shea **11**
Zinc Bistro **8**

Tempe, Mesa & Chandler ▼

98 South **32**
C-Fu Gourmet **35**
Citrus Cafe **33**
Cyclo **34**
Haji Baba **29**
House of Tricks **27**
Landmark **30**
Oregano's **28**
Rosa's Mexican Grill **31**

West Phoenix, Glendale & Litchfield Park ▼

Haus Murphy's **83**
Lily's Cafe **84**
Pepe's Taco Villa **81**
Pho Bang **80**
Silver Dragon **82**

back Rd., Camelback Corridor ☎602/265–2990 ⊟*AE, D, DC, MC, V* ⊘*Closed Sun.*

¢–$ ✕ **Zoës Kitchen.** Cool, clean, fast, inexpensive, and nutritious, this link in a national chain is worth noticing. Hit the Camelback area spas then have a light but filling, Greek-inspired meal without the guilt. Make sure to try the coleslaw with feta cheese. ⊠*1641 E. Camelback Rd., Camelback Corridor* ☎602/263–9637 ⊠*521 W. McDowell Rd., Central Phoenix* ☎602/716–0700 ⊟*AE, D, MC, V.*

> **MORNING GLORY**
>
> Good breakfast and good coffee are hard to find in the same place, and in a town where the distances between destinations can be vast, it's even more crucial. Start your day off right with the simple but exquisite culinary and coffee creations of Phoenix's Drip Coffee Lounge (⊠*2325 N. 7th St.*), **La Grande Orange Grocery** (⊠*4410 N. 40th St.*), or Matt's Big Breakfast (⊠*801 N. 1st St.*).

ITALIAN

$$–$$$$ ✕ **Tomaso's.** In a town where restaurants come and go overnight, Tomaso's has been a favorite since 1977, and for good reason. Chef Tomaso Maggiore learned to cook at the family's restaurant in Palermo, Sicily, and honed his skills at the Culinary Institute of Rome. The result is authentic Italian cuisine that's consistently well prepared and delicious. The house specialty, *osso buco* (braised veal shank), is outstanding. Other notables include risotto and cannelloni. ⊠*3225 E. Camelback Rd., Camelback Corridor* ☎602/956–0836 ⊟*AE, D, DC, MC, V* ⊘*No lunch weekends* ⊠*7341 N. Ray Rd., Chandler* ☎480/940–1200 ⊟*AE, D, MC, V* ⊘*No lunch weekends.*

$$–$$$ ✕ **Daniel's.** Once a year, chef-owner Daniel Malventano takes his cooking crew to Tuscany to train with some of Italy's top chefs, and a visit to his richly romantic restaurant will make you feel like you've been to Italy, too. Indulge in standout Northern Italian creations like veal scaloppine with white-truffle and porcini-mushroom sauce or duck in wild cherry sauce. Finish the meal with *crostata* (Italian pastry filled with pastry cream and sautéed bananas). ⊠*4225 E. Camelback Rd., Camelback Corridor* ☎602/952–1522 ⊟*AE, MC, V* ⊘*No lunch.*

$ ✕ **Postino Winecafé.** Located in a former post office behind La Grande Orange Grocery, Postino is the perfect place to sit on a sofa with a glass of fine wine on a sunny afternoon. If the weather is nice, the makeshift garage doors/windows stay open for people-watching on the patio. Fare is limited to panini sandwiches, salads, and a variety of bruschetta so good you won't mind making a meal out of it: favorites include the prosciutto with figs and mascarpone; Brie with apples and fig spread; and ricotta with dates and pistachios. ⊠*3939 E. Campbell Ave., Camelback Corridor* ☎602/852–3939 ⊟*AE, MC, V* ⊘*Closed Sun.*

MEDITERRANEAN

★ $$$–$$$$ ✕ **T. Cook's at the Royal Palms.** One of the finest restaurants in the Valley, T. Cook's oozes romance, from the floor-to-ceiling windows with dramatic views of Camelback Mountain to its 1930s-style Spanish-colonial architecture and decor. The Mediterranean-influenced menu includes grilled "fireplace" fare like pork chops with polenta dumplings, paella, and a changing variety of enticing entrées. Desserts and pastries are works of art. For special occasion meals, call on the services of maitre d' Paul Xanthopoulos, also known as the Director of Romance. ⊠*Royal Palms Resort & Spa, 5200 E. Camelback Rd., Camelback Corridor* ☎*602/840–3610* ⚐*Reservations essential* ▭*AE, D, DC, MC, V.*

SOUTHWESTERN

$$$–$$$$ ✕ **Vincent on Camelback.** Chef Guerithault is best known for creating French food with a Southwestern touch. You can make a meal of his famous appetizers: corn ravioli with white-truffle oil, or shrimp beignets with lavender dressing. The dessert menu overflows with intoxicating soufflés. ⊠*3930 E. Camelback Rd., Camelback Corridor* ☎*602/224–0225* ⚐*Reservations essential* ▭*AE, D, DC, MC, V* ☯*Closed Sun. No lunch weekends.*

SUSHI

$–$$$ ✕ **Zen 32.** In the ebb and flow of central Phoenix, Zen 32 has managed to stay afloat while just about every other sushi restaurant has sunk—the convenient location, casually chic atmosphere, and consistently creative rolls make it easy to understand why. The soft-shell crab, rainbow, and caterpillar rolls, and the succulent citrus yellowtail are favorites from the sushi menu while the grill produces plenty of tasty nonfish fare. The covered patio faces the zoom and vroom of 32nd Street, but the soothing mist and meditation music create a tranquil, yes, even Zen-like atmosphere. ⊠*3160 E. Camelback Rd., Camelback Corridor* ☎*602/954–8700* ▭*AE, MC, V* ☯*No lunch weekends.*

CENTRAL PHOENIX

AMERICAN

$$–$$$$ ✕ **Durant's Fine Foods.** Durant's has endured since 1950 in the same location with the same menu and even many of the original waitstaff, making it one of Phoenix's legendary eating establishments. Steaks, chops, and fresh seafood, including Florida stone crab, dominate here; when the restaurant once tried to update its menu, regulars protested so furiously the idea was shelved. Those in the know enter through the kitchen door and frequent the Rat Pack–style bar for jumbo martinis fit for ol' Blue Eyes himself. ⊠*2611 N. Central Ave., at Virginia, Central Phoenix* ☎*602/264–5967* ▭*AE, D, DC, MC, V.*

A TOUCH OF PROVENCE

On Saturdays (except in summer) from 9 AM to 1 PM, some of the Valley's tastiest creations, from crepes to paella to *panini*, can be found in the parking lot of Vincent on Camelback, at the Touch of Provence market. Overseen by the restaurant, young Vincent protégés cook up custom orders and people are encouraged to "custom tip" into jars bearing creative causes such as "Saving for MIT" or "Honeymoon Fund." Touch of Provence also features a wine vendor and sellers of independent culinary curios like fresh pesto, honey, and jam.

$–$$$ ✕ **Chelsea's Kitchen.** With its hip, Pacific-Northwest-chic interior and a
Fodor's Choice   patio that feels more like a secret garden, Chelsea's Kitchen can easily
★   make you forget you're dining in the desert. This casually sophisticated
establishment insists on the freshest ingredients (especially fish), used
with equally fresh and flavorful ideas that complement the restaurant's
cool but comfortable style. Specials change frequently but regulars love
the short-rib hash, shrimp ceviche, and signature tacos with tortillas
and corn chips made on-site. ✉ *5040 N. 40th St., Central Phoenix*
☎ *602/957–2555* ▭ *AE, MC, V* ⊗ *No lunch.*

¢–$$ ✕ **La Grande Orange.** This San Francisco–inspired store and eatery sells
Fodor's Choice   artisanal nosh and novelty items, along with a formidable selection
★   of wines. Valley residents flock here to feast on mouthwatering sandwiches, pizzas, salads, and decadent breads and pastries. The small
tables inside fill up quickly at breakfast and lunch but there's also seating on the patio. Try the Commuter Sandwich on a homemade English
muffin or the delicious French pancakes with a Spanish latte that might
be the most memorable cup of *jose* you'll ever have. ✉ *4410 N. 40th
St., Central Phoenix* ☎ *602/840–7777* ▭ *AE, MC, V.*

★ $ ✕ **Pane Bianco.** Chef-owner Chris Bianco spends his evenings turning
out some of the Valley's best pizza at his downtown Pizzeria Bianco,
and his days creating to-die-for focaccia sandwiches at this minimalist
take-out sandwich shop. Order at the counter, pick up your brown-
bagged meal (which always includes a piece of candy), and dine outside
at a picnic table. The menu only has a handful of sandwich selections,
but each features wood-fire focaccia stuffed with farm-fresh ingredients. ✉ *4404 N. Central Ave., Central Phoenix* ☎ *602/234–2100*
▭ *AE, MC, V* ⊗ *Closed Sun. and Mon. No dinner.*

¢–$ ✕ **MacAlpine's Soda Fountain.** Opened in 1928 as a Rexall Drug Store,
this Norman Rockwell–like diner has the oldest operating soda fountain in the Southwest. Wooden booths, worn bar stools, and the vintage soda fountain and jukebox transport diners back to slower times.
Traditional burgers, sandwiches, and salads will make you nostalgic,
even if you weren't around back when. Save room for a decadent
malt, sundae, or ice-cream soda. ✉ *2303 N. 7th St., Central Phoenix*
☎ *602/262–5545* ⌕ *Reservations not accepted* ▭ *AE, D, MC, V.*

CAJUN

¢–$$ ✕ **Baby Kay's.** Named for the Louisiana native who brought her know-
how and love for Creole creations to the Valley, Baby Kay's is one of the
few Phoenix places that specializes in Cajun cuisine. You'll find authen-
tic takes on red beans and rice, gumbo, jambalaya, po'boys, catfish,
and the house specialty: spicy crawfish stew *étouffée*. Baby Kay sold the
restaurant a few years ago but her piquante spirit rolls on. Worthwhile
extras include the green-olive coleslaw. For the cholesterol conscious,
grilled items and spring salads with creole vinaigrette will do in a pinch.
✉ *2119 E. Camelback Rd., Town and Country Shopping Center, Cen-
tral Phoenix* ☎ *602/955–0011* ▭ *AE, MC, V* ⊗ *Closed Sun.*

ECLECTIC

$–$$
Fodor'sChoice
★
✕ **FEZ.** It's not a hat—but it does top the list of new restaurants in central Phoenix. From its sleek interior to its central location and diverse clientele, right down to its affordable lunch, happy hour, dinner, Sunday brunch, and late-night menus, FEZ covers everything. "American fare with a Moroccan flair" means bold culinary leaps, with items like the FEZ Burger, *kisras* (flatbread pizza), and the signature crispy rosemary pomegranate chicken—but it all lands safely

BEST PHOENIX MARGARITAS
Fez, *Central Phoenix*
Via Delosantos, *North Central Phoenix*
Los Dos Molinos, *South Phoenix*
Carlsbad Tavern, *Scottsdale*
Pepe's Taco Villa, *West Phoenix*
Barrio Café, *Downtown*

on the taste buds. Potables include specialty martinis and margaritas and a formidable wine list. ⊠*3815 N. Central Ave., Central Phoenix* ☎*602/287–8700* ⊟*AE, MC, V.*

ITALIAN

$$–$$$
✕ **Avanti.** Owners Angelo Livi and Benito Mellino have been welcoming guests to this romantic Italian restaurant since 1974. Candlelight, a piano bar, and a dance floor are perfect for a special celebration. For starters, try one of the house specialties: potato gnocchi paired with spinach ravioli. The veal dishes, such as saltimbocca or osso buco, are particularly memorable. ⊠*2728 E. Thomas Rd., Central Phoenix* ☎*602/956–0900* ⊟*AE, D, DC, MC, V* ☉*No lunch weekends.*

$–$$$
✕ **La Fontanella.** Quality and value are a winning combination at this outstanding neighborhood restaurant. The interior is reminiscent of an Italian villa, with antiques, crisp table linens, fresh flowers, and windows dressed in lace curtains, and chef-owner Isabelle Bertuccio turns out magnificent food, often using recipes from her Tuscan and Sicilian relatives. The escargot and herb-crusted rack of lamb top the list. Homemade pasta is served with Sicilian semolina bread and homemade sausages or meatballs. For dessert, Isabelle's husband, Berto, creates sumptuous gelato. ⊠*4231 E. Indian School Rd., Central Phoenix* ☎*602/955–1213* ⊟*AE, D, DC, MC, V* ☉*No lunch.*

LATIN AMERICAN

$–$$
✕ **Ticoz Resto-Bar.** The slogan "Urban. Latin. Sexy. Chill" fits this place like a stiletto heel. The colorful but dark interior is sleek and cool, the fare has just the right spice, and the happy-hour mojitos have just the right price, making this one of the hottest new haunts in Central Phoenix. Try the Ticoz lettuce wraps, the empanadas, the sweet-corn tamales, or *barbacoa* (simmered) beef. ⊠*5114 N. 7th St., Central Phoenix* ☎*602/200–0160* ⊟*AE, MC, V.*

SPANISH

¢–$$
✕ **Lola Tapas.** The menu at this tiny tapas bar is about as big as the restaurant itself, but both focus on a delicious and delightful community-oriented dining experience. A long central table and two smaller ones tightly accommodate the steady stream of folks who come for

the cozy, dimly lit Latin atmosphere and the sensible portions of sensational food like garbanzo beans with garlic and sautéed spinach, the Tortilla Española, or the pork skewers. If you can find a space at the tiny bar in back, settle in with a red or white version of what may be the Valley's best sangria while you wait. ⊠ *800 E. Camelback Rd., Central Phoenix* ☎ *602/265–4519* ⌧ *Reservations not accepted* ⊟ *AE, MC, V* ☉ *Closed Sun. and Mon. No lunch.*

DOWNTOWN PHOENIX

AMERICAN

¢–$ ✕ **Mrs. White's Golden Rule Café.** This downtown lunch spot is the best place in town for true Southern cooking. Every entrée—from fried chicken to pork chops—comes with corn bread, and the peach cobbler is legendary. ⊠ *808 E. Jefferson St., Downtown Phoenix* ☎ *602/262–9256* ⌧ *Reservations not accepted* ⊟ *No credit cards* ☉ *Closed Sat. and Sun. No dinner.*

¢–$ ✕ **Welcome Diner.** Sidle up to a bar stool in this tiny vintage 1930s diner for an all-day organic brunch menu featuring hot dogs, hamburgers, tasty egg sandwiches, "a cup of sweet toast," and Nana's Ridiculous Oatmeal Chocolate Chip cookies. This is a welcoming downtown eatery. ⊠ *924 E. Roosevelt, Downtown Phoenix* ☎ *602/495–1111* ⌧ *Reservations not accepted* ⊟ *No credit cards* ☉ *Closed Sun. No dinner.*

CHINESE

¢–$$ ✕ **Gourmet House of Hong Kong.** Traditional Chinatown specialties like *chow fun* (thick rice noodles) are excellent at this simple, diner-style place: try the assorted-meat version, with chicken, shrimp, pork, and squid. Dishes with black-bean sauce are among the menu's best. Delights such as five-flavor frogs' legs, duck feet with greens, and beef tripe casserole are offered, if you're feeling adventurous. ⊠ *1438 E. McDowell Rd., Downtown Phoenix* ☎ *602/253–4859* ⊟ *AE, D, MC, V.*

ECLECTIC

$ ✕ **My Florist Café.** Cool, classic, and supremely stylish, My Florist is a stunning pacesetter for the future of food and fun in the downtown Phoenix area. The sleek, high-ceiling interior, a wall of windows, hardwood floors, and a pristine jazz piano welcome enlightened locals who know good taste and great-tasting food—the menu consists of gourmet salads and sandwiches made with phenomenal breads baked fresh daily at the adjoining Willo Bakery. ⊠ *534 W. McDowell Rd., Downtown Phoenix* ☎ *602/254–0333* ⊟ *AE, D, DC, MC, V.*

MEXICAN

★ $$–$$$ ✕ **Barrio Cafe.** Owners Wendy Gruber and Silvana Salcido Esparza have taken Mexican cuisine to a new level. Expect guacamole prepared tableside and modern Mexican specialties such as *cochinita pibil,* slow-roasted pork with red achiote and sour orange, and *chiles en Nogada,* a delicious traditional dish from Central Mexico featuring a spicy poblano pepper stuffed with fruit, chicken, and raisins. The flavor-packed food consistently draws packs of people but you can drink in the intimate atmosphere—and a specialty margarita—while you wait for a table. ⊠*2814 N. 16th St., Downtown Phoenix* ☎*602/636–0240* ⚲*Reservations not accepted* ▭*AE, MC, V* ☉*Closed Mon.*

NATIVE AMERICAN

¢ ✕ **Fry Bread House.** Indian Fry bread, a specialty of the Native American culture, is a delicious treat—pillows of deep-fried dough topped with sweet or savory toppings and folded in half. Local fry bread fanatics get their fix from chef-owner Cecelia Miller of the Tohono O'odham Nation. Choose from culture-crossing combinations like savory shredded chili beef with cheese, beans, green chiles, veggies, and sour cream, or try the sweeter synthesis of honey and sugar, or chocolate with butter. ⊠*4140 N. 7th Ave., Downtown Phoenix* ☎*602/351–2345* ▭*D, MC, V* ☉*Closed Sun.*

PAN ASIAN

$–$$ ✕ **Fate.** In an old house in the evolving downtown arts district, this funky eatery/art gallery/music salon/well-kept secret turns out some of the Valley's best Asian food. Hong Kong–born chef-owner Johnny Chu pairs simple fresh ingredients with fantastic sauces to create popular dishes such as House Dynamite, a spicy stir-fry of pineapple, veggies, and peanuts in a sweet and spicy sauce. Dinner is served until 3 AM on weekends, accompanied by DJ-spun tunes. ⊠*905 N. 4th St., Downtown Phoenix* ☎*602/254–6424* ▭*MC, V* ☉*Closed Sun.*

PIZZA

$–$$ ✕ **Pizzeria Bianco.** Brooklyn native Chris Bianco makes pizza with a passion in this small establishment on Heritage Square. His wood-fired creations incorporate the finest and freshest ingredients (including homemade mozzarella cheese) in a brick oven imported from Italy. Bar Bianco next door is a good place to relax with a beverage while you wait for your table. ■TIP➔**Arrive a few minutes before they open at 5 PM to avoid the long wait, especially on Friday and Saturday nights.** ⊠*623 E. Adams St., Downtown Phoenix* ☎*602/258–8300* ▭*AE, MC, V* ☉*Closed Sun. and Mon. No lunch.*

NORTH CENTRAL PHOENIX

AMERICAN

$$–$$$ ✕ **Convivo Bistro.** Nestled into the northwest side of the Squaw Peak Promenade shopping center, this restaurant is as close as the desert gets to a Manhattan dining experience: a dozen tables, a tiny kitchen, and a rotating new-American menu featuring fresh seasonal produce. American standards have been given an international flair, so you'll find unexpected flavors in dishes such as seared duck breast with sweet and sour lime sauce. The wine list is thoughtful and not overpriced. Save room for delicious desserts like the lemon tart with Cointreau-soaked berries in a raspberry sauce. ⊠*7000 N. 16th St., North Central Phoenix* ☎*602/997–7676* ▭*AE, MC, V* ☉*Closed Sun. year-round and Mon. May–Nov.*

FRENCH

$$–$$$$　✕ **Coup Des Tartes.** Tables are scattered among three small rooms of an old house at this country French restaurant. It's BYOB, and there's an $8 corkage fee, but all's forgiven when you taste the delicate cuisine prepared in the tiny kitchen. Offerings may include baked Brie, pineapple-caper *escolar* (a delicious, fattier version of sea bass), or herb-crusted chicken with a creamy spinach sauce. The signature dessert, a banana brûlée tart, is delectable. ⊠*4626 N. 16th St., North Central Phoenix* ☎*602/212–1082* ⌂*Reservations essential* ▭*AE, D, MC, V* ⌖*BYOB* ⊘*Closed Sun. and Mon. No lunch.*

INDIAN

$–$$　✕ **Taste of India.** This perennial favorite in the Valley specializes in northern Indian cuisine. Breads here—*bhatura, naan, paratha*—are superb, and vegetarians enjoy wonderful meatless specialties, including the eggplant-based *benghan bhartha,* and *bhindi masala,* a tempting okra dish. Just about every spice in the rack is used for the lamb and chicken dishes, so be prepared to guzzle extra water—or an English beer. If your server says an item is spicy, *trust them.* ⊠*1609 E. Bell Rd., North Central Phoenix* ☎*602/788–3190* ▭*AE, MC, V.*

ITALIAN

$–$$$　✕ **Christo's Ristorante.** Don't judge this book by its cover. Cozy and unassuming in a Phoenix strip mall, Christo's keeps its tables filled with loyal customers who enjoy fine Italian cuisine. Attentive servers ensure your water glass never empties and folks rave about the fresh seafood dishes, the roasted rack of lamb, the veal, and the delicious pasta dishes. Start with the delicious, pan-fried calamari. Dinner's main courses come with soup and salad. ⊠*6327 N. 7th St., North Central Phoenix* ☎*602/264–1784* ▭*AE, D, DC, MC, V* ⊘*Closed Sun.*

MEDITERRANEAN

¢–$$　✕ **Mediterranean House.** The food served here covers an area between Greece and the Middle East. The lentil soup is thick and spicy, and the Egyptian chicken—a huge plate of sliced chicken breast, battered and fried, is delicious. Vegetarians appreciate the combination plate piled with baba ghanoush, hummus, and falafel, served with warm pita and tahini. ⊠*1588 E. Bethany Home Rd., North Central Phoenix* ☎*602/248–8460* ▭*AE, MC, V* ⊘*Closed Sun. No lunch Sat.*

MEXICAN

★ ¢–$$　✕ **Via Delosantos.** The family-owned Via Delosantos looks a little rough around the edges but it's what's inside that counts—an accommodating staff, an enormous and authentic Mexican menu, and one of the best-tasting and best-priced house margaritas in town. Entrées are ample and include more than just tired combinations of beef, beans, and cheese. Try the fajitas *calabacitas* with a yellow- and green-squash succotash; or the delicious chicken *delosantos,* a cheesy chicken breast and tortilla concoction. Expect to wait on weekends, either at the bar or outside, but also expect that the experience will be worth it. ⊠*9120 N. Central Ave., North Central Phoenix* ☎*602/997–6239* ⌂*Reservations not accepted* ▭*AE, D, DC, MC, V.*

PARADISE VALLEY

AMERICAN

$$$–$$$$ ✕ **Lon's at the Hermosa.** In an adobe
FodorsChoice hacienda hand-built by cowboy art-
★ ist Lon Megargee, this romantic spot
has sweeping vistas of Camelback
Mountain and the perfect patio for
after-dinner drinks under the stars.
Megargee's art and cowboy memo-
rabilia decorate the dining room.

**BEST DINING
WITH A VIEW**

T. Cook's at the Royal Palms, *Cam-
elback Corridor*

elements, *Paradise Valley*

Kai, *Chandler*

Mary Elaine's, *Camelback Corridor*

The menu changes seasonally but
includes appetizers like rock shrimp with roasted-corn sauce and juni-
per-smoked wild Chinook salmon. Wood-grilled, melt-in-your-mouth
filet mignon over Gorgonzola mashed potatoes, and more exotic dishes
like pecan-grilled antelope are main course options. Phoenicians love the
Sunday brunch. ⊠*Hermosa Inn, 5532 N. Palo Cristi Dr., Paradise Val-
ley* 🕾*602/955–7878* 🖃*AE, D, DC, MC, V* ☺*No lunch Sat. and Sun.*

ECLECTIC

★ **$$$–$$$$** ✕ **elements.** Perched on the side of Camelback Mountain at the Sanctu-
ary Resort, this stylish, modern restaurant offers breathtaking desert-
sunset and city-light views. There's a cordial community table where
you can sit and order such appetizers as the trilogy of duck, wild escar-
got wontons, and fried calamari with miso-scallion vinaigrette. Entrées
are excellent; among the best is the bacon-wrapped fillet of beef with
Maytag blue cheese and merlot demi-glace. ⊠*Sanctuary on Camelback
Mountain, 5700 E. McDonald Dr., Paradise Valley* 🕾*480/607–2300*
⚑*Reservations essential* 🖃*AE, D, DC, MC, V.*

SCOTTSDALE

Fast-growing Scottsdale can be broken down into roughly three neigh-
borhoods. Downtown encompasses the small area bordered by High-
land Avenue to the north, 56th Street to the west, Thomas Road to
the south, and Scottsdale Road to the east; North Scottsdale includes
everything north of Shea Boulevard; and Central Scottsdale is every-
thing between Downtown and North Scottsdale. The Camelback Cor-
ridor restaurant row runs west–east from Phoenix to Scottsdale, with
64th Street the border between the two.

AMERICAN–CASUAL

★ **$–$$$** ✕ **Bandera.** For a tasty dinner, try this casual, high-volume spot. The
rotisserie chicken is wonderfully moist and meaty; you'll see the birds
spinning in the window before you even walk through the door. Salads,
fresh fish, prime rib, and meat loaf are also on the menu. The mashed
potatoes and grilled artichoke are divine. If you get here during prime
eating hours, especially on weekends, be prepared to wait. ⊠*3821 N.
Scottsdale Rd., Central Scottsdale* 🕾*480/994–3524* ⚑*Reservations
not accepted* 🖃*AE, D, DC, MC, V* ☺*No lunch.*

¢–$$ ✕ **AZ 88.** A great spot for people-watching, this sleek, glassed-in res-
Fodor'sChoice taurant serves some of the Valley's best cocktails and food at affordable
★ prices. Large portions of tasty salads, sandwiches, sumptuous burgers
(try the Au Poivre II), and perfectly poured cosmopolitans never fail to
satisfy. If you're seeking quiet, dine outside on the beautiful patio over-
looking Scottsdale Mall. ⊠ *7353 E. Scottsdale Mall, Central Scottsdale*
☎ *480/994–5576* ⚔ *Reservations not accepted* ☰ *AE, D, DC, MC, V*
⊘ *No lunch weekends.*

¢–$ ✕ **Kashman's Place.** Brooklyn transplants Nancy and Steve Kashman
serve sumptuous omelets with crisp home fries, creatively blended sal-
ads, and piled-high sandwiches to a large following of locals. Every-
thing is deliciously fresh and portions are generous. New York bagels
are done the authentic way—boiled and baked on the premises using
filtered water they've duplicated from NYC water samples. Expect
lines on weekends. ⊠ *32531 N. Scottsdale Rd., at Ashler Hills, North
Scottsdale* ☎ *480/488–5274* ☰ *AE, D, DC, MC, V* ⊘ *No dinner*
⊠ *23425 N. Scottsdale Rd., Suite 6, Pinnacle Peak, North Scottsdale*
☎ *480/585–6221* ☰ *AE, D, DC, MC, V* ⊘ *No dinner.*

¢–$ ✕ **Original Pancake House.** The flapjacks here inspire worship from
locals, who wait patiently for a table on weekends. The signature apple
pancake is made from homemade batter poured over sautéed apples,
then baked to perfection and glazed with cinnamon sugar. Other vari-
eties, such as the Dutch Baby—oven-baked and served with whipped
butter and powdered sugar—are also worth braving the crowds for.
Everything is made from scratch. ⊠ *6840 E. Camelback Rd., Central
Scottsdale* ☎ *480/946–4902* ☰ *No credit cards* ⊘ *No dinner.*

CONTEMPORARY

$$$–$$$$ ✕ **Acacia.** Worth the drive into the foothills of Pinnacle Peak, this res-
taurant is in the Four Seasons Hotel in far North Scottsdale. The menu
includes some exotic offerings like wild boar bacon–wrapped buffalo
tenderloin, but most folks come for the steaks (try the 18-ounce bone-
in rib eye). Seafood is excellent, too, and the Chilled Seafood Pinnacle
(Alaskan king crab legs, jumbo shrimp, seasonal oysters, Maine lobster,
and tuna) is wonderful to share. ⊠ *Four Seasons Scottsdale at Troon
North, 10600 E. Crescent Moon Dr., North Scottsdale* ☎ *480/513–
5086* ☰ *AE, D, DC, MC, V* ⊘ *No lunch.*

$$$–$$$$ ✕ **Michael's at the Citadel.** One of Scottsdale's best-looking restaurants
has a two-story sandstone waterfall, several fireplaces, outdoor seating,
and lush desert landscaping. The contemporary American fare changes
seasonally. Sunday brunch showcases offerings like orange-ricotta
cheese blintzes with lingonberry and cinnamon syrup. For a special
occasion, reserve the chef's table in the kitchen (it accommodates 6 to
10 people) and watch the chefs work their magic. ⊠ *8700 E. Pinnacle
Peak Rd., North Scottsdale* ☎ *480/515–2575* ⚔ *Reservations essen-
tial* ☰ *AE, D, DC, MC, V* ⊘ *No lunch weekends but Sunday brunch
10 AM–2 PM.*

$$–$$$$ ✕ **L'Ecole.** You won't regret putting yourself in the talented hands of
the student chefs at the Valley's premier cooking academy. Choose
from an extensive list of French-inspired entrées or the four-course
prix-fixe menu, available for lunch ($30) and dinner ($35). The menu

1

changes seasonally but expect inventive appetizers such as lobster gratin, stuffed rabbit saddle, ricotta gnocchi, and entrées such as filet mignon. ⊠*Scottsdale Culinary Institute, 8100 E. Camelback Rd., Central Scottsdale* ☎*480/425–3111* ⚍*Reservations essential* ☰*AE, D, DC, MC, V* ⊘*Closed weekends.*

$$–$$$$ ✕ **Razz's Restaurant and Bar.** There's no telling what part of the globe chef-proprietor Erasmo "Razz" Kamnitzer will use for culinary inspiration on any given day, but his creations give dormant taste buds a wake-up call: black-bean paella is a twist on a Spanish theme; South American bouillabaisse is a fragrant fish stew, stocked with veggies; and *bah mie goreng* teams noodles with fish, meat, and vegetables, perked up with dried cranberries and almonds. Count on it—Razz'll dazzle. ⊠*10315 N. Scottsdale Rd., North Scottsdale* ☎*480/905–1308* ☰*AE, D, DC, MC, V* ⊘*Closed Sun. and Mon. and June–Aug. No lunch.*

$$–$$$$ ✕ **Roaring Fork.** Elk-antler chandeliers, earth-tone fabrics and leathers, barbed-wire accessories, and a buffalo skull above the bar add up to a comfortable, rustic restaurant named after the river that winds past Aspen in Colorado. Creations include a pork porterhouse steak and fork-barbecued gulf shrimp on lobster, alongside such mouthwatering side dishes as stone-ground chile cheese grits and green-chile macaroni. The reasonably priced saloon menu is served in the bar from 4 to 7 PM Monday to Saturday. ⊠*Finova Building, 4800 N. Scottsdale Rd., Central Scottsdale* ☎*480/947–0795* ⚍*Reservations essential* ☰*AE, D, DC, MC, V* ⊘*No lunch.*

$–$$$$ ✕ **Cowboy Ciao.** Looking for a culinary kick? This kitchen weds Southwestern fare and Italian flair, and it's no shotgun wedding. The menu changes frequently but offers standby favorites, such as espresso-rubbed filet mignon and elk strip loin with hazelnut pesto. The bread pudding creations are must-trys. The wine list represents more than 40 countries and features 225 grape varietals. Too much to choose from? Ask for the *Nifty Fifty,* a one-page list of guest favorites. ⊠*7133 E. Stetson Dr., Old Town Scottsdale* ☎*480/946–3111* ☰*AE, D, DC, MC, V.*

$$–$$$ ✕ **Rancho Pinot Grill.** The attention to quality paid by the husband-and-wife proprietors here—he manages, she cooks—has made this one of the town's top dining spots. The inventive menu changes daily, depending on what's fresh. If you're lucky, you might come on a day when the kitchen has made *posole,* a mouthwatering broth with hominy, salt pork, and cabbage. Entrées might include quail, chicken with toasted polenta, scallops with edamame tomato relish, grilled sea bass, handmade pasta, or vegetarian antipasto. ⊠*6208 N. Scottsdale Rd., northwest of Trader Joe's in the Lincoln Village Shops, Central Scottsdale* ☎*480/367–8030* ☰*AE, D, DC, MC, V* ⊘*Closed Sun. and Mon. mid-May–Nov. No lunch.*

FodorśChoice ★

FRENCH

$$$$ ✕ **Mary Elaine's.** Formal and elegant, this is the Valley's finest high-end dining experience and the austerity of the restaurant's decor (in the Phoenician Hotel) is a perfect backdrop for dramatic city-light views of Scottsdale from every table. Choose from a seasonally changing three- or six-course prix-fixe or an à la carte menu, and indulge in modern French-inspired offerings such as fricassee of lobster or foie gras

FodorśChoice ★

drizzled with maple syrup and 100-year-old balsamic vinegar. Desserts like the warm chocolate-soufflé tart are breathtaking. An extensive wine cellar, impeccable service, a pleasant jazz vocalist, and view-studded patio seating make this an exceptional dining experience. ⊠ *The Phoenician, 6000 E. Camelback Rd., Scottsdale/Camelback Corridor* ☎ *480/423–2530* ⚑ *Reservations essential* ▤ *AE, D, DC, MC, V* ☾ *Closed Sun. and Mon. No lunch.*

$$–$$$$ ✕ **Zinc Bistro.** No detail was overlooked at this replica of a Parisian bistro, from the zinc-top bar and linen-lined tables topped with butcher paper to the sidewalk café seating and mirrored walls. A Valley local, chef-owner Matt Carter prepares traditional French cuisine almost as if he were a native Frenchman. Bistro classics such as the flatiron steak, cassoulet with duck confit, and the omelet piled high with pommes frites are excellent. Also recommended are the roasted Dungeness crab and mushroom crepes, and the onion soup. The wine list offers a good selection of reasonably priced French wines. ⊠ *15034 N. Scottsdale Rd., Kierland Commons, North Scottsdale* ☎ *480/603–0922* ⚑ *Reservations not accepted* ▤ *AE, DC, MC, V.*

JAPANESE

$$–$$$$ ✕ **Sushi on Shea.** You may be in the middle of the desert, but the sushi here will make you think you're at the ocean's edge. Fresh yellowtail, toro, shrimp, scallops, freshwater eel, and even monkfish liver pâté are among the long list of delights. *Nabemono* (hot pot or meals-in-a-bowl) are prepared at your table. The best dish? Maybe it's the *una-ju* (broiled freshwater eel with a sublime smoky scent) served over sweet rice. The fact that some people believe eel is an aphrodisiac only adds to its charm. ⊠ *7000 E. Shea Blvd., North Scottsdale* ☎ *480/483–7799* ▤ *AE, D, DC, MC, V.*

$–$$ ✕ **Sea Saw.** Chef Nobu Fukada is creating some of the Valley's most
Fodor'sChoice interesting food at this small, simple eatery. "Tapanese" cuisine—small
★ plates of Japanese tapas such as baked black cod marinated in miso, allow you to sample lots of different items. Other delights include the white fish carpaccio (served warm) and the sushi foie gras. If you're feeling really adventurous, try the "Omakase Menu," a 10-course dinner created from what's fresh that day. The few tables and bar seats fill up quickly so if you don't have a reservation, do as the locals do— indulge in a glass of wine next door at Kazmierz wine bar while you wait. ⊠ *7133 E. Stetson Dr., Central Scottsdale* ☎ *480/481–9463* ⚑ *Reservations essential* ▤ *AE, D, DC, MC, V* ☾ *No lunch.*

LATIN

$–$$$ ✕ **Havana Cafe.** Tapas are marvelous here—particularly the shrimp pancakes, ham and chicken croquettes, and Cuban tamales—and there's an intoxicating choice of entrées including paella heaped with a whole Maine lobster. There's something special for vegetarians, too: *cho cho,* a fresh chayote squash stuffed with loads of veggies and topped with a Jamaican curry sauce. ⊠ *6245 E. Bell Rd., North Scottsdale* ☎ *480/991–1496* ⊠ *4225 E. Camelback Rd., Camelback Corridor, Phoenix* ☎ *602/952–1991* ⊠ *4232 E. Chandler Blvd., Ahwatukee* ☎ *480/704–2600* ☾ *No lunch Sun.* ▤ *AE, D, DC, MC, V.*

MEDITERRANEAN

$$$$ ✕ **Marquesa.** Polished marble, antiques, and floor-to-ceiling oil paintings adorn this Spanish colonial–style dining room in the Fairmont Scottsdale Princess Resort. Herbs and flavors indigenous to coastal Spain, France, and Italy season such appetizers as Spanish pequillo peppers stuffed with crab and cheese. Main courses include expertly prepared seafood, meats, and poultry—but the real triumph is the paella, bursting with lobster, chicken, shrimp, escargots, pork, and mussels. A wonderful market-style Sunday brunch can be enjoyed on the garden patio. ⊠ *Fairmont Scottsdale Princess Resort, 7575 E. Princess Dr., North Scottsdale* ☎ *480/585–4848* ⌖ *Reservations essential* ▤ *AE, D, DC, MC, V* ⊘ *Closed Mon. and Tues. Brunch only Sun. No lunch.*

MEXICAN

★ **$$$–$$$$** ✕ **La Hacienda.** La Hacienda is widely considered to be among the finest Mexican-inspired restaurants in North America, and to ensure truly authentic cuisine, executive chef Reed Groban took tasting tours through Mexican villages and towns. You'll find no burritos or tacos here, just appetizers like the crab enchilada with creamy pumpkin-seed sauce and La Hacienda's signature dish—spit-roasted suckling pig marinated in tamarind and bitter orange, carved tableside. The restaurant is on the grounds of the Fairmont Scottsdale Princess Resort. ⊠ *Fairmont Scottsdale Princess Resort, 7575 E. Princess Dr., North Scottsdale* ☎ *480/585–4848* ⌖ *Reservations essential* ▤ *AE, D, DC, MC, V* ⊘ *Closed Wed. No lunch.*

$$ ✕ **Los Sombreros Mexican Cantina.** Los Sombreros is in a converted brick home with lovely patio seating and serves dishes not found in typical Mexican restaurants. Start with the smoked salmon tostada: a crisp corn tortilla spread with cream cheese and chipotle chile, then topped with smoked salmon. Entrées include lamb *adobo*, a shank braised in a piquant sauce of ancho chiles, garlic, and cinnamon. Ice creams are housemade, and the *tamal de chocolate* is made with Mexican chocolate, sugar, and ground almonds. Los Sombreros also serves the best flan you'll find this side of Mexico City. ⊠ *2534 N. Scottsdale Rd., Downtown Scottsdale* ☎ *480/994–1799* ⌖ *Reservations not accepted* ▤ *AE, D, DC, MC, V* ⊘ *Closed Mon. No lunch.*

$–$$ ✕ **Carlsbad Tavern.** This busy New Mexico–style eatery serves big portions of such tasty dishes as a half-pound habanero cheeseburger, green-chile mashed potatoes, chipotle barbecue baby-back ribs, and *carne adovada*, a spicy, slow-roasted pork specialty. They'll custom-mix your margarita with fresh lime and lemon juice and blend it with your choice of some 35 tequilas. There's a late-night menu for the after 10 PM crowd. ⊠ *3313 N. Hayden Rd., Central Scottsdale* ☎ *480/970–8164* ▤ *AE, D, MC, V.*

$–$$ ✕ **Pink Taco.** This Mexican restaurant owned by Harry Morton, the twenty-something heir to the Hard Rock Cafe and Casino throne, blazed onto Scottsdale's chic eatery scene in summer 2006 (the original is in Vegas) and despite furor over the suggestive name (local politicians requested Morton to change it but he refused), the hip hangout continues to be a popular spot for the post-shopping, pre-partying beautiful people of Scottsdale. Main courses tend to be mediocre but the appetizers are tasty and the signature Sandia (watermelon) margarita goes down smooth—and most visitors are here for the people/celebrity watching anyway. ⊠7135 E. Camelback Rd., Scottsdale ☎480/675–7777 ⊕www.pinktaco.com ⚞Reservations not accepted ⊟AE, D, DC, MC, V.

PIZZA

¢–$$ ✕ **Nello's.** Leave it to two brothers from Chicago to come up with some of the best pizza in the Valley. The motto is "In Crust We Trust," and Nello's excels in both thin-crust and deep-dish pies. Try traditional varieties heaped with homemade sausage and mushrooms, or go vegetarian with the spinach pie. Pasta entrées are very good, too, and the family-style salads are inventive and fresh. ⊠8658 E. Shea Blvd., North Scottsdale ☎480/922–5335 ۞Closed Mon. ⊠2950 S. Alma School Dr., Mesa ☎480/820–5995 ۞Closed Mon. ⊠1806 E. Southern Ave., Tempe ☎480/897–2060 ۞Closed Mon. No lunch Sun. ⊠4710 E. Warner Rd., Ahwatukee, Phoenix ☎480/893–8930 ۞Closed Mon. No lunch Sun. ⊟AE, MC, V.

SEAFOOD

$$–$$$$ ✕ **Salt Cellar.** It's rare to find a restaurant in a cellar, especially in the desert. Originally an Arizona State University–frequented hamburger joint, the space has been transformed with crisp linen tablecloths and nautical decor. The kitchen dishes out straightforward, fresh seafood. For starters try Chesapeake Bay crab cakes, oysters Rockefeller, or turtle soup. Move on to entrées such as Idaho trout, Yakimono Hawaiian ahi, or charcoal-broiled king salmon. If you're really hungry, splurge on the 5-pound Maine lobster. ⊠550 N. Hayden Rd., South Scottsdale ☎480/947–1963 ⊟AE, MC, V ۞No lunch.

STEAK

$$–$$$$ ✕ **Don & Charlie's.** A favorite with major-leaguers in town for spring training, this venerable chophouse specializes in prime-grade steak and baseball memorabilia—the walls are covered with pictures, autographs, and uniforms. The New York sirloin, prime rib, and double-thick lamb chops are a hit; sides include au gratin potatoes and creamed spinach. ⊠7501 E. Camelback Rd., Central Scottsdale ☎480/990–0900 ⊟AE, D, DC, MC, V ۞No lunch.

$$–$$$$ ✕ **Morton's of Chicago.** The Windy City chain is famous for exceptional service, immense steaks, and entertaining tableside presentations, but most of all for consistency. If you've been hankerin' for a great, aged prime steak, you won't go wrong here. The monstrous 24-ounce porterhouse or 14-ounce double-cut fillet can satisfy the hungriest cowpoke. The seafood is excellent, too, but plays second fiddle to the beef. ⊠15233 N. Kierland Blvd., North Scottsdale ☎480/951–4440 ⚞Reservations essential ⊟AE, D, DC, MC, V ۞No lunch ⊠2501 E. Camelback Rd., Camelback CorridorPhoenix ☎602/955–9577 ⚞Reservations essential ⊟AE, D, DC, MC, V ۞No lunch.

THAI

$–$$ ✕ **Malee's on Main.** This fashionable, casual eatery in the heart of Scottsdale's Main Street Arts District serves sophisticated, Thai-inspired fare. Try the best-selling crispy *pla:* flash-fried whitefish fillets with fresh cilantro and sweet jalapeño garlic sauce. The spicy garlic sautéed spinach is a must, along with curries made to order with tofu, chicken, beef, pork, or seafood. You specify the spiciness—from mild to flaming, but even "mild" dishes have a bite. ⊠ *7131 E. Main St., Downtown Scottsdale* ☎ *480/947–6042* ⏴ *Reservations essential* ⊟ *AE, DC, MC, V* ⊠ *Desert Ridge Mall, Tatum Blvd. and 101, North Scottsdale* ☎ *480/342–9220* ⊟ *AE, DC, MC, V.*

SOUTH PHOENIX

AMERICAN

$$–$$$$ ✕ **Stockyards Restaurant.** If you're looking for a hearty meal, "Arizona's Original Steak House" is the place to go. Succulent prime rib and steaks, fresh seafood, and poultry are complemented by rib-sticking side dishes such as whiskey-sweet-potato mash, cowboy beans with chorizo, and roasted corn. The handsome dining room decor features Old West heavy wood, etched glass, and pressed-tin ceilings. A beautiful hand-carved mahogany bar and huge cut-glass chandelier adorn the 1889 Saloon in back. ⊠ *5009 E. Washington, South Phoenix* ☎ *602/273–7378* ⊟ *AE, D, DC, MC, V* ⊘ *No lunch weekends.*

BARBECUE

¢–$$ ✕ **Honey Bear's BBQ.** Honey Bear's motto—"You don't need no teeth to eat our meat"—may fall short on grammar, but this place isn't packed with folks looking to improve their language skills. This is Tennessee-style barbecue, which means smoky baby-back ribs basted in a tangy sauce. The sausage-enhanced "cowbro" beans and scallion-studded potato salad are great sides. ⊠ *5012 E. Van Buren St., South Phoenix* ☎ *602/273–9148* ⊠ *2824 N. Central Ave., Phoenix* ☎ *602/279–7911* ⊠ *7670 S. Priest Dr., Tempe* ☎ *480/222–2782* ⏴ *Reservations not accepted* ⊟ *AE, D, MC, V.*

MEXICAN

★ $–$$ ✕ **Los Dos Molinos.** In a hacienda that belonged to silent-era movie star Tom Mix, this fun restaurant focuses on New Mexican–style Mexican food. That means *hot.* New Mexico chiles form the backbone and fiery breath of the dishes, and the green-chile enchilada and beef taco are potentially lethal. The red salsa and enchiladas with egg on top are excellent. There's a funky courtyard where you can sip potent margaritas while waiting for a table. This is a must-do dining experience if you want authentic New Mexican–style food, but be prepared to swig lots of water. ⊠ *8646 S. Central Ave., South Phoenix* ☎ *602/243–9113* ⏴ *Reservations not accepted* ⊟ *AE, D, DC, MC, V* ⊘ *Closed Sun. and Mon.* ⊠ *260 S. Alma School Rd., Mesa* ☎ *480/969–7475* ⏴ *Reservations not accepted* ⊟ *AE, D, DC, MC, V* ⊘ *Closed Sun. and Mon.*

★ ¢ ✕ **Carolina's.** This small, nondescript restaurant in South Phoenix makes the most delicious, thin-as-air flour tortillas imaginable. In-the-know locals and downtown working folk have been lining up at Carolina's for years to partake of the homey, inexpensive Mexican food. The tacos, tamales, burritos, flautas, and enchiladas are served on paper plates. ⊠*1202 E. Mohave St., South Phoenix* ☎*602/252–1503* ⊟*AE, D, DC, MC, V* ☉*Closed Sun. Dinner on weekdays only until 7:30* PM *and Sat. until 6* PM ⊠*2126 E. Cactus Rd., North Central Phoenix* ☎*602/275–8231* ⊟*AE, D, DC, MC, V* ☉*Closed Sun.; dinner on weekdays only until 7:30* PM *and Sat. until 6* PM.

> ### CHANDLER
>
> The residential town of Chandler, south of Tempe, isn't really on the way to anywhere in the Valley, but its days as a destination location are coming around. With improved freeway access, the new Chandler Fashion Square mega-mall, and hip new restaurants like 98 South, Chandler is making its way onto the Phoenix area maps.

TEMPE, MESA & CHANDLER

AMERICAN

$–$$$ ✕ **Landmark.** In a 1908 building that was originally a Mormon church, this family-run restaurant serves all-American home cooking. The traditional dining room is decorated with lace curtains, chandeliers, and white linens, and the food is straightforward and comfy—roast turkey, prime rib, chicken-fried chicken and steak, and seafood dishes. The real draw, though, is the salad *room,* probably the largest salad bar you'll ever see, featuring nearly 100 items that include soups, breads, salad fixings, and hot dishes. Save room for landmark ice-cream pie. ⊠*809 W. Main St., Mesa* ☎*480/962–4652* ⊟*AE, D, MC, V.*

$$ ✕ **98 South Wine Bar & Kitchen.** This cool and relaxing wine bar in historic San Marcos Plaza is the place to sip primo *prosecco* (Italian sparkling wine) or pinot noir while enjoying live music and dining on the fine culinary creations of chef P. T. Barnum. Appetizers such as the cheese plate, the roasted vegetables and hummus, and the skirt steak starter make for a meal on their own, but the dinner and lunch menus feature a full range of delicious entrées with wines to match. ⊠*98 South San Marcos Pl., Chandler* ☎*480/814–9800* ⊟*AE, D, DC, MC, V* ☉*Closed Sun.*

CHINESE

$–$$ ✕ **C-Fu Gourmet.** This is serious Chinese food, the kind you'd expect to find on Mott Street in New York City's Chinatown or Grant Avenue in San Francisco. C-Fu's specialty is fish, and you can watch several species swimming around the big holding tanks. Shrimp are fished out of the tank, steamed, and bathed in a potent garlic sauce. Clams in black-bean sauce and tilapia in a ginger-scallion sauce also hit all the right buttons. If you don't find what you're looking for on the menu, tell them what you want and they'll make it. There's a daily dim sum brunch, too. ⊠*2051 W. Warner Rd., Chandler* ☎*480/899–3888* ⊟*AE, D, DC, MC, V.*

ECLECTIC

$$$–$$$$ ✕ **House of Tricks.** There's nothing up the sleeves of Robert and Robin Trick, who work magic on the eclectic menu that emphasizes the freshest available seafood, poultry, and fine meats, as well as vegetarian selections. One of the Valley's most unique dining venues, the restaurant encompasses a 1920s home and a separate brick- and adobe-style house originally built in 1903, adjoined by an intimate wooden deck and outdoor patio shaded by a canopy of grapevines and trees. At lunch you can't go wrong with the quiche of the day. ⊠ *114 E. 7th St., Tempe* ☎ *480/968–1114* ☐ *AE, D, MC, V* ⊗ *Closed Sun.*

FRENCH

$$–$$$ ✕ **Citrus Cafe.** Elegant yet casual, this small restaurant does everything right, from the romantic candlelit dining room to a daily menu featuring what's freshest from the market. For starters, try the baked Brie with almonds and apples or the superb leek-and-potato soup. Main dishes are pure French comfort food: veal kidneys, sweetbreads, leg of lamb, roast pork, and occasionally rabbit. ⊠ *2330 N. Alma School Rd., Chandler* ☎ *480/899–0502* ☐ *AE, D, DC, MC, V* ⊗ *Closed Mon. No lunch.*

ITALIAN

¢–$$$ ✕ **Oregano's.** Huge portions are an understatement at this casual Chicago-theme eatery. Come hungry and feast on fresh salads, tasty baked sandwiches, pizza (deep-dish, thin crust, or stuffed), and pasta dishes. The young, friendly staff and kitchsy 1950s decor create a fun and comfortable, family-friendly vibe. Save room for the famous pizza cookie: a half-pound of chocolate-chip or white-chocolate macadamia-nut cookie dough, baked on a 6-inch pizza pan and topped with three scoops of vanilla-bean ice cream. ⊠ *523 W. University Dr., Tempe* ☎ *480/858–0501* ⊠ *3622 N. Scottsdale Rd., Downtown Scottsdale* ☎ *480/970–1860* ⊠ *7215 E. Shea Blvd., North Scottsdale* ☎ *480/348–0500* ⊠ *1008 E. Camelback Rd., Central Phoenix* ☎ *602/241–0707* ⊠ *1130 S. Dobson Rd., Mesa* ☎ *480/962–0036* ☐ *AE, D, DC, MC, V* ⌑ *Reservations not accepted.*

MEXICAN

¢–$ ✕ **Rosa's Mexican Grill.** This festive, family-friendly restaurant summons up images of a Baja beach taqueria. The tacos are Rosa's true glory: beef, pork, and chicken are marinated in fruit juices and herbs for 12 hours, slowly oven-baked for another 10, then shredded and charbroiled. The fish taco is in a class by itself. Spoon on one of Rosa's five fresh homemade salsas but beware the fiery habanero version—it might be able to strip the enamel off your teeth. ⊠ *328 E. University Dr., Mesa* ☎ *480/964–5451* ☐ *AE, D, DC, MC, V* ⊗ *Closed Sun.*

MIDDLE EASTERN

¢ ✕ **Haji Baba.** This casual Tempe treasure is a local favorite. It serves hummus, *labni* (fresh cheese made from yogurt), falafel, and kebab plates, and the adjoining store stocks delicious cured olives and hard-to-find Middle Eastern ingredients. ⊠ *1513 E. Apache Blvd., Tempe*

☎480/894–1905 ⚐Reservations not accepted ▤AE, D, MC, V
☉Take-out only on Sun.

NATIVE AMERICAN

$$$$ ✕ **Kai.** Kai (it means "seed" in the Pima language) features innovative
Southwestern cuisine that uses indigenous ingredients from local tribal
farms. The seasonal menu reflects the restaurant's natural setting on
the Gila River Indian Community. Standout appetizers include lobster
tail on Indian fry bread and bacon-wrapped quail. Entrées like seared
duck breast with pheasant sausage and the Cheyenne River buffalo tenderloin are excellent. The restaurant is adorned with Native American
artifacts and has huge windows that showcase gorgeous mountain and
desert views. ⊠Sheraton Wild Horse Pass Resort & Spa, 5594 W. Wild
Horse Pass Blvd., Chandler ☎602/225–0100 ⚐Reservations essential
▤AE, D, DC, MC, V ☉Closed Sun. and Mon.

VIETNAMESE

$–$$ ✕ **Cyclo.** It's always exciting to find an outstanding one-of-a-kind res-
taurant in a town that has more than its fair share of chain establishments, and Cyclo is just that. The friendly and gracious owner Justina
Dwong is as much a draw as the well-prepared Vietnamese food. Try
the bánh xéo, a crispy, turmeric-yellow crepe filled with juicy bites
of pork and shrimp, or crispy cha gío, a spicy lemongrass chicken. A
French-inspired, jasmine-scented crème brûlée provides a perfect ending to the meal. ⊠1919 W. Chandler Blvd., Chandler ☎480/963–
4490 ▤MC, V ☉Closed Sun.

WEST PHOENIX, GLENDALE, LITCHFIELD PARK

CHINESE

$ ✕ **Silver Dragon.** This is one of the best Chinese restaurants in town—if
you order properly. Insist on sitting in the big room to the left as you
walk in the door, and ask for the Chinese menu (it has brief English descriptions). Your boldness will be rewarded with some of the
best Hong Kong–style Chinese fare to be found between New York
and California. Crispy Hong Kong–Style Chicken is a plump whole
bird steamed, flash-fried, and cut into bite-size pieces. Other standouts
include the hot-pot dishes, noodles, fish, and vegetarian dishes—the
Buddhist-style rolls are outstanding. ⊠8946 N. 19th Ave., West Phoenix ☎602/674–0151 ▤AE, MC, V ☉Closed Wed. No lunch Sat.

GERMAN

$–$$$ ✕ **Haus Murphy's.** On weekends you can kick back with the accordion-
ist at this charming storefront restaurant. Schnitzel is a specialty, not
surprisingly, especially the spicy paprika version teamed with crispy
chunks of fried potatoes and green beans. Sauerbraten, paired with
tart red cabbage and two huge potato dumplings, is not for the faint of
appetite. Wash everything down with a German beer—there are eight
on tap—and save room for the homemade apple strudel and Black For-
est torte. ⊠5739 W. Glendale Ave., Glendale ☎623/939–2480 ▤AE,
D, MC, V ☉Closed Mon.

MEXICAN

¢–$ ✕ **Lily's Cafe.** Friendly mom-and-pop proprietors, a jukebox with south-of-the-border hits, and low-priced, fresh, Mexican fare have kept patrons coming back here for almost 50 years. The chimichanga is stuffed with tender beef and covered with cheese, guacamole, and sour cream; fragrant tamales, spunky red-chile beef, and chiles rellenos right out of the fryer also shine. ⊠ *6706 N. 58th Dr., Glendale* ☎ *623/937–7757* ⚖ *Reservations not accepted* ⊟ *No credit cards* ⊘ *Closed Mon., Tues., and Aug.*

¢–$ ✕ **Pepe's Taco Villa.** The neighborhood's not fancy, and neither is this

Fodor's Choice restaurant, but in a town with a lot of gringo-ized south-of-the-border

★ fare, this is the real friendly, real deal. Tacos *rancheros*—spicy, shredded pork pungently lathered with adobo paste—are a dream. So are the green-corn tamales, authentic imported *machacado* (air-dried beef), and chiles rellenos that are perfect with a margarita from the full bar. Don't leave without trying the sensational mole, a rich, exotic sauce fashioned from chiles and chocolate. ⊠ *2108 W. Camelback Rd., West Phoenix* ☎ *602/242–0379* ⊟ *AE, D, MC, V* ⊘ *Closed Tues.*

VIETNAMESE

¢–$$ ✕ **Pho Bang.** What makes this little hole-in-the-wall restaurant so appealing—aside from the prices—is the simplicity and freshness of the food. The house specialty is *tom va bo nuong vi* (#35 on the menu): the server brings three plates, one with transparently thin slices of marinated beef and raw shrimp; another with piles of mint, lettuce, cilantro, pickled leeks, cucumber, and carrot; and the last with rice paper. You fire up the portable grill and cook the beef and shrimp. When they're done, combine with the veggies, fold into rice paper, and start dunking. ⊠ *1702 W. Camelback Rd., West Phoenix* ☎ *602/433–9440* ⊟ *MC, V.*

WHERE TO STAY

Phoenix and Scottsdale have long been the domain of resorts and historic places to stay, and the number of options continues to grow. Competition among the newest megaresorts is fierce and properties vie for family and leisure business with immaculately manicured golf courses and incredible water features—you might be surprised to find rivers, waterfalls, lakes, slides, pools, and even canals replete with gondolas putting the humble hotel pool to shame here in the desert. Resorts come in all shapes and sizes, some consisting of a large main hotel, others spread out in casitas (little houses) surrounding golf courses. Whatever you and your family are looking for, you should be able to find it here.

Downtown Phoenix properties tend to be the business hotels, close to the heart of the city and the convention centers—and often closer to the average vacationer's budget. Many properties here cater to corporate travelers during the week but lower their rates on weekends to entice leisure travelers, so ask about weekend specials when making reservations. With more than 55,000 hotel rooms in the metro area, you can take your pick of anything from a luxurious resort to a guest ranch to an extended-stay hotel. For a true Western experience, guest-ranch territory is 60 mi northwest, in the town of Wickenburg.

Many people flee snow and ice to bask in the warmth of the Valley, so winter is the high season, peaking January through March. Summer season—mid-May through the end of September—is giveaway time, when a night at a resort often goes for half of the winter price, but be forewarned: in the height of summer it can be too hot to do anything beyond your air-conditioned room.

WHAT IT COSTS					
	¢	$	$$	$$$	$$$$
FOR 2 PEOPLE	under $100	$100–$150	$151–$225	$226–$350	over $350

Prices are for a standard double in high season.

CAMELBACK CORRIDOR, PHOENIX

$$$$

Fodor'sChoice

★

Arizona Biltmore. Designed by Frank Lloyd Wright's colleague Albert Chase McArthur, the Biltmore has been Phoenix's premier resort since it opened in 1929. The lobby, with its stained-glass skylights, wrought-iron pilasters, and cozy sitting alcoves, fills with piano music each evening. Guest rooms are spacious, with Southwestern-print fabrics and Mission-style furniture. Accommodating staff are unobtrusive. The Biltmore sits on 39 impeccably manicured acres of cool fountains, open walkways, and colorful flower beds. ⌧*2400 E. Missouri Ave., Camelback Corridor, 85016* ☎*602/955–6600 or 800/950–0086* 🖷*602/381–7600* ⊕*www.arizonabiltmore.com* ⌧*739 rooms, 72 villas* ⌖*In-room: safe, ethernet, Wi-Fi (some), refrigerator. In-hotel: 4 restaurants, bar, tennis courts, pools, gym, spa, bicycles, concierge, children's programs (ages 6–12), laundry service, parking (no fee), no-smoking rooms* ⊟*AE, D, DC, MC, V.*

$$$$

Fodor'sChoice

★

Royal Palms Resort & Spa. Once the home of Cunard Steamship executive Delos T. Cooke, this Mediterranean-style resort has a stately row of the namesake palms at its entrance, courtyards with fountains, and individually designed rooms. Deluxe casitas are all different, though they follow one of three elegant styles—trompe l'oeil, romantic retreat, Spanish colonial. The restaurant, T. Cook's ($$$–$$$$), is renowned and the open-air Alvadora Spa, featuring 7 new spa suites, seems like it has every imaginable amenity, including an outdoor rain shower. In 2007, the resort unveiled its new Montavista collection of rooms, and suites featuring fireplaces and luxury amenities. ⌧*5200 E. Camelback Rd., Camelback Corridor, 85018* ☎*602/840–3610 or 800/672–6011* 🖷*602/840–6927* ⊕*www.royalpalmsresortandspa.com* ⌧*76 rooms, 62 suites, 44 casitas* ⌖*In-room: safe, refrigerator, ethernet, Wi-Fi. In-hotel: restaurant, room service, bar, pool, gym, spa, laundry service, parking (fee), no-smoking rooms* ⊟*AE, D, DC, MC, V.*

$$–$$$$

The Ritz-Carlton, Phoenix. Behind the sand-color facade hides a graceful luxury hotel known for impeccable service. The lobby and spacious public rooms are elegantly inviting, decorated with 18th- and 19th-century European paintings and a handsome china collection. Guest rooms and suites are spacious enclaves of luxury with premium mattresses and pillows, Egyptian-cotton sheets, and downy duvets that are even more inviting after the nightly turn-down service, complete with fine chocolate. A conscientious and attentive staff offers impeccable service and the central location means dining, shopping, and entertainment are within strolling distance. Summer packages are creative, fun, and very affordable. Mountain and city vistas can be appreciated from the second-floor terrace, where there is also a heated pool. ✉2401 E. Camelback Rd., Camelback Corridor, 85016 ☎602/468–0700 or 800/241–3333 ✏602/468–0793 ⊕www.ritzcarlton.com/hotels/phoenix ↩267 rooms, 14 suites △In-room: safe, refrigerator, ethernet, Wi-Fi. In-hotel: restaurant, room service, bar, pool, gym, laundry service, executive floor, parking (fee), no-smoking rooms, public Wi-Fi ▭AE, D, DC, MC, V.

$–$$$ 🏨 **Homewood Suites Phoenix-Biltmore.** This all-suites chain is a major value, especially considering its location in the heart of the upscale Biltmore District and Camelback Corridor. Suites have a spacious living and working area with a sleeper-sofa and one or two separate bedrooms; each has a full kitchen. Every Monday to Thursday evening there is a "Welcome Home" reception—a minifeast featuring anything from a taco bar to baked potatoes with all the trimmings. Guests also get free passes to a nearby fitness club, free breakfast, and transportation within a 5-mi radius of the hotel. ✉2001 E. Highland Ave., Camelback Corridor, 85016 ☎602/508–0937 ✏602/508–0854 ⊕www.phoenixbiltmore.homewood-suites.com ↩124 suites △In-room: kitchen, dial-up, ethernet, Wi-Fi. In-hotel: pool, gym, laundry facilities, laundry service, no-smoking rooms, public Wi-Fi ▭AE, D, DC, MC, V ⦿BP.

$$ 🏨 **Courtyard Phoenix Camelback.** Public areas in this four-story hotel are mostly glass and tile, and filled with greenery. Rooms are tastefully done with light-colored walls and accents like plush new bedding, cherry-wood armoires, and large, pullout desks to accommodate the business traveler. A lap pool and Jacuzzi await in the landscaped courtyard. A small café on premises serves breakfast, and there are more than 50 restaurants within a 1½-mi radius. ✉2101 E. Camelback Rd., Camelback Corridor, 85016 ☎602/955–5200 or 800/321–2211 ✏602/955–1101 ⊕www.camelbackcourtyard.com ↩155 rooms, 12 suites △In-room: refrigerator (some), ethernet. In-hotel: restaurant, pool, gym, laundry facilities, laundry service, parking (no fee) ▭AE, D, DC, MC, V.

$–$$ 🏨 **Phoenix Inn Suites.** Conveniently located and recently remodeled, this Camelback Corridor hotel is a heck of a deal. Done in subtle Southwestern hues, rooms are designed for the business traveler and are spacious, cool, and comfortable. Local calls and high-speed Internet access are free, and several rooms have jetted tubs. The four-story hotel is a block off Camelback Road. ✉2310 E. Highland Ave., Camelback Corridor, 85016 ☎602/956–5221 or 800/956–5221 ✏602/468–7220 ⊕www.phoenixinnsuites.com ↩120 suites △In-room: refrigerator,

WHERE TO STAY IN THE VALLEY OF THE SUN

	HOTEL NAME	Location	Worth Noting	Rooms	Restaurants	Bars	Pools	Spa	Golf Courses	Shopping	Near Major Venues
★ 1	Arizona Biltmore	Camelback Corridor	Quiet and sophisticated	811	4	2	8	yes	2	yes	yes
9	Best Western Inn Suites	Central Phoenix	Well priced, convenient north-central location	109			1			yes	
33	Buttes Marriott Resort	Tempe	Hillside resort near ASU	353	2	3	1	yes		yes	yes
26	Comfort Inn	North Scottsdale	Affordable Scottsdale location	124			1			yes	
20	Copper Wynd Resort and Club	Fountain Hills	Quiet, breathtaking Fountain Hills views	40	2	1	2	yes			
24	Country Inn & Suites	North Scottsdale	Scottsdale residential style	163			1			yes	
5	Courtyard Phoenix Camelback	Camelback Corridor	Great location, Marriott amenities	167	1		1			yes	
19	Crowne Plaza San Marcos Golf Resort	Chandler	Historic golf resort	295	2	2	1	yes	1	yes	
★ 22	Fairmont Scottsdale Princess	North Scottsdale	Home of TPC golf course and 6,300-seat tennis stadium	651	5	6	5	yes	2	yes	yes
★ 28	FireSky Resort & Spa	Scottsdale	Unique, upscale family fun	204	1	2	3			yes	yes
★ 21	Four Seasons Scottsdale at Troon North	North Scottsdale	Remote but luxurious desert mountain getaway	232	3	1	3	yes	1		
27	Gainey Suites Hotel	North Scottsdale	Chic boutique hotel	162	1	1	1			yes	
☆ 7	Hermosa Inn	Paradise Valley	A cozy getaway	35	1	1	1				
13	Hilton Suites	Central Phoenix	Comfortable, central location	226	1	1	1			yes	yes
2	Homewood Suites Phoenix-Biltmore	Camelback Corridor	Residential living, great location	124			1			yes	

★	#	Hotel	Description	Location									
	15	Hotel San Carlos	A historic downtown landmark	Downtown Phoenix	121	1	1					yes	
	31	Hotel Valley Ho	Retro metro chic	Downtown Scottsdale	210	3	3					yes	yes
	16	Hyatt Regency Phoenix	Prime downtown location, revolving rooftop restaurant	Downtown Phoenix	737	4	2	1	yes			yes	yes
	25	Hyatt Regency Scottsdale at Gainey Ranch	3-story waterslide	North Scottsdale	490	4	2	10	yes	3		yes	yes
★	11	JW Marriott Camelback Inn Resort, Golf Club & Spa	Upscale old-time Phoenix in stunning Paradise Valley location	Paradise Valley	480	6	3	3	yes	2		yes	
	12	JW Marriott Desert Ridge Resort & Spa	Luxury accommodations in new development	North Central Phoenix	950	9	3	5	yes	2		yes	
★	29	Phoenician	Luxury with a fabulous location	Camelback Corridor	647	6	2	9	yes	3		yes	yes
	3	Phoenix Inn Suites	Great location	Camelback Corridor	120	1	1	1				yes	
	8	Pointe Hilton at Squaw Peak	Unique, inner-city mountain resort	North Central Phoenix	562	3	3	2	yes			yes	
	18	Pointe South Mountain Resort	Great for families	South Phoenix	640	6	4	7		1		yes	
	30	Ramada Limited Scottsdale	Affordable downtown Scottsdale	Downtown Scottsdale	92	1	1					yes	yes
	4	Ritz-Carlton, Phoenix	In the heart of Camelback Corridor, across from Biltmore Fashion Park	Camelback Corridor	281	1	1	1	yes			yes	
★	6	Royal Palms Resort & Spa	Gorgeous foothill location	Camelback Corridor	182	1	1	1	yes			yes	
★	10	Sanctuary on Camelback Mountain	Modern amenities, spectacular views	Paradise Valley	98	1	1	3	yes			yes	
	17	Sheraton Wild Horse Pass Resort & Spa	Award-winning accommodations and dining	Chandler	500	4	3	4	yes	2		yes	yes
	23	Westin Kierland Resort & Spa	Central to fine shopping and dining	North Scottsdale	827	8	6	4	yes	1		yes	yes
	34	Wigwam Resort	Historic West Valley charm	Litchfield Park	331	2	2	2	yes	3		yes	yes
	14	Wyndham Phoenix	Prime downtown location	Downtown Phoenix	640	1	1	1				yes	yes

Phoenix & Paradise Valley ▼

Best Western Inn Suites Hotel **9**

Crowne Plaza San
Marcos Resort **19**

Hermosa Inn **7**

Hilton Suites **13**

Hotel San Carlos **15**

Hyatt Regency Phoenix **16**

JW Marriott's Camelback Inn **11**

JW Marriott Desert Ridge **12**

Pointe Hilton at Squaw Peak **8**

Pointe South
Mountain Resort **18**

Sanctuary on
Camelback Mountain **10**

Sheraton Wild Horse Pass **17**

Wyndham Phoenix **14**

Camelback Corridor ▼

Arizona Biltmore **1**

Courtyard Phoenix Camelback **5**

Homewood Suites **2**

Phoenix Inn Suites **3**

Ritz-Carlton **4**

Royal Palms **6**

Scottsdale ▼

Comfort Inn **26**

Country Inn & Suites **24**

Fairmont Scottsdale Princess **22**

FireSky Resort and Spa **28**

Four Seasons Scottsdale
at Troon North **21**

Gainey Suites Hotel **27**

Hotel Valley Ho **31**

Hyatt Regency Scottsdale at
Gainey Ranch **25**

The Phoenician **29**

Ramada Ltd. Scottsdale **30**

Westin Kierland **23**

Fountain Hills ▼

Copper Wynd Resort and Club **20**

Tempe ▼

The Buttes Marriot Resort **33**

Tempe Mission Palms Hotel **32**

Litchfield Park ▼

Wigwam Resort **34**

kitchen, dial-up, Wi-Fi. In-hotel: restaurant, bar, room service ⊟*AE, D, DC, MC, V* ⧫*CP.*

CENTRAL PHOENIX

$–$$$ **Hilton Suites.** This practical hotel is a model of excellent design within tight limits. It sits off Central Avenue, 2 mi north of downtown amid the Central Corridor cluster of office towers. The marble-floor, pillared lobby opens into an 11-story atrium with palm trees, natural boulder fountains, glass elevators, and a lantern-lit café. Each suite has a large walk-through bathroom between the living room and bedroom. The hotel offers a full breakfast and if you're up for more than a drink at the inviting lounge bar or dinner at the on-site chain restaurant, you can take the free shuttle service to other area eats and attractions. ⊠*10 E. Thomas Rd., Central Phoenix, 85012* ☏*602/222–1111* 🖷*602/265– 4841* ⊕*www.phoenixsuites.hilton.com* 🛏*226 suites* △*In-room: dial-up, ethernet (some), Wi-Fi. In-hotel: restaurant, room service, bar, pool, gym, concierge, laundry facilities, laundry service, parking (fee), no-smoking rooms, some pets allowed, public Wi-Fi* ⊟*AE, D, DC, MC, V* ⧫*BP.*

¢–$ **Best Western Inn Suites.** Just north of the Pointe Squaw Peak, this affordable all-suites hotel is often overlooked as an option in the neighborhood but it has the same proximity to everything as the Hilton, including great recreation areas (Piestewa Peak Mountain Preserve); great dining options (Convivo is nearby); and it's less than 1 mi from State Route 51, which offers quick and easy access to major freeways, Valley shopping, and Sky Harbor airport. The price is right, especially for the area. ⊠*1615 E. Northern Ave., Central Phoenix, 85020* ☏*602/997–6285* ⊕*www.bwsuite.com* 🛏*77 rooms, 32 2-room suites* △*In-room: ethernet, Wi-Fi. In-hotel: pool, gym, laundry service, parking (no fee), no-smoking rooms, some pets allowed, public Wi-Fi, no elevator* ⊟*AE, D, DC, MC, V.*

DOWNTOWN PHOENIX

$–$$$ **Hotel San Carlos.** Built in 1927 in an Italian Renaissance design, the seven-story San Carlos is the only historic hotel still operating in downtown Phoenix. Among other distinctions, the San Carlos was the Southwest's first air-conditioned hotel, and suites bear the names of such movie-star guests as Marilyn Monroe and Spencer Tracy. Big-band music, wall tapestries, Austrian crystal chandeliers, shiny copper elevators, and an accommodating staff transport you to a more genteel era. The rooms are snug by modern standards but have attractive period furnishings. An off-site fitness center accommodates guests for a small fee. ⊠*202 N. Central Ave., Downtown Phoenix, 85004* ☏*602/253–4121 or 866/253–4121* 🖷*602/253–6668* ⊕*www. hotelsancarlos.com* 🛏*109 rooms, 12 suites* △*In-room: dial-up, Wi-Fi. In-hotel: restaurant, pool, room service, laundry service, parking (fee), public Wi-Fi, no-smoking rooms* ⊟*AE, D, DC, MC, V.*

$-$$$ Hyatt Regency Phoenix. This convention-oriented hotel efficiently handles the arrival and departure of hundreds of business travelers each day. The seven-story atrium has huge sculptures, colorful tapestries, potted plants, and comfortable seating areas. Rooms are spacious, but the atrium roof blocks east views on floors 8 through 10. There's a revolving restaurant with panoramic views of the Phoenix area. ✉ *122 N. 2nd St., Downtown Phoenix, 85004* ☎ *602/252–1234* 📠 *602/254–9472* ⊕ *www.hyatt. com* 🛏 *712 rooms, 25 suites* ⚘ *In-room: dial-up. In-hotel: 4 restaurants, bars, pools, gym, concierge, parking (fee), no-smoking rooms* ☐ *AE, D, DC, MC, V.*

> **BEST LARGE-SCALE RESORTS**
>
> Arizona Biltmore, *Camelback Corridor*
>
> The Phoenician, *Camelback Corridor*
>
> Four Seasons Scottsdale at Troon North, *Scottsdale*
>
> Fairmont Scottsdale Princess, *Scottsdale*
>
> JW Marriott's Camelback Inn Resort, Golf Club & Spa, *Paradise Valley*

$-$$$ Wyndham Phoenix. When Wyndham took over this former Crowne Plaza, the chain invested $6 million to create an appealing mix of classic comfort and modern accommodations. Ideally situated for all things downtown (but little else) the hotel stands, with very little competition, in the center of bustling Copper Square within 1 mi of Heritage and Science Parks, America West Arena, Chase Field, and the Arizona Center. It's also near the light-rail and downtown renovation construction, which, although tedious, gives it a more appealing price tag. Spacious rooms with subtle Southwestern tones are designed for the business traveler, and are relatively quiet (in spite of construction), and well-lit with large desks and ergonomic desk chairs, but they're also kid-friendly, comfortable, and convenient for pro baseball and basketball fans, as well as theater, symphony, convention, and celebrity concert-goers. ■ TIP➔ **Coffee junkies will enjoy the on-site Starbucks.** ✉ *50 E. Adams St., Downtown Phoenix, 85004* ☎ *602/333–0000* ⊕ *www. wyndham.com* 🛏 *532 rooms, 108 suites* ⚘ *In-room: refrigerator (some), ethernet, dial-up, Wi-Fi (some). In-hotel: restaurant, room service, bar, pool, gym, laundry service, parking (fee), no-smoking rooms* ☐ *AE, D, DC, MC, V.*

NORTH PHOENIX

☼ $$-$$$$ JW Marriott Desert Ridge Resort & Spa. Arizona's largest resort has an immense entryway with floor-to-ceiling windows that allow the sandstone lobby, the Sonoran Desert, and the resort's amazing water features to meld together in a single prospect. Four acres of water fun include the popular "lazy river," where you can flop on an inner tube and float the day away. Young 'uns love the Kokopelli Kids program, while adults can rejuvenate at Revive Spa or tee off at the on-site golf courses. Each elegantly decorated room offers a balcony or patio. ✉ *5350 E. Marriott Dr., North Central Phoenix, 85054* ☎ *480/293–*

5000 or 800/835–6206 480/293-3600 *www.jwdesertridgeresort. com* 869 rooms, 81 suites In-room: safe, refrigerator (some), ethernet, dial-up. In-hotel: 9 restaurants, room service, bars, golf courses, tennis courts, pools, spa, bicycles, children's programs (ages 4–12), no-smoking rooms AE, D, DC, MC, V.

$–$$$ **Pointe Hilton at Squaw Peak.** The highlight of the family-oriented Squaw Peak is the 9-acre recreation area *Hole-in-the-Wall River Ranch.* It has swimming pools with waterfalls, a 130-foot water slide, and a 1,000-foot "river" that winds past a miniature golf course, tennis courts, and artificial buttes. Accommodations in the pink-stucco buildings vary from standard two-room suites to a grand three-bedroom house; all have balconies. The resort is adjacent to the Phoenix Mountain Preserve, making it an ideal base for hiking and biking trips. Kids can enjoy the "Coyote Camp" youth programs while adults take in area golf and the Tocasierra Spa. *7677 N. 16th St., North Central Phoenix, 85020* 602/997-2626 or 800/876-4683 602/997-2391 *www.pointehilton.com* 431 suites, 130 casitas, 1 house In-room: kitchen (some), refrigerators (some), dial-up, ethernet (some). In-hotel: 3 restaurants, bars, tennis courts, pools, gym, spa, bicycles, children's programs (ages 6–12), no-smoking rooms, parking (no fee) AE, D, DC, MC, V.

PARADISE VALLEY

★ $$$$ **JW Marriott's Camelback Inn Resort, Golf Club & Spa.** This historic resort is a swank spot for relaxation in the gorgeous valley between Camelback and Mummy mountains. Built on 125 acres in the mid-1930s, the latilla (peeled log) beam buildings ooze Southwestern charm, and the grounds are adorned with stunning cacti and desert flowers. Rooms are spacious, and seven suites have private swimming pools. Visit the spa for a parajoba body wrap or an adobe-mud purification treatment. *5402 E. Lincoln Dr., Paradise Valley 85253* 480/948-1700 or 800/242-2635 480/951-8469 *www.camelbackinn.com* 453 rooms, 27 suites In-room: kitchen (some), ethernet. In-hotel: 6 restaurants, bar, golf courses, tennis courts, pools, spa, children's programs (ages 5–12), parking (no fee), no-smoking rooms AE, D, DC, MC, V.

$$$–$$$$ **Sanctuary on Camelback Mountain.** This luxurious boutique hotel is
Fodor'sChoice the only resort on the north slope of Camelback Mountain. Secluded
★ mountain casitas are painted in desert hues and feature breathtaking views of Paradise Valley. Chic spa casitas surround the pool and are outfitted with contemporary furnishings and private patios. Bathrooms are travertine marble with elegant sinks and roomy tubs. For those who enjoy going *eau* and even *au naturel,* some suites have outdoor tubs. An infinity-edge pool, Zen meditation garden, and Asian-inspired Sanctuary Spa make this a haven for relaxation. The hotel's restaurant, elements ($$$), is the hotspot for cocktails at sunset. *5700 E. McDonald Dr., Paradise Valley 85253* 480/948-2100 or 800/245-2051 480/483-7314 *www.sanctuaryaz.com* 98 casitas In-room: kitchen (some), refrigerator (some), dial-up, ethernet, Wi-Fi.

In-hotel: restaurant, room service, bar, tennis courts, pools, gym, spa, parking (no fee), no-smoking rooms, no elevator, public Wi-Fi ☰*AE, D, DC, MC, V.*

$$–$$$$
Fodor'sChoice
★

Hermosa Inn. The ranch-style lodge at the heart of this small resort was the home and studio of cowboy artist Lon Megargee in the 1930s; today the adobe structure houses Lon's at the Hermosa, justly popular for its new-American cuisine. Villas as big as private homes and individually decorated casitas hold an enviable collection of art. The Hermosa, on 6 acres of lushly landscaped desert, is a blessedly peaceful alternative to some of the larger resorts. ⊠*5532 N. Palo Cristi Rd., Paradise Valley 85253* ☎*602/955–8614 or 800/241–1210* 🖷*602/955–8299* ⊕*www.hermosainn.com* 🛏*4 villas, 3 haciendas, 11 casitas, 17 ranchos* 🖒*In-room: kitchen (some), refrigerator (some), dial-up, Wi-Fi. In-hotel: restaurant, bar, pool, parking (no fee), no-smoking rooms, public Wi-Fi* ☰*AE, D, DC, MC, V* ⚏*CP.*

SCOTTSDALE

☾ ★ **$$$$**

Fairmont Scottsdale Princess. Home of the Tournament Players Club Stadium golf course and the FBR Phoenix Open, this resort covers 450 breathtakingly landscaped acres of desert. Willow Stream Spa, one of the top spa spots in the country, has a dramatic rooftop pool and kids love the fishing pond and water slides. Rooms are done in Southwestern style and service is what you'd expect at a resort of this caliber: excellent and unobtrusive. Even pets get the royal treatment: a specially designated pet room comes with treats and turn-down service. ⊠*7575 E. Princess Dr., North Scottsdale, 85255* ☎*480/585–4848 or 800/344–4758* 🖷*480/585–0091* ⊕*www.fairmont.com* 🛏*458 rooms, 119 casitas, 72 villas, 2 suites* 🖒*In-room: safe, dial-up (some). In-hotel: 5 restaurants, bars, golf courses, tennis courts, pools, gym, spa, children's programs (ages 6–12), parking (no fee), no-smoking rooms, some pets allowed* ☰*AE, D, DC, MC, V.*

☾ ★ **$$$$**

Four Seasons Scottsdale at Troon North. This is a logical choice for serious golfers as it's adjacent to two Troon North premier courses where guests receive preferential tee times and free shuttle service. The resort is tucked in the shadows of Pinnacle Peak, near the Pinnacle Peak hiking trail. Large, casita-style rooms have separate sitting and sleeping areas as well as outdoor garden showers, fireplaces, and balconies or patios. Suites come with telescopes and star charts. Acacia ($$$–$$$$), the hotel's main restaurant, is elegant and accommodating. ⊠*10600 E. Crescent Moon Dr., North Scottsdale, 85262* ☎*480/515–5700 or 888/207–9696* 🖷*480/515–5599* ⊕*www.fourseasons.com* 🛏*210 rooms, 22 suites* 🖒*In-room: safe, refrigerator (some), dial-up, ethernet, Wi-Fi (some). In-hotel: 3 restaurants, bar, tennis courts, pools, gym, golf course, spa, children's programs (ages 5–12), laundry service, parking (no fee), no-smoking rooms* ☰*AE, D, DC, MC, V.*

☾ **$$$$**
Fodor'sChoice
★

The Phoenician. In a town where luxurious, expensive resorts are the rule, the Phoenician still stands apart, primarily in the realm of service. The gilded, marbled lobby with towering fountains is the backdrop for the $25 million fine art collection. Large rooms, in the main

Top Spas in the Valley of the Sun

The Valley of the Sun is all about relaxation and there's no better place for it than at one of Phoenix's rejuvenating resort spas. Many feature Native American–inspired treatments and use indigenous ingredients such as agave, desert clay, and neroli oil (derived from orange blossoms). Try to enjoy not only the treatments but the spa amenities, including pools, whirlpools, eucalyptus steam rooms, and relaxation areas with outdoor fireplaces. *For contact information, see Where to Stay, earlier in this chapter. Prices are subject to change.*

Aji Spa at the Sheraton Wild Horse Pass Resort & Spa. A gem on the grounds of the Gila River Indian community, Aji incorporates its Native American surroundings into every aspect of the spa, from the name ("Aji" is Pima for sanctuary) to its Sonoran design and treatments. The Blue Coyote Wrap ($185 for 80 minutes) begins with a dry brush exfoliation and an application of Azulene mud, and culminates with a cedar–sage oil massage; the 50-minute *Tashogith* white-clay facial ($125) is luxurious. Massages start at 50 minutes for $125.

Alvadora at the Royal Palms Resort & Spa. Romance is not limited to the restaurant and rooms at this Mediterranean-style villa, complete with its own pool and salon, where treatments incorporate herbs, flowers, oils, and minerals indigenous to the Mediterranean. The Orange Blossom Body Buff is a signature treatment: a full body scrub using the *scent*ilating powers of neroli oil, and the Fango Mud Wrap promises good cleansing ($125–$135). The massage menu ranges from a 60-minute classic ($125) to the two-therapist Quattro de Palma ($225) and couples massage sessions ($250–$390). Spa use for nonresort guests is only Sunday through Thursday and requires purchase of a spa package.

Golden Door Spa at The Boulders Resort. If you're seeking the serenity of the desert, this is your place. Influenced by the Asian and Native American cultures, the spa is divided into two wings—east for relaxation and west for activity. Try a Native American–inspired treatment like the Turquoise Wrap ($130 for 50 minutes), which includes a Hopi blue-cornmeal body scrub and a turquoise clay wrap, or surrender to an Asian-inspired 50-minute Shiatsu massage ($140). A 50-minute massage is $130.

The Spa at JW Marriott's Camelback Inn. This is one of the Valley's most popular spas. Aches and pains will melt away with the 60-minute Native Hot Stone Massage (starts at $125); the Sonoran Rose Facial is two treatments in one and incorporates the hands and arms ($135). A 60-minute massage starts at $110. The Comfy leather chairs and a large TV in the men's spa lounge, and private poolside cabanas will make even the most hesitant spa-goer feel at home.

Sanctuary Spa at Sanctuary on Camelback Mountain. This sleek Zen-like spa has 11 Asian-inspired indoor–outdoor treatment rooms nestled against Camelback Mountain. Try a Watsu in-water body massage ($135–$195), a transporting 30-minute Thai Foot Reflexology massage ($135), or a Bamboo Lemongrass Scrub ($85–$195). A 60-minute massage starts at $135. Spa use is restricted to resort guests only.

Willow Stream Spa at the Fairmont Scottsdale Princess. This is one of the Valley's most elaborate spas. Inspired by "Havasupai," a hidden oasis in the Grand Canyon, there's water everywhere—from the rooftop pool to streams that flow throughout the resort's grounds. Amid this luxury, you can splurge for the two-hour Havasupai Body Treatment ($319), in which aches and pains are kneaded away under three waterfalls of varying pressure. It includes a eucalyptus foot massage, a body scrub, a soak in a private tub, and a body, face, and scalp massage. A 60-minute massage starts at about $160.

Avania Spa at the Hyatt Regency Scottsdale at Gainey Ranch. Spa Avania's claim to fame is that it's "the first complete spa experience choreographed to your body's perfect timing": the gorgeous stone-tiled spa seeks to cleanse the body of unnatural stimuli and give equilibrium through the senses, the way nature intended. Specialty treatments include a 60-minute blackberry-balm hand massage ($80) and golfer massage ($140). Two- to four-hour spa packages range from $279 to $468.

VH Spa at the Hotel Valley Ho. After seeing the rebirth of the Hotel Valley Ho, guests should feel comfortable entrusting renovation of the body and soul to the hip, colored-glass VH Spa (VH stands for Vitality and Health). Create your own 60-minute spa experience for $125 or go à la carte with the unique Red Flower Hammam Full-Body Treatment Massage, a Turkish-inspired detoxification that scrubs the skin with coffee, olive stones, and fresh lemon ($95–$185).

Revive Spa at JW Marriott Desert Ridge Resort. A 28,000-square-foot, two-story temple devoted to the health and healing of the human body, Revive at Desert Ridge features 41 luxury treatment rooms, an Olympic-size swimming pool, private balconies for outdoor massages, indoor relaxation rooms with fireplaces, outdoor celestial showers, a rooftop garden with flowing water, a healthful bistro, a fitness center, and a full salon. A pumpkin enzyme peeling masque is just $20; a caviar facial is $195. Massages range $125–$190 and body treatments range $125–$290.

Four Seasons Troon North. The elegant Spa at Four Seasons Troon North is a little bit of heaven, hidden in the serene foothills of the Sonoran desert. The list of massage options seems endless and includes a 50-minute Head Over Heals rub with two therapists at once ($280), or an 80-minute moonlight balcony massage ($275). Body treatments range from $85 to $195. Try the 80-minute, Four Seasons-In-One package with four treatments for $195 or the Golfers Massage in which muscles are kneaded with warmed golf balls.

Jurlique Spa at FireSky Resort and Spa. With its unforgettably elegant and relaxing interior, it's appropriate that Jurlique focuses on repairing and restoring from within. Relying on plant science and a combination of Eastern and Western spa philosophies, the spa brings together some of the best restoration and relaxation money can buy. Try a 90-minute Zen Harmony facial or any 90-minute massage for $190. One-and-a-half- to 6½-hour spa packages range from $175 to $620. The herbal water therapies are heaven "scent."

building and outer-lying casitas are decorated with elegant 1960s furniture and have private patios and oversize marble bathrooms. There's a secluded tennis garden and 27 holes of premier golf. The Centre for Well Being Spa has a meditation atrium and a pool lined with mother-of-pearl tiles where you can drift off to another world. Afterward, you can take in a sophisticated afternoon tea, or save your energy and money for a night at Mary Elaine's ($$$$), one of the finest (and most expensive) restaurants in the state. ⊠6000 E. Camelback Rd., Camelback Corridor, 85251 ☎480/941–8200 or 800/888–8234 ☐480/947–4311

BEST RESORTS WITH KIDS
Fairmont Scottsdale Princess, *Scottsdale*
Westin Kierland Resort & Spa, *Scottsdale*
The Buttes Marriott Resort, *Tempe*
JW Marriott Desert Ridge Resort & Spa, *North Central Phoenix*
Sheraton Wild Horse Pass Resort & Spa, *Chandler*
Pointe Hilton at Squaw Peak, *North Central Phoenix*

⊕www.thephoenician.com ⬭574 rooms, 73 suites ⚘In-room: safe, refrigerator (some), dial-up, ethernet. In-hotel: 6 restaurants, bars, room service, golf courses, tennis courts, pools, gym, children's programs (ages 5–12), parking (no fee), no-smoking rooms, public Wi-Fi ⊟AE, D, DC, MC, V.

☾ ★   🖼 **FireSky Resort & Spa.** The founder of the company that owns this
$$–$$$$ property believed that a hotel should "relieve travelers of their insecurity and loneliness," and this resort prides itself on intimate, eco- and family-friendly boutique environments. An attentive staff focus on even the smallest details—personal and professional—to anticipate and alleviate worries. Luxury rooms with patios have crisp linens, cozy bathrobes, and brand-name bath amenities, and the spa, Jurlique, offers massages and treatments that the muscles will remember fondly. A hosted wine reception is offered to guests nightly from 5 PM to 6 PM. And if that weren't enough to soothe the soul, the resort also soothes the *soles*, with its sand-bottom pool. Kids of all ages love FireSky's "S'more Kits," cooked over the outdoor fire pits. ⊠4925 N. Scottsdale Rd., Scottsdale, 85251 ☎480/945–7666 or 800/528–7867 ☐480/946–4056 ⊕www.fireskyresort.com ⬭196 rooms, 7 suites, 1 presidential suite ⚘In-room: refrigerator (some), Wi-Fi. In-hotel: restaurant, bars, pools, no-smoking rooms, some pets allowed, public Internet, public Wi-Fi, no elevator ⊟AE, D, DC, MC, V.

$$–$$$$ 🖼 **Hotel Valley Ho.** One of Scottsdale's newest hotels is actually one of its oldest. Originally opened in 1956, it was a hangout for celebrities including Natalie Wood, Robert Wagner, and Tony Curtis. After a long stint as a Ramada, the hotel was purchased in 2001 and restored to its former '50s fabulousness—complete with Trader Vic's ($$–$$$), the hotel's original restaurant. A large pool is at the heart of this Frank Lloyd Wright–inspired hotel, surrounded by a two-story, U-shaped building of guest rooms, lush landscaping, and an outdoor grill and dining area. A 6,000-square-foot spa, a fitness center, and 10,000 square feet

of meeting space have been added. ✉ *6850 E. Main St., Downtown Scottsdale, 85251* ☎ *480/248–2000* 🖨 *480/248–2002* ⊕ *www.hotel valleyho.com* ➴ *188 rooms, 6 suites, 16 residential condos.* ⚅ *In-room: dial-up, ethernet, Wi-Fi. In-hotel: 3 restaurants, bars, pool, gym, spa, no-smoking rooms, public Wi-Fi* ☰ *AE, D, DC, MC, V.*

☼ **$$–$$$$** ⊞ **Hyatt Regency Scottsdale at Gainey Ranch.** When you stay here, it's easy to imagine that you're relaxing at an oceanside resort instead of the desert. Shaded by towering palms,

BEST RESORTS FOR GOLFERS

Four Seasons Scottsdale at Troon North, *Scottsdale*

The Phoenician, *Camelback Corridor*

Hyatt Regency Scottsdale at Gainey Ranch, *Scottsdale*

Crowne Plaza San Marcos Golf Resort, *Chandler*

with manicured gardens and paths, the property has water everywhere—a large pool area has a beach, a three-story waterslide, waterfalls, and a lagoon. The two-story lobby, filled with Native American art, opens to outdoor conversation areas where fires burn in stone fireplaces on cool nights. Large rooms have balconies or patios. Three golf courses at nearby Gainey Ranch Golf Club will suit any duffer's fancy. Spa Avania aims to soothe the soul, while kids get their kicks at Camp Hyatt. ✉ *7500 E. Doubletree Ranch Rd., North Scottsdale, 85258* ☎ *480/444–1234 or 800/233–1234* 🖨 *480/483–5550* ⊕ *www.scotts dale.hyatt.com* ➴ *461 rooms, 7 casitas, 22 suites* ⚅ *In-room: dial-up, ethernet, Wi-Fi. In-hotel: 4 restaurants, bars, golf courses, tennis courts, pools, gym, spa, bicycles, children's programs (ages 3–12), executive floor, parking (no fee), no-smoking rooms* ☰ *AE, D, DC, MC, V.*

$–$$$$ ⊞ **Gainey Suites Hotel.** This independently owned boutique hotel is a rare find in both amenities and price. Floorplans vary from studios to two-bedroom suites that sleep eight, all with fully equipped kitchens and flat-panel widescreen TVs. Cozy conversation areas in the lobby and an evening hors d'oeuvres reception create a warm atmosphere. The hotel is directly adjacent to the Gainey Village development, with boutique shopping and upscale dining, as well as a spa. Golfers are not forgotten; the hotel can book tee times at more than 60 courses in the area. ✉ *7300 East Gainey Suites Dr., North Scottsdale, 85258* ☎ *480/922–6969 or 800/970–4666* 🖨 *480/922–1689* ⊕ *www. gaineysuiteshotel.com* ➴ *162 suites* ⚅ *In-room: kitchen, refrigerator, ethernet, dial-up, Wi-Fi. In-hotel: pool, gym, laundry facilities, no-smoking rooms, public Wi-Fi* ☰ *AE, D, MC, V* ⎝⊙⎠ *CP.*

☼ **$–$$$$** ⊞ **Westin Kierland Resort & Spa.** Original artwork by Arizona artists is displayed throughout the Westin Kierland and the spacious rooms all have balconies or patios with views of the mountains or the resort's waterpark and tubing river, where kids can enjoy programs like "Club Teen." Kierland Commons, within walking distance, is a planned village of upscale specialty boutiques and restaurants. Of the eight restaurants, Deseo ($$$–$$$$) is the star, presided over by well-known chef Douglas Rodriguez, regarded as the inventor of Nuevo Latino cuisine.

✉6902 E. Greenway Pkwy., North Scottsdale, 85254 ☎480/624–1000 📠480/624–1001 ⊕www.kierlandresort.com ⛫732 rooms, 63 suites, 32 casitas ⚘In-room: dial-up, refrigerator (some), ethernet, Wi-Fi. In-hotel: 8 restaurants, bars, golf courses, tennis courts, pools, gym, spa, children's programs (ages 4–17), parking (no fee), no-smoking rooms, public Wi-Fi ⊟AE, D, DC, MC, V.

¢–$$ ☷ **Comfort Inn.** This may be one of the nicest Comfort Inns you'll ever lay your eyes on, and it's in a quiet, upscale North Scottsdale neighborhood along the Scottsdale Road corridor. The three-story glass entryway is as welcoming as the enthusiastic staff inside. Rooms are utilitarian but clean and have free HBO. There are trendy restaurants and shopping opportunities within easy walking distance, making this a comfortable, affordable, and family-friendly alternative in a town filled with expensive resorts. ✉7350 E. Gold Dust Rd., at Scottsdale Rd., North Scottsdale, 85258 ☎480/596–6559 or 888/296–9776 📠480/596–0554 ⊕www.comfortinn.com ⛫123 rooms, 1 suite ⚘In-room: refrigerator, dial-up, Wi-Fi. In-hotel: pool, gym, public Wi-Fi, parking (no fee), no-smoking rooms ⊟AE, D, DC, MC, V ⛾CP.

⚘ ¢–$$ ☷ **Country Inn & Suites.** The reasonable price and prime location—within a block of shops and restaurants and a half-block from the Loop 101 Freeway—make this chain outpost a great bargain. The cozy lobby has comfortable seating around a flagstone fireplace. Several specialty suites offer fireplaces and whirlpool baths. A complimentary, 21-item breakfast is offered daily and soup and crackers are served nightly at 9 PM, Monday to Friday. A complimentary shuttle takes guests anywhere within 5 mi of the hotel. ✉10801 N. 89th Pl., North Scottsdale, 85260 ☎480/314–1200 or 800/456–4000 📠480/314–7367 ⊕www.countryinns.com ⛫91 rooms, 72 suites ⚘In-room: refrigerator, kitchen, dial-up, Wi-Fi. In-hotel: pool, gym, parking (no fee), no-smoking rooms, some pets allowed, public Wi-Fi ⊟AE, D, DC, MC, V ⛾CP.

¢–$ ☷ **Ramada Limited Scottsdale.** There are two attractive things about this exterior-corridor, three-story motel: the location, which is within walking distance of Scottsdale's Old Town, and the price, which includes complimentary Continental breakfast. The simple but clean rooms have standard, serviceable furnishings. ✉6935 E. 5th Ave., Downtown Scottsdale, 85251 ☎480/994–9461 or 800/528–7396 📠480/947–1695 ⊕www.RamadaScottsdale.com ⛫92 rooms ⚘In-room: refrigerator, dial-up, Wi-Fi. In-hotel: pool, gym, laundry facilities, parking (no fee), no-smoking rooms, some pets allowed ⊟AE, D, DC, MC, V ⛾CP.

SOUTH PHOENIX

⚘ $$–$$$$ ☷ **Sheraton Wild Horse Pass Resort & Spa.** On the grounds of the Gila River Indian community, 11 mi south of Sky Harbor Airport, the culture and heritage of the Pima and Maricopa tribes are reflected in every aspect of this property. Guest rooms are detailed with Native art and textiles, and Kai (Pima for "seed") Restaurant ($$$–$$$$) combines Southwestern and Native culinary traditions. Families enjoy the Koli Center for on-site equestrian activities and the kids-oriented activity pool. A 2½-mi replica of the Gila River meanders through the property; you can take a boat to the Whirlwind Golf Clubhouse, the nearby Wild Horse Pass Casino, or Rawhide Western Town. Keep your eyes open for the wild horses for which the resort is named—or keep them comfortably closed at the Aji Spa. ☒*5594 W. Wild Horse Pass Blvd., Chandler 85226* ☎*602/225–0100 or 800/325–3535* 🖷*602/225–0300* ⊕*www.wildhorsepassresort.com* 🛏*474 rooms, 26 suites* ♿*In-room: safe, dial-up, ethernet, refrigerator (some). In-hotel: 4 restaurants, bars, golf courses, tennis courts, pools, gym, spa, laundry service, parking (no fee), no-smoking rooms, public Wi-Fi* ⊟*AE, D, DC, MC, V.*

🕑 **$-$$$$** 🏨 **Pointe South Mountain Resort.** This all-suites resort next to South Mountain Park has a golf course and "Oasis," the largest water park in Arizona—guests can tube down a river, splash in the wave pool, or zoom down the nation's tallest water slide. There is a four-story sports center, golf, tennis, horseback riding, and mountain biking. ☒*7777 S. Pointe Pkwy., South Phoenix, 85044* ☎*602/438–9000 or 877/800–4888* 🖷*602/431–6535* ⊕*www.pointesouthmtn.com* 🛏*640 suites* ♿*In-room: dial-up, ethernet, refrigerators (some). In-hotel: 6 restaurants, bars, room service, golf course, tennis courts, pools, gym, bicycles, laundry facilities, public Wi-Fi, parking (no fee)* ⊟*AE, D, DC, MC, V.*

TEMPE, MESA & CHANDLER

$$$-$$$$ 🏨 **Wynd Resort and Club.** Nestled high on a mountain ridge above Scottsdale and Fountain Hills, this secluded resort offers breathtaking views of mountains and the Sonoran Desert. Luxurious guest rooms have imported handmade furniture, granite counters, fireplaces, custom linens, and a private terrace overlooking serene desert vistas. The expansive two- and three-bedroom villas are equipped with kitchens, washers and dryers, and private garages. The Spa at CopperWynd is one of the top spas in the area, and Alchemy, the resort's restaurant ($$$–$$$$), is perfect for a romantic evening. ☒*13225 N. Eagle Ridge Dr., Fountain Hills 85268* ☎*480/333–1900 or 877/707–7760* 🖷*480/333–1901* ⊕*www.copperwynd.com* 🛏*32 rooms, 8 villas* ♿*In-room: dial-up (some), Wi-Fi (some). In-hotel: 2 restaurants, bar, tennis courts, pools, gym, spa, no-smoking rooms, public Wi-Fi* ⊟*AE, D, DC, MC, V.*

🕑 **$$-$$$$** 🏨 **Crowne Plaza San Marcos Golf Resort.** When it opened in 1912, the San Marcos was the first golf resort in Arizona and it's still one of the state's most treasured landmarks. Now part of the Crowne Plaza family, the palm-studded, mission-style San Marcos has undergone luxury upgrades to keep it on par with the competition, while maintaining its historic beauty and charm. Improvements include the Images day spa and restyled rooms with pillow-top mattresses, high-thread-count sheets, and down-filled duvets. Each room and suite has either a balcony or patio and the quiet, single-level golf-course casitas offer patios with "Fore!-star" views. ■**TIP**➡**The resort operates an on-site Starbucks and there's great nearby shopping and dining.** ☒*One San Marcos Pl., Chandler 85225* ☎*480/812–0900* 🖷*480/899–5441* ⊕*www.sanmarcosresort. com* 🛏*238 rooms, 45 casitas, 12 suites* ♿*In-room: ethernet, dial-up.*

In-hotel: 2 restaurants, room service, bars, golf course, pools, spa, parking (no fee), no-smoking rooms ▤*AE, D, DC, MC, V.*

☼ $–$$$ ▦ **The Buttes Marriott Resort.** Two miles east of Sky Harbor airport, nestled in desert buttes at I–10 and AZ 60, this hotel joins dramatic architecture (the lobby's back wall is the volcanic rock itself) and classic Southwest design (pine and saguaro-rib furniture, works by major regional artists) with stunning Valley views. Recently purchased by Marriott, the Buttes is set to become a top relaxation destination with its "Revive"-themed spa facility. "Radial" rooms are the largest; inside rooms face the huge free-form pools with waterfall, hot tubs, and a poolside cantina. The Top of the Rock restaurant is elegant. Kids enjoy summer activities such as Saturday "duck hunts" and cooking with the resort chefs. ✉*2000 Westcourt Way, Tempe 85282* ☎*602/225–9000 or 800/843–1986* 🖷*602/438–8622* ⊕*www.marriott.com.com* ⇆*345 rooms, 8 suites* ♿*In-room: refrigerator (some), dial-up, Wi-Fi. In-hotel: 2 restaurants, bars, tennis courts, pool, gym, spa, laundry service, executive floor, parking (no fee), no-smoking rooms, some pets allowed, public Wi-Fi* ▤*AE, D, DC, MC, V.*

$–$$$ ▦ **Tempe Mission Palms Hotel.** A handsome, casual lobby and an energetic young staff set the tone at this three-story courtyard hotel. Rooms are Southwestern in style, and quite comfortable. Between the Arizona State University campus and Old Town Tempe, this is a convenient place to stay if you're attending ASU sports events, and Harry's Bar becomes a lively sports lounge at game time. ✉*60 E. 5th St., Tempe 85281* ☎*480/894–1400 or 800/547–8705* 🖷*480/968–7677* ⊕*www.missionpalms.com* ⇆*297 rooms, 6 suites* ♿*In-room: refrigerator (some), dial-up, ethernet, Wi-Fi. In-hotel: restaurant, room service, bar, tennis courts, pool, gym, airport shuttle, parking (no fee), no-smoking rooms, public Wi-Fi* ▤*AE, D, DC, MC, V.*

BEST SMALL/ QUIRKY RESORTS
Hermosa Inn, *Paradise Valley*
Sheraton Wild Horse Pass Spa & Resort, *Chandler*
Sanctuary on Camelback Mountain, *Paradise Valley*
Royal Palms Resort & Spa, *Camelback Corridor*
Wigwam Resort, *West Phoenix*

WEST PHOENIX, GLENDALE, LITCHFIELD PARK

$$$$ ▦ **Wigwam Resort.** Built in 1918 as a retreat for executives of the Goodyear Company, the Wigwam has the pleasing feel of an upscale lodge. Casita-style rooms along paths overflowing with cacti, palms, and bougainvillea, are decorated in Southwestern style with distressed-wood furniture, iron lamps, and brightly patterned spreads. Local art adorns the walls, and all rooms have patios. This isolated world of graciousness inspires a fierce loyalty in its guests, some of whom have been returning for more than 50 years. ✉*300 Wigwam Blvd., Litchfield Park 85340* ☎*623/935–3811 or 800/327–0396* 🖷*623/935–3737* ⊕*www.wigwamresort.com* ⇆*261 rooms, 70 suites* ♿*In-hotel: 2 restaurants, bars, golf courses, tennis courts, pools, gym, spa, children's programs (ages 6–12), parking (no fee)* ▤*AE, D, DC, MC, V.*

NIGHTLIFE & THE ARTS

1

THE ARTS

For weekly listings of theater, arts, and music, check out "The Rep Entertainment Guide" in Thursday's *Arizona Republic,* pick up a free issue of the independent weekly *New Times,* the weekly *Get Out* in Thursday's *East Valley Tribune* (or free on newsstands), or check out *Where Phoenix/Scottsdale Magazine,* available free in most hotels. A good online source of information on events in the Valley is ⊕*www. digitalcity.com,* and the online arm of the *Arizona Republic* (⊕*www. azcentral.com*) has extensive nightlife and arts listings.

TICKETS **Arizona State University Public Events Box Office** (☎*480/965–6447* ⊕*www.herbergercollege.asu.edu*) sells tickets for ASU events. **Tickets. com** (⊕*www.tickets.com*) sells tickets for ASU Public Events at Grady Gammage Auditorium, Kerr Theatre, and the Maricopa County Events Center, formerly the ASU Sundome. **Ticketmaster** (☎*480/784–4444* ⊕*www.ticketmaster.com*) sells tickets for nearly every event in the Valley and has outlets at all Robinsons-May department stores, Fry's, Wherehouse, and Tower Records stores.

MAJOR PERFORMANCE VENUES

To feed its growing tourism industry Phoenix has cooked up enticing entertainment venues that attract everything from major league sporting events to the hottest music acts and the most raved about theater productions.

PHOENIX The **Celebrity Theatre** (⊠*440 N. 32nd St., Central Phoenix* ☎*602/267– 1600* ⊕*www.celebritytheatre.com*) is a 2,600-seat theater-in-the-round hosting concerts and other live performances.

Cricket Pavilion (⊠*2121 N. 83rd Ave., West Valley* ☎*602/254–7200* ⊕*www.cricket-pavilion.com*) is an outdoor amphitheater that books live concerts like Counting Crows, the Goo-Goo Dolls, and the annual VANS's Warped Tour.

The **Dodge Theatre** (⊠*400 W. Washington St., Downtown Phoenix* ☎*602/379–2800* ⊕*www.dodgetheatre.com*) is Phoenix's high-tech, state-of-the-art entertainment venue. The space morphs from an intimate Broadway stage setup to a concert hall seating 5,000. There are great views from almost every seat.

The **Herberger Theater Center** (⊠*222 E. Monroe St., Downtown Phoenix* ☎*602/254–7399* ⊕*www.herbergertheater.org*) is the permanent home of the Arizona Theatre Company and Actors Theatre of Phoenix; it also hosts performances of visiting dance troupes, orchestras, and Broadway shows.

The **Mesa Arts Center** (⊠*1 E. Main St., Mesa* ☎*480/644–6500* ⊕*www. mesaartscenter.com*) has risen to the demand for culture and creative art and is fast becoming one of the Valley's top destinations for exhibits, visual art performances, and A-list concerts.

The **Orpheum Theatre** ($\boxtimes$*203 W. Adams St., Downtown Phoenix* ☎*602/534–5600, 602/262–7272 box office*), built in 1927 and renovated throughout the '90s, is a glamorous theater showcasing the Arizona Ballet, children's theater, and film festivals.

Facing the Herberger Theater is **Symphony Hall** ($\boxtimes$*225 E. Adams St., Downtown Phoenix* ☎*602/534–5600* $\oplus$*www.phoenixsymphony. org*), home of the Phoenix Symphony and Arizona Opera.

SCOTTSDALE **Kerr Cultural Center** ($\boxtimes$*6110 N. Scottsdale Rd., Central Scottsdale* ☎*480/965–5377* $\oplus$*www.asukerr.com*) showcases smaller theater and dance performances.

Scottsdale Center for the Arts ($\boxtimes$*7380 E. 2nd St., Downtown Scottsdale* ☎*480/994–2787* $\oplus$*www.scottsdalearts.org*) hosts cultural events on the Scottsdale Mall as well as year-round performances in two intimate theater settings.

TEMPE Frank Lloyd Wright designed the **Gammage Auditorium** ($\boxtimes$*Arizona State University, Mill Ave. at Apache Blvd., Tempe* ☎*480/965–3434* $\oplus$*www.asugammage.com*), where you can see most Broadway shows that reach the area. Note that lines for the ladies' limited restroom facilities are usually long.

Herberger College of Fine Arts at Arizona State University ($\boxtimes$*Arizona State University, Mill Ave. at Apache Blvd., Tempe* ☎*480/965–6447* $\oplus$*www.herbergercollege.asu.edu*) includes Katzin Concert Hall, Lyceum Theatre, Galvin Playhouse, and the Evelyn Smith Music Theatre and Organ Hall, which houses an 1,800-pipe Fritts Organ. Numerous performances are offered during the school year, from September through April, and many are free.

The **Maricopa County Events Center** ($\boxtimes$*19403 R. H. Johnson Blvd., Sun City West* ☎*623/975–1900* $\oplus$*www.maricopa.gov*) sits in the far West Valley yet attracts national tours of comedians and musicians.

CLASSICAL MUSIC

Arizona Opera ($\boxtimes$*4600 N. 12th St., Downtown Phoenix* ☎*602/266–7464* $\oplus$*www.azopera.com*) stages an opera season, primarily classical, in both Tucson and Phoenix. The Phoenix season runs from October to March at Symphony Hall.

Phoenix Symphony Orchestra ($\boxtimes$*Arizona Center, 455 N. 3rd St., Suite 390, Downtown Phoenix* ☎*602/495–1999* $\oplus$*www.phoenixsymphony. org*) is the resident company at Symphony Hall. Its season, which runs September through May, includes orchestral works from classical and contemporary composers, a chamber series, composer festivals, and outdoor Pops concerts.

DANCE

Ballet Arizona (☎*602/381–1096* $\oplus$*www.balletaz.org*), the state's professional ballet company, presents a full season of classical and contemporary works (including pieces commissioned for the company) in Tucson and Phoenix, where it performs at the Orpheum Theater, downtown. The season runs from October through May.

THEATER

Actors Theatre of Phoenix (⌂*Box 1924, Phoenix 85001* ☎*602/253–6701* ⊕*www.atphx.org*) is the resident theater troupe at the Herberger Theater Center. The theater presents a full season of drama, comedy, and musical productions; it runs from September through May.

Arizona Theatre Company (✉*808 N. 1st St.* ☎*602/252–8497* ⊕*www.aztheatreco.org*) is the only resident company in the country with a two-city (Tucson and Phoenix) operation. Productions, held from September through June, range from classic dramas to musicals and new works by emerging playwrights.

Black Theater Troupe (✉*333 E. Portland St., Downtown Phoenix* ☎*602/258–8128*) performs at its own house, the Helen K. Mason Center, a half-block from the city's Performing Arts Building on Deck Park. It presents original and contemporary dramas and musical revues, as well as adventurous adaptations, between September and May.

Ⓒ **Childsplay** (⌂*Box 517, Tempe 85280* ☎*480/350–8101* ⊕*www.childsplayaz.org*) is the state's theater company for young audiences and families, which runs during the school year. Rotating through many a venue, these players deliver high-energy performances.

Ⓒ **Great Arizona Puppet Theatre** (✉*302 W. Latham St., Downtown Phoenix* ☎*602/262–2050* ⊕*www.azpuppets.org*), which performs in a historic building featuring lots of theater and exhibit space, mounts a yearlong cycle of inventive puppet productions that change frequently.

Phoenix Theatre (✉*100 E. McDowell Rd., Downtown Phoenix* ☎*602/254–2151* ⊕*www.phxtheatre.org*), across the courtyard from the Phoenix Art Museum, stages musical and dramatic performances as well as productions for children by the Cookie Company.

Fodor'sChoice **Rawhide Western Town and Steakhouse at the Wildhorse Pass** (✉*5700 West*
★ *North Loop Rd., Gila River Indian Community, Chandler* ☎*480/502–*
Ⓒ *5600* ⊕*www.rawhide.com*) moved from Scottsdale in 2006, and now calls the 2,400-acre master-planned Wild Horse Pass Development in the Gila River Indian Community, home. Large portions of the original Rawhide were moved to the new site, including the legendary steakhouse and saloon, Main Street and all of its retail shops, and the Six Gun Theater. Exciting additions include canal rides along the Gila River Riverwalk, train rides, and a Native American village honoring the history and culture of the Akimel O'othom and Pee Posh Tribes.

Ⓒ **Rockin' R Ranch** (✉*6136 E. Baseline Rd., Mesa* ☎*480/832–1539* ⊕*www.rockinr.net*) includes a petting zoo, a reenactment of a Wild West shoot-out, and—the main attraction—a nightly cookout with a Western stage show. Pan for gold or take a wagon ride until the "vittles" are served, followed by music and entertainment.

NIGHTLIFE

From brewpubs, sports bars, and coffeehouses to dance clubs, megaconcerts, and country venues, the Valley of the Sun offers nightlife of all types. Nightclubs, comedy clubs, upscale lounges, and wine bars abound in downtown Phoenix, along Camelback Road in north-central Phoenix, and in Scottsdale and Tempe, as well as the other suburbs.

Among music and dancing styles, country-and-western has the longest tradition here. Jazz venues, rock clubs, and hotel lounges are also numerous and varied. Phoenix continues to get hipper and more cosmopolitan, so cigar lovers and martini sippers will find plenty of places to indulge. There are also more than 30 gay and lesbian bars, primarily on 7th Avenue, 7th Street, and the stretch of Camelback Road between the two.

You can find listings and reviews in the *New Times* free weekly newspaper, distributed Wednesday, "The Rep Entertainment Guide" of the *Arizona Republic,* or the enter-

> ### EXPERIENCE THE WILD WEST
>
> In addition to the state and county fairs, and some seasonal shows, there are several places in and around Phoenix to get a taste of what the West was like, way back when. Rawhide and the Rockin' R Ranch, closer to town, are the more kid-friendly, while Pioneer Living History Village and Goldfield Ghost Town (*see Side Trips in this chapter*) are more sedate, with a stronger emphasis on authentic historic buildings.

tainment weekly *Get Out* in Thursday's *East Valley Tribune* or free on newsstands (⊕*www.getoutaz.com*). *PHX Downtown,* a free monthly available in downtown establishments, has an extensive calendar of events from art exhibits and poetry readings to professional sports. The local gay scene is covered in *Echo Magazine,* which you can pick up all over town.

BARS & LOUNGES

AZ88 (⊠*7353 Scottsdale Mall, Scottsdale Civic Center, Scottsdale* ☎*480/994–5576*) is great for feasting on huge portions of great food and lavish quantities of liquor, but also for feasting your eyes on the fabulous people who flock here on weekend nights to see and be seen.

Casey Moore's Oyster House (⊠*850 S. Ash Ave., Tempe* ☎*480/968–9935*) is a laid-back institution where rockers, hippies, and families come together in a 1910 house rumored to be haunted by ghosts. Enjoy 28 beers on tap and fresh oysters at this Irish pub–style favorite.

Dos Gringos Trailer Park (⊠*1001 E. 8th St., Tempe* ☎*480/968–7879* ⊠*4209 N. Craftsman Ct., Central Scottsdale, Scottsdale* ☎*480/423–3800*) is a kitschy indoor–outdoor cantina that will remind you of trips over the Mexican border, or at least spring break. Crowds (mostly college students and twentysomethings) swig margaritas and beer amid a multilevel courtyard, TVs, and limestone fountains.

Fez On Central (⊠*3815 N. Central Ave., Central Phoenix* ☎*602/287–8700*) is a stylish restaurant by day and a gay-friendly, hip hot spot by night. The sleek interior and fancy drinks make you feel uptown, while the happy hour prices and location keep this place grounded.

Fox Sports Bar (⊠*16203 N. Scottsdale Rd., North Scottsdale, Scottsdale* ☎*480/368–0369*) is where trendy, stylish sports fans gather to watch live Fox Sports broadcasts on flat-screen TVs, play pool, and socialize in the sleek VIP room.

★ **Jade Bar** (⊠*5700 E. McDonald Dr., Sanctuary on Camelback Resort, Paradise Valley* ☎*480/948–2100*) has spectacular views of Paradise

Valley and Camelback Mountain, an upscale modern bar lined with windows, and a relaxing fire-place-lit patio.

Kazimierz World Wine Bar (✉7137 E. Stetson Dr., Central Scottsdale, Scottsdale ☎480/946–3004) is entered through a door marked THE TRUTH IS INSIDE, beyond which lies a dark, cave-like wine bar with comfy chairs and good music.

Majerle's Sports Grill (✉24 N. 2nd St., Downtown Phoenix, Phoenix ☎602/253–9004), operated by former Suns basketball player Dan Majerle, is within striking distance of the major sports facilities and offers a comprehensive menu for pre- and postgame celebrations.

The Monastery Too (✉4810 E. McKellips, Mesa ☎480/474–4477) is a casual beer and wine pub where you grill your own burgers and nosh on picnic food. You can play horseshoes, chess, or volleyball.

Postino Winebar (✉3939 E. Campbell Ave., Central Phoenix, Phoenix ☎602/852–3939) occupies a former post office in the Arcadia neighborhood. More than 40 wines are poured by the glass. Order a few grazing items off the appetizer menu and settle in, or carry out a bottle of wine, hunk of cheese, and loaf of bread for a twilight picnic.

The Salty Senorita (✉336 N. Scottsdale Rd., Central Scottsdale, Scottsdale ☎480/946–7258) is known more for its extensive margarita selection and lively patio crowd than for its food. The restaurant–bar touts 51 different margaritas—with some recipes so secret they won't tell you what goes in them—try the El Presidente or the Chupacabra.

Seamus McCaffrey's Irish Pub (✉18 W. Monroe St., Downtown Phoenix ☎602/253–6081) is a fun and friendly place to enjoy one of the dozen European brews on draft. A small kitchen turns out traditional Irish fare.

Six Lounge and Restaurant (✉7316 E. Stetson Dr., Central Scottsdale, Scottsdale ☎480/663–6620) is a crowded see-and-be-seen hot spot attracting the Valley's designer-clad jetsetters who groove to the tunes of a DJ.

BLUES, JAZZ & ROCK

Char's Has the Blues (✉4631 N. 7th Ave., Central Phoenix ☎602/230–0205) is one of the Valley's top blues clubs, with nightly bands.

Marquee Theatre (✉730 N. Mill Ave., Tempe ☎480/829–0607) hosts mainly headlining rock-and-roll entertainers.

Mason Jar (✉2303 E. Indian School Rd., Phoenix ☎602/954–0455) draws a mixed crowd to nightly shows, mostly hard rock, in a dark, black-lighted basement.

Old Brickhouse Grill (✉1 E. Jackson St., Downtown Phoenix, Phoenix ☎602/258–7888) is the place to be if you're looking for hip-hop, rap, rock, and the occasional poetry slam.

Remington's Lounge (✉Scottsdale Plaza Resort, 7200 N. Scottsdale Rd., North Scottsdale, Scottsdale ☎480/948–5000) has a popular piano player, Danny Long, who delivers jazz standards as well as ballads to a very appreciative following from Tuesday to Saturday night.

★ **Rhythm Room** (✉1019 E. Indian School Rd., Central Phoenix ☎602/265–4842) attracts excellent local and national rock artists, as well as blues, seven nights a week. The perfect sidekick, Rack Shack

Blues BBQ, in the parking lot, cooks up good barbecue Wednesday through Saturday evenings.

Sugar Daddy's Blues (⊠ *3102 N. Scottsdale Rd., North Scottsdale, Scottsdale* ☎ *480/970–6556*) serves rhythm, blues, and eclectic Cajun-meets-Southwestern food nightly until 2 AM. A gratis graffiti-clad limo will pick you up anywhere within a 7-mi radius of the bar.

CASINOS

There are six casinos on Indian Reservations around the Valley of the sun (three with hotels). Compared with Las Vegas, they offer smaller venues and a low-key atmosphere. The casinos follow Arizona gaming law, such as no betting cash—chips only.

Casino Arizona at Indian Bend (⊠ *9700 E. Indian Bend Rd., North Scottsdale, Scottsdale* ☎ *480/850–8642* ⊕ *www.casinoaz.com*) draws locals for blackjack, poker, keno, more than 200 slot machines, and an off-track betting room that has wide-screen TVs.

Casino Arizona at Salt River (⊠ *Loop 101 and McKellips Rd., South Scottsdale, Scottsdale* ☎ *480/850–7777, 480/850–7790 for free transportation* ⊕ *www.casinoaz.com*) is the largest casino in the area, with five restaurants, four lounges, a sports bar, a 250-seat theater featuring live performances, two large blackjack rooms, and a keno parlor. There's live music and dancing most nights.

Fort McDowell Casino (⊠ *AZ 87 at Fort McDowell Rd., Fountain Hills* ☎ *602/843–3678* or *800/843–3678* ⊕ *www.fortmcdowellcasino. com*) is popular with the resort crowd. In addition to the cards, slot machines, bingo hall, and keno games, off-track greyhound wagering takes place in a classy mahogany room with 18 giant video screens. Take advantage of the free Valley-wide shuttle.

Gila River Casino (⊠ *5550 W. Wildhorse Pass, Chandler* ☎ *480/796–7777 or 800/946–4452* ⊕ *www.wingilariver.com*) near Wildhorse Pass Resort & Spa includes 500 slots, live poker, blackjack, keno, and complimentary soft drinks.

COFFEEHOUSES

Gold Bar Espresso (⊠ *3141 S. McClintock Dr., Suite 6, Tempe* ☎ *480/839–3082*) is an inviting coffeehouse, decorated with funky antiques. The coffee is first-rate, and there's live jazz on weekends.

★ **Lux** (⊠ *4404 N. Central, Downtown Phoenix* ☎ *602/266–6469*), with local art and retro furniture, is an eclectic gathering place for artists, architects, and downtown businesspeople to enjoy excellent classic European espresso drinks.

Paisley Violin European Cafe (⊠ *1030 N.W. Grand Ave., Downtown Phoenix* ☎ *602/254–7843*) is an offbeat, beatnik coffeehouse–café with live local music Wednesday through Saturday nights. Nosh on Mediterranean food and sip a cappuccino amid local art and mismatched furniture.

Willow House (⊠ *149 W. McDowell Rd., Downtown Phoenix* ☎ *602/252–0272*) is a uniquely fun and funky spot in a city not overflowing with great coffeehouses. Thursday-night poetry readings are a big draw. The espresso flows until midnight on weeknights, 1 AM on weekends.

COMEDY

The Comedy Spot (⊠*7117 E. 3rd Ave., Downtown Scottsdale, Scottsdale* ☎*480/945–4422* ⊕*www.thecomedyspot.net*) features local and national stand-up talent. They also offer classes to wanna-be comedians on Sunday.

Rascal's (⊠*100 N. 1st St., Wyndham Hotel, Downtown Phoenix* ☎*602/254–0999*) is part of a chain featuring headline comics. Sunday is open-mike night.

The Tempe Improv (⊠*930 E. University Dr., Tempe* ☎*480/921–9877*), part of a national chain, showcases better-known headliners from Thursday to Sunday. Get there early for good seats.

Theater 168 (⊠*7117 E. McDowell Rd., Central Scottsdale, Scottsdale* ☎*480/423–0120*) has clean, family-friendly comedy shows, performed by Jester'Z Improvisational Troupe on Thursday, Friday, and Saturday nights at 8 PM.

COUNTRY & WESTERN

★ **Greasewood Flats** (⊠*27500 N. Alma School Pkwy., North Scottsdale, Scottsdale* ☎*480/585–7277*) isn't fancy; in fact, it's downright ramshackle, but the burgers are delicious and the crowds friendly. There's a dance floor with live music Thursday through Sunday. In winter, wear jeans and a jacket, since everything is outside; to keep warm, folks congregate around fires burning in halved oil drums.

Handlebar-J (⊠*7116 E. Becker La., Central Scottsdale, Scottsdale* ☎*480/948–0110*) is a lively restaurant and bar with a Western linedancing, 10-gallon-hat–wearing crowd.

DANCE CLUBS

Anderrson's Fifth Estate (⊠*4224 N. Craftsman Ct., Scottsdale* ☎*480/941–9333*), with two DJs and two dance floors, is one hot night spot. There's live music some Fridays, and a retro-dance party airs live on a local radio on Saturday.

★ **Axis/Radius** (⊠*7340 E. Indian Plaza Rd., Central Scottsdale, Scottsdale* ☎*480/970–1112*) is the dress-to-impress locale where you can party at side-by-side clubs connected by a glass catwalk.

Myst (⊠*7340 E. Shoeman La., North Scottsdale, Scottsdale* ☎*480/970–5000*) is an ultraswanky dance club where you can sip cocktails in a sunken lounge or hang out at the white-hot Milk Bar adorned with white leather seating and an all-white bar. Upstairs is the private VIP lounge, complete with sky boxes overlooking the dance floor.

Scorch (⊠*Desert Ridge Marketplace, 21001 N. Tatum Blvd., North Phoenix* ☎*480/513–7211*) is a subterranean dance club and bar, L.A.-style. Dancers behind a translucent screen entertain the crowd with their shadowy forms. Plush booths, lava lights, and a small dance floor complete the scene. It's only open on Friday and Saturday nights.

GAY & LESBIAN BARS

Ain't Nobody's Bizness (⊠*3031 E. Indian School Rd., Central Phoenix* ☎*602/224–9977*) is the most popular lesbian bar in town; you'll also find a few gay men at this male-friendly establishment, well known as one of the most fun in town.

★ **Amsterdam** (✉718 N. Central Ave., Downtown Phoenix ☎602/258–6122) attracts a young crowd that wants to see and be seen; it's where Phoenix's beautiful gay people hang out.

B.S. West (✉7125 E. 5th Ave., Downtown Scottsdale, Scottsdale ☎480/945–9028) is tucked behind a shopping center on Scottsdale's main shopping drag and draws a stylish, well-heeled crowd.

Charlie's (✉727 W. Camelback Rd., West Phoenix ☎602/265–0224), a longtime favorite of local gay men, has a country-western look (cowboy hats are the accessory of choice) and friendly staff.

E Lounge (✉4343 N. 7th Ave.Central Phoenix ☎602/279–0388 ⊕www.eloungephx.com) is for ladies who love live music, drink specials, late-night DJs—and other ladies who love the same.

MICROBREWERIES

★ **Four Peaks Brewing Company** (✉1340 E. 8th St., Tempe ☎480/303–9967) is the former redbrick home of Bordens Creamery. Ten different brews are on tap, and pub grub, pizza, and burgers fill the menu.

Rio Salado Brewing Company (✉1520 W. Mineral Rd., Tempe ☎480/755–1590) brews excellent German-style beers, with at least six on tap regularly. The low-key Tap Room is a great place to relax, shoot darts, or play pool. Complimentary tours of the brewery are available Saturday afternoon.

Rock Bottom Brewery (✉8668 E. Shea Blvd., North Scottsdale, Scottsdale ☎480/998–7777 ✉21001 N. Tatum Blvd., Desert Ridge Mall, North Phoenix, Phoenix ☎480/513–9125 ✉14205 S. 50th St., Ahwatukee, Phoenix ☎480/598–1300) has tasty pub grub (start with the giant soft pretzels served with spicy spinach dip) and beer brewed on the premises. Watch out: the bill tends to rack up quickly.

Zona Brewing Company (✉20751 N. Pima Rd., DC Ranch, North Scottsdale, Scottsdale ☎480/502–5557) has a bar and a beer garden patio where you can sample handcrafted beers and good pub grub.

SPORTS & THE OUTDOORS

The mountains surrounding the Valley of the Sun are among its greatest assets, and outdoor enthusiasts have plenty of options within the city limits to pursue hiking, bird-watching, or mountain biking passions. Piestewa (formerly Squaw) Peak, north of downtown, is popular with hikers, and Camelback Mountain and the Papago Peaks are landmarks between Phoenix and Scottsdale. South of the city are the much less lofty peaks of South Mountain Park, which separates the Valley from the rest of the Sonoran Desert. East of the city, beyond Tempe and Mesa, the peaks of the Superstition Mountains—named for their eerie way of seeming just a few miles away—are the first of a range that stretches all the way into New Mexico.

Central Arizona's dry desert heat imposes particular restraints on outdoor endeavors—even in winter, hikers and cyclists should wear lightweight opaque clothing, a hat or visor, and high-UV-rated sunglasses, and should carry a quart of water for each hour of activity. The intensity of the sun makes strong sunscreen (SPF 15 or higher) a must, and don't

1

forget to apply it to your hands and feet. From May 1 to October 1, you shouldn't jog or hike from one hour after sunrise until a half hour before sunset. During those times, the air is so hot and dry that your body will lose moisture at a dangerous, potentially lethal rate. And don't head out to desert areas at night to jog or hike in summer; that's when rattlesnakes and scorpions are on the prowl.

BICYCLING

There are plenty of gorgeous areas for biking in the Phoenix area, but riding in the streets isn't recommended as there are few adequate bike lanes in the city. **Phoenix Parks and Recreation** (☎ 602/262–6861 ⊕ *www. ci.phoenix.az.us/parks*) has detailed maps of Valley bike paths.

Note that the desert climate can be tough on cyclists, so make sure you're prepared with lots of water.

Pinnacle Peak, about 25 mi northeast of downtown Phoenix, is a popular place to take bikes for the ride north to Carefree and Cave Creek, or east and south over the mountain pass and down to the Verde River, toward Fountain Hills.

Scottsdale's Indian Bend Wash (along Hayden Road, from Shea Boulevard south to Indian School Road) has paths suitable for bikes winding among its golf courses and ponds.

South Mountain Park is the prime site for mountain bikers, with its 40-plus mi of trails—some of them with challenging ascents and all of them quiet and scenic.

Tempe Town Lake (southwest corner of Mill Avenue and Washington Street) has 5 mi of paths for skating, running, bicycling, and walking.

Trail 100 runs throughout the Phoenix Mountain preserve (enter at Dreamy Draw park, just east of the intersection of Northern Avenue and 16th Street); it's just the thing for mountain bikers.

Several area adventure-tour outfits will pick you up at your hotel, supply the bikes, and take you out for excursions at different levels.

ABC/Desert Biking Adventures (☎ 602/320–4602 *or* 888/249–2453 ⊕ *www.desertbikingadventures.com*) offers two-, three-, and four-hour mountain-biking excursions through the McDowell Mountains and the Sonoran Desert.

AOA Adventures (☎ 480/945–2881 ⊕ *www.aoa-adventures.com*) leads half-day, full-day, and multiple-day adventures, with their extremely knowledgeable and personable staff.

Wheels N' Gear (⊠ *16447 N. 91st St., North Scottsdale, Scottsdale* ☎ *480/945–2881*) rents bikes by the day or the week.

FOUR-WHEELING

Taking a jeep or a wide-track Humvee through the backcountry has become a popular way to experience the desert terrain's saguaro-covered mountains and curious rock formations.

Arrowhead Desert Jeep Tours (⊠ *841 E. Paradise La., North Phoenix* ☎ *602/942–3361 or 800/514–9063* ⊕ *www.azdeserttours.com*) offers gold-panning on a private claim, cookouts, cattle drives, river crossings, and Native American–dance demonstrations.

Baseball's Three Seasons

For dyed-in-the-wool baseball fans, there's no better place than the Valley of the Sun. Baseball has become nearly a year-round activity in the Phoenix area, beginning with spring training in late February and continuing through the Arizona Fall League championships in mid-November.

Professional baseball sunk its roots in the warm Sonoran Desert more than a half-century ago, in 1947, when Bill Veeck brought his Cleveland Indians to Tucson and Horace Stoneham brought the New York Giants to Phoenix for spring training. Before 1947, only a few exhibition games had been played in Arizona; most spring-training games took place in the Florida Grapefruit League, as they had since 1914. Some teams trained in California in the 1930s, and a few teams played in such places as San Antonio, Savannah, Puerto Rico, and even Havana, Cuba. In 1951 baseball fans in Arizona watched Joe DiMaggio and rookie Mickey Mantle train and play at the Phoenix Municipal Stadium, when the New York Yankees came over from Florida for a year, brought by owner—and Phoenix resident—Del Webb.

SPRING

Today, the Cactus League consists of 12 major-league teams (9 in the Valley and 3 in Tucson). Ticket prices are reasonable, around $7 to $8 for bleacher seats to $15 for reserved seats. Many stadiums have lawn-seating areas in the outfield, where you can spread a blanket and bring a picnic. Cactus League stadiums are more intimate than big-league parks, and players often come right up to the stands to say hello and to sign autographs. Special events such as fireworks nights, bat and T-shirt giveaway nights, and visits from sports mascots add to the festive feeling during spring training.

Tickets for some teams go on sale as early as December. Brochures listing game schedules and ticket information are available on the Cactus League's Web site (⊕ www.cactus-league.com)

SUMMER

During the regular major-league season, the hometown Arizona Diamondbacks (⊕ www.azdiamondbacks.com) play on natural grass at Chase Field, formerly Bank One Ballpark (BOB), in the heart of Phoenix's Copper Square (the team does spring training in Tucson). The stadium is a technological wonder; if the weather's a little too warm outside, they close the roof, turn on the gigantic air-conditioners, and keep you cool while you enjoy the game. You can tour the stadium, except on afternoon-game days and holidays.

FALL

At the conclusion of the regular season, the Arizona Fall League runs until the week before Thanksgiving. Each major-league team sends six of their most talented young prospects to compete with other young promising players—180 players in all. There are six teams in the league, broken down into two divisions. It's a great way to see future Hall of Famers in their early years. Tickets for Fall League games are $6 for adults, $5 for kids and seniors, or you can get season tickets.

Tickets for most sporting events can be purchased from **Ticketmaster** (☎ 480/784–4444 ⊕ www.ticketmaster.com).

Desert Dog Hummer Adventures (✐*17212 E. Shea Blvd., Fountain Hills* ☎*480/837–3966*) heads out on half- and full-day Hummer tours to the Four Peaks Wilderness Area in Tonto National Forest and the Sonoran Desert. U-Drive desert cars and ATV tours are also available.

Desert Storm Hummer Tours (✉*15525 N. 83rd Way, No. 8, Scottsdale* ☎*480/922–0020 or 866/374–8637* ⊕*www.dshummer.com*) conducts four-hour nature tours for $100 per person (children 12 and under are $80), climbing 4,000 feet up the rugged trails of Tonto National Forest via Hummer.

Wayward Wind Tours (✉*2418 E. Danbury St., Phoenix* ☎*602/867–7825* ⊕*www.waywardwindtours.com*) ventures down to the Verde River on its own trail and offers wilderness cookouts for large groups.

Wild West Jeep Tours (✉*7127 E. Becker La., Suite #74, Scottsdale* ☎*480/922–0144* ⊕*www.wildwestjeeptours.com*) has special permits that allow it to conduct four-wheeler excursions in the Tonto National Forest and to visit thousand-year-old Indian ruins listed on the National Register of Historic Places.

GOLF

Arizona has more golf courses per capita than any other state west of the Mississippi River, making it one of the most popular golf destinations in the United States. It's also one of Arizona's major industries, and green fees can run from $35 at a public course to more than $500 at some of Arizona's premier golfing spots. New courses seem to pop up monthly: there are more than 200 in the Valley (some lit at night), and the PGA's Southwest section has its headquarters here. Call well ahead for tee times during the cooler months. During the summer, fees drop dramatically and it's not uncommon to schedule a round before dawn. ■**TIP➔**Some golf courses offer a discounted twilight rate—and the weather is often much more amenable at this time of day. Check course Web sites for discounts before making your reservations. Also, package deals abound at resorts as well as through booking agencies like **Arizona Golf Adventures** (☎*877/841–6570* ⊕*www.azteetimes.com*), who will plan and schedule a nonstop golf holiday for you. For a copy of the *Arizona Golf Guide*, contact the **Arizona Golf Association** (☎*602/944–3035 or 800/458–8484* ⊕*www.azgolf.org*).

Arizona Biltmore Country Club (✉*Arizona Biltmore Resort & Spa, 24th St. and Missouri Ave., Camelback Corridor* ☎*602/955–9655* ⊕*www.arizonabiltmore.com*), the granddaddy of Valley golf courses, has two 18-hole PGA championship courses, lessons, and clinics. Green fees range from $48 (in summer months) to $175.

Fodor'sChoice **ASU Karsten Golf Course** (✉*1125 E. Rio Salado Pkwy., Tempe* ★ ☎*480/921–8070* ⊕*www.asukarsten.com*) is the Arizona State University 18-hole golf course where NCAA champions train. Green fees are between $30 and $105.

Encanto Park (✉*2775 N. 15th Ave., West Phoenix* ☎*602/253–3963* ⊕*http://phoenix.gov/SPORTS/encant18.html*) has attractive, affordable public 9- and 18-hole courses. Green fees range from $29 to $38, but they might be going up soon.

Fodor's Choice **Gold Canyon Golf Club** (⊠*6100 S.
★ King's Ranch Rd., Gold Canyon*
☎*480/982–9449 or 800/624–6445*
⊕*www.gcgr.com*), near Apache
Junction in the East Valley, offers
fantastic views of the Superstition
Mountains and challenging golf.
Green fees range from $74 to $189.

★ **Grayhawk Country Club** (⊠*8620
E. Thompson Peak Pkwy., North
Scottsdale, Scottsdale* ☎*480/502–
1800* ⊕*www.grayhawk.com*),
a 36-hole course, has beautiful
mountain views. The cost for 18

> **WHAT TO GET FOR
> THE GOLFER WHO
> HAS EVERYTHING?**
>
> The latest trend in specialty
> massages is the "golf ball mas-
> sage" offered by the spa at Four
> Seasons Troon North (⊕ *www.
> fourseasons.com/scottsdale/spa*):
> the knotted, sore muscles are
> kneaded with warmed golf balls.
> No joke.

holes ranges from $50 (summer) to $220; 36 holes is $325.

Hillcrest Golf Club (⊠*20002 Star Ridge Dr., Sun City West* ☎*623/584–
1500* ⊕*www.hillcrestgolfclub.com*) is the best course in the Sun Cities
development, with 18 holes on 179 acres of well-designed turf. Green
fees range from $34 to $69.

Lookout Mountain Golf Club (⊠*Pointe Hilton at Tapatio Cliffs, 1111
N. 7th St., North Central Phoenix* ☎*602/866–6356* ⊕*www.pointe
hilton.com*) has one 18-hole, par-72 course. Green fees range from
$129 to $144.

Marriott's Camelback Golf Club (⊠*Marriott's Camelback Inn, 7847 N. Mock-
ingbird La., Paradise Valley* ☎*480/596–7050* ⊕*www.camelbackinn.
com*) has two 18-hole courses. Green fees range from $39 (summer
twilight) to $179.

Ocotillo Golf Resort (⊠*3751 S. Clubhouse Dr., Chandler* ☎*480/917–
6660* ⊕*www.ocotillogolf.com*) is designed around 95 acres of man-
made lakes; there's water in play on nearly all 27 holes. Green fees are
$35 (summer twilight) to $175.

Papago Golf Course (⊠*5595 E. Moreland St., North Central Phoenix*
☎*602/275–8428* ⊕*http://phoenix.gov/SPORTS/papago.html*) is a
low-priced 18 holes and Phoenix's best municipal course. Green fees
are $30 to $50.

★ **The Phoenician Golf Club** (⊠*The Phoenician, 6000 E. Camelback Rd.,
Camelback Corridor* ☎*480/423–2449* ⊕*www.thephoenician.com*)
has a 27-hole course. Green fees are $79 to $199. Summer fees after
11 AM start at $29.

Raven Golf Club at South Mountain (⊠*3636 E. Baseline Rd., South Phoenix* ☎*602/243–3636* ⊕*www.ravenatsouthmountain.com*) has thousands of Aleppo pines and Lombardy poplars, making it a cool, shady
18-hole haven for summertime golfers. Eighteen holes range from $69
to $180. Call or visit the Web site for other Raven golf properties.

SunRidge Canyon (⊠*13100 N. SunRidge Dr., Fountain Hills* ☎*480/837–
5100* ⊕*www.sunridgegolf.com*), east of Scottsdale, is a great 18-hole
course for both the low handicapper and those who score above 100.
The incredible mountain views are almost distracting. Green fees are
$65 (summer) to $175.

★ **Tournament Players Club of Scottsdale** (✉*Fairmont Scottsdale Princess Resort, 17020 N. Hayden Rd., North Scottsdale, Scottsdale* ☎*480/585–3600* ⊕*www.tpc.com*), a 36-hole course by Tom Weiskopf and Jay Morrish, is the site of the PGA FBR Open, which takes place in January. Green fees range from $67 to $249.

Fodor'sChoice **Troon North** (✉*10320 E. Dynamite Blvd., North Scottsdale, Scottsdale*
★ ☎*480/585–7700* ⊕*www.troonnorthgolf.com*) is a challenge for the length alone (7,008 yards). The million-dollar views add to the experience at this perfectly maintained 36-hole course. Green fees are $75 to $295.

Wigwam Golf and Country Club (✉ *Wigwam Resort, 300 Wigwam Blvd., Litchfield Park* ☎*623/935–3811* ⊕*www.wigwamresort.com*) is the home of the famous Gold Course, as well as two other 18-hole courses. Green fees range from $64 to $162.

HIKING

One of the best ways to see the beauty of the Valley of the Sun is from above, so hikers of all calibers seek a vantage point in the mountains surrounding the flat Valley.

The city's **Phoenix Mountain Preserve System** (⌖*Phoenix Mountain Preservation Council, Box 26121, Phoenix 85068* ☎*602/262–6861* ⊕*www.phoenixmountains.org*) administers the mountainous regions that surround the city and has its own park rangers who can help plan your hikes. It also publishes a book, *Day Hikes and Trail Rides in and around Phoenix.* ■TIP➜No matter the season, be sure to bring sunscreen, a hat, plenty of water, and a camera to capture a dazzling sunset. When hiking in Arizona it's a good idea to tell someone where you'll be and when you plan to return.

The wonderful folks at **AOA Adventures** (☎*480/945–2881* ⊕*www. aoa-adventures.com*) cater to hikers at different levels of expertise on their half-day, full-day, and multiple-day hikes. The guides are extremely knowlegdeable about local flora and fauna.

★ **Camelback Mountain and Echo Canyon Recreation Area** (✉*Tatum Blvd. and McDonald Dr., Paradise Valley* ☎*602/256–3220 Phoenix Parks & Recreation Dept.*) has intermediate to difficult hikes up the Valley's most outstanding central landmark.

☾ **The Papago Peaks** (✉ *Van Buren St. and Galvin Pkwy., Central Scottsdale, Scottsdale* ☎*602/256–3220 Phoenix Parks & Recreation Dept. Eastern and Central District*) were sacred sites for the Tohono O'odham. The soft-sandstone peaks contain accessible caves, some petroglyphs, and splendid views of much of the Valley. This is a good spot for family hikes.

Piestewa Peak Summit Trail (✉*2701 E. Piestewa [formerly Squaw] Peak Dr., Paradise Valley* ☎*602/262–7901 North Mountain Preserves Ranger Station*), just north of Lincoln Drive, ascends the landmark mountain at a steep 19% grade, but children can handle the 1¼-mi hike if adults take it slowly—allow about 1½ hours for each direction. No dogs are allowed on the trail.

Pinnacle Peak Trail (✉ *26802 N. 102nd Way, 1 mi south of Dynamite and Alma School Rds., North Scottsdale, Scottsdale* ☎ *480/312–0990*) is a well-maintained trail offering a moderately challenging 3½-mi round-trip hike or horseback experience, for those who care to round up a horse at the local stables. Interpretive programs and trail signs along the way describe the geology, flora, fauna, and cultural history of the area.

WORD OF MOUTH

"You should hike up Camelback for an amazing 360 degree look at the Valley of the Sun. Even if you only climb a short way up you can get a great view south over the Phoenician Hotel and much of Phoenix. If you are in good shape and aren't afraid of heights, climbing to the top is a blast."
—amwosu

★ **South Mountain Park** (✉ *10919 S. Central Ave., South Phoenix* ☎ *602/534–6324*) is the jewel of the city's Mountain Park Preserves. Its mountains and arroyos contain more than 60 mi of marked and maintained trails—all open to hikers, horseback riders, and mountain bikers. It also has three car-accessible lookout points, with 65-mi sight lines. Rangers can help you plan hikes to view some of the 200 petroglyph sites.

☺ **Waterfall Trail** (✉ *13025 N. White Tank Mountain Rd., Waddell* ☎ *623/935–2505*) is a short and easy trail. Part of the 25 mi of trails available at the White Tanks Regional Park, it's kid-friendly, and strollers and wheelchairs roll along easily to Petroglyph Plaza, which boasts 1,500-year-old boulder-carvings—dozens are in clear view from the trail. From there the trail takes a rockier but manageable course to a waterfall, which, depending on area rainfall, can be cascading, creeping, or completely dry. Stop at the visitor center to view desert reptiles such as the king snake and a gopher snake in the aquariums.

HORSEBACK RIDING

More than two dozen stables and equestrian-tour outfitters in the Valley attest to the saddle's enduring importance in Arizona—even in this auto-dominated metropolis. Stables offer rides for an hour, a whole day, and even some overnight adventures.

Cowboy College (✉ *30208 N. 152nd St., North Scottsdale, Scottsdale* ☎ *480/471–3151 or 888/330–8070* ⊕ *www.cowboycollege.com*) has wranglers who will teach you everything you need to know about ridin', ropin', and ranchin'.

MacDonald's Ranch (✉ *26540 N. Scottsdale Rd., North Scottsdale, Scottsdale* ☎ *480/585–0239* ⊕ *www.macdonaldsranch.com*) offers one- and two-hour trail rides and guided breakfast, lunch, and dinner rides through desert foothills above Scottsdale.

★ **OK Corral & Stable** (✉ *2655 E. Whiteley St., Apache Junction* ☎ *480/982–4040* ⊕ *www.okcorrals.com*) offers one-, two-, and four-hour horseback trail rides and steak cookouts as well as one- to five-day horse-packing trips. Ron Feldman, an authority on the history and secrets of the Lost Dutchman Mine, is the guide for historical pack trips through the Superstition Mountains.

BALLOONING

A sunrise or sunset hot-air-balloon ascent is a remarkable desert sightseeing experience. The average fee—there are more than three dozen Valley companies to choose from—is $135 per person, and hotel pickup is usually included. Since flight paths and landing sites vary with wind speeds and directions, a roving land crew follows

> **WAY UP HIGH**
>
> Taking a balloon trip is one of the most awe-inspiring ways to see the desert. There's nothing quite like being way up high above it all, and several of the local ballooning outfits serve champagne on touchdown; uplifting!

each balloon in flight. Time in the air is generally between 1 and 1½ hours, but allow 3 hours for the total excursion.

Adventures Out West and Unicorn Balloon Company (☎480/991–3666 or 800/755–0935 ⊕www.adventuresoutwest.com) has horseback riding, jeep tours, and hot-air-balloon flights that conclude with complimentary champagne, a flight certificate, and video.

The Hot Air Balloon Company (☎602/482–6030 or 800/843–5987 ⊕www.arizonaballooning.com) offers private and group sunrise and sunset flights with sparkling beverages and fresh pastries served on touchdown.

Hot Air Expeditions (☎480/502–6999 or 800/831–7610 ⊕www.hotairexpeditions.com) is the best ballooning in Phoenix. Flights are long, the staff is charming, and the gourmet snacks, catered by the acclaimed Vincent restaurant, are out of this world.

SAILPLANING–SOARING

Arizona Soaring Inc. (⊠Maricopa ☎480/821–2903 or 800/861–2318 ⊕www.azsoaring.com), at the Estrella Sailport in Maricopa, 35 mi south of Phoenix off I-10, gives sailplane rides in a basic trainer or high-performance plane. The adventuresome can opt for a wild 15-minute acrobatic flight.

TENNIS

With all of the blue sky and sunshine in the Valley, it's a perfect place to play tennis or watch the pros. The Fairmont Scottsdale Princess hosts several national championships, including the annual Franklin Templeton Men's Classic and the State Farm Women's Tennis Championship. Major resorts, such as the Radisson, Phoenician, Wigwam, Fairmont Princess, and JW Marriott Desert Ridge (and many smaller properties), have tennis courts. Granted, tennis plays second fiddle to golf here—but many of the larger resorts offer package tennis deals. If you're not staying at a resort, there are more than 60 public facilities in the area.

Camelback Village Racquet & Health Club (⊠4444 E. Camelback Rd., Camelback Corridor ☎602/840–6412 ⊕www.dmbclubs.com ⊠7477 E. Doubletree Ranch Rd., Scottsdale ☎602/609–6979) is a private tennis facility, health club, and spa featuring lighted courts, ball-machine clinics, and lessons. Visitors can enjoy club amenities for $17 a day.

Kiwanis Park Recreation Center (⊠ *6111 S. All America Way, Tempe* ☎ *480/350–5201*) has 15 lighted premier-surface courts (all for same-day or one-day-advance reserve).

Mountain View Tennis Center (⊠ *1104 E. Grovers Ave., Phoenix* ☎ *602/534–2500*), just north of Bell Road, has 20 lighted courts and group lessons. Court fees are $1.50 per person for 90 minutes.

Phoenix Tennis Center (⊠ *6330 N. 21st Ave., West Phoenix* ☎ *602/249–3712*) is a city facility with 22 lighted hard courts.

Scottsdale Ranch Park (⊠ *10400 E. Via Linda, North Scottsdale, Scottsdale* ☎ *480/312–7774* ⊕ *www.scottsdaleaz.gov/econnect*) is a city facility with 12 lighted courts. Lessons are available here, too.

TUBING

The Valley may not be known for its wealth of water, but locals manage to make the most of what there is. A popular summer stop is the northeast side of the Salt River, where sun worshippers can rent an inner tube and float down the river for an afternoon. Tubing season runs from May to September. Several Valley outfitters rent tubes. Make sure you bring lots of sunscreen, a hat, water—and a rope to attach your cooler to a tube.

Salt River Recreation (⊠ *Usery Pass and Power Rds., Mesa* ☎ *480/984–3305* ⊕ *www.saltrivertubing.com*), offers shuttle-bus service to and from your starting point and rents tubes for $14 (cash only) for the day.

SHOPPING

Since its resorts began multiplying in the 1930s and '40s, Phoenix has acquired many high-fashion clothiers and leisure-wear boutiques, but you can still find the Western clothes that in many parts of town still dominate the fashion. Jeans and boots, cotton shirts and dresses, 10-gallon hats, and bola ties (the state's official neckwear) are still the staples. On the scene as well are the arts of the Southwest's true natives—Navajo weavers, sand painters, and silversmiths; Hopi weavers and katsina-doll carvers; Pima and Tohono O'odham (Papago) basket makers and potters; and many more. Inspired by the region's rich cultural traditions, contemporary artists have flourished here, making Phoenix—particularly Scottsdale, a city with more art galleries than gas stations—one of the Southwest's largest art centers (alongside Santa Fe, New Mexico).

Today's shoppers find the best of the old and the new—all presented with Southwestern style. Upscale stores, one-of-a-kind shops, and outlet malls sell the latest fashions, cowboy collectibles, hand-woven rugs, traditional Mexican folk art, and contemporary turquoise jewelry.

Most of the Valley's power shopping is concentrated in central Phoenix, downtown Scottsdale, and the Kierland area in North Scottsdale but auctions and antiques shops cluster in odd places—and as treasure hunters know, you've always got to keep your eyes open.

SHOPPING CENTERS

Arizona Mills (⊠ *5000 Arizona Mills Circle, I–10 and Baseline Rd., Tempe* ☎ *480/491–7300*), a mammoth "value-oriented retail and entertainment mega mall," features more than 175 outlet stores and sideshows, including Off 5th–Saks Fifth Avenue, Kenneth Cole, and Last Call from Neiman Marcus. When you tire of bargain-hunting relax in the food court, cinemas, or faux rain forest.

> ### WANT TO BEAT THE HEAT?
>
> Looking for some relief from the midday desert heat? Cool stores with icy air-conditioning can be just the ticket. Although many of Phoenix's malls are gorgeously landscaped, outdoor areas, Fashion Square and Arizona Mills are indoor complexes.

★ **Biltmore Fashion Park** (⊠ *24th St. and Camelback Rd., Camelback Corridor* ☎ *602/955–8400*) has a posh, parklike setting. Macy's, Saks Fifth Avenue, and Borders are the anchors for more than 70 stores and upscale shops, such as Betsey Johnson and Cartier. It's accessible from the Camelback Esplanade and the Ritz Carlton by a pedestrian tunnel that runs beneath Camelback Road.

The Borgata (⊠ *6166 N. Scottsdale Rd., Central Scottsdale, Scottsdale*), an outdoor re-creation of the Italian village of San Gimignano, with courtyards, stone walls, turrets, and fountains, is a lovely setting for browsing upscale boutiques or just sitting at an outdoor café.

Cofco Chinese Cultural Center (⊠ *668 N. 44th St., Phoenix* ☎ *602/273-7268*) is adorned with replicas of pagodas, statues, and traditional Chinese gardens. It's the place to find Asian restaurants, gift shops, and the *Super L,* a huge Asian grocery store. Take a stroll through the market's fish department—you'll forget you're in the desert.

☾ **Desert Ridge Marketplace** (⊠ *Tatum Blvd. and Loop 101, North Phoenix* ☎ *480/513–7586*), an outdoor megamall, has more than 1 million square feet of shops and restaurants, but it's also a family entertainment destination, with an 18-theater cineplex, bowling alley, rock-climbing wall, and Dave & Buster's, a multivenue entertainment center with a virtual-reality game room and dance club.

★ **Kierland Commons** (⊠ *Greenway Pkwy. at Scottsdale Rd., North Scottsdale, Scottsdale* ☎ *480/348–1577*), next to the Westin Kierland Resort, is one of the city's newest shopping areas. "Urban village" is the catchphrase for this outdoor pedestrian mall with restaurants and upscale chain retailers, among them J. Crew, and Tommy Bahama.

★ **Mill Avenue Shops** (⊠ *Mill Avenue, between Rio Salado Pkwy. and University Dr., Downtown, Tempe* ☎ *480/967–4877*), named for the landmark Hayden Flour Mill, is an increasingly commercial area, but it's still a fun-filled walk-and-shop experience. Directly west of the Arizona State University campus, Mill Avenue is an active melting pot of students, artists, residents, and tourists. Shops include Borders, Urban Outfitters, a few remaining locally owned clothing and curio stores, and countless bars and restaurants. The Valley Art Theater is a Mill Avenue institution and Tempe's place for indie cinema. Twice a year (in early December and March/April), the Mill Avenue area is the place to find indie arts and crafts when it hosts the Tempe Festival of the Arts.

★ **Old Town Scottsdale** (⊠*Between Goldwater Blvd., Brown Ave., 5th Ave. and 3rd St., Downtown, Scottsdale* ☎*800/737–0008*) is the place to go for authentic Southwest-inspired gifts, clothing, art, and artifacts. Despite its massive modern neighbors, this area and its merchants have long respected and maintained the single-level brick storefronts that embody Scottsdale's upscale cowtown charm. More than 100 businesses meet just about any aesthetic want or need, including Gilbert Ortega, one of the premiere places for fine Native American jewelry and art. Some of Scottsdale's best restaurants are also tucked in this pleasing maze of merchants.

★ **Scottsdale Fashion Square** (⊠*Scottsdale and Camelback Rds., Central Scottsdale, Scottsdale* ☎*480/949–0202*) has a retractable roof and many specialty shops unique to Arizona. There are also Nordstrom, Dillard's, Neiman Marcus, Macy's, Juicy Couture, Anthropologie, Z Gallerie, Louis Vuitton, Tiffany, and Arizona's only Gucci store. A huge food court, restaurants, and a cineplex complete the picture.

★ **The Shops at Gainey Village** (⊠*8787 N. Scottsdale Rd., North Scottsdale, Scottsdale* ☎*480/458–8064*), near historic Gainey Ranch, makes for stiff shopping competition in the area. Composed primarily of upscale boutiques, this stylish strip mall also features fine dining at hot spots like Bloom and Thai Foon and nosh spots like Paradise Bakery, the Coffee Bean, and Pei Wei Asian Café.

OPEN-AIR MARKETS

It can be a real treat to visit a farmers market even if you're not a local doing grocery shopping. Phoenix markets often feature funky tortillas and Mexican wares so you can sample some goodies and maybe find some presents to take home. Two of metropolitan Phoenix's best markets are in the tiny town of Guadalupe, which is tucked around I–10, Baseline Road, and Warner Road. Take I–10 south to Baseline Road, go east ½ mi, and turn south on Avenida del Yaqui to find open-air vegetable stalls, roadside fruit stands, and tidy houses covered in flowering vines. To find the fresh wares of a Valley farmers market, visit ⊕*www.arizonafarmersmarkets.com*, a comprehensive calendar listing started and maintained by longtime market coordinators Dee and John Logan.

Guadalupe Farmer's Market (⊠*9210 S. Ave. del Yaqui, Guadalupe* ☎*480/730–1945*) has all the fresh ingredients you'd find in a rural Mexican market—tomatillos, varieties of chile peppers (fresh and dried), fresh-ground *masa* (cornmeal) for tortillas, spices like cumin and cilantro, and on and on. It's open every day year-round: from 9 AM to 6 PM in fall, winter, and spring; to 7 PM in summer; and to 5 PM Sunday.

Mercado Mexico (⊠*8212 S. Ave. del Yaqui, Guadalupe* ☎*480/831–5925*) carries ceramics, paper-, tin-, and lacquerware, all at unbeatable prices. Stock up from 10 AM to 6 PM daily, year-round.

SPECIALTY SHOPS

ANTIQUES & COLLECTIBLES

The central Phoenix corridor, between 7th Street and 7th Avenue, has many antiques stores. Most shops sit north of Thomas and south of Camelback. Prices, though reasonable, are firm at most shops. A surprise to many visitors is the old-town district of suburban Glendale, with more than 80 antiques and collectibles shops nestled around Historic Old Towne and Catlin Court, which are listed on the National Register of Historic Places.

Antique Centre (⊠2012 N. Scottsdale Rd., Central Scottsdale, Scottsdale ☎480/675–9500) has a hodgepodge of collectibles and trinkets.
Glendale Old Towne & Catlin Court (⊠59th and Glendale Aves., Glendale) antiques district has a plethora of shops and restaurants in colorful, century-old bungalows. Stop in at antique-filled Aunt Pittypat's Kitchen for breakfast or lunch or have a cup of tea at the Spicery, which is in an 1895 Victorian home.

ARTS & CRAFTS

Art One (⊠4120 N. Marshall Way, Central Scottsdale, Scottsdale ☎480/946–5076) carries works by students as well as local and emerging artists.
Cosanti Originals (⊠6433 Doubletree Ranch Rd., Paradise Valley, Scottsdale ☎480/948–6145) is the studio where architect Paolo Soleri's famous bronze and ceramic wind chimes are made and sold. You can watch the craftspeople at work, then pick out your own—prices are surprisingly reasonable.
Drumbeat Indian Arts (⊠4143 N. 16th St., Central Phoenix ☎602/266–4823) is a small, interesting shop specializing in Native American music, movies, books, drums, and crafts supplies. If you're lucky, you might find authentic fry bread and Navajo tacos being cooked in the parking lot on weekends.
★ **The Heard Museum Shop** (⊠2301 N. Central Ave., Downtown Phoenix ☎602/252–8344) is hands-down the best place in town for Southwestern Native American and other crafts, both traditional and modern. Prices tend to be high, but quality is assured, with many one-of-a-kind items among the collection of rugs, katsina dolls, pottery, and other crafts; there's also a wide selection of lower-priced gifts.
Trailside Galleries (⊠7330 Scottsdale Mall, Downtown Scottsdale, Scottsdale ☎480/945–7751) has been showcasing works by members of the Cowboy Artists of America for more than 40 years and specializes in traditional American paintings and sculptures.
Fodor'sChoice **Wilde Meyer Galleries** (⊠4142 N. Marshall Way, Downtown Scottsdale, Scottsdale ☎480/945–2323 ⊠Colores by Wilde Meyer: 7100 E.
★ Main St., Downtown Scottsdale, Scottsdale ☎480/947–1489 ⊠Wilde Meyer Discoveries: 8777 N. Scottsdale Rd., Shops at Gainey Ranch, Scottsdale ☎480/488–3200) has three locations around the Valley of the Sun and is the place to go for the true colors of the Southwest. In addition to one-of-a-kind paintings, the galleries also feature rustic, fine art imports from around the state and the world, including furniture, sculptures, and jewelry. Look for Linda Carter Holman's "Latin

Ladies" paintings and works by Scottsdale's own Sherri Belassen whose unique cowboys and cattle will leave you with a colorful new Western perspective.

BOOKS

The major U.S. chains—Barnes & Noble, B. Dalton, Borders, and Waldenbooks—are all represented in the Valley, but there are still some interesting independents.

Brentano's Bookstore (⊠ *Scottsdale Fashion Square South, 7014–590 E. Camelback Rd., Camelback Corridor* ☎ *480/423–8717*) is a small bookstore with an assortment of stationery and cards.

Changing Hands Bookstore (⊠ *6428 S. McClintock Dr., Tempe* ☎ *480/730–0205*) has a large selection of new and used books.

ART FESTIVALS

Art Link's First Fridays & Art Detour is an excellent way to check out the Phoenix arts scene: Galleries stay open late and crowds converge to view the work of emerging and established artists, listen to live music, and see impromptu street performances. ☎ *602/256–7539* ⊕ *www.artlinkphoenix.com.*

Art Walk (☎ *480/990–3939*), every Thursday 7–9 PM year-round (except Thanksgiving), is perfect for checking out the Scottsdale galleries: Locals and tourists browse Main Street and Marshall Way, the two major gallery strips, and the atmosphere is a party.

Gifts Anonymous (⊠ *4524 N. 7th St., Central Phoenix* ☎ *602/277–5256*) carries books and gifts exclusively for those in 12-step, recovery, and life issue programs.

Guidon (⊠ *7117 W. Main St., Downtown Scottsdale, Scottsdale* ☎ *480/945–8811*), a small, independent bookshop in Scottsdale's art district, specializes in out-of-print and hard-to-find Western fiction and nonfiction titles.

The Poisoned Pen (⊠ *4014 N. Goldwater Blvd., Central Scottsdale, Scottsdale* ☎ *480/947–2974*) specializes in mysteries.

Those Were the Days (⊠ *516 S. Mill Ave., Tempe* ☎ *480/967–4729*) sells used and rare books.

FOOD SHOPS

★ **AJ's Fine Foods** (⊠ *5017 N. Central Ave., Phoenix* ☎ *602/230–7015* ⊠ *4430 E. Camelback Rd., Phoenix* ☎ *602/522–0956* ⊠ *7141 E. Lincoln Dr., Scottsdale* ☎ *480/998–0052* ⊠ *7131 W. Ray Rd., Chandler* ☎ *480/705–0011* ⊠ *20050 N. 67th Ave., Glendale* ☎ *623/537–2310* ⊠ *23251 N. Pima Rd., North Scottsdale* ☎ *480/563–5070*) is the Valley's grandest upscale grocery store and a great place to fill your basket with exclusive local creations ranging from Goldwater's salsas and sauces (created by the daughters of the late senator Barry Goldwater), to Sada's Pepper Melody and Rene's Desert Rub spice mixes, and creative gift items like handbags, high-end bath products, and festive Southwestern wear. It's possible to spend hours here, and it's also possible to spend far more money than you would at an average grocery store, but the vast inventory of unique items not found together anywhere else and the first-class, one-stop shopping experience make it all worthwhile. Be sure to partake of the fresh, chef-prepared food offerings, like homemade soups, salad, pizza, specialty sandwiches, and gourmet take-out entrées from the bistro.

★ **Sportsman's Fine Wine & Spirits** (✉3205 E. Camelback Rd., Phoenix ☎602/955–WINE [9463] ✉10802 N. Scottsdale Road, Scottsdale ☎480/948–0520 ✉6685 W. Beardsley Rd., Glendale ☎623/572–9463) is the place to go to "lift your spirits." Sportsman's stocks fine wines and rare beverage finds from both local and international sources. They also sell cheeses and other delicious wine accompaniments including panini sandwiches, roasted garlic, hummus, bruschetta, baked feta, and warm pretzels.

★ **T'z Marketplace** (✉58 San Marcos Pl., San Marcos Plaza, Chandler ☎480/857–2088) brings Old World charm and style to Old Town Chandler with epicurean delights from all over the map. Enjoy unique non-alcoholic beverages along with fine wines, meats, cheeses, and other tantalizing food choices like savory sandwiches, gelato, chocolates, cookies, crackers, and more.

VINTAGE CLOTHING & FURNITURE

In certain parts of the Valley, "old" is the new "new." The Melrose District, on 7th Avenue between Indian School and Camelback Roads in central Phoenix, is banking on its old Phoenix charm in a slow but steady race to become the next hip historic neighborhood. New faces on old buildings are the perfect welcome mat for progress with forthcoming lofts, condos, eateries, and big plans for public art, but the overall charm is anchored by its variety of vintage stores. Open hours are generally 11–6 and some stores are closed Monday.

7th Heaven Vintage & More (✉4200 N. 7th Ave., Melrose District, Phoenix ☎602/277–4405) could be considered chicken soup for the collector's soul. Offering an eclectic mix of 1940s through '70s furniture and accessories, 7th Heaven encourages customers to "let their homes envelope them in the comfort time provides."

Figs (✉4501 N. 7th Ave., Melrose District, Phoenix ☎602/279–1443) carries a wealth of stylish interior, architectural, and garden elements. Owner John Douglas prides himself on being a direct importer of east Asian furniture, antiques, and accessories. Closed Monday.

Home Again (✉4955 N. 7th Ave., Melrose District, Phoenix ☎602/424–0488) is a down-home store that buys and sells vintage and modern home furnishings and antiques. A registered antiques dealer, Home Again welcomes dealers. Open Mondays "by chance."

Melrose Vintage (✉4238 N. 7th Ave., Melrose District, Phoenix ☎602/636–0300) has a cheerful, dollhouse-like yellow exterior and that's not the only thing that makes it memorable. The no-nonsense staff knows its stuff, which includes tasteful and fun low- to high-end shabby chic furnishings: everything from ribbon to armoires. It's closed Monday and Tuesday.

Phoenix Metro Retro (✉708 W. Montecito Ave., Melrose District, Phoenix ☎602/ 279–0702): is it a hip New York loft? No, it's a vintage, mid-century, and modern furniture store. Cool and inviting, Metro Retro aptly exhibits the talent and time it takes for people like owner Carl Reese to find those "perfect" pieces for your purchasing pleasure.

■TIP➡Post-shopping you can pick up some other "pleasure pieces" at the Urban Cookie Company next door. Metro Retro is closed Monday and Tuesday.

Retro Redux (⊠4303 N. 7th Ave., Melrose District, Phoenix ☎602/234–0120) has a selection of vintage clothing, costume jewelry, period pictures, furnishings, and accessories that's as fun and funky as its name. It's closed Monday.

Vintage Solutions (⊠4302 N. 7th Ave., Melrose District, Phoenix ☎602/604–1831) is the place for sweet deals on deco and mid-century furniture, collectibles, and accessories that stand the test of time. A local newspaper recently called the owners and operators of Vintage Solutions "eagle-eye tchotchke aficionados who know a good deal when they see one, and aren't above passing their savings on to you." Closed Monday.

SIDE TRIPS NEAR PHOENIX

The following sights are within a 1- to 1½-hour drive of Phoenix. To the north, the thriving artist communities of Carefree and Cave Creek are popular Western attractions. Arcosanti and Wickenburg are half- or full-day trips from Phoenix. Stop along the way to visit the petroglyphs of Deer Valley Rock Art Center and the reenactments of Arizona territorial life at the Pioneer Living History Village. You also might consider Lake Pleasant, Arcosanti, and Wickenburg as stopovers on the way to or from Flagstaff, Prescott, or Sedona.

South of Phoenix, an hour's drive takes you back to prehistoric times and the site of Arizona's first known civilization at Casa Grande Ruins National Monument, a vivid reminder of the Hohokam who began farming this area more than 1,500 years ago.

DEER VALLEY ROCK ART CENTER

㉝ *15 mi north of downtown Phoenix on I–17. Exit at W. Deer Valley Rd. and drive 2 mi west.*

Deer Valley Rock Art Center has the largest concentration of ancient petroglyphs in the metropolitan Phoenix area. Some 1,500 of the cryptic symbols are here, left behind by Native American cultures that lived in the Valley (or passed through) during the last 1,000 years. After watching a video about the petroglyphs, pick up a pair of binoculars ($1) and an informative trail map and set out on the ¼-mi path. Telescopes point to some of the most well-formed petroglyphs; they range from human and animal forms to more abstract figures. *For more information about petroglyphs, see The Writing on the Wall CloseUp box in Chapter 5.* ⊠3711 W. Deer Valley Rd., North Phoenix ☎623/582–8007 ⊕www. asu.edu/clas/shesc/dvrac ☎$5 ⊗May–Sept., Tues.–Fri. 8–2, Sat. 9–5, Sun. noon–5; Oct.–Apr., Tues.–Sat. 9–5, Sun. noon–5.

PIONEER LIVING HISTORY VILLAGE

✋ ㉞ *25 mi north of downtown Phoenix on I–17 (Exit 225, Pioneer Rd.), just north of Carefree Hwy. (AZ 74).*

The Pioneer Arizona Living History Museum contains 28 original and reconstructed buildings from throughout territorial Arizona. Costumed guides filter through the bank, schoolhouse, and print shop, as well as the Pioneer Opera House, where classic melodramas are performed daily. It's popular with the grade-school field-trip set, and it's your lucky day if you can tag along for their tour of the site—particularly when John the Blacksmith forges, smelts, and answers sixth-graders' questions that adults are too know-it-all to ask. ✉ *3901 W. Pioneer Rd., North Phoenix, Phoenix* ☎ *623/465–1052* ⊕ *www. pioneer-arizona.com* 💲 *$7* ☉ *Oct.–May, Wed.–Sun. 9–5; June–Sept., Wed.–Sun. 8–2.*

CAVE CREEK & CAREFREE

㉟ *15 mi north of downtown Phoenix on I–17. Exit at Carefree Hwy. (AZ 74) and turn right, then go 12 mi. Turn left onto Cave Creek Rd. and go 3 mi to downtown Cave Creek then another 4 mi on Cave Creek Rd. to Carefree.*

Some 30 mi north of Phoenix, resting high in the Sonoran Desert at an elevation of 2,500 feet, the towns of Cave Creek and Carefree look back to a lifestyle far different from that of their more populous neighbors to the south.

Cave Creek got its start with the discovery of gold in the region. When the mines and claims "played out," the cattlemen arrived, and the sounds of horse hooves and lowing cattle replaced those of miners' picks. The area grew slowly and independently from Phoenix to the south, until a paved road connected the two in 1952. Today the mile-long main stretch of town on Cave Creek Road is a great spot to have some hot chili and cold beer, try on Western duds, or learn the two-step in a "cowboy" bar. You're likely to run into folks dressed in cowboy hats, boots, and bold belt buckles. Horseriders and horse-drawn wagons have the right of way here and the 25-mph speed limit is strictly enforced by county deputies. You can amble up the hill and rent a horse for a trip into the Tonto National Forest in search of some long-forgotten native petroglyphs, or take a jeep tour out to the forest. Some tours include a stop at the world's largest saguaro: the 46-foot "Grand One," with a base circumference of 7 feet, 10 inches, was partially burned during the 2005 Cave Creek Complex Fire.

Just about the time the dirt road–era ended in Cave Creek, planners were sketching out a new community, which became neighboring Carefree. The world's largest sundial, at the town's center, is surrounded by crafts shops, galleries, artists' workshops, and cafés. Today Cave Creek and Carefree sit cheek by jowl—but the one has beans, beef, biscuits, and beer, while the other discreetly orders up a notch or two.

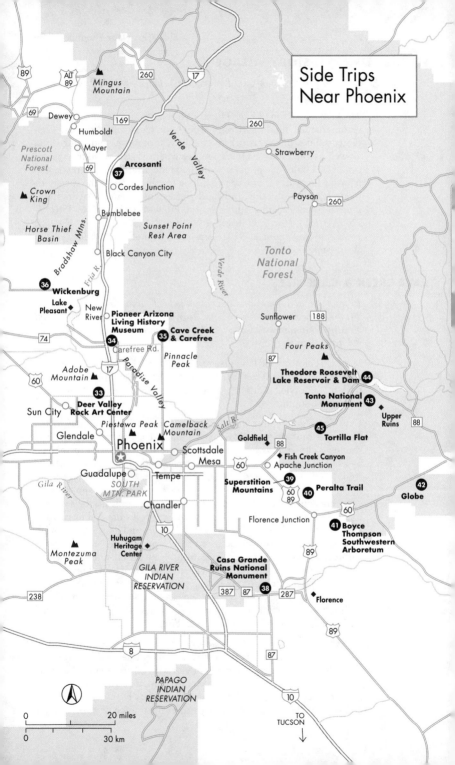

Side Trips Near Phoenix

89
ALT 89
Mingus Mountain
260
17

Dewey **69**
Humboldt
169
260
Strawberry
Mayer

Prescott National Forest
69
Arcosanti
37
Cordes Junction
Verde Valley
Payson **260**

Crown King
Bumblebee
Sunset Point Rest Area

Horse Thief Basin
Bradshaw Mtns.
Black Canyon City
Verde River

Tonto National Forest

Frid R.
36 **Wickenburg**
Lake Pleasant
New River
Pioneer Arizona Living History Museum **34**
188

74
Cave Creek & Carefree **35**
Sunflower
87

Carefree Rd.
Pinnacle Peak
Four Peaks

Adobe Mountain
17
60
Theodore Roosevelt Lake Reservoir & Dam **44**

Deer Valley Rock Art Center **33**
Paradise Valley
Tonto National Monument **43**

Sun City
Piestewa Peak
Camelback Mountain
Upper Ruins

Glendale
Salt R.
88

Phoenix
Goldfield
88
45 **Tortilla Flat**

Scottsdale
Mesa
60
Fish Creek Canyon

Guadalupe
Apache Junction

SOUTH MTN. PARK
Tempe
Superstition Mountains
39
40 **Peralta Trail**
42 **Globe**

Gila River
60
89

Chandler
Florence Junction
60

10
41 **Boyce Thompson Southwestern Arboretum**

Montezuma Peak
Huhugam Heritage Center
89

GILA RIVER INDIAN RESERVATION
Casa Grande Ruins National Monument

238
387 **87** **38**
287
Florence

8
87
89

PAPAGO INDIAN RESERVATION
10

N

0   20 miles
0   30 km

TO TUCSON

Pick up maps and information about the area at the **Carefree–Cave Creek Chamber of Commerce.** ✉748 *Easy St., No. 9, Carefree 85377* ☎480/488–3381 ⊕*www.carefreecavecreek.com* ☉ *Weekdays 8–4.*

Exhibits at the **Cave Creek Museum** depict pioneer living, mining, and ranching. See the last original 1920s tuberculosis cabin and a collection of Indian artifacts from the Hohokam and Yavapai tribes. ✉*6140 E. Skyline Dr., Cave Creek* ☎480/488–2764 ⊕*www.cavecreekmuseum.org* ✑*$3* ☉*Oct.–May, Wed.–Sun. 1–4:30.*

☽ Pseudo-Western **Frontier Town** (✉*6245 E. Cave Creek Rd., Cave Creek*) has wooden sidewalks, ramshackle buildings, and souvenir shops. Grab a sandwich and a bottle of Cave Creek Chili Beer (with a real chile pepper in each bottle) at **Crazy Ed's Satisfied Frog** (✉*6245 E. Cave Creek Rd., Cave Creek* ☎480/488–3317).

The **Heard Museum North,** a satellite of the big Heard in downtown Phoenix, has one gallery with its own small, permanent collection of Native American art. It also hosts two rotating exhibits during the year. The gift shop is well stocked with expensive, high-quality items. ✉*32633 N. Scottsdale Rd., at Carefree Hwy., Scottsdale* ☎480/488–9817 ⊕*www.heard.org* ✑*$3* ☉*Mon.–Sat. 10–5:30, Sun. noon–5.*

> **WORD OF MOUTH**
>
> "If you are looking for different, try Carefree and Cave Creek in Northern Phoenix. Carefree is beautiful desert. It usually blooms in April. There are hiking trails in Cave Creek and you can also climb a trail winding around Pinnacle Peak. Cave Creek is a small cowboy town with a funky hotel. There are lots of Mexican, Southwest, and western shops and also great cowboy restaurants. Carefree is artsy…It is very friendly and relaxed."
>
> –Skooger

NEED A BREAK?

Bakery Café at el Pedregal Marketplace (✉*34505 N. Scottsdale Rd., at Carefree Hwy., Carefree* ☎*480/488–4100*). Adjacent to the Boulders Resort (and not far from the Heard Museum North), this is a good place to pick up a breakfast or lunch of fresh-baked goods or to take a shopping break with a sandwich and a cool drink.

SPORTS & THE OUTDOORS

TENNIS & GOLF The **Boulders Resort Golf Club** (✉*The Boulders, 34631 N. Tom Darlington Dr., Carefree* ☎480/488–9028 *or* 866/397–6520 ⊕*www.theboulders.com*) has two championship 18-hole, par-72 courses, and 8 tennis courts.

HORSEBACK RIDING **Spur Cross Stable** (✉*44029 Spur Cross Rd., Cave Creek* ☎480/488–9117 *or* 800/758–9530 ⊕*www.horsebackarizona.com*) has well-cared-for horses that will take you on one- to seven-hour rides to the high Sonoran Desert of the Spur Cross Preserve and the Tonto National Forest. Some rides include visits to petroglyph sites and a saddlebag lunch.

WHERE TO STAY & EAT

$$–$$$ ✕ **Tonto Bar & Grill at Rancho Manana.** Old West ambience oozes from every corner of the Tonto Bar & Grill, from the hand-carved beams of the ceiling to the latilla (stick)-covered patios with views of the pristine Sonoran Desert. Try the cowboy Cobb salad or the Tonto burger piled with fried onions and Tillamook cheddar for lunch; lamb chops with leek fondue or grilled grouper with orange-tomato salsa are good choices at dinner. ⊠ *5736 E. Rancho Manana Blvd., Cave Creek* ☎ *480/488–0698* ⊟ *AE, D, DC, MC, V.*

$–$$$ ✕ **Horny Toad Restaurant.** The Horny Toad is a rustic spot for barbecued pork ribs and steak, but the real star is the fried chicken. ⊠ *6738 E. Cave Creek Rd., Cave Creek* ☎ *480/488–9542* ⊟ *AE, D, DC, MC, V.*

$$–$$$$ ▦ **The Boulders Resort and Golden Door Spa.** One of the country's top

Fodor's Choice resorts hides amid hill-size, 12-million-year-old granite boulders and

★ the lush Sonoran Desert. Casitas snuggled against the rocks have exposed log-beam ceilings and curved, pueblo-style half-walls. Each has a patio with a view, a wood-burning fireplace, and a spacious bathroom with deep soaking tub. El Pedregal Marketplace, an upscale mall, adjoins the resort, and there are two golf courses. The Golden Door spa is one of the best in the state. ⊠ *34631 N. Tom Darlington Dr., Carefree 85377* ☎ *480/488–9009 or 800/553–1717* ⊟ *480/488–4118* ⊕ *www.theboulders.com* ⇆ *160 casitas, 46 patio homes* ⌂ *In-room: safe, kitchen (some), refrigerator, Wi-Fi (some), ethernet. In-hotel: 5 restaurants, room service, golf courses, tennis courts, pools, gym, spa, concierge, parking (no fee), no elevator* ⊟ *AE, D, DC, MC, V.*

$ ▦ **Cave Creek Tumbleweed Hotel.** Innkeepers Gary and Jeri Rust have kept the 1950s flavor of this western hotel intact. There's a fireplace in the lobby and a quiet pool outside. Red-and-tan rooms have Southwestern and cowboy accents. The hotel is a short walk from restaurants and shops in town. ⊠ *6333 E. Cave Creek Rd., Cave Creek 85327* ☎ *480/488–3668* ⊕ *www.tumbleweedhotel.com* ⇆ *32 rooms, 8 casitas* ⌂ *In-room: kitchen (some). In-hotel: pool, no-smoking rooms, no elevator* ⊟ *AE, MC, V.*

NIGHTLIFE

Watch real cowboys and cowgirls two-step to live music at **Buffalo Chip Saloon** (⊠ *6811 E. Cave Creek Rd., Cave Creek* ☎ *480/488–9118*), where you can also chow down on mesquite-grilled chicken and buffalo chips (hot, homemade potato chips). Reservations are suggested for the all-you-can-eat Friday night fish fry that draws crowds. There's live music and dancing Thursday through Saturday. At **Crazy Ed's Satisfied Frog Restaurant and Goatsucker Saloon** (⊠ *6245 E. Cave Creek Rd., Cave Creek* ⊕ *www.satisfiedfrog.com* ☎ *480/488–3317*) you can sing along with Jack "Fast Fingers" Fairclough as he plays the honky-tonk piano. **Harold's Cave Creek Corral** (⊠ *6895 E. Cave Creek Rd., Cave Creek* ☎ *480/488–1906* ⊕ *www.haroldscorral.com*) is just across the dirt parking lot from the Buffalo Chip Saloon. Harold's has two full bars, a restaurant (serving some of the best ribs in the Valley), a huge dance floor with live bands on weekends, a game room, and 15 TVs.

SHOPPING

Cave Creek and Carefree have a thriving arts community with hundreds of artists and dozens of galleries. **El Pedregal Festival Marketplace** (⊠*Scottsdale Rd. and Carefree Hwy., Carefree* 📞*480/488–1072*) is a two-tier shopping plaza at the foot of a 250-foot boulder formation. In spring and summer there are open-air Thursday-night concerts in the courtyard amphitheater. In addition to its posh boutiques and specialty stores, el Pedregal houses Roberts Gallery, the exclusive dealer of artist Virgil Walker's exquisite and must-see feathered sculptures. **Spanish Village** (⊠*Ho and Hum Rds., Carefree* 📞*480/488–0350*), an outdoor shopping area, is complete with bell tower, fountains, courtyards, and winding alleyways. You can while away an afternoon browsing 30 shops, then contemplate dinner at one of several casual restaurants.

WICKENBURG

36 *70 mi from Phoenix. Follow I–17 north for about 25 mins to Carefree Hwy. (AZ 74) junction. About 30 mi west on AZ 74, take U.S. 89/93 north and go another 10 mi to Wickenburg.*

This town, land of guest ranches and tall tales, is named for Henry Wickenburg, whose nearby Vulture Mine was the richest gold strike in the Arizona Territory. In the late 1800s, Wickenburg was a booming mining town on the banks of the Hassayampa River, with a seemingly endless supply of gold, copper, and silver. Nowadays, Wickenburg's Old West history attracts visitors to its sleepy downtown and Western museum. There's a group of good antiques shops, most of which are on Tegner and Frontier streets.

On the northeast corner of Wickenburg Way and Tegner Street, check out the **Jail Tree,** to which prisoners were chained, the desert heat sometimes finishing them off before their sentences were served.

Maps for self-guided walking tours of the town's historic buildings are available at the **Wickenburg Chamber of Commerce** (⊠*216 N. Frontier St.* 📞*928/684–5479* ⊕*www.wickenburgchamber.com*), in the city's old Santa Fe Depot.

The **Desert Caballeros Western Museum** has one of the best collections of Western art in the nation with paintings and sculpture by Remington, Bierstadt, Joe Beeler (founder of the Cowboy Artists of America), and others. Kids enjoy the re-creation of a turn-of-the-20th-century Main Street that includes a general store, period clothing, and a large collection of cowboy gear. ⊠*21 N. Frontier St.* 📞*928/684–2272* ⊕*www. westernmuseum.org* 💲*$7.50* ⊙*Mon.–Sat. 10–5, Sun. noon–4.*

The self-guided trails of **Hassayampa River Preserve** wind through lush cottonwood-willow forests, mesquite trees, and around a 4-acre, spring-fed pond and marsh habitat. Waterfowl, herons, and Arizona's rarest raptors shelter here. ⊠*3 mi southeast of Wickenburg on U.S. 60* 📞*928/684–2772* 💲*$5* ⊙*Mid-Sept.–mid-May, Wed.–Sun. 8–5; Summer hours vary depending on fire danger and weather. Call to check.*

🕙 **Robson's Mining World** is a replica of a 19th-century mining town that has the world's largest collection of antique mining equipment, the Nellie Meda gold mine, more than 30 buildings, a restaurant, a saloon, and a general store. Visitors can stay at the old mining hotel ($) which has 26 rooms. Attractions include hanging out in town, panning for gold, or hiking in the desert or the nearby Harcuvar Mountains. The restaurant serves juicy prime rib and a miner's pie filled with meat, potatoes, and vegetables, baked in pastry. ⊠ *29 mi west of Wickenburg on U.S. 60 to AZ 71, Box 3465, Wickenburg* ☎ *928/685–2609* 🖷 *928/685–4164* ⊕ *www.robsonsminingworld.com* 🎫 *$5* ⊙ *Oct.–Apr., weekdays 10–4, weekends 9–5.*

The **Vulture Mine** was once the largest producing gold mine in Arizona, though its vein has long since run out. A small town originally grew up around the mine, but the only things left today are a few storage buildings and a home where caretakers live. The self-guided tour through this "ghost town" wanders past mining memorabilia; old buildings including bunkhouses, the jail, and a blacksmith shop; the mine shaft itself; and the infamous hanging tree where more than a dozen ore thieves (high graders) were hanged. ∎TIP→**Vulture Mine offers no protective safeguards for its aged buildings, shafts, and equipment. Wander at your own risk and keep an eye on children.** Head west from Wickenburg on U.S. 60 for about 6 mi; then turn left onto Vulture Mine Road and travel 12 mi to the mine at the end of the pavement. ⊠ *Vulture Mine Rd., Vulture Mine* ☎ *602/859–2743* 🎫 *$7* ⊙ *Sept.–May, daily 9–4.*

WHERE TO STAY & EAT

¢–$$ ✕ **Anita's Cocina.** Reliable Tex-Mex fare is served at Anita's. The fresh tamales are tasty, for lunch or dinner. Try a fruit burrito for dessert. ⊠ *57 N. Valentine St.* ☎ *928/684–5777* ▤ *MC, V.*

🕙 $$$$ 🛏 **Rancho de los Caballeros.** This 20,000-acre property combines the
Fodor's Choice   guest-ranch experience with first-class amenities. Meals are served in
★   the lodge's bright, festive dining room, and everyone is asked to dress for each night's sit-down dinner. Rooms are spacious and done in low-key Southwestern style. Some contain two queen-size beds and can be creatively configured through a system of adjoining doors to annex separate living rooms or sleeping quarters for children. Activities ranging from skeet-shooting to horseback riding are available. The Los Caballeros Golf Club course is considered one of the country's top resort courses. ⊠ *1551 S. Vulture Mine Rd., 85390* ☎ *928/684–5484 or 800/684–5030* 🖷 *928/684–2267* ⊕ *www.sunc.com* ➹ *79 rooms* 🛆 *In-hotel: restaurant, bar, golf course, spa, tennis courts, pool, bicycles, children's programs (ages 5–12), no elevator* ▤ *MC, V* ⊙ *Closed mid-May–early Oct.*

$$$–$$$$ 🛏 **Kay El Bar Ranch.** On the National Register of Historic Places, this remote guest ranch is personable and low-key. Some of the biggest mesquite trees in Arizona shade the lodge, a family cottage with private patio (built in 1914), two separate casitas, and a charming adobe cookhouse. In the evening everyone gathers in the living room by the stone fireplace for cocktails and homemade hors d'oeuvres. ⊠ *37500 S. Rincon Rd.* ◌ *Box 2480, 85358* ☎ *928/684–7593 or 800/684–*

7583 ⊕*www.kayelbar.com* ⤴*8 rooms, 1 house, 2 casitas* ⚲*In-room: no phone, no TV. In-hotel: restaurant, pool, no elevator* ☰*MC, V* ⊙*Closed May–mid-Oct.* ℱ*FAP.*

NIGHTLIFE
The **Rancher Bar** (⊠*910 W. Wickenburg Way* ☎*928/684–5957)* is a modern-day saloon where real live wranglers and cowboys meet up to shoot some pool, and the breeze, after a hard day's work.

ARCOSANTI

 65 mi north of Phoenix on I–17, near exit for Cordes Junction (AZ 69).

Two miles down a partly paved road northeast from the gas stations and cafés, the evolving complex and community of Arcosanti was masterminded by Italian architect Paolo Soleri to be a self-sustaining habitat in which architecture and ecology function in symbiosis. Building began in 1970 but Arcosanti is a bit tired-looking these days and hasn't quite achieved Soleri's original vision. It's still worth a stop to take a tour, have a bite at the café, and purchase one of the hand-cast bronze wind-bells made at the site. The town is off I–17 at Cordes Junction, near the town of Mayer. ☎*928/632–7135* ⊕*www.arcosanti.org* ᴿ*Tour $8* ⊙*Daily 9–5; tours hourly 10–4.*

CASA GRANDE RUINS NATIONAL MONUMENT

38 *Take U.S. 60 east (Superstition Freeway) to Florence Junction (U.S. 60 and AZ 89) and head south 16 mi on AZ 89 to Florence. Casa Grance is 9 mi west of Florence on AZ 287 or, from I–10, 16 mi east on AZ 387 and AZ 87. Note: follow signs to ruins, not to town of Casa Grande. When leaving the ruins, take AZ 87 north 35 mi back to U.S. 60.*

The ruins of Casa Grande, whose original purpose still eludes archaeologists, were unknown to European explorers until Father Kino, a Jesuit missionary, first recorded their existence in 1694. The ruins were set aside as federal land in 1892 and named a national monument in 1918. Although only a few prehistoric sites can be viewed, more than 60 are in the monument area, including the 35-foot-tall (that's four stories) Casa Grande (Big House). The tallest Hohokam building known, Casa Grande was built in the early 14th century and is believed by some to have been an ancient astronomical observatory or a center of government, religion, trade, or education. Allow an hour to explore the site, longer if park rangers are giving a talk or leading a tour.

■**TIP➡On your way out, cross the parking lot by the covered picnic grounds and climb the platform for a view of a ball court and two platform mounds, said to date from the 1100s.** ⊠*AZ 87, Coolidge* ☎*520/723–3172* ⊕*www.nps.gov/cagr* ᴿ*$5* ⊙*Daily 8–5.*

THE APACHE TRAIL

Fodor'sChoice
★
President Roosevelt called this 150-mi drive "the most awe-inspiring and most sublimely beautiful panorama nature ever created." A stretch of winding highway, the AZ 88 portion of the Apache Trail closely follows the route forged through wilderness in 1906 to move construction supplies for building the Roosevelt Dam, which lies at the northernmost part of the loop. Although the drive itself can be completed in one day, it's advisable to spend a night in Globe, continuing the loop back to Phoenix the following day.

From the town of Apache Junction, you can choose to drive the trail in either direction; there are advantages to both. If you begin the loop going clockwise—heading eastward on AZ 88 to the Superstition Mountains, the Peralta Trail, Boyce Thompson Arboretum, Globe, Tonto National Monument, Theodore Roosevelt Lake Reservoir & Dam, and Tortilla Flat—your drive may be more relaxing; you'll be on the farthest side of this narrow dirt road some refer to as the "white-knuckle route," with its switchbacks and drop-offs straight down into spectacular Fish Creek Canyon. ■TIP➔This 42-mi-long drive is not for someone who is afraid of heights. But if you follow the route counterclockwise—continuing on U.S. 60 past the town of Apache Junction—you'll be able to appreciate each attraction better.

SUPERSTITION MOUNTAINS

39 *From Phoenix, take I–10 and then U.S. 60 (the Superstition Freeway) east through suburbs of Tempe, Mesa, and Apache Junction.*

As the Phoenix metro area gives way to cactus- and creosote-dotted desert, the massive escarpment of the Superstition Mountains heaves into view and slides by to the north. The Superstitions are supposedly where the legendary Lost Dutchman Mine is, the location—not to mention the existence—of which has been hotly debated since pioneer days (⇨ *The Lost Dutchman Mine CloseUp*).

The best place to learn about the "Dutchman" Jacob Waltz and the Lost Dutchman Mine is at **Superstition Mountain Museum** (⌧*4087 N. Apache Trail, AZ 88, Apache Junction* ☎*480/983–4888* ⊕*www.superstitionmountainmuseum.org* ⌧*$5* ⊙*Daily 9–4*). The museum exhibits include a collection of mining tools, historical maps, and artifacts relating to the "gold" age of the Superstition Mountains.

Goldfield became an instant city of about 4,000 residents after a gold strike in 1892; the town dried up five years later when the gold mine flooded. Today, **Goldfield Ghost Town** (⌧*4650 N. Mammoth Mine Rd., 4 mi northeast of Apache Junction on AZ 88, Goldfield* ☎*480/983–0333* ⊕*www.goldfieldghosttown.com*) is an interesting place to grab a cool drink, pan for gold, go for a mine tour, or take a desert jeep ride or horseback tour of the area. The ghost town's shops are open daily 10 to 5, the saloon daily 10 to 8.

PERALTA TRAIL

40 *About 11½ mi southeast of Apache Junction, off U.S. 60, take Peralta Trail Rd., just past King's Ranch Rd., an 8-mi, rough gravel road that leads to the start of the Peralta Trail.*

The 4-mi round-trip Peralta Trail winds 1,400 feet up a small valley for a spectacular view of **Weaver's Needle,** a monolithic rock formation that is one of Arizona's more famous sights. Allow a few hours for this rugged and challenging hike, bring plenty of water, sunscreen, a hat, and a snack or lunch, and don't hike it in the middle of the day in summer.

BOYCE THOMPSON ARBORETUM

★ **41** *12 mi east of Florence Junction (U.S. 60 and AZ 89).*

At the foot of Picketpost Mountain in Superior, the Boyce Thompson Arboretum is often called an oasis in the desert: the arid rocky expanse gives way to lush riparian glades home to 3,200 different desert plants and more than 230 bird and 72 terrestrial species. The arboretum offers a living album of the world's desert and semiarid region plants, including exotic species such as Canary Islands date palms and Australian eucalyptus. Trails offer breathtaking scenery in the gardens and the exhibits, especially during the spring wildflower season. A variety of unique tours are offered year round. Benches with built-in misters offer relief from the heat. Bring along a picnic and enjoy the beauty. ✉*37615 U.S. 60, Superior* ☎*520/689–2811* ⊕*www.ag.arizona.edu/ bta* ☜*$7.50* ☉*May–Aug., daily 6 AM–3 PM; Sept.–Apr., daily 8–5.*

EN ROUTE A few miles past the arboretum, **Superior** is the first of several modest mining towns and the launching point for a dramatic winding ascent through the Mescals to a 4,195-foot pass that affords panoramic views of this copper-rich range and its huge, dormant, open-pit mines. Collectors will want to watch for antiques shops through these hills, but be forewarned that quality varies considerably. A gradual descent will take you into **Miami** and **Claypool**, once-thriving boomtowns that have carried on quietly since major-corporation mining ground to a halt in the 1970s. Working-class buildings are dwarfed by the mountainous piles of copper tailings to the north. At a stoplight in Claypool, AZ 88 splits off northward to the Apache Trail, but continue on U.S. 60 another 3 mi to make the stop in the city of Globe.

GLOBE

42 *U.S. 60, 51 mi east of Apache Junction, 25 mi east of Superior, and 3 mi east of Claypool's AZ 88 turnoff.*

In the southern reaches of Tonto National Forest, Globe is the most cosmopolitan of the area's mining towns. Initially, it was gold and silver that brought miners here—the city allegedly got its name from a large, circular boulder of silver, with lines like continents, found by prospectors—although the region is now known for North America's

The Lost Dutchman Mine

Not much is known about Jacob "the Dutchman" Waltz, except that he was born around 1808 in Germany (he was "Deutsch," not "Dutch") and emigrated to the United States, where he spent several years at mining camps in the Southeast, in the West, and finally in Arizona. There's documentation that he did indeed have access to a large quantity of gold, though he never registered a claim for the mine that was attributed to him.

In 1868 Waltz appeared in the newly developing community of Pumpkinville, soon to become Phoenix. He kept to himself on his 160-acre homestead on the banks of the Salt River. From time to time, he would disappear for a few weeks and return with enough high-quality ore to keep him in a wonderful fashion. Soon word was out that "Crazy Jake" had a vast gold mine in the Superstition Mountains, east of the city near the Apache Trail.

At the same time, stories about a wealthy gold mine discovered by the Peralta family of Mexico were circulating. Local Apaches raided the mine, which was near their sacred Thunder Mountain, in what became known as the Peralta Massacre, and the Peraltas and more than 100 people working for them at the mine were killed. Rumors soon spread that Waltz had saved the life of a young Mexican who was part of Peralta's group—one of few who had escaped—and was shown the Peralta's mine as a reward.

As the legend of the Dutchman's mine grew, many opportunists attempted to follow Waltz into the Superstition Mountains. A crack marksman, Waltz quickly discouraged several who tried to track him. The flow of gold continued for several years.

In 1891 the Salt River flooded, badly damaging Waltz's home. When the floodwaters receded, neighbors found Waltz there in a weakened condition. He was taken to the nearby home and boarding house of Julia Thomas, who nursed the Dutchman for months. When his death was imminent, he reportedly gave Julia the directions to his mine.

Julia and another boarder searched for the mine fruitlessly. In her later years, she sold maps to the treasure, based upon her recollections of Waltz's description. Thousands have searched for the lost mine; many losing their lives—either to the brutality of fellow searchers or that of the rugged desert—in the process and more than a century later, gold seekers are still trying to connect the pieces of the puzzle.

There's no doubt that the Dutchman had a source of extremely rich gold ore but was it in the Superstition Mountains, the nearby Goldfields, or maybe even in the Four Peaks region? Wherever it was, it's still hidden. Perhaps the best-researched books on the subject are T. E. Glover's *The Lost Dutchman Mine of Jacob Waltz* and the companion book, *The Holmes Manuscript*. Ron Feldman of OK Corral (☎ 480/982–4040 ⊕ *www.okcorrals. com*) in Apache Junction has become an expert on the subject during his 30-plus years in the region. He leads adventurers on pack trips into the mysterious mountains to relive the lore and legends.

richest copper deposits. ■TIP→**If you're driving the Apache Trail loop, stop in Globe to fill up the tank; it's the last chance to gas up until looping all the way back to U.S. 60 at Apache Junction.** Globe is worth more than a quick pit stop, though; its charm is its lack of prestige—and, in some cases, modernity.

At the **Globe Chamber of Commerce** (✉*1360 N. Broad St., Globe, 1¼ mi north of downtown on U.S. 60* ☎*928/425–4495 or 800/804–5623* ⊕*www.globemiamichamber.com*), open weekdays 8–5, Saturday 10–2, Sunday 11–2, you can pick up brochures detailing the self-guided Historic Downtown Walking Tour.

A good place to begin a visit to Globe is the **Gila County Historical Museum** (✉*1330 N. Broad St.* ☎*928/425–7385*), where you can see the collection of memorabilia from the area's mining days. The museum, which is free, is open Monday to Saturday, 9 to 4.

The restored late-19th-century Gila County Courthouse houses the **Cobre Valley Center for the Arts** (✉*101 N. Broad St.* ☎*928/425–0884*) and showcases works by local artists. It's open Monday to Saturday, 10 to 4.

For a step 800 years back in time, tour the 2 acres of excavated Salado Indian ruins on the southeastern side of town at the **Besh-Ba-Gowah Archaeological Park.** After a trip through the small museum and a video introduction, enter the area full of remnants of more than 200 rooms occupied here by the Salado during the 13th and 14th centuries. Public areas include the central plaza (also the principal burial ground), roasting pits, and open patios. Besh-Ba-Gowah is a name given by the Apaches, who, arriving in the 17th century, found the pueblo abandoned and moved in—loosely translated, the name means "metal camp," and remains left on the site point to it as part of an extensive commerce and trading network. ✉*150 N. Pine St.* ☎*928/425–0320 or 800/804–5623* ⊕*www.jqjacobs.net/southwest/besh_ba_gowah.html* 🎫*$3* ⊙*Daily 9–5.*

WHERE TO STAY & EAT

¢–$ ✕ **Chalo's.** This roadside spot offers top-notch Mexican and Tex-Mex food. Try the savory stuffed sopaipillas, filled with pork and beef, beans, and red or green chiles. ✉*902 E. Ash St.* ☎*928/425–0515* ▤*AE, D, MC, V.*

¢–$ ⬚ **Noftsger Hill Inn.** Built in 1907, this B&B was originally the North Globe Schoolhouse; now classrooms serve as guest rooms, filled with mining-era antiques and affording fantastic views of the Pinal Mountains and historic Old Dominion Mine. All rooms have private baths; one has air-conditioning, and the rest have evaporative coolers, which work well at this higher elevation. You can walk off "miner-size" breakfasts on the enjoyable hike through the scenic Copper Hills behind the old school. ✉*425 North St., 85501* ☎*928/425–2260 or 877/780–2479* ⊕*www.noftsgerhillinn.com* ⇆*6 rooms* ⌂*In-room: no a/c (some), VCR (some), no TV (some). In-hotel: no-smoking rooms, no elevator* ▤*MC, V* ⏀*BP.*

¢   🏨 **El Rey Motel.** Hosts Rebecca and Ricardo Bernal operate this quintessential roadside motel, where wagon wheels and potted plants pepper the grounds. This vintage motor court offers small, immaculate rooms, covered parking spaces, and a shared central picnic and barbecue area. ✉1201 E. Ash St., 85501 ☎928/425–4427 🖷928/402–9147 ⛶23 rooms ♿In-hotel: no elevator ⊟AE, D, MC, V.

NIGHTLIFE

Run by the San Carlos Apache tribe, **Apache Gold** (✉U.S. 70, 5 mi east of Globe ☎928/425–7800 or 800/272–2433 ⊕www.apachegoldcasinoresort.com) has more than 500 slots, blackjack, keno, bingo, and video and live poker. Call about the free shuttle from most of Globe's hotels and motels. The Apache Grill Restaurant offers gourmet dishes and the Wickiup Buffet serves authentic Apache and Southwestern cuisine.

SHOPPING

Broad Street, Globe's main drag, is lined with antiques and gift shops. On Ash, between Hill and South East streets, **Copper City Rock Shop** (✉566 Ash St. ☎928/425–7885) specializes in mineral products, many from Arizona. **Past Times** (✉150 W. Mesquite ☎928/425–2220) carries antiques. **True Blue Jewelry** (✉200 N. Willow St. ☎928/425–8361) carries high-quality jewelry made with turquoise supplied by Globe's Sleeping Beauty Mine. Ask to watch the five-minute video about turquoise mining and preparing it for use. Try **Turquoise Ladies** (✉996 N. Broad St. ☎928/425–6288) for owner June Stratton's collection of uniquely Globe souvenirs and stories.

EN ROUTE   At the stoplight 3 mi south of Globe on U.S. 60, AZ 88 splits off to the northwest. About 25 mi later on AZ 88, heading toward the Tonto National Monument, you'll see towering quartzite cliffs about 2 mi in the distance—look up and to the left for glimpses of the 40-room **Upper Ruins,** 14th-century condos left behind by the Salado people. They can't be seen from within the national monument, so make sure you've got binoculars.

TONTO NATIONAL MONUMENT

43 *30 mi northeast of the intersection of U.S. 60 and AZ 88.*

This well-preserved complex of 13th-century Salado cliff dwellings is worth a stop. There's a self-guided walking tour of the Lower Cliff Dwellings, but if you can, take a ranger-led tour of the 40-room Upper Cliff Dwellings, offered on selected mornings from November to April. Tour reservations are required and should be made as far as a month in advance. ✉AZ 88, Roosevelt ⌂HC 02, Box 4602, 85545 ☎928/467–2241 ⊕www.nps.gov/tont 🎫$3 ⊙Daily 8–5.

THEODORE ROOSEVELT LAKE RESERVOIR & DAM

44 *5 mi northwest of Tonto National Monument on AZ 88.*

Flanked by the desolate Mazatzal and Sierra Anchas mountain ranges, this aquatic recreational area is a favorite with bass anglers, water-skiers, and boaters. This is the largest masonry dam on the planet, and the massive bridge is the longest two-lane, single-span, steel-arch bridge in the nation.

EN ROUTE Past the reservoir, AZ 88 turns west and becomes a meandering dirt road, eventually winding its way back to Apache Junction via the magnificent, bronze-hue volcanic cliff walls of **Fish Creek Canyon**, with views of the sparkling lakes, towering saguaros, and, in the springtime, vast fields of wildflowers.

TORTILLA FLAT

45 *AZ 88, 38 mi southwest of Roosevelt Dam; 18 mi northeast of Apache Junction.*

Close to the end of the Apache Trail, this old-time restaurant and country store are what is left of an authentic stagecoach stop. This is a fun place to stop for a well-earned rest and refreshment—miner- and cowboy-style grub, of course—before heading back the last 18 mi to civilization. Enjoy a hearty bowl of killer chili and some prickly-pear-cactus ice cream while sitting at the counter on a saddle barstool.

VALLEY OF THE SUN ESSENTIALS

To research prices, get advice from other travelers, and book travel arrangements, visit ⊕*www.fodors.com.*

TRANSPORTATION

BY AIR

Phoenix Sky Harbor International Airport (PHX) is served by most major airlines; it's a hub for US Airways and Southwest Airlines. Just 3 mi east of downtown Phoenix, it's surrounded by freeways linking it to almost every part of the metro area. The "Stage & Go Lot," west of the Terminal 2 parking garage, allows drivers to wait in their cars free of charge as an alternative to circling the terminals. The new "pet park" with restroom facilities and water for Fido is outside the west-end baggage claim level at Terminal 4.

It's easy to get from Sky Harbor to downtown Phoenix (3 mi west) and Tempe (3 mi east). The airport is also only about 30 minutes by freeway from Glendale (to the west) and Mesa (to the east). Scottsdale (to the northeast) can be reached by AZ 101; depending on your destination and your time of arrival, expect the trip to take anywhere from 25 minutes to downtown Scottsdale to an hour to North Scottsdale.

Valley Metro buses can get you directly from Terminal 2, 3, or 4 to the bus terminal downtown (at 1st and Washington streets) or to Tempe (Mill and University avenues). With free transfers, the bus can take you from the airport to most other Valley cities (Glendale, Sun City, Scottsdale, etc.), but the trip is likely to be slow unless you take an express.

Red Line buses (part of Valley Metro) originate at the downtown terminal and run westbound to Phoenix every half hour from about 6 AM until after 9 PM weekdays. Saturday, take Bus 13 and transfer at Central Avenue to Bus 0 north. The Red Line runs eastbound to Tempe every half hour from 3:30 AM to 7 PM; 25 minutes later, it goes to downtown Mesa. Fares range from $.60 to $1.75.

The blue vans of SuperShuttle cruise Sky Harbor, each taking up to seven passengers to their individual destinations, with no luggage fee or airport surcharge. Wheelchair vans are also available. Drivers accept credit cards and expect tips. Fares are $7 to downtown Phoenix, around $16 to most places in Scottsdale, and $20 to $35 to places in far north Scottsdale or Carefree. SuperShuttle also operates the upscale and personalized ExecuCar service.

Only a few taxi firms (Checker/Yellow Cab and Courier Cab are good options) are licensed to pick up at Sky Harbor's commercial terminals. All add a $1 surcharge for airport pickups, don't charge for luggage, and are available 24 hours a day. A trip to downtown Phoenix can cost from $8 to $12. The fare to downtown Scottsdale averages about $25. If you're headed to the East Valley, expect to shell out more than $30.

A few limousine firms cruise Sky Harbor, and many more provide airport pickups by reservation. Scottsdale Limousine requires reservations but offers a toll-free number; rates start at $65 (plus tip).

Contacts ExecuCar (☎602/232–4600 or 800/410–4444 ⊕ www.supershuttle. com). **Scottsdale Limousine** (☎480/946–8446 or 800/747–8234). **Sky Harbor International Airport (PHX)** (☎602/273–3300 ⊕ www.phxskyharbor.com). **SuperShuttle** (☎602/244–9000 or 800/258–3826 ⊕ www.supershuttle.com). **Valley Metro buses** (☎602/253–5000).

BY BUS

Greyhound Lines has statewide and national routes from its main terminal near Sky Harbor airport.

Valley Metro routes service most of the Valley suburbs, but these routes are not really suitable for vacationers and offer limited service evenings and weekends.

Phoenix runs a free Downtown Area Shuttle (DASH), with purple minibuses circling the area between the Arizona Center and the state capitol at 15-minute intervals from 6:30 AM to 11 PM weekdays and from 11 AM to 11 PM weekends; this system also serves major thoroughfares in several suburbs—Glendale, Scottsdale, Tempe, Mesa, and Chandler. The city of Tempe operates the Free Local Area Shuttle (FLASH), which serves the downtown Tempe and Arizona State University area from

7 AM until 8 PM. Check the Valley Metro Web site for all public transit options (including DASH and FLASH) in the Valley.

Contacts Greyhound Lines (✉ *2115 E. Buckeye Rd., Phoenix* ☎ *602/389–4200 or 800/229–9424* ⊕ *www.greyhound.com*). **Valley Metro** (☎ *602/262–7433* ⊕ *www.valleymetro.org*).

BY CAR

To get around Phoenix, *you will need a car.* Only the major down-town areas (Phoenix, Scottsdale, Tempe, and Glendale) are pedestrian-friendly. There's no mass transit beyond a commuter-bus system. At the airport most rental companies offer shuttle services to their lots.
■ TIP➔ **Don't expect to nab a rental car without a reservation, however, especially in the high season, from January to April.**

If you're driving to Phoenix and coming from the west, you'll prob-ably come in on I–10. The trip from the Los Angeles basin, via Palm Springs, takes six to seven hours, depending on where you start. From San Diego, I–8 slices across the low desert to Yuma and on toward the Valley on what the Spanish called El Camino del Diablo (the Devil's Highway); at Gila Bend, take AZ 85 up to I–10. The trip takes six to seven hours. From the east, I–10 takes you from El Paso, across south-ern New Mexico, and through Chiricahua Apache country into Tuc-son, then north to Phoenix (a total of about six to seven hours).

From the northwest, I–40 crosses over from California and runs along old Route 66 to Flagstaff. East of Kingman, however, U.S. 93 branches off diagonally to the southeast, becoming U.S. 60 at Wickenburg and continuing into Phoenix.

The northeastern route, I–40 from Albuquerque, crosses Hopi and Navajo historic lands to Flagstaff, where I–17 takes you south to Phoe-nix—an eight-hour journey. For a scenic shortcut, take AZ 377 south at Holbrook to Heber and the pines of the Mogollon Rim; then take AZ 260 down the 2,000-foot drop to Payson and AZ 87 through the forests of saguaro cactus into Phoenix.

Around downtown Phoenix, AZ 202 (Papago Freeway), AZ 143 (Hohokam Freeway), and I–10 (Maricopa Freeway) make an elongated east–west loop, encompassing the state capitol area to the west and Tempe to the east. At mid-loop, AZ 51 (Piestewa—formerly Squaw—Peak Parkway) runs north into Phoenix. From AZ 202 east, the AZ 101 runs north to Scottsdale and makes a loop west through Glendale, Peoria, Sun City, and Avondale and connects to I–10. And from the loop's east end, I–10 runs south to Tucson, 100 mi away (although it's still referred to as I–10 East, as it's eventually headed that way); U.S. 60 (Superstition Freeway) branches east to Tempe and Mesa.

Roads in Phoenix and its suburbs are laid out on a single, 800-square-mi grid. Even the freeways run predominantly north–south and east–west. (Grand Avenue, running about 20 mi from northwest downtown to Sun City, is the *only* diagonal.)

Central Avenue is the main north–south grid axis: all roads parallel to and west of Central are numbered *avenues*; all roads parallel to and east of Central are numbered *streets*. The numbering begins at Central and increases in each direction.

RULES OF THE ROAD
Camera devices are mounted on several streetlights and select freeways to catch speeders and red-light runners, and their locations are constantly changing. You may think you've gotten away with a few miles over the limit and return home only to find a ticket waiting for you.

Many accidents in the Valley are created as a result of confusion in the left-turn lanes. Each individual jurisdiction varies: in some, the left-turn arrow precedes the green light and in other jurisdictions it follows the green light. As well, the yellow lights tend to be shorter than most drivers are accustomed to so be prepared for sudden stops and watch intersections for yellow-light runners. Weekdays 6 AM to 9 AM and 4 PM to 6 PM, the center or left-turn lanes on the major surface arteries of 7th Street and 7th Avenue become one-way traffic-flow lanes between McDowell Road and Dunlap Avenue. These specially marked lanes are dedicated mornings to north–south traffic (into downtown) and afternoons to south–north traffic (out of downtown).

BY TAXI
Taxi fares are unregulated in Phoenix, except at the airport. The 800-square-mi metro area is so large that one-way fares in excess of $50 are not uncommon; it's a good idea to ask what the damages will be before you get in, since it will often be cheaper to rent a car, even if you are renting for only a day. Except within a compact area, such as central Phoenix, travel by taxi is not recommended.

Taxis charge about $3 for the first mile and $1.50 per mile thereafter (not including tips).

Contacts Checker/Yellow Cab (☎ 602/252–5252). **Courier Cab** (☎ 602/232–2222).

BY TRAIN
Amtrak provides train service in Arizona with bus transfers to Phoenix. Eastbound train passengers will stop in Flagstaff, where Amtrak buses depart for Phoenix each morning. Westbound train travelers will likely make the transfer in Tucson, where Amtrak-run buses have limited service to Phoenix on Sunday, Tuesday, and Thursday nights. What used to be Phoenix's downtown train terminal is now the Amtrak Thruway Bus Stop.

Information Amtrak (✉ *4th Ave. and Harrison St.* ☎ *602/253–0121 or 800/872–7245* ⊕ *www.amtrak.com*).

CONTACTS & RESOURCES

EMERGENCIES

Emergencies Ambulance, Fire, and Police Emergencies (☎ *911*).

Hospitals Maricopa County Medical Center (✉ *2601 E. Roosevelt St., Central Phoenix* ☎ *602/344–5011*). Scottsdale Memorial Hospital (✉ *7400 E. Osborn Rd., Central Scottsdale, Scottsdale* ☎ *480/481–4000 or 480/860–3000*). Doctor Referral (☎ *602/252–2844*).

INTERNET

These days, wireless Internet (Wi-Fi) is widely available throughout the Valley of the Sun, including Sky Harbor Airport and the state capitol complexes downtown. To attract customers, many businesses offer it for free while some, like Starbucks charge a tidy sum to sip and surf. Most hotels have grown hip to the benefit of offering hot spots, especially for business travelers and, while most of them charge for the service, others will offer it free in public areas. For those traveling without a laptop, cyberspace is still just a click away on public computers for a fee. Larger hotels and resorts generally have business centers with computer and Internet service.

TOUR OPTIONS

Reservations for tours are a must all year, with seats often filling up quickly in the busy season, October through April. All tours provide pickup service at area resorts, but some offer lower prices if you drive to the tour's point of origin.

BIKING, HIKING & RAFTING TRIPS

Arizona Outback Adventures leads hiking, biking, and rafting tours around the state. Cimarron Adventures and River Co. arranges half-day float trips down the Salt and Verde rivers; trips cost about $35 per person. Desert Voyages specializes in raft and kayak trips.

Contacts Arizona Outback Adventures (☎ *480/945–2881* ⊕ *www.aoa-adventures.com*). Cimarron Adventures and River Co. (☎ *480/994–1199* ⊕ *www.cimarronadventures.com*). Desrt Voyages (☎ *480/998–7238* ⊕ *www.desertvoyagers.com*).

ORIENTATION TOURS

Gray Line Tours gives seasonal, three-hour narrated tours including downtown Phoenix, the Arizona Biltmore hotel, Camelback Mountain, mansions in Paradise Valley, Arizona State University, Papago Park, and Scottsdale's Old Town; the price is about $40.

Open Road Tours offers excursions to Sedona and the Grand Canyon, Phoenix city tours, and Native American–culture trips to the Salt River Pima–Maricopa Indian Reservation.

For $38, Vaughan's Southwest Custom Tours gives a 4½-hour city tour for 11 or fewer passengers in custom vans, stopping at the Pueblo Grande Museum, the Arizona Biltmore, and the state capitol. Vaughan's will also take you east of Phoenix on the Apache Trail. The tour is offered on Tuesday, Friday, and Saturday; the cost is $75.

Contacts **Gray Line Tours** (☎ *602/495–9100 or 800/732–0327* ⊕ *www. graylinearizona.com*). **Open Road Tours** (☎ *602/997–6474 or 800/766–7117* ⊕ *www.openroadtours.com*). **Vaughan's Southwest Custom Tours** (☎ *602/971– 1381 or 800/513–1381* ⊕ *www.southwesttours.com*).

VISITOR INFORMATION

The Native American Tourism Center aids in arranging tourist visits to reservation lands; it can't afford to send information packets, but you can call or stop in weekdays 8 to 5.

Contacts **Arizona Office of Tourism** (☎ *602/364–3730 or 888/520–3444* ⊕ *www. arizonaguide.com*). **Native American Tourism Center** (⊠ *4130 N. Goldwater Blvd., Phoenix* ☎ *480/945–0771* 🖷 *480/945–0264*).

Greater Phoenix Convention and Visitors Bureau (☎ *602/254–6500* ⊕ *www. phoenixcvb.com*). **Scottsdale Convention and Visitors Bureau** (☎ *480/421–1004 or 800/782–1117* ⊕ *www.scottsdalecvb.com*).

Grand Canyon National Park

Grand Canyon

WORD OF MOUTH

"When we were there we viewed the sunset from the main area outside Bright Angel lodge—beautiful! We caught the sunrise from the South Kaibab trailhead—beautiful! Storm rolled in that night, no sunset just thunder and lightning—awesome! Next day, cloudy, misty, light rain, sun peeking though clouds—beautiful! I guess what I am saying is don't get too hung up on being at the right spot for the sunrise/sunset, it's all spectacular!"

—BlackandGold

WELCOME TO GRAND CANYON NATIONAL PARK

Visitors at sunset viewing Grand Canyon from Mather Point on the South Rim

TOP REASONS TO GO

★ **Its status:** This is one of those places you really want to be able say, "Been there, done that!"

★ **Awesome Vistas:** Painted desert, sandstone canyon walls, pine and fir forests, mesas, plateaus, volcanic features, the Colorado River, streams, and waterfalls make for some jaw-dropping moments.

★ **Year-round adventure:** Outdoor junkies can bike, boat, camp, fish, hike, ride mules, whitewater raft, watch birds and wildlife, cross-country ski, and snowshoe.

★ **Continuing education:** Adults and kids can get schooled, thanks to free park-sponsored nature walks and interpretive programs.

★ **Sky-high and river-low experiences:** Experience the canyon via plane, train, and automobile, as well as helicopter, boat, bike, mule, or on foot.

1 North Rim. Of the nearly 5 million people who visit the park annually, 90% enter at the South Rim, but many believe the North Rim is even more gorgeous—and worth the extra effort. Accessible only from mid-May to mid-October (or the first good snowfall), the North Rim has legitimate bragging rights: at more than 8,000 feet above sea level (and 1,000 feet higher than the South Rim), it offers precious solitude and three developed viewpoints. Rather than staring into the canyon's depths, you get a true sense of its expanse.

2 South Rim. The South Rim, on the other hand, is where the action is: Grand Canyon Village's lodging, camping, eateries, stores, and museums, plus plenty of trailheads into the canyon. Visitor services and facilities are open and available every day of the year, including holidays. Three shuttle routes, all free, cover 30-some stops, and visitors who'd rather relax than rough it can treat themselves to comfy hotel rooms and elegant restaurant meals (lodging and camping reservations are essential).

Map labels: Kanab Canyon, Colorado River, KANAB PLATEAU, Great Thumb Mesa, Tuweep, The Dome, Supai, Havasu Canyon, Toroweap Overlook, 3, 18, HAVASUPAI INDIAN RESERVATION, 0 10 mi, 0 10 km

Visitors viewing a winter cloud inversion from Mather Point on the South Rim

2

GETTING ORIENTED

Grand Canyon National Park is a superstar—biologically, historically, and recreationally. One of the world's best examples of arid-land erosion, the canyon provides a record of three of the four eras of geological time. In addition to its diverse fossil record, the park reveals prehistoric traces of human adaptation to an unforgiving environment. It's also home to several major ecosystems, five of the world's seven life zones, three of North America's four desert types, and all kinds of rare, endemic, and protected plant and animal species.

3 West Rim. Though technically not in Grand Canyon National Park the west rim of the canyon has some spectacular scenery, and some of the most gorgeous waterfalls in the United States. The recently opened Skywalk, part of the Hualapai Tribe's efforts to expand its tourism offerings on the West Rim, is a U-shaped glass bridge suspended above the Colorado River—not for the faint of heart.

Desert View Watchtower overlooks the eastern end of Grand Canyon

GRAND CANYON NATIONAL PARK PLANNER

When to Go

There's no bad time to visit the canyon, though the busiest times of year are summer and spring break. Visiting during these peak seasons, as well as holidays, requires patience and a tolerance for crowds. Note that weather changes on a whim in this exposed high-desert region. *You cannot visit the North Rim in the winter due to weather conditions and related road closures.*

AVG. HIGH/LOW TEMPS

SOUTH RIM

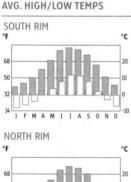

NORTH RIM

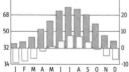

INNER CANYON

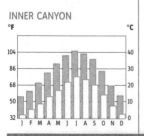

Flora & Fauna

Eighty-eight mammal species inhabit Grand Canyon National Park, as well as 300 species of birds, 24 kinds of lizards, and 24 kinds of snakes. The rare Kaibab squirrel is found only on the North Rim—you can recognize them by their all-white tails and the long tufts of white hair on their ears. The pink Grand Canyon rattlesnake lives at lower elevations within the canyon.

Hawks and ravens are visible year-round. The endangered California condor has been reintroduced to the canyon. Park rangers give daily talks on the magnificent birds, whose wingspan measures 9 feet.

In spring, summer, and fall, mule deer, recognizable by their large antlers, are abundant at the South Rim. Don't be fooled by gentle appearances; these guys can be aggressive. It's illegal to feed them, as it will disrupt their natural habitats, and increase your risk of getting bitten.

The South Rim's Coconino Plateau is fairly flat, at an elevation of about 7,000 feet, and covered with stands of pinyon and ponderosa pines, junipers, and Gambel's oak trees. On the Kaibab Plateau on the North Rim, Douglas fir, spruce, quaking aspen, and more ponderosas prevail. In spring you're likely to see asters, sunflowers, and lupine in bloom at both rims.

Festivals to Plan Your Trip Around

May: Williams Rendezvous Days. A black powder shooting competition, 1800s-era crafts, and a parade fire up Memorial Day weekend in honor of Bill Williams, the town's namesake mountain man. ☎ 928/635–4061 ⊕ www.williamschamber.com.

Sept.: Grand Canyon Music Festival. Three weekends of "mostly chamber" music fills the Shrine of Ages at Grand Canyon Village. ☎ 928/638–9215 or 800/997–8285 ⊕ grandcanyonmusicfest.org.

Dec.: Mountain Village Holiday. Williams hails the holidays with a parade of lights, ice skating rink, Polar Express train rides, and live entertainment. ☎ 928/635–4061 ⊕ www.williamschamber.com.

Getting There & Around

The best route into the park from the east or south is from Flagstaff. Take U.S. 180 northwest to the park's southern entrance and Grand Canyon Village. To go on to the North Rim, go north from Flagstaff on U.S. 89 to Bitter Springs, then take U.S. 89A to the junction of Highway 67 and travel south on the highway for about 40 mi. From the west on Interstate 40, the most direct route to the South Rim is on U.S. 180 and Highway 64.

The South Rim is open to car traffic year-round, though access to Hermits Rest is limited to shuttle buses from March through November. Parking is free once you pay the $25 park entrance fee, but it can be hard to find a spot. Try the large lot in front of the general store near Yavapai Lodge or the Maswik Transportation Center lot. If you visit from October through April, traffic will be lighter parking less of a problem.

There are three free shuttle routes in the Grand Canyon: The Hermits Rest Route operates March through November, between Grand Canyon Village and Hermits Rest. The Village Route operates year-round in the village area; it provides the easiest access to the Canyon View Information Center. The Kaibab Trail Route goes from Canyon View Information Center to Yaki Point, including a stop at the South Kaibab Trailhead. In summer, South Rim roads are congested, and it's easier, and sometimes required, to park your car and take the free shuttle. Running from one hour before sunrise until one hour after sunset, shuttles arrive every 15 to 30 minutes. The roughly 30 stops are clearly marked throughout the park.

The more remote North Rim is off limits during winter. From mid-October (or the first heavy snowfall) through mid-May, there are no services, and Highway 67 south of Jacob Lake is closed.

Planning Your Time

The park is most crowded near the entrances and in Grand Canyon Village, as well as on the scenic drives, especially the 25-mi Desert View Drive. To avoid crowds, go farther into the canyon, and try the mostly paved Rim Trail. See the "Tips for Avoiding Canyon Crowds" box in this chapter for more info.

The best time of day to see the canyon is before 10 AM and after 2 PM, when the angle of the sun brings out the colors of the rock, and clouds and shadows add dimension.

Plan ahead: especially if you want to go down the canyon on a mule: mule rides require at least a six-month advance reservation, and up to one or two year's notice for the busy season (they can be reserved up to 23 months in advance). Sometimes cancellations allow riders to join at the last minute, but don't count on it. For camping and lodging in the park, reservations are also essential; they're taken up to 13 months in advance.

Perhaps the easiest way to visit the West Rim from Vegas is with a tour. The 14-mi, dirt access road is rough, and high-clearance vehicles are a necessity, but **Bighorn Wild West Tours** (702/385–4676 or 888/385–4676) will pick you up in a Hummer at your Vegas hotel for an all-day trip that includes the shuttle-bus package and lunch, for $239.

By Jill Koch   **WHEN IT COMES TO THE GRAND CANYON**, there are statistics, and there are sensations. While the former are impressive—the canyon measures in at an average width of 10 mi, length of 277 mi, and depth of a mile—they don't truly prepare you for that first impression. Seeing the canyon for the first time is an astounding experience—one that's hard to wrap your head around. In fact, it's more than an experience, it's an emotion, one that is only just beginning to be captured with the superlative "Grand."

Nearly 5 million visitors come to the park each year. They can access the canyon via two main points: the South Rim and the North Rim. The width from the North Rim to the South Rim varies from 600 feet to 18 mi, but traveling between rims by road requires a 215-mi drive. Hiking arduous trails from rim to rim is a steep and strenuous trek of at least 21 mi, but it's well worth the effort. You'll travel through five of North America's seven life zones. (To do this any other way, you'd have to travel from the Mexican desert to the Canadian woods.) In total, 630 mi of trails traverse the canyon, 51 of those miles maintained. West of Grand Canyon National Park, the tribal lands of the Hualapai and the Havasupai lie on the West Rim of the canyon.

GRAND CANYON'S SOUTH RIM

Visitors to the canyon converge mostly on the South Rim, and mostly during the summer. Grand Canyon Village is here, with most of the park's lodging and camping, trailheads, restaurants, stores, and museums, along with a nearby airport and railroad depot. Believe it or not, the average stay in the park is a mere four hours; this is not advised! You need to spend several days to truly appreciate this marvelous place, but at the very least, give it a full day. Hike down into the canyon, or along the rim, to get away from the crowds and experience nature at its finest.

SCENIC DRIVE

Hermit Road. The Santa Fe Company built Hermit Road, formerly known as West Rim Drive, in 1912 as a scenic tour route. Ten overlooks dot this 8-mi stretch, each worth a visit. The road is filled with hairpin turns, so make sure you adhere to posted speed limits. From March through November, Hermit Road is closed to private auto traffic because of congestion; during this period, a free shuttle bus will carry you to all the overlooks. Riding the bus round-trip without getting off at any of the viewpoints takes 75 minutes; the return trip stops only at Mohave and Hopi points. ■**TIP➡ Take plenty of water with you for the ride—the only water along the way is at Hermits Rest.**

GREAT ITINERARIES

2

GRAND CANYON IN 1 DAY

Start early, pack a picnic lunch, and take the shuttle to **Canyon View Information Plaza** just north of the south entrance, to pick up information and see your first incredible view at **Mather Point.** Continue east along **Desert View Drive** for about 2 mi to **Yaki Point,** your first stop. Next, hop back on the shuttle to head 7 mi east to **Grandview Point,** for a good view of the buttes Krishna Shrine and Vishnu Temple. Go 4 mi east and catch the view at **Moran Point,** then 3 mi to the **Tusayan Ruin and Museum,** where a small display is devoted to the history of the Ancestral Puebloans. Continue another mile east to **Lipan Point** to view the Colorado River. In less than a mile, you'll arrive at **Navajo Point,** the highest elevation on the South Rim. **Desert View and Watchtower** are the final stops along the shuttle route.

On the return shuttle, hop off at any of the picnic areas for lunch. Once back at Grand Canyon Village, walk the paved **Rim Trail** to **Maricopa Point.** Along the way, pick up souvenirs in the village and stop at the historic **El Tovar Hotel** to make dinner reservations. If you have time, take the shuttle on **Hermit Road** to **Hermits Rest,** 8 mi away. It's a good place to watch the sunset.

GRAND CANYON IN 3 DAYS

On Day 1, follow the one-day itinerary for the morning, but spend more time exploring Desert View Drive and enjoy a leisurely picnic or lunch in Grand Canyon Village. Travel Hermit Road on your second morning, and drive to Grand Canyon Airport for a late morning small plane or heli-

copter tour of the area. Have lunch in **Tusayan** and cool off during the IMAX film *Grand Canyon—The Hidden Secrets.* Back in the Village, take in a free ranger-led program. On your third day, hike **Bright Angel Trail** into the canyon. It takes twice as long to hike back up, so plan accordingly. Pick up trail maps at **Canyon View Information Plaza,** and bring plenty of water.

Alternatively, spend days 2 and 3 exploring **Grand Canyon West.** Fill the first day with a Hummer tour along the rim, a helicopter ride into the canyon, or a pontoon boat ride on the Colorado River, and fill up on Hualapai tacos at the Hualapai Lodge's Diamond Creek Restaurant. The next day, raft the Class V and VI rapids or hike 8 mi into **Havasu Canyon** to the small village of Supai and the Havasupai Lodge. You'll need a Havasupai tribal permit to hike here.

GRAND CANYON IN 5 DAYS

Between May and October, you can visit the North Rim as well as the South. Follow the three-day South Rim itinerary and, early on your fourth day, start the long but rewarding drive to the North Rim, where you can spend the last couple of days of your trip. The most popular trails here are **Transept Trail,** which starts near the Grand Canyon Lodge, and **Cliff Springs Trail,** which starts near **Cape Royal.** Before leaving the area, drive Cape Royal Road 11 mi to **Point Imperial**—at 8,803 feet, it's the highest vista on either rim.

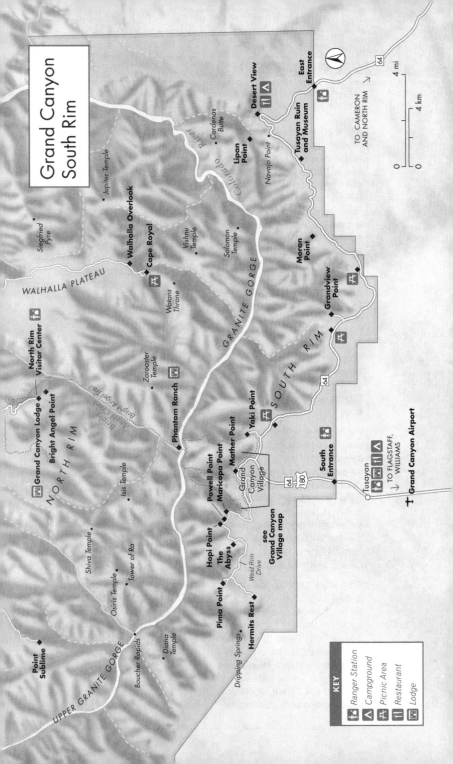

Grand Canyon South Rim

KEY

Ranger Station
Campground
Picnic Area
Restaurant
Lodge

4 mi
4 km

TO CAMERON
AND NORTH RIM

Colorado River

East Entrance
Desert View
Tusayan Ruin and Museum

Cardenas Butte
Lipan Point
Navajo Point

Moran Point

Grandview Point

GRANITE GORGE

SOUTH RIM

Walhalla Overlook
Cape Royal

WALHALLA PLATEAU

Vishnu Temple
Solomon Temple
Wotans Throne

Jupiter Temple

Siegfried Pyre

North Rim Visitor Center

Grand Canyon Lodge
Bright Angel Point

NORTH RIM

Zoroaster Temple
Phantom Ranch

Bright Angel Trail
Bright Angel Creek

Yaki Point
Mather Point

Grand Canyon Village

South Entrance
Tusayan

TO FLAGSTAFF, WILLIAMS

Grand Canyon Airport

Isis Temple

Shiva Temple
Tower of Ra

Osiris Temple

Diana Temple

Point Sublime

UPPER GRANITE GORGE

Boucher Rapids

Dripping Springs

Powell Point
Maricopa Point

Hopi Point
The Abyss

West Rim Drive

Pima Point
Hermits Rest

see Grand Canyon Village map

Tips for Avoiding Canyon Crowds

"I find that in contemplating the natural world, my pleasure is greater if there are not too many others contemplating it with me, at the same time."—Edward Abbey

It's hard to commune with nature while you're searching for a parking place, dodging video cams, and stepping away from strollers. However, this scenario is likely to occur only during the very peak months of mid-May through mid-October. One option is to bypass Grand Canyon National Park altogether and head to the West Rim of the canyon, tribal land of the Hualapai and Havasupai. If only the park itself will do, the following tips will help you to keep your distance and your cool.

TAKE ANOTHER ROUTE

Avoid road rage by choosing a different route to the South Rim, foregoing the traditional highways 64 and U.S. 180 from Flagstaff. Take U.S. 89 north from Flagstaff instead, passing near Sunset Crater and Wupatki national monuments. When you reach the Cameron Trading Post at the junction with Highway 64, take a break—or stay overnight. This is a good place to shop for Native American artifacts, souvenirs, and the usual postcards, dream-catchers, recordings, and T-shirts. There are also high-quality Navajo rugs, jewelry, and other authentic handicrafts, and you can sample Navajo tacos. U.S. 64 to the west takes you directly to the park's east entrance; the scenery along the Little Colorado River Gorge en route is eye-popping. It's 25 mi from the Grand Canyon east entrance to the visitor center at Canyon View Information Plaza.

BYPASS THE SOUTH RIM ALTOGETHER

Although the North Rim is just 10 mi across from the South Rim, the trip to get there by car is a five-hour drive of 215 mi. At first it might not sound like the trip would be worth it, but the payoff is huge. Along the way, you will travel through some of the prettiest parts of the state and be granted even more stunning views than those on the more easily accessible South Rim. Those who make the North Rim trip often insist it offers the canyon's most beautiful views and best hiking. To get to the North Rim from Flagstaff, take U.S. 89 north past Cameron, turning left onto U.S. 89A at Bitter Springs. En route you'll pass the area known as Vermilion Cliffs. At Jacob Lake, take Highway 67 directly to the Grand Canyon North Rim. The road to the North Rim closes from around mid-October through mid-May because of heavy snow, but in summer months and early fall, it's a wonderful way to beat the crowds at the South Rim.

RIDE THE RAILS

There is no need to deal with all of the other drivers racing to the South Rim. Forget the hassle of the twisting rim roads, jaywalking pedestrians, and jammed parking lots and sit back and relax in the comfy train cars of the Grand Canyon Railway. Live music and storytelling enliven the trip as you journey past the breathtaking landscape. The train departs from the depot every morning between 8:30 and 10:30 AM, depending on the season, and makes the 65-mi journey in 2¼ hours. You can do the round-trip in a single day; however, you may choose to stay overnight at the South Rim and return to Williams the following afternoon.

WHAT TO SEE

HISTORIC SITES

Kolb Studio. Built in 1904 by the Kolb brothers as a photographic workshop and residence, this building provides a view of Indian Gardens, where, in the days before a pipeline was installed, Emery Kolb descended 3,000 feet each day to get the water he needed to develop his prints. Kolb was doing something right; he operated the studio until he died in 1976 at age 95. The gallery here has changing exhibitions of paintings, photography, and crafts. There's also a bookstore. ⊠ *Grand Canyon Village, near Bright Angel Lodge* ⊙ *Daily, 8–6.*

Lookout Studio. Built in 1914 to compete with the Kolbs' photographic studio, the building was designed by architect Mary Jane Colter. The combination lookout point and gift shop has a collection of fossils and geologic samples from around the world. An upstairs loft provides another excellent overlook into the gorge below. ⊠ *About ¼ mi west of Hermit Road Junction on Hermit Rd.*

Powell Memorial. A granite statue honors the memory of John Wesley Powell, who measured, charted, and named many of the canyons and creeks of the Colorado River. It was here that the dedication ceremony for Grand Canyon National Park took place on April 3, 1920. ⊠ *About 3 mi west of Hermit Road Junction on Hermit Rd.*

SCENIC STOPS

The Abyss. At an elevation of 6,720 feet, the Abyss is one of the most awesome stops on Hermit Road, revealing a sheer drop of 3,000 feet to the Tonto Platform, a wide terrace of Tapeats sandstone layers about two-thirds of the way down the canyon. From the Abyss you'll also see several isolated sandstone columns, the largest of which is called the Monument. ⊠ *About 5 mi west of Hermit Road Junction on Hermit Rd.*

Desert View and Watchtower. From the top of the 70-foot stone-and-mortar watchtower, even the muted hues of the distant Painted Desert to the east and the Vermilion Cliffs rising from a high plateau near the Utah border are visible. In the chasm below, angling to the north toward Marble Canyon, an imposing stretch of the Colorado River reveals itself. Up several flights of stairs, the Watchtower houses a glass-enclosed observatory with powerful telescopes. ⊠ *About 23 mi east of Grand Canyon Village on Desert View Dr.* ☎ *928/638–2736* ⊙ *Daily 8–7, hours may vary.*

Grandview Point. At an elevation of 7,496 feet, the view from here is one of the finest in the canyon. To the northeast is a group of dominant buttes, including Krishna Shrine, Vishnu Temple, Rama Shrine, and Shiva Temple. A short stretch of the Colorado River is also visible. Directly below the point, and accessible by the steep and rugged Grandview Trail, is Horseshoe Mesa, where you can see the ruins of Last Chance Copper Mine. ⊠ *About 12 mi east of Grand Canyon Village on Desert View Dr.*

Hopi Point. From this elevation of 7,071 feet, you can see a large section of the Colorado River; although it appears as a thin line, the river is nearly 350 feet wide below this overlook. Across the canyon to the north is Shiva Temple, which remained an isolated section of the Kaibab Plateau until 1937. That year, Harold Anthony of the American Museum of Natural History led an expedition to the rock formation in the belief that it supported life that had been cut off from the rest of the canyon. Imagine the expedition members' surprise when they found an empty Kodak film box on top of the temple. Directly below Hopi Point lies Dana Butte, named for a prominent 19th-century geologist. In 1919, an entrepreneur proposed connecting Hopi Point, Dana Butte, and the Tower of Set across the river with an aerial tramway, a technically feasible plan that fortunately has not been realized. ⊠*About 4 mi west of Hermit Road Junction on Hermit Rd.*

★ **Hermits Rest.** This westernmost viewpoint and Hermit Trail, which descends from it, were named for "hermit" Louis Boucher, a 19th-century French-Canadian prospector who had a number of mining claims and a roughly built home down in the canyon. Views from here include Hermit Rapids and the towering cliffs of the Supai and Redwall formations. The stone building at Hermits Rest sells curios and refreshments. ⊠*About 8 mi west of Hermit Road Junction on Hermit Rd.*

Lipan Point. Here, at the canyon's widest point, you can get an astonishing visual profile of the gorge's geologic history, with a view of every eroded layer of the canyon. You can also see Unkar Delta, where a creek joins the Colorado to form powerful rapids and a broad beach. Ancestral Puebloan farmers worked the Unkar Delta for hundreds of years, growing corn, beans, and melons. ⊠*About 25 mi east of Grand Canyon Village on Desert View Dr.*

Maricopa Point. This site merits a stop not only for the arresting scenery, which includes the Colorado River below, but also for its view of a defunct mine. On your left, as you face the canyon, are the Orphan Mine, a mine shaft, and cable lines leading up to the rim. The mine, which started operations in 1893, was worked first for copper and then for uranium until the venture came to a halt in 1969. The Battleship, the red butte directly ahead of you in the canyon, was named during the Spanish-American War, when battleships were in the news. ⊠*About 2 mi west of Hermit Road Junction on Hermit Rd.*

★ **Mather Point.** You'll likely get your first glimpse of the canyon from this viewpoint, one of the most impressive and accessible on the South Rim. Named for the National Park Service's first director, Stephen Mather, this spot yields extraordinary views of the Grand Canyon, including deep into the Inner Gorge and numerous buttes: Wotan's Throne, Brahma Temple, and Zoroaster Temple, among others. The Grand Canyon Lodge, on the North Rim, is almost directly north from Mather Point and only 10 mi away—yet you have to drive 215 mi to get from one spot to the other. ⊠*Near Canyon View Information Plaza.*

TRIP PLANNING

Before you go, request the complimentary *Trip Planner*, updated regularly by the National Park Service, by writing to: Trip Planner, Grand Canyon National Park, Box 129, Grand Canyon, AZ 86023. You can also get the trip planner on-line at ⊕ *www.nps.gov/grca/grandcanyon/trip_planner.htm*. Several Web sites also are useful for trip-planning, including the National Park Service's Web site, ⊕ www.nps.gov, as well as ⊕ www.thecanyon.com, a commercial site with information on lodging, dining, and general park basics.

Once you arrive at the park, pick up *The Guide*, a free newspaper with a detailed area map and a schedule of free park programs. The park also distributes *The Grand Canyon Accessibility Guide*, also free, which can be picked up at visitor centers.

Mohave Point. From here you can view the 5,401-foot Cheops Pyramid, a grayish rock formation behind Dana Butte, plus some of the strongest rapids on the Colorado River. The Granite and Salt Creek rapids are navigable, but not without plenty of effort. ⊠ *About 5 mi west of Hermit Road Junction on Hermit Rd.*

Moran Point. This point was named for American landscape artist Thomas Moran, who was especially fond of the play of light and shadows from this location. He first visited the canyon with John Wesley Powell in 1873. "Thomas Moran's name, more than any other, with the possible exception of Major Powell's, is to be associated with the Grand Canyon," wrote noted canyon photographer Ellsworth Kolb. It's fitting that Moran Point is a favorite spot of photographers and painters. ⊠ *About 17 mi east of Grand Canyon Village on Desert View Dr.*

Navajo Point. A possible site of the first Spanish view into the Canyon in 1540, this peak is also at the highest elevation (7,498 feet) on the South Rim. ⊠ *About 21 mi east of Grand Canyon Village on Desert View Dr.*

Pima Point. Enjoy a bird's-eye view of Tonto Platform and Tonto Trail, which winds its way through the canyon for more than 70 mi. Also to the west, two dark, cone-shaped mountains—Mount Trumbull and Mount Logan—are visible on the North Rim on clear days. They rise in stark contrast to the surrounding flat-top mesas and buttes. ⊠ *About 7 mi west of Hermit Road Junction on Hermit Rd.*

Trailview Overlook. Look down on a dramatic view of the Bright Angel and Plateau Point trails as they zigzag down the canyon. In the deep gorge to the north flows Bright Angel Creek, one of the region's few permanent tributary streams of the Colorado River. Toward the south is an unobstructed view of the distant San Francisco Peaks, as well as Bill Williams Mountain (on the horizon) and Red Butte (about 15 mi south of the canyon rim). ⊠ *About 2 mi west of Hermit Road Junction on Hermit Rd.*

Yaki Point. Stop here for an exceptional view of Wotan's Throne, a flat-top butte named by François Matthes, a U.S. Geological Survey scientist who developed the first topographical map of the Grand Canyon. ⊠ *2 mi east of Grand Canyon Village on Desert View Dr.*

Yavapai Observation Station. A panorama of the canyon is visible through the building's large windows. The station has new geological displays opening in 2007. ⊠ *Adjacent to Grand Canyon Village* ⊠ *Free.*

VISITOR CENTERS

Canyon View Information Plaza. The park's main orientation center near Mather Point provides pamphlets and resources to help plan your sightseeing. Park rangers are on hand to answer questions and aid in planning canyon excursions. A bookstore is stocked with books covering all topics on the Grand Canyon, and a daily schedule of ranger-led hikes and evening lectures is posted on a bulletin board inside. A shuttle bus will get you there. ⊠ *East side of Grand Canyon Village* ☎ *928/638–7888* ⊙ *Daily 8–5, outdoor exhibits may be viewed anytime.*

Desert View Information Center. ⊠ *East entrance* ☎ *800/858–2808* ⊙ *Daily 9–5; hours vary in winter.*

Yavapai Observation Station. Shop in the bookstore, catch the park shuttle bus, or pick up information for the Rim Trail here. ⊠ *1 mile east of Market Plaza* ☎ *928/638–7888* ⊙ *Daily 8–8; hours vary in winter.*

SPORTS & THE OUTDOORS

AIR TOURS

★ Flights by plane and helicopter over the canyon are offered by a number of companies, departing for the Grand Canyon Airport at the south end of Tusayan. Prices and lengths of tours vary, but you can expect to pay about $109–$120 per adult for short plane trips and approximately $130–$235 for brief helicopter tours.

OUTFITTERS & EXPEDITIONS   Companies worth noting are **Air Grand Canyon** (⊠ *Grand Canyon Airport, Tusayan* ☎ *928/638–2686 or 800/247–4726* ⊕ *www.air grandcanyon.com*), **Grand Canyon Airlines** (⊠ *Grand Canyon Airport, Tusayan* ☎ *928/638–2407 or 866/235–9422* ⊕ *www.grandcanyonairlines.com*), **Grand Canyon Helicopters** (⊠ *Grand Canyon Airport, Tusayan* ☎ *928/638–2764 or 800/541–4537* ⊕ *www.grandcanyon helicoptersaz.com*), **Maverick-AirStar Helicopters** (⊠ *Grand Canyon Airport, Tusayan* ☎ *928/638–2622 or 800/962–3869* ⊕ *www.maverick. com*), and **Papillon Grand Canyon Helicopters** (⊠ *Grand Canyon Airport, Tusayan* ☎ *928/638–2419 or 800/528–2418* ⊕ *www.papillon.com*).

BICYCLING

The South Rim's limited opportunities for off-road biking, narrow shoulders on park roads, and heavy traffic may disappoint hard-core cyclists. Bicycles are permitted on all park roads and on the multi-use Greenway System, currently under development. Bikes are prohibited on all other trails, including the Rim Trail. Mountain bikers visiting the South Rim may be better off meandering through the ponderosa pine forest on the Tusayan Bike Trail. No rentals are available at the canyon.

HIKING

Although permits are not required for day hikes, you must have a backcountry permit for longer trips (⇨ *Permits in the Grand Canyon Essentials section at the end of chapter*). Some of the more popular trails are listed in this chapter; more detailed information and maps can be obtained from the Backcountry Information Center. Also, rangers can help design a trip to suit your abilities.

Remember that the canyon has significant elevation changes and, in summer, extreme temperature ranges, which can pose problems for people who aren't in good shape or who have heart or respiratory problems. **Carry plenty of water and energy foods.** The majority of each year's 400 search-and-rescue incidents result from hikers underestimating the size of the canyon, hiking beyond their abilities, or not packing sufficient food and water.

Under no circumstances should you attempt a day hike from the rim to the river and back. Remember that when it's 80°F on the South Rim, it's 110°F on the canyon floor. Allow two to three days if you want to hike rim to rim (it's easier to descend from the North Rim, as it is more than 1,000 feet higher than the South Rim).

Fodor'sChoice **Rim Trail.** The South Rim's most popular walking path is the 13-mi (one-★ way) Rim Trail, which runs along the edge of the canyon from Mather Point (the first overlook on Desert View Drive) to Hermits Rest. This walk, which is paved to Maricopa Point, visits several of the South Rim's historic landmarks. Allow anywhere from 15 minutes to a full day; the Rim Trail is an ideal day hike, as it varies only a few hundred feet in elevation from Mather Point (7,120 feet) to the trailhead at Hermits Rest (6,640 feet). The trail also can be accessed from the major viewpoints along Hermit Road, which are serviced by shuttle buses during the busy summer months.

★ **Bright Angel Trail.** Well-maintained, this is one of the most scenic hiking paths from the South Rim to the bottom of the canyon (9 mi each way). Rest houses are equipped with water at the 1½- and 3-mi points from May through September and at Indian Garden (4 mi) year-round. Water is also available at Bright Angel Campground, 9¼ mi below the trailhead. Plateau Point, about 1½ mi below Indian Garden, is as far as you should attempt to go on a day hike; plan on spending six to nine hours. Bright Angel Trail is the easiest of all the footpaths into the canyon, but because the climb out from the bottom is an ascent of 5,510 feet, the trip should be attempted only by those in good physical condition and should be avoided in midsummer due to extreme heat. The top of the trail, a tight set of switchbacks called Jacob's Ladder, can be icy in winter. Originally a bighorn sheep path and later used by the Havasupai, the trail was widened late in the 19th century for prospectors and is now used for both mule and foot traffic. Hikers going

CLOSE UP

Park Insider: Chuck Wahler

When Chuck Wahler tells people to "take a hike," he means it in the most helpful, encouraging sense. A 16-year employee at Grand Canyon National Park, Wahler knows the lay of the land, and he encourages folks to get a feel for it on foot. A hike "either along the rim or into the canyon" ranks among his top "must-do" suggestions for park visitors.

As Chief of the Operations Branch for the park's Division of Interpretation and Resource Education, Wahler manages front-line operations for the division. "The staff that works with me operates the park visitor centers and museums, and presents interpretive programs to our visitors," he explains.

Those programs include the popular "Junior Ranger" activities, which also make Wahler's must-do list: "If there are children in your group, have them participate."

Variety is the spice of park life, as far as Wahler is concerned, and the range of activities is his favorite thing about his workplace. "It is a constantly changing place," he says, "different from minute to minute, day to day, and season to season." That diversity inspires another suggestion: "Views of the canyon from along Hermit Road are very different from those along Desert View Drive," explains Wahler. "If you have the time, plan to experience both areas of the park."

Navigating the 1,904-square-mile park is a sizeable task, but it's made easier by the free shuttle system. The buses stop at 30-some points of interest, and Wahler advocates hopping aboard whenever possible. "You'll spend more of your time exploring the park and less time looking for a place to park."

For another insider tip, he touts the park's aptly named newspaper. "*The Guide* provides visitors with all the basic information they need to plan their visit to the park. Taking a few minutes to read the newspaper will help make a visit more enjoyable." Distributed at the entrance station, *The Guide* is printed in English, French, German, Japanese, and Italian.

Wahler also urges travelers to consider coming during "the off-season" (late fall through early spring). "The weather can delightful, and the park is often less crowded than in the summer."

No matter the season, Wahler's final must-do is a simple one: "Find a quiet place along the rim, and just sit and enjoy the canyon."

2

Hopi
Point
Powell Point
Kolb Studio
Maricopa Point
TO
HERMITS REST 5mi
Trailview
Overlook
Bright Angel
Lodge
Bright Angel Trailhead
El Tovar
Train Depot
Ranger Office
Maswik
Lodge
Center Rd
Rowe Well Rd
Bright Angel
Trail
Indian
Garden
RIM TRAIL
Park
Headquarters
Mather
Campground
South Entrance Road
Plateau Point
Yavapai
Observation Station
Greenway
Mather Point
Canyon View
Information
Plaza
Yavapai Ladge
RIM TRAIL
Pipe Creek
Vista
TO
EAST ENTRANCE &
DESERT VIEW
Colorado
River
180
64
Grand Canyon
Village &
The Rim Trail
TO
SOUTH ENTRANCE,
TUSAYAN, & FLAGSTAFF
scale varies in this perspective

downhill should yield to those going uphill. Also note that mule trains have the right-of-way—and sometimes leave unpleasant surprises in your path.

DIFFICULT   **Clear Creek Trail.** Make this 9-mi hike only if you are prepared for a multiday trip. The trail departs from Phantom Ranch at the bottom of the canyon and leads across the Tonto Platform to Clear Creek, where drinking water is usually available, but should be treated.

Grandview Trail. Accessible from the parking area at Grandview Point, the trailhead is at 7,400 feet. The path heads down into the canyon for 4⁸⁄₁₀ mi to the junction and campsite at East Horseshoe Mesa Trail. Classified as a wilderness trail, the route is aggressive and not as heavily traveled as some of the more well-known trails, such as Bright Angel and Hermit; allow six to nine hours, round-trip. There is no water available along the trail, which follows a steep descent to 4,800 feet at Horseshoe Mesa, where Hopi Indians once collected mineral paints.

Hermit Trail. Beginning on the South Rim just west of Hermits Rest (and 8 mi west of Grand Canyon Village), this steep, 9.3-mi (one-way) trail drops more than 5,000 feet to Hermit Creek, which usually flows year-round. It's a strenuous hike back up and is recommended for experienced long-distance hikers only; plan for six to nine hours. There's an

GRAND CANYON NATIONAL PARK: TOP PICKS HIKING TRAILS

	Grade	Miles (one way)	Beginning Elevation	Ending Elevation	Mules	Campground	Open Info	Water Shuttle	Access/Ranger Station	Toilet/Restroom	Emergency Telephone	Hiking Level	Trail Conditions
South Rim													
Bright Angel Trail South	Steep	9.6 mi	6785 ft	2480 ft (Colorado River)	Y	Y	Y/R	(Seasonal)	Y	Y	Y	Intermediate-Experienced	Maintained
Grandview Trail	Very Steep	3.2 mi	7400 ft	4800 ft (Horseshoe Mesa)		Y	Y/R		Y	Y		Experienced	Maintained
Hermit Trail	Steep	9.3 mi	6640 ft	2400 ft (Colorado River)			Y/R	(Untreated)	Y	Y**	Y**	Experienced	Unmaintained
New Hance Trail	Steep	8 mi	7000 ft	2600 ft (Colorado River)			Y/R					Experienced	Unmaintained
Rim Trail	Level	9 mi	6640 ft	7120 ft (Mather Point)			Y/R	Y	Y	Y	Y	Beginner-Experienced	Maintained
South Kaibab Trail	Steep	7.1 mi	7100 ft	2546 ft (Phantom Ranch)	Y	Y	Y/R	Y**	Y	Y	Y	Experienced	Unmaintained
North Rim													
Ken Patrick Trail	Level/Incline	10 mi	8250 ft	8803 ft (Point Imperial)			mid-May–mid-Oct.		Y			Beginner-Experienced	Unmaintained
North Kaibab Trail	Steep	7.1 mi	8255 ft	2400 ft (Colorado River)	Y		mid-May–mid-Oct.	Y	Y	Y		Intermediate-	Maintained
Transept Trail	Level	1.5 mi	8255 ft	8200 ft (Campground)			mid-May–mid-Oct.			Y		Beginner	Maintained
Uncle Jim Trail	Level	2.5 mi	8300 ft	8244 ft (Uncle Jim Point)	Y		mid-May–mid-Oct.					Beginner-Experienced	Maintained
Widforss Trail	Level/Incline	4.9 mi	8080 ft	7900 ft (Widforss Point)			mid-May–mid-Oct.				Y	Beginner-Experienced	Unmaintained

*(South Rim trails occasionally close due to weather or trail conditions) **(Trailhead) Y/R = year-round

2

abundance of lush growth and wildlife, including desert bighorn sheep, along this trail.

The trail descends from the trailhead at 6,640 feet to the Colorado River at 2,400 feet. Day hikers should not go past Santa Maria Springs at 4,880 feet. For much of the year, no water is available along the way; ask a park ranger about the availability of water at Santa Maria Springs and Hermit Creek before you set out. All water from these sources should be treated before drinking. The route leads down to the Colorado River and has inspiring views of Hermit Gorge and the Redwall and Supai formations. Six miles from the trailhead are the ruins of Hermit Camp, which the Santa Fe Railroad ran as a tourist camp from 1911 until 1930.

★ **South Kaibab Trail.** This trail starts at Yaki Point on Desert View Drive, 4 mi east of Grand Canyon Village. Because the trail is so steep—descending from the trailhead at 7,260 feet down to 2,480 feet at the Colorado River—and has no water, many hikers return via the less-demanding Bright Angel Trail; allow four to six hours. During this 6.5-mi trek to the Colorado River, you're likely to encounter mule trains and riders. At the river, the trail crosses a suspension bridge and runs on to Phantom Ranch. Along the trail there is no water and very little shade. There are no campgrounds, though there are portable toilets at Cedar Ridge (6,320 feet), 1½ mi from the trailhead. Toilets and an emergency phone are also available at the Tipoff, 4½ mi down the trail (3 mi past Cedar Ridge). The trail corkscrews down through some spectacular geology. Look for (but don't remove) fossils in the limestone when taking water breaks.

Tonto Trail. A very strenuous 13.8-mi loop, Tonto Trail should be attempted only in cool weather; summer temperatures on the trail often reach 100 degrees. It parallels the Colorado River from South Kaibab Trailhead to Bright Angel Trailhead, and there's little shade.

NEED A BREAK? If you've been driving too long and want some exercise, along with great views of the canyon, it's an easy 1¼-mi-long hike from the **Information Plaza** to **El Tovar Hotel.** The path runs through a quiet wooded area for about ½ mi, and then along the rim for another ¾ mi.

JEEP TOURS

Grand Canyon Jeep Tours & Safaris. If you'd like to get off the pavement and see parts of the park that are accessible only by dirt road, a jeep tour can be just the ticket. From March through October, Grand Canyon Outback leads daily, 1½- to 4½-hour, off-road tours within the park, as well as in Kaibab National Forest. The rides are bumpy and are not recommended for people with back injuries. Combo tours adding helicopter and airplane rides are available. ☐ Box 1772, Grand Canyon 86023 ☎ 928/638–5337 or 800/320–5337 ⊕ www.grandcanyonjeeptours. com ☑ $45–$199 ☐ AE, MC, V ☜ Reservations essential.

Marvelous Marv's Private Grand Canyon Tours. For a personalized experience, take this private tour of the Grand Canyon and surrounding sights any time of year. Rides can be rough; if you have had back injuries, check with your doctor before taking a jeep tour. ⌂ *Box 544, Williams 86046* ☎*928/635–4948 or 928/707–0291* ⊕*www.marvelous marv.com* ▤*$85* ▤*No credit cards* ⌂*Reservations essential.*

MULE RIDES

★ Mule rides provide an intimate glimpse into the canyon for those who have the time, but not the stamina to see the canyon on foot. Reservations are essential and are accepted up to 23 months in advance, or you can check the waiting list for last-minute cancellations.

These trips have been conducted since the early 1900s. A comforting fact as you ride the narrow trail: No one's ever been killed while riding a mule that fell off a cliff. (Nevertheless, the treks are not for the faint of heart or people in questionable health.)

ARRANGING TOURS

Transportation-services desks are maintained at El Tovar, Bright Angel, Maswik Lodge, and Yavapai Lodge (closed in winter) in Grand Canyon Village. The desks provide information and handle bookings for sightseeing tours, taxi and bus services, mule and horseback rides, and accommodations at Phantom Ranch (at the bottom of the Grand Canyon). The concierge at El Tovar can also arrange most tours, with the exception of mule rides and lodging at Phantom Ranch. On the North Rim, Grand Canyon Lodge has general information about local services.

OUTFITTERS **Grand Canyon National Park Lodges Mule Rides.** These trips delve into the canyon from the South Rim. Riders must be at least 55 inches tall, weigh less than 200 pounds, and understand English. Children under 15 must be accompanied by an adult. Riders must be in fairly good physical condition, and pregnant women are advised not to take these trips. The all-day ride to Plateau Point costs $142.21 (box lunch included). An overnight with a stay at Phantom Ranch at the bottom of the canyon is $369.54 ($651.80 for two riders). Two nights at Phantom Ranch, an option available from November through March, will set you back $517.82 ($879.63 for two). Meals are included. ⌂*6312 S. Fiddlers Green Circle, Ste. 600, N. Greenwood Village, CO 80111* ☎*303/297–2757 or 888/297–2757* ▤*303/297–3175* ⊕*www.grand-canyonlodges.com* ⊙*May–Sept., daily.*

SKIING

Although you can't schuss down into the Grand Canyon, you can cross-country ski in the woods near the rim when there's enough snow, which has been lacking the last few seasons. The best time for cross-country skiing is mid-December though early March. Trails, suitable for beginner and intermediate skiers, begin ³⁄₁₀mi north of the Grandview Lookout and travel through the Kaibab National Forest. Contact the **Tusayan Ranger District** (⌂*Box 3088, Grand Canyon 86023* ☎*928/638–2443* ⊕*www.fs.fed.us/r3/kai*) for details.

Freebies at the Canyon

While you're here, be sure to take advantage of the many freebies offered at Grand Canyon National Park. The most useful of these services is the system of free shuttle buses at the South Rim; it caters to the road-weary, with three routes winding through the park—Hermits Rest Route, Village Route, and Kaibab Trail Route. Of the bus routes, the Hermits Rest Route runs only from March through November; the other two run year-round, and the Kaibab Trail Route provides the only access to Yaki Point. Hikers coming or going from the Kaibab Trailhead can catch the Hikers Express, which departs three times each morning from the Bright Angel Lodge, makes a quick stop at the Backcountry Office, and then heads out to the South Kaibab Trailhead.

Ranger-led programs are always free and offered year-round, though more are scheduled during the busy spring and summer seasons. These programs might include activities such as stargazing and topics such as geology and the cultural history of prehistoric peoples. Some of the more in-depth programs may include a fossil walk or a condor talk. Check with the visitor center for seasonal programs including wildflower walks and fire ecology.

Kids ages 4 to 14 can get involved with the park's Junior Ranger program, with ever-changing activities including hikes and hands-on experiments.

Despite all of these options, rangers will tell you that the best free activity in the canyon is watching the magnificent splashes of color on the canyon walls during sunrise and sunset.

EDUCATIONAL OFFERINGS

Grand Canyon Field Institute. Instructors lead guided educational tours, hikes around the canyon, and weekend programs at the South Rim. Tour topics include everything from archaeology and backcountry medicine to photography and natural history. Contact GCFI for a schedule and price list. ✉ *Box 399, Grand Canyon 86023* ☎ *928/638–2485 or 866/471–4435* 🖷 *928/638–2484* ⊕ *www.grandcanyon.org/fieldinstitute* ☎ *$95–$2,150* ▤ *DC, MC, V* ⚒ *Reservations essential.*

Interpretive Ranger Programs. The National Park Service sponsors all sorts of orientation activities, such as daily guided hikes and talks, at both the North and South rims. The focus may be on any aspect of the canyon—from geology and flora and fauna to history and early inhabitants. For schedules on the South Rim, go to Canyon View Information Plaza, pick up a free copy of *The Guide* to the South Rim, or check online. ☎ *928/638–7888* ⊕ *www.nps.gov/grca* ☎ *Free.*

Junior Ranger Program for Families. Children ages 4 to 14 can take part in these hands-on educational programs. ☎ *928/638–7888* ⊕ *www.nps. gov/grca/pphtml/forkids.html* ☎ *Free.*

Fossil Walk: Remnant Impressions. The walk, ½-mile one way, explores an exposed fossil bed along the rim, where you'll see the remains of brachiopods, sponges, and other marine creatures. Departs from the Patio of Bright Angel Lodge.

Spirit of Sunset Walk. Explore the ever-changing colors of the canyon at sunset on this ½-mile walk. Meet at Desert View and Watchtower; allow 40 minutes. ☎928/638–7888 ⊗*Daily, 1 hr before sunset* ✉*Box 129, Grand Canyon 86023* ☎928/638–7888 ⊕*www.nps.gov/grca* ✉*Free.*

☾ **Way Cool for Kids.** Rangers coordinate these free, hour-long introductions to the park for children ages 7–11, daily at 9 AM. Kids and rangers walk around the Village Rim area and talk about local plants and animals, history, or archaeology. Programs are subject to change. ✉*South Rim Park Headquarters, Parking Lot A* ☎928/638–7888 ✉*Free.*

> ## PETS AT THE CANYON
>
> Pets are allowed in Grand Canyon National Park; however, they must be on a leash at all times. With the exception of service animals, pets are not allowed below the rim or on park shuttles. A **kennel** (☎928/638–0534), near the Maswik Lodge, houses cats and dogs. It is open daily from 7:30–5. Reservations are strongly recommended.

BUS TOURS

Xanterra Motorcoach Tours. Narrated by knowledgeable guides, tours include the Hermits Rest Tour, which travels along the old wagon road built by the Santa Fe Railway; the Desert View Tour, which glimpses the Colorado River's rapids and stops at Lipan Point; and Sunrise and Sunset Tours. (✉*6312 S. Fiddlers Green Circle, Ste. 600, N. Greenwood Village, CO 80111* ☎*303/297–2757 or 888/297–2757* ⊕*www. grandcanyonlodges.com* ✉*$13.50 to $38 per person; children 16 and younger free when accompanied by a paying adult*).

ARTS & ENTERTAINMENT

★ The **Grand Canyon Music Festival** (☎*928/638–9215 or 800/997–8285* ⊕*www.grandcanyonmusicfest.org*) is held each September at the Shrine of Ages amphitheater and stages nearly a dozen concerts. In the early 1980s, music aficionados Robert Bonfiglio and Clare Hoffman hiked through the Grand Canyon and decided the stunning spectacle should be accompanied by the strains of a symphony. One of the park rangers agreed, and the wandering musicians performed an impromptu concert. Encouraged by the experience, Bonfiglio and Hoffman started the Grand Canyon Music Festival. Concerts are held on three consecutive weekends.

SHOPPING

Nearly every lodging facility and retail store at the South Rim stocks Native American arts and crafts and Grand Canyon books and souvenirs. Prices are comparable to other souvenir outlets, though you may find some better deals in Williams. However, a portion of the proceeds from items purchased at Hopi House, Desert Watchtower, and the visitor center go to the Grand Canyon Association.

Desert View Trading Post (⊠ *Desert View Dr., near the Watchtower at Desert View, Grand Canyon* ☎928/638–2360) sells a mix of traditional Southwestern souvenirs and authentic Native American arts and crafts.

★ **Hopi House** (⊠ *West Rim Dr., east of El Tovar Hotel, Grand Canyon Village* ☎928/638–2961) has the widest selection of Native American handicrafts in the vicinity.

GRAND CANYON'S NORTH RIM

The North Rim stands 1,000 feet higher than the South Rim and has a more alpine climate, with twice as much annual precipitation. Here, in the deep forests of the Kaibab Plateau, the crowds are thinner, the facilities fewer, and the views even more spectacular. Due to snow, the north Rim is off-limits in the winter.

Lodgings are available but limited. Your best bet may be to pack your camping gear and hiking boots and take several days to explore the lush Kaibab Forest. The canyon's highest, most dramatic rim views also can be enjoyed on two wheels (via primitive dirt access roads) and on four legs (courtesy of a trusty mule).

SCENIC DRIVE

★ **Highway 67.** Open mid-May to mid-October (and often until Thanksgiving), the two-lane paved road climbs 1,400 feet in elevation as it passes through the Kaibab National Forest. Point Imperial and Cape Royal can be reached by spurs off this scenic drive running from Jacob Lake to Bright Angel Point.

WHAT TO SEE

HISTORIC SITES

Grand Canyon Lodge. Built in 1928 by the Union Pacific Railroad, the massive stone structure is listed on the National Register of Historic Places. Its huge sunroom has hardwood floors, high-beam ceilings, and a marvelous view of the canyon through plate-glass windows. On warm days, visitors sit in the sun and drink in the surrounding beauty on an outdoor viewing deck, where National Park Service employees deliver free lectures on geology and history *(⇨ Educational Offerings).* ⊠ *Off Hwy. 67, near Bright Angel Point.*

SCENIC STOPS

★ **Bright Angel Point.** The trail, which leads to one of the most awe-inspiring overlooks on either rim, starts on the grounds of the Grand Canyon Lodge and runs along the crest of a point of rocks that juts into the canyon for several hundred yards. The walk is only ½ mi round-trip, but it's an exciting trek accented by sheer drops on each side of the trail. In a few spots where the route is extremely narrow, metal railings ensure visitors' safety. The temptation to clamber

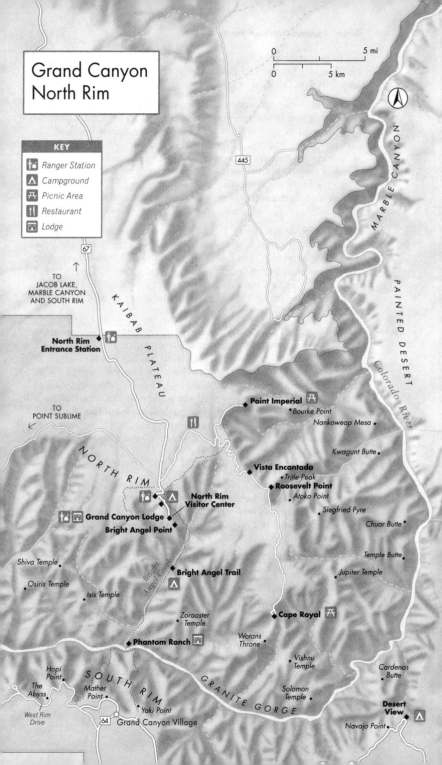

Grand Canyon
North Rim

KEY

🏕	Ranger Station
△	Campground
⛱	Picnic Area
🍴	Restaurant
🏠	Lodge

5 mi
5 km

445

67

TO
JACOB LAKE,
MARBLE CANYON
AND SOUTH RIM

North Rim
Entrance Station

K A I B A B

P L A T E A U

TO
POINT SUBLIME

N O R T H   R I M

MARBLE CANYON

P A I N T E D   D E S E R T

Colorado River

Point Imperial

Bourke Point

Nankoweap Mesa

Kwagunt Butte

Vista Encantada

Tritle Peak

Roosevelt Point

Atoko Point

Siegfried Pyre

Chuar Butte

North Rim
Visitor Center

Grand Canyon Lodge
Bright Angel Point

Shiva Temple

Osiris Temple

Isis Temple

Bright Angel Trail

Bright Angel Creek

Zoroaster
Temple

Temple Butte

Jupiter Temple

Cape Royal

Wotans
Throne

Phantom Ranch

Vishnu
Temple

Solomon
Temple

Cardenas
Butte

Hopi
Point

The
Abyss

West Rim
Drive

S O U T H   R I M

Mather
Point

Yaki Point

G R A N I T E   G O R G E

Desert
View

Navajo Point

64

Grand Canyon Village

out to precarious perches to have your picture taken could get you killed—every year several people die from falls at the Grand Canyon. ⊠*North Rim Dr., Grand Canyon.*

Cape Royal. A popular sunset destination, **Cape Royal** showcases the canyon's jagged landscape; you'll also get a glimpse of the Colorado River, framed by a natural stone arch called "the Angels Window." In autumn, the aspens turn a beautiful gold, adding even more color to an already magnificent scene of the forested surroundings. At Angels Window Overlook, **Cliff Springs Trail** starts its 1-mi route (round-trip) through a forested ravine. The trail terminates at Cliff Springs, where the forest opens to another impressive view of the canyon walls. ⊠*Cape Royal Scenic Dr., 23 mi southeast of the Grand Canyon Lodge.*

Point Imperial. At 8,803 feet, Point Imperial has the highest vista point at either rim; it offers magnificent views of both the canyon and the distant country: the Vermilion Cliffs to the north, the 10,000-foot Navajo Mountain to the northeast in Utah, the Painted Desert to the east, and the Little Colorado River Canyon to the southeast. ⊠*2⁷/₁₀ mi left off Cape Royal Scenic Dr., 11 mi northeast of the Grand Canyon Lodge.*

FodorsChoice   **Point Sublime.** Talk about solitude. Here you can camp within feet of the
★   canyon's edge. Sunrises and sunsets are spectacular. The winding road, through gorgeous high country, is only 17 mi, but it will take you at least two hours, one-way. The road is intended only for vehicles with high-road clearance (pickups and four-wheel-drive vehicles). It is also necessary to be properly equipped for wilderness road travel. Check with a park ranger or at the information desk at Grand Canyon Lodge before taking this journey. You may camp here only with a permit from the Backcountry Office. ⊠*North Rim Dr., Grand Canyon; about 20 mi west of North Rim Visitor Center.*

VISITOR CENTER

North Rim Visitor Center. View exhibits, peruse the bookstore, and pick up useful maps and brochures. Interpretive programs are often scheduled in the summer. If you're craving coffee, it's a short walk from here to the Grand Canyon Lodge. ⊠*Near the parking lot on Bright Angel Peninsula* ☎*928/638–7888* ☉*Mid-May–mid-Oct., daily 8006.*

SPORTS & THE OUTDOORS

BICYCLING

Mountain bikers can test the many dirt access roads found in this remote area, including the 17-mi trek to Point Sublime. It's rare to spot other people on these primitive roads. Note that you must bring your own bikes, as rentals are unavailable in the park. Bicycles and leashed pets are allowed on the 1²/₁₀ mi (one-way) **Bridle Trail,** which follows the road from Grand Canyon Lodge to the North Kaibab Trailhead. Watch for construction on this hard-packed trail.

HIKING

EASY **Cliff Springs Trail.** An easy 1-mi (round-trip), 1-hour walk near Cape Royal, Cliff Springs Trail leads through a forested ravine to an excellent view of the canyon. The trailhead begins across from Angels Window Overlook. Narrow and precarious in spots, it passes ancient dwellings, winds beneath a limestone overhang, and ends at Cliff Springs.

ℭ **Transept Trail.** This 3-mi (round-trip), 1½-hour trail begins at 8,255 feet near the Grand Canyon Lodge's east patio. Well-maintained and marked, it has little elevation change, sticking near the rim before reaching a dramatic view of a large stream through Bright Angel Canyon. The route leads to a side canyon called Transept Canyon, which geologist Clarence Dutton named in 1882, declaring it "far grander than Yosemite." Check the posted schedule to find a Ranger Talk along this trail; it's also a great place to view fall foliage.

MODERATE **Ken Patrick Trail.** This primitive trail begins at a trailhead on the east side of the North Kaibab trailhead parking lot. It travels 10 mi one way (allow 6 hours) from the trailhead at 8,250 feet to Point Imperial at 8,803 feet. It crosses drainages and occasionally detours around fallen trees. The end of the road brings the highest views from either rim. Note that there is no water along this trail.

Uncle Jim Trail. This 5-mi, 3-hour loop trail that starts at the North Kaibab Trail parking lot at 8,300 feet and winds south through the forest, past Roaring Springs Canyon and Bright Angel Canyon. The highlight of this rim hike is Uncle Jim Point, which, at 8,244 feet, overlooks the upper sections of the North Kaibab Trail.

Widforss Trail. Round-trip, Widforss Trail is 9⁸⁄₁₀ mi, with an elevation change of 200 feet. The trailhead, at 8,100 feet, is across from the North Kaibab Trail parking lot. Allow 6 hours for the hike, which passes through shady forests of pine, spruce, fir, and aspen on its way to Widforss Point, at 7,900 feet. You are likely to see wildflowers in summer, and this is a good trail for viewing fall foliage. It's named in honor of artist Gunnar M. Widforss, renowned for his paintings of National Park landscapes.

DIFFICULT **North Kaibab Trail.** At 8,250 feet, the trailhead to North Kaibab Trail is about 2 mi north of the Grand Canyon Lodge and is open only from May through October. It is recommended for experienced hikers only, who should allow four days for the full hike. The long, steep path drops 5,840 feet over a distance of 14½ mi to the Colorado River, so the National Park Service suggests that day hikers not go farther than Roaring Springs (5,020 feet) before turning to hike back up out of the canyon. After about 7 mi, Cottonwood Campground (4,080 feet) has drinking water in summer, restrooms, shade trees, and a ranger. It leads to Phantom Ranch.

MULE RIDES

ℭ **Canyon Trail Rides.** This company leads mule rides on the easier trails of the North Rim. A one-hour ride (minimum age 7) runs $30. Half-day trips on the rim or into the canyon (minimum age 10) cost $65; full-day trips (minimum age 12) go for $125. Weight limits vary from 200 to 220 pounds. Available daily from May 15 to October 15, these excursions are popular, so make reservations in advance. ☎435/679–8665 ⊕www.canyonrides.com.

RAFTING

Fodor'sChoice ★ Those who have taken a white-water raft trip down the Colorado River often say it as one of their most memorable life experiences. Most trips begin at Lees Ferry, a few miles below the Glen Canyon Dam near Page. There are tranquil half- and full-day float trips from the Glen Canyon Dam to Lees Ferry, as well as raft trips that run from seven to 18 days. Many of these voyages end at Phantom Ranch at the bottom of the Grand Canyon at river mile 87. You'll encounter some good white water along the way, including Lava Falls, listed in the *Guinness Book of World Records* as "the fastest navigable white water stretch in North America."

Sixteen companies (at the time of this writing) offer motorized and oar-powered excursions, but reservations for raft trips (excluding smooth-water, one-day cruises) often need to be made more than six months in advance. Prices for river-raft trips vary greatly, depending on type and length. Half-day trips on smooth water run as low as $62 per adult/$52 for children. Trips that negotiate the entire length of the canyon and take as long as 12 days can cost more than $3,000.

OUTFITTERS & EXPEDITIONS Reputable outfitters include **Arizona River Runners** (☎602/867–4866 or 800/477–7238 ⊕www.raftarizona.com), **Canyoneers, Inc.** (☎928/526–0924, 800/525–0924 outside Arizona ⊕www.canyoneers.com), **Diamond River Adventures, Inc.** (☎928/645–8866 or 800/343–3121 ⊕www.diamondriver.com), **Grand Canyon Expeditions Company** (☎435/644–2691 or 800/544–2691 ⊕www.gcex.com), **Tour West, Inc.** (☎801/225–0755 or 800/453–9107 ⊕www.twriver.com), and **Wilderness River Adventures** (☎928/645–3279 or 800/992–8022 ⊕www.riveradventures.com).

EDUCATIONAL OFFERINGS

Interpretive Ranger Programs. Daily guided hikes and talks may focus on any aspect of the canyon—from geology and flora and fauna to history and the canyon's early inhabitants. For schedules, go to the Grand Canyon Lodge or pick up a free copy of *The Guide* to the North Rim. ☎928/638–7888 ⊕www.nps.gov/grca.

GRAND CANYON: THE WEST RIM

West of Grand Canyon National Park, the tribal lands of the Hualapai and the Havasupai lie on the West Rim of the Canyon.

The Hualapai tribe has been attempting to foster tourism to the little known West Rim, where a road travels through their reservation lands down to the Colorado River. This is a launch point for the region's river runners but because few others know about the road, traffic is a rarity.

Some 12,000 people a year hike, ride, or fly deep into the Grand Canyon to visit the more well-known Havasupai, the "people of the blue green waters." Dubbed the "Shangri-la of the Grand Canyon," the remote, inaccessible Indian reservation includes some of the world's most beautiful and famous waterfalls, together with streams and pools tinted a mystical blue green by dissolved travertine.

THE HUALAPAI TRIBE & GRAND CANYON WEST

78 mi west of Williams via Interstate 40 and AZ 66.

The Hualapai Tribe is expanding its tourism offerings on the West Rim, but you still won't be shoulder to shoulder with other visitors. Hualapai guides add Native American perspective to a canyon trip that you won't find on North and South Rim tours. **Diamond Creek Road,** directly north of the Hualapai Lodge in Peach Springs, is the access point for adventures in this developing section of the Grand Canyon, and winds past Diamond Peak to the Colorado River above Diamond Creek Rapid. The road is at river mile 226, which is 138 mi downstream from Phantom Ranch (as the crow flies the distance is about half of that). Diamond Creek Road can be braved by high clearance passenger vehicles, but your best bet is four-wheel-drive, especially in summer when storms are common.

More than 30 tour and transportation companies service Grand Canyon West from Las Vegas, Phoenix, and Sedona by airplane, helicopter, coach, SUV, and Hummer. Local Hualapai guides add a Native American perspective to a canyon trip that you won't find on North and South rim tours.

The Hualapai Tribe's efforts to expand its tourism offerings on the West Rim include the new **Skywalk,** a cantilever-shaped glass bridge suspended 4,000 feet above the Colorado River and extending 70 feet from the edge of the Grand Canyon—talk about a cliffhanger! Located at Eagle Point, it opened in early 2007. The Skywalk is approximately 10 feet wide, and the bridge's deck, made of tempered glass several inches thick, has five-foot glass railings on each side. A three-level, 6,000-square-foot visitor's center includes a museum, movie theater, VIP lounge, gift shop, and several restaurants and bars. The high-end Skywalk Café has an outdoor patio and rooftop seating on the edge of the canyon.

The Hualapai Tribe requires visitors to obtain permits to travel on tribal lands, although no permit is required to drive to the West Rim if you take a tour while there. ✉ *Hualapai Tourist Information, Peach Springs, on the West Rim of the Canyon, 86434* ☎ *928/769–2230 or 888/255–9550* ⊕ *www.destinationgrandcanyon.com* 🎟 *$15–$17; Skywalk $75* ⊙ *Daily.*

THE HAVASUPAI TRIBE & HAVASU CANYON

141 mi from Williams (to head of Hualapai Trail), west on I-40 and AZ 66, north on Indian Hwy. 18. Note: last gas is at junction of AZ 66 and Indian Hwy. 18.

Havasu Canyon, south of the middle part of the national park and away from the crowds, is the home of the Havasupai, a tribe that has lived in this isolated area for centuries. Their name means "people of the blue green waters," and you'll know why when you see the canyon's waterfalls, as high as 200 feet, cascading over red cliffs into travertine pools surrounded by thick foliage and sheltering trees.

The striking falls, plunging into deep turquoise pools, seem like something from Hawaii or Shangri La. The travertine in the water coats the walls and lines the pools with bizarre, drip-castle rock formations. Centuries of accumulated travertine formations in some of the most popular pools were washed out in massive flooding decades ago, destroying some of the otherworldly scenes pictured in older photos but the place is still magical.

The 500 tribal members now live in the village of Supai, accessible only down the 8-mi-long **Hualapai Trail,** which drops 3,000 feet. The quiet and private Havasupai mostly remain apart from the modest flow of tourists, which nevertheless plays a vital role in the tribal economy.

To reach Havasu's waterfalls, you must hike downstream from the village of Supai. The first fall, 1½ mi from Supai, is the 75-foot-high **Navajo Falls,** named after a 19th-century Havasupai chief who was abducted as a child and raised by the Navajo until he eventually discovered his origin and returned to his tribe as an adult. Navajo Falls rushes over red-wall limestone and collects in a beautiful blue-green pool perfect for swimming. Not much farther downstream, the striking **Havasu Falls** dashes over a ledge into another pool of refreshing 70°F water. The last of the enchanting waterfalls is **Mooney Falls,** 2 mi down from Navajo Falls. Mooney Falls, named after a prospector who fell to his death here in 1880, plummets 196 feet down a sheer travertine cliff. The hike down to the pool below is a steep descent down slippery rocks with only the assistance of chains suspended along a series of iron stakes.

The Havasupai restrict the number of visitors to the canyon; you must have reservations. They ask that hikers call ahead before taking the trek into the canyon. Hualapai Trail leaves from Hualapai Hilltop, 63 mi north on Indian Route 18 from Route 66. From an elevation of 5,200 feet, the trail travels down a moderate grade to Supai village at 3,200 feet. Bring plenty of water and avoid hiking during the middle of the day, when canyon temperatures can reach into the 100s. If you'd rather ride, you can rent a horse for the trip down for $150 round-trip, or $75 one-way. Riders must be able to mount and dismount by themselves; be at least 4 feet, 7 inches; and weigh less than 250 pounds. Reservations must be made at least six weeks in advance with Havasupai Tourist Enterprise, which requires a 50% deposit. You'll need to spend the night if you're hiking or riding.

Another option is a helicopter ride into the canyon with **Air West Helicopters** (☎623/516–2790). Flights leave from Hualapai Hilltop and cost $85 per person each way. They do not accept reservations. There's a $30 entrance fee for visiting the Havasupai tribal lands. You're expected to respect the land and its people. The tribe does not allow alcohol, drugs, pets, or weapons. ⊠*Havasupai Tourist Enterprise, Supai 86435* ☎*928/448–2141 general information, 928/448–2111 lodging reservations* ⊕*www.havasupaitribe.com.*

SPORTS & THE OUTDOORS

TOURS Shuttle bus, helicopter, boat trips, and food are available at the West Rim. Visitors aren't allowed to travel in their own vehicles once they reach the West Rim, but must purchase tour packages on **Grand Canyon West Tours** (⊠*887 Rte. 66, Peach Springs 86434* ☎*928/769–2230 or 888/255–9550* ⊕*www.destinationgrandcanyon.com*). For an extra cost you can add a helicopter trip into the canyon, a boat trip on the Colorado, or a walk on the Skywalk. Depending on the package you purchase, Hualapai guides will take you to canyon viewpoints (Quarter Master, Eagle Point, and Guano Point) and Hualapai Ranch (western town) or the Indian Village. The tour includes a barbecue lunch.

RAFTING One-day river trips are offered by the Hualapai tribe through the **Hualapai River Runners** (⊠*887 Rte. 66, Peach Springs 86434* ☎*928/769–2230 or 888/255–9550* ⊕*www.destinationgrandcanyon.com*) from March through October. The trips, which cost $290 (plus 7% tax) paid in advance, leave from the Hualapai Lodge at 8 AM and return between 6:30 and 8:30 PM. Lunch, snacks, and beverages are provided. Children must be eight or older to take the trip, which runs several rapids with the most difficult rated as Class V or VI, depending on the river flow.

EDUCATIONAL OFFERINGS

☘ **Grand Canyon West** (☎702/878–9378, 877/716–9378 ⊕*www.destinationgrandcanyon.com*) Depending on the package (starting at $30), Hualapai guides will take you to attractions including Eagle Point, where the Indian Village walking tour visits authentic dwellings of the Hualapai, Havasupai, Navajo, Plains, and Hopi; Hualapai Ranch, site of western performances, cookouts, and horseback and wagon rides; and Guano Point, where the "High Point Hike" offers panoramic views of the Colorado River. Park & Ride services are available from Dolan Springs, Arizona, for a nominal fee; reservations are required.

WHAT'S NEAR THE GRAND CANYON?

The northwest section of Arizona is geographically fascinating. In addition to the Grand Canyon, it's home to national forests, national monuments, and national recreation areas. Towns, however, are small and scattered. Many of them cater to visiting adventurers, and Native American reservations dot the map.

NEARBY TOWNS & ATTRACTIONS

NEARBY TOWNS

Towns near the canyon's South Rim include the park's gateway, Tusayan, 3 mi south and Williams, 58 mi south. Flagstaff is 80 mi southeast and Tuba City is about 50 mi from the canyon's east entrance.

Tusayan has the basic amenities and an airport that serves as a starting point for airplane and helicopter tours of the canyon. The cozy mountain town of **Williams,** founded in 1882 when the railroad passed through, was once a rough-and-tumble joint, replete with saloons and bordellos. Today it reflects a much milder side of the Wild West, with 3,000 residents and 1,512 motel rooms. Wander along main street—part of historic Route 66, but locally named, like the town, after trapper Bill Williams—and indulge in Route 66 nostalgia inside antiques shops or souvenir and T-shirt stores.

The communities closest to the North Rim include Fredonia, 76 mi north; Marble Canyon, 80 mi northeast; Lees Ferry, 85 mi east; and Jacob Lake, 45 mi north.

Fredonia, a small community of about 1,200, approximately an hour's drive north of the Grand Canyon, is often referred to as the gateway to the North Rim; it's also relatively close to Zion and Bryce Canyon national parks. **Marble Canyon,** to the north of Tuba City, marks the geographical beginning of the Grand Canyon at its northeastern tip. It's a good stopping point if you are driving U.S. 89 to the North Rim. En route from the South Rim to the North Rim is **Lees Ferry,** where most of the area's river rafts start their journey. The tiny town of **Jacob Lake,** nestled high in pine country at an elevation of 7,925 feet, was named after Mormon explorer Jacob Hamblin, also known as the "Buckskin Missionary." It has a hotel, café, campground, and lush mountain countryside.

NEARBY ATTRACTIONS

Planes of Fame Museum. A good stop 30 mi north of Williams, at the junction of U.S. Highway 180 and State Route 64 in Valle, this satellite of the Air Museum Planes of Fame in Chino, California, chronicles the history of aviation with an array of historic and modern aircraft. One of the featured pieces is a C-121A Constellation "Bataan," the personal aircraft of General MacArthur used during the Korean War. Visitors are not allowed inside the cockpits. ⊠ *755 Mustang Way, Valle* ☎ *928/635–1000* ⊕ *www.planesoffame.org* ☎ *$5.95* ⊙ *Daily 9–5.*

★ **Vermilion Cliffs.** West from the town of Marble Canyon are these spectacular cliffs, more than 3,000 feet high in many places. Keep an eye out for condors; the giant endangered birds were reintroduced into the area in the winter of 1996–97. Reports suggest that the birds, once in captivity, are surviving well in the wilderness.

SCENIC DRIVES & VISTAS

U.S. 89. The route north from Cameron Trading Post (Cameron, AZ) on U.S. 89 offers a stunning view of the **Painted Desert** to the right. The desert, which covers thousands of square miles stretching to the south and east, is a vision of subtle, almost harsh beauty, with windswept plains and mesas, isolated buttes, and barren valleys in pastel patterns. About 30 mi north of Cameron Trading Post, the Painted Desert country gives way to sandstone cliffs that run for miles. Brilliantly hued and ranging in color from light pink to deep orange, the **Echo Cliffs** rise to more than 1,000 feet in many places. They are essentially devoid of vegetation, but in a few high places, thick patches of tall cottonwood and poplar trees, nurtured by springs and water seepage from the rock escarpment, manage to thrive.

U.S. 89A. At Bitter Springs, Aria., 60 mi north of Cameron, U.S. 89A branches off from U.S. 89, running north and providing views of **Marble Canyon,** the geographical beginning of the Grand Canyon. Like the Grand Canyon, Marble Canyon was formed by the Colorado River. Traversing a gorge nearly 500 feet deep is **Navajo Bridge,** a narrow steel span built in 1929 and listed on the National Register of Historic Places. Formerly used for car traffic, it now functions only as a pedestrian overpass.

AREA ACTIVITIES

SPORTS & THE OUTDOORS

AIR TOURS At **National Geographic Visitor Center Grand Canyon** (✉ *Hwy. 64/U.S. 180, 2 mi south of the Grand Canyon's south entrance, Tusayan* ☎ *928/638–2203 or 928/638–2468* ⊕ *www.explorethecanyon.com* ☉ *Mar.–Oct., daily 8:30–8:30; Nov.–Feb., daily 10:30–6:30*) you can schedule and purchase tickets for air tours and daily Colorado River trips; buy a national park pass, and access the park by special entry lanes.

Rangers say the best bet for bikers—and only experienced ones should attempt it—is the **Rainbow Rim Trail** (☎ *928/643–7395*), an 18-mi, one-way trail that begins at Parissawampitts. It travels past four other fantastic viewpoints—Fence, Locust, North Timp, and Timp—and winds through a ponderosa pine forest and up and down through side canyons, aspen groves, and pristine meadows. Located in the **Kaibab National Forest,** the trail is open to hikers and bikers and stays within 200 feet of its 7,550 feet elevation.

Pedal the depths of the Kaibab National Forest on the **Tusayan Bike Trail** (✉ *Tusayan Ranger District, Tusayan* ☎ *928/638–2443*). Following linked loop trails at an elevation of 6,750 feet, you can bike as few as 3 mi or as many as 32 mi round-trip along old logging roads through ponderosa pine forest. Keep an eye out for elk, mule deer, hawks, eagles, pronghorn antelope, turkeys, coyote, and porcupines. Open for biking year-round (but most feasible March through October), the trail is accessed on the west side of Hwy. 64, a half-mile north of Tusayan.

Cyclists also can enjoy the scenery along abandoned sections of Route 66 on the **Historic Route 66 Mountain Bike Tour.** Maps of the tour, which include the 6-mi **Ash Fork Hill Trail** and the 5-mi **Devil Dog Trail,** are available at the Williams Visitor Center.

FISHING   Fish for trout, crappie, catfish, and smallmouth bass at a number of lakes surrounding Williams. To fish on public land, anglers ages 14 and older are required to obtain a fishing license from the **Arizona Game and Fish Department** (⌂*3500 S. Lake Mary Rd., Flagstaff 86001* ☎*928/774–5045* ⊕*www.gf.state.az.us.*).

The stretch of ice-cold, crystal-clear water at Lees Ferry off the North Rim provides arguably the best trout fishing in the Southwest. Many rafters and anglers stay the night in a campground near the river or in nearby Marble Canyon before hitting the river at dawn. Marble Canyon Lodge (☎*928/355–2225*) sells Arizona fishing licenses, as does **Lees Ferry Anglers** (✉*Milepost 547, N. U.S. 89A, Marble Canyon* ☎*928/355–2261, 800/962–9755 outside Arizona* ⊕*www.leesferry. com*), which also operates guided trips, starting from $300 per person per day.

Arizona Raft Adventures (✉*4050 E. Huntington Rd., Flagstaff 86004* ☎*928/526–8200 or 800/786–7238* 🖷*928/526–8246* ⊕*www.azraft. com*) organizes 6- to 16-day paddle and/or motor trips for all skill levels. Trips, which run $1,600 to $3,450, depart April through October.

With a reputation for high quality and a roster of 3- to 13-day trips, **Canyoneers** (⌂*Box 2997, Flagstaff 86003* ☎*928/526–0924 or 800/525–0924* 🖷*928/527–9398* ⊕*www.canyoneers.com*) is popular with those who want to do some hiking as well. The five-day trip "Best of the Grand" trip includes a hike down to Phantom Ranch. Three- to 14-day trips, available April through September, cost between $925 and $3,150.

Owned and operated by a mother-and-daughters team, **Diamond River Adventures** (⌂*Box 1300, Page 86040* ☎*928/645–8866 or 800/343– 3121* 🖷*928/645–9536* ⊕*www.diamondriver.com*) offers both oar-powered and motorized river trips from 4 to 14 days from May through early October. Prices range from $830 to $2,600.

You can count on **Grand Canyon Expeditions** (⌂*Box O, Kanab, UT 84741* ☎*435/644–2691 or 800/544–2691* 🖷*435/644–2699* ⊕*www. gcex.com*) to take you down the Colorado River safely and in style: They limit the number of people on each boat to 14, and evening meals might include filet mignon, pork chops, or shrimp. The April through mid-September trips cost $2,145 to $3,500 for 8 to 16 days.

CLOSE UP Rafting Basics

So you're ready to tackle the churning white water of the Colorado River as it rumbles and hisses its way through the Grand Canyon? Well, you're in good company: The crafty, one-armed Civil War veteran John Wesley Powell first charted these dangerous rapids during the summer of 1869. It wasn't until 1938, though, that the first commercial river trip made its way down this fearsome corridor. Running the river has come a long way since then—and since Norman Neville made the first trip by kayak, in 1941, in a craft he built out of scrap lumber salvaged from an outhouse and a run-down barn.

White-water rafting still offers all the excitement of those early days—without the danger and discomfort. Professional river runners lead journeys ranging from relaxing half-day float trips to adventurous 18-day oar excursions. Lifejackets, beverages, tents, sheets, tarps, sleeping bags, wet bags, first aid, and food are provided—but you'll still need to plan ahead by packing clothing, hats, sunscreen, toiletries, and other sundries. Keep in mind that seats fill up fast due to the restricted number of visitors allowed on the river each season by the National Park Service. But once you've secured your seat, all that's left to do is pack your bags and get geared up for an experience of a lifetime. Lots of people book trips for summer's peak period: June through August. If you're flexible, take advantage of the Arizona weather; May to early June and September are ideal rafting times in the Grand Canyon.

NEED A BREAK? The **Grand Canyon Railway,** first established in 1901 and reopened in 1989, transports passengers in railcars that date from the 1920s. The scenic, narrated train ride (2¼ hours each way) runs from the Williams Depot to the South Rim of the Grand Canyon. The vintage 1923 train travels 65 mi through prairie, ranch, and national park land to the log-cabin train station in Grand Canyon Village. You won't see the Grand Canyon from the train, but you can walk or catch the shuttle at the restored, historic Grand Canyon Railway Station. On board, Wild West characters entertain. Specialty tours include the Polar Express, a wintertime train ride that has often been sold out. If you have a pet, it can stay at the Pet Resort while you ride the train. ⊠ *Williams Depot, 233 N. Grand Canyon Blvd. at Fray Marcos Blvd.* ☎ *800/843–8724 railway reservations and information* ⊕ *www.thetrain. com* ⊠ *$60–$155 round-trip, not including 9.525% tax and national park entrance fee. Youth and child rates available* ⊙ *Departs daily from Williams between 8:30 and 10:30* AM, *depending on the season, and from the South Rim between 3 and 4:30* PM.

You can rent horses at the **Apache Stables** (⊠*Hwy. 64/U.S. 180* ☎*928/638–2891* ⊕*www.apachestables.com*) for $30.50 an hour or $55.50 for a two-hour guided tour of the Kaibab National Forest. A four-hour ride through Long Jim Canyon ($95.50) will take you through rugged canyon country to the viewpoint on the rim. The stables open in March, and rides are offered, weather permitting, through the end of November.

🌣 **Elk Ridge Ski and Outdoor Recreation** (✉ *Off I–40* ☎ *7596 Buckridge Dr., 86046* ☎ *928/234–6587* ⊕ *www.elkridge.com*) is usually open from mid-December through much of March, weather permitting. There are four groomed runs (including one for beginners), areas suitable for cross-country skiing, and a hill set aside for tubing. The lodge rents skis, snowboards, and inner tubes. From Williams, take South 4th Street for 2 mi, and then turn right at the sign and go another 1½ mi.

EDUCATIONAL OFFERINGS

🌣 **Grand Canyon West** (☎ *702/878–9378,* *877/716–9378* ⊕ *www. destinationgrandcanyon.com*). Depending on the package (starting at $30), Hualapai guides will take you to attractions including Eagle Point, where the Indian Village walking tour visits authentic dwellings of the Hualapai, Havasupai, Navajo, Plains, and Hopi; Hualapai Ranch, site of western performances, cookouts, and horseback and wagon rides; and Guano Point, where the "High Point Hike" offers panoramic views of the Colorado River. Park & Ride services are available from Dolan Springs, Arizona, for a nominal fee; reservations are required.

ARTS & ENTERTAINMENT

🌣 At the **National Geographic Visitor Center Grand Canyon** in Tusayan, discover the canyon's natural history in the 35-minute film *Grand Canyon: The Hidden Secrets,* on an IMAX screen that stands seven stories high. ✉ *Hwy. 64/U.S. 180, 2 mi south of the south entrance, Tusayan* ☎ *928/638–2203 or 928/638–2468* ⊕ *www.explorethecanyon.com* 🎫 *$10.65 for adults, $7.46 for children (tickets purchased online cost $7.99 for adults, $5.59 for kids)* ⊙ *Mar.–Oct., daily 8:30–8:30; Nov.–Feb., daily 10:30–6:30; shows every hr on the ½ hr.*

WHERE TO STAY & EAT

ABOUT THE RESTAURANTS

Inside the park, you can find everything from cafeteria food to casual café fare to elegant evening specials. There's even a coffeehouse brewing organic joe. Reservations are accepted (and recommended) only at El Tovar Dining Room; they can be made 6 months in advance with El Tovar room reservations, 30 days in advance without. The dress code is casual across the board, but El Tovar is your best option if you're looking to dress up a bit and thumb through an extensive wine list. On the North Rim there is just one restaurant. Drinking water and restrooms are not available at most picnic spots. Options outside the park range from fast food to nice sit-down restaurants. Near the park, even the priciest places allow casual dress.

ABOUT THE HOTELS

The park's accommodations include three "historic rustic" facilities and four motel-style lodges. Of the 922 rooms, cabins, and suites, only 203, all at the Grand Canyon Lodge, are located at the North Rim. Outside of El Tovar Hotel, the canyon's architectural crown jewel, frills are hard to find. Rooms are basic but comfortable, and most guests would agree that the best in-room amenity is a view of the canyon. Though rates vary widely, most rooms fall in the $125 to $136 range.

Reservations are a must, especially during the busy summer season. If you want to get your first choice (especially Bright Angel Lodge or El Tovar), make reservations as far in advance as possible; they're taken up to 13 months ahead. You might find a last-minute cancellation, but you shouldn't count on it. Although lodging at the South Rim will keep you close to the action, the frenetic activity and crowded facilities are off-putting to some. With short notice, the best time to find a room on the South Rim is during winter. And though the North Rim is less crowded than the South Rim, lodging (remember that rooms are limited) is available only from mid-May through mid-October.

Outside the park, Tusayan's hotels offer a convenient location but no bargains, while Williams and Flagstaff can provide price breaks on food and lodging, as well as a respite from the crowds. Extra amenities (e.g., swimming pools and Internet access) are also more abundant. Reservations are always a good idea.

ABOUT THE CAMPGROUNDS

Inside the park, camping is permitted only in designated campsites. Some campgrounds charge nightly camping fees in addition to entrance fees, and some accept reservations up to five months in advance. Others are first-come, first-served. The South Rim has three campgrounds, one with RV hookups. The North Rim's single in-park campground does not offer hookups. All four campgrounds are near the rims and easily accessible. In-park camping in a spot other than a developed rim campground requires a permit from the Backcountry Information Center, which also serves as your reservation. Permits can be requested by mail or fax; applying well in advance is recommended. Call 928/638–7875 for information. Numerous backcountry campsites dot the canyon—be prepared for a considerable hike. The three established backcountry campgrounds require a trek of 4$^{6}/_{10}$ to 16$^{6}/_{10}$ mi.

Outside the park, two campgrounds, one with hookups, are located within 7 mi of the South Rim, and two are located within about 45 mi of the North Rim. At the time of this writing one is closed for renovations; the other has hookups and accepts reservations. Developed and undeveloped campsites are available, first-come, first-served, in the Kaibab National Forest.

WHERE TO EAT

IN THE PARK: SOUTH RIM

$–$$$ ✗**Arizona Room.** The canyon views from this casual Southwestern-style steak house are the best of any restaurant at the South Rim. The menu includes chicken, steak (there's good prime rib), and seafood (including salmon), as well as vegetarian options. It's open for lunch from 11:30–3 and for dinner starting at 4:30; seating is first-come, first served, so arrive early to avoid the crowds. ⊠*Bright Angel Lodge, West*

Rim Dr., Grand Canyon Village 928/638–2961 *Reservations not accepted* AE, D, DC, MC, V *Closed Jan.–mid-Feb.*

$–$$$
Fodor's Choice
★

✕ **El Tovar Dining Room.** Modeled after a European hunting lodge, this rustic 19th-century dining room built of hand-hewn logs is worth a visit. Breakfast, lunch, and dinner are served beneath the beamed ceiling. The cuisine is modern Southwestern, and the menu includes such dishes as sautéed rainbow trout served with a wild rice salad and grilled New York strip steak with buttermilk-cornmeal onion rings and pepper jack au gratin potatoes. It's the best restaurant for miles. ⊠ *El Tovar Hotel, West Rim Dr., Grand Canyon Village* 303/297–2757 or 888/297–2757 *(reservations only), 928/638–2961* *Reservations essential* AE, D, DC, MC, V.

> **TOP PICNIC SPOTS**
>
> **Buggeln,** 15 mi east of Grand Canyon Village on Desert View Drive, has some secluded, shady spots and is wheelchair accessible, with assistance. **Cape Royal,** 23 mi south of the North Rim Visitor Center, is the most popular designated picnic area on the North Rim due to its panoramic views. **Grandview Point** has, as the name implies, grand views; it's 12 mi east of the Village on Desert View Drive. **Point Imperial,** 11 mi northeast of the North Rim Visitor Center, has shade and some privacy.

¢–$ ✕ **Bright Angel Restaurant and Fountain.** The draw here is casual, affordable dining. No-surprises dishes will fill your belly at breakfast, lunch, or dinner. ⊠ *Bright Angel Lodge, Grand Canyon Village* 928/638–2961 *Reservations not accepted* AE, D, DC, MC, V.

¢–$ ✕ **Maswik Cafeteria.** You can get up a burger or Mexican fare at this food court. ⊠ *Maswik Lodge, Grand Canyon Village* 928/638–2961 *Reservations not accepted* AE, D, DC, MC, V.

¢ ✕ **Yavapai Canyon Café.** Fast-food favorites here include pastries, burgers, and pizza. Open for breakfast, lunch, and dinner, the cafeteria also serves specials, chicken potpie, fried catfish, and fried chicken. ⊠ *Grand Canyon Village* 928/638–2961 *Reservations not accepted* AE, D, DC, MC, V *Closed mid-Dec.–Feb.*

IN THE PARK: NORTH RIM

★ **$–$$$** ✕ **Grand Canyon Lodge Dining Room.** The historic lodge has a huge, high-ceilinged dining room with spectacular views and very good food; you might find pork medallions, red snapper, and spinach linguine with red clam sauce on the dinner menu. It's also open for breakfast and lunch. ⊠ *Grand Canyon Lodge, Bright Angel Point (North Rim)* 928/638–2611 *Reservations essential* AE, D, DC, MC, V *Closed mid-Oct. to mid-May.*

¢ ✕ **Deli in the Pines.** Dining choices are very limited on the North Rim, but this is your best bet for a meal on a budget. Selections include pizza, salads, deli sandwiches, hot dogs, and ice cream. ⊠ *Grand Canyon Lodge, Bright Angel Point (North Rim)* 928/638–2611 *Reservations not accepted* AE, D, DC, MC, V *Closed mid-Oct. to mid-May.*

OUTSIDE THE PARK

◐ ★ $$-$$$ ✕**Canyon Star Restaurant and Saloon.** Relax in the rustic dining room at the Grand Hotel for breakfast, lunch, or dinner. The dinner menu includes prime rib, bison, and salmon. Every evening there's entertainment: live music, karaoke, or Native American dance performances—all great for families. There's even a kids' menu. In the summer, be sure to reserve a table. ⊠*Hwy. 64/U.S. 180, Tusayan* ☎928/638–3333 ⊟*AE, DC, MC, V.*

$$-$$$ ✕**The Coronado Room.** When pizza and burgers just won't do, the restaurant at the Best Western Grand Canyon Squire Inn is the best upscale choice in Tusayan. The menu encompasses everything from escargot to elk steak. Even though the Coronado Room takes pride in its fine-dining atmosphere, dress is casual and comfortable. Reservations are a good idea, particularly in the busy season. ⊠*Hwy. 64/U.S. 180, Tusayan* ☎928/638–2681 ⊟*AE, D, DC, MC, V* ⊗*No lunch.*

★ $-$$ ✕**Pancho McGillicuddy's.** Established in 1893 as the Cabinet Saloon, this restaurant is on the National Register of Historic Places. Gone are the spittoons and pipes—the smoke-free dining area now has Mexican-inspired decor and such specialties as "armadillo eggs," the local name for deep-fried jalapeños stuffed with cheese. Other favorites include fish tacos, buzzard wings—better known as hot wings—and pollo verde (chicken breasts smothered in a sauce of cheese, sour cream, and green chiles). The bar has TVs tuned to sporting events and pours more than 30 tequilas. ⊠*141 Railroad Ave., Williams* ☎928/635–4150 ⊟*AE, D, MC, V.*

¢-$$ **Café Tusayan.** Homemade pies and local microbrews from Sedona, Flagstaff, and Tucson brighten the menu of standard fare—omelets, salads, burgers, salmon, and prime rib—at this basic restaurant. ⊠*Hwy. 64/ U.S. 180, Tusayan* ☎928/638–2151 ⊟*MC, V.*

◐ ¢-$$ ✕**Cruisers Café 66.** Talk about nostalgia. Imagine your favorite '50s-style, high school hangout—with cocktail service. Good burgers, salads, and malts are family-priced, but a choice steak is available, too, for $30. Stuffed buffalo, a large mural of the town's heydey along the "Mother Road," and historic cars out front make this a Route 66 favorite. Kids enjoy the relaxed atmosphere and jukebox tunes. ⊠*233 W. Rte. 66, Williams* ☎928/635–2445 ⊟*AE, DC, MC, V.*

Fodor'sChoice ★

¢ ✕**Grand Canyon Coffee Café.** You'll find good espresso drinks here, along with English-style fish and chips, and wonderful sandwiches on home-made focaccia. The mountain man sandwich is piled high with roast beef, cheddar and onions. On display are a few Harley-Davidson artifacts, some for sale. ⊠*125 W. Rte. 66, Williams* ☎928/635–1255 ⊟*AE, MC, V* ⊗*Closed Jan.–Feb.*

¢ ✕**Twisters.** Kick up some Route 66 nostalgia at this old-fashioned soda fountain and gift shop. Dine on hamburgers and hot dogs, a famous Twisters sundae, Route 66 Beer Float, or cherry phosphate—all to the sounds of '50s tunes. The adjoining gift shop is a blast from the past, with Route 66 merchandise, classic Coca-Cola memorabilia, and fanciful items celebrating the careers of such characters as Betty Boop, James Dean, Elvis, and Marilyn Monroe. ⊠*417 E. Rte. 66, Williams* ☎928/635–0266 ⊕*www.route66place.com* ⊟*AE, D, MC, V.*

WHERE TO STAY

IN THE PARK: SOUTH RIM

$$–$$$$
Fodor'sChoice
★

El Tovar Hotel. A registered National Historic Landmark, El Tovar was built in 1905 of Oregon pine logs and native stone. The hotel's proximity to all of the canyon's facilities, its European hunting-lodge atmosphere, and its renowned dining room make it the best place to stay on the South Rim. It's usually booked well in advance (up to 13 months ahead), though it's easier to get a room during winter months. Three suites and several rooms have canyon views (these are booked early), but you can enjoy the view anytime from the cocktail-lounge back porch. ⊠ *West Rim Dr., Grand Canyon Village* ☜*Box 699, Grand Canyon 86023* ☏*303/297–2757 or 888/297–2757 (reservations only), 928/638–2961* 🖷*303/297–3175 (reservations only)* ⊕*www.grandcanyonlodges.com* ⟿*70 rooms, 12 suites* ☖*Restaurant, room service, refrigerators, cable TV, bar, a/c, no smoking* ▤*AE, D, DC, MC, V.*

$$

Kachina Lodge. Located on the rim halfway between El Tovar and Bright Angel Lodge, this motel-style lodge has many rooms with partial canyon views ($10 extra). Although lacking the historical charm of the neighboring lodges, these rooms are a good bet for families and are within easy walking distance of dining facilities at El Tovar and Bright Angel Lodge. There are also several rooms for people with physical disabilities. There's no air-conditioning, but evaporative coolers keep the heat at bay. Check in at El Tovar Hotel to the east. ⊠ *West Rim Dr., Grand Canyon Village* ☜*Box 699, Grand Canyon 86023* ☏*303/297–2757 or 888/297–2757 (reservations only), 928/638–2961* 🖷*303/297–3175 (reservations only)* ⊕*www.grandcanyonlodges.com* ⟿*50 rooms* ☖*Refrigerators, cable TV, in-room data ports, ironing boards, safes, coffeemakers, hairdryers, no-smoking rooms* ▤*AE, D, DC, MC, V.*

$$

Thunderbird Lodge. This motel with comfortable, no-nonsense rooms is next to Bright Angel Lodge in Grand Canyon Village. For $10 more, you can get a room with a partial view of the canyon. Rooms have either two queen beds or one king. Check in at Bright Angel Lodge, the next hotel to the west. Some rooms do not have a/c, but instead have evaporative coolers. ⊠ *West Rim Dr., Grand Canyon Village* ☜*Box 699, Grand Canyon 86023* ☏*303/297–2757 or 888/297–2757 (reservations only), 928/638–2961* 🖷*303/297–3175 (reservations only)* ⊕*www.grandcanyonlodges.com* ⟿*55 rooms* ☖*Refrigerators, ironing boards, safes, coffeemakers, hairdryers, no-smoking rooms, no a/c (some)* ▤*AE, D, DC, MC, V.*

☾ $–$$

Bright Angel Lodge. Famed architect Mary Jane Colter designed this 1935 log-and-stone structure, which sits within a few yards of the canyon rim and blends superbly with the canyon walls. It offers a similar location to El Tovar for about half the price. Accommodations are in motel-style rooms or cabins. Lodge rooms don't have TVs, and some rooms do not have private bathrooms. Scattered among the pines, 50 cabins, some with fireplaces, have TVs and private baths. Expect historic charm but not luxury. The Bright Angel Dining Room serves family-style meals all day and a Warm Apple Grunt dessert large enough to share. The Arizona Room serves dinner only. Adding to

2

the experience are an ice-cream parlor, gift shop, and small history museum with exhibits on Fred Harvey and Mary Jane Colter. ⊠ *West Rim Dr., Grand Canyon Village* ⌂ *Box 699, Grand Canyon 86023* ☎ *303/297–2757, 888/297–2757 (reservations only), 928/638–2961* 🖷 *303/297–3175 (reservations only)* ⊕ *www.grandcanyonlodges.com* ⇄ *39 rooms, 6 with shared toilet and shower, 13 with shared shower; 50 cabins* ⓑ *Restaurant, coffee shop, bar, Internet room, shop, no a/c, no TV in some rooms.* ⊟ *AE, D, DC, MC, V.*

☼ **$–$$** 🍴 **Maswik Lodge.** The lodge, named for a Hopi Kachina who is said to guard the canyon, is ¼ mi from the rim. Accommodations, nestled in the ponderosa pine forest, range from rustic cabins to more modern rooms, refurbished in 2006. The cabins are the cheapest option but are available only spring through fall. Some rooms have air conditioning, and the rest have ceiling fans. Maswik Cafeteria offers sandwiches, salads, snack foods, and a choice of several hot meals. Teenagers like the lounge, where they can shoot pool, throw darts, or watch the big-screen TV. There is also an Internet room. Kids under 16 stay free. ⊠ *Grand Canyon Village* ⌂ *Box 699, Grand Canyon 86023* ☎ *303/297–2757 or 888/297–2757 (reservations only), 928/638–2961* 🖷 *303/297–3175 (reservations only)* ⊕ *www.grandcanyonlodges.com* ⇄ *250 rooms, 28 cabins* ⓑ *Cafeteria, sports bar, shop, no-smoking rooms, no a/c (some)* ⊟ *AE, D, DC, MC, V.*

$–$$ 🍴 **Yavapai Lodge.** The largest motel-style lodge in the park is tucked in a piñon and juniper forest at the eastern end of Grand Canyon Village, near the RV park. The basic rooms are near the park's general store, the visitor center (½ mi), and the rim (¼ mi). The cafeteria, open for breakfast, lunch, and dinner, serves standard park service food. An Internet room is available to guests. ⊠ *Grand Canyon Village* ⌂ *Box 699, Grand Canyon 86023* ☎ *303/297–2757 or 888/297–2757 (reservations only), 928/638–2961* 🖷 *303/297–3175 (reservations only)* ⊕ *www.grandcanyonlodges.com* ⇄ *358 rooms* ⓑ *Restaurant, refrigerators, coffeemakers, no-smoking rooms* ⊟ *AE, D, DC, MC, V* ⊘ *Closed Jan. and Feb.*

¢–$ 🍴 **Phantom Ranch.** In a grove of cottonwood trees on the canyon floor, Phantom Ranch is accessible only to hikers and mule trekkers. The wood-and-stone buildings originally made up a hunting camp built in 1922. There are 40 dormitory beds and 14 beds in cabins, all with shared baths. Seven additional cabins are reserved for mule riders, who buy their trips as a package. The mess hall-style restaurant, one of the most remote eating establishments in the United States, serves family-style meals, with breakfast, dinner, and box lunches available. Reservations, taken up to 13 months in advance, are a must. ⊠ *On canyon floor, at intersection of the Bright Angel and Kaibab trails* ☎ *303/297–2757 or 888/297–2757* 🖷 *303/297–3175 (reservations only)* ⊕ *www. grandcanyonlodges.com* ⇄ *4 dormitories and 2 cabins for hikers, 7 cabins with outside showers for mule riders* ⓑ *Dining room, no a/c, no room phones, no room TVs* ⊟ *AE, D, DC, MC, V.*

$$ ⛺ **Mather Campground.** Mather has RV and tent sites but no hookups.
Fodor's Choice No reservations are accepted from December to March, but the rest
★ of the year, especially during the busy spring and summer seasons,

they are a good idea, and can be made up to five months in advance. Ask at the campground entrance for same-day availability. ⊠ *Off Village Loop Dr., Grand Canyon Village* ☎ *National Park Reservation Service* 🕾 *800/365–2267* ⊕ *reservations.nps.gov/index.cfm* ⤵ *308 sites for RVs and tents* ♿ *Flush toilets, pay phones, drinking water, guest laundry, showers, fire grates, picnic tables, dump station* ☉ *Open year-round.*

$ 🚐 **Desert View Campground.** Popular for spectacular views of the canyon from the nearby Watchtower, this campground fills up fast in summer. Fifty RV (without hookups) and tent sites are available on a first-come, first-served basis. ⊠ *Desert View Dr., 23 mi east of Grand Canyon Village off Hwy. 64* ☎ *Backcountry Office, Box 129, Grand Canyon 86023* 🕾 *928/638–7875* 🖷 *928/638–2125* ♿ *Grills, flush toilets, drinking water, picnic tables* ⤵ *50 campsites* ⚠ *Reservations not accepted* ☉ *Mid-May–mid-Oct.*

¢ 🚐 **Bright Angel Campground.** This campground is near Phantom Ranch on the South and North Kaibab trails, at the bottom of the canyon. There are toilet facilities and running water, but no showers. A backcountry permit, which serves as your reservation, is required to stay here. ⊠ *Intersection of South and North Kaibab trails, Grand Canyon* ☎ *Backcountry Office, Box 129, Grand Canyon 86023* 🕾 *928/638–7875* 🖷 *928/638–2125* ⤵ *32 tent sites* ♿ *Flush toilets, drinking water, picnic tables* ⚠ *backcountry permit required* ☉ *Open year-round.*

¢ 🚐 **Indian Garden.** Halfway down the canyon is this campground, en route to Phantom Ranch on the Bright Angel Trail. Running water and toilet facilities are available, but not showers. A backcountry permit, which serves as a reservation, is required. ⊠ *Bright Angel Trail, Grand Canyon* ☎ *Backcountry Office, Box 129, Grand Canyon 86023* 🕾 *928/638–7875* 🖷 *928/638–2125* ♿ *Vault toilets, drinking water, picnic tables* ⤵ *15 tent sites* ⚠ *Reservations essential* ☉ *Open year-round.*

INSIDE THE PARK: NORTH RIM

$–$$
Fodor'sChoice
★
🏨 **Grand Canyon Lodge.** This historic property, constructed mainly in the 1920s and '30s, is the premier lodging facility in the North Rim area. The main building has limestone walls and timbered ceilings. Lodging options include small, rustic cabins; larger cabins (some with a canyon view and some with two bedrooms); and newer, traditional motel rooms. You might find marinated pork kebabs or linguine with cilantro on the dining room's dinner menu ($–$$$). Dining room reservations are essential and should be made as far in advance as possible. ⊠ *Hwy. 67, North Rim, Grand Canyon National Park 86052* 🕾 *303/297–2757 or 888/297–2757 (reservations only), 928/638–2611* 🖷 *303/297–3175 (reservations only)* ⊕ *www.grandcanyonnorthrim. com* ⤵ *44 rooms, 157 cabins* ♿ *Cafeteria, dining room, bar, shop, laundry facilities, no a/c, no room TVs, no-smoking rooms* ⊟ *AE, D, MC, V* ☉ *Closed mid-Oct.–mid-May.*

$$ 🚐 **North Rim Campground.** The only designated campground at the North Rim of Grand Canyon National Park sits 3 mi north of the rim, and has 83 RV and tent sites (no hookups). You can reserve a site up to five months in advance. ⊠ *Hwy. 67, Grand Canyon* ☎ *National*

Park Reservation Service ☎*800/365–2267* ⊕*reservations.nps.gov* ⬑*83 campsites* ⚴*Flush toilets, dump station, drinking water, guest laundry, showers, fire grates, picnic tables, general store* ⚴*Reservations essential* ⊙*Generally open mid-May–mid-Oct., possibly later, weather permitting.*

2

OUTSIDE THE PARK

$–$$$

Fodors̓Choice

★

✕🖼**Cameron Trading Post.** Fifty-four miles north of Flagstaff, this trading post dates back to 1916. Southwestern-style rooms have carved-oak furniture, tile baths, and balconies overlooking the Colorado River. Native-stone landscaping—including fossilized dinosaur tracks—and a small, well-kept garden are pleasant. Make your reservations far in advance for high season. The dining room's delicious homemade green chili and fry bread, Navajo tacos, and hamburgers are worth the stop alone (¢–$$). Satellite TV is in the rooms. ⊠*U.S. 89* 🕮*Box 339, Cameron 86020* ☎*928/679–2231 or 800/338–7385, Ext. 414 (for hotel)* 🖷*928/679–2350* ⊕*www.camerontradingpost.com* ⬑*62 rooms, 4 suites* ⚴*Restaurant* ☰*AE, D, DC, MC, V.*

$–$$

✕🖼**Jacob Lake Inn.** The bustling lodge at Jacob Lake Inn is a popular stop for those heading to the North Rim; it has a grocery store, coffee shop, restaurant, and gift shop. Even if you don't stay here, stop for one of their famous malts or milk shakes (¢–$). The five-acre complex in Kaibab National Forest has basic cabins and standard motel rooms that overlook the highways; 25 rooms added in 2006 have TVs, phones, and in-room broadband. ⊠*Hwy. 67/U.S. 89A, 86022* ☎*928/643–7232* ⊕*www.jacoblake.com* ⬑*14 rooms, 22 cabins* ⚴*Restaurant, café, some room phones, some room TVs, Wi-Fi (some), ethernet (some); no a/c (some)* ☰*AE, D, MC, V.*

☾ ★ $$–$$$$

🖼**Best Western Grand Canyon Squire Inn.** About 2 mi south of the park's south entrance, this motel lacks the historic charm of the older lodges at the canyon rim, but has more amenities, including a small cowboy museum in the lobby and an upscale gift shop. Children enjoy the bowling alley, arcade, and outdoor swimming pool. Rooms are spacious and furnished in Southwestern style. Those in the rear have a view of the woods. The Coronado Dining Room has an adventurous menu and good service. Wireless Internet service is available in the lobby, and all rooms have broadband. There also are billiards, bowling, and a video game room. ⊠*100 Hwy. 64, Grand Canyon 86023* ☎*928/638–2681 or 800/622–6966* 🖷*928/638–2782* ⊕*www.grandcanyonsquire.com* ⬑*250 rooms, 4 suites* ⚴*Restaurant, coffee shop, outdoor pool, gym, hot tub, sauna, ethernet, concierge, meeting rooms, no-smoking rooms* ☰*AE, D, DC, MC, V.*

★ $$$

🖼**The Grand Hotel.** At the south end of Tusayan, this popular hotel has bright, clean rooms decorated in Southwestern colors. The lobby has a stone-and-timber design, cozy seating areas, and Wi-Fi access. Good steaks, Mexican fare, and barbecue are on the restaurant's menu, and a Starbucks in the lobby is a bonus. At the bar, you can sit on a saddle that was once used for canyon mule trips. ⊠*Hwy. 64/U.S. 180, Tusayan* ☎*928/638–3333* 🖷*928/638–3131* ⊕*www.grandcanyongrandhotel. com* ⬑*119 rooms, 2 suites* ⚴*Restaurant, satellite TV, Wi-Fi in lobby,* *indoor pool, gym, hot tub, laundry facilities, bar, meeting rooms, some pets allowed (fee), no-smoking rooms* ▤*AE, D, DC, MC, V.*

★ $$-$$$ ⊞ **Sheridan House Inn.** Nestled among two acres of pine trees near Route 66, this B&B has decks looking to the tall ponderosa pines and a flagstone patio with a hot tub. Average-size bedrooms all have king beds and marble bathrooms. The game room has puzzles, board games, and VCRs, and the entertainment room has a pool table and piano. Hearty breakfasts—scrambled eggs, fruit plates, bacon, sausage, potatoes, eggs Benedict, and buttermilk pancakes—will ready you for the hour-long drive to the canyon. K. C. and Mary Seidner are gracious hosts who will gladly help guests plan itineraries. ⊠*460 E. Sheridan Ave., Williams, AZ 86046* ☎*928/635–9441 or 888/635–9345* ↩*6 rooms, 2 suites* ⚲*In-room VCRs, hot tub, Wi-Fi, no a/c* ▤*AE, D, MC, V* ⏍*BP.*

★ $-$$$ ⊞ **Grand Canyon Railway Hotel and Resort.** This hotel was designed to resemble the train depot's original Fray Marcos lodge. Neoclassical Greek columns flank the grand entrance, which leads to a lobby with maplewood balustrades, an enormous flagstone fireplace, and oil paintings of the Grand Canyon by local artist Kenneth McKenna. Original bronzes by Frederic Remington, from the private collection of hotel owners Max and Thelma Biegert, also adorn the lobby. The pleasant Southwestern-style accommodations have large bathrooms. Adjacent to the lobby is Spenser's, a pub with an ornate 19th-century hand-carved bar. ⊠*235 N. Grand Canyon Blvd., Williams 86046* ☎*928/635–4010 or 800/843–8724* ⊕*www.thetrain.com* ↩*288 rooms, 10 suites* ⚲*Indoor pool, gym, hot tub, bar, meeting room, no-smoking rooms* ▤*AE, D, MC, V.*

$$ ✕⊞ **Havasupai Lodge.** These are fairly spartan accommodations, but you won't notice it too much when you see the natural beauty surrounding you. The lodge and restaurant are at the bottom of Havasu Canyon and are operated by the Havasupai tribe. The restaurant serves three meals a day, mostly sandwiches and fast-food-type fare, and a daily special ($). In addition to the room rate, there is a $30 per-person tribal entry fee. ⊠*Supai 86435* ☎*928/448–2111 or 928/448–2201* ⊕*www. havasupaitribe.com* ↩*24 rooms* ⚲*Restaurant, no room phones, no room TVs, no-smoking rooms* ▤*MC, V.*

$$ ⊞ **Red Feather Lodge.** This motel and adjacent hotel are a good value, with an outdoor pool and seasonal hot tub. All rooms were remodeled in 2005, with a Southwestern theme in the large rooms. The lodge's Café Tusayan serves standard American food. The motel portion of the lodge is closed January through March, except to guests with pets and smokers. The rooms have cable TV with movies and video games, and there is Internet access in the rooms and lobby, though there is a fee to use the service. ⊠*Hwy. 64/U.S. 180, Tusayan* ☎*928/638–2414 or 800/538–2345* 🖷*928/638–9216* ⊕*www.redfeatherlodge.com* ↩*212 rooms, 1 suite* ⚲*Restaurant, pool, gym, hot tub, Internet, pets (fee), no-smoking rooms* ▤*AE, D, DC, MC, V* ⏍*CP.*

$-$$ ⊞ **Mountainside Inn, Gateway to the Grand Canyon.** At the east entrance to town, this basic motel has comfortable rooms, a good American restaurant called Miss Kitty's Steakhouse, and country-western bands in summer. ⊠*642 E. Rte. 66, William s86046* ☎*928/635–4431 or*

800/462–9381 🖷*928/635–2292* ☎*95 rooms, 1 suite* ♨*Restaurant, pool, hot tub* ▤*AE, D, MC, V.*

$$ 🎫**Red Garter.** This restored saloon and bordello from 1897 now houses a small, antique-filled B&B. Guest rooms are on the second floor; ask for the "Best Gal's Room," which has its own sitting room overlooking the train tracks. All four rooms (two are interior, with skylights) are very quiet, as the only train traffic is the Grand Canyon Railway. Even if you don't stay here, the fresh pastries served in the first-floor coffee shop are worth a stop. ✉*137 W. Railroad Ave., Williams 86046* ☎*928/635–1484 or 800/328–1484* ⊕*www.redgarter.com* ☎*4 rooms* ♨*Coffee shop, Wi-Fi, ethernet, no kids under 8, no-smoking rooms* ▤*D, MC, V* ⫢*CP* ⊘*Closed Dec.–mid-Feb.*

☾ **$–$$** 🎫**The Canyon Motel and Railroad RV Park.** Rail cars, cabooses, and cottages make up this 13-acre property on the outskirts of Williams. The best room is the 1929 Santa Fe red caboose ($121): It's family-friendly, with two sides separated by a bathroom, giving parents a little privacy. The original wooden floor and tool equipment add to the authenticity. The other caboose looks much like a standard hotel room inside, as do the flagstone cottage rooms built from the local sandstone known for its variegated colors. A Pullman passenger car ($105) holds three rooms (rail-car suites), each with their own bathroom. The motel also has a few dry campsites (no water available) and a 47-space RV park with full hookups, opened in 2006. Guests have access to hiking, horseshoes, and a playground. ✉*1900 E. Rodeo Rd., Williams, AZ 86046* ☎*928/635–9371 or 800/482–3955* 🖷*928/635–4138* ⊕*www. thecanyonmotel.com* ☎*18 rooms, 5 rail-car suites* ♨*Microwaves, refrigerators, VCRs (some), grills (RV park), indoor pool, no a/c (some), no room phones* ▤*D, MC, V* ⫢*CP.*

★ **$–$$** 🎫**Marble Canyon Lodge.** This Arizona Strip lodge opened in 1929 on the same day the Navajo Bridge was dedicated. Three types of accommodations are available: rooms in the original building, standard motel rooms in the newer building, and two-bedroom apartments. You can play the 1920s piano or sit on the porch swing of the native-rock lodge and look out on Vermilion Cliffs and the desert. Zane Grey and Gary Cooper are among well-known past guests. The restaurant serves steaks, pasta, and sandwiches ($–$$$$). There is an airstrip here, too. ✉*¼ mi west of Navajo Bridge on U.S. 89A* ⬚*Box 6001, Marble Canyon 86036* ☎*928/355–2225 or 800/726–1789* 🖷*928/355–2227* ☎*46 rooms, 8 apartments* ♨*Restaurant, lounge, shop, meeting room, some pets allowed* ▤*AE, D, MC, V.*

¢–**$** ✗🎫**Hualapai Lodge.** Located at Peach Springs, the hotel has a comfortable lobby with a large fireplace that is welcoming on chilly nights. The rooms are clean but basic. The Diamond Creek Café offers standard American fare, including hamburgers and sandwiches, along with specialties such as Hualapai tacos, which are worth a stop on their own. ✉*900 Rte. 66, Peach Springs 86434* ☎*928/769–2230 or 888/255–9550* ⊕*www.grandcanyonresort.com* ☎*55 rooms* ♨*Restaurant, cable TV, saltwater pool, gym, spa, shop, laundry facilities, no-smoking rooms, a/c* ▤*AE, D, MC, V.*

Diamond Creek. The Hualapai permit camping on their tribal lands here, with an overnight camping permit of $20 per person per night, which can be purchased at the **Hualapai Lodge** (✉ *900 Rte. 66, Peach Springs 86434* ☎ *928/769–2230 or 888/255–9550*). Camping on the beach of the Colorado is accessed by Diamond Creek Road. The camping area is primitive, with only a picnic table and pit toilets. No fires are allowed, but grills may be used, and rock pit barbecues are available.

For information about camping in Havasu Canyon, call the **Havasupai Tourist Enterprise** (☎ *928/448–2141*). You can stay in the primitive campgrounds for $12 (plus 8% tax) per person per night, in addition to the $30 per person entry fee.

GRAND CANYON ESSENTIALS

TRANSPORTATION

BY AIR
Several carriers fly to the Grand Canyon Airport from Las Vegas, including Air Vegas, Scenic Airlines, and Vision Air.

North Las Vegas Airport in Las Vegas is the primary air hub for flights to Grand Canyon Airport. You can also make connections into the Grand Canyon from Sky Harbor International Airport in Phoenix.

Xanterra Transportation Company offers 24-hour taxi service at Grand Canyon Airport, Grand Canyon Village, and the nearby village of Tusayan. Taxis also make trips to other destinations in and around Grand Canyon National Park.

Contacts Air Vegas (☎ *800/940–2550* ⊕ *www.airvegas.com*). **Grand Canyon National Parks Airport** (☎ *928/638–2446*). **North Las Vegas Airport** (☎ *702/261–3806*). **Phoenix Sky Harbor International Airport (PHX)** (☎ *602/273–3300*). **Scenic Airlines** (☎ *800/634–6801* ⊕ *www.scenic.com*). **Vision Air** (☎ *702/261–3850* ⊕ *www.visionholidays.com*). **Xanterra Transportation Company** (☎ *928/638–2822*).

BY BUS
There's no public bus transportation to the Grand Canyon. Greyhound Lines provides bus service to Williams, Flagstaff, and Kingman. Schedules change frequently; call or check the Web site for information.

Within the park, there are three free shuttle routes. Hermits Rest Route operates from March through November between Grand Canyon Village and Hermits Rest; it runs every 15 to 30 minutes one hour before sunrise until one hour after sunset, depending on the season. The Village Route operates year-round in the village area from one hour before sunrise until after dark; it is the easiest access to the Canyon View Information Center. The Kaibab Trail Route travels from Canyon View Information Center to Yaki Point, including a stop at the South Kaibab Trailhead.

From mid-May to late October, the Trans Canyon Shuttle leaves Bright Angel Lodge at 1:30 PM and arrives at the North Rim's Grand Canyon Lodge about 6 PM. The return trip leaves the North Rim each morning at 7 AM, arriving at the South Rim at about noon. One-way fare is $65, round-trip $120. A 50% deposit is required two weeks in advance.

Contact Trans Canyon Shuttle (☏ *928/638–2820*).

BY CAR

Most of Arizona's scenic highlights are many miles apart, and a car is essential for touring the state. However, you won't really need one if you're planning to visit only the Grand Canyon's most popular area, the South Rim. Some people choose to fly to the Grand Canyon and then hike, catch a shuttle or taxi, or sign on for bus tours or mule rides.

If you're driving to Arizona from the east, or coming up from the southern part of the state, the best access to the Grand Canyon is from Flagstaff. You can take U.S. 180 northwest (81 mi) to Grand Canyon Village on the South Rim. Or, for a scenic route with stopping points along the canyon rim, drive north on U.S. 89 from Flagstaff, turn left at the junction of AZ 64 (52 mi north of Flagstaff), which merges with U.S. 180 at Valle, and proceed north and west for an additional 57 mi until you reach Grand Canyon Village on the South Rim.

To visit the North Rim of the canyon, proceed north from Flagstaff on U.S. 89 to Bitter Springs. Then take U.S. 89A to the junction of AZ 67. Travel south on AZ 67 for approximately 40 mi to the North Rim, which is 210 mi from Flagstaff.

If you're crossing Arizona on Interstate 40 from the west, your most direct route to the South Rim is on AZ 64 (U.S. 180), which runs north from Williams for 58 mi to Grand Canyon Village.

GASOLINE The only gas station inside the national park on the South Rim is at Desert View, and this station operates only from March 31 to September 30 depending on snowfall. Gas is available year-round near the South Entrance at Moqui Lodge (though the lodge itself is now closed), in Tusayan, and at Cameron, to the east.

At the South Rim, in Grand Canyon Village, the Public Garage is a fully equipped AAA garage that provides auto repair daily 8 to noon and 1 to 5 as well as 24-hour emergency service. This is a garage for repairs only and does not sell gasoline.

At the North Rim, the Chevron service station, which repairs autos, is inside the park on the access road leading to the North Rim Campground. No diesel fuel is available at the North Rim.

ROAD CONDITIONS When driving off major highways in low-lying areas, watch for rain clouds. Flash floods from sudden summer rains can be deadly.

The South Rim stays open to auto traffic year-round, although access to Hermits Rest is limited to shuttle buses in summer because of congestion. Roads leading to the South Rim near Grand Canyon Village and the parking areas along the rim are congested in summer as well. If you visit from October through April, you can experience only light to moderate traffic and have no problem with parking.

Reaching elevations of 8,000 feet, the more remote North Rim has no services available from late October through mid-May. AZ 67 south of Jacob Lake is closed by the first heavy snowfall in November or December and remains closed until early to mid-May.

To check on Arizona road conditions, call the Arizona Department of Transportation's recorded hotline.

Automobile Service Stations **Jacob Lake Inn** (⊠ *Hwy. 67/U.S. 89A, Fredonia 86022* ☎ *928/643–7232).* **Conoco Station** (⊠ *Grand Canyon Village* ☎ *928/638–2608).*

CONTACTS & RESOURCES

ADMISSION FEES
A fee of $25 per vehicle is collected at the east entrance near Cameron and at the south entrance near Tusayan; pedestrians and cyclists pay $12 per person. The fee pays for up to one week's access. The Grand Canyon Pass, available for $50, gives unlimited access to the park for 12 months from the purchase date.

ADMISSION HOURS
The South Rim is open 24/7, year-round. The North Rim is open mid-May through mid-October, depending on the weather. Highway 67 from Jacob Lake is closed due to snowfall from around mid-October to mid-May, and during these times all facilities at the North Rim are closed. The entrance gates are open 24 hours, but are generally staffed from about 7 AM to 7 PM. If you arrive when there's no one at the gate, you may enter legally without paying. The park is in the Mountain time zone.

BANKS
There is an ATM at the South Rim office in Market Plaza near the General Store and at Maswik Lodge. Near the North Rim, there's an ATM at Jacob lake Inn.

EMERGENCIES
In case of a fire or medical emergency, dial 911; from in-park lodgings, dial 9-911. To report a security problem, contact the Park Police (☎928/638–7805), stationed at all visitor centers. There are no pharmacies at the North or South Rim. Prescriptions can be delivered daily to the South Rim Clinic from Flagstaff. A health center is staffed by physicians from 8 AM–6 PM, seven days a week (reduced hours in winter). Emergency medical services are available 24 hours a day.

Contacts **Emergency services** (☎ *911, 9–911 in park lodgings).* **Grand Canyon Walk-in Clinic** (⊠ *Grand Canyon Village* ☎ *928/638–2551).*

The **North Country Community Health Center** (✉ *1 Clinic Rd., Grand Canyon* ☎ *928/638–2551*).

LOST & FOUND

Report lost or stolen items or turn in found items at Canyon View Information Plaza or Yavapai Observation Station (☎ 928/638–7798). For items lost or found in hotels, restaurants, or lounges, call ☎ 928/638–2631, Ext. 6503.

PERMITS

Hikers descending into the canyon for an overnight stay need a back-country permit ($10, plus $5 per person per night), which can be obtained in person, by mail, or faxed by request. Permits are limited, so make your reservation as far in advance as possible (they're taken up to four months ahead of arrival). A visit to the park's Web site will go far in preparing you for the permit process. Day hikes into the canyon or anywhere else in the national park do not require a permit; overnight stays at Phantom Ranch require reservations but no permits. Overnight camping in the national park is restricted to designated campgrounds.

Contacts Backcountry Information Center (✉ *Box 129, Grand Canyon 86023* ☎ *928/638–7875* 🖨 *928/638–2125* 🌐 *www.nps.gov/grca*).

PETS

Pets are allowed in Grand Canyon National Park; however, they must be on a leash at all times. Pets are not allowed below the rim or on the park buses, with the exception of service animals. There's a kennel, near the Maswik Lodge, which houses cats and dogs. It's open daily from 7:30 AM to 5 PM. Reservations are highly recommended.

Contact Grand Canyon Kennel (☎ *928/638–0534*).

POST OFFICE

The Market Plaza shopping center near Yavapai Lodge has a post office that is open weekdays 9 to 4:30 and Saturday 11 to 1.

PUBLIC TELEPHONES

There are public telephones at all visitor centers and lodgings. Cell-phone reception is not possible in many areas of the park.

RESTROOMS

All visitor centers, lodgings, and restaurants have restrooms.

SHOPS & GROCERIES

The Canyon Village Marketplace has three locations in the South Rim: at Grand Canyon Village, in nearby Tusayan, and at Desert View near the park's east entrance. The main store, in Grand Canyon Village, is a department store selling a full line of camping, hiking, and backpacking supplies, in addition to groceries. The store also rents hiking supplies including backpacks, tents, and walking sticks.

The North Rim General Store, inside the park at the North Rim Camp-ground, carries groceries, some clothing, and travelers' supplies.

Contacts **Canyon Village Marketplace** (✉ *Grand Canyon Village* ☎ *928/638–2262* ✉ *Tusayan* ☎ *928/638–2854* ✉ *Desert View* ☎ *928/638–2393*). **North Rim General Store** (✉ *North Rim Campground, Grand Canyon North Rim* ☎ *928/638–2611*).

TOURS

AIR TOURS Flights by plane and helicopter over the canyon are offered by a number of companies, departing for the Grand Canyon Airport at the south end of Tusayan. Prices and lengths of tours vary, but you can expect to pay about $75–$100 per adult for short plane trips and approximately $100–$150 for a brief helicopter tour.

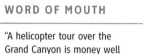

Contacts **Air Grand Canyon** (✉ *Grand Canyon Airport, Tusayan* ☎ *928/638–2686* ⊕ *www.airgrandcanyon.com*). **AirStar Helicopters/Airlines** (✉ *Grand Canyon Airport, Tusayan* ☎ *928/638–2622 or 800/962–3869* ⊕ *www.airstar.com*). **Grand Canyon Airlines** (✉ *Grand Canyon Airport, Tusayan* ☎ *928/638–2463 or 866/235–9422* ⊕ *www.grandcanyonairlines.com*). **Grand Canyon Helicopters** (✉ *Grand Canyon Airport, Tusayan* ☎ *928/638–2764 or 800/541–4537* ⊕ *www. grandcanyonhelicoptersaz.com*). **Papillon Helicopters** (✉ *Grand Canyon Airport, Tusayan* ☎ *928/638–2419 or 800/528–2418* ⊕ *www.papillon.com*).

Contact **Xanterra Motorcoach Tours** (✉ *Grand Canyon Village* ☎ *928/638–2631 or 928/638–3283*).

HIKING TOURS The Grand Canyon Field Institute leads a full program of educational guided hikes around the canyon year-round. Topics include everything from archaeology and backcountry medicine to photography and natural history. Reservations are essential and cost from $85 to $1,200. For a personalized tour of the Grand Canyon and surrounding sacred sites, contact Marvelous Marv, whose knowledge of the area is as extensive as his repertoire of local legends.

Contacts **The Grand Canyon Field Institute** (✉ *Box 399, Grand Canyon 86023* ☎ *928/638–2485 or 866/471–4435* ⊕ *www.grandcanyon.org/fieldinstitute*). **Marvelous Marv** (✉ *Box 544, Williams 86046* ☎ *928/635–4948* ⊕ *www. marvelousmarv.com*).

JEEP TOURS If you'd like to get off the pavement and see parts of the park that are accessible only by dirt road, a jeep tour can be just the ticket. Rides can be rough; if you have had back injuries, check with your doctor before taking a jeep tour. From March through October, Grand Canyon Outback Jeep Tours leads daily 1½- to 4½-hour off-road tours within the park, as well as in Kaibab National Forest. Expect to pay from $40 to $94, and reservations are essential.

Information **Grand Canyon Outback Jeep Tours** (✉ *Box 1772, Grand Canyon 86023* ☎ *928/638–5337 or 800/320–5337* ☎ *928/638–5337* ⊕ *www.grand canyonjeeptours.com*).

RAFTING
TOURS

Nearly two dozen companies currently offer excursions, but reservations for raft trips (excluding smooth-water, one-day cruises) often need to be made more than six months in advance. A complete list of concessionaires offering trips on the Colorado River is available on the Grand Canyon National Park Web site. National Park Service white-water concessionaires include Arizona River Runners, Canyoneers, Diamond River Adventures, Grand Canyon Expeditions, and Tour West. For a smooth-water, one-day trip check out Wilderness River Adventures. Prices for river-raft trips vary greatly, depending on type and length. Half-day trips on smooth water run as low as $54 per person. Trips that negotiate the entire length of the canyon and take as long as 12 days can cost more than $2,000.

Contacts Arizona River Runners (☎ 602/867–4866 or 800/477–7238 ⊕ www. raftarizona.com). **Canyoneers, Inc.** (☎ 928/526–0924, 800/525–0924 outside Arizona ⊕ www.canyoneers.com). **Diamond River Adventures, Inc.** (☎ 928/645–8866 or 800/343–3121 ⊕ www.diamondriver.com). **Grand Canyon Expeditions** (☎ 435/644–2691 or 800/544–2691 ⊕ www.gcex.com). **Tour West, Inc.** (☎ 801/225–0755 or 800/453–9107 ⊕ www.twriver.com). **Wilderness River Adventures** (☎ 928/645–3279 or 800/992–8022 ⊕ www.riveradventures.com).

SPECIAL
INTEREST
TOURS

The National Park Service sponsors all sorts of free Ranger Programs at both the South and the North rims. These orientation activities include daily guided hikes and talks. The focus may be on any aspect of the canyon—from geology, flora, and fauna to history and early inhabitants. Programs change seasonally. For schedules, go to Canyon View Information Plaza on the South Rim or the Grand Canyon Lodge on the North Rim.

Several of the free programs are designed especially for children. Children ages 9 to 11 use field guides, binoculars, magnifying glasses, and other exploration tools on the one-hour Junior Ranger Discovery Pack Program. Park rangers also coordinate Way Cool for Kids, free, hour-long introductions to the park for ages 7 to 11. Kids and rangers walk around the Village Rim area and talk about local plants and animals, history, or archaeology. These two programs are only offered in the summer; check for times at the Canyon View Information Plaza.

Information Ranger Programs (✉ Box 129, Grand Canyon 86023 ☎ 928/638–7888 ⊕ www.nps.gov/grca).

VISITOR INFORMATION

Every person arriving at the South or North Rim is given a detailed map of the area. Centers at both rims also publish a free newspaper, the *Guide*, which contains a detailed area map; it's available at the visitor center, entrance stations, and many of the lodging facilities and stores. The park also distributes *Accessibility Guide,* a free newsletter that details the facilities accessible to travelers with disabilities. Grand Canyon National Park is the contact for general information. Write ahead for a complimentary *Trip Planner,* updated regularly by the National Park Service.

Several Web sites are useful for trip-planning information, including the National Park Service's Web site, which has information on fees and permits. Try thecanyon.com, a commercial site where you'll find information on lodging, dining, and general park information. You can use the Xanterra Parks & Resorts Grand Canyon Web site to make reservations for park lodging, mule rides, bus tours, and some smooth-water rafting trips. The park service allows camping reservations to be made online as well, through the campground reservation vendor.

In summer, transportation-services desks are maintained at El Tovar, Bright Angel, Maswik Lodge, and Yavapai Lodge in Grand Canyon Village; in winter, the one at Yavapai is closed. The desks provide information and handle bookings, sightseeing tours, taxi and bus services, mule and horseback rides, and accommodations at Phantom Ranch (at the bottom of the Grand Canyon). The concierge at El Tovar can also arrange most tours, with the exception of mule rides and lodging at Phantom Ranch.

Grand Canyon Lodge has general information about local services available in summer when the North Rim is open.

The Williams and Forest Service Visitor Center, run by the U.S. Forest Service and the Williams Chamber of Commerce, offers information on the Kaibab National Forest and the entire Grand Canyon region.

Grand Canyon Contacts **Grand Canyon Chamber of Commerce** (☎ *928/638-2901* ⊕ *www.grandcanyonchamber.com*). **Grand Canyon National Park** (☎ *928/638-7888 recorded message* 🖷 *928/638-7797* ⊕ *www.nps.gov/grca*). **Grand Canyon National Park Lodges** (☎ *303/297-2757* 🖷 *303/297-3175* ⊕ *www.grandcanyonlodges.com*). **Navajo Nation Tourism Dept. (Tuba City)** (☎ *928/871-6436* ⊕ *www.discovernavajo.com*). **North and South Rim Camping** (☎ *800/365-2267* ⊕ *http://reservations.nps.gov/index.cfm*). **Williams and Forest Service Visitor Center** (☎ *928/635-4061*).

Williams Visitor Center (✉ *200 W. Railroad Ave., at Grand Canyon Blvd.* ☎ *928/635-1418 or 800/863-0546* ⊕ *www.williamschamber.com* ✆ *Spring, fall, and winter, daily 8–5; summer, daily 8–6:30*).

North-Central Arizona

Hopi Lizard and Manawgya Kachina dolls, Museum of Northern Arizona, Flagstaff Arizona

WORD OF MOUTH

"Go to the Northern Arizona Museum outside of Flagstaff...it will give you a good overview of the native population and beautiful crafts."

—Vera

WELCOME TO NORTH-CENTRAL ARIZONA

Mountain biking in Sedona

TOP REASONS TO GO

★ **Mother Nature:** Stunning red rocks, snow-capped mountains, and crisp country air rejuvenate the most cynical city dwellers.

★ **Father Time:** Ancient Native American ruins, such as Walnut Canyon and Montezuma's Castle, show life before Columbus "discovered" America. You can learn their history in the excellent National Monument visitor centers.

★ **Main Street charm:** Jerome and Prescott exude small-town hospitality with turn-of-the-century architecture and charming bed-and-breakfasts.

★ **Beat the heat:** It's the high desert, but a very cool place; temperatures throughout north-central Arizona are typically 20 degrees cooler than in the Phoenix area.

★ **Let your aura out:** The free spirit and energy of Sedona is delightfully infectious, even for skeptics.

Sedona, Oak Creek Canyon

1 Flagstaff. College-town enthusiasm and high-country charm combine to make this one of Arizona's most outdoors-friendly towns. Hiking, biking, skiing, and climbing are local passions, and there are state and national parks to explore.

2 Sedona. Surrounded by the Coconino National Forest, Sedona's residents call their home a museum without walls. The town's red rocks lure visitors from around the world. You'll enjoy breathtaking views, fantastic cuisine, and a dash of New Age whimsy.

Sedona

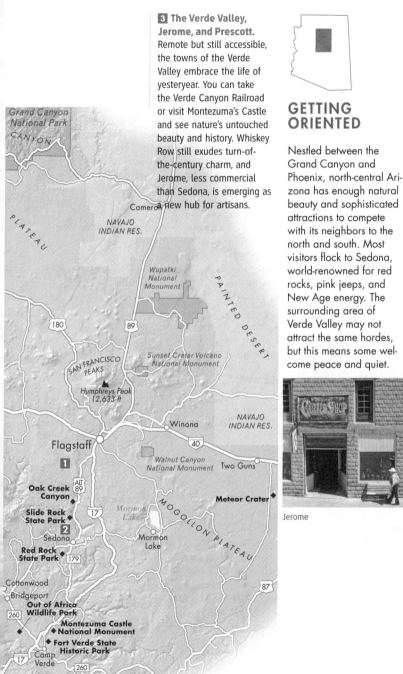

3 **The Verde Valley, Jerome, and Prescott.** Remote but still accessible, the towns of the Verde Valley embrace the life of yesteryear. You can take the Verde Canyon Railroad or visit Montezuma's Castle and see nature's untouched beauty and history. Whiskey Row still exudes turn-of-the-century charm, and Jerome, less commercial than Sedona, is emerging as a new hub for artisans.

GETTING ORIENTED

Nestled between the Grand Canyon and Phoenix, north-central Arizona has enough natural beauty and sophisticated attractions to compete with its neighbors to the north and south. Most visitors flock to Sedona, world-renowned for red rocks, pink jeeps, and New Age energy. The surrounding area of Verde Valley may not attract the same hordes, but this means some welcome peace and quiet.

Jerome

Map labels

Grand Canyon National Park

CANYON

PLATEAU

Cameron

NAVAJO INDIAN RES.

Wupatki National Monument

PAINTED DESERT

180

89

SAN FRANCISCO PEAKS

Sunset Crater Volcano National Monument

Humphreys Peak 12,633 ft

Winona

NAVAJO INDIAN RES.

Flagstaff **1**

40

Walnut Canyon National Monument

Two Guns

Oak Creek Canyon

ALT 89

17

Mormon Lake

MOGOLLON PLATEAU

Meteor Crater

Slide Rock State Park

2

Sedona

Mormon Lake

Red Rock State Park

179

Cottonwood

Bridgeport

Out of Africa Wildlife Park

260

Montezuma Castle National Monument

Fort Verde State Historic Park

17

Camp Verde

260

87

3

NORTH CENTRAL ARIZONA PLANNER

Getting Here & Around

Don't plan on flying into Flagstaff, Sedona, or Prescott: commercial flights are limited, and besides, getting here is half the fun; the scenery is gorgeous. You'll definitely want a car, and North-central Arizona is only two hours from Phoenix. Avoid interstates when possible; the back ways can be more direct and have the best views of the stunning landscape.

If you're driving to or from Phoenix, stop at Montezuma's Castle, and if you have time, ride the Verde Canyon Railroad for an off-road look at the terrain.

If you're driving from Sedona to Flagstaff or the Grand Canyon, head north through the wooded Oak Creek Canyon: it's the most scenic route.

Making the Most of Your Time

Sedona will probably occupy most of your time, so plan to spend at least two days there, hiking or shopping. Any turn off the main drag is almost certain to lead somewhere worthwhile, but Oak Creek Canyon and Chapel of the Holy Cross are must-sees. Then, depending on your preferences, spend your time looking (window shopping or star gazing) or doing (hiking, exploring). If you can, plan to be in Sedona midweek, when the weekend crowds aren't around. A Red Rock Pass is required to park in the Coconino National Forest.

Outdoors enthusiasts should head to Flagstaff for a day to enjoy the Mount Elden Trail System or hit the slopes at Arizona Snowbowl. Flagstaff also has the Lowell Observatory.

Prescott and Jerome can be combined for a day or less, or choose one or the other. You can check out the pulse of downtown Prescott's museum and famous Whiskey Row then spend a night in an historic hotel; Jerome has several quaint bed-and-breakfasts, as well as a Main Street shopping district that may offer more affordable treasures than those at Sedona's boutiques.

For scenic views, nothing beats the Verde Canyon Railroad. Native American historic sites such as Montezuma's Castle and Tuzigoot National Monument offer perspective on native life centuries ago.

Tour Operators

Pink Jeep Tours offers the quintessential Sedona experience. Tours go through remote areas and let visitors focus on the scenery instead of steering. Costs start at $50 per person. ✉ *204 N. AZ 89A, Sedona* ☎ *928/282–5000 or 800/873–3662* ⊕ *www.pinkjeep.com.*

Sample Itineraries

Have an extra half-day? Here are some ideas for how to spend it:

Nature lovers should visit either the Coconino or Prescott national forests. Stop in at a local coffee house and get sandwiches for a picnic, then head out on a scenic trail to enjoy some solitude.

History buffs have a host of choices for half-day trips, whether it's Walnut Canyon, the Mine Museum in Jerome, Meteor Crater or Fort Verde State Historic Park.

Bargain hunters might not fare so well in the luxury boutiques of Sedona, but artisans and antiques dealers have enclaves in Jerome, Prescott, and Flagstaff.

Local Food and Lodging

You'll find lots of American comfort food in this part of the country: barbecue restaurants, steak houses, and burger joints predominate. If you're looking for something different, Sedona and Flagstaff have the majority of good, multiethnic restaurants in the area, and if you're craving Mexican, you're sure to find something authentic and delicious (note that burritos are often called "burros" around here). Sedona is the best place in the area for fine dining, but foodies can savor meals in neighboring towns as well. Some area restaurants close in January and February—the slower months in the area—so call ahead. Reservations are suggested from April through October.

Flagstaff and Prescott have the more affordable lodging options, with lots of comfortable motels and bed-and-breakfasts, but no real luxury. The opposite is true in Sedona, which is filled with opulent resorts and hideaways, most offering solitude and spa services—just don't expect a bargain. Reservations are essential for Sedona and suggested for Flagstaff and Prescott. Little Jerome has a few B&Bs but call ahead if you think you might want to spend the night. If you're in for a thrill, many of the historic hotels in north-central Arizona have haunted rooms that can be booked on request.

What It Costs

	¢	$	$$	$$$	$$$$
Restaurants	under $8	$8–$12	$13–$20	$21–$30	over $30
Hotels	under $70	$70–$120	$121–$175	$176–$250	over $250

Restaurant prices are per person for a main course at dinner. Hotel prices are for a standard double in high season, excluding taxes and service charges.

Into Thin Air

It's wise, especially if you're an outdoors enthusiast, to start in the relatively lowland areas of Prescott and the Verde Valley, climbing gradually to Sedona and Flagstaff—it can take several days to grow accustomed to the high elevation in Flagstaff.

When to Go

Autumn, when the wet season ends, the stifling desert temperatures moderate (it's 20 degrees cooler than Phoenix), and the mountain aspens reach their full golden splendor, is a great time to visit this part of Arizona. During the summer months many Phoenix residents travel north to escape the 100-degree temperatures, meaning excessive traffic along Interstate 17 just north of Phoenix on Friday and Sunday evenings. Hotels are less expensive in winter, but mountain temperatures dip below zero, and snowstorms can occur weekly, especially near Flagstaff.

Sedona has springlike temperatures even in January, when it's snowing in Flagstaff, but summer temperatures above 90°F are common.

Prescott and Flagstaff hold most of their festivals and cultural events in summer. Sedona's biggest event, the Jazz on the Rocks Festival, takes place in September.

Updated by
Cara LaBrie

RED-ROCK BUTTES ABLAZE IN THE slanting light of late afternoon, the San Francisco Peaks tipped white from a fresh snowfall, pine forests clad in dark green needles—north-central Arizona is rich in natural attractions, a landscape of vast plateaus punctuated by steep ridges and canyons. To the north of Flagstaff the San Francisco Peaks, a string of tall volcanic mountains, rises over 12,000 feet, tapering to the 9,000-foot Mount Elden and a scattering of diminutive cinder cones. To the south, a seemingly endless stand of ponderosa pines covers this part of the Colorado Plateau before the terrain plunges dramatically into Oak Creek Canyon. The canyon then opens to reveal red buttes and mesas in the high-desert areas surrounding Sedona. The desert gradually descends to the Verde Valley, crossing the Verde River before reaching the 7,000-foot Black Range, over which lies the Prescott Valley.

Flagstaff, the hub of this part of Arizona, was historically a way station en route to southern California. First the railroads, then Route 66 carried westbound traffic right through the center of town. Many of those who were "just passing through" stayed and built a community, revitalizing downtown with cafés, an activity-filled square, eclectic shops, and festivals. The town's large network of bike paths and parks abuts hundreds of miles of trails and forest roads, an irresistible lure for outdoors enthusiasts. Not surprisingly, the typical resident of Flagstaff is outdoorsy, young, and has a large, friendly dog in tow.

Down AZ 89A in Sedona, the average age and income rises considerably. This was once a hidden hamlet used by Western filmmakers but New Age enthusiasts flocked to the region in the 1980s believing it was the center of spiritual powers. Well-off executives and retirees followed soon after, building clusters of McMansions throughout the area. Sophisticated restaurants, upscale shops, luxe accommodations, and New Age entrepreneurs cater to both these populations, and to the tourist trade which brings close to 5 million visitors a year. It can be difficult, though not impossible, to find a moment of serenity, even in wilderness areas. A hike into apparently remote territory is often disturbed by a tour plane buzzing above or a gonzo mountain biker who brakes for no one. Despite these quibbles, the beauty here is unsurpassed. For this reason, Sedona and much of north-central Arizona attracts more than its share of artists and galleries.

Pioneers and miners are now part of north-central Arizona's past, but the wild and woolly days of the Old West are not forgotten. The preserved fort at Camp Verde recalls frontier life, and the decrepit facades of the funky former mining town of Jerome have an infectious charm. The many Victorian houses in temperate Prescott attest to the attempt to bring "civilization" to Arizona's territorial capital.

North-central Arizona is also rich in artifacts from its earliest inhabitants: several national and state parks—among them Walnut Canyon, Wupatki, Montezuma Castle, and Tuzigoot national monuments—hold well-preserved evidence of the architectural accomplishments of Native American Sinagua and other ancestral Puebloans who made their homes in the Verde Valley and the region near the San Francisco Peaks.

FLAGSTAFF

146 mi northwest of Phoenix, 27 mi north of Sedona via Oak Creek Canyon.

Few travelers slow down long enough to explore Flagstaff, a town of 54,000, known locally as "Flag"; most stop only to spend the night at one of the town's many motels before making the last leg of the trip to the Grand Canyon, 80 mi north. Flag makes a good base for day trips to Native American ruins and the Navajo and Hopi reservations, as well as to the Petrified Forest National Park and the Painted Desert, but the city is a worthwhile destination in its own right. Set against a lovely backdrop of pine forests and the snowcapped San Francisco Peaks, downtown Flagstaff retains a frontier flavor.

In summer, Phoenix residents head here, seeking relief from the desert heat, since at any time of the year temperatures in Flagstaff are about 20°F cooler than in Phoenix. They also come to Flagstaff in winter: to ski at the small Arizona Snowbowl, about 15 mi northeast of town among the San Francisco Peaks.

EXPLORING FLAGSTAFF

Numbers in the margin correspond to numbers on the Flagstaff, Sedona, and Prescott maps.

WHAT TO SEE

❽ Arizona Snowbowl. Although still one of Flagstaff's largest attractions, years of drought have made snowy slopes a luxury. Fortunately, visitors can enjoy the beauty of the area year-round. The Agassiz ski lift climbs to a height of 11,500 feet in 25 minutes, and doubles as a sky ride through the Coconino National Forest in summer. From this vantage point, you can see up to 70 mi; views may even include the North Rim of the Grand Canyon. There's a lodge at the base with a restaurant and bar. To reach the ski area, take U.S. 180 north from Flagstaff; it's 7 mi from the Snowbowl exit to the skyride entrance. ⊠ *Snowbowl Rd., North Flagstaff* ☎ *928/779–1951* ⊕ *www.arizonasnowbowl.com* ⌨ *Skyride $10* ⊗ *Skyride: Memorial Day–early Sept., daily 10–4; early Sept.–mid-Oct., Fri.–Sun. 10–4, weather permitting.*

❶ Historic Downtown District. Storied Route 66 runs right through the heart of downtown Flagstaff. The late-Victorian, Tudor Revival, and early–art deco architecture in this district recalls the town's heyday as a logging and railroad center. A walking-tour map of the area is available at the visitor center in the Tudor Revival–style **Santa Fe Depot** (⊠ *1 E. Rte. 66, Downtown*), an excellent place to begin sightseeing.

Highlights include the 1927 **Hotel Monte Vista** (⊠ *100 N. San Francisco St., Downtown* ⊕ *www.hotelmontevista.com*), built after a community drive raised $200,000 in 60 days. The construction was promoted as a way to bolster the burgeoning tourism in the region, and the hotel was held publicly until the early 1960s. The 1888 **Babbitt Brothers Building** (⊠ *12 E. Aspen Ave., Downtown*) was constructed as a building-sup-

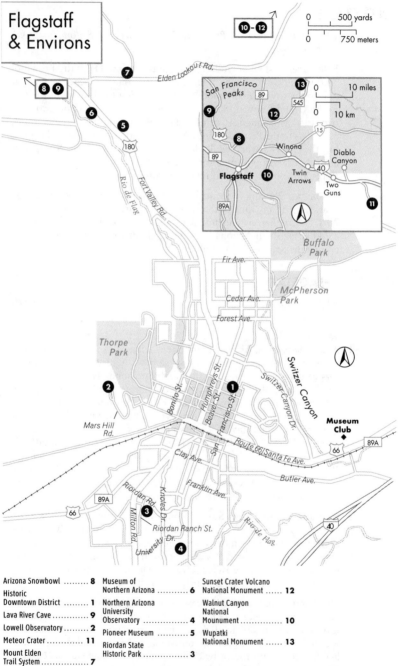

Flagstaff & Environs

Arizona Snowbowl **8**	Museum of Northern Arizona **6**	Sunset Crater Volcano National Monument **12**
Historic Downtown District **1**	Northern Arizona University Observatory **4**	Walnut Canyon National Mounument **10**
Lava River Cave **9**		
Lowell Observatory **2**	Pioneer Museum **5**	Wupatki National Monument **13**
Meteor Crater **11**	Riordan State Historic Park **3**	
Mount Elden Trail System **7**		

FLAGSTAFF TIPS

■ You can see most of Flagstaff's attractions in a day—especially if you visit the Lowell Observatory or the Northern Arizona University Observatory in the evening, which is also when the Museum Club is best experienced.

■ Consult the schedule of tour times if you want to visit the Riordan State Historic Park.

■ Devote at least an hour to the excellent Museum of Northern Arizona.

■ The Historic Railroad District is a good place for lunch.

■ If you're a skier, spend part of a winter's day at Arizona Snowbowl; in summer you can spend a couple of hours on the sky ride and scenic trails at the top.

■ Take your time enjoying the trails on Mount Elden and remember to pace yourself in the higher elevations; allow a full day for hiking.

■ The Lava River Cave is an easy—if dark—hike that can be comfortably done in an hour.

ply store and then turned into a department store by David Babbitt, the mastermind of the Babbitt empire. The Babbitts are one of Flagstaff's wealthiest founding families. Bruce Babbitt, the most recent member of the family to wield power and influence, was the governor of Arizona from 1978 through 1987 and Secretary of the Interior under President Clinton (1993–2001). Most of the area's first businesses were saloons catering to railroad construction workers, which was the case with the 1888 **Vail Building** (⊠*5 N. San Francisco St., Downtown*), a brick art deco–influenced structure covered with stucco in 1939. It now houses Crystal Magic, a New Age shop. ⊠*Downtown Historic District, Rte. 66 north to Birch Ave., and Beaver St. east to Agassiz St.*

NEED A BREAK?

The town's most interesting shops are concentrated downtown, and there are a couple of brewpubs and some spots where you can grab a quick bite. Students, skiers, new and aging hippies, and just about everyone else who likes good coffee jam into **Macy's European Coffee House and Bakery** (⊠*14 S. Beaver St., Downtown* ☏*928/774–2243*) for the best cup in town. The **Black Bean** (⊠*12 E. Rte. 66, Downtown* ☏*928/779–9905*) is the place for do-it-yourself burritos, as healthful or as guacamole-smothered as you like.

❾ **Lava River Cave.** Subterranean lava flow formed this mile-long cave roughly 700,000 years ago. Once you descend into its boulder-strewn maw, the cave is spacious, with 40-foot ceilings, but claustrophobes take heed: about halfway through, the cave tapers to a 4-foot-high squeeze that can be a bit unnerving. A 40°F chill pervades the cave throughout the year so take warm clothing. To reach the turnoff for the cave, go approximately 9 mi north of Flagstaff on U.S. 180, then turn west onto FR 245. Turn left at the intersection of FR 171 and look for the sign to the cave. The trip is approximately 45 minutes from Flagstaff. Although the cave is on National Forest Service property, the only thing here is an interpretive sign, so it's definitely something you tackle at your own risk. ■TIP→Pack a flashlight (or two). ✉ *FR 171B.*

🔥 ★ ❷ **Lowell Observatory.** In 1894, Boston businessman, author, and scientist Percival Lowell founded this observatory from which he studied Mars. His theories of the existence of a ninth planet sowed the seeds for the discovery of Pluto at Lowell in 1930 by Clyde Tombaugh.

> **PLANET PLUTO?**
>
> Modern scholars of the heavens may now categorize Pluto as a "dwarf" planet but Flagstaff locals are very clear on their opinion: once a planet, always a planet. Visit the Lowell Observatory for a look.

The 6,500-square-foot Steele Visitor Center hosts exhibits and lectures and has a gift shop. Several interactive exhibits—among them Pluto Walk, a scaled-down version of the solar system—appeal to children. A new Discovery Channel telescope is anticipated for 2009 and you are invited, on some evenings, to peer through the 24-inch Clark telescope. Day and evening viewings are offered year-round, but call ahead for a schedule. ■TIP→**The observatory dome is open and unheated, so dress for the outdoors.** To reach the observatory, less than 2 mi from downtown, drive west on Route 66, which resumes its former name, Santa Fe Avenue, before it merges into Mars Hill Road. ✉ *1400 W. Mars Hill Rd., West Flagstaff* ☎ *928/774–3358* ⊕ *www.lowell.edu* 💲 *$6* ☉ *Visitor center and night viewing hrs change seasonally; call ahead.*

❼ **Mount Elden Trail System.** Most trails in the 35-mi-long Mount Elden Trail System lead to views from the dormant volcanic field, across the vast ponderosa pine forest, all the way to Sedona. The most challenging trail in the Mount Elden system, which happens to be the route with the most rewarding views, is along the steep switchbacks of the **Elden Lookout Trail** (✉ *Off U.S. 89, 3 mi east of downtown Flagstaff*). If you traverse the full 3 mi to the top, keep your focus on the landscape rather than the tangle of antennae and satellite dishes that greet you at the top. The 4-mi-long **Sunset Trail** (✉ *Off U.S. 180, 3 mi north of downtown Flagstaff, then 6 mi east on FR 420 [Schultz Pass Rd.]*) proceeds with a gradual pitch through the pine forest, emerging onto a narrow ridge nicknamed the Catwalk. By all means take pictures of the stunning valley views, but make sure your feet are well placed. ■TIP→**The access road to this trail is closed in winter.**

NEED A BREAK?

Museum Club Roadhouse and Danceclub. For real Route 66 color, check out this local institution fondly known as the Zoo because the building housed an extensive taxidermy collection in the 1930s. Most of the stuffed animals are gone, but some owls still perch above the dance floor of what is now a popular country-and-western club. Even if you don't like crowds or country music, it's worth stopping in for a drink and to see this gigantic log cabin constructed around five trees; the entryway is a huge wishbone-shaped pine. ✉ *3404 E. Rte. 66, Downtown* ☎ *928/526-9434* ⊕ *www.museumclub.com* 💲 *Free* ☉ *Daily 11 AM–2 AM.*

🌀 ★ ❻ **Museum of Northern Arizona.** This institution, founded in 1928, is respected worldwide for its research and its collections centering on the natural and cultural history of the Colorado Plateau. Among the permanent exhibitions are an extensive collection of Navajo rugs and a Hopi kiva (men's ceremonial chamber). A gallery devoted to area geology is usually a hit with children: it includes a life-size model dilophosaurus, a carnivorous dinosaur that once roamed northern Arizona. Outdoors, a life-zone exhibit shows the changing vegetation from the bottom of the Grand Canyon to the highest peak in Flagstaff. A nature trail, open only in summer, heads down across a small stream into a canyon and up into an aspen grove. In summer the museum hosts exhibits and the works of Native American artists, whose wares are also sold in the museum gift shop. ✉*3101 N. Fort Valley Rd., North Flagstaff* ☎*928/774–5213* ⊕*www.musnaz.org* 💲*$5* 🕑*Daily 9–5.*

❹ **Northern Arizona University Observatory.** The observatory, with its 24-inch telescope, was built in 1952 by Dr. Arthur Adel, a scientist at Lowell Observatory whose study of infrared astronomy pioneered research into molecules that absorb light passing through the Earth's atmosphere. Today's studies of Earth's shrinking ozone layer rely on some of Dr. Adel's early work. Visitors to the observatory—which houses one of the largest telescopes that the public is allowed to move and manipulate—are usually hosted by friendly students and faculty members of the university's Department of Physics and Astronomy. ✉*Bldg. 47, Northern Arizona Campus Observatory, Dept. of Physics and Astronomy, S. San Francisco St., just north of Walkup Skydome, University* ☎*928/523–8121 weekdays, 928/523–7170 Fri. night* 💲*Free* 🕑*Viewings Fri. 7:30–10* PM*, weather permitting.*

❺ **Pioneer Museum.** The Arizona Historical Society operates this museum in a volcanic-rock building constructed in 1908. The structure was Coconino County's first hospital for the poor, and the current displays include one of the depressingly small nurses' rooms, an old iron lung, and a reconstructed doctor's office. Most of the exhibits, however, touch on more cheerful aspects of Flagstaff history—like road signs and children's toys. The museum holds a folk-crafts festival on July 4, with blacksmiths, weavers, spinners, quilters, and candle makers. Their crafts, and those of other local artisans, are sold in the museum's gift shop. The museum is part of the Fort Valley Park complex, in a wooded residential section at the northwest end of town. ✉*2340 N. Fort Valley Rd., North Flagstaff* ☎*928/774–6272* 💲*$3* 🕑*Mon.–Sat. 9–5.*

❸ **Riordan State Historic Park.** This must-see artifact of Flagstaff's logging heyday is near Northern Arizona University. The centerpiece is a mansion built in 1904 for Michael and Timothy Riordan, lumberbaron brothers who married two sisters. The 13,300-square-foot, 40-room log-and-stone structure—designed by Charles Whittlesley, who was also responsible for the El Tovar Hotel at the Grand Canyon—contains furniture by Gustav Stickley, father of the American Arts and Crafts design movement. One room holds "Paul Bunyan's shoes," a 2-foot-long pair of boots made by Timothy in his workshop. Everything on display is original to the house. The mansion may be explored on a guided tour only, and reservations are suggested. ⊠*409 W. Riordan Rd., University* ☎*928/779–4395* ⊕*www.pr.state.az.us* ⬜*$6* ⊙*May–Oct., daily 8:30–5, with tours on the hr 9–4; Nov.–Apr., daily 10:30–5, with tours on the hr 11–4.*

SPORTS & THE OUTDOORS

HIKING & ROCK CLIMBING

You can explore Arizona's alpine tundra in the San Francisco Peaks, part of the Coconino National Forest, where more than 80 species of plants grow on the upper elevations. The habitat is fragile, so hikers are asked to stay on established trails (there are lots of them). The altitude here will make even the hardiest hikers breathe a little harder, so anyone with cardiac or respiratory problems should be cautious about overexertion. ■TIP➔**Flatlanders should give themselves at least a day or two to adjust to the altitude.**

The rangers of the **Coconino National Forest** (⊠*1824 S. Thompson St., North Flagstaff* ☎*928/527–3600* ⊕*www.fs.fed.us/r3/coconino*) maintain many of the region's trails and can provide you with details on hiking in the area; the forest's main office is open weekdays 7:30 to 4:30.

Flagstaff is in the **Peaks District** (⊠*Peaks Ranger Station, 5075 N. U.S. 89, East Flagstaff* ☎*928/526–0866*) of the Coconino National Forest, and there are many trails to explore. The **Humphreys Peak Trail** (⊠*Trailhead: Snowbowl Rd., 7 mi north of U.S. 180*) is 9 mi round-trip, with a vertical climb of 3,843 feet to the summit of Arizona's highest mountain (12,643 feet). Those who don't want a long hike can do just the first mile of the adjacent, 5-mi-long **Kachina Trail** (⊠*Trailhead: Snowbowl Rd., 7 mi north of U.S. 180*); gently rolling, this route is surrounded by huge stands of aspen and offers fantastic vistas. In fall, changing leaves paint the landscape shades of yellow, russet, and amber.

Vertical Relief Rock Gym (⊠*205 S. San Francisco St., Downtown* ☎*928/556–9909*) has the tallest indoor climbing walls in the Southwest as well as climbing excursions throughout the Flagstaff area.

HORSEBACK RIDING

The wranglers at **Hitchin' Post Stables** (⊠*4848 Lake Mary Rd., South Flagstaff* ☎*928/774–1719*) lead rides into Walnut Canyon and operate horseback or horse-drawn wagon rides with sunset barbecues. In winter they'll take you through Coconino National Forest on a sleigh.

MOUNTAIN BIKING

With more than 30 mi of challenging trails a short ride from town, it was inevitable that one of Flagstaff's best-kept secrets would leak out. The mountain biking on Mount Elden is on par with that of more celebrated trails in Colorado and Utah.

The **Coconino National Forest** has some of the best trails in the region. A good place to start is the **Lower Oldham Trail** (⊠*Trailhead: Cedar St.*), which originates on the north end of Buffalo Park in Flagstaff; there's a large meadow with picnic areas and an exercise path. The terrain rolls, climbing about 800 feet in 3 mi, and the trail is technical in spots but easy enough to test your tolerance of the elevation. Many fun trails spur off this one. They're all hemmed in by roads and cabins so it's difficult to get too lost.

The very popular **Schultz Creek Trail** (⊠ *Trailhead: Schultz Pass Rd., near intersection with U.S. 180*) is fun and suitable for strong beginners, although seasoned experts will be thrilled as well. Most opt to start at the top of the 600-foot-high hill and swoop down the smooth, twisting path through groves of wildflowers and stands of ponderosa pines and aspens, ending at the trailhead four giddy miles later.

The **Sunset Trail** (⊠ *Trailhead: Elden Lookout Rd., 7 mi from intersection with Schultz Pass Rd.*), near the summit of Mount Elden, affords amazing views off the ridge rendered barren by a 1977 fire. The trail narrows into the aptly nicknamed Catwalk, with precipitous drops a few feet on either side. ■TIP➜**Fear, either from the 9,000-foot elevation or the sheer exposure, is not an option. You need to be an at least moderately experienced mountain biker to attempt this trail.** When combined with Elden Lookout Road and Schultz Creek Trail, the usual loop, the trail totals 15 mi and climbs almost 2,000 feet. You can avoid the slog up Mount Elden by parking one vehicle at the top of Elden Lookout Road, at the trailhead, and a friend's vehicle at the bottom.

You can rent mountain bikes, get good advice, and purchase trail maps at **Absolute Bikes** (⊠ *18 N. San Francisco St., Downtown* ☏ *928/779–5969*). From mid-June through mid-October, the **Flagstaff Nordic Center** (⊠ *U.S. 180, 16 mi north of Flagstaff, North Flagstaff* ☏ *928/220–0550* ⊕ *www.flagstaffnordiccenter.com*) opens its cross-country trails to mountain bikers. **Mountain Sports** (⊠ *24 N. San Francisco St., Downtown* ☏ *928/226–2885 or 800/286–5156*) has competitive rates for bike rentals. A map of the **Urban Trails System,** available at the Flagstaff Visitor Center (⊠ *1 E. Rte. 66, Downtown* ☏ *928/774–9541 or 800/842–7293*), details biking options in town.

SKIING & SNOWBOARDING

The ski season usually starts in mid-December and ends in mid-April. The **Arizona Snowbowl** (⊠ *Snowbowl Rd., North Flagstaff* ☏ *928/779–1951, 928/779–4577 snow report* ⊕ *www.arizonasnowbowl.com*), 7 mi north of Flagstaff off U.S. 180, has 32 downhill runs (37% beginner, 42% intermediate, and 21% advanced), four chairlifts, and a vertical drop of 2,300 feet. There are a couple of good bump runs, but it's better for beginners or those with moderate skill; serious area skiers take a road trip to Teluride. Still, it's a fun place to spend the day. Snowboarders share trails with downhill skiers. The Hart Prairie Lodge has an equipment-rental shop and a SKIwee center for ages 4 to 7. All-day adult lift tickets are $46. Half-day discounts are available, and group-lesson packages (including two hours of instruction, an all-day lift ticket, and equipment rental) are a good buy at $68. A children's program (which includes lunch, progress card, and full supervision 9–3:30) runs $70. Many Flagstaff motels offer ski packages, including transportation to Snowbowl.

The **Flagstaff Nordic Center** (⊠ *U.S. 180, 16 mi north of Flagstaff, North Flagstaff* ☎ *928/220–0550* ⊕ *www.flagstaffnordiccenter.com*) is 9 mi north of Snowbowl Road. There are 25 mi of well-groomed cross-country trails here that are open from 8 to 4 daily, with longer hours on Friday (6 to 9). Coffee, hot chocolate, and snacks are served at the lodge. You can also rent sleds for a nearby run called Crowley Pit. A day pass for skiing costs $12 on weekdays and $15 on weekends. An instruction package costs $40 on weekdays and $45 on weekends, including equipment. Friday evening trail passes cost $10. To rent equipment by itself is $15.

WHERE TO STAY & EAT

★ $$$–$$$$ ✕ **Cottage Place.** Regarded by locals as one of the best fine dining venues in the area, this restaurant in a cottage built in 1909 has intimate dining rooms and an extensive wine list. The menu strays slightly from Continental to include some classic American dishes, such as char-broiled lamb chops. The grilled herb salmon and the chateaubriand for two are recommended. Dinner includes soup and salad, but save room for Chocolate Decadence. ⊠ *126 W. Cottage Ave., Downtown* ☎ *928/774–8431* ⊟ AE, MC, V ⊘ *Closed Mon. and Tues. No lunch* ⊕ *www.cottageplace.com.*

$$–$$$$ ✕ **Black Bart's Steakhouse Saloon & Old West Theater.** The Wild West decor at this rollicking, brightly lit barn of a restaurant is a bit cornball, but the barbecued chicken is tender and flavorful; don't expect to see vegetables on your plate unless they're deep-fried. Northern Arizona University music students entertain while they wait on tables, so don't be surprised if your server suddenly jumps onstage to belt out a couple of show tunes. ⊠ *2760 E. Butler Ave., Downtown* ☎ *928/779–3142 or 800/574–4718* ⊕ *www.blackbartssteakhouse.com* ⊟ AE, D, DC, MC, V ⊘ *No lunch.*

$$–$$$ ✕ **Buster's Restaurant.** At lunchtime, families and students from nearby Northern Arizona University settle into comfy booths to enjoy fresh seafood, homemade soups, salads, giant burgers, and steaks. What better environment to ask Mom or Dad for some extra money, or to discuss that first semester's report card? Try the *lahvosh* appetizer—a huge cracker heaped with toppings ranging from smoked salmon to mushrooms—or the Caesar salad with grilled Cajun chicken. At night, single professionals and skiers crowd the bar and work through its impressive beer selection. ⊠ *1800 S. Milton Rd., University* ☎ *928/774–5155* ⊟ AE, D, DC, MC, V.

$–$$ ✕ **Beaver Street Brewery and Whistle Stop Cafe.** Popular among the wood-fired pizzas is the Enchanted Forest, with Brie, portobello mushrooms, roasted red peppers, spinach, and artichoke pesto. Whichever pie you order, expect serious amounts of garlic. Sandwiches, such as the South-western chicken with three types of cheese, come with a hefty portion of tasty fries. You won't regret ordering one of the down-home desserts, like the super-gooey chocolate bread pudding. Among the excellent microbrews usually on tap, the raspberry ale is a local favorite. ⊠ *11 S. Beaver St., Downtown* ☎ *928/779–0079* ⊕ *www.beaverstreetbrewery. com* ⊟ AE, D, DC, MC, V.

¢–$$ ✕ **Salsa Brava.** This cheerful Mexican restaurant, with light-wood booths and colorful designs, eschews heavy Sonoran-style fare in favor of the grilled dishes found in Guadalajara. It's considered the best Mexican food in town—but there's not much competition. The fish tacos are particularly good. On weekends come for a huevos rancheros breakfast. ⊠*2220 E. Rte. 66, East* ☎*928/779–5293* ⊕*www.salsabravaflagstaff.com* ▤AE, D, MC, V.

¢–$ ✕ **Bun Huggers.** Since 1979, the best burger in town is flipped over a mesquite-fired grill. Also try the tasty, if decadent, deep-fried zucchini served with shredded cheddar cheese and ranch dressing. There's a small salad bar here, but it seems like an afterthought, existing only to heal guilty consciences. ⊠*901 S. Milton Rd., University* ☎*928/779–3743* ▤AE, D, MC, V.

¢–$ ✕ **Café Espress.** The menu is largely vegetarian at this natural-foods restaurant. Stir-fried vegetables, pasta, Mediterranean salads, tempeh burgers, pita pizzas, fish or chicken specials, and wonderful baked goods made on the premises all come at prices that will make you feel good, too. This is a hip place (the work of local artists hangs on the walls) but friendly, and it opens for breakfast every day at 7. ⊠*16 N. San Francisco St., Downtown* ☎*928/774–0541* ▤AE, MC, V.

★ ¢ ✕ **La Bellavia.** At this favorite bohemian breakfast and lunch nook, the trout and eggs platter is the standard—two eggs served with Idaho trout flavored with a hint of lemon, rounded off by a buttermilk pancake. Other options include Swedish oat pancakes, seven-grain French toast, and nine varieties of eggs Benedict. A palette of creative sandwiches and familiar salads makes this a worthwhile lunch stop as well. The café doubles as a gallery for local artists whose work hangs on the walls. If you like your pancakes, you can buy a package of the mix to take home. ⊠*18 S. Beaver St., Downtown* ☎*928/774–8301* ▤MC, V ⊗*No dinner.*

★ $$–$$$ ▦ **Inn at 410.** An inviting alternative to the chain motels in Flagstaff, this B&B has a convenient but quiet downtown location. All the accommodations in the beautifully restored 1907 residence are suites with private baths. Monet's Garden is a lovely Jacuzzi suite with fireplace. Pancakes with blue cornmeal and piñon nuts, and curried cornbread pudding with pumpkin sauce highlight a tantalizing breakfast menu. No kids allowed in some rooms. ⊠*410 N. Leroux St., Downtown, 86001* ☎*928/774–0088 or 800/774–2008* ☐*928/774–6354* ⊕*www.inn410.com* ⇗*9 suites* ⚲*In-room: no phone, refrigerator, VCR/DVD. In-hotel: no-smoking rooms, no elevator* ▤MC, V †⊙*BP.*

★ $$ ▦ **Little America of Flagstaff.** The biggest hotel in town is deservedly popular. It's far from the roar of the trains, the grounds are surrounded by evergreen forests, and it's one of the few places in Flagstaff with room service. Plush rooms have comfortable sitting areas with French provincial–style furniture. Other pluses are courtesy van service to the airport and the Amtrak station, and a gift shop with great Southwestern stuff. Don't miss the famous Sunday Brunch with breakfast fare alongside prime rib, seafood, and European-style pastries. ⊠*2515 E. Butler Ave., Downtown, 86004* ☎*928/779–2741 or 800/352–4386* ☐*928/779–7983* ⊕*www.flagstaff.littleamerica.com* ⇗*248 rooms*

&In-room: *kitchen, refrigerator, safe. In-hotel: restaurant, room service, bar, pool, gym, laundry facilities, laundry service, public Wi-Fi, no elevator* ⊟AE, D, DC, MC, V.

$$ ⊡ **Sled Dog Inn.** This inn is on 4 acres, but its grounds seem vastly larger, since the land borders the immense Coconino National Forest. A big draw here, as the name implies, are the owners' Siberian huskies, which are lovingly cared for. Rooms are contemporary rustic. ⊠*10155 Mountainaire Rd., South Flagstaff, 86001* ☎*928/525–6212 or 800/754–0064* ⊕*www.sleddoginn.com* ⇆*8 rooms, 2 suites* &*In-room: no TV. In-hotel: no kids under 10, no-smoking rooms, no elevator, public Wi-Fi* ⊟AE, D, MC, V ❘○❘*CP.*

$$ ⊡ **Starlight Pines Bed and Breakfast.** If you prefer the clean lines of 1920s design to Victorian froufrou, consider staying at this stylish B&B. Rooms in this residence on the city's east side are lovely, with art deco pieces including Tiffany lamps and other antiques; one room has a private porch, another a fireplace. ⊠*3380 E. Lockett Rd., East Flagstaff, 86004* ☎*928/527–1912 or 800/752–1912* ⊕*www.starlightpinesbb.com* ⇆*4 rooms* &*In-room: no TV. In-hotel: no-smoking rooms, no elevator, public Wi-Fi* ⊟D, MC, V ❘○❘*BP.*

$–$$ ⊡ **Hotel Monte Vista.** Over the years many Hollywood stars, including Bob Hope and Spencer Tracy, have stayed at this downtown hotel, which is celebrating its 80th anniversary in 2008. It's a quirky, fun place, but renovations have not yet restored it to its heyday. Funky room designs might have golden cherubs descending from an azure ceiling—in the Air Supply Room—or are inspired by the famous guests: framed antique postcards of Western novel book covers hang in the Zane Grey Room. Enjoy live music every Friday and Saturday night. ⊠*100 N. San Francisco St., Downtown, 86001* ☎*928/779–6971 or 800/545–3068* ⊜*928/779–2904* ⊕*www.hotelmontevista.com* ⇆*48 rooms* &*In-hotel: restaurant, bars, laundry service, some pets allowed* ⊟AE, D, MC, V.

$ ⊡ **Hotel Weatherford.** With a columned veranda, this hotel, built in 1897, is a dramatic presence at the hub of town. Imbued with a creaky charm, the rooms are spartan and a bit worn around the edges but comfortable. Forgo TV and a telephone for a taste of the Old West. The Exchange Pub downstairs has a bustling nightlife scene. ⊠*23 N. Leroux St., Downtown, 86001* ☎*928/779–1919* ⊜*928/773–8951* ⊕*www.weatherfordhotel.com* ⇆*10 rooms, 7 with bath* &*In-room: no a/c, no phone, no TV. In-hotel: restaurant, bars, no elevator* ⊟AE, D, DC, MC, V.

NIGHTLIFE & THE ARTS

NIGHTLIFE   Flagstaff's large college contingent has plenty of places to gather after dark; most are in historic downtown and most charge little or no cover. It's easy to walk from one rowdy spot to the next. For information on what's going on, pick up the free *Flagstaff Live.*

The **Hotel Weatherford** (⊠*23 N. Leroux St., Downtown* ☎*928/779–1919*) has a double bill: Charly's hosts late-night jazz and blues bands; the Exchange Pub tends to attract folksy ensembles. The **Mogollon**

Brewing Company (⊠*15 N. Agassiz St., Downtown* ☎*928/773–8950*) rolls out live music and hardy stout. The **Monte Vista Lounge** (⊠*100 N. San Francisco St., Downtown* ☎*928/774–2403*) packs 'em in with nightly live blues, jazz, classic rock, and punk. **San Felipe's Coastal Cantina** (⊠*103 N. Leroux, Downtown* ☎*928/779–6000*) is the place for tequila, fish tacos, dancing, and a raucous Spring Break atmosphere.

THE ARTS There is no shortage of cultural entertainment in Flagstaff, including several summer festivals.

Flagstaff Cultural Partners/Coconino Center for the Arts (⊠*2300 N. Fort Valley Rd., North Flagstaff* ☎*928/779–2300* ⊕*www.culturalpartners. org*) has gallery space for exhibitions, a theater, and performance space. The **Flagstaff Symphony Orchestra** (☎*928/774–5107* ⊕*www.flagstaff symphony.org*) has year-round musical events. The 1917 **Orpheum Theater** (⊠*15 W. Aspen St., Downtown* ☎*928/556–1580* ⊕*www.orpheum presents.com*) features music acts, films, lectures, and plays. **Theatrikos Theatre Company** (⊠*11 W. Cherry Ave., Downtown* ☎*928/774–1662* ⊕*www.theatrikos.com*) is a highly regarded performance art group.

A Celebration of Native American Art (⊠*3101 N. Fort Valley Rd., North Flagstaff* ☎*928/774–5211*), featuring exhibits of work by Zuni, Hopi, and Navajo artists, is held at the Museum of Northern Arizona from late May through September.

The **Festival of Science** (☎*800/842–7293* ⊕*www.scifest.org*), in September, is made stellar by Flagstaff's observatories.

SHOPPING

For fine arts and crafts—everything from ceramics and stained glass to weaving and painting—visit the **Artists Gallery** (⊠*17 N. San Francisco St., Downtown* ☎*928/773–0958*), a local artists' cooperative. **Babbitt's Backcountry Outfitters** (⊠*12 E. Aspen Ave., Downtown* ☎*928/774–4775*) is the place to pick up any sporting goods needs. The **Black Hound Gallerie** (⊠*120 N. Leroux St., Downtown* ☎*928/774–2323*) specializes in posters, prints, and funky kitsch of all kinds. **Bookman's** (⊠*1520 S. Riordan Ranch Rd., University* ☎*928/774–0005*) is packed solid with used books on every topic; a cybercafé and live folk music occupy a corner of the store. **Carriage House Antique & Gift Mall** (⊠*413 N. San Francisco St., Downtown* ☎*928/774–1337*) has 20-odd vendors selling vintage clothing and jewelry, furniture, fine china, and other collectibles. The **Museum of Northern Arizona Gift Shop** (⊠*3101 N. Fort Valley Rd., University* ☎*928/774–5213*) carries high-quality jewelry and crafts. **Winter Sun Trading Company** (⊠*107 N. San Francisco St., Downtown* ☎*928/774–2884*) sells medicinal herbs, jewelry, and crafts. **Zani** (⊠*9 N. Leroux St., Downtown* ☎*928/774–9409*) stocks hip home furnishings and greeting cards in addition to futons.

SIDE TRIPS NEAR FLAGSTAFF

Travelers heading straight through town bound for the Grand Canyon often neglect the area north and east of Flagstaff but a detour has its rewards. If you don't have time to do everything, take a quick drive to Walnut Canyon—it's only about 15 minutes out of town.

EAST OF FLAGSTAFF

★ ⑩ **Walnut Canyon National Monument** consists of a group of cliff dwellings constructed by the Sinagua people, who lived and farmed in and around the canyon starting around AD 700. The more than 300 dwellings here were built between 1080 and 1250 and abandoned, like those at so many other settlements in Arizona and New Mexico, around 1300. The Sinagua traded far and wide with other Native Americans, including people at Wupatki. Even macaw feathers, which would have come from tribes in what is now Mexico, have been excavated in the canyon. Early Flagstaff settlers looted the site for pots and "treasure"; Woodrow Wilson declared the site a national monument in 1915, which began a 30-year process of stabilizing the ruins.

> **WORD OF MOUTH**
>
> "Walnut Canyon was amazing—the cliffs are very protected so the cliff dwellings have been well preserved as compared to some of the sites we have visited which were just out on the open mesa. It is a reasonable hike to the bottom of the canyon, but very worthwhile."
>
> –mykidssherpa

Part of the fascination of Walnut Canyon is the opportunity to enter the dwellings, stepping back in time to an ancient way of life. Some of the Sinagua homes are in near-perfect condition in spite of all the looting, because of the dry, hot climate and the protection of overhanging cliffs. You can reach them by descending 185 feet on the 1-mi stepped **Island Trail,** which starts at the visitor center. As you follow the trail, look across the canyon for other dwellings not accessible on the path.

Island Trail takes about an hour to complete at a normal pace. Those with health concerns should opt for the easier ½-mi **Rim Trail,** which has overlooks from which dwellings, as well as an excavated, reconstructed pit house, can be viewed. Picnic areas dot the grounds and line the roads leading to the park. ■**TIP➜Wear layers, as the climate can change quickly.** Guides conduct tours on Wednesday, Saturday, and Sunday from late May through early September. ✉ *Walnut Canyon Rd., 3 mi south of I–40, Exit 204, Winona* ☎*928/526–3367* ⊕*www.nps.gov/waca* 🖃*$5* ☉*Nov.–Apr., daily 9–5; May–Oct., daily 8–5.*

⑪ **Meteor Crater,** a natural phenomenon in a privately owned park 43 mi east of Flagstaff, is impressive if for no other reason than its sheer size. A hole in the ground 600 feet deep, nearly 1 mi across, and more than 3 mi in circumference, Meteor Crater is large enough to accommodate the Washington Monument or 20 football fields. It was created by a meteorite crash 49,000 years ago. The area looks so much like the surface of the moon that NASA made it one of the official training sites for the Project Apollo astronauts. You can't descend into the crater because of the efforts of its owners to maintain its condition—scientists consider this to be the best-preserved crater on Earth—but guided rim tours, given every hour on the hour from 9 to 3, give useful background information. There's a small snack bar, and the Rock Shop sells specimens from the area and jewelry made from native stones. Take I–40 east of Flagstaff to Exit 233, then drive 6 mi south on Meteor Crater Road. ⊠ *Meteor Crater Rd., 43 mi east of Flagstaff* ☎ *928/289–5898 or 800/289–5898* ⊕ *www.meteor crater.com* ✉ *$15* ⊙ *Memorial Day–Labor Day, daily 7–7; Labor Day–Memorial Day, daily 8–5.*

> ## THE SINAGUA PEOPLE
>
> The achievements of the Sinagua people, who lived in north-central Arizona from the 8th through the 15th centuries, reached their height in the 12th and 13th centuries, when related groups occupied most of the San Francisco Volcanic Field and a large portion of the upper and middle Verde Valley. The Sinagua sites around modern-day Camp Verde, Clarkdale, and Flagstaff provide a window onto this remarkable culture. Some of the best examples of surviving Sinagua architecture can be found at Walnut Canyon and Wupatki National Monument, northeast of Flagstaff.

SAN FRANCISCO VOLCANIC FIELD

The San Francisco Volcanic Field north of Flagstaff encompasses 2,000 square mi of fascinating geological phenomena, including ancient volcanoes, cinder cones, valleys carved by water and ice, and the San Francisco Peaks themselves, some of which soar to almost 13,000 feet. There are also some of the most extensive Native American ruins in the Southwest: don't miss Sunset Crater and Wupatki. These national monuments can be explored in relative solitude during much of the year. ■ TIP→ The area is short on services, so fill up on gas and consider taking a picnic.

Sunset Crater Volcano National Monument lies 14 mi northeast of Flagstaff off U.S. 89. Sunset Crater, a cinder cone that rises 1,000 feet, was an active volcano 900 years ago. Its final eruption contained iron and sulfur, which give the rim of the crater its glow and thus its name. You can walk around the base, but you can't descend into the huge, fragile cone. The **Lava Flow Trail**, a half-hour, mile-long, self-guided walk, provides a good view of the evidence of the volcano's fiery power: lava formations and holes in the rock where volcanic gases vented to the surface.

If you're interested in hiking a volcano, head to **Lenox Crater**, about 1 mi east of the visitor center, and climb the 280 feet to the top of the cinder cone. The cinder is soft and crumbly so wear closed, sturdy shoes. From **O'Leary Peak**, 5 mi from the visitor center on Forest Route 545A, great views can be had of the San Francisco Peaks, the Painted Desert, and beyond. The road is unpaved and rutted, though, so it's advisable to take only high-clearance vehicles, especially in winter. In addition, there's a gate, about halfway along the route, which is usually closed, and when it is, it means a steep 2½-mi hike to the top on foot. To get to the area from Flagstaff, take Santa Fe Avenue east to U.S. 89, and head north for 12 mi; turn right onto the road marked Sunset Crater and go another 2 mi

to the visitor center. ⊠ *Sunset Crater–Wupatki Loop Rd., 14 mi northeast of Flagstaff* ☎ *928/556–0502* ⊕ *www.nps.gov/sucr* ⚑ *$5, including Wupatki National Monument and Doney Mountain* ☉ *Nov.–Apr., daily 9–5; May–Oct., daily 8–5.*

★ ⑬ Families from the Sinagua and other ancestral Puebloans are believed to have lived together in harmony on the site that is now **Wupatki National Monument,** farming and trading with one another and with those who passed through. The eruption of Sunset Crater may have influenced migration to this area a century after the event, as freshly laid volcanic cinders held in moisture needed for crops. Although there's evidence of earlier habitation, most of the settlers moved here around 1100 and left the pueblo by about 1250. The 2,700 identified sites contain archaeological evidence of a Native American settlement.

The site for which the national monument was named, the Wupatki (meaning "tall house" in Hopi), was originally three stories high, built above an unexplored system of underground fissures. The structure had almost 100 rooms and an open ball court—evidence of Southwestern trade with Mesoamerican tribes for whom ball games were a central ritual. Next to the ball court is a blowhole, a geologic phenomenon in which air is forced upward by underground pressure.

Other ruins to visit are Wukoki, Lomaki, and the Citadel, a pueblo on a knoll above a limestone sink. Although the largest remnants of Native American settlements at Wupatki National Monument are open to the public, other sites are off-limits. If you're interested in an in-depth tour, consider a ranger-led overnight hike to the **Crack-in-Rock Ruin.** The 14-mi (round-trip) trek covers areas marked by ancient petroglyphs and dotted with well-preserved ruins. The trips are conducted in April and October; call by February or August if you'd like to take part in the lottery for one of the 100 available places on these $50 hikes. Between the Wupatki and Citadel ruins, the **Doney Mountain** affords 360-degree views of the Painted Desert and the San Francisco Volcanic Field. It's a perfect spot for a sunset picnic. In summer, rangers give lectures. ⊠ *Sunset Crater–Wupatki Loop Rd., 19 mi north of Sunset Crater visitor center* ☎ *928/679–2365* ⊕ *www.nps.gov/wupa* ⚑ *$5, including Wupatki National Monument and Doney Mountain* ☉ *Daily 9–5.*

Vortex Tour

What is a vortex? The word "vortex" comes from the Latin *vertere*, which means "to turn or whirl." In Sedona, a vortex is a funnel created by the motion of spiraling energy. Sedona has long been believed to be a center for spiritual power because of the vortices of subtle energy in the area. This energy isn't described as electricity or magnetism, though it's said to leave a slight residual magnetism in the places where it's strongest.

New Agers believe there are four major vortices in Sedona: Airport, Red Rock Crossing/Cathedral Rock, Boynton Canyon, and Bell Rock. Each manifests a different kind of energy, and this energy interacts with the individual in its presence. People come from all over the world to experience these energy forms, hoping for guidance in spiritual matters, health, and relationships.

Juniper trees, which are all over the Sedona area, are said to respond to vortex energy in a way that reveals where this energy is strongest. The stronger the energy, the more axial twist the junipers bear in their branches.

Airport Vortex is said to strengthen one's "masculine" side, aiding in self-confidence and focus. Red Rock Crossing/Cathedral Rock Vortex nurtures one's "feminine" aspects, such as patience and kindness. You'll be directed to Boynton Canyon Vortex if you're seeking balance between the masculine and feminine. And finally, Bell Rock Vortex, the most powerful of all, strengthens all three aspects: masculine, feminine, and balance.

These energy centers are easily accessed, and vortex maps are available at crystal shops all over Sedona.

SEDONA & OAK CREEK CANYON

119 mi north of Phoenix, I–17 to AZ 179 to AZ 89A; 60 mi northeast of Prescott, U.S. 89 to AZ 89A; 27 mi south of Flagstaff on AZ 89A.

It's easy to see what draws so many people to Sedona. Red-rock buttes—Cathedral Rock, Bear Mountain, Courthouse Rock, and Bell Rock, among others—reach up into an almost always blue sky, and both colors are intensified by dark-green pine forests. Surrealist Max Ernst, writer Zane Grey, and many filmmakers drew inspiration from these vistas—more than 80 Westerns were shot in the area in the 1940s and '50s alone.

These days, Sedona lures enterprising restaurateurs and gallery owners from the East and West coasts. New Age followers, who believe that the area contains some of the Earth's more important vortices (energy centers), also come in great numbers believing that the "vibe" here confers a sense of balance and well-being, and enhances creativity. Vortex maps of the area are available at most of Sedona's New Age stores.

Expansion since the early 1980s has been rapid, and lack of planning has taken its toll in unattractive developments and increased traffic. The town has been chosen to take part in the federally sponsored Main Street program, which means, among other things, that a number of

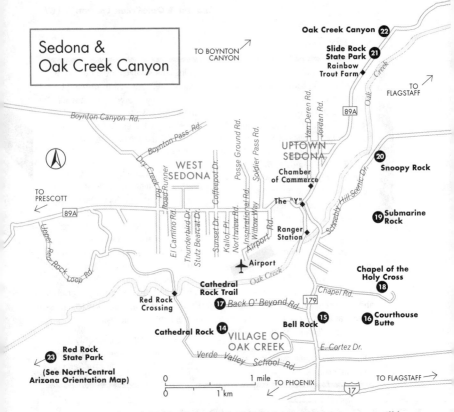

Sedona & Oak Creek Canyon

TO BOYNTON CANYON

Oak Creek Canyon 22

Slide Rock State Park 21
Rainbow Trout Farm ◆

TO FLAGSTAFF

Boynton Canyon Rd.

Boynton Pass Rd.

Dry Creek Rd.

Road Runner

Van Deren Rd.

Jordan Rd.

89A

UPTOWN SEDONA

Chamber of Commerce

The "Y"

WEST SEDONA

El Camino Rd.

Thunderbird Dr.

Stutz Bearcat Dr.

Coffeepot Dr.

Sunset Dr.

Kallof Pl.

Northview Rd.

Posse Ground Rd.

Soldier Pass Rd.

Inspirational Rd.

Willow Way

Airport Rd.

Ranger Station

Snoopy Rock 20

Schnebly Hill Scenic Dr.

Submarine Rock 19

TO PRESCOTT

89A

Upper Red Rock Loop Rd.

Airport

Oak Creek

Cathedral Rock Trail

Red Rock Crossing

17 Back O' Beyond Rd.

Chapel Rd.

179

Chapel of the Holy Cross 18

Cathedral Rock 14

VILLAGE OF OAK CREEK

Bell Rock 15

16 Courthouse Butte

E. Cortez Dr.

Red Rock State Park 23

Verde Valley School Rd.

(See North-Central Arizona Orientation Map)

0 — 1 mile — TO PHOENIX

0 — 1 km

TO FLAGSTAFF →

17

Red Rock Territorial–style buildings in the Uptown section will be preserved and that a separate parking district will be built.

The town itself is young and there are few historic sites; the main downtown activity is shopping, mostly for Southwestern-style paintings, clothing, rugs, jewelry, and Native American artifacts. Just beyond the shops and restaurants, however, canyons, creeks, Indian ruins, and the red rocks beckon. The area is easy to hike or bike, or you can take a jeep tour.

Sedona is roughly divided into three neighborhoods: Uptown, which is a walkable shopping district; West Sedona, which is a 4-mi-long commercial strip; and Central Sedona, which encompasses everything south of the "Y" where AZ 179 and AZ 89A intersect.

EXPLORING SEDONA

MAIN ATTRACTIONS

15 **Bell Rock.** With its distinctive shape right out of your favorite Western film and its proximity to the main drag ensuring a steady flow of admirers, you may want to arrive early to see this popular butte. The parking lot next to the Bell Rock Pathway often fills by mid-morning even midweek. The views from the parking lot are good, but an easy and fairly accessible path follows mostly gentle terrain for 1 mi to the base of the butte. Mountain bikers, parents with all-terrain baby strollers, and not-so-avid hikers should have little problem getting there. No official paths climb the rock itself, but many forge their own routes (at their own risk). ⊠*AZ 179, several hundred yards north of Bell Rock Blvd., Village of Oak Creek.*

⓮ Cathedral Rock. It's almost impossible not to be drawn to this butte's towering, variegated spires. The approximately 1,200-foot-high Cathedral Rock looms dramatically over town. When you emerge from the narrow gorge of Oak Creek Canyon, this is the first recognizable formation you'll spot. ■**TIP➡The butte is best seen toward dusk from a distance.** Hikers may want to drive to the Airport Mesa and then hike the rugged but generally flat path that loops around the airfield. The trail is a ½ mi up Airport Road off AZ 89A in West Sedona; the reward is a panoramic view of Cathedral Rock without the crowds. Those not hiking should drive through the Village of Oak Creek, and 5 mi west on Verde Valley School Road to its end, to a small park called *Red Rock Crossing* and a picnic area on the other side of the creek named Crescent Moon Park, where you can view the butte from a beautiful streamside vantage point and take a dip in Oak Creek if you wish. ⊠*5 mi to end of Verde Valley School Rd., west off AZ 179, Village of Oak Creek.*

⓱ Cathedral Rock Trail. A vigorous but nontechnical 1½-mi scramble up the slickrock, this path leads to a nearly 360-degree view of red-rock country. Follow the cairns (rock piles marking the trail) and look for the footholds in the rock. Carry plenty of water: though short, the trail offers little shade and the pitch is steep. You can see the Verde Valley and Mingus Mountain in the distance. Look for the barely discernible "J" etched on the hillside marking the former ghost town of Jerome 30 mi distant. ⊠*Trailhead: About ½ mi down Back O' Beyond Rd. off AZ 179, 3 mi south of Sedona.*

⓲ Chapel of the Holy Cross. You needn't be religious to be inspired by the setting and the architecture here. Built in 1956 by Marguerite Brunwige Staude, a student of Frank Lloyd Wright, this modern landmark, with a huge cross on the facade, rises between two red-rock peaks. Vistas of the town and the surrounding area are spectacular. There are no regular services, but anyone is welcome for quiet meditation. A small gift shop sells religious artifacts and books. A trail east of the chapel leads you—after a 20-minute walk over occasional loose-rock surfaces—to a seat sur-

---

SEDONA IN A NUTSHELL

There might only be 30 mi separating Flagstaff and Sedona, but they're very different places. Flagstaff's natural terrain and earthiness lend a "granola-y" feel to the city, and the Northern Arizona University students here enhance it. Meanwhile, Sedona's beauty is no secret, and residents (full- and part-time) pay a premium to enjoy it. A recent phrase circulated through town: "When a woman meets a man in Scottsdale, she asks if he has a home in California. When a woman meets a man in Sedona, she asks if he has a home in Paris."

SEDONA TIPS

■ In warmer months visit air-conditioned shops at midday and do hiking and jeep tours in the early morning or late afternoon, when the light is softer and the heat less oppressive.

■ Many of the most memorable spots in Sedona are considered energy centers; vortex maps of the area are available at most of Sedona's New Age stores.

■ The vistas of Sedona from **Airport Mesa** at sunset can't be beat.

■ The **Upper Red Rock Loop** will likely consume a roll or two of film.

■ You might want to drive out to **Boynton Canyon**, sacred to the Yavapai Apache, who believe it was their ancient birthplace. This is also the site of the Enchantment Resort, where all are welcome to hike the canyon and stop in for lunch or a late-afternoon drink.

rounded by voluptuous red-limestone walls, worlds away from the bustle and commerce around the chapel. ⊠ *Chapel Rd., off AZ 179, Village of Oak Creek* ☎ *928/282–4069* ⊕ *www.chapeloftheholycross. com* ☜ *Free* ☉ *Daily 9–5.*

★ **Oak Creek Canyon.** Whether you want to swim, hike, picnic, or enjoy beautiful scenery framed through a car window, head north through the wooded Oak Creek Canyon. It's the most scenic route to Flagstaff and the Grand Canyon, and worth a drive-through even if you're not heading north. The road winds through a steep-walled canyon, where you crane your neck for views of the dramatic rock formations above. Although the forest is primarily evergreen, the fall foliage is glorious. Oak Creek, which runs along the bottom, is lined with tent campgrounds, fishing camps, cabins, motels, and restaurants. ⊠ *AZ 89A, beginning 1 mi north of Sedona, Oak Creek Canyon.*

❤ ㉑ **Slide Rock State Park.** A good place for a picnic, Slide Rock is 7 mi north of Sedona. On a hot day you can plunge down a natural rock slide into a swimming hole (bring an extra pair of jeans or a sturdy bathing suit and river shoes to wear on the slide). The site started as an early-20th-century apple orchard and the natural beauty attracted Hollywood—a number of John Wayne and Jimmy Stewart flicks were filmed here. A few easy hikes run along the rim of the gorge. Fly-fishing for trout is possible when it's too cold for swimming. One downside is the traffic, particularly on summer weekends; you might have to wait to get in. Unfortunately, the popularity of the stream has led to the occasional midsummer closing due to E. coli–bacteria infestations; the water is tested daily. ⊠ *6871 N. AZ 89A, Oak Creek Canyon* ☎ *928/282–3034* ⊕ *www.pr.state. az.us* ☜ *$10 per vehicle for up to*

WORD OF MOUTH

"If your kids are young enough the Slide Rock Park in Oak Creek will be fun. A hint: do your sliding in clothing (jeans type) that won't come off as you go down!"

–John_T_Cuttino

Red Rock Geology

It's hard to imagine that the land-locked desert surrounding Sedona was, for much of prehistoric time, an area of dunes and swamps on the shore of an ancient sea. The ebb and flow of this sea shaped the land. When the sea rose, it planed the dunes before dropping more sediment on top. The process continued for a few hundred million years. Eventually the sediment hardened into gray layers of limestone on top of the red sandstone. When North America collided with another continental plate, the land buckled and lifted, forming the Rocky Mountains and raising northern Arizona thousands of feet. Volcanoes erupted in the area, capping some of the rock with erosion-resistant basalt.

Oak Creek started flowing at this time, eroding through the layers of sandstone and limestone. Along with other forces of erosion, the creek carved out the canyons and shaped the buttes. Sedona's buttes stayed intact because a resilient layer of lava had hardened on top and slowed the erosion process considerably. As iron minerals in the sandstone were gradually exposed to the elements, they turned red in a process similar to rusting. The iron minerals, in turn, stained the surrounding colorless quartz and grains of sand—it only takes 2% red iron materials to give the sandstone its red color.

Like the rings of a tree, the striations in the rock document the passage of time and the events, limestone marking the rise of the sea, sandstone when the region was coastline.

---

4 persons ⊗ *Labor Day–Memorial Day, daily 8–5; Memorial Day–Labor Day, daily 8–7.*

 ❷⓪ Snoopy Rock. Kids love this: when you look almost directly to the east, this butte really does look like the famed Peanuts beagle lying atop red rock instead of his doghouse. You can distinguish the formation from several places around town including the mall in Uptown Sedona, but to get a clear view, venture up Schnebly Hill Road. Park by the trailhead on the left immediately before the paved road deteriorates to dirt. Marg's Draw, one of several trails originating here, is worthwhile, gently meandering 100 feet down-canyon, through the tortured desert flora to Morgan Road. Backtrack to the parking lot for close to a 3-mi hike. Always carry plenty of water, no matter how easy the hike appears. ⊠*Schnebly Hill Rd., off AZ 179, Central.*

ALSO WORTH SEEING

⓰ Courthouse Butte. The red sandstone seems to catch on fire toward sunset when this monolith is free of shadow. From the highway, Courthouse Butte sits in back of Bell Rock and can be viewed without any additional hiking or driving. ⊠*AZ 179, Village of Oak Creek.*

❷③ Red Rock State Park. Two miles west of Sedona via AZ 89A is the turnoff for this 286-acre state park, a less-crowded alternative to Slide Rock State Park, though without the possibility for swimming. The 5 mi of interconnected park trails are well marked and provide beautiful vistas. There are daily ranger-guided nature walks, bird-watching excursions on Wednesday and Saturday, and a guided hike to Eagle's Nest scenic overlook—the highest point in the park—every Saturday. Call ahead for times, which change with the season. ⊠ *4050 Red Rock Loop Rd., West* ☎ *928/282–6907* ⊕ *www.pr.state.az.us* ⊠ *$6 per car* ☉ *Oct.–Mar., daily 8–5; Apr. and Sept., daily 8–6; May–Aug., daily 8–8.*

⑲ Submarine Rock. This elongated vessel of a rock has an interesting shape, but isn't as photogenic as others in the area: nestled in the canyon and colored in beige tones, it doesn't catch the sunlight in the same way. Getting to Submarine Rock, though, is more interesting than seeing it. You can drive up FR 179F, a very technical jeep trail that should be attempted only by highly skilled off-road-vehicle drivers, or you can take a jeep tour offered in town. For experienced mountain bikers, Broken Arrow Trail, used heavily by cyclists and hikers, rolls across washes, red clay, and large mounds of slickrock. The 2-mi hike is moderate but best done in the early morning in summer. Note that Submarine Rock is not the best retreat for serenity seekers: the rock abuts the jeep trail, which is clogged with tour jeeps revving over the rugged terrain. ⊠ *End of Morgan Rd., off AZ 179, Central.*

> **SOMETHING FISHY?**
>
> North-central Arizona may not be the most obvious fishing destination, but **Rainbow Trout Farm** is a fun way to spend a few hours if you're so inclined. Anglers young and old almost always enjoy a sure catch and you can rent a cane pole here with a hook and bait for $1. There's no charge if your catch is under 8 inches; above that it's $8 to $12, depending on the length. The real bargain is that the staff will clean and pack your fish for 50¢ each. ⊠ *3500 N. AZ 89A, 3 mi north of Sedona, Oak Creek Canyon* ☎ *928/282–5799* ☉ *Daily 9–5.*

SPORTS & THE OUTDOORS

The Brins fire consumed 4,500 acres in Sedona in 2006. Although no people or structures were harmed, the human-ignited fire threatened the Oak Creek Canyon area and serves as a reminder for fire safety. Take precautions and use common sense. Extinguish all fires with water. Never toss a cigarette butt. And don't hesitate to ask questions of local park rangers.

■ **TIP→** A Red Rock Pass is required to park in the Coconino National Forest from Oak Creek Canyon through Sedona and the Village of Oak Creek.

GOLF

The **Oak Creek Country Club** (⊠ *690 Bell Rock Blvd., Village of Oak Creek* ☎ *928/284–1660* ⊕ *www.oakcreekcountryclub.com*) is a good semiprivate course.

Fodor's Choice **Sedona Golf Resort** (⊠ *35 Ridge Trail Dr., Village of Oak Creek* ★ ☎ *928/284–9355* ⊕ *www.sedonagolfresort.com*) was designed by Gary Panks to take advantage of the many changes in elevation and scenery;

golf courses are a dime a dozen in Arizona, but this one is regarded as one of the best in the state.

HIKING & BACKPACKING

For free detailed maps, hiking advice, and information on campgrounds, contact the rangers of the **Coconino National Forest** (⊠*Sedona Ranger District, 250 Brewer Rd., West, 86339* ☎*928/282–4119* ⊕*www. fs.fed.us/r3/coconino* ⊗*Weekdays 8–4:30*). Ask here or at your hotel for directions to trailheads for Doe's Mountain (an easy ascent, with many switchbacks), Loy Canyon, Devil's Kitchen, and Long Canyon.

> **WORD OF MOUTH**
>
> "Sedona has lots of excellent hiking, from very basic to much more advanced; tons of shopping; and good restaurants. We had never hiked before and really enjoyed that. "
>
> –tdoubrava

Among the paths in Coconino National Forest, the popular **West Fork Trail** (⊠*Trailhead: AZ 89A, 9½ mi north of Sedona*) traverses the Oak Creek Canyon for a 3-mi hike. A walk through the woods in the midst of sheer red-rock walls and a dip in the stream is a great summer combo. The trailhead is about 3 mi north of Slide Rock State Park.

Any backpacking trip in the **Secret Mountain Wilderness** near Sedona guarantees stunning vistas, otherworldly rock formations, and zenlike serenity, but little water, so pack a good supply. ■**TIP➔Plan your trip for the spring or fall: summer brings 100°F heat and sudden thunderstorms that flood canyons without warning.** Most individual trails in the wilderness are too short for anything longer than an overnighter, but several trails can be linked up to form a memorable multiday trip. Contact the Sedona Ranger District for full details.

HORSEBACK RIDING

Among the tour options at **Trail Horse Adventures** (⊠*85 Five J La., Lower Red Rock Loop Rd., West* ☎*800/723–3538* ⊕*www.trailhorse adventures.com*) are a midday picnic, an Oak Creek swim, and a full-moon ride with a campfire cookout. Rides range from about $60 for an hour to in the neighborhood of $200 for an entire day.

MOUNTAIN BIKING

Given the red-rock splendor, challenging terrain, miles of single track, and mild weather, you might think Sedona would be a mountain-biking destination on the order of Moab or Durango. Inexplicably, you won't find the lycra-clad throngs patronizing pasta bars or throwing back microbrews on the Uptown mall, but all the better for you: the mountain-biking culture remains fervent but low-key. A few strategically located, excellent bike shops can outfit you and give advice.

As a general rule, mountain bikes are allowed on all trails and jeep paths unless designated as wilderness or private property. The rolling terrain, which switches between serpentine trails of buff red clay and mounds of slickrock, has few sustained climbs but ■**TIP➔be careful of blind drop-offs that often step down several feet in unexpected places.** The thorny trailside flora makes carrying extra inner tubes a must, and an inner tube sealant is a good idea, too. If you plan to ride for several hours, pack a gallon of water and start early in the morning on hot days. Shade is rare, and with the nonpotable exception of Oak Creek, water is nonexistent.

For the casual rider, **Bell Rock Pathway** (⊠*Trailhead: 5 mi south of Sedona on AZ 179*) is a scenic and easy ride traveling 3 mi through some of the most breathtaking scenery in red-rock country. Several single-track trails spur off this one making it a good starting point for many other rides in Sedona. **Submarine Rock Loop** is perhaps the most popular single-track loop in the area, and for good reason. The 10-mi trail is a heady mixture of prime terrain and scenery following slickrock and twisty trails up to Chicken Point, a sandstone terrace overlooking colorful buttes. The trail continues as a bumpy romp through washes almost all downhill. Be wary of blind drop-offs in this section. It wouldn't be overly cautious to scout any parts of the trail that look sketchy.

A few hundred yards south of Bell Rock Pathway, **Bike and Bean** (⊠*6020 AZ 179, Village of Oak Creek* ☎*928/284–0210* ⊕*www. bike-bean.com*) offers rentals, tours, their own blend of coffee, and advice on trails and conditions.

WHERE TO STAY & EAT

Some Sedona restaurants close in January and February, so call before you go; if you're planning a visit in high season (April to October), make reservations.

★ $$$–$$$$ ✕ **L'Auberge.** The most formal dining room in Sedona, on the L'Auberge de Sedona resort property, promises a quiet, civilized evening of indulgence. Chef Jonathan Agelman offers a fusion of American cuisine with French influences, and among the house favorites is the venison accompanied by wild game cassoulet and broccolini. You can make the most of L'Auberge's 1,200-bottle wine cellar by enjoying the seven-course wine-paired meal for $105. The lavish Sunday brunch ($$$$) is well worth the splurge. ⊠*L'Auberge de Sedona, 241 AZ 89A, Uptown* ☎*928/282–1667* ⊟AE, D, DC, MC, V.

$$$–$$$$ ✕ **Shugrue's Hillside.** Almost everything is good here, which has made this one of the most popular restaurants in Sedona, but the salads and meats are particularly noteworthy. The Caesar salad is refreshingly traditional and the inventive ginger-walnut chicken salad is large enough to share. Rack of lamb and filet mignon are prepared and presented simply. There's a small, well-priced wine list. ⊠*671 AZ 179, Central* ☎*928/282–5300* ⊟AE, DC, MC, V.

$$–$$$$ ✕ **Cowboy Club.** At this upscale restaurant, you can hang out in the casual Cowboy Club or dine in the more formal Silver Saddle Room, where suede booths are surrounded by cowboy art and a pair of large cow horns. High-quality cuts of beef are the specialty, but the fried chicken served with cumin–mashed potatoes is delish, too. ⊠*241 AZ 89A, Uptown* ☎*928/282–4200* ⊟AE, D, DC, MC, V.

$$–$$$$ ✕ **René at Tlaquepaque.** Ease into the plush banquettes at this lace-curtained restaurant for classic Continental dishes. Recommended starters include French onion soup and the spinach and wild mushroom salad in a hazelnut vinaigrette. Rack of lamb is the house specialty, and the Dover sole is a real find, far from the white cliffs. Crêpes suzette for two, prepared table-side, is an impressive dessert. There's a well-selected wine list, too. Service is formal but resort-casual attire is acceptable. ⊠ *Tlaquepaque Arts & Crafts Village, Unit B–117, AZ 179, Central* ☎ *928/282–9225* ⊟ AE, MC, V.

★ **$$–$$$** ✕ **Dahl & DiLuca.** Andrea DiLuca and Lisa Dahl have created one of the most popular Italian restaurants in town: Andrea runs the kitchen, and Lisa meets and greets diners. Lisa also slips into the kitchen every day to make delicious homemade soups like white bean with ham and hearty minestrone. Renaissance reproductions and café seating give the impression of having been transported to a Roman piazza. ⊠ *2321 W. AZ 89A, West* ☎ *928/282–5219* ⊟ AE, D, MC, V ⊘ *No lunch.*

★ **$$–$$$** ✕ **Heartline Café.** Fresh flowers and innovative cuisine that even the staff struggles to characterize are this attractive café's hallmarks. Local ingredients pepper the menu, giving a Sedona twist to Continental fare, and favorites include pecan-crusted trout with Dijon sauce and oak-grilled salmon marinated in tequila and lime. Appealing vegetarian plates are also available. Desserts include a phenomenal crème brûlée, as well as homemade truffles at the chef's whim. A gourmet take-out restaurant next door is perfect prep for picnics under the red rocks. ⊠ *1610 W. AZ 89A, West* ☎ *928/282–0785* ⊟ AE, D, MC, V.

$$–$$$ ✕ **Takashi.** Those seeking serenity and a respite from heavy meals will enjoy this Japanese restaurant, which provides aesthetic pleasure in everything from tea (with little bits of floating popcorn and brown rice) to dessert (sweet ginger or red-bean ice cream). Salads include spicy sushi tuna with Japanese mayonnaise on a bed of cabbage and fresh vegetables. Combination dinners such as sashimi with tempura or teriyaki let you sample a bit of everything. ⊠ *465 Jordan Rd., Uptown* ☎ *928/282–2334* ⊟ AE, DC, MC, V ⊘ *Closed Mon. No lunch weekends.*

$–$$ ✕ **Oaxaca Restaurant.** Tasty standards complement some of the best uptown canyon vistas at this modern Mexican restaurant with a lovely balcony. The smoky kick of the salsa, along with the old-world Mexican decor and sun-kissed scenery may transport you south of the border, but dishes are prepared under the auspices of owner Carla Butler, a dietitian who shuns the traditional use of lard and cholesterol-containing oils in favor of healthier options—with delicious results. ⊠ *321 N. AZ 89A, Uptown* ☎ *928/282–4179* ⊟ AE, DC, MC, V.

$ ✕ **Thai Spices.** This small restaurant has a loyal following of vegetarians and health-food enthusiasts, though not everything is meatless. The curries, especially red curry with tempeh, are delicious and can be prepared at the spice level of your choice. Traditional pad thai with chicken is satisfyingly homey and the spicy beef salad, a house specialty only for the brave, will make your hair stand on end. ⊠ *2986 W. AZ 89A, West* ☎ *928/282–0599* ⊟ MC, V.

¢–$ ✕ **Coffee Pot Restaurant.** Locals and tourists alike swarm to this spacious diner for scrumptious breakfast and brunch food served by a brisk and friendly waitstaff. One hundred and one omelet options are the stars of the show, and include such concoctions as the quirky peanut butter and jelly or the basic ham and cheese. Warm homemade biscuits always hit the spot. An extensive lunch menu that includes everything from Mexican dishes to a Greek salad round out the offerings. ⊠ *2050 W. 89A, West* ☎ *928/282–6626* ▭ *D, MC, V* ⊗ *No dinner.*

★ ¢–$ ✕ **Sally's Mesquite Grill and BBQ.** Although it offers limited indoor seating, this Uptown hideaway behind a long row of tourist shops is worth a visit. It's super casual, with just an ordering window where you can select pulled pork sandwiches and homemade comfort food such as beans or cole slaw. The BBQ sauce has a bit of a kick, and the french fries (also made from scratch) are fabulous. Hours vary with the season, so call ahead. ⊠ *250 Jordan Rd., No. 9, Uptown* ☎ *928/282–6533* ▭ *MC, V.*

¢–$ ✕ **Sedona Coffee Roasters.** Not only does this café serve the best coffee in town by a mile, but the lunch sandwiches are perfect fare before, during (you can get 'em to go), or after a red-rock hike. Daily specials might include a healthful tuna salad with sprouts or a more decadent jumbo beef Polish hot dog. You can also choose your own sandwich fixings from a list of fresh ingredients. ⊠ *2155 W. AZ 89A, West* ☎ *928/282–0282* ▭ *MC, V* ⊗ *No dinner.*

$$$$ ▦ **Enchantment Resort.** The rooms and suites at this resort are tucked into pueblo-style buildings in serene Boynton Canyon. Accommodations come in many configurations, some with kitchens, separate living and dining areas, and multiple bedrooms which can be joined to create large, elaborate suites. All have beehive gas fireplaces and superb views. The Yavapai Room serves excellent Southwestern cuisine and the resort's spa, Mi Amo, offers treatments like hot stone massage. ⊠ *525 Boynton Canyon Rd., West, 86336* ☎ *928/282–2900 or 800/826–4180* ⊟ *928/282–9249* ⊕ *www.enchantmentresort.com* ↩ *107 rooms, 115 suites* ♺ *In-room: safe, ethernet, kitchen (some). In-hotel: 2 restaurants, bar, tennis courts, pools, gym, spa, bicycles, children's programs (ages 4–12), no elevator* ▭ *AE, D, MC, V.*

★ $$$$ ▦ **El Portal Sedona.** This stunning hacienda is one of the most beautifully designed hotels in the Southwest. Decor accents include authentic Tiffany and Roycroft pieces, French doors leading to balconies or a grassy central courtyard, stained-glass windows and ceiling panels, river-rock or tile fireplaces, and huge custom-designed beds. All rooms have flat-screen TVs with DVD players, and guests can enjoy gym, spa, and pool privileges next door at Los Abrigados Resort. Wine and hors d'oeuvres are served in the afternoon, and the inn also serves dinner Wednesday through Saturday evenings. ⊠ *95 Portal La., Central, 86336* ☎ *928/203–9405 or 800/313–0017* ⊟ *928/203–9401* ⊕ *www.elportalsedona.com* ↩ *11 rooms, 1 suite* ♺ *In-room: refrigerator, DVD, Wi-Fi. In-hotel: no-smoking rooms, no elevator, some pets allowed* ▭ *AE, D, MC, V* ⦿ *BP.*

★ $$$–$$$$ ▦ **Alma de Sedona.** The Alma de Sedona continues to be one of Sedona's most enchanting B&Bs, with spectacular views, and ultracomfortable beds. The inn was built well off the main drag and in the shadow of the buttes for views and privacy. Understated, elegant, and inviting rooms all have private entrances and patios; bath salts and candles await in the bathrooms. ⊠*50 Hozoni Dr., West, 86336* ☎*928/282–2737 or 800/923–2282* 🖷*928/203–4141* ⊕*www.almadesedona.com* ⇥*12 rooms* ⌂*In-room: refrigerator; In-hotel: pool, no-smoking rooms, public Wi-Fi, no elevator* ⊟MC, V ⎮◎⎮*BP.*

$$$–$$$$ 🏨 **Briar Patch Inn.** This B&B in a verdant canyon with a rushing creek has rooms in wooden cabins, some with decks overlooking Oak Creek. On summer mornings you can sit outside and enjoy home-baked breads and fresh egg dishes while listening to live classical music. New Age and crafts workshops are sometimes held on the premises. Winter is equally beautiful; request a cabin with a fireplace and wake to see icicles hanging from the trees. ⊠*3190 N. AZ 89A, Oak Creek Canyon, 86336* ☎*928/282–2342 or 888/809–3030* 🖷*928/282–2399* ⊕*www.briar patchinn.com* ⇥*18 cottages* ⌂*In-room: refrigerator, kitchen (some), TV (some). In-hotel: no-smoking rooms* ⊟AE, MC, V ⎮◎⎮*BP.*

★ **$$$–$$$$** 🏨 **Graham Inn and Adobe Village.** Some of the rooms at this inn south of Sedona have Jacuzzi tubs and balconies that look out onto the red rocks. Each of the four individually decorated casitas on the lot next door has a gas fireplace that opens into both the sitting area and the bathroom area, which is outfitted with a two-person Jacuzzi tub. What makes this place really special, though, are the impeccable yet casual service and the French chef who makes breakfasts worth the price of admission. The owners are committed to always having at least one room under $200. ⊠*150 Canyon Circle Dr., Village of Oak Creek, 86351* ☎*928/284–1425 or 800/228–1425* 🖷*928/284–0767* ⊕*www. sedonasfinest.com* ⇥*6 rooms, 1 suite, 4 private villas* ⌂*In-room: kitchen (some), refrigerator (some), VCR. In-hotel: pool, no-smoking rooms, no elevator* ⊟AE, D, MC, V ⎮◎⎮*BP.*

$$$–$$$$ 🏨 **Junipine Creekside Retreat.** These one- and two-bedroom cabins— here called creek houses—nestled in a juniper and pine forest (hence the name) are spacious and airy, with vaulted ceilings and fireplaces. An excellent value for groups of four or more, some of the cabins are more than 1,400 square feet and sleep up to eight people. Junipine's most enchanting feature might be the sound of Oak Creek roaring below, though, lulling you to sleep by the fire. ⊠*8351 N. AZ 89A, Oak Creek Canyon, 86336* ☎*928/282–3375 or 800/742–7463* 🖷*928/282–7402* ⊕*www.junipine.com* ⇥*50 suites* ⌂*In-room: kitchen, TV (some), DVD/VCR (some). In-hotel: restaurant, no-smoking rooms, no elevator* ⊟AE, D, MC, V.

★ **$$$–$$$$** 🏨 **L'Auberge de Sedona.** This hillside resort consists of a central lodge building; a creek-side lodge; a four-bedroom home with a living room, dining room, and kitchen; and—the major attraction—cabins in the woods along Oak Creek. Rooms in the lodge are decorated in lush Country European style and the cabins have wood-burning fireplaces. Phoenix couples flock to this country-French hideaway and dine in the hotel's French restaurant, one of the most romantic eateries in Arizona. ⊠*301 L'Auberge La., Uptown* 🖃*Box B, 86336* ☎*928/282–1661 or 800/272–6777* 🖷*928/282–2885* ⊕*www.lauberge.com* ⇥*21 rooms,*

31 cottages; ⟨⟩*In-room: refrigerator, safe. In-hotel: 2 restaurants, pool, public Wi-Fi, spa* ☰AE, D, DC, MC, V.

$$-$$$$ ▦ **Boots & Saddles.** Irith and Sam are the worldly and consummate hosts at this quiet inn tucked behind the main street in West Sedona. The rooms are decorated in an upscale Western motif, complete with genuine cowboy artifacts, and the Sacred Feather room has unparalleled red-rock views and a telescope for stargazing. ✉*2900 Hopi Dr., West, 86336* ☎*928/282–1944 or 800/201–1944* ⊕*www.oldwestbb. com* ⟨*6 rooms* ⟨⟩*In-room: refrigerator, TV, DVD/VCR. In-hotel: no-smoking rooms, no elevator* ☰AE, D, MC, V ⟨⟩|*BP.*

$$-$$$ ▦ **Amara Resort.** You might not expect to find such an urbane boutique hotel in small, outdoorsy Sedona, but Amara fits right in with its ochre-and-tan–sandstone exterior and secluded setting adjacent to gurgling Oak Creek. Sleek rooms deviate from the usual Sedona look, with low-slung beds and work desks with ergonomic seating. Other cushy extras include in-room DVD players and Aveda bath products. Step out onto your room's private balcony or terrace to take in expansive red-rock views. The Amara Grille, on the property, serves globally inspired contemporary victuals. ✉*310 N. AZ 89, Village of Oak Creek, 86336* ☎*928/282–4828 or 866/455–6610* ⊟*928/282–4825* ⊕*www.amararesort.com* ⟨*92 rooms, 8 suites* ⟨⟩*In-room: dial-up. In-hotel: 3 restaurants, bar, concierge, no-smoking rooms, public Internet, gym* ☰AE, D, DC, MC, V.

$$-$$$$ ▦ **Boots & Saddles.** Irith and Sam are the worldly and consummate hosts at this quiet inn tucked behind the main street in West Sedona. The rooms are decorated in an upscale Western motif, complete with genuine cowboy artifacts, and the Sacred Feather room has unparalleled red-rock views and a telescope for stargazing. ✉*2900 Hopi Dr., West, 86336* ☎*928/282–1944 or 800/201–1944* ⊕*www.oldwestbb. com* ⟨*6 rooms* ⟨⟩*In-room: refrigerator, TV, DVD/VCR. In-hotel: no-smoking rooms, no elevator* ☰AE, D, MC, V ⟨⟩|*BP.*

$$-$$$ ▦ **Lodge at Sedona.** Rooms in this rambling wood-and-stone house have a refined rustic style; some have fireplaces, redwood decks, or hot tubs. For solitude, walk the seven-path classic labyrinth (made of local rock) and through the gardens. A chef prepares a five-course breakfast each morning. ✉*125 Kallof Pl., West, 86336* ☎*928/204–1942 or 800/619–4467* ⊟*928/204–2128* ⊕*www.lodgeatsedona.com* ⟨*5 rooms, 9 suites* ⟨⟩*In-room: Wi-Fi, no phone, VCR (some), TV (some). In-hotel: restaurant, pool, gym, concierge, no-smoking rooms, no elevator* ☰D, MC, V ⟨⟩|*BP.*

$-$$$ ▦ **Sky Ranch Lodge.** There may be no better vantage point in town from which to view Sedona's red-rock canyons than the private patios and balconies at Sky Ranch Lodge, near the top of Airport Mesa. Some rooms have stone fireplaces and some have kitchenettes. Paths on the grounds wind around fountains and, in summer, through colorful flower gardens. This is an excellent value, primarily because of the views. ✉*Top of Airport Rd., West, 86339* ☎*928/282–6400* ⊟*928/282–7682* ⊕*www.skyranchlodge.com* ⟨*92 rooms, 2 cottages* ⟨⟩*In-room: kitchen (some), refrigerator (some). In-hotel: pool, no-smoking rooms, no elevator, some pets allowed* ☰AE, MC, V.

★ $$ ⚅ **The Canyon Wren.** The best value in the Oak Creek Canyon area, this small B&B has free-standing cabins with views of the canyon walls, and Milena and Mike (she's Slovenian, he's Floridian) regard guests' privacy first and foremost. It's likely that their two lovable dogs, Zoey and Wookiee, will greet you on

arrival. Cabins have private decks and fireplaces. Breakfast is a selection of delicious baked goods from Milena's kitchen. ⊠*6425 N. AZ 89A, Oak Creek Canyon, 86336* ☎*928/282–6900 or 800/437–9736* 🖷*928/282–6978* ⊕*www.canyonwrencabins.com* ⇌*4 cabins* ♿*In-room: no phone, kitchen, no TV. In-hotel: no-smoking rooms, no elevator* ⊟*AE, D, MC, V* ⦿❙*CP.*

$–$$ ⚅ **Desert Quail Inn.** Close to a lion's share of the trailheads but out of the main flow of tourist traffic, this is a good base for outdoor adventures and the front desk has plenty of maps and advice on offer. Rooms are spacious and bright, and the in-room refrigerators are stocked with fresh fruit—a nice touch. ⊠*6626 AZ 179, Village of Oak Creek, 86351* ☎*928/284–1433 or 800/385–0927* 🖷*928/284–0487* ⊕*www. desertquailinn.com* ⇌*41 rooms* ♿*In-room: refrigerator. In-hotel: pool, laundry facilities, no elevator* ⊟*AE, D, DC, MC, V.*

$ ⚅ **Sedona Motel.** Built on a terrace removed from the highway in order to afford it the same expansive red-rock views as the pricier resorts, this motel is pretty typical in all other respects. It's within easy reach of most of Sedona's attractions, and the rooms are well kept. ⊠*218 AZ 179, Central, 86336* ☎*928/282–7187 or 877/828–7187* ⇌*16 rooms* ♿*In-room: refrigerator* ⊟*D, MC, V.*

NIGHTLIFE & THE ARTS

Nightlife in Sedona tends to be sedate although on high-season weekends, there's usually live music at the Enchantment Resort. Shugrue's Hillside also regularly presents local musicians. Offerings vary from jazz to rock and pop; in all cases, call ahead. Find out about cultural events in Sedona at the **Book Loft** (⊠*175 AZ 179, just south of the "Y," Central* ☎*928/282–5173*), which often hosts poetry readings, theatrical readings, book signings, and lectures. The Sedona **Jazz on the Rocks Festival** (☎*928/282–1985* ⊕*www.sedonajazz.com*), held every September, always attracts a sellout crowd that fills the town to capacity. The **Sedona Arts Center** (⊠*N. AZ 89A and Art Barn Rd., Uptown* ☎*928/282–3809* ⊕*www.sedonasculpturewalk.com*) sponsors events ranging from classical concerts to plays; there's an innovative and growing film festival every March.

The closest thing to a rollicking cowboy bar in Sedona is **Rainbow's End** (⊠*3235 W. AZ 89A, West* ☎*928/282–1593*), a steak house with a dance floor. Call to find out when country-and-Western bands are scheduled.

SHOPPING

With a few exceptions, most of the stores in what is known as the Uptown area (north of the "Y," running along AZ 89A to the east of its intersection with AZ 179) cater to the tour-bus trade with Native American jewelry and New Age souvenirs. If this isn't your style, the largest concentration of stores and galleries is in Central Sedona, along AZ 179, south of the "Y," with plenty of offerings for serious shoppers.

There are three main art gallery complexes in Sedona—Hillside Courtyard & Marketplace, Hozho Center, and Tlaquepaque Arts & Crafts Village. Each has smaller galleries within the larger complex; several are listed below. Hozho and Tlaquepaque are the best of the three, though Hillside is very close to Hozho. The **Hillside Courtyard & Marketplace** (⊠ *671 AZ 179, Central* ☎ *928/282–4500*) has several galleries. The **Hozho Center** (⊠ *431 AZ 179, Central* ☎ *928/204–2257*), a minute or two north of Hillside on AZ 179, is a small, upscale complex in a beige Santa Fe–style building, with galleries and fine-art souvenirs. **Tlaquepaque Arts & Crafts Village** (⊠ *AZ 179, just south of "Y," Central* ☎ *928/282–4838*) is home to more than 100 shops and galleries, and remains one of the best places for travelers to find treasures from their trip to Sedona. The complex of clay-tile-roofed buildings arranged around a series of courtyards shares its name and architectural style with a crafts village just outside Guadalajara. It's a lovely place to browse, but beware: prices tend to be high, and locals joke that it's pronounced "to-lock-your-pocket."

STORES & GALLERIES

Souvenirs in Sedona run the gamut, from authentic Southwestern art to jewelry, and more than enough crystals to bring you inner harmony.

Canyon Outfitters (⊠ *2701 W. 89A, West* ☎ *928/282–5293*) is good for gearing up with maps, clothing, and camping equipment before your outdoor adventures. **Clay Pigeon** (⊠ *Hillside Courtyard & Marketplace, 671 AZ 179, Central* ☎ *928/282–2845*) carries boldly designed dishes and sculptures with a Western accent. **Crystal Magic** (⊠ *2978 W. 89A, West* ☎ *928/282–1622* ⊕ *www.crystalmagicsedona.com*) dabbles in the metaphysical with crystals, jewelry, and books for the new age. **El Prado Galleries** (⊠ *Tlaquepaque, AZ 179, No. 101, Bldg. E, Central* ☎ *928/282–7390* ⊕ *www.elpradogalleries.com*) is a good bet for Southwestern art. **Esteban's** (⊠ *Tlaquepaque, AZ 179, No. 103, Bldg. B, Central* ☎ *928/282–4686*) focuses on ceramics and Native American crafts. **Garland's Navajo Rugs** (⊠ *411 AZ 179, Central* ☎ *928/282–4070* ⊕ *www.garlandsrugs.com*) has a collection of new and antique carpets, as well as Native American katsina dolls, pottery, and baskets. **Isadora** (⊠ *Tlaquepaque, AZ 179, No. 120, Bldg. A, Central* ☎ *928/282–6232*) has beautiful handwoven jackets and shawls. **James Ratliff Gallery** (⊠ *431 AZ 179, Central* ☎ *928/282–1404* ⊕ *www.jamesratliffgallery.com*) has fun and functional pieces by not-yet-established artists. **Kuivato Glass Gallery** (⊠ *Tlaquepaque, AZ 179, No. 122, Bldg. B, Central* ☎ *928/282–1212*) carries gorgeous glassware. **Lanning Gallery** (⊠ *Ho-*

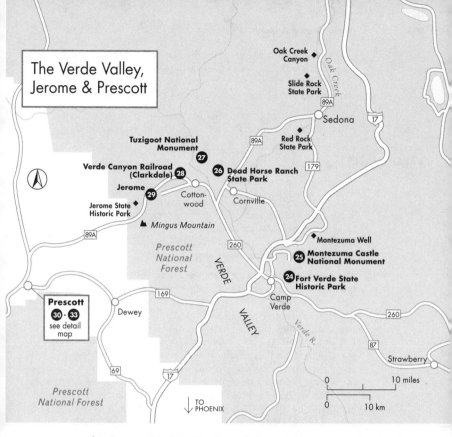

The Verde Valley,
Jerome & Prescott

Oak Creek Canyon

Slide Rock
State Park

89A

Sedona

17

89A

Red Rock
State Park

179

Tuzigoot National
Monument

27

Verde Canyon Railroad
(Clarkdale)

28

26 Dead Horse Ranch
State Park

Jerome

29

Cotton-
wood

Cornville

Jerome State
Historic Park

Mingus Mountain

89A

Prescott
National
Forest

260

VERDE

Montezuma Well

25 Montezuma Castle
National Monument

24 Fort Verde State
Historic Park

Prescott

30 - 33

see detail
map

169

Dewey

VALLEY

Camp
Verde

Verde R.

260

87

Strawberry

69

17

TO
PHOENIX

Prescott
National Forest

0   10 miles

0   10 km

zho Center, 431 AZ 179, Central ☎928/282–6865 ⊕www.lanning
gallery.com) sells Southwestern art and jewelry. **Looking West** (✉242 N.
AZ 89A, Uptown ☎928/282–4877) sells the spiffiest cowgirl-style get-
ups in town. **Sedona Pottery** (✉411 AZ 179, Central ☎928/282–1192)
sells unusual pieces, including flower-arranging bowls, egg separators,
and life-size ceramic statues by shop owner Mary Margaret Sather.

THE VERDE VALLEY, JEROME & PRESCOTT

About 90 mi north of Phoenix, as you round a curve approaching
Exit 285 of I–17, the valley of the Verde River suddenly unfolds in a
panorama of grayish-white cliffs, tinted red in the distance and dotted
with desert scrub, cottonwood, and pine. For hundreds of years many
Native American communities, especially those of the southern Sinagua people, lined the Verde River. Rumors of great mineral deposits
brought Europeans to the Verde Valley as early as 1583, when Hopi
Indians guided Antonio de Espejo here, but it wasn't until the second
half of the 19th century that this wealth was commercially exploited.
The discovery of silver and gold in the Black Hills, which border the
valley on the southwest, gave rise to such boomtowns as Jerome—and
to military installations such as Fort Verde, set up to protect the white

settlers and wealth seekers from the Native American tribes they displaced. Mineral wealth was also the impetus behind the establishment of Prescott as a territorial capital by President Lincoln and other Unionists who wanted to keep the riches out of Confederate hands.

Numbers in the text correspond to numbers in the margin and on the North-Central Arizona, Prescott, Sedona, and Flagstaff maps.

VERDE VALLEY

94 mi north of Phoenix on I–17.

Often overlooked by travelers on trips to Prescott or Flagstaff, the Verde Valley offers several enjoyable diversions, including the historical wonders at Montezuma Castle and Tuzigoot. And if you're tired of the car, the Verde Canyon Railroad in Clarkdale is a great way to get off road without doing the driving.

24 The military post for which **Fort Verde State Historic Park** is named was built between 1871 and 1873 as the third of three fortifications in this part of the Arizona Territory. To protect the Verde Valley's farmers and miners from Tonto Apache and Yavapai raids, the fort's administrators oversaw the movement of nearly 1,500 Native Americans to the San Carlos and Fort Apache reservations. A museum details the history of the area's military installations, and three furnished officers' quarters show the day-to-day living conditions of the top brass—it's a good break from the interstate if you've been driving for too long. Signs from any of Interstate 17's three Camp Verde exits will direct you to the 10-acre park. ⊠ *125 E. Hollomon St.* ☎ *928/567–3275* ⊕ *www.pr.state. az.us* ✉ *$2* ⊗ *Daily 8–5.*

25 The five-story, 20-room cliff dwelling at **Montezuma Castle National Monument** was named by explorers who believed it had been erected by the Aztecs. Southern Sinagua Native Americans actually built the roughly 600-year-old structure, which is one of the best-preserved prehistoric ruins in North America—and one of the most accessible. An easy paved trail (1/3 mi round-trip) leads to the dwelling and to adjacent Castle A, a badly deteriorated 6-story living space with about 45 rooms. No one is permitted to enter the ruins, but the viewing area is close by. From Camp Verde, take Main Street to Montezuma Castle Road.

Somewhat less accessible than Montezuma's Castle—but equally striking—is the **Montezuma Well** (☎ *928/567–4521*), a unit of the national monument. Although there are some Sinagua and Hohokam ruins here, the limestone sinkhole with a limpid blue-green pool lying in the middle of the desert is the

> ### WORD OF MOUTH
>
> "I love Montezuma's Castle. It is a very easy walk and impressive. But I like even more the section a few miles away called Montezuma's Well. It's a big sinkhole with a few small cliff dwellings on the cliff above the well. You can hike down into the well. You can also hike to where the water comes out of the well and see how they irrigated 800 years ago."
>
> –bigtyke

park's main attraction. This cavity— 55 feet deep and 365 feet across—is all that's left of an ancient subterranean cavern; the water remains at a constant 76°F year-round. It's a short hike up here, but the peace, quiet, and the views of the Verde Valley reward the effort. To reach Montezuma Well from Montezuma Castle, return to I–17 and go north to Exit 293; signs direct you to the well, which is 4 mi east of the freeway. The drive includes a short section of dirt road. ⊠*Montezuma Castle Rd., 7 mi northeast of Camp Verde* ☎928/567–3322 *Montezuma Castle, 928/567–3322 Ext. 15 bookstore* ⊕*www.nps.gov/ moca* ⊠*$5* ⊘*Labor Day–Memorial Day, daily 8–5; Memorial Day– Labor Day, daily 8–6.*

> ### DID SOMEONE SAY DEAD HORSES?
>
> In the late 1940s, when Calvin "Cap" Ireys asked his family to help him choose among the ranches he was thinking about buying in the Verde Valley, his son immediately picked "the one with the dead horse on it." Ireys sold the land to the state in 1973 at one-third of its value, with the stipulation that the park into which it was to be converted retain the ranch's colorful name.

26 The 423-acre spread of **Dead Horse Ranch State Park,** which combines high-desert and wetlands habitats, is a pleasant place to while away the day. You can fish in the Verde River or the well-stocked Park Lagoon, or hike on some 6 mi of trails that begin in a shaded picnic area and wind along the river; adjoining forest service pathways are available for those who enjoy longer treks. Birders can check off more than 100 species from the Arizona Audubon Society lists provided by the rangers. Bald eagles perch along the Verde River in winter, and the common black hawks—a misnomer for these threatened avians—nest here in summer. It's 1 mi north of Cottonwood, off Main Street. ⊠*675 Dead Horse Ranch Rd., Cottonwood* ☎928/634–5283 ⊕*www.pr.state. az.us* ⊠*Day use $6 per car; camping without electricity $15, with electricity $25* ⊘*Daily 8–5.*

27 **Tuzigoot National Monument** isn't as well preserved as Montezuma Castle but it's more impressive in scope. Tuzigoot is another complex of ruins of the Sinagua people, who lived on this land overlooking the Verde Valley from about AD 1000 to 1400. The pueblo, constructed of limestone and sandstone blocks, once rose three stories and housed 110 rooms. Inhabitants were skilled dry farmers and traded with peoples hundreds of miles away. Items used for food preparation, as well as jewelry, weapons, and farming tools excavated from the site, are displayed in the visitor center. Within the ruins, you can step into a reconstructed room. ⊠*3 mi north of Cottonwood on Broadway Rd., between Cottonwood's Old Town and Clarkdale, Clarkdale* ☎928/634–5564 ⊕*www.nps.gov/tuzi* ⊠*$5* ⊘*Labor Day–Memorial Day, daily 8–5; Memorial Day–Labor Day, daily 8–6.*

★ ❷ Train buffs come to the Verde Valley to catch the 22-mi **Verde Canyon Railroad,** which follows a dramatic route through the Verde Canyon, the remains of a copper smelter, and much unspoiled desert that is inaccessible by car. The destination—the city of Clarkdale, might not be that impressive, but the ride is undeniably scenic. Knowledgeable announcers regale riders with the area's colorful history and point out natural attractions along the way—in winter, you're likely to see bald eagles. This trip, which takes about four hours, is especially popular in fall-foliage season and in spring, when the desert wildflowers bloom; make reservations well in advance. Round-trip rides cost $54.95. For $79.95 you can ride the much more comfortable living-room-like first-class cars, where hot hors d'oeuvres, coffee, and a cocktail are included in the price. ■TIP→**Reservations are required.** ⊠*Arizona Central Railroad, 300 N. Broadway, Clarkdale* ☎*800/320–0718* ⊕*www. verdecanyonrr.com.*

WHERE TO EAT

$$ ✕ **Kramer's at the Manzanita Restaurant & Lounge.** You might not expect to find sophisticated cooking in Cornville, 6 mi east of Cottonwood, but a European-born chef prepares Continental fare here, using organic produce and locally raised meat whenever possible. Roast duckling à l'orange and rack of lamb are beautifully presented; try the mushroom soup if it's available. The hours are not as cosmopolitan as the food: dinner ends at 8 PM. ⊠*11425 E. Cornville Rd., Cornville* ☎*928/634–8851* ⊟MC, V ۞*Closed Mon. and Tues.*

$$ ✕ **Page Springs Restaurant.** Come to these two rustic, wood-paneled rooms in Cornville, on the loop to the town of Page Springs—off AZ 89A—for down-home Western chow: great chili, burgers, and steaks. You'll get an Oak Creek view for much less than you'd pay closer to Sedona. ⊠*1975 N. Page Springs Rd., Cornville* ☎*928/634–9954* ⊟No credit cards.

¢ ✕ **Gabriela's Mexican Food.** Off the main Camp Verde drag, this tiny eatery serves traditional Mexican food. Try the *carne asada* (marinated, grilled beef) tacos and the chicken *burros* (what burritos are often called in this part of Arizona). ⊠*154 W. Holliman St., Camp Verde* ☎*928/567–6300* ⊟AE, D, MC, V ۞*Closed Sun.*

SPORTS & THE OUTDOORS

The **Verde Ranger District** office of the **Prescott National Forest** (⊠*300 E. AZ 260, Camp Verde* ☎*928/567–4121* ⊕*www.fs.fed.us/r3/prescott*) is a good resource for places to hike, fish, and boat along the Verde River.

The **Black Canyon Trail** (⊠*AZ 260, 4 mi south of Cottonwood, west on FR 359 4½ mi*) is a bit of a slog, rising more than 2,200 feet in 6 mi, but the reward is grand views from the gray cliffs of Verde Valley to the red buttes of Sedona to the blue range of the San Francisco Peaks.

JEROME

★ ㉙ *3½ mi southwest of Clarkdale, 20 mi northwest of Camp Verde, 33 mi northeast of Prescott, 25 mi southwest of Sedona on AZ 89A.*

Jerome was once known as the Billion Dollar Copper Camp, but after the last mines closed in 1953 the booming population of 15,000 dwindled to 50 determined souls, earning Jerome the "ghost town" designation it still holds, although its population has risen back to almost 500. It's hard to imagine this town was once the location of Arizona's largest JCPenney store and one of the state's first Safeway supermarkets! Jerome saw its first revival during the mid-1960s, when hippies arrived and turned it into an arts colony of sorts, and it has since become a tourist attraction. In addition to its shops and historic sites, Jerome is worth visiting for its scenery: it's built into the side of Cleopatra Hill, and from here you can see Sedona's red rocks, Flagstaff's San Francisco Peaks, and even eastern Arizona's Mogollon Rim country.

> ## WORD OF MOUTH
>
> "Jerome has the feeling of what Sedona used to be before it became a major tourist destination. Jerome was once a mining town; now it is full of small art galleries and funky shops; it's perched on the side of a mountain. Definitely within reach if you're doing Sedona. I stayed in the Grand Hotel there, which used to be the hospital for the miners, and is supposedly haunted. The restaurant is really wonderful."
> –robhart

Jerome is about a mile above sea level, but structures within town sit at elevations that vary by as much as 1,500 feet, depending on whether they're on Cleopatra Hill or at its foot. Blasting at the United Verde (later Phelps Dodge) mine regularly shook buildings off their foundations—the town's jail slid across a road and down a hillside, where it sits today. And that's not all that was unsteady about Jerome. In 1903 a reporter from a New York newspaper called Jerome "the wickedest town in America," due to its abundance of drinking and gambling establishments; town records from 1880 list 24 saloons. Whether by divine retribution or drunken accidents, the town burned down several times.

Jerome currently has around 50 retail establishments (that's more than one for every 10 residents). You can get a map of the town's shops and its attractions at the visitor-information trailer on AZ 89A. Except for the state-run historic park, attractions and businesses don't always stay open as long as their stated hours if things are slow.

Of the three mining museums in town, the most inclusive is part of **Jerome State Historic Park.** Just outside town, signs on AZ 89A will direct you to the turnoff for the park, reached by a short, precipitous road. The museum occupies the 1917 mansion of Jerome's mining king, Dr. James "Rawhide Jimmy" Douglas Jr., who purchased Little Daisy Mine in 1912. You can see some of the tools and heavy equipment used to grind ore, but accounts of the town's wilder elements—such as the House of Joy brothel—are not so prominently displayed. ⊠*State Park Rd.* ☎*928/634–5381* ⊕*www.pr.state.az.us* ⊠*$3* ⊙*Daily 8–5.*

The **Mine Museum** in downtown Jerome is staffed by the Jerome Historical Society. The museum's collection of mining stock certificates alone is worth the (small) price of admission—the amount of money that changed hands in this town 100 years ago boggles the mind. ⊠*200 Main St.* ☎*928/634–5477* ⊠*$2* ⊙*Daily 9–5.*

WHERE TO STAY & EAT

$–$$ ✕ **Haunted Hamburger/Jerome Palace.** After the climb up the stairs from Main Street to this former boarding house, you'll be ready for the hearty burgers, chili, cheese steaks, and ribs that dominate the menu. Lighter fare, including such meatless selections as the guacamole quesadilla, is also available. An outdoor deck overlooks Verde Valley. ⊠*410 Clark St.* ☎*928/634–0554* ▭MC, V.

¢ ✕ **Flatiron Cafe.** Ask where to have lunch or a late-afternoon snack, and nearly every Main Street shop owner will direct you to a tiny eatery at the fork in the road. The menu includes healthful sandwiches, such as black-bean hummus with feta cheese, and many coffee drinks. Breakfast is also served. ⊠*416 Main St.* ☎*928/634–2733* ▭No credit cards ⊙*Closed Wed. and Thurs. No dinner.*

¢ ✕ **Red Rooster Café.** The old Safeway is now a café with tin ceilings and country accents, yet the delicious meat-loaf sandwich is nontraditional, served on whole-wheat bread with Dijon mustard *sans* mashed potatoes. A compact but eclectic lunch menu includes green-chile quiche and a turkey pita topped with bacon, avocado, and chipotle mayonnaise. Leave room for the delicate bread pudding made from croissants. ⊠*363 S. Main St.* ☎*928/634–7087* ▭MC, V ⊙*No dinner.*

$–$$ ▦ **Ghost City Inn.** The outdoor veranda at this 1898 B&B affords sweeping views of the Verde Valley and Sedona. Most rooms are decorated in Victorian style, but one has contemporary Western touches and another has a rustic appeal. All rooms have private baths. Afternoon tea with cookies is an unexpected luxury for this formerly rough-and-ready town. ⊠*541 N. Main St., 86331* ☎☎*928/634–4678 or 888/634–4678* ⊕*www.ghostcityinn.com* ⟿*6 rooms* ⚼*In-room: VCR. In-hotel: no kids under 14, no-smoking rooms, some pets allowed, no elevator* ▭AE, D, MC, V ⍟*BP.*

$–$$ ▦ **Jerome Grand Hotel.** This full-service hotel is housed in a former hospital built in 1927. Rooms are comfy, with homey furnishings that part with the institutional past, and many have splendid views. ⊠*200 Hill St., 86331* ☎*928/634–8200 or 888/817–6788* ▤*928/639–0299* ⊕*www.jeromegrandhotel.net* ⟿*22 rooms, 1 suite* ⚼*In-room: VCR. In-hotel: restaurant, bar, elevator* ▭D, MC, V.

★ $–$$ ▦ **Surgeon's House.** Plants, knickknacks, bright colors, and plenty of sunlight make this Mediterranean-style home a welcoming place to stay and the friendly ministrations of innkeeper Andrea Prince enhance the experience. Multicourse breakfasts might include overstuffed burritos or a marinated fruit compote. There are two suites and two rooms, including a former chauf-feur's quarters that has a skylight and private patio. All have private bathrooms. Knockout vistas can be seen from almost everywhere in the house. ✉*101 Hill St., 86331* ☎*928/639–1452 or 800/639–1452* ⊕*www.surgeonshouse.com* 🛏*2 rooms, 2 suites* ♿*In-room: kitchen (some), no TV. In-hotel: some pets allowed, no elevator* ☐*MC, V* 🍴*BP*.

NIGHTLIFE

Jerome's a ghost town, so don't expect a hopping nightlife, although there are some places to have fun. **Paul & Jerry's Saloon** (✉*Main St.* ☎*928/634–2603*) attracts a (relative) crowd to its two pool tables and old wooden bar. On weekends there's live music and a lively scene at the **Spirit Room** (✉*Main St. and AZ 89A* ☎*928/634–8809*); the mural over the bar harks back to the days when it was a dining spot for the prostitutes of the red-light district.

SHOPPING

Jerome has its share of art galleries (some perched precariously on Cleopatra Hill), along with boutiques, and they're funkier than those in Sedona. Main Street and, just around the bend, Hull Avenue are Jerome's two primary shopping streets. Your eyes may begin to glaze over after browsing through one boutique after another, most offering tasteful Southwestern paraphernalia.

Aurum (✉*369 Main St.* ☎*928/634–3330*) focuses on contemporary art jewelry in silver and gold; about 30 artists are represented. **Designs on You** (✉*233 Main St.* ☎*928/634–7879*) carries attractively styled women's clothing. **Jerome Artists Cooperative Gallery** (✉*502 Main St.* ☎*928/639–4276*) specializes in jewelry, sculpture, painting, and pottery by local artists. **Nellie Bly** (✉*136 Main St.* ☎*928/634–0255*) stocks perfume bottles and outstanding kaleidoscopes. **Raku Gallery** (✉*250 Hull Ave.* ☎*928/639–0239*) stocks the work of 300 artists; you'll find wrought-iron furniture, free-blown glass, and fountains. **Sky Fire** (✉*140 Main St.* ☎*928/634–8081*), the most sophisticated shop in Jerome, has two floors of items to adorn your person and your house, from Southwestern-pattern dishes to handcrafted Mission-style hutches.

EN ROUTE

The drive down a mountainous section of AZ 89A from Jerome to Prescott is gorgeous (if somewhat harrowing in bad weather), filled with twists and turns through **Prescott National Forest.** A scenic turnoff near Jerome provides one last vista and a place to apply chains during surprise snowstorms. There's camping, picnicking, and hiking at the crest of Mingus Mountain. If you're coming from Phoenix, the route that crosses the Mogollon Rim, overlooking the Verde Valley, is scenic and less precipitous.

PRESCOTT

33 mi southwest of Jerome on AZ 89A to U.S. 89, 100 mi northwest of Phoenix via I–17 to AZ 69.

In a forested bowl 5,300 feet above sea level, Prescott is a prime summer refuge for Phoenix-area dwellers. It was proclaimed the first capital of the Arizona Territory in 1864 and settled by Yankees to ensure that gold-rich northern Arizona would remain a Union resource. (Tucson and southern Arizona were strongly pro-Confederacy.) Although early territorial settlers thought that ruins in the area were of Aztec origin, today it's believed that ancestors of the Yavapai, whose reservation is on the outskirts of town, were the area's original inhabitants. The Aztec theory—inspired by *The History and Conquest of Mexico,* a popular book by historian William Hickling Prescott, for whom the town was named—has left its mark on such street names as Montezuma, Cortez, and Alarcon.

> **PRESCOTT TIP**
>
> Tourism in Prescott can be bustling but is rarely overwhelming. Any day will do to tour the Victorian homes and antiques shops, but if you enjoy museums, avoid going on Sunday. The museum hours are stunted on this day, and you won't want to be rushed through the extensive grounds of the Sharlot Hall Museum. Devoting a full day to tour Prescott is plenty, with time left over, perhaps, to watch the sunset from Thumb Butte.

Despite a devastating downtown fire in 1900, Prescott remains the Southwest's richest treasure trove of late-19th-century New England–style architecture (some have called it the "West's most Eastern town"). With two institutions of higher education, Yavapai College and Prescott College, Prescott could be called a college town, but it doesn't really feel like one, perhaps because so many retirees also reside here, drawn by the temperate climate and low cost of living.

The 1916 Yavapai County Courthouse stands in the heart of Prescott, bounded by Gurley, Goodwin, Cortez, and Montezuma streets, and guarded by an equestrian bronze of turn-of-the-20th-century journalist and lawmaker Bucky O'Neill, who died while charging San Juan Hill in Cuba with Teddy Roosevelt during the Spanish-American War. The city's main drag is Gurley Street. Those interested in architecture should get a map of the Victorian neighborhoods. Most are within walking distance of the chamber office. Many Queen Annes have been beautifully restored, and a number are now B&Bs. Antiques and collectibles shops line Cortez Street to the north of the courthouse.

WHAT TO SEE

㉝ Phippen Museum of Western Art. The paintings and bronze sculptures of George Phippen, along with works by other artists of the West, form the permanent collection of this museum, about 5 mi north of downtown. Phippen met with a group of prominent cowboy artists in 1965 to form the Cowboy Artists of America, a group dedicated to preserv-

Phippen
Museum of
Western Art ... **33**

Sharlot Hall
Museum **31**

Smoki
Museum **32**

Whiskey
Row **30**

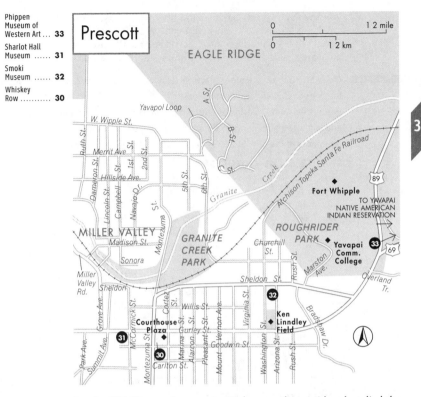

ing the Old West as they saw it. He became the president but died the next year. A memorial foundation set up in his name opened the doors of this museum in 1984. ⊠*4701 U.S. 89 N* ☎*928/778–1385* ⊕*www. phippenartmuseum.org* ⊒*$5* ⊗*Tues.–Sat. 10–4, Sun. 1–4.*

☾ **③①** **Sharlot Hall Museum.** Local history is documented at this remarkable museum. Along with the original ponderosa-pine log cabin, which housed the territorial governor, and the museum, named for historian and poet Sharlot Hall, the parklike setting contains three fully restored period homes and a transportation museum. Territorial times are the focus, but natural history and artifacts of the area's prehistoric peoples are also on display. ⊠*415 W. Gurley St., 2 blocks west of Courthouse Plaza, Downtown* ☎*928/445–3122* ⊕*www.sharlot.org* ⊒*$5* ⊗*Mon.–Sat. 10–4, Sun. noon–4.*

③② **Smoki Museum.** The 1935 stone-and-log building, which resembles an Indian pueblo, is almost as interesting as the Native American artifacts inside. Baskets, katsinas, pottery, rugs, and beadwork make up the collection, which represents Native American culture from the pre-Columbian period to the present. ⊠*147 N. Arizona St., Downtown* ☎*928/445–1230* ⊕*www.smokimuseum.org* ⊒*$5* ⊗*Mon.–Sat. 10–4, Sun. 1–4.*

③ Whiskey Row. Twenty saloons and houses of pleasure once lined this stretch of Montezuma Street, along the west side of Courthouse Plaza. Social activity is more subdued these days, and the historic bars provide an escape from the street's many boutiques. ⊠ *Downtown.*

NEED A BREAK?

Caffe St. Michael's a great place to relax over a coffee or grab a bowl of black-bean chili and watch the people on Whiskey Row. The café and bar has been restored to its original 1901 style. The service at the counter is brisk and will leave you plenty of time for antiquing or museum browsing for the remainder of the day. ⊠ *205 W. Gurley St., Downtown* ☎ *928/778–2500.*

SPORTS & THE OUTDOORS

HIKING & CAMPING

More than a million acres of national-forest land surround Prescott. Thumb Butte is a popular hiking spot, but there are lots of other trekking and overnighting options. Contact the **Bradshaw Ranger District** (⊠ *2230 E. AZ 69, Hwy. 69* ☎ *928/443-8000* ⊕ *www.fs.fed.us/r3/ prescott*) for information about hiking trails and campgrounds in the Prescott National Forest south of town down to Horse Thief Basin. Campgrounds near Prescott are generally not crowded.

The **Thumb Butte Loop Trail** (⊠ *Thumb Butte Rd., 3 mi west of Prescott following Gurley St.—which turns into Thumb Butte*), a 2-mi trek on a paved yet steep loop, takes you 600 feet up near the crest of its namesake. The vistas are large, but you won't be alone on this popular trail.

HORSEBACK RIDING

Granite Mountain Stables (⊠ *2400 W. Shane Dr., 7 mi northeast of Prescott* ☎ *928/771–9551* ⊕ *www.granitemountainstables.com*) has daily guided rides as well as group specials, such as hay-wagon outings. Hour-long rides or lessons cost about $35.

WHERE TO STAY & EAT

$$–$$$ ✕ **Murphy's.** Mesquite-grilled meats and beer brewed exclusively for the restaurant are the specialties here. The baby-back ribs, fresh steamed clams, and fresh fried catfish are your best bets. ⊠ *201 N. Cortez St., Downtown* ☎ *928/445–4044* ☐ AE, D, MC, V.

$$ ✕ **The Palace.** Legend has it that the patrons who saved the Palace's ornately carved 1880s Brunswick bar from a Whiskey Row fire in 1900 continued drinking at it while the rest of the row burned across the street. Whatever the case, the bar remains the centerpiece of the beautifully restored turn-of-the-20th-century structure, with a high, pressed-tin ceiling. Steaks and chops are the stars here, but the grilled fish and hearty corn chowder are fine, too. ⊠ *120 S. Montezuma St., Downtown* ☎ *928/541–1996* ☐ AE, MC, V.

$–$$ ✕ **Genovese.** Low-price, classic southern-Italian fare makes this restaurant near Courthouse Plaza a local favorite. Try the cannelloni stuffed with shrimp, crab, ricotta cheese, and spinach. ⊠ *217 W. Gurley St., Downtown* ☎ *928/541–9089* ☐ AE, MC, V.

¢–$$ ✕ **Prescott Brewing Company.** Good beer, good food, good service, and good prices—for a casual meal, it's hard to beat this cheerful restaurant. In addition to chili, fish-and-chips, and British-style bangers and mash, vegetarian enchiladas made with tofu, and pasta salad are on the menu. Fresh-baked beer bread comes with many entrées. ⊠*130 W. Gurley St., Downtown* ☎928/771–2795 ⊟AE, D, DC, MC, V.

¢–$ ✗ **El Charro Restaurant.** This is the best Mexican food in town: mostly heavy Sonoran food, and most of it homemade. The restaurant has been open since 1959, and the enchiladas, fajitas, and basic soft tacos are perennial customer favorites. The salsa has been tamed over the years, but ask for hot sauce and your wish will be granted. ⊠*120 N. Montezuma St., Downtown* ☎928/445–7130 ⊟AE, MC, V.

¢   ✗ **Kendall's Famous Burgers and Ice Cream.** A great diner, replete with booths and a 1950s-style soda fountain, Kendall's serves hamburgers cooked to order with your choice of 14 condiments. Make sure to try the homemade french fries. ⊠*113 S. Cortez St., Downtown* ☎928/778–3658 ⊟D, MC, V.

$$–$$$ ▥ **Prescott Resort Conference Center and Casino.** On a hill on the outskirts of town, this upscale property has views of the mountain ranges surrounding Prescott and the Valley, although many guests hardly notice, so riveted are they by the poker machines and slots in Arizona's only hotel casino. There are plenty of recreational facilities to occupy those able to resist the one-armed bandits. ⊠*1500 AZ 69, 86301* ☎928/776–1666 or 800/967–4637 ⊟928/776–8544 ⊕*www.prescottresort.com* ⊅*161 rooms* ☖*In-room: refrigerator. In-hotel: restaurant, bar, tennis courts, pool, gym, no-smoking rooms, public Wi-Fi* ⊟AE, D, DC, MC, V.

★ $–$$$ ▥ **Hassayampa Inn.** Built in 1927 for early automobile travelers, the Hassayampa Inn oozes character. The ceiling in the lobby is hand-painted, and some rooms still have the original furnishings. A free full breakfast of your choice at the restaurant gilds the lily of reasonable rates. The Peacock Room, the hotel's pretty—if overly formal—dining room, has tapestried booths, dim lighting, and better-than-average Continental food. ⊠*122 E. Gurley St., Downtown, 86301* ☎928/778–9434 or 800/322–1927 ⊟928/445–8590 ⊕*www.hassayampainn.com* ⊅*58 rooms, 10 suites* ☖*In-hotel: restaurant, bar* ⊟AE, D, DC, MC, V ℟*BP.*

$–$$ ▥ **Hotel Vendome.** This World War I–era hostelry has seen miners, health seekers, and such celebrities as cowboy star Tom Mix walk through its doors. Old-fashioned touches, including the original claw-foot tubs, remain and, like many other historic hotels, the Vendome has its obligatory resident ghost (her room costs slightly more). Only a block from Courthouse Plaza, this is a good choice for those who want to combine sightseeing, modern comforts, and good value. ⊠*230 Cortez St., Downtown, 86303* ☎928/776–0900 or 888/468–3583 ⊟928/771–0395 ⊕*www.vendomehotel.com* ⊅*16 rooms, 4 suites* ☖*In-hotel: bar, no-smoking rooms, no elevator* ⊟AE, D, DC, MC, V ℟*CP.*

¢–$ ▥ **Hotel St. Michael.** Don't expect serenity on the busiest corner of Courthouse Plaza, but for low rates and historic charm it's hard to beat this hotel in operation since 1900. Rooms have 1920s–40s-era antiques; some face the plaza and others look out on Thumb Butte. The first-floor Caffe St. Michael serves great coffee and croissants. ⊠*205 W. Gurley St., Downtown, 86303* ☎928/776–1999 or 800/678–3757 ⊟928/776–7318 ⊕*www.stmichaelhotel.com* ⊅*71 rooms* ☖*In-hotel: restaurant* ⊟AE, D, DC, MC, V.

NIGHTLIFE & THE ARTS

Prescott's popular **Bluegrass Festival on the Square** takes place in June. The town, which had its first organized cowboy competition in 1888, lays claim to having the world's oldest rodeo: the annual **Frontier Days** roundup, held on July 4 weekend at the Yavapai County Fairgrounds. In August the **Cowboy Poets Gathering** brings together campfire bards from around the country.

The **Prescott Fine Arts Association** (⊠*208 N. Marina St., Downtown* ☎*928/445–3286* ⊕*www.pfaa.net*) sponsors musicals and dramas, plays for children, and a concert series. The association's gallery also presents rotating exhibits by local, regional, and national artists. The **Prescott Jazz Society** (⊠*129½ N. Cortez St., Downtown* ☎*928/772–5019* ⊕*www.pjazz.org*) has an intimate storefront lounge. The **Yavapai Symphony Association** (⊠*228 N. Alarcon St., Suite B, Downtown* ☎*928/776–4255*) hosts performances by the Phoenix and Flagstaff symphonies; call ahead for schedules and venues.

Montezuma Street's Whiskey Row, off Courthouse Plaza, is nowhere near as wild as it was in its historic heyday, but most bars have live music—and a lively crowd—on the weekends. The **Hassayampa Inn** (⊠*122 E. Gurley St., Downtown* ☎*928/778–9434*) is an upscale, art-nouveau piano bar; there's always someone tickling the ivories on the weekend. **Hooligan's Pub** (⊠*112 Montezuma St., Downtown* ☎*928/771–0997*), above Matt's Saloon, has live entertainment nightly and a large dance floor. The Brunswick bar at **Lyzzard's Lounge** (⊠*120 N. Cortez St., Downtown* ☎*928/778–2244*) was shipped from England via the Colorado River.

SHOPPING

Shops selling antiques and collectibles line Cortez Street, just north of Courthouse Plaza. You'll find fun stuff—especially Western kitsch—as well as some good buys on valuable pieces. Many of the stores gather together groups of retailers. Courthouse Plaza, especially along Montezuma Street, is lined with specialty and gift shops. Many match those in Sedona for quality and price. Be sure to check out **Arts Prescott** (⊠*134 S. Montezuma St., Downtown* ☎*928/776–7717* ⊕*www.artsprescott. com*), a cooperative gallery of talented local craftspeople and artists. **Bashford Courts** (⊠*130 Gurley St., Downtown* ☎*928/445–9798*) has three floors of artsy stores. At 14,000 square feet, the **Merchandise Mart Antique Mall** (⊠*205 N. Cortez St., Downtown* ☎*928/776–1728*) is the largest of the town's collections of collectors. To get your fill of Old West kitsch, stop at **Prescott Museum & Trading Company** (⊠*142 S. Montezuma St., Downtown* ☎*928/776–8498*), which also displays vintage boots, saddles, and taxidermy. **Sun West Gallery** (⊠*152 S. Montezuma St., Downtown* ☎*928/778–1204*) has artwork, furnishings, and Native American Zapotec rugs.

NORTH-CENTRAL ARIZONA ESSENTIALS

To research prices, get advice from other travelers, and book travel arrangements, visit ⊕ *www.fodors.com.*

TRANSPORTATION

BY AIR

Most visitors reach this area of Central Arizona by car, but there are several nearby airports. Prescott Municipal Airport is 8 mi north of town on U.S. 89. Flagstaff Pulliam Airport is 3 mi south of town off I–17 at Exit 337. Sedona Airport is in West Sedona.

US Airways Express flies from Phoenix to Flagstaff Pulliam Airport. Sedona Airport is a base for several air tours but has no regularly scheduled flights. United Airlines and Frontier Airlines offer connecting service to Prescott Municipal Airport from Phoenix.

A taxi from the airport to downtown should cost about $8 to $10. Cabs are not regulated; some, but not all, have meters, so it's wise to agree on a rate before you leave for your destination.

Contacts Flagstaff Pulliam Airport (☎ *928/556–1234*). **Prescott Municipal Airport** (☎ *928/445–7860*). **Sedona Airport** (☎ *928/282–4487*).

BY BUS

Greyhound Lines has daily connections from throughout the West to Flagstaff, but none to Sedona. Buses also run between Prescott and Phoenix Sky Harbor International Airport.

The Sedona/Phoenix Shuttle makes eight trips daily between those cities; the fare is $45 one-way, $85 round-trip. You can also get on or off at Camp Verde, Cottonwood, or the Village of Oak Creek. The bus leaves from three terminals of Sky Harbor International Airport in Phoenix. Reservations are required.

Contacts Greyhound Lines (☎ *800/231–2222* ⊕ *www.greyhound.com*). **Sedona/ Phoenix Shuttle Service** (☎ *928/282–2066, 800/448–7988 in Arizona* ⊕ *www. sedona-phoenix-shuttle.com*).

BY CAR

It makes sense to rent a car in this region since trails and monuments stretch miles past city limits and many area towns cannot be reached by the major bus companies. The major rental agencies have offices in Flagstaff, Prescott, and Sedona. If you want to explore the red rocks of Sedona, you can rent a four-wheel-drive from one of the local agencies such as Canyon Jeep Rentals or Sedona Car Rental.

A Red Rock Pass is required to park anywhere in the Coconino National Forest from Oak Creek Canyon through Sedona. Passes cost $5 for the day, $15 for the week, or $20 for an entire year and can be purchased at four visitor centers surrounding and within Sedona. Passes are also available from vending machines at popular trailheads including Boynton Canyon, Bell Rock, and Huckaby. Locals widely resent the pass, feeling that free access to National Forests is a right. The Forest Service counters that it doesn't receive enough federal funds to maintain the land surrounding Sedona, trampled by 5 million visitors each year, and that a parking fee is the best way to raise revenue.

Flagstaff lies at the intersection of Interstate 40 (east–west) and I–17 (running south from Flagstaff), 134 mi north of Phoenix via I–17. The most direct route to Prescott from Phoenix is to take I–17 north for 60 mi to Cordes Junction and then drive northwest on AZ 69 for 36 mi into town. I–17, a four-lane divided highway, has several steep inclines and descents (complete with a number of runaway-truck ramps), but it's generally an easy and scenic thoroughfare. If you want to take the more leisurely route through Verde Valley to Prescott, continue north on I–17 another 25 mi past Cordes Junction until you see the turnoff for AZ 260, which will take you to Cottonwood in 12 mi. Here you can pick up AZ 89A, which leads southwest to Prescott (41 mi) or northeast to Sedona (19 mi).

Sedona stretches along AZ 89A, its main thoroughfare, which runs roughly east–west through town. To reach Sedona more directly from Phoenix, take I–17 north for 113 mi until you come to AZ 179; it's another 15 mi on that road into town. The trip should take about 2½ hours. The 27-mi drive from Sedona to Flagstaff on AZ 89A, which winds its way through Oak Creek Canyon, is breathtaking.

■TIP➔Weekend traffic near Sedona, especially during the high season, can approach gridlock on the narrow highways. Leave for your destination at first light to bypass the day-trippers, late risers, and midday heat.

Contacts **Canyon Jeep Rentals** (✉ *Oak Creek Terrace Resort, 4548 AZ 89A, Sedona* ☎ *928/282–6061 or 800/224–2229*). **Red Rock Pass** (☎ *928/282–4119 information only* ⊕ *www.redrockcountry.org*). **Sedona Car Rental** (✉ *Sedona Airport, Sedona* ☎ *928/282–2227 or 800/879–5337* ⊕ *www.sedonacarrental.com*).

BY TAXI

In Sedona, try Bob's Sedona Taxi. A Friendly Cab and Sun Taxi are also options. A–1 Quick Cab & Tours in Flagstaff provides local and long-distance service.

Information **A-1 Quick Cab & Tours** (☎ *928/527–0686*). **A Friendly Cab** (☎ *928/774–4444*). **Bob's Sedona Taxi** (☎ *928/282–1234*). **Sun Taxi** (☎ *928/774–7400*).

BY TRAIN

Amtrak comes into the downtown Flagstaff station twice daily. There's no rail service into Prescott or Sedona.

Information **Amtrak** (☎ *928/774–8679* ⊕ *www.Amtrak.com*).

CONTACTS & RESOURCES

EMERGENCIES
Ambulance, Fire & Police **Ambulance, Fire, and Police Emergencies** (☎ *911*).

Hospitals Flagstaff Medical Center (✉1200 N. Beaver St., Flagstaff ☎928/779–3366). The **Verde Valley Medical Center Sedona Campus** (✉3700 W. AZ 89A, Sedona ☎928/204–3000). **Yavapai Regional Medical Center** (✉1003 Willow Creek Rd., Prescott ☎928/445–2700).

Pharmacies in Flagstaff Most grocery stores have in-house pharmacies, and Flagstaff, Sedona, and Prescott are home to most national pharmacy chains. **Flagstaff Medical Center Pharmacy** (✉1200 N. Beaver St., Flagstaff ☎928/779–3366).

Pharmacy in Prescott Goodwin Street Pharmacy (✉406 W. Goodwin St., Prescott ☎928/445–3550).

Pharmacies in Sedona Walgreens (✉1995 W. AZ 89A, Sedona ☎928/282–2528).

TOUR OPTIONS

IN FLAGSTAFF The Ventures program, run by the education department of the Museum of Northern Arizona, offers tours of the area led by local scientists, artists, and historians. Trips might include rafting excursions down the San Juan River, treks into the Grand Canyon or Colorado Plateau backcountry, or bus tours into the Navajo reservation to visit with Native American artists. Prices start at about $160 for cultural tours and go up to $1,250 for outdoor adventures, with most tours in the $750 to $850 range.

IN SEDONA Sedona Trolley offers two types of daily orientation tours, both departing from the main bus stop in Uptown and lasting less than an hour. One goes along AZ 179 to the Chapel of the Holy Cross, with stops at Tlaquepaque and some galleries; the other passes through West Sedona to Boynton Canyon (Enchantment Resort). Rates are $10 for one or $19 for both.

Several jeep-tour operators headquartered along Sedona's main Uptown drag conduct excursions, some focusing on geology, some on astronomy, some on vortices, some on all three. You can even find a combination jeep tour and horseback ride.

The ubiquitous Pink Jeep Tours are a popular choice. Sedona Red Rock Jeep Tours is also a reliable operator. Prices start at about $50 per person for two hours and go upward of $100 per person for four hours. Although all the excursions are safe, many are not for those who dislike heights or bumps.

Prices for hot-air-balloon tours generally start at $190 per person for one to two hours. The only two companies with permits to fly over Sedona are Northern Light Balloon Expeditions and Red Rock Balloon Adventures.

> **WORD OF MOUTH**
>
> "My husband and I were in Sedona last June and I would definitely recommend the Pink Jeep tour. It takes you on 'roads' that no car can travel on and you see some wonderful scenery. You also make a couple of stops to walk around and see breathtaking views. Plus the ride itself is great! It was a lot of fun and one of our best memories of that trip. I highly recommend it."
> —teddysmom

A Day in the West will take you to all the prime spots and help you take your best (photographic) shot. Rates are $55 per person for a basic two-hour tour.

Contacts A Day in the West (☎ *928/282-4320 or 800/973-3662* ⊕ *www.aday inthewest.com*). **Museum of Northern Arizona** (☎ *928/774-5213* ⊕ *www.musnaz. org*). **Northern Light Balloon Expeditions** (☎ *928/282-2274 or 800/230-6222* ⊕ *www.northernlightballoon.com*). **Pink Jeep Tours** (✉ *204 N. AZ 89A, Sedona* ☎ *928/282-5000 or 800/873-3662* ⊕ *www.pinkjeep.com*). **Red Rock Balloon Adventures** (☎ *928/284-0040 or 800/258-3754* ⊕ *www.redrockballoons.com*). **Sedona Red Rock Jeep Tours** (✉ *270 N. AZ 89A, Sedona* ☎ *928/282-6826 or 800/848-7728* ⊕ *www.redrockjeep.com*). **Sedona Trolley** (☎ *928/282-4211* ⊕ *www.sedonatrolley.com*).

VISITOR INFORMATION

Information Camp Verde Chamber of Commerce (☎ *928/567-9294* ⊕ *www. campverde.org*). **Clarkdale Chamber of Commerce** (☎ *928/634-9438* ⊕ *www. clarkdalechamber.com*). **Cottonwood Chamber of Commerce** (☎ *928/634-7593* ⊕ *www.cottonwood.verdevalley.com*). **Flagstaff Visitors Center** (☎ *928/774-9541 or 800/842-7293* ⊕ *www.flagstaffarizona.org*). **Jerome Chamber of Commerce** (☎ *928/634-2900* ⊕ *www.jeromechamber.com*). **Prescott Chamber of Commerce** (☎ *928/445-2000 or 800/266-7534* ⊕ *www.prescott.org*). **Sedona-Oak Creek Canyon Chamber of Commerce** (☎ *928/282-7722 or 800/288-7336* ⊕ *www.sedonachamber.com*).

Northeast Arizona

A visitor to the Lower Antelope Canyon

WORD OF MOUTH

"Antelope Canyon...I remembered to take with my tripod and it was needed. I must have taken more than 30 photos. The midday sun bouncing off the canyon walls and the hanging dust were truly amazing.... The canyon is about 200 yards long and almost perfectly level from front to back. A very easy meandering walk and photo session. The curved walls and reflecting light made for quite a sight that should not be missed by anybody passing through the area."

—Myer

WELCOME TO NORTHEAST ARIZONA

TOP REASONS TO GO

★ **Drive the Rim Roads at Canyon de Chelly:** Visit one of the most spectacular natural wonders in the Southwest, rivaling the Grand Canyon for beauty. It's a must for photography buffs.

★ **Go Boating at Glen Canyon:** Get to know this stunning, mammoth reservoir by taking a boat out on Lake Powell, amid the towering cliffs.

★ **Explore Hubbell Trading Post:** Take the self-guided tour to experience the relationship between the Native people and the Indian traders.

★ **Shop for Handmade Crafts on the Hopi Mesas:** Pick up crafts by some of Arizona's leading artisans among the Hopi, who sustain their culture through the continuous occupation of the ancient villages on these mesas.

★ **Take a Jeep Tour Through Monument Valley:** On an excursion through this this 92,000-acre area, see the landscape depicted in such iconic western films as *Stagecoach* and *The Searchers*.

1 Navajo Nation East. Vastly underrated Canyon de Chelly National Monument offers some of the most spectacular panoramas in the world, and Window Rock is the governmental and cultural hub of the Navajo people.

2 The Hopi Mesas. An artistically rich and dramatically situated tribal land entirely surrounded by Navajo Nation, the Hopi Mesas rise above the high-desert floor, rife with trading posts and art galleries selling fine weavings, jewelry, and crafts.

3 Navajo Nation West. Just 80 mi east of the Grand Canyon's South Rim, the bustling community of Tuba City anchors the western portion of Navajo Nation— it's an excellent base for checking out the region's painted-desert landscapes and Navajo trading posts.

4 Monument Valley. You've probably seen images of this ancestral Puebloan stomping ground in everything from classic Western movies to Ansel Adams photos; you can explore this sweeping valley on a variety of Indian-led tours.

5 Glen Canyon Dam & Lake Powell. The one section of northeastern Arizona not set on Indian lands is dominated by the nation's second-largest man-made body of water, Lake Powell, and 710-foot-tall Glen Canyon Dam; it's a boating paradise, and the town of Page has the greatest number of hotels and restaurants in the region.

Monument Valley, Navajo Tribal Park

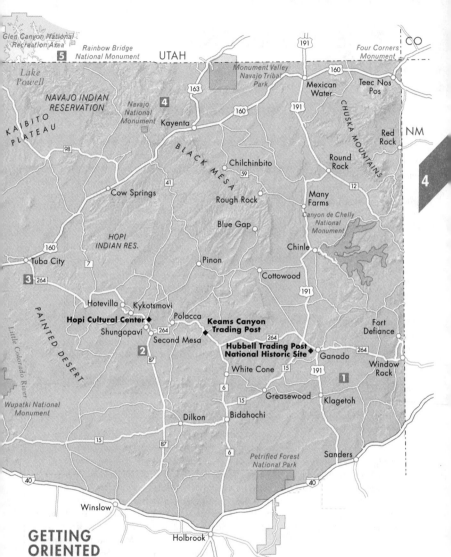

GETTING ORIENTED

Relatively few visitors experience the vast, sweeping northeast quadrant of Arizona, which comprises the Navajo and Hopi reservations but efforts to spend a few days here are rewarded with stunning scenery and the chance to learn about some of the world's most vibrant indigenous communities. This is part of the West's great Four Corners Region, home to the underrated and spectacular Canyon de Chelly National Monument as well as the dramatic buttes and canyons of Monument Valley. The one portion of the area outside tribal lands is Page, the anchor for exploring the 200 mi of shoreline that fringe crystalline Lake Powell.

NORTHEAST ARIZONA PLANNER

Getting Here & Around

It's possible to fly into Page's small airport from Phoenix and rent a car, but most travelers arrive by car, either from Phoenix (220 mi to Tuba City, 330 mi to Window Rock) or some destination on the way, such as Sedona (100 mi to Tuba City) or the South Rim of the Grand Canyon (80 mi to Tuba City). Many visitors see northeastern Arizona as part of a road-tripping adventure through the Four Corner Region, perhaps combining a visit here with trips to the national parks of southern Utah and southwestern Colorado. This "en route" road-tripping strategy makes the most sense for most travelers, especially given the region's stunningly scenic drives.

It's virtually impossible to see much of northeastern Arizona without a car—this is your best bet not only for getting here, but also for visiting attractions and communities throughout the region.

Making the Most of Your Time

Northeastern Arizona encompasses an enormous area but relatively few key attractions, so it's best to use one or two primary communities (Page or Tuba City on the west side, Kayenta on the north, and Chinle or Window Rock on the east) as bases for day trips to outlying attractions. If your time is limited, put Canyon de Chelly and Monument Valley at the top of your list—if you're ambitious, you could explore these two sites on consecutive days, spending the night in either Chinle or Kayenta. Focus on the South Rim Drive at Canyon de Chelly, and in Monument Valley, book a jeep tour with the highly respected Sacred Monument Tours. On travel days from one base community to another, plan a scenic drive, such as AZ 264 from Tuba City to Window Rock (don't miss the great crafts shopping at Second Mesa), or AZ 98 to U.S. 160 to U.S. 191 from Page to Chinle. Give yourself at least two days to get to know any one part of the region, and as much as a week to 10 days to fully explore all of it.

If You Like Hiking

Some of the best hikes in this region are in Canyon de Chelly, up the streambed between the soaring vermilion, orange, and white sandstone cliffs, with the remains of the ancient ancestral Puebloan communities frequently in view. Mummy Cave is especially worth a look, its three-story watchtower nearly perfectly preserved. The more weathered Antelope House and White House stand against the sweeping canyon cliffs as impressive reminders of a bygone era. The Navajo National Monument offers impressive hikes to two ruins: Beta-Takin, a settlement dating back to AD 1250, and Keet Seel, which dates back as far as AD 950. Both are in alcoves at the base of gigantic overhanging cliffs. Remember, you cannot hike or camp on private property or tribal land without a backcountry permit.

Local Food & Lodging

Northeastern Arizona is a vast area with small hamlets and towns scattered miles apart, and there are few stores or restaurants along the highway. With the exception of Page, which has more culinary variety, most of the region's restaurants serve basic but tasty Native American and Southwestern cuisine. Navajo and Hopi favorites include mutton stew, Hopi *piki* (paper-thin, blue-corn bread), and Navajo fry bread. Navajo tacos are fry bread piled with refried beans, ground beef, lettuce, tomato, scallions, cheese, avocado, sour cream, and salsa. Top the fry bread with butter, honey, and confectioner's sugar for a delicious dessert.

Page also has the area's greatest concentration of lodgings, most of them fairly standard chain motels and hotels, but this base camp for exploring Lake Powell also has several bed-and-breakfasts as well as houseboat rentals. You'll find a handful of well-maintained chains in the Navajo Nation, mostly in Kayenta, Chinle, Tuba City, and Window Rock. This is also a popular area for both tent and RV camping—you can obtain a list of campgrounds from the Page/Lake Powell Chamber of Commerce and the Navajo Nation Visitor Center.

Festivals to Plan a Trip Around

A number of festivals and events take place among the Navajo and Hopi communities.

The Navajo Nation Annual Tribal Fair takes place the first weekend of September after Labor Day, at Window Rock. It's the world's largest Native American fair and includes a rodeo, traditional Navajo music and dances, food booths, and an intertribal powwow.

The Hopi Harvest Festival, in August and September, is a celebration featuring Harvest and Butterfly social dances.

The Central Navajo Fair is in late August, in Chinle.

What It Costs

	¢	$	$$	$$$	$$$$
Restaurants	under $8	$8–$12	$13–$20	$21–$30	over $30
Hotels	under $70	$70–$120	$121–$175	$176–$250	over $250

Restaurant prices are per person for a main course at dinner. Hotel prices are for a standard double in high season, excluding taxes and service charges.

What Time Is It?

Unlike the rest of Arizona (including the Hopi Reservation), the Navajo Reservation observes daylight saving time. Thus for half the year—April to October—it's an hour later on the Navajo Reservation than everywhere else in the state.

Updated
by Andrew
Collins

NORTHEAST ARIZONA IS A VAST and magnificent land of lofty buttes, towering cliffs, and turquoise skies so clear that horizons appear endless. Most of the land in the area belongs to the Navajo and Hopi peoples, who cling to ancient traditions based on spiritual values, kinship, and an affinity for nature. In many respects life on the Hopi Mesas has changed little during the last two centuries, and visiting this land can feel like traveling to a foreign country. In such towns as Tuba City and Window Rock it's not uncommon to hear the gliding vowels and soft consonants of the Navajo language, a tongue as different from Hopi as English is from Chinese. As you drive in the vicinity, tune your AM radio to 660 KTNN, the Voice of the Navajo Nation since 1985. You'll quickly understand why the U.S. Marine Navajo "code talkers" communicating in their native tongue were able to devise a code within their language that was never broken by the Japanese.

The Navajo Nation encompasses more than 27,000 square mi, an area that would rank it larger than 10 of the 50 states. In its approximate center sits the nearly 3,000-square-mi Hopi Reservation, a series of adobe villages built on high mesas overlooking the cultivated land. On Arizona's northern and eastern borders, where the Navajo Nation continues into Utah and New Mexico, the Navajo and Canyon de Chelly national monuments contain haunting cliff dwellings of ancient people who lived in the area some 1,500 years ago. Glen Canyon Dam, which abuts the far northwestern corner of the reservation on U.S. 89, holds back more than 200 mi of emerald waters known as Lake Powell.

Most of northeast Arizona is desert country, but it's far from boring: eerie and spectacular rock formations as colorful as desert sunsets highlight immense mesas, canyons, and cliffs; towering stands of ponderosa pine cover the Chuska Mountains to the north and east of Canyon de Chelly. Navajo Mountain to the north and west in Utah soars more than 10,000 feet, and the San Francisco Peaks climb to similar heights to the south and west by Flagstaff. According to the Navajo creation myth, these are two of the four mountainous boundaries of the sacred land where the Navajo first emerged from Earth's interior.

NAVAJO NATION EAST

Land has always been central to the history of the Navajo people: it's embedded in their very name. The Tewa were the first to call them *Navahu*—which means "large area of cultivated land." But according to the Navajo creation myth, they were given the name *ni'hookaa diyan diné*—"holy earth people"—by their creators. Today, among tribal members, they call themselves the Diné. The eastern portion of the Arizona Navajo Nation (in Navajo, *diné bikéyah*) is a dry but often surprisingly green land, especially in the vicinity of the aptly named Beautiful Valley, south of Canyon de Chelly along U.S. 191. A landscape of rolling hills, wide arroyos, and small canyons, the area is dotted with traditional Navajo hogans, sheepfolds, cattle tanks, and wood racks. The region's easternmost portion is marked by tall mountains

GOOD DRIVING TOURS

IF YOU HAVE 2 DAYS

If you're just driving through the area on your way across the state, you might start off in ⌂ **Window Rock ❶** ⌐. From here, it's an easy drive to some of the most interesting sights in northeastern Arizona. On your first day, visit **Canyon de Chelly ❷**. On the second, set out for the **Hopi Mesas ❺–❼**, stopping along the way at **Hubbell Trading Post National Historic Site ❸** and, perhaps, **Keams Canyon Trading Post ❹** for a mid-morning snack. If you're headed next toward the Grand Canyon, continue toward the **Hopi Mesas ❺–❼** and into **Tuba City ❽**. If you're planning to continue across toward Flagstaff or Sedona, you can head south from Keams Canyon Area toward I–40.

IF YOU HAVE 5 DAYS

If you plan to spend a bit more time exploring the region after a trip to the Grand Canyon, head north on U.S. 89 on your first day to ⌂ **Tuba City ❽** ⌐. Along the way, stop by **Cameron Trading Post ❾** for a light lunch and some shopping. Explore Tuba City and relax here the night. On the second day, head east at Moenkopi on AZ 264 for the **Hopi Mesas ❺–❼**. (And fill your tank before you leave since Tuba City is the last stop for gas before the mesas.) Have lunch at the **Hopi Cultural Center,** then return to Tuba City and head northeast on U.S. 160 toward ⌂ **Kayenta ❿**, where you can spend your second night. Get up early the next day to visit the **Navajo National Monument ⓮**, hiking to Beta-Takin or Keet Seel pueblo (remember you need to make reservations in advance). Spend your third night at the lodge at ⌂ **Goulding's Trading Post ⓭** in Monument Valley. The next day, visit **Monument Valley Navajo Tribal Park ⓫**, and then take U.S. 160 north to U.S. 191 and head south for Chinle, a good base for touring ⌂ **Canyon de Chelly ❷**.

and towering sandstone cliffs cut by primitive roads that are generally accessible only by horse or four-wheel-drive vehicles.

Numbers in the margin correspond to numbers on the Northeast Arizona map.

WINDOW ROCK

⌐ ❶ *192 mi from Flagstaff, east 160 mi on I–40, then north on Hwy. 12; 26 mi from Gallup, New Mexico, north on U.S. 491 and west on NM 264 (which becomes AZ 264).*

Named for the immense arch-shaped "window" in a massive sandstone ridge above the city, Window Rock is the capital of the Navajo Nation and the center of its Tribal Government. With a population of around 3,000, this community serves as the business and social center for Navajo families throughout the reservation. Window Rock is a good place to stop for food, supplies, and gas.

The **Navajo Nation Council Chambers** is a handsome structure that resembles a large ceremonial hogan. The murals on the walls depict scenes

Reservation Rules

Visitors to the Navajo Nation and Hopi Reservation should observe several rules, as follows:

Alcohol & Drugs: The possession and consumption of alcoholic beverages or illicit drugs is illegal on Hopi and Navajo land. You can't purchase alcohol legally while you are on the reservations, and you shouldn't bring any with you.

Camping: No open fires are allowed in reservation campgrounds; you must use grills or fireplaces. You may not gather firewood on the reservation—bring your own. Camping areas have quiet hours from 11 PM to 6 AM. Pets must be kept on a leash or confined. Don't litter.

Hopi Shrines: Hopi spirituality is intertwined with daily life, and objects that seem ordinary to you may have deeper significance. If you come upon a collection of objects at or near the Hopi Mesas do not disturb them.

Permits & Permissions: No off-trail hiking, rock climbing, or other off-road travel is allowed unless you are accompanied by a local guide. A tribal permit is required for fishing. Violations of fish and game laws are punishable by heavy fines, imprisonment, or both.

Photography: Always ask permission before taking photos of locals. Even if no money is requested, consider offering a dollar or two to the person whose photo you have taken. The Navajo are very open about photographs; the Hopi do not allow photographs at all, including videos, tape recordings, notes, or even sketches.

Religious Ceremonies: Should you see a ceremony in progress, look for posted signs indicating who is welcome. If there are no signs, check with local shops or the village community to see if the ceremony is open to the public. Unless you're specifically invited, stay out of kivas (ceremonial rooms) and stay on the periphery of dances or processions.

Respect for the Land: Do not wander through residential areas or disturb property. Do not disturb or remove animals, plants, rocks, petrified wood, or artifacts. They are protected by Tribal Antiquity and federal laws.

in the history of the tribe, and the bell beside the entrance was a gift to the tribe by the Santa Fe Railroad to commemorate the thousands of Navajos who worked to build the railroad. Visitors can observe sessions of the council, where 88 delegates representing 110 reservation chapters meet on the third Monday of January, April, July, and October. Turn east off Indian Highway 12, about ½ mi north of AZ 264, to reach the Council Chambers. **Window Rock Navajo Tribal Park & Veteran's Memorial,** near the Council Chambers, is a memorial park honoring Navajo veterans, including the famous World War II code talkers. ⊠*AZ 264* ☎*928/871–6647, 928/871–6417 for guided tours* ⊕*www.navajonationparks.org.*

The **Navajo Museum,** on the grounds of the former Tse Bonito Park off AZ 264, is devoted to the art, culture, and history of the Navajo people and has an excellent library on the Navajo Nation. The museum hosts exhibitions of Native artists each season; call for a list of shows.

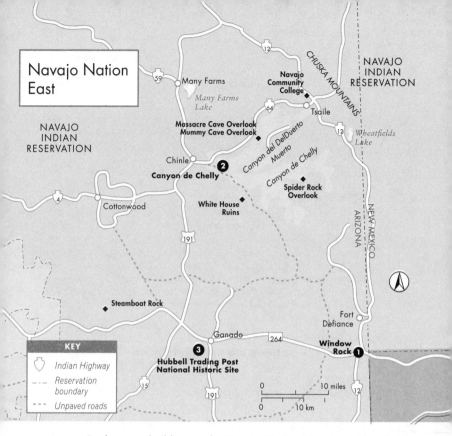

NAVAJO
INDIAN
RESERVATION

NAVAJO
INDIAN
RESERVATION

CHUSKA MOUNTAINS

Many Farms

Many Farms
Lake

Navajo
Community
College

Tsaile

Massacre Cave Overlook
Mummy Cave Overlook

Wheatfields
Lake

Chinle

2

Canyon de Chelly

Canyon del DelDuerto
Muerto

Canyon de Chelly

Spider Rock
Overlook

Cottonwood

White House
Ruins

ARIZONA

NEW MEXICO

Steamboat Rock

Fort
Defiance

Ganado

Window
Rock **1**

KEY

Indian Highway

Reservation
boundary

Unpaved roads

3

Hubbell Trading Post
National Historic Site

0   10 miles

0   10 km

In the same building as the Navajo Nation Museum is the **Navajo Nation Visitor Center,** a great resource for all sorts of information on reservation activities. Within walking distance of the Navajo Museum, the **Navajo Arts and Crafts Enterprises** (⊕*www.gonavajo.com/navajoart*) displays local artwork, including pottery, jewelry, and blankets. ⊠*AZ 264, next to Quality Inn Navajo Nation* ☎*928/871–7941* ⊕*www. discovernavajo.com* ⊠*Free* ⊘*Mon. and Sat. 8–5, Tues.–Fri. 8–8.*

☾ Amid the sandstone monoliths on the border of Arizona and New Mexico, the **Navajo Nation Botanical and Zoological Park** displays about 30 species of domestic and native animals, birds, and amphibians that figure in Navajo legends, as well as examples of plants used by traditional people. Most of the animals here were brought in as orphans or after sustaining injuries. It's the only Native American–owned-and-operated zoo in the United States. ⊠*AZ 264, northeast of Navajo Nation Museum* ☎*928/871–6573* ⊕*www.discovernavajo.com* ⊠*Free* ⊘*Wed.–Sun. 10–5.*

Many all-Indian rodeos are held near the center of downtown at
☾ the **Navajo Tribal Fairgrounds.** The community hosts the annual Fourth of July celebration, with a major rodeo, ceremonial dances, and a parade. The Navajo Nation Tribal Fair, much like a traditional state fair, is held in early September. It offers standard county-fair rides,

midway booths, contests, powwow competitions, and an all-Indian rodeo. ✉*AZ 264* ☎*928/871–6647 Navajo Nation Fair Office* 🌐*www.navajonationfair.com.*

WHERE TO STAY

¢–$ **Navajo Land Days Inn.** This well-kept, affordable chain property in St. Michaels, 3 mi west of Window Rock, has standard rooms decorated in Southwestern style. ✉*392 W. AZ 264, St. Michaels 86511* ☎*928/871–5690 or 800/329–7466* 🌐*www.daysinn.com* *65 rooms, 8 suites* *In-room: Wi-Fi. In-hotel: restaurant, pool, gym, some pets allowed* *AE, D, MC, V.*

¢–$ **Quality Inn Navajo Nation Capital.** Rooms in this two-story beam-and-stucco hotel are decorated with a Navajo-style palette of tan, orange, and yellow that complements the basic pine furniture. The Diné Restaurant ($–$$)serves Navajo and Southwestern fare (you can build your own Navajo tacos) plus a handful of American standards, and the gift shop sells authentic Navajo jewelry. The hotel is within walking distance of Navajo Nation Museum. ✉*48 W. AZ 264, at Hwy. 12, 86515* ☎*928/871–4108 or 800/662–6189* 🌐*www.explorenavajo.com* *56 rooms* *In-hotel: restaurant, public Internet, some pets allowed* *AE, D, MC, V* *CP.*

SHOPPING

★ An outlet of the **Navajo Arts and Crafts Enterprises** (✉*AZ 264 at Hwy. 12, next to Quality Inn Navajo Nation Capital* ☎*928/871–4090 or 866/871–4095* 🌐*www.gonavajo.com/navajoart*) stocks tribal art purchased from craftspeople across the reservation, including stunning silverwork, traditional Navajo dolls, pottery, and rugs. Local artisans are occasionally at work here. Major credit cards are accepted.

CANYON DE CHELLY

❷ *30 mi west of Window Rock on AZ 264, then north 25 mi on U.S. 191.*

Fodor's Choice ★

Home to ancestral Puebloans from AD 350 to 1300, the nearly 84,000-acre Canyon de Chelly (pronounced d'*shay*) is one of the most spectacular natural wonders in the Southwest. On a smaller scale, it rivals the Grand Canyon for beauty. Its main gorges—the 26-mi-long Canyon de Chelly ("canyon in the rock") and the adjoining 35-mi Canyon del Muerto ("canyon of the dead")—comprise sheer, heavily eroded sandstone walls that rise to 1,100 feet over dramatic valleys. Ancient pictographs and petroglyphs decorate some of the cliffs, and within the canyon complex there are more than 7,000 archaeological sites. Stone walls rise hundreds of feet above streams, hogans, tilled fields, and sheep-grazing lands.

The first inhabitants of the canyons arrived more than 2,000 years ago—anthropologists call them the basket makers because baskets were the predominant artifacts they left behind. By AD 750, however, the basket makers had disappeared—their reason for leaving the region is unknown, but some speculate they were forced to leave because of encroaching cultures or climatic changes—and they were replaced by Pueblo tribes who constructed stone cliff dwellings. The departure of the Pueblo people around AD 1300 is widely believed to have resulted from changing climatic conditions, soil erosion, dwindling local resources, disease, and internal conflict. Present-day Hopi see these people as their ancestors. Beginning around AD 780, Hopi farmers settled here, followed by the Navajo around 1300. The Navajo migrated from far northern Canada; no one is sure when they first arrived in the Southwest. Despite evidence to the contrary, most Navajos hold that their people have always lived here and that the Diné passed through three previous underworlds before emerging into this, the fourth or Glittering World.

> **WORD OF MOUTH**
>
> "Canyon de Chelly and Moab were real highlights for me. We hiked de Chelly with a guide arranged through the visitor center…He was wonderful!!! We learned so much and saw the canyon intimately—hiking, climbing on the rocks, sometimes using footholds that had been carved out centuries before. The hike was filled with ruins, petroglyphs, vegetation and lore. Don't miss Canyon de Chelly, it's not just another canyon."
> —thelmaandlouise

You can view prehistoric ruins near the base of cliffs and perched on high, sheltering ledges, some of which you can access from the park's two main drives along the canyon rims. The dwellings and cultivated fields of the present-day Navajo lie in the flatlands between the cliffs, and those who inhabit the canyon today farm much the way their ancestors did. Most residents leave the canyon in winter but return in early spring to farm.

The **visitor center** has exhibits on the history of the cliff dwellers and provides information on scheduled hikes, tours, and National Park Service programs offered throughout the summer months.

Both Canyon de Chelly and Canyon del Muerto have a paved rim drive with turnoffs and parking areas. Each drive takes a minimum of two hours—allow more if you plan to hike to White House Rim, picnic in a parking area, or spend time photographing the sites. Overlooks along the rim drives provide incredible views of the canyon; be sure to stay on trails and away from the canyon edge, and to control children and pets at all times.

★ The **South Rim Drive** (36 mi round-trip with seven overlooks) of Canyon de Chelly starts at the visitor center and ends at **Spider Rock Overlook,** where cliffs plunge 1,000 feet to the canyon floor. The view here is of two pinnacles, Speaking Rock and Spider Rock; the latter rises about 800 feet from the canyon floor and is considered a sacred place. Other highlights on the South Rim Drive are Junction Overlook, where Canyon del Muerto joins Canyon de Chelly; White House Overlook, from which a 2½-mi round-trip trail leads to the **White House Ruin,** with dwelling remains of nearly 60 rooms and several kivas; and Sliding House Overlook, where you can see ruins on a narrow, sloped ledge across the canyon. The carved and sometimes narrow trail down the canyon side to White House Ruin is the only access into Canyon de Chelly without a guide—but if you have a fear of heights, this may not be the hike for you.

The **North Rim Drive** (34 mi round-trip with four overlooks) of Canyon del Muerto also begins at the visitor center and continues northeast on Indian Highway 64 toward the town of Tsaile. Major stops include Antelope House Overlook, the site of a large ruin named for the animals painted on an adjacent cliff; the Mummy Cave Overlook, where two mummies were found inside a remarkably unspoiled pueblo dwelling; and Massacre Cave Overlook, which marks the spot where an estimated 115 Navajo were killed by the Spanish in 1805. (The rock walls of the cave are still pockmarked from the Spaniards' ricocheting bullets.) ⊠ *Indian Hwy. 7, 3 mi east of U.S. 191, Chinle* ☎ *928/674–5500 visitor center* ⊕ *www.nps.gov/cach* ☎ *Free* ☉ *Daily 8–5.*

In Tsaile, Navajo medicine men worked with architects to design the town's six-story **Diné College,** the first Native American–owned community college in the country. Because all important Navajo activities traditionally take place in a circle (a hogan is essentially circular), the campus was laid out in the round, with the buildings inside its perimeter covered in reflective glass to mirror the piñon-covered landscape surrounding the campus. Diné College's **Hatathli Museum and Art Gallery** contains art and exhibits on Navajo culture as well as intertribal exhibits from across the United States. ⊠ *Indian Hwy. 12, south of Indian Hwy. 64, Tsaile* ☎ *928/724–3311 college, 928/724–6654 museum* ☎ *By donation* ☉ *Museum weekdays 8:30–4.*

To the north of Tsaile are the impressive **Chuska Mountains,** covered with sprawling stands of ponderosa pine. There are no established hiking trails in the Chuska Mountains, but up-to-date hiking information and backcountry-use permits (rarely granted if a Navajo guide does not accompany the trip) can be obtained through the Navajo Nation. ⊠ *Navajo Nation Parks and Recreation Department, Bldg. 36A, E. AZ 264, Window Rock* ☎ *928/871–6647* ⊕ *www.navajonationparks.org.*

SPORTS & THE OUTDOORS

HIKING   From late May through early September, free three-hour ranger-led hikes depart from the visitor center at 9 AM. Also in summer, two four-hour hikes (about $10 per person) leave from the visitor center in the morning and afternoon. Some trails are strenuous and steep; others are easy or moderate. Those with health concerns or a fear of heights should proceed with caution. Call ahead: hikes are occasionally canceled due to local customs or events.

Only one hike within Canyon de Chelly National Monument—the **White House Ruin Trail** on the South Rim Drive—can be undertaken without an authorized guide. The trail starts near White House Overlook and runs along sheer walls that drop about 550 feet. If you have concerns about height, be aware that the path gets narrow and somewhat

PLANNING FOR CANYON DE CHELLY

To get even a basic sense of the park's scope and history, plan to spend at least a full day here. If time is short, the best strategy is to spend some time at the visitor center and then drive the most magnificent of the two park roads, South Rim Drive. You could, theoretically, drive both park roads in one day, but it's better to set aside a second day for North Rim Drive. From the different overlooks along the park roads, you'll be treated to amazing photo ops of the valley floors below, and you can also access certain ruins. For a more in-depth look at Canyon de Chelly, con-sider one of the guided hiking, jeep, or horseback tours into the canyon.

Guided tours all allow visits directly into the canyons, not just the park drives high above them; jeep tours even have the option of camping overnight. Each kind of tour has its pros and cons: you'll cover the most ground in a jeep; horseback trips get you close to one of the park's most notable geological formations, Spider Rock; and guided walks provide the most leisurely pace and an excellent opportunity to interact with your guide and ask questions. You can also plan a custom treks lasting up to a week.

slippery along the way. The hike is 2½ mi round-trip, and hikers should carry their own drinking water.

Private, guided hikes to the interior of the canyons cost about $15 per hour with a three-hour minimum for groups of up to four people. (Don't venture into the canyon without a guide or you'll face a stiff fine.) For overnights, you'll need a guide as well as permission to stay on private land. If you have a four-wheel-drive vehicle and want to drive yourself, guides will accompany you for a charge of about $15 an hour with a three-hour minimum for up to three vehicles. All Navajo guides are members of the **Tsegi Guide Association** (⊠*Canyon de Chelly Visitor Center, Indian Hwy. 7, Chinle* ☎*928/674–5500*). You can hire a guide on the spot at the visitor center, or you can call ahead and make a reservation.

HORSEBACK RIDING
★
Totsonii Ranch (⊠*South Rim Dr.Chinle* ☎*928/755–6209* ⊕*www. totsoniiranch.com*), 13 mi from the visitor center at the end of the paved road, offers several types of tours into different parts of Canyon de Chelly: Canyon Rim (two hours), Three Turkey Ruins (four hours), Spider Rock (four hours), White House Ruins (six to seven hours), Canyon de Chelly overview (eight to nine hours), and one- and two-night treks. Some of these trips are geared only toward skilled adult riders, such as the Canyon Rim trips, which encounter steep terrain and offer amazing views. Spider Rock is a great choice for virtually any skill level and can be done in a half day—the ride leads right to the base of this 800-foot iconic pillar. Rates are $15 per hour per person plus $15 per hour per guide.

JEEP TOURS
Canyon de Chelly Tours (☎*928/674–3772* ⊕*www.canyondechellytours. com*) offers private jeep tours into Canyon de Chelly and arranges group tours and overnight camping in the canyon as well as late afternoon

and evening tours. Entertainment such as storytellers, music, and Navajo legends can be arranged with advance reservation. Rates begin around $50 per person for three-hour tours, or $25 per hour per car if you use your own SUV. Treks with **Thunderbird Lodge Canyon Tours** (✉*Thunderbird Lodge Gift Shop, Indian Hwy. 7, Chinle* ☎928/674–5841 or 800/679–2473 ⊕*www.tbirdlodge.com*), in six-wheel-drive vehicles, are available from late spring to late fall. Half-day tours are $41 and start at 9 AM and 1 or 2 PM daily; all-day tours cost $67 and include lunch.

> **WORD OF MOUTH**
>
> "Don't obsess too much over accommodations at Canyon de Chelly—they're all pretty basic without much ambience. The main experience is the Canyon itself."
> —Cher

WALKING TOURS   **Footpath Journey Tours** (☎928/724–3366 ⊕*www.footpathjourneys.com*) offers custom weeklong treks into the canyon for $750, not including food.

WHERE TO STAY & EAT

Chinle is the closest town to Canyon de Chelly. There are good lodgings with restaurants, as well as a supermarket and a campground. Be aware that you'll probably be approached by panhandlers in the grocery store parking lot. In late August each year, Chinle is host to the Central Navajo Fair, a public celebration complete with a rodeo, carnival, and traditional dances.

$–$$ ✕🏠 **Holiday Inn Canyon de Chelly.** Once Garcia's Trading Post, this hotel near Canyon de Chelly is less generic than you might expect: the exterior is territorial fort in style, although the rooms are predictably pastel and contemporary. The lobby restaurant (¢–$$), low-key by most standards, is the most upscale eatery in the area, serving well-prepared specialties such as mutton stew with fry bread and honey. They also sell a box picnic for guests and there is a gift shop stocked with local Native American arts and crafts. ✉*Indian Hwy. 7* 🏠*Box 1889, Chinle 86503* ☎928/674–5000 or 888/465–4329 ⊕*www.holidayinn.com* 🛏*108 rooms* ⚑*In-room: Wi-Fi. In-hotel: restaurant, gym, pool* ▤*AE, D, DC, MC, V.*

$ ✕🏠 **Best Western Canyon de Chelly Inn.** This two-story motel about 3 mi from Canyon de Chelly has cheerful rooms with modern oak furnishings. All rooms have coffeemakers. The on-site Junction restaurant ($–$$) opens for breakfast at 7 AM; traditional Navajo, Italian, Mexican, and American fare is served until 10 PM. ✉*100 Main St.* 🏠*Box 295, Chinle 86503* ☎928/674–5288 or 800/327–0354 ⊕*www.bestwestern.com* 🛏*102 rooms* ⚑*In-room: ethernet. In-hotel: restaurant, pool* ▤*AE, D, DC, MC, V.*

★ $ ✕🏠 **Thunderbird Lodge.** In an ideal location within the national monument's borders, this pleasant establishment has stone-and-adobe units that match the site's original 1896 trading post. The cafeteria ($–$$) is in the original trading post and serves reasonably priced soups, salads, sandwiches, and entrées, including charbroiled steaks. The lodge also offers jeep tours of Canyon de Chelly and Canyon del Muerto.

⊠*Indian Hwy. 7* ⌂*Box 548, Chinle 86503* ☎*928/674–5841 or 800/679–2473* ⊕*www.tbirdlodge. com* ⇆*73 rooms* ⅃*In-hotel: restaurant* ⊟*AE, D, DC, V.*

¢ 🏠 **Many Farms Inn.** Many Farms High School runs this facility, which is staffed by Navajo students of hotel management. It's not fancy, but rooms are pleasant and contain two single beds, which means single or double occupancy only. Bathrooms are shared, and you have to go to the first floor to use pay phones or watch TV. ⊠*U. S. 191 and Indian Hwy. 59* ⌂*Box 307, Many Farms 86538* ☎*928/781–6362* ⊕*www.manyfarms.bia. edu* ⇆*30 rooms* ⅃*In-room: no phone, refrigerator, no TV. In-hotel: gym* ⊟*No credit cards* ⊗*Closed weekends Aug.–May.*

HUBBELL TRADING POST NATIONAL HISTORIC SITE

❸ *40 mi south of Canyon de Chelly, off AZ 264; 30 mi west of Window Rock.*

John Lorenzo Hubbell, a merchant and friend of the Navajo, established this trading post in 1876. Hubbell taught, translated letters, settled family quarrels, and explained government policy to the Navajo, and during an 1886 smallpox epidemic, he turned his home into a hospital and ministered to the sick and dying. He died in 1930 and is buried near the trading post.

The National Park Service Visitor Center exhibits illustrate the post's history, and you can take a self-guided tour of the grounds and Hubbell home and visit the Hubbell Trading Post, which contains a fine display of Native American artistry. The visitor center has a fairly comprehensive bookstore specializing in Navajo history, art, and culture; local weavers often demonstrate their craft on site.

The **Hubbell Trading Post Store** is famous for "Ganado red" Navajo rugs, which are sold at the store here. The quality is outstanding and prices are high but fair—rugs can cost anywhere from $100 to more than $30,000. Considering the time that goes into weaving each one, the prices are quite reasonable. It's hard to resist the beautiful designs and colors, and it's a pleasure just to browse around this rustic spot, where Navajo artists frequently show their work. Documents of authenticity are provided for all works. Note: when photographing weavers, ask permission first. They expect a few dollars in return. ⊠*AZ 264, 1 mi west of town, Ganado* ☎*928/755–3475 park office, 928/755–3254 store* ⊕*http://www.nps.gov/hutr* ⌸*Free; $2 to tour Hubbell home* ⊗*Late May–early Sept., daily 8–6; mid-Sept.–mid-May, daily 8–5.*

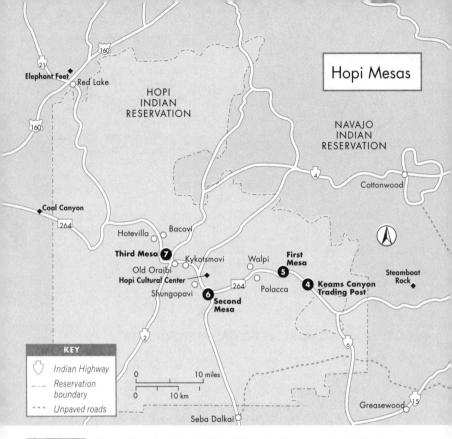

EN
ROUTE

About 20 mi west of Hubbell Trading Post on AZ 264 is **Steamboat Rock**, an immense, jutting peninsula of stone that resembles an early steamboat, complete with a geologically formed waterline. At Steamboat Rock you are only 5 mi from the eastern boundary of the Hopi Reservation.

THE HOPI MESAS

The Hopi occupy 12 villages in regions referred to as First Mesa, Second Mesa, and Third Mesa. Although these areas have similar languages and traditions, each has its own individual features. Generations of Hopitu, "the peaceful people," much like their Puebloan ancestors, have lived in these largely agrarian settlements of stone-and-adobe houses, which blend in with the earth so well that they appear to be natural formations. Television aerials, satellite dishes, and automobiles notwithstanding, these Hopi villages still exude the air of another time.

Descendants of the ancient Hisatsinom, the Hopi number about 12,000 people today. Their culture can be traced back 2,000 years, making them one of the oldest known tribes in North America. They successfully developed "dry farming" and grow many kinds of vegetables and corn (called maize) as their basic food—in fact the Hopi are often called the "corn people." They incorporate nature's cycles into most of their religious rituals. In the celebrated Snake Dance ceremony, dancers carry venomous snakes in their mouths to appease the gods and to bring rain. In addition to farming the land, the Hopi create fine pottery and basketwork and excel in wood carving of katsina dolls.

Although you do not need permission before entering the Hopi Reservation, you must obtain a permit to visit certain areas. Since all Hopi villages are separate and autonomous, each has its own governing policies, which are sometimes posted at the entrance to the village. Many villages don't allow cars, and some close to the public when they are participating in religious ceremonies. Lodging is available on Second Mesa and recommended if you wish to see the Hopi Mesas at a leisurely pace.

KEAMS CANYON TRADING POST

❹ *43 mi west of Hubbell Trading Post on AZ 264.*

The trading post established by Thomas Keam in 1875 to do business with local tribes is now the area's main tourist attraction, offering a primitive campground, restaurant, service station, and shopping center, all set in a dramatic rocky canyon. An administrative center for the Bureau of Indian Affairs, Keams Canyon also has a number of government buildings. A road, accessible by passenger car, winds northeast 3 mi into the 8-mi wooded canyon. At **Inscription Rock,** about 2 mi down the road, frontiersman Kit Carson engraved his name in stone. There are several picnic spots in the canyon.

WHERE TO EAT

¢–$$ ✕ **Keams Canyon Restaurant.** A typical no-frills roadside diner with Formica tabletops, Keams offers both American and Native American dishes, including Navajo tacos heaped with ground beef, chile, beans, lettuce, and grated cheese. Daily specials, offered at $1 to $2 off the regular price, may include anything from barbecued ribs to lamb chops to crab legs. There's also an ice-cream stand in the same building. ⊠*Keams Canyon Shopping Center, AZ 264, Keams Canyon* ☎*928/738–2296* ▭*D, MC, V* ☉*No dinner weekends.*

SHOPPING

Keams Canyon Arts and Crafts and McGee's Art Gallery (⊠*AZ 264, Keams Canyon* ☎*928/738–2295*), upstairs from the Keams Canyon Restaurant, sells first-rate, high-quality Hopi crafts such as handcrafted jewelry, pottery, beautiful carvings, basketry, and artwork.

FIRST MESA

★ **❺** *11 mi west of Keams Canyon, on AZ 264.*

First Mesa villages are renowned for their polychrome pottery and katsina-doll carvings. The first village that you approach is Polacca; the older and more impressive villages of Hano, Sichomovi, and Walpi are at the top of the sweeping mesa. From Polacca, a paved road (off AZ

264) angles up to a parking lot near the village of Sichomovi, and to the Punsi Hall Visitor Center. You must get permission at Punsi Hall to take the guided walking tour of Hano, Sichomovi, and Walpi. Admission is by tour only, so call ahead to find out when they're offered.

WORD OF MOUTH
"I recommend visiting the Hopi mesas ... The ancient town of Walpi is perched on the top of First Mesa—very dramatic—and the town is still used for ceremonies."
–lisatravels

The older Hopi villages have structures built of rock and adobe mortar in simple architectural style. **Hano** actually belongs to the Tewa, a New Mexico Pueblo tribe. In 1696 the Tewa Indians sought refuge with the Hopi on First Mesa after an unsuccessful rebellion against the Spanish in the Rio Grande Valley. Today, the Tewa live close to the Hopi but maintain their own language and ceremonies. **Sichomovi** is built so close to Hano that only the residents can tell where one ends and the other begins. Constructed in the mid-1600s, this village is believed to have been built to ease overcrowding at Walpi, the highest point on the mesa. **Walpi** (☎ *928/737–9556* ⊕ *hopibiz.com/walpi.html*), built on solid rock and surrounded by steep cliffs, frequently hosts ceremonial dances. It's the most pristine of the Hopi villages, with cliff-edge houses and vast scenic vistas. Inhabited for more than 1,100 years (dating back to 900 AD), Walpi's cliff-edge houses seem to grow out of the nearby terrain. Today, only about 10 residents occupy this settlement, which has neither electricity nor running water; one-hour guided tours of the village are available. Note that Walpi's steep terrain makes it a less than ideal destination for acrophobes. ✉ *Punsi Hall Visitor Center, First Mesa* ☎ *928/737–2262* ⊕ *hopibiz.com/tour.html* ✉ *Guided First Mesa tours $8, Walpi tours $5* ⊙ *First Mesa tours Nov.–mid-Mar., daily 9:30–4; mid-Mar.–Oct., daily 9–5, except when ceremonies are being held; Walpi tours weekdays 8:30–4, weekends by appointment.*

SECOND MESA

6 *8 mi southwest of First Mesa, on AZ 264.*

The Mesas are the Hopi universe, and Second Mesa is the "Center of the Universe." **Shungopavi,** the largest and oldest village on Second Mesa, which was founded by the Bear Clan, is reached by a paved road angling south off AZ 264, between the junction of AZ 87 and the Hopi Cultural Center. The villagers here make silver overlay jewelry and coil plaques. Coil plaques are woven from galleta grass and yucca and are adorned with designs of katsinas, animals, and corn. The art of making the plaques has been passed from mother to daughter for generations, and fine coil plaques have become highly sought-after collector's items. The famous Hopi snake dances (closed to the public) are held here in August during even-numbered years. Two smaller villages are off a paved road that runs north from AZ 264, about 1/5 mi east of the Hopi Cultural Center. **Mishongnovi,** the easternmost settlement, was established in the late 1600s. For permission to visit **Sipaulovi,** which was originally at the base of the mesa before being moved to its present site in 1680, call the Sipaulovi Village Community Center (☎928/737–2570).

At the **Hopi Museum and Cultural Center,** you can stop for the night, learn about the people and their reservation, and eat authentic Hopi cuisine. The museum here is dedicated to preserving the Hopi traditions and to presenting those traditions to non-Hopi visitors. A gift shop sells works by local Hopi artisans at reasonable prices, and a modest picnic area on the west side of the building is a pleasant spot for lunch with a view of the San Francisco Peaks. ⊠*AZ 264, Second Mesa* ☎*928/734–2401* ⊕*www. hopiculturalcenter.com* ⊠*Museum $3* ⊙*Mid-Mar.–Oct., weekdays 8–4:30, weekends 9–3; Nov.–mid-Mar., weekdays 8–4:30.*

> ## HOPI CEREMONIES
>
> The Hopi are known for their colorful ceremonial dances, many of which are supplications and appreciations for rain, fertile crops, and harmony with nature. Most of the ceremonies take place in village plazas and kivas (underground ceremonial chambers) and last two days or longer; outsiders are sometimes permitted to watch segments of some ceremonies but are never allowed into kivas unless invited. Seasonal katsina dances performed at agricultural ceremonies may be restricted, ask upon, or before, arrival.

WHERE TO STAY & EAT

$ ✕🖼 **Hopi Cultural Center Restaurant and Motel.** This Hopi-run establishment is the only place to eat or sleep in the immediate area, but because of its remote location it almost always has vacant rooms. The attractive, adobe building with a tan and reddish-brown exterior contains clean, quiet, moderately priced rooms with coffeemakers. The restaurant (¢–$) serves traditional Hopi dishes, including Indian tacos, Hopi blue-corn pancakes, fry bread (delicious with honey or salsa), and *nok qui vi* (a tasty stew made with tender bits of lamb, hominy, and mild green chiles). ⊠*5 mi west of AZ 87 on AZ 264, Second Mesa 86403* ☎*928/734–2401* ⊕*www.hopiculturalcenter.com* ⇋*33 rooms* ⌂*In-hotel: no elevator* ▤*DC, MC, V.*

SHOPPING

The **Hopi Arts and Crafts/Silvercrafts Cooperative Guild** (⊠*AZ 264, Second Mesa* ☎*928/734–2463*), west of the Hopi Cultural Center, hosts craftspeople selling their wares; you might even see silversmiths at work here. Shops at the **Hopi Cultural Center** (⊠*AZ 264, Second Mesa* ☎*928/734–2401*) carry the works of local artists and artisans. At **Hopi Fine Arts** (⊠*AZ 264 at AZ 87, Second Mesa* ☎*928/737–2222* ⊕*www. hopifinearts.net*), proprietor and musician Alph Secakuku is a native of the Hopi Pueblo and an authority on all arts and crafts of the Hopi people. He represents about 75 active artisans in his user-friendly gallery. **Tsakurshovi** (⊠*AZ 264, Second Mesa* ☎*928/734–2478*), 1½ mi east of the Hopi Cultural Center, is a small shop where Hopi come to buy bundles of sweet grass and sage, deer hooves with which to make rattles, and ceremonial belts adorned with seashells. The proprietor's wife, Janice Day, is a renowned Hopi basket maker. The shop has one of the largest collections of Hopi baskets in the Southwest.

THIRD MESA

❼ *12 mi northwest of Second Mesa, on AZ 264.*

Third Mesa villages are known for their agricultural accomplishments, textile weaving, wicker baskets, silver overlay, and plaques. You'll find crafts shops and art galleries, as well as occasional roadside vendors, along AZ 264. The Hopi Tribal Headquarters and Office of Public Relations in Kykotsmovi should be visited first for necessary permissions to visit the villages of Third Mesa.

Kykotsmovi, at the eastern base of Third Mesa, is literally translated as "ruins on the hills" for the many ruin sites on the valley floor and in the surrounding hills. Present-day Kykotsmovi was established by Hopi people from Oraibi—a few miles west—who either converted to Christianity or who wished to attend school and be educated. Kykotsmovi is the seat of the Hopi Tribal Government.

Old Oraibi, a few miles west and on top of Third Mesa at about 7,200 feet in elevation, is believed to be the oldest continuously inhabited community in the United States, dating from around AD 1150. It was also the site of a rare, bloodless conflict between two groups of the Hopi people; in 1906, a dispute, settled uniquely by a "push of war" (a pushing contest), sent the losers off to establish the town of Hotevilla. Oraibi is a dusty spot, and, as an act of courtesy, tourists are asked to park their cars outside and approach the village on foot.

Hotevilla and **Bacavi** are about 4 mi west of Oraibi, and their inhabitants are descended from the former residents of that village. The men of Hotevilla continue to plant crops and beautiful gardens along the mesa slopes. ✉*Cultural Preservation Office, AZ 264* 📪*Box 123, Kykotsmovi 86039* 📞*928/734–3000 or 928/734–2441* 🌐*www.nau. edu/~hcpo-p* 🕐 *Weekdays 8:30–5.*

EN ROUTE Beyond Hotevilla, AZ 264 descends from Third Mesa, exits the Hopi Reservation, and crosses into Navajo territory, past **Coal Canyon,** where Native Americans have long mined coal from the dark seam just below the rim. The colorful mudstone, dark lines of coal, and bleached white rock have an eerie appearance, especially by the light of the moon. Twenty miles west of Coal Canyon, at the junction of AZ 264 and U.S. 160, is the town of Moenkopi, the last Hopi outpost. Established as a farming community, it was settled by the descendants of former Oraibi residents.

NAVAJO NATION WEST

The Hopi Reservation is like a doughnut hole surrounded by the Navajo Nation. If you approach the Grand Canyon from U.S. 89, via Flagstaff, north of the Wupatki National Monument, you'll find two significant sites in the western portions of the Navajo Reservation, the

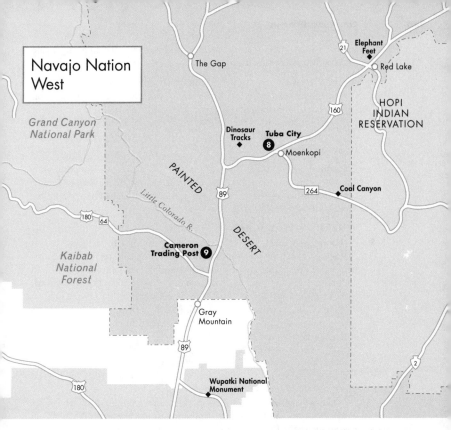

Navajo Nation West

Grand Canyon National Park

The Gap

Elephant Feet

21

Red Lake

HOPI INDIAN RESERVATION

160

Dinosaur Tracks

Tuba City

8

Moenkopi

PAINTED

264

Coal Canyon

Little Colorado R.

89

DESERT

180   64

Kaibab National Forest

Cameron Trading Post

9

Gray Mountain

89

2

Wupatki National Monument

180

Cameron Trading Post and Tuba City. Situated 45 mi west of the Hopi town of Hotevilla, Tuba City is a good stop over if you're traveling east to the Hopi Mesas or northeast to Page.

At Cameron, the turnoff point for the South Rim of the Grand Canyon, the Cameron Trading Post was built in 1916 and commemorates Ralph Cameron, a pre-statehood territorial-legislative delegate. The sheer walls of the Little Colorado River Canyon about 10 mi west of U.S. 89 along AZ 64 are quite impressive and also worth a stop.

TUBA CITY

▶ **8** *52 mi northwest of Third Mesa on AZ 264.*

Tuba City, believed to be named after a Hopi chief "Tsuve," has about 10,500 permanent residents and is the administrative center for the western portion of the Navajo Nation. In addition to a hotel, hostel, and a few restaurants, this small town has a hospital, a bank, a trading post, and a movie theater. In late October, Tuba City hosts the Western Navajo Fair, a celebration combining traditional Navajo song and dance with a parade, pageant, and countless arts-and-crafts exhibits.

The octagonal **Tuba City Trading Post** (⊠ *Main St.* ☎ *928/283–5441*), founded in the early 1870s, sells groceries and authentic, reasonably priced Navajo rugs, pottery, baskets, and jewelry—it's adjacent to the Quality Inn Navajo Nation.

About 5½ mi west of Tuba City, between mileposts 316 and 317 on U.S. 160, is a small sign for the **Dinosaur Tracks.** More than 200 million years ago, dilophosaurus—a carnivorous bipedal reptile over 10 feet tall—left tracks in mud that turned to sandstone. There's no charge for a look. Ask the locals about guiding you to the nearby petroglyphs and freshwater springs.

Four miles west of the dinosaur tracks on U.S. 160 is the junction with U.S. 89. This is one of the most colorful regions of the **Painted Desert,** with amphitheaters of maroon, orange, and red rocks facing west; it's especially glorious at sunset.

WHERE TO STAY & EAT

$-$$ ✕ **Hogan Restaurant.** The fare at this spot adjacent to the Quality Inn Navajo Nation is mostly Southwestern and Mexican, but the menu also lists basic American and Navajo dishes. The chicken enchiladas and beef tamales are as good as any south of the border. Breakfast is served, too. ⊠*Main St. (AZ 264)* ☎*928/283–5260* ▭*AE, D, DC, MC, V.*

¢–$ ✕ **Kate's Cafe.** A favorite of locals, this all-American café serves break-fast—try the vegetarian omelet—lunch, and dinner. At lunch choose from hearty burgers, Kate's club sandwich, grilled chicken, or salads. Dinner selections include five daily pasta specials and a charbroiled New York–strip steak. There may be a wait, but for local color and fine food at reasonable prices, this is the place to go. ⊠*Main St. (AZ 264)* ☎*928/283–6773* ▭*No credit cards.*

$ ▥ **Quality Inn Navajo Nation.** This hotel has a trading post and shops for essentials, gifts, and souvenirs. Standard rooms are spacious and well maintained, fine for an overnight stop before or after a visit to the Hopi Mesas. The on-site Hogan Restaurant serves basic fare. ⊠*Main St. at Moenave Rd.* ⌂*Box 247, 86045* ☎*928/283–4545 or 800/644–8383* ⊕*www.qualityinntubacity.com* ⟋*78 rooms, 2 suites* ⌖*In-room: Wi-Fi. In-hotel: restaurant, laundry facilities, some pets allowed* ▭*AE, D, DC, MC, V.*

¢ ▥ **Grey Hills Inn.** Hotel management students at Grey Hills High School run this unusual lodging, a former dormitory with large, clean rooms and comfortable beds. Warm service, paintings, and other touches add character to otherwise plain rooms and the rather drab, institutional setting. Bathrooms and showers are down the hall, but the rates are reasonable. A share of the inn's profits helps support the students' class. ⊠*Grey Hills High School, U.S. 160, ½ mi north of AZ 264* ⌂*Box 160, 86045* ☎*928/283–4450* ⟋*32 rooms with shared bath* ▭*MC, V.*

SHOPPING

The **Native American swap meet** (⊠*Main St.*), behind the community center and next to the baseball field, held every Friday from 8 AM on, has great deals on jewelry, jewelry-making supplies, semiprecious stones, rugs, pottery, and other arts and crafts; there are also food concessions and booths selling herbs. The **Toh Nanees Dizi Shopping Center** (⊠*U.S. 160*), ½ mi northeast of town, has a pizza parlor, Chinese restaurant, supermarket, and the Silver Screen Cinema.

CAMERON TRADING POST

❾ *25 mi southwest of Tuba City on U.S. 89.*

Cameron Trading Post and Motel, established in 1916 overlooking a spectacular gorge and vintage suspension bridge, is one of the few remaining authentic trading posts in the Southwest. A convenient stop if you're driving from the Hopi Mesas to the Grand Canyon, it has reasonably priced dining, lodging, camping, and shopping *(⇨ the listing in Chapter 2 for more detailed information).* Fine authentic Navajo products are sold at an outlet of the **Navajo Arts and Crafts Enterprises** (✉ *U.S. 89 at AZ 64, Cameron* ☎928/679–2244). ✉*U.S. 89, Cameron* ☎928/679–2231 ⊕*www.gonavajo.com/navajoart.*

EN ROUTE

As you proceed toward Kayenta, 22 mi northeast of Tuba City on U.S. 160, you'll come to the tiny community of Red Lake. Off to the left of the highway is a geologic phenomenon known as **Elephant Feet.** These massive eroded-sandstone buttes offer a great family photo opportunity: pose under the enormous columns. Northwest of here at the end of a graded dirt road in Navajo backcountry is **White Mesa Natural Bridge,** a massive arch of white sandstone that extends from the edge of White Mesa. The long **Black Mesa** plateau runs for about 15 mi along U.S. 160. Above the prominent escarpments of this land formation, mining operations—a major source of revenue for the Navajo Nation—delve into the more than 20 billion tons of coal deposited there.

MONUMENT VALLEY

The magnificent Monument Valley stretches to the northeast of Kayenta into Utah. At a base altitude of about 5,500 feet, the sprawling, arid expanse was once populated by ancestral Puebloan people (more popularly known by the Navajo word *Anasazi,* which means both "ancient ones" and "enemy ancestors") and in the last few centuries has been home to generations of Navajo farmers. The soaring red buttes, eroded mesas, deep canyons, and naturally sculpted rock formations of Monument Valley are easy to enjoy on a leisurely drive.

IF IT LOOKS FAMILIAR...

If Monument Valley looks familiar, it probably should. Scenes from many movies, including *National Lampoon's Vacation, How the West Was Won, Forrest Gump, Stagecoach, 2001: A Space Odyssey,* and *Wind Talkers*—have been filmed here. It's also the world's most popular backdrop for TV and magazine advertisements.

At U.S. 163 and the Monument Valley entrance is a street of disheveled buildings called Vendor Village. Here you can purchase trinkets and souvenirs without paying sales tax. Bartering is perfectly acceptable and expected.

KAYENTA

🔟 *75 mi northeast of Tuba City, on U.S. 160, 22 mi south of Monument Valley.*

Kayenta, a small town with a couple of convenience stores, three chain motels, and a hospital, is a good base for exploring nearby Monument Valley Navajo Tribal Park and the Navajo National Monument. The Burger King in town has an excellent Navajo Code Talker exhibit with lots of memorabilia relative to this heroic World War II marine group.

Take a self-guided walking tour through the small outdoor cultural park, the **Navajo Cultural Center of Kayenta,** which describes the beliefs and traditions that have shaped North America's largest Native American tribe. ⊠ *U.S. 160 between Hampton Inn and Burger King* 🕾 *928/697–3170* ⊕ *www.kayenta.nndes.org* ✉ *Free* ☉ *Daily 7 AM–sunset.*

> ### WORD OF MOUTH
>
> "My wife and I visited Monument Valley. It was great. We decided to go on one of the tours offered by the native guides there. They have a booth in the middle of the parking lot and use large 4-wheel drive vehicles. It was great. The 2½-hour tour was well worth the $40 pp. In addition to not having to worry about the bad road the guide gave us all kinds of information on the land and native peoples. He took us into the beautiful back country to see several arches and rock formations which were far more breathtaking than anything off the public road."
>
> –nuggetboy

WHERE TO STAY & EAT

★ ¢–$ ✗ **Amigo Cafe.** The tables are packed with locals who frequent this small, clean establishment where everything is made from scratch. The delicious fry bread is the real drawing card. If you've never had a Navajo taco or Navajo hamburger, this is a good place to be initiated. The café also serves excellent Mexican fare and traditional American dishes. ⊠ *North of U.S. 160 on U.S. 163* 🕾 *928/697–8448* ▭ *MC, V* ☉ *Closed Sun.*

¢–$ ✗ **Golden Sands.** The decor and the service at this local café next to the Best Western Wetherill Inn are equally unrefined, but you can fuel up on hamburgers, Navajo tacos, and other regional specialties. It's also a good place to learn about the area from residents who stop in for coffee. ⊠ *U.S. 163* 🕾 *928/697–3684* ▭ *No credit cards* ☉ *Closed Mon.*

★ $–$$ ✗🏨 **Hampton Inn of Kayenta.** This warm and inviting hotel is the best accommodation in the area, although it's little different from any other in the chain. The functional, comfortable rooms and lobby are tastefully decorated with Southwest textures, and the on-site restaurant (¢–$$) is staffed by Native Americans wearing traditional Navajo garb. Stick with the Native American cuisine; a good choice is the Sheepherder's Taco. There's a free Continental-breakfast bar, a patio with a beehive fireplace, and a gift shop with top-quality Native American art and unique gifts. ⊠ *U.S. 160* 🕾 *Box 1219, 86033* 🕾 *928/697–3170* 🖷 *928/697–3189* ⊕ *www.hamptoninn.com* ⇴ *73 rooms* ⚲ *In-room:*

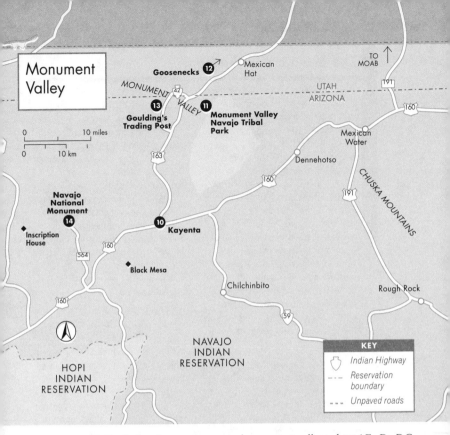

Wi-Fi. *In-hotel: restaurant, pool, some pets allowed* ⊟*AE, D, DC, MC, V* Ⓞ*CP.*

$-$$ 🏨 **Holiday Inn Monument Valley.** This contemporary hotel has everything you would expect from a Holiday Inn. The on-site Wagonwheel Restaurant, one of the few dining options in these parts, offers both standard and Native American fare, and the gift shop offers traditional local arts and crafts. ⊠*U.S. 160 at U.S. 163* ⬚*Box 307, 86033* ☎*928/697–3221 or 888/465–4329* ⊕*www.holidayinn.com* ⬎*160 rooms* ⌂*In-hotel: restaurant, pool, gym, laundry facilities* ⊟*AE, D, DC, MC, V.*

$ 🏨 **Best Western Wetherill Inn.** This clean two-story motel has Southwestern decor and a well-stocked gift shop. ⊠*U.S. 163* ⬚*Box 175, 86033* ☎*928/697–3231 or 800/528–1234* ⊕*www.bestwestern.com* ⬎*54 rooms* ⌂*In-hotel: pool, public Wi-Fi* ⊟*AE, D, DC, MC, V.*

MONUMENT VALLEY NAVAJO TRIBAL PARK

🌀 ⑪ *24 mi northeast of Kayenta, off U.S. 163.*

Fodor'sChoice
★ For generations, the Navajo have grown crops and herded sheep in Monument Valley, considered to be one of the most scenic and mesmerizing destinations in the Navajo Nation. Within Monument Valley

The Navajo and the Hopi

Both the Navajo and Hopi base their culture on the land around them, but they are very different from one another. The Navajo refer to themselves as the Diné (pronounced din-*eh*)—"the people"—and live on 17 million acres in Arizona, New Mexico, Utah, and Colorado. The Hopi trace their roots back to the original settlers of the area, whom they call the *Hisatsinom*, or "people of long ago"—they are also known as Anasazi, meaning both "ancient ones" and "ancient enemies." Hopi culture is more formal and structured than that of the Navajo, and their religion has remained stronger and purer. For both tribes, unemployment is high on the reservation, and poverty a constant presence.

The Navajos use few words and possess a subtle sense of humor that can pass you by quickly if you're not a good listener. From childhood they are taught not to talk too much, be loud, or show off. Eye contact is considered impolite. If you're conversing with Navajos, some may look down or away even though they are paying attention to you. Likewise, touching is seen differently; handshaking may be the only physical contact that you see. When shaking hands, a light touch is preferred to a firm grip which is considered overbearing.

Although most Navajos speak English with varying degrees of mastery, listen closely to the language of the Diné.

Stemming from the Athabascan family of languages, it is difficult for outsiders to learn because of subtle accentuation. The famous Marine Corps Navajo "Code Talkers" of World War II saved thousands of lives in the South Pacific by creating a code within their native Navajo language. Their unbreakable radio messages mystified the Japanese, and got through safely and accurately to American troops. These Native Americans are true patriots who today speak humbly of their accomplishments. Many "Code Talkers" still alive today reside in the area around Tuba City.

Hopi mythology holds that a white-skinned people will save the tribe from its difficult life. Long ago, however, in the face of brutal treatment by whites, most Hopi became convinced that salvation would originate elsewhere. (Some Hopi now look to the Dalai Lama for redemption.) Although not easy to witness, the disappointment of the Hopi and the despair of the Navajo are easy to understand after a visit to the reservation.

Most Navajo and Hopi disapprove of the practice, but some panhandlers cluster at shopping centers and view sites, hoping to glean a few tourist dollars. Visitors should respond to panhandlers with a polite but firm "no." If you wish to help, make a donation to a legitimate organization that raises funds at reservation grocery stores.

---

lies the 30,000-acre Monument Valley Navajo Tribal Park, where eons of wind and rain have carved the mammoth red-sandstone monoliths into memorable formations. The monoliths, which jut hundreds of feet above the desert floor, stand on the horizon like sentinels, frozen in time and unencumbered by electric wires, telephone poles, or fences...a scene virtually unchanged for centuries. These are the very same nostalgic images so familiar to movie buffs who recall the early Western films of John Wayne. A 17-mi self-guided driving tour on a dirt road (there's only one road, so you can't get lost) passes the memorable **Mittens** and **Totem Pole** formations, among others. Drive slowly, and be sure to walk (15 minutes round-trip) from North Window around the end of Cly Butte for the views. The park has a 99-site campground, which closes from early October through April. Call ahead for road conditions in winter.

> **DID YOU KNOW?**
>
> Filmed in and around Monument Valley in 1939, *Stagecoach* has come to be regarded as one of the great Hollywood Westerns of all time. The iconic John Wayne–Claire Trevor film earned Oscars for Best Supporting Actor (Thomas Mitchell) and Best Music, as well as several nominations, including Best Director for Ford.

The **Monument Valley Visitor Center** has a small crafts shop and exhibits devoted to ancient and modern Native American history. Most of the independent guided tours here use enclosed vans and charge about $20 for 2½ hours. You can generally find Navajo Native American guides—who will escort you to places that you are not allowed to visit on your own—in the center or through the booths in the parking lot. ✉ *Visitor Center, off U.S. 163, 24 mi north of Kayenta, Monument Valley* ✆ *Box 2520, Window Rock 86515* ☎ *435/727–5874 park visitor center, 928/871–6647 Navajo Parks & Recreation Dept.* ⊕ *www.navajonationparks.org* 💲 *$5* ⊗ *Visitor center May–Sept., daily 6 AM–8 PM; Mar. and Apr., daily 7–7; Oct.–Feb., daily 8–5.*

SPORTS & THE OUTDOORS

HIKING, HORSEBACK RIDING & JEEP TOURS

Jeep tours of the valley, from hour-long to overnight, can be arranged through Roland Cody Dixon at **Roland's Navajoland Tours** (☎ 520/697–3524 *or 800/368–2785*); he offers cultural tours with crafts demonstrations, camping, and photography. **Sacred Monument Tours** (☎ *435/727–3218 or 928/380–4527* ⊕ *www.monumentvalley.net*) has hiking, jeep, photography, and horseback riding tours into Monument Valley. **Simpson's Trailhandler Tours** (☎ *435/727–3362* ⊕ *www.trailhandlertours.com*) offers four-wheel-drive jeep tours as well as photography and hiking tours. **Totem Pole Tours** (☎ *435/727–3313* ⊕ *www.moab-utah.com/totempole*) offers jeep tours, some including entertainment and outdoor barbecues.

OFF THE BEATEN PATH

Four Corners Monument. An inlaid brass plaque marks the only point in the United States where four states meet: Arizona, New Mexico, Colorado, and Utah. Despite the Indian wares and booths selling greasy food, there's not much else to do here but pay a fee and stay long enough to snap a photo; you'll see many a twisted tourist trying to get an arm or a leg in each state. The monument is a 75-mi drive from Kayenta and is administered by the Navajo Nation Parks & Recreation Department. ✉ *7 mi northwest of the U.S. 160 and U.S. 64 junction, Teec Nos Pos* ☎ *928/871–6647 Navajo Parks & Recreation Dept.* ⊕ *www.navajonationparks.org* 💲 *$3* ⊗ *Sept.–May, daily 8–5; Apr.–Aug., daily 7 AM–8 PM.*

GOOSENECKS REGION, UTAH

FodorśChoice
★

12 *33 mi north of Monument Valley Navajo Tribal Park, on UT 316.*

Monument Valley's scenic route, U.S. 163, continues from Arizona into Utah, where the land is crossed, east to west, by a stretch of the San Juan River known as the Goosenecks—named for the myriad twists and curves it takes. This barren, erosion-blasted gorge has a stark beauty. This spot is a well-known take-out point for white-water runners on the San Juan, a river that vacationing sleuths will recognize as the setting of many of Tony Hillerman's Jim Chee mystery novels. The scenic overlook for the Goosenecks is reached by turning west from U.S. 163 onto UT 261, 4 mi north of the small community of **Mexican Hat**, then proceeding on UT 261 for 1 mi to a directional sign at the road's junction with UT 316. Turn left onto UT 316 and proceed 4 mi to the vista-point parking lot.

WHERE TO STAY & EAT

★ $ ✕▣ **San Juan Inn & Trading Post.** The inn's Southwestern-style, rustic rooms overlooking the river at Mexican Hat are clean and well-maintained. Diners can watch the river at the Old Bridge Grille ($–$$), which serves great grilled steak and juicy hamburgers, fresh trout, and inexpensive Navajo dishes. ⊠ *U.S. 163* ⓓ *Box 310276, Mexican Hat, UT d84531* ☎ *435/683–2220 or 800/447–2022* ⊕ *www.sanjuaninn. net* ➳ *36 rooms* ⚒ *In-hotel: restaurant, gym, laundry facilities* ▭ *AE, D, DC, MC, V.*

GOULDING'S TRADING POST

13 *1 mi west of Monument Valley Navajo Tribal Park, off U.S. 163 on Indian Hwy. 42.*

Established in 1924 by Harry Goulding and his wife "Mike," this trading post provided a place where Navajos could exchange livestock and handmade goods for necessities. Goulding's is probably best known, though, for being used as a headquarters by director John Ford when he filmed the Western classic *Stagecoach*. Today the compound has a lodge, restaurant, museum, gift shop, grocery store, and campground. The Goulding Museum displays Native American artifacts and Goulding family memorabilia as well as an excellent multimedia show about Monument Valley.

WHERE TO STAY & EAT

$$ ✕▣ **Goulding's Lodge.** There are spectacular views of Monument Valley from each room's private balcony and all the rooms have coffeemakers and hair dryers. The on-premises Stagecoach restaurant (¢–$$), serving American fare, is decorated with Western movie memorabilia. Goulding's also conducts custom guided tours of

> **WORD OF MOUTH**
>
> "The best way to start your Monument Valley experience is to stay overnight at Goulding's Lodge, wake up early, go out on your balcony and watch the sun rise over the monuments."
>
> –HowardR

Monument Valley and provides Navajo guides into the backcountry. The lodge is 2 mi off U.S. 163, at the Monument Valley Navajo Tribal Park turnoff. ⊠ *Off U.S. 163, 24 mi north of Kayenta* ✉ *Box 360001, Monument Valley, UT 84536* ☎ *435/727–3231* ⊕ *www.gouldings.com* ⌨ *62 rooms* ⚷ *In-room: VCR. In-hotel: restaurant, pool, laundry facilities* ⊟ *AE, D, DC, MC, V.*

NAVAJO NATIONAL MONUMENT

⓮ *53 mi southwest of Goulding's Trading Post, 21 mi west of Kayenta.*
Fodor's Choice *From Kayenta, take U.S. 160 southwest to AZ 564, and follow signs*
★ *9 mi north to monument.*

At the Navajo National Monument, two unoccupied 13th-century cliff pueblos, Betatakin and Keet Seel, stand under the overhanging cliffs of Tsegi Canyon. The largest ancient dwellings in Arizona, these stone-and-mortar complexes were built by ancestral Puebloans, obviously for permanent occupancy, but abandoned after less than half a century.

The well-preserved, 135-room **Betatakin** (Navajo for "ledge house") is a cluster of cliff dwellings that seem to hang in midair before a sheer sandstone wall. When discovered in 1907 by a passing American rancher, the apartments were full of baskets, pottery, and preserved grains and ears of corn—as if the occupants had been chased away in the middle of a meal. For an impressive view of Betatakin, walk to the rim overlook about ½ mi from the visitor center. Ranger-led tours (a 5-mi, four-hour, strenuous round-trip hike including a 700-foot descent into the canyon) leave once a day from late May to early September at 8 AM and return between noon and 1 PM. No reservations are accepted; groups of no more than 25 form on a first-come, first-served basis.

Keet Seel (Navajo for "broken pottery") is also in good condition in a serene location, with 160 rooms and five kivas. Explorations of Keet Seel, which lies at an elevation of 7,000 feet and is 8½ mi from the visitor center by foot, are restricted: only 20 people are allowed to visit per day, and only between late May and early September, when a ranger is present at the site. A permit—which also allows campers to stay overnight near the ruins—is required. Trips to Keet Seel are very popular, so reservations are taken up to two months in advance. Anyone who suffers from vertigo might want to avoid this trip: the trail leads down a 1,100-foot near-vertical rock face.

The **visitor center** houses a small museum, exhibits of prehistoric pottery, and a good crafts shop. Free campground and picnic areas are nearby, and rangers sometimes present campfire programs in summer. No food, gasoline, or hotel lodging is available at the monument. AZ 564 turns north off U.S. 160 at the Black Mesa gas station and convenience store and leads to the visitor center. ⊠ *AZ 564, Black Mesa* ✉ *HC 71, Box 3, Tonalea 86044* ☎ *928/672–2700* ⊕ *www.nps.gov/ nava* ▣ *Free* ☉ *Apr.–Oct., weekdays 8–5, weekends 8–7; Nov.–Mar., daily 9–5; tours late May–early Sept.*

SPORTS & THE OUTDOORS

HIKING Hiking is the best way for adventurous souls to see Keet Seel at the Navajo National Monument. It's a fairly strenuous hike to the ruins, but if you're fit and leave early enough, it's well worth it to visit some of the best-preserved ruins in the Southwest. It's free, but the trail is open only from late May through early September, and you

> **WORD OF MOUTH**
>
> "If you get a chance, stop at Navajo National Monument...there's a wonderful little museum and an informative film...and you can walk to see cliff dwellings."
>
> –desertduds

need to call ahead to make a reservation, usually at least two months in advance. *Navajo National Monument, HC 71, Box 3, Tonalea 86044* *928/672–2366* *Free* *Apr.–Oct., weekdays 8–5, weekends 8–7; tours late May–early Sept.*

WHERE TO STAY & EAT

$ ✕⊡ **Anasazi Inn–Tsegi Canyon.** On U.S. 160, 10 mi east of Black Mesa and 9 mi west of Kayenta, this is the closest lodging to Navajo National Monument. The one-story property offers basic, clean accommodations with exterior entrances and commanding views of Tsegi Canyon. There's also a well-stocked gift shop and a restaurant that serves sandwiches, burgers, and basic Navajo fare—it's decent if nothing special, but it's also the only dining option for miles around. ⊠ *Off U.S. 160, 9 mi west of Kayenta* *Box 1543, Kayenta, AZ 86033* *928/697–3793* *www.anasaziinn.com/tsegicanyon* *57 rooms* *In-hotel: restaurant* *AE, D, MC, V.*

GLEN CANYON DAM & LAKE POWELL

Lake Powell is the heart of the huge 1,254,429-acre Glen Canyon National Recreation Area. Created by the barrier of Glen Canyon Dam in the Colorado River, Lake Powell is ringed by red cliffs that twist off into 96 major canyons and countless inlets (most accessible only by boat) with huge, red-sandstone buttes randomly jutting from the sapphire waters. It extends through terrain so rugged it was the last major area of the United States to be mapped. You could spend 30 years exploring the lake and still not experience everything there is to see. The Sierra Club has started a movement to drain the lake to restore water-filled Glen Canyon, which some believe was more spectacular than the Grand Canyon, but the lake is likely to be around for years to come.

South of Lake Powell the landscape gives way to **Echo Cliffs,** orange-sandstone formations rising 1,000 feet and more above the highway in places. At **Bitter Springs,** the road ascends the cliffs and provides a spectacular view of the 9,000-square-mi Arizona Strip to the west and the 3,000-foot Vermilion Cliffs to the northwest.

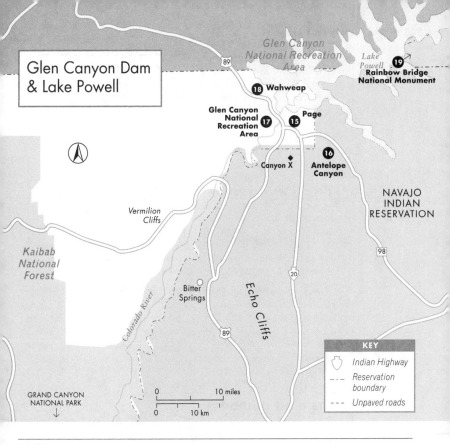

Glen Canyon Dam
& Lake Powell

Glen Canyon
National Recreation
Area

Lake
Powell **19** ↗
**Rainbow Bridge
National Monument**

18 Wahweap

**Glen Canyon
National
Recreation
Area** **17**   **15**   **Page**

16

Canyon X ◆   **Antelope
Canyon**

**NAVAJO
INDIAN
RESERVATION**

Vermilion
Cliffs

Kaibab
National
Forest

98

Bitter
Springs

Echo Cliffs

20

Colorado River

89

KEY
⌂ Indian Highway
--- Reservation
boundary
--- Unpaved roads

GRAND CANYON
NATIONAL PARK
↓

0 ——— 10 miles
0 ——— 10 km

PAGE

15 *90 mi west of the Navajo National Monument, 136 mi north of Flagstaff on U.S. 89.*

Built in 1957 as a Glen Canyon Dam construction camp, Page is now a
tourist spot and a popular base for day trips to Lake Powell; it has also
become a major point of entry to the Navajo Nation. The nearby Vermilion Cliffs are where the California condor, an endangered species,
has been successfully reintroduced into the wild. The town's human
population of nearly 7,000 makes it the largest community in far-
northern Arizona, and most of the motels, restaurants, and shopping
centers are concentrated along **Lake Powell Boulevard,** the name given to
U.S. 89 as it loops through the business district. Each year, more than
3 million people come to play at Lake Powell.

At the corner of North Navajo Drive and Lake Powell Boulevard is
the **John Wesley Powell Memorial Museum,** whose namesake led the first
known expeditions down the Green River and the rapids-choked Colorado through the Grand Canyon between 1869 and 1872. Powell
mapped and kept detailed records of his trips, naming the Grand Can-

yon and many other geographic points of interest in northern Arizona. Artifacts from his expeditions are displayed in the museum. The museum also doubles as the town's visitor information center. A travel desk dispenses information and allows you to book boating tours, raft trips, scenic flights, accommodations in Page, or Antelope Canyon tours. When you sign up for tours here, concessionaires give a donation to the nonprofit museum with no extra charge to you. ⊠ 6 N. Lake Powell Blvd. ☎ 928/645–9496 or 888/597–6873 ⊕ www.powellmuseum.org ⊠$5 ⊗ Weekdays 9–5, Memorial Day–Labor Day also open Sat., call for hrs.

> **LAKE POWELL FAST FACTS**
>
> Lake Powell is 185 mi long with 2,000 mi of shoreline—longer than America's Pacific coast.
>
> This is the second-largest man-made lake in the nation and it took 17 years to fill.
>
> The Glen Canyon Dam is a 710-foot-tall wall of concrete.

☼ The **Navajo Village Heritage Center** imparts an understanding of life on the reservation. You can take a guided tour of a traditional Navajo hogan and bread oven. For $55 per person (or $150 per family), the village hosts a 3½-hour "Evening with the Navajo–Grand Tour," which includes two hours of cultural entertainment and a Navajo taco dinner around a campfire. Less extensive (and expensive) versions of the tour are also available. ⊠ 531 Haul Rd. ☎ 928/660–0304 ⊕ www.navajo-village.com ⊠$5 ⊗ Apr.–Oct., daily 10–3.

SPORTS & THE OUTDOORS
For water sports on Lake Powell, see Wahweap below.

FLOAT TRIPS **Colorado River Discovery** (☎ 888/522–6644 ⊕ www.raftthecanyon.com) offers waterborne tours, including a 5½-hour guided rafting excursion down a calm portion of the Colorado River on comfortable, safe boats ($64). The scenery—multicolor-sandstone cliffs adorned with Native American petroglyphs—is spectacular. The trips are offered daily from May through September, and one trip is available March, April, October, and November (no tours in winter).

GOLF **Lake Powell National Golf Course** (⊠ 400 Clubhouse Dr., off U.S. 89 ☎ 928/645–2023 ⊕ www.golflakepowell.com) has wide fairways, tiered greens with some of the steepest holes in the Southwest, and a generous lack of hazards. A round at this 18-hole, par-72 course costs $60 (including cart); from the fairways you can enjoy vistas of Glen Canyon Dam and Lake Powell. There's a 9-hole, par-36 municipal course here as well.

HIKING The **Glen Canyon Hike** (⊠ Off U.S. 89), a short walk from the parking lot down a flight of uneven rock steps, takes you to a viewpoint on the canyon rim high above the Colorado River and provides fantastic views of the Colorado as it flows through Glen Canyon. To reach the parking lot, turn west on Scenic View Drive, 1½ mi south of Carl Hayden Visitor Center.

The **Horse Shoe Bend Trail** (✉ *Off U.S. 89*) has some steep up and down paths and a bit of deep sand to maneuver; however, the views are well worth the hike. The trail leads up to a bird's-eye view of Glen Canyon and the Colorado River downstream from Glen Canyon Dam. There are some sheer drop-offs here, so watch children. To reach the trail, drive 4 mi south of Page on U.S. 89 and turn west onto a blacktop road 2/10 mi south of mile marker 545. It's a ¾-mi hike from the parking area to the top of the canyon.

WHERE TO STAY & EAT

★ **$-$$$** ✕ **Dam Bar and Grille.** Although the Grille's vaguely industrial-looking decor resembles a construction site more than a restaurant, the food is good, well prepared, and filling—consider the 8-ounce cowboy steak topped with sautéed mushrooms and Swiss cheese, the smoked baby-back ribs, or the burger topped with bacon and cheddar. ✉ *644 N. Navajo Dr.* ☎*928/645–2161* ⊕*www.damplaza.com* ▤*AE, MC, V.*

$-$$ ✕ **Zapata's.** Specials include green chile and home-style enchiladas, not to mention very good margaritas. Everything is made from scratch using family recipes. The basic, clean restaurant is decorated with Mexican blankets, *ristras* (strings of dried red chiles), and pottery. ✉*614 N. Navajo Dr.* ☎*928/645–9006* ▤*AE, D, MC, V.*

$-$$ ▥ **Courtyard by Marriott.** An attractive hotel on the grounds of Lake Powell National Golf Course, the Courtyard has airy rooms decorated in a Southwestern motif with plush bedding and 25-inch TVs, health and fitness facilities, and dining at Peppers ($–$$), which serves predictable but reliable American and Mexican standards. ✉*600 Clubhouse Dr.* ☏*Box 4150, 86040* ☎*928/645–5000 or 888/236–2427* ⊕*www. courtyard.com* ⤢*153 rooms* ⌂*In-room: Wi-Fi. In-hotel: restaurant, bar, pool, gym, laundry facilities* ▤*AE, D, DC, MC, V.*

$ ▥ **Best Western Arizonainn.**On a bluff at the northern end of Page, this modern, well-run motel has large rooms with queen-size beds and Southwestern-print bedspreads and has fantastic views of Lake Powell, just 2 mi away. Butterfield Steakhouse serves Southwestern and standard American fare. ✉*716 Rim View Dr.* ☏*Box 250, 86040* ☎*928/645–2466 or 800/826–2718* ⊕*www.bestwestern.com* ⤢*103 rooms* ⌂*In-room: ethernet. In-hotel: restaurant, bar, pool, gym, laundry facilities, some pets allowed* ▤*AE, D, DC, MC, V* ⅋*CP.*

$ ▥ **Best Western at Lake Powell.** The newer of the two Best Westerns in town is a modern, three-story motel on a high bluff overlooking Glen Canyon Dam with dazzling views of the Vermilion Cliffs. The large rooms are functional, and the beds are comfortable. ✉*208 N. Lake Powell Blvd., 86040* ☎*928/645–5988 or 888/794–2888* ⊕*www. bestwestern.com/atlakepowell* ⤢*132 rooms* ⌂*In-room: Wi-Fi. In-hotel: pool, gym, laundry facilities* ▤*AE, D, DC, MC, V* ⅋*CP.*

★ **$** ▥ **Canyon Colors B&B.** Run by New England transplants Bev and Rich Jones, this desert-country B&B offers travelers a personal touch. The Sunflower and Paisley rooms, which can accommodate three and two, respectively, have queen beds and wood-burning stoves. The B&B also has an extensive video library, including many videos of Lake Powell and the Navajo Nation. Reservations, necessary in summer, can be made up to a year in advance. ✉*225 S. Navajo Dr.* ☏*Box 3657,*

86040 ☎928/645–5979 or 800/536–2530 ⊕www.canyoncolors.com ⇥2 rooms ♿In-room: refrigerator, VCR. In-hotel: public Internet, pool ☰AE, D, DC, MC, V ⊚BP.

NIGHTLIFE

The **Bowl** (⊠24 N. Lake Powell Blvd. ☎928/645–2682) is a 10-lane bowling alley with an outdoor patio, billiards, and coffee shop. **Gunsmoke Saloon & Eatery** (⊠644 N. Navajo Dr. ☎928/645–1888) is a spot where you can dance to live music, play billiards and video games, watch sports on TV, and munch on chicken wings until 1 AM. **Ken's Old West Restaurant & Lounge** (⊠718 Vista Ave. ☎928/645–5160 ⊕www. kensoldwest.net) has country-and-western music and dancing; you can also get good steak, prime rib, seafood, or a barbecue-chicken dinner.

SHOPPING

There are numerous gift shops and clothing stores in the downtown area along Lake Powell Boulevard. There's lots of junk, but you can find authentic Native American arts and crafts, too. **Big Lake Trading Post** (⊠1501 AZ 98 ☎928/645–2404) has a gas station, convenience store, car wash, and coin laundry. **Blair's Dinnebito Trading Post** (⊠626 Navajo Dr. ☎928/645–3008 ⊕www.blairstradingpost.com) has been around for more than half a century. Authentic Native American arts and crafts are only a small part of what this store sells. Need tack equipment, rodeo ropes, rugs, saddlery, pottery? It's all here and reasonably priced. Wander upstairs and visit the Elijah Blair collection and memorabilia rooms. The gift shop at **Lake Powell Resort** (⊠100 Lake Shore Dr., Wahweap ☎928/645–2433 ⊕www.lakepowell.com) carries authentic Native American rugs, pottery, jewelry, and baskets as well as tourist T-shirts and postcards.

ANTELOPE CANYON

★ ⑯ *4 mi east of Page on the Navajo Reservation, on AZ 98.*

You've probably seen dozens of photographs of Antelope Canyon, a narrow, red-sandstone slot canyon with convoluted corkscrew formations, dramatically illuminated by light streaming down from above. And you're likely to see assorted shutterbugs waiting patiently for just the right shot of these colorful, photogenic rocks, which are actually petrified-sand dunes of a prehistoric ocean that once filled this portion of North America. The best photos are taken at high noon, when light filters through "the slot" in the canyon surface. This is one place that you'll need to protect your camera equipment against blowing dust. Access to the canyon is limited to those on licensed tours. ⊠AZ 98, Page ✉Box 2520, Window Rock 86515 ☎928/871–6647 Navajo Parks & Recreation Dept. ⊕www.navajonationparks.org ☞$6, included in tour cost.

ANTELOPE CANYON TOURS

Access to Antelope Canyon is restricted by the Navajo Tribe to licensed tour operators. The tribe charges a $6 per-person fee, included in the price

Tribes & Their Crafts

There are 21 Native American tribes in Arizona, and many of the craftspeople on the reservations sell their wares, with specialties that include pottery, turquoise and sterling-silver jewelry, handwoven baskets, and Navajo wool rugs.

As the Spanish ventured northward from Mexico in the late 1500s and early 1600s, they taught the Native Americans their silvercrafting skills, while tribes specializing in pottery and weaving carry on a tradition that began hundreds of years ago. Generally, tribes used indigenous ingredients and supplies that were at hand: those living along rivers and waterways were more apt to produce baskets since reeds were plentiful; tribes that required water to be carried to their village were most likely to create pottery.

Once the railroads were built and travelers started coming west by train, Fred Harvey, who had set up fine eating establishments at railroad stops along the route, realized that the easterners were looking for souvenir handicrafts to take home with them. He encouraged Navajo weavers to create large pieces, like rugs and wall hangings. Navajos wove blankets from wool using natural plant dyes for color and each community is known for specific colors and designs that are passed down from mother to daughter, for generations. A medium-size rug (5 feet by 7 feet) with a complex pattern may require more than half a year to create, so don't be shocked if the price tag reads above $30,000.

Native beadwork traces its origins to trades with early trappers and explorers. Trade beads, as they were known, often came from Europe and became popular adornments for clothing and everyday items. Beaded fetishes, drums, rattles, and dolls were often part of spiritual ceremonies. Navajo silver and turquoise jewelry is often sought out by shoppers. The famous squash blossom necklaces, if completely handmade, can run more than $1,000, especially if the silver beads are made as two separate hemispheres. Proud craftsmen have individual logos or personal marks that are put into each piece. Authentic pieces will also indicate that the silver is Sterling.

Your best bet for big ticket items is to buy directly from the native craftsmen themselves or from a reputable dealer. If you're traveling in Navajoland, the Cameron Trading Post north of Flagstaff, or the Hubbell Trading Post south of Canyon de Chelly at Ganado are two spots where you can find exemplary rugs, jewelry, and craft items. In Phoenix, the gift shop at the famed Heard Museum offers some of the finest Native American handicrafts at reasonable prices. You can be certain that each and every piece of jewelry and art sold there is 100% native crafted.

Most products sold on the Hopi and Navajo reservations are authentic, but fakes are not unheard of. Trading posts are very reliable, as are most roadside stands, which can offer some outstanding values, but be wary of solo vendors hanging around parking lots. If you're planning on shopping on the Hopi Reservation or elsewhere outside the Navajo trading posts, it's a good idea to carry cash or traveler's checks, as not all vendors accept credit cards.

of tours offered by the licensed concessionaires in Page. The easiest way to book a tour is in town at the John Wesley Powell Memorial Museum Visitor Center; you pay nothing extra for the museum's service. If you'd like to go directly to the tour operators, you can do that, too; visit ⊕ *www.navajonationparks. org/htm/antelopecanyon.htm* for a list of approved companies. Most companies offer 1½-hour sightseeing tours for about $25 to $30, or longer photography tours for $50. The best time to see the canyon is between 8 AM and 2 PM.

Antelope Canyon Adventures (☎*928/ 645–5501 or 866/645–5501* ⊕*www.jeeptour.com*) offers 1½-hour sightseeing tours and 2-hour photography tours.

> ## SLOT CANYONS
>
> Slot canyons are unique to the Southwest. Carved through sandstone by wind and water, they are narrow at the top—some are only a foot wide on the surface—and wider at the bottom, which can be more than 100 feet below ground level. The play of light as it filters down through the slot onto the sandstone walls makes them remarkable subjects for photographs, but they are dangerous, particularly during the summer rainy season when flash floods can rush through them and sweep away an unwary hiker. Before hiking into a slot canyon, consult with locals and pay attention to weather forecasts.

John Wesley Powell Memorial Museum Visitor Center (☎*928/645–9496* ⊕*www.powellmuseum.org*) arranges and books 1½-hour tours and 2-hour photography tours. Photo tours leave from Page at 8 and 9:30 AM and return about 2 PM. The shorter sightseeing tours leave frequently between 8 AM and 4 PM.

Overland Canyon Tours (☎*928/608–4072* ⊕*www.overlandcanyontours. com*) is one of only a few Native American–operated tour companies in Page. Tours include a narrative explaining the canyon's history and geology.

Antelope Canyon Tours (☎*928/645–9102 or 866/645–9102* ⊕*www. antelopecanyon.com*) offers several tours daily from 8 AM to 3 PM for sightseers and photographers. The photo tour gives serious and amateur photographers the opportunity to wait for the "right light" to photograph the canyon and get basic information on equipment setup.

CANYON X
TOURS
On private property, the isolated slot canyon known as Canyon X can be toured only by Navajo guide Harley Klemm and his company, Overland Canyon Tours, which also operates popular tours to Antelope Canyon. Only one tour is given per day—departure times vary—and tours are offered by advance reservation only, with a limit of six participants. Because the area is rugged, children are not allowed, and participants should have good physical mobility to climb crevasses and some rough terrain.

GLEN CANYON NATIONAL RECREATION AREA

⑰ *2 mi west of Page on U.S. 89.*

Once you leave the Page business district heading northwest, the Glen Canyon Dam and Lake Powell behind it immediately become visible. This concrete-arch dam—all 5 million cubic feet of it—was completed in September 1963, its power plant an engineering feat that rivaled the Hoover Dam. The dam's crest is 1,560 feet across and rises 710 feet from bedrock and 583 feet above the waters of the Colorado River. When Lake Powell is full, it's 560 feet deep at the dam. The plant generates some 1.3 million kilowatts of electricity when each generator's 40-ton shaft is producing nearly 200,000 horsepower. Power from the dam serves a five-state grid consisting of Colorado, Arizona, Utah, California, and New Mexico and provides energy for some 1.5 million users.

With only 8 inches of annual rainfall, the Lake Powell area enjoys blue skies nearly year-round. Summer temperatures range from the 60s to the 90s. Fall and spring are usually balmy, with daytime temperatures often in the 70s and 80s, but chilly weather can set in. Nights are cool even in the summer, and in winter the risk of a cold spell increases, but all-weather houseboats and tour boats make for year-round cruising.

Boaters and campers should note that regulations require the use of portable toilets on the lake and lakeshore to prevent water pollution.

Just off the highway at the north end of the bridge is the **Carl Hayden Visitor Center,** where you can learn about the controversial creation of Glen Canyon Dam and Lake Powell and enjoy panoramic views of both. To enter the visitor center, you must go through a metal detector. Absolutely no bags are allowed inside. ✉*U.S. 89, 2 mi west of town, Page* ☏*928/608–6404* ⊕*www.nps.gov/glca* ☏*$15 per vehicle or $7 per person (entering on foot or by bicycle), good for up to seven days, $16 per week boating fee* ☉ *Visitor Center Memorial Day–Labor Day, daily 8–6; Labor Day–Nov. and Mar.–Memorial Day, daily 8–5; Dec.–Feb., daily 8–4.*

WAHWEAP

⑱ *5 mi north of Glen Canyon Dam on U.S. 89.*

Most waterborne-recreational activity on the Arizona side of the lake is centered on this vacation village, where everything needed for a lakeside holiday is available: tour boats, fishing, boat rentals, dinner cruises, and more. The Lake Powell Resort has excellent views of the lake area and you can take a boat tour from the Wahweap Marina.

★ **⑲** A boat tour to **Rainbow Bridge National Monument** is a great way to see the enormity of the lake and its incredible, rugged beauty. This 290-foot red-sandstone arch is the world's largest natural bridge and can be reached by boat or strenuous hike *(⇨ Hiking).* The lake level is down due to the prolonged drought throughout the region, so expect a 1½-mi hike from the boat dock to the monument. The bridge can also be viewed by air. To the Navajos, this is a sacred area with deep religious and spiritual significance, so outsiders are asked not to hike underneath the arch itself. ☎928/608–6200 ⊕*www.nps.gov/rabr.*

SPORTS & THE OUTDOORS

BOATING One of the most scenic lakes of the American West, Lake Powell has 186 mi of clear sapphire waters

WORD OF MOUTH

"Rainbow Bridge is really a great experience. The trip there and back on the tour boat really lets you see a lot of the lake, buttes and mesas you can't see from land."

–utahtea

edged with vast canyons of red and orange rock. Ninety-six major side canyons intricately twist and turn into the main channel of Lake Powell, into what was once the main artery of the Colorado River through Glen Canyon. In some places the lake is 500 feet deep, and by June the lake's waters begin to warm and stay that way well into October.

An $80 million project begun in 2003 and under construction in four phases, **Antelope Point Marina** (⌖*BIA Hwy. N22B, Mile Marker 4, Navajo Nation 86040* ☎602/952–0114 ⊕*www.azmarinas.com*) will include a Navajo Cultural Center, artist studios, more than 400 wet slips for houseboats and watercraft, a floating marina village and restaurant, 225 luxury casitas, and an RV park and campground. As of this writing, the first two phases (infrastructure and the marina village) had been completed; the campground is slated to open in 2008, and the luxury casitas and cultural center in 2010. At **Aramark's Lake Powell Resorts & Marinas** (☎928/645–1004 or 800/528–6154 ⊕*www. visitlakepowell.com*) houseboat rentals range widely in size, amenities, and price, depending upon season. *For more information on houseboats, see Housebaating in Where to Stay & Eat, below.* You may want to rent a powerboat or personal water craft along with a houseboat to explore the many narrow canyons and waterways on the lake. A 19-foot powerboat for eight passengers runs approximately $330 per day and up.

Stateline Marina (✉*U.S. 89, State Line, UT* ☎928/645–1111), 1½ mi north of Lake Powell Resort, is part of Aramark's Lake Powell Resorts & Marinas and site of the boat-rental office. It's here that you pick up rental houseboats, powerboats, kayaks, Jet Skis, and personal water craft. There's also a public launch ramp if you're towing your own boat. **Wahweap Marina** (✉*100 Lake Shore Dr., Wahweap* ☎928/645–2433) is the largest of the four full-service Lake Powell marinas run by Aramark's Lake Powell Resorts & Marinas. There are 850 slips and the most facilities, including a decent diner, public launch ramp, fishing dock, and a marina store where you can buy fishing licenses and other necessities. It's the only full-service marina on the Arizona side of the lake (the other three marinas—Hite, Bullfrog, and Halls Crossing—are in Utah).

BOAT TOURS Excursions on double-decker scenic cruisers piloted by experienced guides leave from the dock of Lake Powell's **Lake Powell Resort** (✉*100 Lake Shore Dr., Wahweap* ☎928/645–2433 or 800/528–6154). The most popular tour is the full-day trip to Rainbow Bridge National

Monument for $119 (a box lunch is included). There's also a 2½-hour sunset dinner cruise ($61) featuring a prime-rib dinner—vegetarian lasagna meals are available if ordered in advance. It's served on the fully enclosed decks of the 95-foot *Canyon King* paddle wheeler, a reproduction of a 19th-century bay boat.

FISHING Anglers delight in the world-class bass fishing on Lake Powell. You'll hear over and over how the big fish are "biting in the canyons," so you'll need a small vessel if you plan on fishing for the big one. Landing a 20-pound striper isn't unusual (the locals' secret is to use anchovies for bait). Fishing licenses for both Arizona and Utah are available at the **Marina Store at Wahweap Marina** (⊠ *100 Lake Shore Dr., Wahweap* ☎ *928/645–1136*). **Stix Bait & Tackle** (⊠ *5 S. Lake Powell Blvd., Page* ☎ *928/645–2891*) can recommend local fishing guides.

> ## WORD OF MOUTH
>
> "I could not get enough of Lake Powell. We rented a houseboat, and then rented jet skis for a half day. On a jet ski, you can go way up all the little shallow crevices left by the drought. I understand there are petroglyphs back up in there that have only recently been uncovered with the receding waterline. And on a jet ski, you can go where ever you want and stop where ever you want."
>
> –waikikigirl

HIKING Bring plenty of water and electrolyte-rich beverages such as Gatorade when hiking, and drink often. It's important to remember when hiking at Lake Powell to watch the sky for storms: it may not be raining where you are but flooding can occur in downstream canyons—particularly slot canyons—from a storm miles away.

Only seasoned hikers in good physical condition will want to try either of the trails leading to **Rainbow Bridge**; both are about 26 to 28 mi round-trip through challenging and rugged terrain. This site is considered sacred by the Navajo, and it's requested that visitors show respect by not walking under the bridge. Take Indian Highway 16 north toward the Utah state border. At the fork in the road, take either direction for about 5 mi to the trailhead leading to Rainbow Bridge. Excursion boats pull in at the dock at the arch, but no supplies are sold there.

Navajo Nation Parks and Recreation Department (⊠ *Bldg. 36A, E. AZ 264* 🖃 *Box 2520, Window Rock 86515* ☎ *928/871–6647* ⊕ *www.navajonationparks.org*) provides backcountry permits (a small fee is charged), which must be obtained before hiking to Rainbow Bridge. Write to the office, and allow about a month to process the paperwork.

WHERE TO STAY & EAT

$$–$$$ ✕🛏 **Lake Powell Resort.** This sprawling one-story lodge, run by Aramark, sits on a promontory above Lake Powell and serves as the center

Fodor'sChoice for recreational activities in the area. The brightly colored Southwest-

★ ern-style suites in the newest building are particularly attractive. The Rainbow Room restaurant ($–$$$) offers an extensive Southwestern, American, and Continental menu and breakfast buffet, all with panoramic views of Lake Powell. In season there are also decent pizzas from Bene Pizza. ✉ *100 Lake Shore Dr., 7 mi north of Page off U.S. 89, Wahweap* ⌂ *Box 1597, Page 86040* ☎ *928/645–2433 or 800/528–6154* ⊕ *www.lakepowell.com* ⇝ *350 rooms* ♿ *In-room: refrigerator. In-hotel: 2 restaurants, bar, pools, some pets allowed* ▱ *AE, D, DC, MC, V.*

Without a doubt, the most popular and fun way to vacation on Lake Powell is to rent a houseboat. Houseboats, ranging in size from 36 to 59 feet and sleeping 6 to 12 people, come complete with marine radios, fully equipped kitchens, and bathrooms with hot showers; you need only bring sheets and towels. The larger, deluxe boats are a good choice in hot summer months since they have air-conditioning. **Aramark's Lake Powell Resorts & Marinas** (☎ *800/528–6154* ⊕ *www.lakepowell.com*) is the only concessionaire that rents boats on Lake Powell. There are many vacation packages available. One houseboat that sleeps 10 runs from $865 for three nights in winter to about $3,000 for seven nights during the summer peak. At the other end of the spectrum, 75-foot luxury houseboats, which sleep 12, cost as much as $12,000 for seven nights. You receive hands-on instruction before you leave the marina.

NORTHEAST ARIZONA ESSENTIALS

To research prices, get advice from other travelers, and book travel arrangements, visit ⊕ *www.fodors.com.*

TRANSPORTATION

BY AIR
The only airline that offers service directly to northeastern Arizona is Great Lakes Aviation, which flies into Page Municipal Airport from Phoenix.

Contacts Great Lakes Aviation (☎ *800/554–5111* ⊕ *www.greatlakesav.com*). **Page Municipal Airport** (☎ *928/645–4337* ⊕ *www.cityofpage.org/airport.htm*).

BY BUS
In the unlikely event you end up in this part of the world without a car, bus travel is an option, albeit a not particularly practical one. The Navajo Transit System has extensive, fixed routes throughout the Navajo Reservation. The buses are modern, in good condition, and generally on time, but they do not make frequent runs, and when they do run they can be slow. Fares range from 50¢ for local rides to a high of $13.05 (Window Rock to Tuba City). This can be an up-close-and-personal way to travel through the Navajo Nation and meet the people who live here as they go about their daily business.

Contacts Navajo Transit System (☎ *928/729–4002* ⊕ *www.nts.navajo.org*).

BY CAR
The only practical way to tour the Navajo and Hopi nations is by car. If you're arriving from Southern California or other parts of Arizona, Flagstaff is the best jumping-off point. If you're traveling from Utah or

Nevada, you might come in from Utah on U.S. 89, starting your tour at Page. From Colorado, logical entry points are Farmington and Shiprock, New Mexico, via U.S. 64 (what looks like a more direct route to Canyon de Chelly through Red Rock ends up crossing an unimproved road). Gallup, New Mexico, to the east, is also a convenient starting point for exploring if you're coming from the Albuquerque area.

A tour of Navajo-Hopi country can involve driving significant distances among widely scattered communities, so a detailed, up-to-date road map is essential. Gas stations carry adequate state maps, but two other maps are particularly recommended: the AAA guide to Navajo-Hopi country or the excellent map of the northeast prepared by the Navajo Nation Tourism Office.

Most of the 25,000 square mi of the Navajo Reservation and other areas of northeastern Arizona are off the beaten track. It's prudent to stay on the well-maintained paved thoroughfares. If you don't have the equipment for wilderness travel—including a four-wheel-drive vehicle and provisions—and do not have backcountry experience, stay off the dirt roads unless they are signed and graded and the skies are clear. Be on the lookout for ominous rain clouds in summer or signs of snow in winter. Never drive into dips or low-lying areas during a heavy rainstorm. If you heed these simple precautions, car travel through the region will be as safe as anywhere else. While driving around the Navajo Nation, tune in to 660 AM (KTNN) for local news and weather.

Road service, auto repairs, and other automotive services are few and far between, so service your vehicle before venturing into the Navajo and Hopi reservations (or do so in the larger communities, such as Tuba City, Kayenta, and Window Rock), and carry emergency equipment and supplies. If you need assistance, ask a local for the nearest auto-repair service. Diamond Towing offers a 24-hour emergency road service.

Contact Diamond Towing (⊠ *Kayenta* ☎ *928/697–8437*).

BY TRAIN
No passenger trains enter the Navajo or Hopi Reservation or stop at any of the other towns along its perimeter, but Amtrak calls on Winslow and Flagstaff, from which you can rent a car to explore the region.

CONTACTS & RESOURCES

EMERGENCIES
Dial 911 for emergencies on reservation lands.

Ambulance & Fire Kayenta Ambulance (☎ *928/697–4074*). **Page Ambulance** (☎ *928/645–2461*).

Hospitals Monument Valley Health Center (⊠ *4 Rock Door Canyon, Monument Valley, UT 84536* ☎ *435/727–3241*). **Page Hospital** (⊠ *501 N. Navajo Ave., Page* ☎ *928/645–2424*). **Sage Memorial Hospital** (⊠ *Ganado* ☎ *928/755–3411*). **U.S. Public Health Service Indian Hospital** (⊠ *Chinle* ☎ *928/674–7001* ⊠ *Fort*

Defiance ☎ *928/729–5741* ✉ *Keams Canyon* ☎ *928/738–2211* ✉ *Tuba City* ☎ *928/283–2501*).

Pharmacies **Safeway Pharmacy** (✉ *Page Plaza, Page* ☎ *928/645–5714*). **Wal-Mart Pharmacy** (✉ *Gateway Plaza, Page* ☎ *928/645–2917*).

Police **Canyon de Chelly Police** (☎ *928/674–2111 or 928/674–2112*). **Hopi tribal police: Hopi Mesas** (☎ *928/738–2233 or 928/738–2234*). **Navajo tribal police** (✉ *Chinle* ☎ *928/674–2111 or 928/674–2112* ✉ *Tuba City* ☎ *928/283–3111 or 928/283–3112* ✉ *Window Rock* ☎ *928/871–6111 or 928/871–6112* ✉ *Kayenta* ☎ *928/697–5600*). **Page Police** (☎ *928/645–2463*).

TOUR OPTIONS

AIR TOURS Page-based American Aviation offers flightseeing tours of Monument Valley, Lake Powell and Rainbow Bridge, and Bryce. Gallup Flying Service offers photo and scenic aerial tours of Navajoland from Gallup, New Mexico.

Information **American Aviation** (☎ *928/608–1060 or 866/525–3247* ⊕ *www. americanaviationwest.com*). **Gallup Flying Service** (☎ *505/863–6606* ⊕ *www. gallupflyingservice.com*).

VISITOR INFORMATION

Information **Glen Canyon Recreation Area** (☎ *928/608–6200* ⊕ *www.nps. gov/glca*). **Inter Tribal Council of Arizona: Hopi Tribe** (☎ *928/734–3000* ⊕ *www.itcaonline.com/tribes_hopi.html*). **Navajo Nation Tourism Office** (☎ *928/810–8501* ⊕ *www.discovernavajo.com*). **Page/Lake Powell Chamber of Commerce** (✉ *Box 727, 86040* ☎ *928/645–2741 or 888/261–7243* ⊕ *www. pagelakepowelltourism.com*).

Eastern Arizona

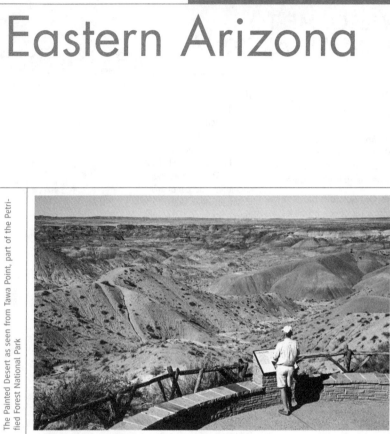

The Painted Desert as seen from Tawa Point, part of the Petrified Forest National Park

WORD OF MOUTH

"My family and I really liked the Painted Desert/Petrified Forest. I saw landscapes there the likes of which I have never seen before and they change drastically throughout the park."

—lisatravels

WELCOME TO EASTERN ARIZONA

Chinle formation in Petrified Forest National Park

TOP REASONS TO GO

★ **Salt River Canyon:** Watch the desert's cacti disappear as the country's pine delights your senses.

★ **Get outside:** No place for couch potatoes, eastern Arizona is home to some of the state's best recreation areas for skiing, fishing, golfing, camping, and exploring.

★ **Be petrified:** Marvel at huge petrified logs and the dazzling colors of nature at Petrified Forest National Park.

★ **Hit the road:** Whether you're traveling the Colorado Trail National Scenic Byway or getting your kicks on Route 66, these roads were made for travelers.

★ **Discover native traditions:** The rich culture and heritage of Native American tribes permeates this area.

1 **The White Mountains.** In a state known for its extreme temperatures, residents of the White Mountains are proud of their home's relatively staid climate. The comfortable conditions and panoramic mountain views draw thousands here in the summer, making the region a playground for golfers, hikers, and fishermen. But there's plenty to do if you don't want to get your hands dirty.

2 **The Petrified Forest.** Forget about a Hollywood sci-fi thriller—the Petrified Forest actually takes you back in time. One of Arizona's most unique sites, the park has yielded fossils dating back 225 million years. A visit to the forest is like exploring an outdoor museum. It's worth the hike, especially if you catch the brilliant colors of the Painted Desert at midday.

Chinle shale mounds at the Blue Mesa in Petrified Forest NP

Springtime at Petrified Forest
National Park

GETTING ORIENTED

Eastern Arizona is a large, somewhat loosely defined series of small towns and historic sites. Visitors searching for an escape from the desert heat head for the White Mountains and its majestic vistas of ponderosa pines. Others seek history and head northeast to the 186,000-acre Petrified Forest National Park. No matter the destination don't forget to stop and experience the area's local flavor, whether it's a museum of Native American crafts or a drive through a town whose name was derived from a losing hand of cards.

The newly renovated Painted Desert Inn was built in 1924

EASTERN ARIZONA PLANNER

Getting Here & Around

There isn't much choice: you'll be driving to and around eastern Arizona. Greyhound and Amtrak offer limited service, but they aren't that helpful for travelers. Part of the experience in eastern Arizona is the drive. Rent a car in Phoenix or Tucson, or even Flagstaff, and enjoy the open road.

When to Go

If you're a skier, winter is the time to tour the White Mountains. Sunrise Park Resort has 10 lifts and 65 trails, and a private snowboarders' park.

If you're not a winter sports enthusiast, it's probably best to plan your trip to Eastern Arizona for the high season (May through October). Residents of Phoenix and Tucson flock here to escape unbearably hot temperatures, but you can still find some solitude if you rent a cabin or choose a smaller, more remote resort or bed-and-breakfast.

Eastern Arizona is enjoyable year-round, but many lodging facilities and tourist attractions are closed in autumn and winter, so call ahead.

Making the Most of Your Time

The Petrified Forest is the main attraction for most of Eastern Arizona's visitors. Plan to reserve a day for the forest and the Painted Desert, with one or two additional days to explore the neighboring towns. If solitude is your goal, consider staying at a lodge surrounded by private forest.

Pinetop-Lakeside offers the best base for your trip, with a wide range of lodging facilities and amenities. Neighboring area towns, such as Snowflake-Taylor or Holbrook, have storied motels and bed-and-breakfasts.

Depending on your preferences, you can add day trips and excursions. Fans of the great outdoors have their choice of activities like fishing, skiing, hiking, and biking in the White Mountains. Those who like a little less sweat in their vacations can hit the open road and explore historic Route 66 or the Colorado Trail.

Sample Itineraries

If an outdoors adventure is the plan, head to Pinetop-Lakeside, Greer, or Springerville-Eagar and enjoy a day or two of hiking, biking, and fishing. In winter, hit the slopes or put on a pair of snowshoes.

Is your destination Petrified Forest National Park? Make the most of it by checking out neighboring towns during your journey. Spend a night at one of Snowflake-Taylor's quaint inns, then head for the park. Spend a second night in one of the historic hotels in Winslow or Holbrook, and head back to the city by way of Show Low on your third day.

If you have more time, there are more natural wonders: At Springerville-Eagar, you can connect to U.S. 191, also known as the Coronado Trail Scenic Byway. Towering over this southern part of the White Mountains is Mount Baldy, an 11,590-foot extinct volcano considered sacred by the Apache. Also worth exploring is the Mogollon Rim, a limestone escarpment that extends 200 mi southwest of Flagstaff to the White Mountains.

Paradise for Outdoors Enthusiasts

Like hiking? Hikers and mountain bikers of all abilities enjoy the White Mountains' 225 mi of interconnecting loop trails, open to those on foot or on non-motorized wheels. Ranger stations have maps. Allow an hour for each 2 mi of trail, plus an additional hour for every 1,000 feet gained in altitude. Carry water and watch out for poison ivy.

Like fishing? Anglers flock to the more than 65 lakes, streams, and reservoirs in the White Mountains. In winter only artificial lures and flies are permitted. An Arizona fishing license is required; on tribal land, you'll also need a White Mountain Apache fishing license. Want an easier catch? Some lodges have private lakes stocked with trout.

Like golfing? The High Country's links draw golfers from all over and these mountain fairways angle through lush forests and past lakes and springs.

Like skiing? The 11,000-foot White Mountains offer hilly, wooded landscapes that invite downhill and cross-country skiing adventurers. Greer's nearby Pole Knoll Trail System and surrounding Forest Service roads make for 33 mi of cross-country trails. No matter where you stay in the White Mountains, Sunrise Park Resort is never more than an hour's drive away.

Local Food & Lodging

Luxury travel this is not. Some local lodges, such as the Greer Lodge Resort, are expanding and offering more luxury services such as massages. Most places, however, offer clean rooms without many frills. Fine dining is difficult to find; home-style cooking, steak houses, and the occasional authentic Mexican joint pepper most towns. Reservations are suggested during the busy summer months.

What It Costs

	¢	$	$$	$$$	$$$$
Restaurants	Under $7	$7–$12	$13–$18	$19–$25	over $25
Hotels	Under $50	$50–$90	$91–$130	$131–$175	over $175

Restaurant prices are per person for a main course at dinner. Hotel prices are for a standard double in high season, excluding taxes and service charges.

Native American Sites

North of Springerville-Eagar, Casa Malpais Archaeological Park is a prehistoric pueblo site with construction characteristics of both the ancient Puebloan and Mogollon peoples. Nearby Lyman Lake State Park has petroglyph trails with some of the region's more accessible rock art. West of Holbrook, Homolovi Ruins State Park is home to a large complex of Hopi ancestral pueblos. Petroglyphs and pueblos dating back more than 600 years can be found at stops along the 28-mi park road in the Petrified Forest National Park.

5

Updated by
Cara LaBrie

IN A STATE OF DRAMATIC natural wonders, eastern Arizona is often overlooked—truly a tragedy, as it's one of Arizona's great outdoor playgrounds. In the White Mountains, northeast of Phoenix, you can hike amid the largest stand of ponderosa pine in the world, fish for trout in babbling brooks, swim in clear reservoirs fed by unsullied mountain streams, and, at night, gaze upward at millions of twinkling stars. The region's winter sports are just as varied: you can ski downhill or cross country, snowboard, snowshoe, and snowmobile on hundreds of miles of designated trails.

The White Mountains are unspoiled high country at its best. Certain areas have been designated as primitive wilderness and remain preserved. In these vast tracts, the air is rent with piercing cries of hawks and eagles, and majestic herds of elk graze in verdant, wildflower-laden meadows. Past volcanic activity has left the land strewn with cinder cones, and the whole region is bounded by the Mogollon Rim (pronounced *muh*-gee-on)—a 200-mi geologic upthrust that splits the state—made famous as the "Tonto Rim" in Zane Grey's books. Much of the plant life is unique to this region; this is one of the few places in the country where such desert plants as juniper and manzanita grow intermixed with mountain pines and aspen.

The human aspects of the landscape are equally appealing. Historic Western towns are friendly outposts of down-home hospitality, and the many prehistoric ruins are reminders of the native cultures that once flourished here, and are still a vital presence. The Fort Apache Reservation, home to the White Mountain Apache Tribe, is north of the Salt River, and the San Carlos Apache Tribal Reservation is south of the river. Visitors are welcome to explore most reservation lands. All that's required is a permit, easily obtained from tribal offices.

Historic sites and natural wonders also attract visitors to eastern Arizona. To the north, along historic Route 66, are the Painted Desert and Petrified Forest National Park, and Homolovi Ruins State Park. The austere mesas of the Painted Desert are famous for their multihued sedimentary layers. Nature also has worked wonders on the great fallen logs of the Petrified Forest National Park. In Triassic times, the park was a great, steamy swampland; some 225 million years ago, seismic activity forced the swamp's decaying plant matter (and a number of deceased dinosaurs) deep underground, where it eventually turned to stone. Fifty miles west of these unusual geologic remains, Homolovi Ruins State Park marks the site of four major ancestral Hopi pueblos, two of which contain more than 1,000 rooms.

THE WHITE MOUNTAINS

With elevations climbing to more than 11,000 feet, the White Mountains of east-central Arizona are a winter wonderland and a summer haven from the desert heat. In the 1870s, U.S. soldier and diarist John Gregory Bourke labeled the White Mountains region "a strange upheaval, a freak of nature, a mountain canted up on one side; one

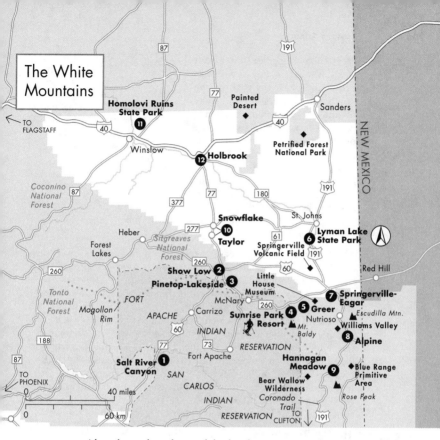

The White
Mountains

Homolovi Ruins
State Park 11

Painted
Desert

Sanders

TO
FLAGSTAFF 40

Winslow

Holbrook 12

Petrified Forest
National Park

NEW MEXICO

Coconino
National
Forest 87

377

St. Johns

Snowflake

Taylor 10

Springerville
Volcanic Field

Lyman Lake
State Park 6

Heber

Sitgreaves
National
Forest

Forest
Lakes

260

260

Show Low 2

Pinetop-Lakeside 3

Little
House
Museum

Red Hill

Tonto
National
Forest

Mogollon
Rim

FORT

APACHE

Carrizo

McNary

260

Sunrise Park
Resort 4

Greer 5

Nutrioso

Mt.
Baldy

Springerville-
Eagar 7

Escudilla Mtn.

Williams Valley

188

60

INDIAN

77

73

RESERVATION

Fort Apache

Alpine 8

87

TO
PHOENIX

40 miles

SAN

CARLOS

Hannagan
Meadow 9

Bear Wallow
Wilderness

Blue Range
Primitive
Area

0

60 km

INDIAN

RESERVATION

Coronado
Trail
TO
CLIFTON

Rose Peak

191

Salt River
Canyon 1

rides along the edge and looks down two or three thousand feet
into...a weird scene of grandeur and rugged beauty." The area is still
grand and rugged, carved by deep river canyons and tall cliffs covered
with ponderosa pine. It's also much less remote than it was in Bourke's
time, with a full-scale real-estate boom now under way.

Winter travelers in the White Mountains should be aware that weather
conditions can change without notice. Call for weather information
before heading out on area highways.

SALT RIVER CANYON

❶ *40 mi north of Globe on U.S. 60.*

Exposing a time lapse of 500 million years, the multicolor spires,
buttes, mesas, and walls of the **Salt River Canyon** have inspired its nickname, the mini–Grand Canyon. Approaching the Salt River Canyon
from Phoenix, U.S. 60 climbs through rolling hills, and the terrain
changes from high desert with cactus and mesquite trees to forests of
ponderosa pine. After entering the San Carlos Indian Reservation, the
highway drops 2,000 feet and makes a series of hairpin turns to the
Salt River. Stop at the viewing and interpretive display area before

crossing the bridge to stretch your legs. Wander along the banks below and enjoy the rock-strewn rapids. On hot days slip your shoes off and dip your feet into the chilly water. The river and canyon are open to hiking, camping, fishing, and white-water rafting, but you need a permit as this is tribal land. For information and recreational permits, contact the **San Carlos Apache Tribe** (☎928/475–2343 or 888/475–2344 ⊕*www.sancarlos apache.com*) or the **White Mountain Apache Tribe** (☎928/338–4385 ⊕*www.wmat.nsn.us*).

> **WORD OF MOUTH**
>
> "The Salt River has rafting trips that are very mild. Note that the season is very short. Tubing the Salt River is another option during the summer—it's great fun, by the way."
>
> –jkgourmet

The Apache people migrated to the Southwest around the 10th century. Divided into individual bands instead of existing as a unified tribe, they were a hunting and gathering culture, moving with the seasons to gather food, and their crafts—baskets, beadwork, and cradleboards—were compatible with their mobile lifestyle. The U.S. government didn't understand that different Apache bands might be hostile to each other and tried to gather separate tribes on one reservation, compounding relocation problems. Eventually, the government established San Carlos Apache Indian Reservation in 1871 and Fort Apache Indian Reservation in 1897. Both tribes hold fiercely to their cultures. The native language is still spoken and taught in schools and tribal ceremonies continue to be held. Both tribes have highly acclaimed "hot-shot" crews that immediately respond to forest fires throughout the West.

The Salt River forms the boundary between these two large Apache reservations of eastern Arizona.

The **San Carlos Apache Indian Reservation** (☎928/475–2361 *for tribal offices*), established in 1871 for various Apache tribes, covers 1.8 million acres southeast of Salt River Canyon. One third of the reservation is covered with forest, and the rest is desert. The San Carlos Apaches number about 12,500 and are noted for their beadwork and basketry. Peridot, a beautiful yellow-green stone resembling the emerald, is mined near the town of Peridot and made into jewelry.

The **Cultural Center** houses displays of Apache history and culture, along with explanations of cultural traditions like Changing Women Ceremony, a girls' puberty rite. Crafts are sold here. ✉*Hwy. 70, Milepost 272, Peridot* ☎928/475–2894 💲$3 ⊗ *Weekdays 9–5.*

The 1.6-million-acre **Fort Apache Indian Reservation** (☎928/338–1230 *for tribal tourism*) is the ancestral home of the White Mountain Apache Tribe. The elevation of the tribal lands ranges from 3,000 feet at the bottom of Salt River to 11,000 feet in the White Mountains and provides some of the best outdoor recreation in the state. Most of the over 12,000 tribal members live in nine towns, with the largest, Whiteriver (population 2,500), serving as tribal headquarters. Tribal enterprises include Sunrise Ski Resort, Hon-Dah Resort Casino, cattle ranching, and lumber.

Apache Cultural Museum. The entrance price buys access to three great places to visit on the Fort Apache Indian Reservation. The museum explains the history, culture, and artistic traditions of the Apaches, and sells local crafts and books. The **Fort Apache Historical Park** harks back to cavalry days with horse barns, parade grounds, log cabins, and officers' homes. **Kinishba Ruins,** 5 mi west of Fort Apache (get directions and a map at the Cultural Center) is a partly restored sandstone pueblo and the only Native American ruin on the reservation that is open to visitors. ⌧ ½ *mi east of junction of State Rte. 73 and Indian Rte. 46, 5 mi south of White River* ☎ *928/338–4625* ⌧ *$3* ☺ *Sept.– May, weekdays 8–5; June–Aug., Mon.–Sat. 8–5.*

EN ROUTE

The road out of the Salt River Canyon climbs along the canyon's northern cliffs, providing views of this truly spectacular chasm, unfairly overlooked in a state full of world-famous gorges. The highway continues some 50 mi northward to the **Mogollon Rim**—a huge geologic ledge that bisects much of Arizona—and its cool upland pine woods.

5

SHOW LOW

❷ *60 mi north of the Salt River Canyon on U.S. 60.*

Show Low has little of the charm of its neighboring White Mountains communities, but it's the main commercial center for the High Country. Additionally, the city is a crossing point for east–west traffic along the Mogollon Rim and traffic headed for Holbrook and points north. If you're heading up to the Painted Desert and Petrified Forest from Phoenix, you might want to spend the night here.

Look around the collectibles shop **Painted Nest** for antiques and unusual crafts. The owners turn used furniture into shabby chic, and you might pick up some decorating ideas. ⌧ *1191 E. Deuce of Clubs* ☎ *928/537– 2755* ☺ *Closed Sun. and Mon.*

SPORTS & THE OUTDOORS

FISHING **Fool Hollow Lake Recreational Area** (⌧ *2 mi north of U.S. 60 off AZ 260* ☺ ☎ *928/537–3680*) is open year-round for camping, fishing, and boating. Set amid a piney 800 acres, the lake is stocked with rainbow trout, walleye, and bass, and the surrounding area provides wonderful opportunities for wildlife viewing. **Show Low Lake** (⌧ *Show Low Lake Rd.* ☎ *928/537–4126*), south of town and 1 mi off AZ 260, holds the state record for the largest walleye catch and is well stocked with largemouth bass, bluegill, and catfish. Lucky anglers have pulled out 9-pound rainbow trout. Facilities include a bait shop, marina with boat rentals, and campsites with bathrooms and showers. **Troutback Flyfishing** (⌧ *Box 864, Show Low 85902* ☎ *928/532–3474 or 800/903–4092* ⊕ *www. troutback.com*) has access to some of the most scenic lakes and private waters in the region. From April through October, this fishing-guide company specializes in fly-fishing instruction, guided walk-wades, and float-tube and boating trips.

GOLF **Bison Golf & Country Club** (⌧ *860 N. 36th Dr., at AZ 260* ☎ *928/537– 4564*) is a par-70 course with a back nine in the pines and a front nine in a more open meadow setting. Need to practice driving or putting? You can do it here. The course is open year-round.

Silver Creek Golf Club (✉*2051 Silver Lake Blvd.* ☎*928/537–2744* ⊕*www.silvercreekgolfclub.com*), 5 mi east of town on U.S. 60, then 7½ mi north on Bourdon Ranch Road, is an 18-hole championship golf course. The course opened to rave reviews in the 1980s, and was voted by the PGA as one of the top 10 golf courses in Arizona— no small feat in a state that lives and breathes golf. It's also one of the more affordable courses in the area. Given its lower elevation, this course is usually a few degrees warmer than Show Low and stays open year-round. Greens fees change seasonally; call for details.

> ### WHAT AN ODD NAME!
>
> Yes, Show Low *is* an odd name. Legend has it that two partners, Clark and Cooley, homesteaded the area in 1870 but wanted to dissolve the partnership some years later after an argument. They decided to play cards—the winner would buy out the loser. On the last hand of the night, Cooley was a point behind when Clark allegedly offered "show low and you win." Cooley cut the deck and came up with the deuce of clubs, winning the game and the land. Part of the partners' then-ranch is now the town of Show Low, and the main drag through town is called Deuce of Clubs.

WHERE TO STAY & EAT

$–$$$$ ✗ **Native New Yorker.** If you want to catch your favorite sporting event, this restaurant has eight TVs in the dining room and nine TVs in the adjacent sports bar. They're famous for their wings, but the soup in the sourdough bread bowl is good, too. A steak dinner runs about $33. ✉*391 W. Deuce of Clubs* ☎*928/532–5100* ▭AE, D, MC, V.

¢–$$ ✗ **High in the Pines Deli.** Locals flock to this deli and coffeehouse for tasty specialty sandwiches—the roasted pork tenderloin is out of this world. European-style charcuterie boards include selections of pâtés, meats, and cheeses served with fresh baguette bread. On a cold day, try the Show Low hot chocolate or steaming homemade soups. Box lunches are available. ✉*1191 E. Hall St.* ☎*928/537–1453* ▭AE, D, MC, V ☉*Closed Sun. No dinner.*

★ ¢–$$ ✗ **Licano's Mexican Food and Steakhouse.** Licano's serves what locals claim are the best enchiladas on the mountain, along with prime rib and lobster tail. The spacious lounge, with a weekday happy hour from 4:30 to 6:30, stays open to 9:30 nightly. ✉*573 W. Deuce of Clubs* ☎*928/537–8220* ▭AE, D, MC, V.

$$–$$$ ▦ **Holiday Inn Express.** Larger rooms and more conveniences than its Show Low neighbors make for a comfortable night's rest. All rooms were recently renovated and include microwaves and refrigerators. Feel like working out? Check out the cardio equipment, and cool off with a complimentary bottle of water and a dip in the indoor pool. ✉*151 W. Deuce of Clubs, 85901* ☎*928/537–5115* ▤*928/537–2929* ⊕*www. hiexpress.com* ⤴*71 rooms* ⌂*In-room: refrigerator, Wi-Fi. In hotel: pool, gym, laundry facilities* ▭AE, D, DC, MC, V ℟CP.

$ 🏨 **Best Western Paint Pony Lodge.** Spacious rooms have wood accents and picture windows overlooking Arizona's pine-studded high country. Suites and some rooms include fireplaces, and use of an off-property gym is free for hotel guests. ⊠*581 W. Deuce of Clubs, 85901* ☎*928/537–5773* ⊕*www.bestwestern.com* ☞*48 rooms, 2 suites* ♿*In-room: refrigerator, Wi-Fi. In-hotel: no-smoking rooms, some pets allowed, no elevator* ⊟AE, D, DC, MC, V ⦿CP.

$ 🏨 **KC Motel.** Victorian decor, including four-poster beds, and large rooms make this a not-so-typical motel. ⊠*60 W. Deuce of Clubs, 85901* ☎*928/537–4433 or 800/531–7152* 🖷*928/537–0106* ⊕*www.kcmotelinshowlow.com* ☞*37 rooms* ♿*In-room: refrigerator, Wi-Fi. In hotel: no elevator* ⊟AE, D, DC, MC, V ⦿CP.

PINETOP-LAKESIDE

❸ *15 mi southeast of Show Low on AZ 260.*

5

At 7,200 feet, the community of Pinetop-Lakeside borders the world's largest stand of ponderosa pine. Two towns, Pinetop and Lakeside, were incorporated in 1984 to form this municipality—although they still retain separate post offices. The modest year-round population is 4,200, but in summer months it can jump as high as 30,000. Once popular only with the retirement and summer-home set, the city now lures thousands of "flatlanders" up from the Valley of the Sun with its gorgeous scenery, excellent multiuse trails, premier golf courses, and temperatures rarely exceeding 85°F. The main drag is known as both AZ 260 and White Mountain Boulevard.

SPORTS & THE OUTDOORS

BICYCLING & HIKING Ranked No. 3 in the country's "Top Ten Trail Towns" by the American Hiking Society, Pinetop-Lakeside is the primary trailhead for the White Mountains Trails System, roughly 200 mi of interconnecting multiuse loop trails spanning the White Mountains. All these trails are open to mountain bikers, horseback riders, and hikers.

Half a mile off AZ 260 on Woodland Road, **Big Springs Environmental Study Area** is a ½-mi loop trail that wanders by riparian meadows, two streams, and a spring-fed pond. A series of educational signs is devoted to the surrounding flora and fauna. The trailhead for **Country Club Trail** is at the junction of Forest Service roads 182 and 185; these 3½ mi of moderately difficult mountain-biking and hiking trails can be spiced up by following the spur-trail to the top of Pat Mullen Mountain and back. The well-traveled and very easy **Mogollon Rim Interpretive Trail** follows a small part of the 19th-century **Crook Trail** along the Mogollon Rim; the ¼-mi path, with a trailhead just west of the Pinetop-Lakeside city limits, is well marked with placards describing local wildlife and geography. The 8-mi **Panorama Trail,** rated moderate, affords astonishing views from the top of extinct double volcanoes known as the Twin Knolls and passes though a designated wildlife habitat area; the trailhead is 6 mi east on Porter Mountain Road, off AZ 260.

You can get trail brochures or other information from the **Apache-Sitgreaves National Forest** (⊠*Lakeside Ranger Station, 2022 W. White Mountain Blvd., Lakeside 85929* ☎*928/368–5111* ⊕*www.fs.fed.us/r3/asnf*), including a $2 booklet on the White Mountains Trail System.

FISHING East of Pinetop-Lakeside and 9 mi south of AZ 260, 260-acre **Hawley Lake** (⊠*AZ 473, Hawley Lake* ☎*928/338–4385*) sits on Apache territory and yields mostly rainbow trout; rental boats are available in the marina. Tribal permits are required for all recreational activities: contact **White Mountain Apache Fish & Game Department** (☎*928/338–4385*) for details. **Paradise Creek Anglers** (⊠*560 W. White Mountain Blvd., Lakeside* ☎*928/367–6200 or 800/231–3831* ⊕*www.paradisecreekanglers.com*) offers fishing advice and lessons, as well as equipment rentals.

GOLF **Pinetop Lakes Golf & Country Club** (⊠*4643 Buck Springs Rd., Pinetop* ☎*928/369–4184* ⊕*www.pinetoplakesgolf.com*) has fewer trees than other area courses, but it offers several water hazards to compensate. The shorter course is wonderful for public play. The club has a driving range, putting greens, and tennis courts, not to mention a restaurant and lounge. It's open April to October. Green fees range from $29 to $44 for 18 holes.

HORSEBACK RIDING **Porter Mountain Stables** (⊠*4048 Porter Mountain Rd., Lakeside* ☎*928/368–5306*) offers one-hour to all-day horseback trips in the summer.

SKIING & SNOWBOARDING The **Skier's Edge** (⊠*560 W. White Mountain Blvd., Pinetop* ☎*928/367–6200 or 800/231–3831* ⊕*www.skiersedgepinetop.com*) has cross-country and downhill skis as well as snowboards and boots. **Snowriders** (⊠*857 E. White Mountain Blvd., Pinetop* ☎*800/762–0256* ⊕*www.azsnowriders.com*) sells and rents skis and snowboards and offers special seasonal rental packages for children 12 and under. It's open December through March 15, weather permitting.

WHERE TO STAY & EAT

★ $$–$$$$ ✕ **Christmas Tree.** Year-round festive lights and displays of colorful ornaments inside this restaurant highlight a theme that's been at work here since 1977. Chicken and dumplings are the house specialty, but beef Stroganoff and honey duck served with fried apples are also highly recommended. Steaks, chops, lamb, and seafood are available as well, along with a children's menu. Save room for a piece of the Christmas Tree's famous fresh-baked fruit cobbler or Texas sheet cake à la mode. Reservations are a good idea. ⊠*455 N. Woodland Rd., near AZ 260, Lakeside* ☎*928/367–3107* ⊟D, MC, V ⊘*Closed 3rd wk in Oct.–Thanksgiving. Closed Mon. and Tues. No lunch.*

$–$$$$ ✕ **Charlie Clark's Steak House.** From golfers relishing a successful day on the links to locals in search of decent chow, Charlie Clark's has been the meeting place of the White Mountains since it opened in 1938. Prime rib is the house specialty—a delicate "ladies cut" is available for those with smaller appetites. Minnesota walleye pike adds a Midwestern spin to the menu. ✉*1701 E. White Mountain Blvd., Pinetop* ☎*928/367–4900* ⊕*www.charlieclarks.com* ☰AE, D, MC, V.

¢–$$ ✕ **Los Corrales.** Bright yellows and oranges make for a cheerful family-style eatery, which attracts locals with Mexican seafood dishes such as *Camarones a la Crema* (shrimp and mushrooms in cream sauce) and luncheon specials. Dessert specialties include fried ice cream and apple chimichanga. A small bar serves drinks. ✉*845 E. White Mountain Blvd.* ☎*928/367–5585* ☰AE, D, DC, MC, V.

$$–$$$$ ⊡ **Northwoods Resort.** Each of the 14 fully furnished cottages at this mountain retreat has its own covered porch and barbecue. Inside, natural wood paneling, brick fireplaces, and wall-to-wall carpeting add to the homey feel. Full electric kitchens have refrigerators, ovens, microwaves, and adjacent dinette sets. Proprietors here keep their promise to provide "meticulously maintained" accommodations, all the way down to a daily replenishment of firewood. The honeymoon cabin has an indoor spa, and the two-story cabins can accommodate up to 18 people. ✉*AZ 260, Milepost 352* ⊘*Box 397N, Pinetop 85935* ☎*928/367–2966 or 800/813–2966* 🖷*928/367–2969* ⊕*www.northwoodsaz.com* ☞*14 cabins* ⌂*In-room: no a/c, kitchen. In-hotel: laundry facilities, no-smoking rooms* ☰D, MC, V.

$$ ⊡ **Hon-Dah Resort Casino and Conference Center.** Stuffed high-country creatures atop a mountain of boulders welcome you to Apache Tribe–operated Hon-Dah. The main draw is the casino, with hundreds of slot machines, live poker and blackjack, and weekend entertainment. Large rooms all have coffeemakers and wet bars. A high-roof atrium holds the pool and hot tub. The Indian Pine Restaurant serves three daily meals, and a small gift shop sells local Apache crafts. ✉*777 AZ 260, Pinetop 85935* ☎*928/369–0299 or 800/929–8744* 🖷*928/369–7405* ⊕*www.hon-dah.com* ☞*126 rooms, 2 suites* ⌂*In-room: refrigerator, ethernet. In-hotel: restaurant, bars, pool, no-smoking rooms* ☰AE, D, DC, MC, V.

$$ ⊡ **Lake of the Woods Resort.** Janet Pierson was so taken with Lakeside after her first visit that she and two friends decided to buy Lake of the Woods Resort. Situated on the resort's private lake, guests can fish for trout, hike, rent a boat, and enjoy the natural surroundings of the area. Novice fishermen take note: Pierson and crew stock the lake a half-dozen times a year with trout. It's almost as easy as shooting fish in a barrel. ✉*2244 W. White Mountain Blvd., Lakeside 85929* ☎*928/368–5353* ⊕*www.lakeofthewoodsaz.com* ☞*26 cabins, 7 houses* ⌂*In room: kitchen, no phone. In hotel: no elevator, some pets allowed.* ☰MC, V ⏏❙BP.

$$ ⊡ **Whispering Pines Resort.** These well-maintained cabins have fireplaces (wood or natural gas), grills, and double sofa beds. One-, two-, and three-bedroom units—some with second bathrooms—have either handsome knotty-pine or more modern wood-panel interiors. The four log cabins, three of them studio units, have that cabiny-hideaway vibe. Couples may want to request one of the alpine suites, with whirlpool tubs. On 12 acres bordering the Apache-Sitgreaves National Forest, cabins are in walking distance of Woodland Lake and Walnut Creek. It'll feel like home after a while: the resort doesn't offer daily housekeep-

ing. ⊠*AZ 260, just beyond Milepost 352* ☐*Box 1043, Pinetop85935*
☎*928/367–4386 or 800/840–3867* 🖷*928/367–3702* ⊕*www.whis-peringpinesaz.com* ↪*38 cabins* ☖*In-room: no a/c, kitchen (some).*
*In-hotel: laundry facilities, no-smoking rooms, some pets allowed, no
elevator* ⊟AE, D, MC, V.

NIGHTLIFE

There isn't much nightlife in the White Mountains area, but **Charlie Clark's Steakhouse** (⊠*1701 E. White Mountain Blvd., Pinetop*
☎*928/367–4900*) has a lounge with a full bar, pool tables, and a
bouncing jukebox that stays open until 1 AM on weekends. **Hon-Dah
Resort Casino** (⊠*777 AZ 260, Pinetop* ☎*928/369–0299 or 800/929–
8744* ⊕*www.hon-dah.com*) is the spot where you can always find live
music, concerts, and comedy. Check the Web site or call the casino to
find out about upcoming performances.

SHOPPING

Antique Mercantile Company (⊠*2106 W. White Mountain Blvd., Lakeside* ☎*928/368–9090*) has century-old collectibles ranging from first-
edition law encyclopedias to working Victrolas. Upscale-quality glass,
china, furniture, military items, and vintage sports and camera equipment are all for sale. In winter it's open by appointment only. The log-
cabin **Harvest Moon Antiques** (⊠*392 W. White Mountain Blvd., Pinetop*
☎*928/367–6973*), open Memorial Day through Thanksgiving weekend, specializes in Old West relics, ranging from buckskins and Apache
wares to old guns and U.S. Cavalry items. This is an excellent place
to find affordable Native American jewelry and Navajo rugs. **Orchard
Antiques** (⊠*1664 W. White Mountain Blvd., Lakeside* ☎*928/368–
6563*), open from April to October and on all major holidays, is a reliable purveyor of high-quality furniture, glass, china, and sterling, and
deals in some quilts and vintage clothing.

SUNRISE PARK RESORT

☙ ❹ *17 mi southeast of McNary, 7 mi south of AZ 260 on AZ 273.*

In winter and early spring, skiers and other snow lovers flock to this ski
area. There's plenty more than downhill and cross-country skiing here,
including snowboarding, snowmobiling, snowshoeing, ice-fishing, and
sleigh rides. The resort has 10 lifts and 65 trails on three mountains
rising to 11,000 feet. Eighty percent of the downhill runs are for beginning or intermediate skiers, and many less-intense trails begin at the top
so skiers of varying skill levels can enjoy riding the chairlifts together.
There's a "ski-wee" hill for youngsters. The Sunrise Express high-speed
chairlift anchors the 10 lifts and has an uphill skier capacity of 16,000
skiers per hour. One-day lift tickets are $45. Sunrise's Snowboard Park
features jumps of all difficulty levels and its own sound system, and is
exclusively for snowboarders—so there's no tension on the hill between
boarders and skiers. Cross-country skiers enjoy 13½ mi of interconnecting trails. You can rent equipment at the ski shop. In summer a
marina is open for boat rentals on Sunrise Lake. ⊠*AZ 273, 7 mi south*

of AZ 260 ⏏*Box 117, Greer 85927* ☎*928/735–7669, 800/772–7669 hotel reservations and snow reports* ⏣*www.sunriseskipark.com* ▤AE, D, MC, V.

WHERE TO STAY

$–$$ 🏨 **Sunrise Park Lodge.** Catering to those who want to be as close as possible to the lifts, this hotel runs a shuttle to the slopes every half hour, has comfortable rooms with ski racks, and offers lodging and lift-ticket packages. The VIP Suite, with its wet bar, refrigerator, microwave oven, and hot tub, comes with two lift tickets that grant the holders line-cutting privileges on the slopes. In summer you can enjoy boating on Sunrise Lake, "3-D" archery, scenic chairlift rides, horseback riding, and mountain biking on designated trails. Call ahead because the lodge closes from the end of ski season until Memorial Day weekend in spring and then closes again in fall from mid-October until the first heavy snowfall. ⊠*AZ 273, 7 mi south of AZ 260* ⏏*Box 117, Greer 85927* ☎*928/735-7669 or 800/772-7669* 🖷*928/735-7315* ⏣*www. sunriseskipark.com* ⇆*100 rooms, 1 suite* ♿*In-room: no a/c, refrigerator (some). In-hotel: 2 restaurants, bar, pool, no-smoking rooms, no elevator* ▤AE, D, DC, MC, V.

GREER

★ ❺ *35 mi southeast of Pinetop-Lakeside and 15 mi southwest of Eagar on AZ 260, 8 mi east of AZ 273 turnoff, via AZ 373 south.*

The charming community of Greer sits just south of AZ 260 among pine, spruce, willow, and aspen on the banks of the Little Colorado River. At an elevation of 8,500 feet, this portion of gently sloping national forest land is covered with meadows and reservoirs and is dominated by 11,590-foot Baldy Peak. Much of the surrounding area remains under the control of the Apache tribe, so visitors must take care to respect Apache law and land. AZ 373 is also Greer's "Main Street," which winds through the village and crosses the Little Colorado River, eventually coming to a dead end. It's affectionately called the Road to Nowhere.

Listed on the National Register of Historic Places, the **Butterfly Lodge Museum** was built as a hunting lodge in 1914 by John Butler, the husband of "Aunt Molly" (of Molly Butler Lodge fame), for author James Willard Schultz and his artist son, Lone Wolf, a prolific painter of Indian and Western scenes. There's a small gift shop. Take time to watch the surrounding meadow come to life with beautiful butterflies, from which the lodge got its name. ⊠*AZ 373 at CR 1126* ☎*928/735-7514* ⏣*www.wmonline.com/butterflylodge.htm* ▤*$2* ⏱*Memorial Day–Labor Day, Thurs.–Sun. 10–5.*

SPORTS & THE OUTDOORS

The **Tin Star Trading Post** (⊠*38940 AZ 373* ☎*928/735-7540*) sells sleds in winter and tackle the rest of the year. Fishing licenses, groceries, and camping supplies are also for sale. You can grab a cup of Joe at the Post's coffee shop.

FISHING   The three Greer Lakes are actually the Bunch, River, and Tunnel reservoirs. Bait and fly-fishing options are scenic and plentiful, and there are several places to launch a boat. Winding through Greer, the Little Colorado River's West Fork is well stocked with brookies and rainbows and has 23 mi of fishable waters.

HIKING   The difficult but accessible **Mount Baldy Trail** begins at **Sheeps Crossing,** southwest of Greer on AZ 273. In just under 8 mi (one-way), the trail climbs the northern flank of 11,590-foot Mount Baldy, the second-highest peak in Arizona. Note that the summit of Baldy is on the White Mountain Apache Reservation. Considered sacred land, this final ¼ mi is off-limits to non-Apaches. The boundary is clearly marked; please respect it, no matter how much you wish to continue to the peak.

SKIING   Cross-country skiers find Greer an ideally situated hub for some of the mountain's best trails. About 2½ mi west of AZ 373 on AZ 260, a trailhead marks the starting point for the **Pole Knoll Trail System,** nearly 30 mi of well-marked, groomed cross-country trails interlacing through the Apache-Sitgreaves National Forest and color-coded by experience level. Trail maps are available from the **Apache-Sitgreaves National Forest** (⊠*Springerville Ranger District, 165 S. Mountain Ave., Springerville 85938* ☎*928/333–4372* ⊕*www.fs.fed.us/r3/asnf*).

WHERE TO STAY & EAT

¢–$$ ✕ **Rendezvous Diner.** The diner has earned a reputation for serving up some of Greer's tastiest dishes, not to mention the area's best hot spiced cider. Of particular note are the pineapple teriyaki, green-chile burgers, and generous portions of homemade cobblers. It's open year-round for breakfast and lunch. ⊠*117 Main St.* ☎*928/735–7483* ⊟MC, V ⊙*Closed Tues. No dinner.*

¢–$ ✕ **Greer Mountain Resort Country Cafe.** This plant-hung diner-café is open from 7 AM to 3 PM. Grab a seat by the fireplace and sample the homemade ranch beans, a signature grilled-cheese sandwich with green chiles and tomato, or fresh-baked cobbler. ⊠*AZ 373, 1½ mi south of AZ 260* ☎*928/735–7560* ⊟MC, V ⊙*Closed Wed. No dinner.*

$–$$ ✕▥ **Molly Butler Lodge.** Colorful quilts and wood furnishings fill the comfortable rooms at Arizona's oldest lodge. There are no phones or TVs in the rooms, but both are available in the main building. The menu in the restaurant ($–$$) is divided between entrées that are "upstream" (sautéed scallops, halibut, trout amandine) and "downstream" (prime rib au jus, "hot dang" chili), but it's the aged steaks that draw locals. No need to worry about holidays: the restaurant is open 365 days a year. Enjoy sweeping views of Greer's pristine wilderness amid the lodge's cozy, rustic decor, with kerosene lamps on the tables and mounted hunting trophies on the walls. There's a two-night minimum. ⊠*109 Main St., 85927* ☎*928/735–7226* ⊕*www.mollybutlerlodge.com* ⤴*17 rooms* ⚱*In-room: no a/c, no phone, no TV. In-hotel: bar, some pets allowed* ⊟AE, D, MC, V.

★ $$–$$$$ ▥ **Greer Lodge Resort.** Designed for travelers on all budgets, the Greer Lodge Resort offers accommodations that range from basic rooms to luxury cabins. Situated on a mile-long property that continues to expand as the years go on—the owner has invested $28 million and purchased neighboring lodges to add more than 100 rooms—the resort now incorporates the former Red Setter Inn and Four Seasons Resort. Guests can enjoy fly-fishing in three private trout ponds or fish along the Little Colorado River, and a dining room and bar, plus a spa, make it unnecessary to leave the property—but hiking, cross-country skiing, and opportunities for viewing wildlife are close by. Children under 16 are welcome in the cabins but not allowed in the luxury lodge rooms. Plans for additional expansion include restaurants, dance facilities, and more luxury spa amenities. ⊠*44 Main St.* ⌂*Box 244, 85927* ☎*928/735–7216* ⊕*www.greerlodgeaz.com* ➔*140 rooms* ⚲*In-room: no a/c (some), no TV (some), no phone (some). In-hotel: restaurant, bar, spa, no elevator, public Wi-Fi, some pets allowed* ⊟AE, D, DC, MC, V ⍥*EP.*

$$–$$$$ ⚏ **White Mountain Lodge.** On the banks of the Little Colorado River, this charming lodge is the oldest building in Greer. The lodge holds three suites and six cabins with kitchens and gas fireplaces; most have whirlpool tubs. Wildlife-watching in Greer Meadow is a popular pastime, as is just sitting on a bench next to the beaver pond. ⊠*140 Main St.* ☎*928/735–7568 or 888/493–7568* ⨮*928/735–7498* ⊕*www. wmlodge.com* ➔*3 suites, 6 cabins* ⚲*In-room: no a/c, kitchen, VCR. In-hotel: no elevator* ⊟AE, D, DC, MC, V ⍥*BP.*

$$–$$$ ⚏ **Greer Mountain Resort.** Budget travelers and families appreciate these cabin-style accommodations. Each unit is different, but most can sleep up to six people and contain either a fireplace or a gas- or wood-burning stove. The smallest, one-bedroom, knotty-pine units have no fireplaces, but they're reasonably priced and good for couples. You may want to enjoy breakfast or lunch at the resort's roadside restaurant, or you can whip up your own feast in the fully equipped kitchens. ⊠*AZ 373, 1½ mi south of AZ 260* ⌂*Box 145, Greer 85927* ☎⨮*928/735– 7560* ⊕*www.greermountainresort.com* ➔*8 units* ⚲*In-room: no a/c, kitchen, no TV* ⊟MC, V.

$ ⚏ **Downs' Ranch Hide-Away.** Looking for a vacation that is really back-of-beyond? For stress relief, do as the locals do and go "down on the Blue." Blue, Arizona, on the Blue River in the Blue Range Primitive Area, along the Arizona–New Mexico border, is one of the most remote sections of the state and a sure cure for the city-life blues. The road to Blue is dirt, and mail is delivered only three days a week, so relax and enjoy the solitude. Try hiking or horseback riding to explore Blue River, pine forests, canyons, Native American ruins, wildlife—or just sit on the porch and enjoy a hefty helping of serenity. Cabins have complete kitchens, and owners Bill and Mona Bunnell suggest you bring food. Ask in advance if you need meals arranged. Doubles are $60 per night for two, with a $20 per extra person surcharge, or $250 a week plus $30 per additional person. Note that credit cards are not accepted at the ranch; you may pay with cash, check, traveler's check, or money order. ⌂*Box 77, Blue 85922* ☎*928/339–4952* ⊕*www.dcoutfitters. com, downsranchhideaway@frontiernet.net* ➔*4 cabins.*

The Writing on the Wall

The rock art of early Native Americans is carved or painted on basalt boulders, on canyon walls, and on the underside of overhangs throughout eastern Arizona. Designs pecked or scratched into the stone are called petroglyphs; those that are painted on the surface are pictographs. Few pictographs remain because of the deleterious effects of weathering, but the more durable petroglyphs number in the thousands. No one knows the exact meaning of these signs, and interpretations vary from use in shaman or hunting rituals to clan signs, maps, or even indications of visits by extra-terrestrials.

It's just as difficult to date a "glyph" as it is to understand it. Archaeologists try to determine a general time frame by judging the style, the date of the ruins and pottery in the vicinity, the amount of patination (formation of minerals) on the design, or the superimposition of newer images on top of older ones. Most of eastern Arizona's rock art is estimated to be at least 1,000 years old, and many of the glyphs were created even earlier.

Some glyphs depict animals like big horn sheep, deer, bear, and mountain lions; others are geometric patterns. The most unusual are the anthropomorphs, strange humanlike figures with elaborate headdresses. A concentric circle is a common design. A few of these circles served as solstice signs, indicating summer and winter solstice and other important dates. At a certain time in the year, when the angle of the sun is just right, a shaft of light shines through a crack in a nearby rock, illuminating the center of the circle. Archaeologists believe these solar calendars helped determine the time for ceremonies and planting. Many solstice signs are in remote regions, but you can visit the Petrified Forest National Park around June 20 to see a concentric circle illuminated during the summer solstice. The glyph, reached by paved trail just a few hundred yards from the parking area, is visible year-round, but a finger of light shines directly in the center during the week of the solstice. The phenomenon occurs at 9 AM, a reasonable hour for looking at the calendar.

Damaged by vandalism, many rock-art sites are not open to the public, but Hieroglyphic Point in Salt River Canyon, Five-Mile Canyon in Snowflake, Lyman Lake State Park, and Petrified Forest National Park are all good spots to view petroglyphs. Do not touch petroglyphs or pictographs—the oils from your hands can cause damage to the image.

NIGHTLIFE

Tiny Greer's nightlife can be found in the bar and lounge of the **Molly Butler Lodge** (✉ *109 Main St.* ☎ *928/735–7226*), where you can listen to vintage tunes on the jukebox, sink into a cozy seat near the fireplace, play an arcade game, or challenge a local to a game of pool or darts.

LYMAN LAKE STATE PARK

6 *18 mi north of Springerville on U.S. 180/191, 55 mi southeast of National Park on U.S. 180.*

Created in 1915, when the Little Colorado River was dammed for irrigation purposes, the 3-mi-long **Lyman Lake** reservoir is popular for boating, waterskiing (a permit is required for the exclusive waterskiing course on the dam end), windsurfing, and sailing. Designated swimming beaches accommodate those who prefer to stick closer to shore.

A buoyed-off "no-wake" area at the lake's west end ensures that fishing efforts there won't be disturbed by passing speedboats and water-skiers. Bait your hook for largemouth bass as well as the good-size (6 to 8 pounds) channel catfish that can be pulled up from May to August. Locals recommend early spring for walleye—the tastiest catch of all; Lyman Lake also has lots of crawfish, aka "poor man's shrimp."

Between early May and late October, ranger-led pontoon-boat tours go across Lyman Lake to the **Ultimate Petroglyph Trail,** where some of the state's most wondrous and accessible Native American rock art lies chiseled in basalt. Check out the Rattlesnake Point Pueblo site, which dates to the 14th century and has three rooms and a kiva.

Other attractions in the 1,200-acre park include a volleyball court, horseshoe pits, and a water-ski slalom course. There's also a campground, along with several log cabins and yurts for rent, and a camping supply and boat rental store, but no gasoline for cars is sold here. In nearby St. Johns, there are lodging, restaurants, gasoline, and an airfield and fuel for planes. ✉ *U.S. 180/191, 18 mi north of Springerville/Eagar* 📭 *Box 1428, St. Johns 85936* ☎ *928/337–4441* 🌐 *www.pr.state.az.us* 💲 *$5.*

EN ROUTE The junction of U.S. 180/191 and U.S. 60, just north of Springerville, is the perfect jumping-off spot for a driving tour of the **Springerville Volcanic Field.** On the southern edge of the Colorado Plateau, it covers a total area larger than the state of Rhode Island and is spread across a high-elevation plain similar to the Tibetan Plateau. Six miles north of Springerville on U.S. 180/191 are sweeping westward views of the **Twin Knolls**—double volcanoes that erupted twice here about 700,000 years ago. As you travel west on U.S. 60, Green's Peak Road and various south-winding Forest Service roads make for a leisurely, hour-long drive past **St. Peter's Dome** and a stop for impressive views from **Green's Peak,** the topographic high point of the Springerville Field. A free detailed driving-tour brochure of the Springerville Volcanic Field is available from the **Springerville-Eagar Regional Chamber of Commerce** (✉ *318 Main St.* 📭 *Box 31, Springerville 85938* ☎ *928/333–2123* 🌐 *www.springerville-eagarchamber.com*).

SPRINGERVILLE-EAGAR

❼ *45 mi east of Pinetop-Lakeside on AZ 260, 67 mi southeast of Petrified Forest National Park on U.S. 180.*

Sister cities Springerville and Eagar are tucked into a circular, high mountain basin christened "Valle Redondo," or Round Valley, by Basque settlers in the late 1800s. Nestled on the back side of massive 10,912-foot Escudilla Mountain, this self-proclaimed "Gateway to the White Mountains" sits in a different climate belt from nearby Greer and Sunrise Resort; insulated by its unique geography, Springerville-Eagar has markedly less severe winter temperatures and lighter snowfall than neighboring mountain towns. Geographically, the Round Valley also served as a unique Old West haven for the lawless—a great place to conceal stolen cattle and hide out for a while. Butch Cassidy, the Clantons, and the Smith gang all spent time here. So did the late John Wayne, whose former 26-Bar Ranch lies just west of Eagar off AZ 260.

The Round Valley is the favorite of skiers in the know, who appreciate the location as they commute to the lifts at Sunrise with the sun always at their back—important when you consider the glare off those blanketed snowscapes between the resort and Pinetop-Lakeside—and the dramatically lighter traffic on this less-icy stretch of AZ 260.

The 14½-acre **Casa Malpais Archaeological Park** pueblo complex is piquing the interest of a growing number of anthropologists and astronomers. The "House of the Badlands" (a sobriquet for the rough-textured ground's effect on bare feet) has a series of narrow terraces lining eroded edges of basalt (hardened lava flow) cliff, as well as an extensive system of subterranean rooms nestled within Earth's fissures underneath. Strategically designed gateways in the walls of the complex allow streams of sunlight to precisely illuminate significant petroglyphs prior to the setting equinox or solstice sun. Casa Malpais's Great Kiva (any kiva over 30 feet is considered great) is square cornered instead of round, consistent with Ancestral Puebloan heritage. Some archaeologists believe the pueblo served as a regional ceremonial center for the Mogollon people. Both Hopi and Zuni tribes trace their history to Casa Malpais. The site has a small museum in town, with artifacts from the Casa Malpais ruin, a butterfly collection, and items from early-days Springerville; a small gift shop offers Native American jewelry and local history books. The site itself may only be visited on a tour; these leave from the museum at 9, 11, and 2. ⊠ *318 E. Main St., Springerville* ☎ *928/333–5375* ⌧ *$7* ☉ *Museum open daily 8–4.*

The **Little House Museum** has a collection of local pioneer and ranching memorabilia, but it's the mesmerizing tones from a rare collection of automatic musical instruments that you remember—that, and the museum's colorful curator, Wink Crigler, with her tales of this region's lively past. Tours to archaeological digs and petroglyphs are available by appointment. To reach the ranch, go 10 mi southwest of Eagar on AZ 260, turn south onto South Fork Road, and go 3 mi. ⊠ X *Diamond Ranch, S. Fork Rd., 10 mi southwest of Eagar* ☎ *928/333–2286* ⊕ *www.xdiamondranch.com* ⌧ *$8* ☉ *By reservation only.*

The **Renée Cushman Art Collection Museum** is open to the public only by special appointment, but a visit is worth the effort. Renée Cushman's extensive collection of objets d'art—some acquired on her travels, some collected with the accumulated resources of three wealthy husbands, and some willed to her by her artistic father—is administered by the Church of Latter-day Saints. Her treasure includes a Rembrandt engraving, Tiepolo pen-and-inks, and an impressive collection of European antiques, some dating back to the 15th century. Call the **Springerville-Eagar Regional Chamber of Commerce** (☎928/333–2123) to arrange your visit.

SPORTS & THE OUTDOORS

For your mountain-sport needs the **Sweat Shop** (⊠74 N. Main St., Eagar ☎928/333–2950) rents skis, snowboards, and mountain bikes.

FISHING **Becker Lake** (⊠U.S. 60, 2 mi northwest of Springerville, Becker Lake ☎928/367–4281) is a "specialty lake" for trout fishing; call for seasonal bait requirements. **Big Lake** (⊠AZ 273, 24 mi south of AZ 260, Big Lake ☎928/735–7313), known to many as the "queen of all trout lakes," is stocked each spring and fall with rainbow, brook, and cutthroat trout. **Nelson Reservoir** (⊠U.S. 191, Nutrioso), between Springerville-Eagar and Alpine, is well stocked with rainbow, brown, and brook trout. The **Speckled Trout** (⊠224 E. Main St., Springerville ☎928/333–0852 ⊕www.cybertrails.com/~cltrout) offers fishing guide services and sells Orvis-licensed fly-fishing equipment. A small gift shop features books, linens, and wind chimes, along with nonalcoholic drinks like espresso and fruit smoothies. **Sport Shack** (⊠329 E. Main St., Springerville ☎928/333–2222) sells camping equipment, fishing tackle, and hunting and fishing licenses. **Troutback** (✉Box 864, Show Low 85901 ☎928/532–3474 ⊕www.troutback.com) is a fly-fishing guide service that will create half- or full-day fishing trips for novices and seasoned anglers alike throughout the White Mountains. Equipment, including boats, waders, fly rods and reels, and float tubes, is available for rent. **Western United Drug** (⊠105 E. Main St., Springerville ☎928/333–4321) stays open 365 days a year and has a well-stocked sporting-goods and outdoor-equipment section.

WHERE TO STAY & EAT

¢–$$ ✕ **Booga Reds.** The delicious home-style cooking, such as fish-and-chips and roast-beef dinner, is worth a stop. Should your palate demand something spicier, try one of the many Mexican dishes—the enchiladas are wonderful. Save room for the daily fruit or cream pie. Booga Reds opens at 6 AM for an early breakfast but closes relatively early—at 9 PM—so make your dinner an early one, too. ⊠521 E. Main St., Springerville ☎928/333–2640 ⊟MC, V.

¢–$ ✕ **Java Blues.** Not your typical mountain eatery, Java Blues oozes a coffeehouse vibe with its overstuffed couches and stained-glass windows. Salads, soups, sandwiches, and a Greek Board—a variety of Greek meats and cheeses served with toasted baguette—are on the menu. Locals swear by the grilled roast beef and Brie sandwich and the grilled chicken and bacon chef salad. The restaurant opens early and closes early (weekdays 6 AM–7 PM, Saturday 6 AM–6 PM, and Sunday 7 AM–3 PM), so plan accordingly. Hear live bluegrass every Sunday afternoon. ✉ *341 E. Main St., Springerville* 🕾 *928/333–5282* ▭ MC, V.

★ $$–$$$ ▣ **✕ Diamond & MLY Ranch.** This magnificent ranch has log cabins complete with porches, fireplaces, and full kitchens. Most sleep two to six, but the Butler House sleeps eight and has an atrium and private yard. Activities include fly-fishing, horseback riding, and tours of Little Bear archaeological site—in June you can even take part in the excavation yourself. Nonguests are welcome to participate in activities. ✉ *South Fork Rd., 10 mi southwest of Eagar off AZ 260* ✆ *Box 791, Springerville 85938* 🕾 *928/333–2286* 🖷 *928/333–5009* ⊕ *www. xdiamondranch.com* ⇆ *7 cabins* ⚭ *In-room: no a/c, kitchen. In-hotel: no-smoking rooms* ▭ AE, D, MC, V.

★ $–$$ ▣ **Paisley Corner B & B.** From pressed-tin ceilings and stained-glass windows in the parlor to an authentic soda shop re-creation replete with Wurlitzer jukebox, not a detail has been overlooked in this restored 1910 colonial revival–style home. Rooms have antique beds and armoires, old-fashioned showers, and pull-chain commodes. Lush terry robes, wine, baskets of fresh fruit, and homemade munchies are included. The owners operate a coffeehouse 2 mi away where guests can have breakfast (included in the room price). ✉ *287 N. Main St., Springerville 85938* 🕾 *928/333–4665* ⇆ *4 rooms* ⚭ *In-room: no phone. In-hotel: no-smoking rooms no elevator* ▭ MC, V ⧉ *BP.*

$ ▣ **Rode Inn.** Don't let the John Wayne motif scare you away—two cardboard figures of "The Duke" in full cowboy regalia are perched on a walkway above the lobby, and his photos decorate the walls; the rooms and service here are excellent. John Wayne did in fact stay here (when it was a Ramada Inn), and the room in which he slept has been converted into a plush suite. ✉ *242 E. Main St., Springerville 85938* 🕾 *928/333–4365* ⊕ *www.rodeinn.com* ⇆ *60 rooms, 3 suites* ⚭ *In-room: refrigerator, Wi-Fi. In-hotel: laundry facilities, no-smoking rooms, no elevator* ▭ AE, D, DC, MC, V ⧉ *CP.*

¢–$ ▣ **Reed's Lodge.** It's an older motel, but a town favorite. The rooms of this mostly single-story motel have Western accents such as knotty-pine paneling and Navajo-print bedspreads. Perks include a recreation room with pool table, video games, and a pinball machine; movie rentals for a nominal fee; a gift shop; and complimentary bicycles. Proprietor Roxanne Knight will arrange visits for guests on a working cowboy-style (not dude) ranch, cattle drives, horseback adventures, four-wheel-drive tours, wildlife and petroglyph-viewing trips, or fossil-hunting expeditions. ✉ *514 E. Main St., Springerville 85938* 🕾 *928/333–4323 or 800/814–6451* 🖷 *928/333–5191* ⊕ *www.k5reeds.com* ⇆ *45 rooms, 5 suites* ⚭ *In-room: refrigerator (some), VCR. In hotel: no-smoking rooms, no elevator, some pets allowed* ▭ AE, D, DC, MC, V.

NIGHTLIFE

Springerville and Eagar aren't known for their nightlife, but **Tequila Red's** (✉ *521 E. Main St., Springerville* 🕾 *928/333–5036*) is the best place around to catch a televised sporting event. It's behind Booga Reds restaurant.

SHOPPING
K-5 Western Gallery (⊠*Reed's Lodge, 514 E. Main St., Springerville* ☎*928/333–4323*) sells wares created by White Mountains artists and local craftspeople, including those from nearby reservations. The gallery teems with Western-theme paintings, books on local history, wildlife, and cowboy poetry, and even John Wayne paper dolls.

CORONADO TRAIL

The 127-mi stretch of U.S. 191 from Springerville to Clifton.

Surely one of the world's curviest roads, this steep, winding portion of U.S. 191 was referred to as the Devil's Highway in its prior incarnation as U.S. 666. More significantly, the route parallels the one allegedly followed more than 450 years ago by Spanish explorer Francisco Vásquez de Coronado on his search for the legendary Seven Cities of Cibola, where the streets were reputedly paved with gold and jewels.

This 127-mi stretch of highway is renowned for the transitions of its spectacular scenery over a dramatic 5,000-foot elevation change—from rolling meadows to spruce- and ponderosa pine–covered mountains, down into the Sonoran Desert's piñon pine, grassland savannas, juniper stands, and cacti. A trip down the Coronado Trail crosses through Apache-Sitgreaves National Forest, as well as the White Mountain Apache and San Carlos Apache Indian reservations.

■ TIP→**Allow a good four hours to make the drive, more if you plan to stop and leisurely explore—which you should.**

Pause at **Blue Vista,** perched on the edge of the Mogollon Rim, about 30 mi outside Alpine, to take in views of the Blue Range Mountains to the east and the succession of tiered valleys dropping some 4,000 feet back down into the Sonoran Desert. Still above the rim, this is one of your last opportunities to enjoy the blue spruce, ponderosa pine, and high-country mountain meadows.

About 17 mi south of Blue Vista, the Coronado Trail continues to twist and turn, eventually crossing under 8,786-foot **Rose Peak.** Named for the wild roses growing on its mountainside, Rose Peak is also home to a fire lookout tower from which peaks more than 100 mi away can be seen on a clear day. This is a great picnic-lunch stop.

After Rose Peak, enjoy the remaining scenery some 70 more mi until you reach the less scenic towns of Clifton and Morenci, homes to a massive copper mine. U.S. 191 then swings back west, links up with U.S. 70, and provides a fairly straight shot to Globe.

ALPINE

❽ *27 mi south of Springerville-Eagar on U.S. 191.*

Known as the Alps of Arizona, the tiny, scenic village of Alpine promotes its winter recreation opportunities, but outdoors enthusiasts will find that the town, sitting on the lush plains of the San Francisco River, is an ideal base for hiking, fishing, and mountain-biking excursions during the warmer months. With summer cabins tucked in the pines, campgrounds, 11 lakes, and 200 mi of trout streams within a 30-mi radius, outdoor recreation drives this mountain burg.

SPORTS & THE OUTDOORS

BICYCLING   The 8-mi **Luna Lake Trail** (⊠ *U.S. 180, Alpine*), 5 mi east of U.S. 191, is a good two-hour cruise for beginner and intermediate cyclists. The trailhead is on the north side of the lake, before the campground entrance.

FISHING   A divergence of the San Francisco River's headwaters, 80-acre **Luna Lake** (⊠ *U.S. 180, Alpine*), 5 mi east of U.S. 191, is well stocked with rainbow trout. **Tackle Shop** (☎ *928/339–4338*), at the junction of U.S. 180 and 191, carries trout and fly-fishing supplies. **Arizona Mountain Flyfishing** (☎ *928/339–4829* ⊕ *www.azmtflyfishing.com*) guides anglers to top fishing streams and teaches novices.

GOLF   **Alpine Country Club** (⊠ *58 County Rd. 2122* ⚐ *Box 526, Alpine* ☎ *928/339–4944* ⊕ *www.geocities.com/alpinecountryclub*) is off U.S. 180, 3 mi east of U.S. 191. At 8,500 feet above sea level, it's one of the highest golf courses in the Southwest. Even if you don't play golf, stop in for New Mexican–style food—enchiladas here are stacked, not rolled—and breathtaking scenery at the club's Aspen Room Restaurant. It's 1 mi south of Alpine on Blue River Road. The course is closed in winter, and the restaurant is closed Mondays.

HIKING   The **Escudilla National Recreation Trail** (⊠ *U.S. 191, Hulsey Lake*) is more idyllic than arduous; the 3-mi trail wends through the Escudilla Wilderness to the summit of towering 10,912-foot **Escudilla Mountain,** Arizona's third-tallest peak. The trail climbs 1,300 feet to a fire tower ¼ mi from the summit. From Alpine, take U.S. 191 north and follow the signs to Hulsey Lake (about 5 mi).

SKIING   **Williams Valley Winter Sports Area** (⊠ *FSR 249, Alpine* ☎ *928/339–4384*), 2½ mi west of town, has 12½ mi of cross-country trails of varying difficulty maintained by the Alpine Ranger District. Toboggan Hill is a favorite for families, with sleds, toboggans, and tubes. Shelters, picnic facilities, and toilets are available.

Trails begin just off Forest Service Road 249, on the west side of **Williams Valley Winter Sports Area** (⊠ *FSR 249, Alpine* ☎ *928/339–4384*), and the network of snow-covered Forest Service roads extends for miles. Pick up an Apache-Sitgreaves National Forest map and Winter Sports brochure from the Alpine Ranger District, and call for conditions prior to heading out, as weak links in longer routes sometimes "burn out."

WHERE TO STAY & EAT

★ $–$$ ✕ ▯ **Tal-Wi-Wi Lodge.** This lodge draws many repeat visitors to its lush meadows, a favorite for bird-watchers. Motel-style rooms are simple and clean, with three of the most popular rooms offering wood-burning fireplace-stoves, indoor hot tubs, or both. In the evening stroll the grounds and gaze at the Milky Way in the brilliant night sky. With satellite TV and live country music on weekends, the lodge saloon draws a loyal local following. The cozy, casual restaurant is open May through November and serves breakfast on weekends and dinner Thursday through Saturday. Prime rib is the house specialty but they also serve pizza and home-made pies. ⊠ *U.S. 191* ⇧ *Box 169, Alpine 85920* ☎ *928/339–4319 or 800/476–2695* 🖶 *928/339–1962* ⊕ *www.talwiwilodge.com* ⋐ *20 rooms* ⚭ *In-room: no a/c, no TV. In-hotel: restaurant, bar, some pets allowed, public Wi-Fi, no-smoking rooms* ▤ MC, V.

OFF THE BEATEN PATH

Blue Range Primitive Area. Directly east of Hannagan Meadow, these unspoiled 170,000 acres, lovingly referred to by locals as "The Blue," comprise the last designated primitive area in the United States. The diverse terrain surrounds the Blue River and is crossed by the Mogollon Rim from east to west. No motorized or mechanized equipment is allowed—including mountain bikes; passage is restricted to foot or horseback. Many trails interlace the Blue: prehistoric paths of the ancient native peoples, cowboy trails to move livestock between pastures and water sources, access routes to lookout towers and fire trails. Avid backpackers and campers may want to spend a few days exploring the dozens of hiking trails. Even though trail access is fairly good, hikers need to remember that this is primitive, rough country, and it's essential to carry adequate water supplies.

HANNAGAN MEADOW

★ ❾ *50 mi south of Springerville-Eagar on U.S. 191, 23 mi south of Alpine on U.S. 191.*

Surely one of the state's most remote places, Hannagan Meadow is a pastorally mesmerizing location. Lush and isolated at a 9,500-foot-plus elevation, the meadow is home to elk, deer, and range cattle, as well as blue grouse, wild turkey, and the occasional eagle. Adjacent to the meadow, the Blue Range Primitive Area gives access to miles of untouched wilderness and some beautiful rugged terrain, and it's a designated recovery area for the endangered Mexican gray wolf. It's believed that Francisco Vásquez de Coronado and his party came through the meadow on their famed expedition in 1540 to find the Seven Cities of Cibola.

SPORTS & THE OUTDOORS

Want to get away from it all? The **Apache Ranger District** of the Apache-Sitgreaves National Forest offers secluded spaces for outdoors adventures year-round. Hikers and anglers can check out the 11,000-acre **Bear Wallow Wilderness Area** (west of U.S. 191 and bordered by FSR 25 and 54), which has cool, flowing streams stocked with native Apache trout. The **Rose Spring Trail** is a pleasant 5½-mi hike with a moderate gradient and magnificent views from the Mogollon Rim's edge; the trailhead is at the end of Forest Service Road 54. **Reno Trail** and

Gobbler Trail both drop into the main canyon from well-marked trail-heads off Forest Service Road 25. Reno Trail meanders 2 mi through conifer forest and aspen, while Gobbler Trail is 2½ mi long with views overlooking the Black River and Fort Apache Indian Reservation. This designated wilderness (and some of its trails) borders the San Carlos Apache Indian Reservation, where an advance permit is required for entry. In the winter, try the 8½ mi of groomed cross-country trails of the **Hannagan Meadow Winter Recreation Area** (⊠ *U.S. 191, Hannagan Meadow*), which also is part of the Apache-Sitgreaves forest. The 4½-mi **Clell Lee Loop** is an easy route; the advanced-level, ungroomed **KP Rim Loop** traverses upper elevations of the Blue Primitive Range and provides some of the most varied (and tranquil) remote skiing in the state. The area just northeast of U.S. 191 is a snowmobiling play-ground. Trailheads are at U.S. 191 and Forest Service Road 576. There are no rental shops nearby, so bring your own equipment.

Contact **Apache-Sitgreaves National Forest** (⊠ *Alpine Ranger District, U.S. 191* ⌂ *Box 469, Alpine 85920* ☎ *928/339–4384* ⊕ *www.fs.fed. us/r3/asnf*) for trail maps and information.

WHERE TO STAY

★ $–$$ ⌂ **Hannagan Meadow Lodge.** Antiques and floral prints impart a gen-teel, Victorian feel to this lodge. The dining room has hewn-log beams and a glass wall that overlooks a pristine meadow; room rates include breakfast (unless you stay in the cabins). Log cabins are more rustic; some have full kitchens and fireplaces, whereas others are equipped with microwaves, stove tops, and wood-burning stoves. The solitude of the area is enhanced by the absence of phones and TVs in rooms and cab-ins. The general store sells sundries as well as fishing supplies and rents snowshoes, cross-country skis, and mountain bikes. ⊠ *U.S. 191, 22 mi south of Alpine, Hannagan Meadow* ⌂ *HC 61, Box 335, Alpine 85920* ☎ *928/339–4370* ⊕ *www.hannaganmeadow.com* ⇆ *8 rooms, 10 cabins* ⌂ *In-room: no a/c, no phone, kitchen (some), no TV. In-hotel: restaurant, bicycles, some pets allowed, no elevator* ☰ MC, V ⦿ CP.

THE PETRIFIED FOREST & THE PAINTED DESERT

Only about 1½ hours from Show Low and the lush, verdant forests of the White Mountains, Arizona's diverse and dramatic landscape changes from pine-crested mountains to the sunbaked terrain of the Petrified Forest and lunarlike landscape of the Painted Desert.

PETRIFIED FOREST NATIONAL PARK

Updated by
John Blodgett

Northern Entrance: 54 mi east of Homolovi Ruins State Park and 27 mi east of Holbrook on I–40; Southern Entrance: 18 mi east of Hol-brook on U.S. 180.

⊠ *North Entrance: I–40, Milepost 311, 27 mi east of Holbrook, Petri-fied Forest* ☎ *928/524–6228* ⊕ *www.nps.gov/pefo* ⌧ *$10 per vehicle or $5 per person on foot, bicycle, motorcycle, or bus, valid for seven*

Petrified Forest Flora & Fauna

There are few places where the span of geologic and human history is as wide or apparent as it is at Petrified Forest National Park. Fossilized trees and countless other fossils date back to the Triassic Period, while a stretch of the famed Route 66 is protected within park boundaries. The park's 218,533 acres, which include portions of the Painted Desert, are covered with petrified tree trunks whose wood cells were fossilized over centuries by brightly hued mineral deposits—silica, iron oxide, carbon, manganese, aluminum, copper, and lithium. Petrified logs scattered about a vast pink-hued lunarlike landscape resemble a fairly-tale forest turned to stone. The park holds plenty of other fossils; ancestors of the Hopi, Zuni, and Navajo left petroglyphs, pottery, and even structures built of petrified wood. Remnants of humans and their artifacts have been recovered at more than 500 sites in the park. Nine park sites are on the National Register of Historic Places; one, the Painted Desert Inn, is one of only 3% of such sites that are also listed as a National Historic Landmark.

Engelmann asters and sunflowers are among the blooms in the park each summer. Juniper trees, cottonwoods, and willows grow along Puerco River Wash, providing shelter for all manner of wildlife. You might spot mule deer, coyotes, prairie dogs, and foxes, while other inhabitants, like porcupines and bobcats, tend to hide. Bird-watchers should keep an eye out for mockingbirds, red-tailed and Swainson's hawks, roadrunners, swallows, and hummingbirds. Look for all three kinds of lizards—collared, side-blotched, and southern prairie—in rocks.

Beware of rattlesnakes. They are common but can generally be avoided by using common sense: watch where you step, and don't step anywhere you can't see. If you do come across a rattler, give it plenty of space, and let it go its way before you continue yours. Other reptiles—and there are plenty—are just as common but not as worrisome. The gopher snake looks similar to a rattlesnake, but is nonpoisonous. The collared lizard, with its yellow head, can be seen scurrying out of your way just about everywhere in bursts measured at up to 15 mph. They are not poisonous, but will bite in the rare instance of being caught.

days ☾ *Daily 8–5 except for Christmas Day. Extended summer hours; call for information.*

WHAT TO SEE

Though named for its famous fossilized trees, Petrified Forest has something to see for history buffs of all stripes, from a segment of Route 66 to ancient dwellings to even more ancient fossils. And the good thing is, much of Petrified Forest's treasures can easily be viewed without a great amount of athletic conditioning. You can see a lot just by driving along the main road, from which historic sites are readily accessible. By combining a drive along the park road with a short hike here and there, and a visit to one of the park's landmarks, much can be seen in as little as half a day for those with limited time.

Petrified Forest National Park

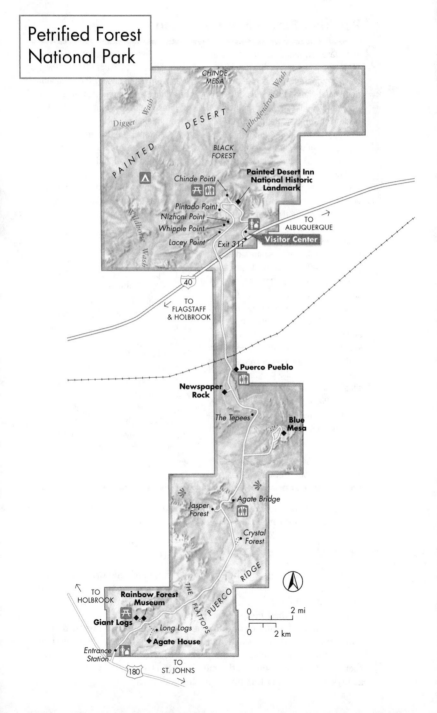

PETRIFIED FOREST IN ONE DAY

A nonstop drive through the park (28 mi) takes only 45 minutes, but you can spend most of a day exploring if you stop along the way. From almost any vantage point you can see the multicolored rocks and hills that were home to prehistoric humans and ancient dinosaurs.

Entering the park from the north, stop at **Painted Desert Visitor Center** and see a 20-minute introductory film. **Painted Desert Inn visitor center,** 2 mi south of the north entrance, provides further orientation in the form of guided ranger tours. Drive south 8 mi to reach **Puerco Pueblo,** a 100-room pueblo built before 1400. Continuing south you'll find Puebloan petroglyphs at **Newspaper Rock** and, just beyond, **The Tepees,** cone-shaped rock forma-

tions covered with manganese and other minerals.

Blue Mesa is roughly the midpoint of the drive, and the start of a 1-mi, moderately steep loop hike that leads you around badland hills made of bentonite clay. Drive on for 5 mi until you come to **Jasper Forest,** just past **Agate Bridge,** with views of the landscape strewn with petrified logs. **Crystal Forest,** 18 mi south of the north entrance, is named for the smoky quartz, amethyst, and citrine along the 8/10-mi loop trail. **Rainbow Forest Museum,** at the park's south entrance, has restrooms, a bookstore, and exhibits. Just behind Rainbow Forest Museum is **Giant Logs,** a 4/10-mi loop that takes you to "Old Faithful," the largest log in the park, estimated to weigh 44 tons.

HISTORIC SITES

Agate House. This eight-room pueblo is thought to have been built entirely of petrified wood 700 years ago. Researchers believe it might have been used as a temporary dwelling by seasonal farmers or traders from one of the area tribes. ⊠*Rainbow Forest Museum parking area.*

Newspaper Rock. See huge boulders covered with petroglyphs believed to have been carved by the Pueblo Indians more than 500 years ago. ⊠*6 mi south of Painted Desert Visitor Center on the main park road.*

Painted Desert Inn National Historic Site. You'll find cultural history exhibits as well as the murals of Fred Kabotie, a popular 1940s artist whose work was commissioned by Mary Jane Colter. Native American crafts are displayed in this museum and mini visitor center. Check the schedule for daily events. ⊠*2 mi north of Painted Desert Visitor Center on the main park road* ☎*928/524–6228* ⊕*www.nps.gov/pefo* ⊠*Free* ☉*Daily 8–4.*

Puerco Pueblo. This is a 100-room pueblo, built before 1400 and said to have housed ancestral Puebloan people. Many visitors come to see petroglyphs, as well as a solar calendar. ⊠*10 mi south of the Painted Desert Visitor Center on the main park road.*

SCENIC STOPS

★ **Agate Bridge.** Here you'll see a 100-foot log spanning a 40-foot-wide wash. ⊠*19 mi south of Painted Desert Visitor Center on the main park road.*

Crystal Forest. Before they were "mined" by looters, the fragments of petrified wood strewn here once held clear quartz and amethyst crystals. ⊠ *20 mi south of Painted Desert Visitor Center on the main park road.*

★ **Giant Logs.** A short walk leads you past the park's largest log, known as "Old Faithful." It's considered the largest because of its diameter (9 feet, 9 inches), as well as how tall it once was. ⊠ *28 mi south of Painted Desert Visitor Center on the main park road.*

Jasper Forest. More of an overlook than a forest, this spot has a large concentration of petrified trees in jasper or red. ⊠ *17 mi south of Painted Desert Visitor Center on the main park road.*

The Tepees. Witness the effects of time on these cone-shaped rock formations colored by iron, manganese, and other minerals. ⊠ *8 mi south of Painted Desert Visitor Center on the main park road.*

> **GUILT TRIPS**
>
> In 1906, President Theodore Roosevelt made the area a national monument to protect the petrified wood, which many looters were hauling away in large quantities. Since then, it has been illegal to remove even a small sliver of petrified wood from the park. Those who have say it's brought them all sorts of problems. "Guilt Books" at the Rainbow Forest Museum, located at the park's south entrance, preserve letters from guilt-ridden former visitors anxiously returning their purloined souvenirs and detailing directly attributable hexes—from runs of bad luck to husbands turning into "hard-drinking strangers."

SCENIC DRIVE

Painted Desert Scenic Drive. A 28-mi scenic drive takes you through the park from one entrance to the other. If you begin from the north, the first 5 mi of the drive takes you along the edge of a high mesa, with spectacular views of Painted Desert. Beyond lies the desolate Painted Desert Wilderness Area. After the 5 mi point, the road crosses I–40, then swings south toward Perco River across a landscape covered with sagebrush, saltbrush, sunflowers, and Apache plume. Past the river, the road climbs onto a narrow mesa leading to Newspaper Rock, a panel of Pueblo Indian rock art. Then the road bends southeast, enters a barren stretch, and passes tepee-shaped buttes in the distance. Next you come to Blue Mesa, roughly the park's midpoint and a good place to stop for views of petrified logs. The next stop on the drive is Agate Bridge, really a 100-foot log over a wide wash. The remaining overlooks are Jasper Forest and Crystal Forest, where you can get a further glimpse at the accumulated petrified wood. On your way out of the park, stop at the Rainbow Forest Museum for a rest and to shop for a memento. ⊠ *Begins at Painted Desert Visitor Center.*

VISITOR CENTERS

Painted Desert Visitor Center. This is the place to go for general park information and an informative 20-minute film on the park. Proceeds from books purchased here fund the continuing research and interpretive activities for the park. ⊠ *North entrance, off I–40, 27 mi east of Holbrook* ☎ *928/524–6228* ⊕ *www.nps.gov/pefo* ☉ *Daily 8–5.*

Rainbow Forest Museum and Visitor Center. The museum houses artifacts of early reptiles, dinosaurs, and petrified wood. Be sure to see Gertie, the skeleton of a phytosaur, a crocodile-like carnivore. ✉*South entrance, off U.S. 180, 18 mi southeast of Holbrook* ☎*928/524–6228* *Free* ⌚*Daily 8–5.*

PERMITS

Permits are required for backcountry hiking and camping, and are free (limit 15 days) at Painted Desert Visitor Center or Rainbow Forest Museum and Visitor Center before 4 PM.

SPORTS & THE OUTDOORS

As with visits to all national parks, you don't get the full experience unless you take time to smell the roses—or in this case, get close enough to see the multihued lines streaking a petrified log. However, because the park goes to great pains to maintain the integrity of the fossil- and artifact-strewn landscape, sports and outdoor options in the park are limited. Off-highway activity is restricted to on-trail hiking and horseback riding.

5

BICYCLING

Bikes are allowed on the 28-mi paved drive only. There are no rentals within the park, so bring your own equipment.

HIKING

All trails begin off the main road, with restrooms at or near the trailheads. Most maintained trails are relatively short, paved, clearly marked, and, with a few exceptions, easy to moderate in difficulty. Hikers with greater stamina can make their own trails in the wilderness area, located just north of the Painted Desert Visitor Center. Watch your step for rattlesnakes, which are common in the park—if left alone and given a wide berth, they are easily negotiated.

EASY **Crystal Forest.** The easy 8/10-mi loop leads you past petrified wood that once held quartz crystals and amethyst chips. ✉*20 mi south of the Painted Desert Visitor Center.*

Giant Logs. At 4/10 mi, Giant Logs is the park's shortest trail. The loop leads you to "Old Faithful," the park's largest log—it's 9 feet, 9 inches at its base, weighing 44 tons. ✉*Directly behind Rainbow Forest Museum, 28 mi south of Painted Desert Visitor Center.*

Long Logs. While barren, the easy 6/10-mi loop reveals the largest concentration of wood in the park. ✉*26 mi south of Painted Desert Visitor Center.*

Puerco Pueblo. A relatively flat and interesting 3/10-mi trail takes you past remains of an ancestral home of the Pueblo people, built before 1400. The trail is paved and handicapped accessible. ✉*10 mi south of Painted Desert Visitor Center.*

MODERATE **Agate House.** A fairly flat 1-mi trip takes you to an eight-room pueblo sitting high on a knoll. *See Historic Sites, What to See.* ✉*26 mi south of Painted Desert Visitor Center.*

Blue Mesa. Although it's only 1 mi long and it's significantly steeper than the rest, this trail at the park's midway point is one of the most popular. ⊠*14 mi south of Painted Desert Visitor Center.*

Painted Desert Rim. The 1-mi trail is at its best in early morning or late afternoon, when the sun accentuates the brilliant red, blue, purple, and other hues of the desert and petrified forest landscape. ⊠*Tawa Point and Kachina Point, 1 mi north of Painted Desert Visitor Center.*

DIFFICULT **Kachina Point.** This is the trailhead for wilderness hiking. A 1-mi trail leads to the Wilderness Area, but from there you're on your own. With no developed trails, hiking here is cross-country style, but expect to see strange formations, beautifully colored landscape, and maybe, just maybe, a pronghorn antelope. ⊠*On the northwest side of the Painted Desert Inn Museum.*

HORSEBACK RIDING

Horseback riding in Petrified Forest is limited mostly to the wilderness area (paved roads and trails are off-limits), but that doesn't mean it's a limiting experience. Although there are no outfitters in the park who provide horses or guides, you can load/unload and park your trailer on the northwest side of Painted Desert Inn, 2 mi north of the Painted Desert Visitor Center.

There are no maintained trails in this section of the park, but riders are advised to stick to dry washes as much as possible so as to minimize impact to the fragile desert ecosystem. The first switchback into the Wilderness Area is steep, sometimes unstable, and often exposed; so some riders lead their horses down on foot. Once you reach the desert floor, the grade is relatively flat and easy to ride. If you want to camp overnight, you'll need to get a free permit, available at either visitor center. A designated zone north of Lithodendron Wash is set aside for camping, though no campsites are maintained. Group camping is limited to eight people and four horses.

EDUCATIONAL OFFERINGS

FILMS

Timeless Impressions. At the Painted Desert Visitor Center, a 20-minute educational film serves as an introduction to the park. It covers the highlights, briefly explaining the sights you'll see and their archaeological significance. The film runs continuously, starting every half hour. ⊠*Painted Desert Visitor Center* ☎*928/524–6228* ☉*Daily 8–5.*

RANGER PROGRAMS

Children 12 and younger can learn more about the park's extensive human, animal, and geologic history as they train to become a Junior Ranger.

Park Rangers lead regular **20-minute tours** along the Great Logs trail, inside the Painted Desert Inn Museum, and to the Puerco Pueblo. Ask at either visitor center for the availability of **special tours,** such as the after-hours lantern tour of the Painted Desert Inn Museum.

WHERE TO STAY & EAT

There is no lodging or campgrounds within the Petrified Forest. Backcountry camping is allowed if you obtain a free permit at the visitor center or museum; the only camping allowed is minimal-impact camping in a designated zone north of Lithodendron Wash in the Wilderness Area. Group size is limited to 8. RVs are not allowed. There are no fire pits or designated sites, nor is any shade available. Also note that if it rains, that pretty Painted Desert formation turns to sticky clay.

Dining in the park is limited to a cafeteria in the Painted Desert Visitor Center and snacks in the Rainbow Forest Museum. You may want to pack a lunch and eat at one of the park's picnic areas.

WHERE TO EAT

¢ ✕ **Painted Desert Visitor Center Cafeteria.** This is the only place in the park where you can get a full meal. Offerings are standard cafeteria fare. ⊠ *North entrance, off I–40, 27 mi east of Holbrook* ☎ *928/524–6228* ⊟ MC, V.

¢ ✕ **Rainbow Forest Museum Snack Bar.** Quick snacks are available at the museum. ⊠ *South entrance, off U.S. 180, 18 mi southeast of Holbrook* ☎ *928/524–6228* ⊟ MC, V.

PICNIC AREAS **Chinde Point Picnic Area.** This small picnic area is near the north entrance and has picnic tables and restrooms. ⊠ *2 mi north of Painted Desert Visitor Center.*

Rainbow Forest Museum Picnic Area. This small picnic area is near the south entrance and has picnic tables and restrooms. ⊠ *South entrance, off I–40, 27 mi east of Holbrook.*

SNOWFLAKE-TAYLOR

🔟 *15 mi north of Show Low on AZ 77.*

Snowflake-Taylor is a good jumping-off point for exploring eastern Arizona; it's an easy day trip to the Homolovi Ruins or the Petrified Forest. The towns are also a less-crowded alternative for summer excursions in the nearby White Mountains. Most Phoenix weekenders head for the higher towns, so Snowflake and Taylor avoid the crush of summer visitors that results in higher prices at hotels and restaurants. Sandwiched between the White Mountains and the Colorado Plateau, the communities enjoy year-round pleasant weather with summer highs in the 90s. Yes, it snows in Snowflake, but it seldom lasts more than a day.

Snowflake and Taylor were settled by Mormons in the 1870s and named for Mormon church leaders. Snowflake's unusual name is a combination of Erastus Snow, an apostle in the early Mormon church of Salt Lake City, Utah, and William Flake, one of the town founders. One Arizona's two Mormon temples sits on Temple Hill west of Snowflake, and the towns still have a large Mormon contingent in their combined population of 9,000. You can take a walking tour of Snowflake's historical district, with pioneer homes and antiques stores.

The **Stinson Museum** once served as a schoolhouse. James Stinson, the first rancher in the valley, was the original resident of the small adobe home. William J. Flake bought out Stinson's holdings and founded the town of Snowflake. Flake added on to the structure, which today is a museum containing pioneer memorabilia, quilts, Native American artifacts, and a small gift shop. Check with the Chamber of Commerce (☎928/536–4331) for seasonal winter hours. ⊠*102 N. 1st St.* ☎*928/536–4881* *$1* ☉*Mon.–Sat. 10–2.*

The **Taylor Museum,** a small local museum with pioneer and Native American exhibits, celebrates July 4 by "firing the anvil" at sunrise. At 4 AM, revelers place an anvil on the ground, a newspaper and gun powder on top, then another anvil. When the gunpowder is lit, the anvil flies 3 feet into the air with a deafening bang. The rest of the year, the anvil resides at the museum along with the Jennings drum, which was brought to town by early Mormon settlers. ⊠*2 N. Main St.* ☎*928/536–6649* *Donations accepted* ☉*Mon.–Sat. 10–2.*

SPORTS & THE OUTDOORS

GOLF One of the least expensive golf courses in the White Mountains, the 27-hole **Snowflake Municipal Golf Course** (⊠*90 N. Country Club Dr.* ☎*928/536–7233*) is open year-round. Especially scenic with red rocks and waterfalls, the course includes a driving range and water hazard. The restaurant is open May through October. Green fees are $18 for 9 holes with a cart, and $36 for 18 holes with a cart; rates are lower November through April.

HIKING At the junction of Silver Creek Canyon and Five-Mile Canyon, 5 mi north of Snowflake, ancient peoples left petroglyphs carved through the dark desert varnish revealing the light sandstone of the canyon walls. **Petroglyph Hike** (⊠*Silver Creek Canyon*), the trail from the canyon top down to the petroglyphs, is short but steep. Trail access is regulated by the city of Snowflake. To check-in and get directions, contact the **Snowflake-Taylor Chamber of Commerce** (☎*928/536–4331 or 928/536–4881*).

WHERE TO STAY & EAT

★ $–$$ ✕ **La Cocina de Eva.** If you like Mexican food, stop here. The green-corn tamales and enchiladas are delicious, and locals go for the bean burro smothered in green chile sauce. Portions are large and service is friendly. A combination of Mexican knickknacks and Western paintings gives this popular spot a homey feel. ⊠*201 N. Main St., Snowflake* ☎*928/536–7683* ▭MC, V ☉*Closed Sun.*

¢–$$ ✕ **Enzo's Ristorante Italiano.** Behind Heritage Antiques, in the historic district of Snowflake, is the only Italian restaurant in town. Sauces and breads are homemade, and although they may take a while, the minestrone soup, baked pastas, and shrimp Alfredo are worth the wait. ⊠*50 E. 1st St. N, Snowflake* ☎*928/243–0450* ▭No credit cards ☉*Closed Mon. and Tues. No lunch.*

¢–$$ ✕ **Trapper's Cafe.** Opened in 1973 by "Trapper" Hatch and still family-owned, this hometown diner is decorated with Hatch's old trapping equipment and animal paintings by local artists. Chicken-fried steak and homemade barbecue sauce draw a loyal crowd. People drive out of their way just to stop for a piece of Trapper's pies, especially banana cream. Have a slice at the counter with a cup of coffee. ⊠ *9 S. Main St., Taylor* ☎ *928/536–7758* ▤ *MC, V* ⊘ *Closed Sun.*

$–$$ ▦ **Comfort Inn.** The Comfort Inn is the only hotel in either Snowflake or Taylor with a pool. The pool, the large rooms, and the complimentary Continental breakfast make the inn a great deal for families. A large river-rock fireplace and rustic furniture adorn the comfortable lobby. ⊠ *2055 S. Main St., Snowflake 85937* ☎ *928/536–3888 or 877/505–3888* ▤ *928/536–3888* ⊕ *www.comfortinn.com* ➴ *64 rooms* ◌ *In-room: refrigerator (some), Wi-Fi. In-hotel: pool, laundry facilities, no-smoking rooms, gym, no elevator, some pets allowed* ▤ *AE, D, MC, V* ⏍*CP.*

$ ▦ **Osmer D. Heritage Inn.** Elegantly furnished with period antiques, this redbrick home with a white-picket fence was built in 1890 by Mormon pioneer Osmer D. Flake. Filled with pioneer style, Osmer D's is next door to Heritage Antiques and between two restaurants—making it the best place to start Snowflake's historic walking tour. ⊠ *161 N. Main St., Snowflake 85937* ☎ *928/536–3322 or 866/486–5947* ⊕ *www.heritage-inn.net* ➴ *9 rooms, 2 suites* ◌ *In-room: Wi-Fi. In-hotel: no-smoking rooms, no elevator* ▤ *AE, D, MC, V* ⏍*BP.*

$ ▦ **Rodeway Silver Creek Inn.** Simply furnished, clean, and near fast-food restaurants, Silver Creek sees many "regulars" who travel through the area often. There's ample parking for RVs and trailers, and it's close to Taylor's only grocery store. ⊠ *825 N. Main St., Taylor 85939* ☎ *928/536–2600* ➴ *42 rooms* ◌ *In-room: refrigerator. In-hotel: no elevator* ▤ *AE, D, DC, MC, V* ⏍*CP.*

HOMOLOVI RUINS STATE PARK

★ ⓫   *53 mi east of Flagstaff, 33 mi west of Holbrook. Exit 257 off I–40.*

Homolovi is a Hopi word meaning "place of the little hills." The pueblo sites here are thought to have been occupied between AD 1200 and 1425 and include 40 ceremonial kivas and two pueblos containing more than 1,000 rooms each. The Hopi believe their immediate ancestors inhabited this place and still hold the site to be sacred. Many rooms have been excavated and recovered for protection. Weekdays in June and July you can see archaeologists working the site. Mobility-impaired persons should check with the ranger station for alternate access information; rangers conduct guided tours. The Homolovi Visitor Center has a small museum with Hopi pottery and ancestral Puebloan artifacts; it also hosts workshops on native art, ethnobotany, and traditional foods. ⊠ *AZ 87, 5 mi northeast of Winslow* ⏍ *HCR 63, Box 5, Winslow 86047* ☎ *928/289–4106* ⊕ *www.pr.state.az.us.*

The Ancestral Puebloan petroglyphs of **Rock Art Ranch,** in Chevelon Canyon, are startlingly vivid after more than 1,000 years. Brantly Baird, owner of this working cattle ranch, will guide you along the ¼-mi trail, explaining western and archaeological history. It's mostly easy walking, except for the climb in and out of Chevelon Canyon, where there are hand rails. Baird houses his Native American artifacts and pioneer farming items in his own private museum. It's out of the way and on a dirt road, but you'll see some of the best rock art in northern Arizona. Reservations are required. ⊠ *Off AZ 87, 13 mi southeast of Winslow* ✉ *Box 224, Joseph City 85032* ☎ *928/288–3260* ⬚ *$20* ⊙ *May–Oct. by appointment only.*

WHERE TO STAY

Homolovi Ruins State Park is 5 mi northeast of the town of Winslow. Frequent flooding on the Little Colorado River frustrated the attempts

> ### MARY COLTER
>
> Pick a historic hotel or site of significance built in the late 19th or early 20th century in northern or eastern Arizona, and there's a chance architect Mary Colter was part of it. Colter designed the La Posada in Winslow, the Painted Desert Inn, several structures at the Grand Canyon including the Hopi House, and decorated the historic El Tovar Hotel, also at the Grand Canyon. Her work now is being emulated in housing developments across the Southwest, as architects embrace the charm of centuries-old design.

of Mormon pioneers to settle here, but with the coming of the railroad the town roared into life. Later, Route 66 sustained the community until I–40 passed north of town. New motels and restaurants sprouted near the interstate exits, and downtown was all but abandoned. Downtown Winslow is now revitalizing, with La Posada Hotel as its showpiece, but dining options are still scarce.

$$ 🏨 **La Posada Winslow.** One of the great railroad hotels, La Posada (it means "resting place") exudes the charm of an 18th-century Spanish hacienda. Architect Mary Colter, famous for her work at the Grand Canyon, designed and decorated the 68,000-square-foot hotel. Spanish and Native American furniture, antiques, and art permeate her designs. The lobby is a gallery for paintings by Tina Mion, one of the owners. Individually decorated rooms are restored to 1930s style and the lush gardens are a swath of green in the red-rock Colorado Plateau. If you can't spend the night, take the self-guided tour ($2 donation). ⊠ *303 E. 2nd St., Winslow 86047* ☎ *928/289–4366* 🖨 *928/289–3873* ⊕ *www. laposada.org* ⮑ *37 rooms* ⬚ *In-room: no phone. In-hotel: restaurant, bar, no-smoking rooms, no elevator* ⊟ AE, D, MC, V.

HOLBROOK

⑫ *35 mi east of Homolovi State Park via I–40.*

Downtown Holbrook is a monument to Route 66 kitsch. The famous "Mother Road" traveled through the center of Holbrook before I–40 replaced it as the area's major east–west artery, and remnants of the "good ole days" can be found all over town. Route 66 itself still runs through Holbrook, following Navajo Boulevard and Hopi Drive. It makes a sharp corner at the intersection of these two roads, and used to cause traffic jams. The Downtowner, a popular coffee shop on this corner, served simple meals and coffee to sleepy truck drivers. As if traffic weren't already scrambled enough, crowds from the movie theater at what is today East Hopi Drive brought Route 66 to a standstill. Moviegoers, who filled the streets at the end of the show, considered it their right to block traffic; after all, many had traveled over 100 mi to see the movie.

Before Route 66 rolled into Holbrook, the town was a notorious hangout for cowboys from the vast Aztec Land and Cattle Company, better known as the Hashknife Outfit for the shape of their brand. Pick up a walking tour at the Chamber of Commerce and see the sites, including the infamous Bucket of Blood Saloon.

★ The **Old Courthouse Museum** (☎ *800/524–2459* ⊕ *www.ci.holbrook. az.us* ✉ *Free* ☉ *Weekdays 8–5, weekends 8–4*), at the corner of Arizona Street and Navajo Boulevard, holds memorabilia from the Route 66 heyday along with Old West and railroad records. Near the railroad tracks you'll be surprised by models of bright green dinosaurs glaring down at you. The Indian Rock Shop makes dinosaurs, and their wares are stored outside. The shop isn't open to the public, but it's hard to find a place to store a dinosaur.

WHERE TO STAY & EAT

$–$$ ✗ **Mesa Italiana Restaurant.** While getting your kicks on Route 66, stop by to enjoy a hearty meal at one of Holbrook's most popular restaurants, where the chef prepares authentic-tasting traditional Italian dishes. Locals recommend the fresh pastas, calzones, spaghetti with Italian mushrooms, and salads. Don't forget the spumoni for dessert. ✉ *2318 E. Navajo Blvd.* ☎ *928/524–6696* ▭ AE, D, MC, V ☉ *No weekend lunch*.

$ ▦ **Holbrook Days Inn.** A heated indoor pool and hot tub, free Continental breakfast and local phone calls, and proximity to local restaurants make this a pleasant, convenient choice. Rooms have coffeemakers, hair dryers, and cable TV. ✉ *2601 Navajo Blvd., Holbrook 86025* ☎ *928/524–6949* ⊕ *www.daysinn.com* ⌔ *51 rooms, 3 suites* ⚒ *In-room: refrigerator (some). In-hotel: pool, public Wi-Fi, laundry facilities* ▭ AE, D, DC, MC, V ⦿ CP.

★ ¢–$ ▦ **Wigwam Motel.** One of the iconic images of Route 66 and listed on the National Register of Historic Places, the Wigwam consists of 15 bright-white concrete tepees where you can sleep inexpensively, in a quirky environment. As you might expect, wigwams are phoneless, but—here's to Mother Progress—these have cable TV. A small lobby museum exhibits Mexican, Native American, and military relics collected by the owner's family. The 180-pound, polished petrified wood sphere is one of the largest in the Southwest. All of the classic cars parked by the tepees also belong to the owners. ✉ *711 W. Hopi Dr., Holbrook 86025* ☎ *928/524–3048* ▤ *928/524–9335* ⊕ *www.galerie-kokopelli. com/wigwam* ⌔ *15 rooms* ⚒ *In-room: no phone* ▭ MC, V.

SHOPPING

McGees Beyond Native Tradition (⊠*2114 E. Navajo Blvd., Holbrook* ☎*928/524–1977 or 800/524–9183* ⊕*www.hopiart.com*) is the area's premier source of high-quality Native American jewelry, rugs, Hopi baskets, and katsina dolls. The owners have long-standing relationships with reservation artisans and a knowledgeable staff that adroitly assists first-time buyers and seasoned collectors.

EASTERN ARIZONA ESSENTIALS

To research prices, get advice from other travelers, and book travel arrangements, visit ⊕*www.fodors.com.*

BY BUS

White Mountain Passenger Lines has service between Phoenix and Show Low; one-way fares are around $48. Greyhound Lines travels from Phoenix to Winslow, 50 mi west of Petrified Forest National Park, for around $45.

Information **Greyhound Lines** (⊠*816 Transcon La., Winslow* ☎*928/289–2171* ⊕ *www.greyhound.com*). **White Mountain Passenger Lines** (⊠*1041 E. Hall St., Show Low* ☎*928/537–4539* ⊠*319 S. 24th St., Phoenix* ☎*602/275–4245* ⊕ *www.wmlines.com*).

BY CAR

A car is essential for touring eastern Arizona, especially because most of the region's top scenic attractions are between towns. Rental facilities are few and far between in these parts, so rent a car from your departure point, whether it's Phoenix, Flagstaff, or Albuquerque.

If you're arriving from points west via Flagstaff, I–40 leads directly to Holbrook, where drivers can take AZ 77 south into Show Low or U.S. 180 southeast to Springerville-Eagar. Those departing from the metropolitan Phoenix area should take the scenic drive northeast on U.S. 60, or the only slightly faster AZ 87 north to AZ 260 east, both of which lead to Show Low. From Tucson, AZ 77 north connects with U.S. 60 at Globe and continues through Show Low up to Holbrook. From New Mexico, drivers can enter the state on I–40 and take U.S. 191 south into Springerville-Eagar, or continue on to Holbrook and reach the White Mountains via AZ 77. For those who want to drive the Coronado Trail south-to-north, U.S. 70 and AZ 78 link up with U.S. 191 from Globe to the west and New Mexico to the east, respectively.

ROAD CONDITIONS In winter, motorists should travel prepared, with jumper cables, a shovel, tire chains, and—for tire traction on icy roads—a bag of cat litter. Chain requirements apply to all vehicles, including those with four-wheel drive. Bridges and overpasses freeze first and are often slicker than normal road surfaces; never assume sufficient traction simply because a road appears to be sanded. Drivers who must travel in poor visibility conditions should turn on the headlights and always keep the highway's white reflectors to their right. For road conditions throughout the region, call the White Mountains Road and Weather Information Line.

Contact White Mountains Road and Weather Information Line (☎ *928/537–7623).*

BY TRAIN

Amtrak trains depart daily at 6:01 AM from Flagstaff to Winslow. There's no train service to Phoenix; those traveling from Phoenix will need to take the Amtrak shuttle—which departs Phoenix-area bus stations four times daily bound for Flagstaff—and stay overnight in Flagstaff to catch the early-morning train to Winslow. From Albuquerque, Winslow is only a four-hour ride, leaving daily at 4:45 PM.

Contact Amtrak (☎ *928/774–8679 in Flagstaff).*

CAMPING

Call or write the Apache-Sitgreaves National Forest for a brochure listing all public camping facilities in the region, most of which operate from April to November. To ensure a site at a fee campground, call the National Recreation Reservation Service, which charges a reservation fee of $10 per transaction. Book your campground site well in advance with the Game and Fish Division of the White Mountain Apache Tribe.

Contacts Apache-Sitgreaves National Forest (☎ *928/368–5111* ⊕ *www. fs.fed.us/r3/asnf).* National Recreation Reservation Service (☎ *877/444–6777* ⊕ *www.reserveusa.com).* White Mountain Apache Tribe (☎ *928/338–4385* ⊕ *www.wmat.nsn.us).*

EMERGENCIES

Ambulance & Fire Ambulance and Fire Emergencies (☎ *911).*

Hospitals Navapache Regional Medical Center (✉ *2200 E. Show Low Lake Rd., Show Low* ☎ *928/537–4375* ⊕ *www.nrmc.org).* White Mountain Regional Medical Center (✉ *118 S. Mountain Ave., Springerville* ☎ *928/333–4368* ⊕ *www.wmrmc.com).*

Police Police Emergencies (☎ *911).*

VISITOR INFORMATION

Contacts Alpine Chamber of Commerce (☎ *928/339–4330* ⊕ *www. alpinearizona.com).* Holbrook Chamber of Commerce (☎ *928/524–6558 or 800/524–2459* ⊕ *www.ci.holbrook.az.us).* Pinetop-Lakeside Chamber of Commerce (☎ *928/367–4290 or 800/573–4031* ⊕ *www.pinetoplakesidechamber.com).* Show Low Chamber of Commerce (☎ *928/537–2326 or 888/746–9569* ⊕ *www. showlowchamberofcommerce.com).* Snowflake/Taylor Chamber of Commerce (☎ *928/536–4331* ⊕ *www.snowflaketaylorchamber.org).* Springerville-Eagar Regional Chamber of Commerce (☎ *928/333–2123* ⊕ *www.springerville-eagar chamber.com).* White Mountain Apache Office of Tourism (☎ *928/338–1230* ⊕ *www.wmat.nsn.us).*

Contacts Apache-Sitgreaves National Forest (☎ *928/333–4301* ⊕ *www.fs.fed. us/r3/asnf).* Alpine Ranger District (☎ *928/339–4384 Lakeside Ranger District*

☎ *928/368–5111).* **Springerville Ranger District** (☎ *928/333–4372).* **Arizona Game & Fish Department** (☎ *928/367–4281* ⊕ *www.gf.state.az.us).* **Petrified Forest National Park** (☎ *928/524–6228* ⊕ *www.nps.gov/pefo).* **San Carlos Apache Tribe** (☎ *928/475–2361).* **White Mountain Apache Fish & Game Department** (☎ *928/338–4385).*

Tucson

Saguaro Cactus, Saguaro National Park

WORD OF MOUTH

"If you want nightlife and shopping, go to Phoenix. If you want quiet, laid-back, beautiful surroundings with fabulous hiking opportunities, try Tucson."

—tucsonartist

WELCOME TO TUCSON

TOP REASONS TO GO

★ **Cacti:** Unique to this region, the saguaro cactus is the quintessential symbol of the Southwest. The best places to check out saguaros up close are at Saguaro National Park East or West and Sabino Canyon.

★ **Mexican food:** Tucson boasts that it's the "Mexican Food Capital," and you won't be disappointed at any of the Mexican restaurants listed in this chapter.

★ **The Arizona-Sonora Desert Museum:** Anyone who thinks that museums are boring hasn't been to this one, where you can learn about the wildlife, plants, and geology of the region in a gorgeous, mostly outdoors, setting. Don't miss one of the daily hawk- or falcon flying demonstrations.

★ **Mission San Xavier del Bac:** The "White Dove of the Desert" is the oldest building in Tucson. Ornate carvings and frescoes inside add to the mystical quality of this active parish on the Tohono O'odham reservation.

1 Downtown. Three historic districts—Barrio Historico, El Presidio, and Armory Park—encompass the downtown area.

2 The University of Arizona. The 353-acre campus, classified as an arboretum, houses several top-rated museums. At the west entrance, University Boulevard is lined with boutiques, cafés, and bookstores.

3 Central and East Tucson. This mostly residential area is home to Tucson's zoo, its largest indoor shopping mall (Park Place), and its best municipal golf course (Randolph Park).

4 The Catalina Foothills. North of River Road the landscape becomes hilly

GETTING ORIENTED

The metropolitan Tucson area covers more than 500 square mi in a valley ringed by mountains—the Santa Catalinas to the north, the Santa Ritas to the south, the Rincons to the east, and the Tucson Mountains to the west. Saguaro National Park bookends Tucson, with one section on the far east side and the other out west near the world-class Arizona-Sonora Desert Museum. The central portion of the city has most of the shops, restaurants, and businesses, but not many tourist sights. Downtown's historical district and the neighboring University area are much smaller and easily navigated on foot. Up north in the Catalina Foothills, you'll find first-class resorts, restaurants, and hiking trails, most with spectacular views of the entire valley.

and streets wind up to beautiful homes and resorts. At the east end, Sabino Canyon offers prime hiking.

5 Northwest. Suburban sprawl at it finest, this part of town just keeps growing. Two dude ranches are holdouts from a quieter era.

6 Westside. The untamed Tucson Mountain region, embraces miles of saguaro forests, the Arizona-Sonora Desert Museum, and Mission San Xavier del Bac on the Tohono O'odham reservation.

7 Saguaro National Park. Saguaro National Park, is made up of two sections: the western section is the smaller—and more heavily visited area.

TUCSON PLANNER

Getting Here & Getting Around

You can fly to Tucson International Airport but cheaper, non-stop flights into Phoenix are often easier to find; the drive (or shuttle) is two hours down I-10 to Tucson. Once in town, a car is essential.

When to Go

Summer lodging rates (late May–September) are hugely discounted, even at many of the resorts, but there's a good reason: summer in Tucson is hot! Swimming and indoor activities like museums (and spa treatments) are doable; but only the hardiest hikers and golfers stay out past noon in summer.

Tucson averages only 12 inches of rain a year. Winter temperatures hover around 65°F during the day and 38°F at night. Summers are unquestionably hot—July averages 104°F during the day and 75°F at night—but, as Tucsonans are fond of saying, "it's a dry heat."

International Gem and Mineral Show descends on Tucson in February; book your hotel in advance or you'll be hard pressed to find a room.

What to Do and Where to Do It

Fall, winter, and spring in Tucson are mild with little rainfall, making the Tucson area wonderful for outdoor sports. The city has miles of bike paths (shared by joggers and walkers) and plenty of open spaces with memorable desert views, and some of the best golf courses in the country. Hikers enjoy the desert trails in Saguaro National Park, Sabino Canyon, and Catalina State Park—all within 20 minutes of central Tucson; in summer, there are cooler treks in nearby mountain ranges (Mt. Lemmon to the north and Madera Canyon to the south). Equestrians can find scenic trails at one of the many area stables or dude ranches.

Making the Most of Your Time

Even if you have only one day, you can experience both the wild and developed parts of Tucson. You can visit the Arizona-Sonora Desert Museum in the morning and combine it with a stop at Mission San Xavier del Bac or Old Tucson Studios. On the way back to town, stop in downtown's Barrio Historico and El Presidio neighborhoods to meander the adobe-lined streets, then have dinner at one of the outstanding Mexican restaurants in downtown or South Tucson.

Another option is spending a half day in Saguaro National Park. Set out in the early morning when it's cooler and the liveliest time for wildlife. If you're based in the Foothills, you can choose Sabino Canyon instead; the saguaros are almost as plentiful and the vistas are equally rewarding. Nature in the morning can be combined with an afternoon in the University area: Visit any of the five campus museums, then stroll University Boulevard and 4th Avenue for ethnic eats and vintage boutiques.

If you have another day for exploring and like to shop, head south to the Mexican border. If you haven't seen Mission San Xavier yet, it's directly en route to Tubac, an artists' colony with historic sights as well as galleries. You can then venture farther south for bargain hunting in Nogales, Mexico (park on the U.S. side and walk across); or head back toward Tucson, stopping at the Titan Missile Museum or at one of the casinos.

Native Cultures

Mexican Americans make up about 30% of Tucson's population and play a major role in all aspects of daily life. The city's south-of-the-border soul is visible in its tile-roof architecture, mariachi festivals, and abundance of Mexican restaurants. Native Americans have a strong presence in the area as well: the Tohono O'odham reservation borders Tucson, and the Pascua Yaqui have their villages within the city limits. Mission San Xavier del Bac, a thriving reservation parish, is a good spot to experience religious festivals around Christmas and Easter, and to sample fry bread, a favorite Indian snack. Native American crafts include exquisite jewelry and basketry as well as the more pedestrian (but still authentic) tourist trinkets.

Dining and Lodging

Tucson boldly proclaims itself to be the "Mexican Food Capital of the United States" and most of the Mexican food in town is Sonoran style—native to the adjoining Mexican state of Sonora. This means prolific use of cheese, mild peppers, corn tortillas, pinto beans, and beef or chicken. If Mexican's not your thing, there are plenty of other options: you won't have any trouble finding sushi, Indian, Italian, Thai, and Greek food. There are some exemplary Southwestern restaurants in the area, too, for sampling innovative local cuisine.

When it comes to places to spend the night, the options in Tucson run the gamut: there are luxurious desert resorts, bed-and-breakfasts ranging from bedrooms in modest homes to private cottages nestled on wildlife preserves, as well as small to medium-size hotels and motels. For a unique experience, you can check into a Southwestern-style "dude" ranch—some of them former cattle ranches from the 1800s—on the outskirts of town (unless otherwise indicated, price categories for guest ranches include all meals and most activities).

What It Costs

	¢	$	$$	$$$	$$$$
Restaurants	Under $8	$8–$12	$13–$20	$21–$30	over $30

Restaurant prices are per person for a main course at dinner. Hotel prices are for a standard double in high season, excluding taxes and service charges.

Festivals & Events

Jan.–Feb. **Tucson Gem, Mineral and Fossil Showcase.** This huge trade show, the largest of its kind in the world, offers everything from precious stones to geodes to beads. ☎800/638–8350.

Feb. **La Fiesta de los Vaqueros.** America's largest outdoor midwinter rodeo, with more than 600 events, takes place on the Tucson Rodeo Grounds. ☎520/741–2233.

Apr. **Fiesta de Saguaro.** This celebration of the Hispanic culture and heritage is held at the Rincon Mountain District in Saguaro National Park. ☎520/733–5153.

July **Saguaro Harvest Celebration.** Held at Colossal Cave Mountain Park in Vail, AZ, this celebrations centers on the majestic saguaro and the summer harvest of its fruit. ☎520/647–7121.

Updated by
Mara Levin

THE OLD PUEBLO, AS TUCSON is affectionately known, is built upon a deep Native American, Spanish, Mexican, and Old West foundation. Arizona's second-largest city is both a bustling center of business and a relaxed university and resort town. Metropolitan Tucson has more than 850,000 residents, including thousands of snowbirds who flee colder climes to enjoy the sun that shines on the city more than 340 days out of 365.

The city has a tri-cultural (Hispanic, Anglo, Native American) population, and the chance to see how these cultures interact—and to sample their cuisines—is one of the pleasures of a visit. The city is particularly popular among golfers, but the area's many hiking trails will keep nonduffers busy, too. If the weather is too hot to stay outdoors comfortably, museums like the Arizona State Museum and the Center for Creative Photography offer a cooler alternative.

This college town has Mexican and Native American cultural influences, a striking landscape, and all the amenities of a resort town, as well as its fair share of ubiquitous strip malls and tract-home developments. High-tech industries have moved into the area, but the economy still relies heavily on tourism and the university—although, come summer, you'd never guess; when the snowbirds and students depart, Tucson can be a sleepy place.

EXPLORING TUCSON

GETTING YOUR BEARINGS

The central portion of Tucson—which has most of the shops, restaurants, and businesses—is roughly bounded by Craycroft Road to the east, Oracle Road to the west, River Road to the north, and 22nd Street to the south. The older downtown section, east of I–10 off the Broadway-Congress exit, is smaller and easy to navigate on foot. Streets downtown don't run on any sort of grid, however, and many are one-way, so it's best to get a good, detailed map. The city's Westside area is the vast region west of I–10 and I–19, which includes the western section of Saguaro National Park and the San Xavier Indian Reservation.

DOWNTOWN

The area bordered by Franklin Street on the north, Cushing Street on the south, Church Avenue on the east, and Main Avenue on the west contains over two centuries of Tucson's history, dating from the original walled El Presidio de Tucson, a Spanish fortress built in 1776, when Arizona was still part of New Spain. A good deal of the city's history was destroyed in the 1960s, when large sections of downtown's barrio were bulldozed to make way for the Tucson Convention Center, high-rises, and parking lots. However, within the area's three small historic districts it's still possible to explore Tucson's architectural and cultural past.

El Presidio Historic District, north of the Convention Center and the government buildings that dominate downtown, is an architectural thumbnail of the city's former self. The north–south streets Court, Meyer, and Main are sprinkled with traditional Mexican adobe houses sitting cheek by jowl with territorial-style houses, with wide attics and porches. Paseo Redondo, once called Snob Hollow, is the wide road along which wealthy merchants built their homes. The area most closely resembling 19th-century Tucson is the **Barrio Historico,** also known as Barrio Viejo. The narrow streets of this neighborhood, including Convent Avenue, have a good sampling of thick-wall adobe houses. The houses are close to the street, hiding the yards and gardens within. To the east of the Barrio Historico, across Stone Avenue, is the **Armory Park** neighborhood, mostly constructed by and for the railroad workers who settled here after the 1880s. The brick or wood territorial-style homes here were the Victorian era's adaptation to the desert climate.

Numbers in the text correspond to numbers in the margin and on the What to See in Downtown Tucson map.

MAIN ATTRACTIONS

➊ **"A" Mountain.** The original name of this mountain, Sentinel Peak, west of downtown came from its function as a lookout point for the Spanish, though the Pima village and cultivated fields that once lay at the base of the peak are long gone. In 1915 fans of the University of Arizona football team whitewashed a large "A" on its side to celebrate a victory, and the tradition has been kept up ever since—the permanent "A" is now red, white, and blue. During the day, the peak's a great place to get an overview of the town's layout; at night the city lights below form a dazzling carpet, but the teenage hangout–makeout scene may make some uncomfortable. ⊠ *Congress St. on Sentinel Peak Rd., Downtown.*

➍ **El Tiradito** *(The Castaway).* No one seems to know the details of the story behind this little shrine, but everyone agrees a tragic love triangle was involved. A bronze plaque indicates only that it's dedicated to a sinner who is buried here on unconsecrated ground. The candles that line the cactus-shrouded spot attest to its continuing importance in local Catholic lore. People light candles and leave *milagros* (literally, "miracles"; little icons used in prayers for healing) for loved ones. A modern-day miracle: the shrine's inclusion on the National Register of Historic Places helped prevent a freeway from plowing through this section of the Barrio Historico. ⊠ *Main Ave. south of Cushing St., Downtown.*

LONG LIVE ADOBE!

Adobe—brick made of mud and straw, cured in the hot sun—was used widely as a building material in early Tucson because it provides natural insulation from the heat and cold and because it's durable in Tucson's dry climate. When these buildings are properly made and maintained, they can last for centuries. Driving around downtown Tucson, you'll see adobe houses painted in vibrant hues such as bright pink and canary yellow.

"A" Mountain
(Sentinel Peak) . **1**

El Tiradito
(The
Castaway) **4**

Pima County
Courthouse **8**

Santa Cruz
River Park **2**

Sosa-Carillo-
Fremont
House **3**

St. Augustine
Cathedral **5**

Tucson
Children's
Museum **6**

Tucson
Museum
of Art and Historic
Block **7**

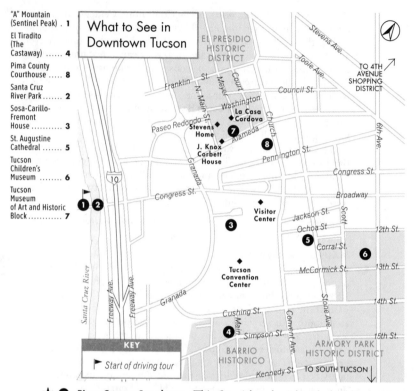

What to See in Downtown Tucson

KEY

⚑ *Start of driving tour*

★ **⑧ Pima County Courthouse.** This Spanish colonial–style building with a mosaic-tile dome is among Tucson's most beautiful historic structures. Still in use, it was built in 1927 on the site of the original single-story adobe court of 1869; a portion of the old presidio wall can be seen in the south wing of the courthouse's second floor. At the side of the building, the county assessor's office has a diorama depicting the area's early days. ⊠ *115 N. Church Ave., between Alameda and Pennington Sts., Downtown* ⊕ *www.jp.co.pima.az.us* ☞ *Free* ⊙ *Weekdays 8–4:30, Sat. 8–noon.*

⏚ **⑥ Tucson Children's Museum.** Youngsters are encouraged to touch and explore the science, language, and history exhibits here. They can key in on Little Tikes IBM computers or turn on the electricity in the streets of a model town. Dinosaur Canyon has mechanical prehistoric creatures, and there's a bubble room where children can place themselves in the middle of a large vertical soap bubble. ⊠ *200 S. 6th Ave., Downtown* ☎ *520/792–9985* ⊕ *www.tucsonchildrensmuseum.org* ☞ *$5.50* ⊙ *Tues.–Sat. 10–5, Sun. noon–5.*

★ **⑦ Tucson Museum of Art and Historic Block.** The five historic buildings on this block are listed in the National Register of Historic Places. You can enter La Casa Cordova, the Stevens Home, the J. Knox Corbett House, and the Edward Nye Fish House but the Romero House, believed to

A DRIVING TOUR OF DOWNTOWN

This 30-minute driving tour is a great overview of the different historical neighborhoods and architecture of Tucson. Leave yourself extra time if you plan to stop in any of the museums. Drive up to "A" Mountain (Sentinel Peak) **1** ➤ for a great perspective of downtown Tucson (if you're squeamish about heights, be aware that the narrow, winding road has no guard rails). Come down from on high and head east along Congress Street, stopping at Santa Cruz River Park to view the religious sculptures and mosaics by local artists before crossing the usually dry **Santa Cruz River 2**. Turn right (heading south) on Granada, passing the new Federal Court Building. The **Sosa-Carillo-Fremont House 3** is on the left. Continuing south on Granada, turn left onto Cushing Street, then right onto Main, to see the shrine of **El Tiradito (The Castaway) 4**, next to the El Minuto Restaurant's parking lot.

To see the brightly-colored adobe houses in the Barrio Historico neighborhood, turn right onto Simpson, left onto Samaniego, left onto 17th Street, and left onto Convent, which becomes Church. One-way streets require you to drive north on Church, east on Broadway Boulevard, and then south on Stone Avenue to see **St. Augustine Cathedral 5**. Head east on McCormick to 6th Avenue, in the Armory Park District, where the kids may want to check out the hands-on activities at the **Tucson Children's Museum 6**. To get to the **Tucson Museum of Art and Historic Block 7**, take 6th Avenue north to Congress Street, where you'll see the historic Hotel Congress on the right. This stretch of Congress was once Tucson's bustling center, before suburban growth supplanted it. Drive west on Congress to Church Avenue, head north to Alameda, then west to Main, where you'll enter the El Presidio neighborhood and find convenient public parking. The museum and historic complex include La Casa Cordova, the J. Knox Corbett House, and the Stevens Home. After your museum tour, walk east on Alameda and then south on Church to reach the **Pima County Courthouse 8**, downtown's architectural jewel.

6

incorporate a section of the presidio wall, is not open to the public. In the center of the museum complex, connecting the modern buildings to the surrounding historic houses, is the Plaza of the Pioneers, honoring Tucson's early citizens. The museum building, the only modern structure of the complex, houses a permanent collection of modern and contemporary art and hosts traveling shows.

Permanent and changing exhibitions of Western art fill the **Edward Nye Fish House,** an 1868 adobe that belonged to an early merchant, entrepreneur, and politician, and his wife. The building is notable for its 15-foot beamed ceilings and saguaro cactus–rib supports. There are free docent tours of the museum, and you can pick up a self-guided tour map of the El Presidio district. **La Casa Cordova,** one of the oldest buildings in Tucson, is also one of the best local examples of a Sonoran row house. This simple but elegant design is a Spanish style adapted to adobe construction. The oldest section of La Casa

Cordova, constructed around 1848, has been restored to its original appearance and is the Mexican Heritage Museum. Furnishings of the Native American and pioneer settlers and an exhibit on the presidio's history are inside. The **J. Knox Corbett House** was built in 1906–07, and occupied by members of the Corbett family until 1963. The original occupants were J. Knox Corbett, successful businessman, postmaster, and mayor of Tucson, and his wife Elizabeth Hughes Corbett, an accomplished musician and daughter of Tucson pioneer Sam Hughes. Tucson's Hi Corbett field (the spring training field for the Colorado Rockies) is named for their grandnephew, Hiram. The two-story, Mission Revival–style residence has been furnished with Arts and Crafts pieces: Stickley, Roycroft, Tiffany, and Morris are among the more famous manufacturers represented. The **Stevens Home** was where the wealthy politician and cattle rancher Hiram Stevens and his Mexican wife, Petra Santa Cruz, entertained many of Tucson's leaders during the 1800s. A drought brought the Stevens's cattle ranching to a halt in 1893 and Stevens killed himself in despair after unsuccessfully attempting to shoot his wife (the bullet was deflected by the comb she wore in her hair). The 1865 house was restored in 1980 and now houses the Tucson Museum of Art's permanent collections of pre-Columbian, Spanish colonial, and Latin American folk art. ■**TIP**➔**There's free parking in a lot behind the museum at Washington and Meyer streets.** ✉*140 N. Main Ave., Downtown* ☎*520/624–2333* ⊕*www.TucsonMuseumofArt.org* ✏*$8, includes Museum and all four homes; free 1st Sun. of every month; tours free* ⊘*Tues.–Sat. 10–4, Sun. noon–4. Guided tours Oct.–May, Tues.–Sun.*

NEED A BREAK?

On the patio of the Stevens Home, part of the Tucson Museum of Art and Historic Block, Cafe A La C'Arte (✉*150 N. Main Ave., Downtown* ☎*520/628–8533*) serves fanciful salads, soups, and sandwiches on weekdays from 11 to 3.

ALSO WORTH SEEING

❸ Sosa-Carillo-Fremont House. One of Tucson's oldest adobe residences, this was the only building spared when the surrounding barrio was torn down to build the Tucson Convention Center. The restored house, now a branch of the Arizona Historical Society, is furnished in 1880s fashion and has changing displays of territorial life. The house is in the Convention Center complex. ✉*151 S. Granada Ave., Downtown* ☎*520/622–0956* ⊕*www.arizonahistoricalsociety.org* ✏*$3; guided walking tours of Presidio and Tucson Historic District $10* ⊘*Wed.–Sat. 10–4; walking tours Nov.–Apr., Sat. at 10.*

❺ St. Augustine Cathedral. Although the imposing white-and-beige, late-19th-century, Spanish-style building was modeled after the Cathedral of Queretaro in Mexico, a number of its details reflect the desert setting: above the entryway, next to a bronze statue of St. Augustine, are carvings of local desert scenes with saguaro cacti, yucca, and prickly pears—look closely and you'll find the horned toad. Compared with the magnificent facade, the modernized interior is a bit disappointing. ■**TIP**➔**For a distinctly Southwestern experience, attend the maria-**

chi mass celebrated Sunday at 8 AM. ✉*192 S. Stone Ave., Downtown* ☎*520/623–6351* ✉*Free* ⊙*Daily 7–6.*

❷ Santa Cruz River & River Park. When Europeans arrived in what is now Arizona, the Santa Cruz River had wide banks suitable for irrigation; over time its banks have been narrowed and contained and are now lined by River Park. These days it's a dry wash, or arroyo, most of the year, but sudden summer thunderstorms and rainwater from upper elevations can turn it into a raging river in a matter of hours. It's a favorite spot for walkers, joggers, bicyclists, and horseback riders. The park has a bike path, restrooms, drinking fountains, and sculptures created by local artists.

THE UNIVERSITY OF ARIZONA

The U of A (as opposed to rival ASU, in Tempe) is a major economic influence in Tucson, with a student population of more than 34,000. The land for the university was "donated" by a couple of gamblers and a saloon owner in 1891—their benevolence reputedly inspired by a bad hand of cards—and $25,000 of territorial (Arizona was still a territory back then) money was used to build Old Main, the original building, and hire six faculty members. Money ran out before Old Main's roof was placed, but a few enlightened citizens pitched in funds to finish it. Most of the city's populace was less than enthusiastic about the institution: they were disgruntled when the 13th Territorial Legislature granted the University of Arizona to Tucson and awarded Phoenix what was considered the real prize—an insane asylum and a prison.

The university's flora is impressive—it represents a collection of plants from arid and semiarid regions around the world. An extremely rare mutated, or "crested," saguaro grows at the northeast corner of the Old Main building. The long, grassy Mall in the heart of campus—itself once a vast cactus garden—sits atop a huge underground student activity center, and makes for a pleasant stroll on a balmy evening.

Numbers in the text correspond to numbers in the margin and on the University of Arizona map.

MAIN ATTRACTIONS

❾ Arizona Historical Society's Museum. Flanking the entrance to the museum are statues of two men: Father Kino, the Jesuit who established San Xavier del Bac and a string of other missions, and John Greenaway, indelibly linked to Phelps Dodge, the copper-mining company that helped Arizona earn statehood in 1912. The museum houses the headquarters of the state Historical Society and has exhibits exploring the history of southern Arizona, the Southwest United States, and northern Mexico, starting with the Hohokam Indians and Spanish explorers. The harrowing "Life on the Edge: A History of Medicine in Arizona" exhibit gives a new appreciation of modern drugstores in present-day Tucson. Children enjoy the exhibit on copper mining (complete with an atmospheric replica of a mine shaft and camp) and the stagecoaches in the transportation area. The library has an extensive collection of his-

A Campus Tour

This tour takes in the highlights of the University area: Start at the northwest corner of campus, at Euclid and 2nd streets, at the public parking garage, then walk a half-block east on 2nd Street to the **Arizona Historical Society's Museum** ❾ ☞ to see how far the Old Pueblo has come in 100 years. A block south on Park Avenue, just inside the main gate of the university, is the **Arizona State Museum** ❿, the place to explore Native American culture. Heading east on University Boulevard and deeper into the campus, you'll pass Old Main and the crested saguaro. As the road curves to the left, University Boulevard turns into the campus mall. The Student Union and University Bookstore are on your left; the sculpture in front of the complex depicts Arizona–Mexico border struggles. Cross over to the south side of the mall (watch out for Frisbees) and take a peek inside the old Gymnasium, then continue east, passing the steps leading down to the underground activity center, and you'll come to the **Flandrau Science Center and Planetarium** ⓫. Check telescope-viewing schedules, see a light show, or stock up on science-oriented gifts here.

Walk north on Cherry, then turn left onto 2nd Street, passing several fraternity and sorority houses. Turn right on Olive Road to find the **Center for Creative Photography** ⓬, home to most of photographer Ansel Adams's negatives and a slew of other exhibits in this medium. Across from the center is the **University of Arizona Museum of Art** ⓭. From here it's a short walk west on Speedway Boulevard to Park Avenue, where you can go south to 2nd Street and return to the Arizona Historical Society's Museum and the parking lot.

For more college culture, continue down Park to University Boulevard and turn right. This area is the hub of off-campus activity, with restaurants, cafés, and trendy boutiques. You can walk—or on weekends ride the **Old Pueblo Trolley** ⓮—along University to **4th Avenue** ⓯, Tucson's last bastion of bohemia, for shopping and people-watching.

TIPS: If you drive, leave your car in a university garage or lot; those on 2nd Street at Mountain Avenue, on Speedway Boulevard at Park Avenue, on Tyndall Avenue south of University Boulevard, and on 2nd Street at Euclid Avenue are the most convenient. Parking is free on weekends and holidays.

Call ahead to verify hours for the university's museums, as yearly budget revisions often cause schedule changes. Visit the University of Arizona Web site (⊕ *www.arizona.edu*) for parking maps and the latest visitor information.

---

toric Arizona photographs and sells inexpensive reprints. You can park in the garage at the corner of 2nd and Euclid streets and get a free parking pass in the museum. ✉ *949 E. 2nd St., University* ☎ *520/628–5774* ⊕ *www.arizonahistoricalsociety.org* 🖾 *$5; free 1st Sat. of every month* ☉ *Tues.–Sat. 10–4; library weekdays 10–3, Sat. 10–1.*

❿ **Arizona State Museum.** Inside the main gate of the university is Arizona's oldest museum, dating from territorial days (1893) and recognized as one of the world's most important resources for the study of South-

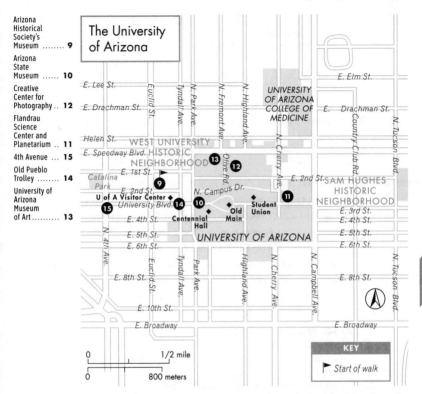

Arizona Historical Society's Museum **9**

Arizona State Museum **10**

Creative Center for Photography .. **12**

Flandrau Science Center and Planetarium .. **11**

4th Avenue ... **15**

Old Pueblo Trolley **14**

University of Arizona Museum of Art **13**

The University of Arizona

western cultures. Exhibits in the original (south) building focus on the state's ancient history, including fossils and a fascinating sample of tree-ring dating. "Paths of Life: American Indians of the Southwest" is a permanent exhibit that explores the cultural traditions, origins, and contemporary lives of 10 native tribes of Arizona and Sonora, Mexico. ✉ *Park Ave. at University Blvd., University* 🕾 *520/621–6302* ⊕ *www. statemuseum.arizona.edu* 🎟 *Free* ☉ *Mon.–Sat. 10–5, Sun. noon–5.*

★ ⑫ **Center for Creative Photography.** Ansel Adams conceived the idea of a photographer's archive and donated the majority of his negatives to this museum. In addition to its superb collection of his work, the center has works by other major photographers including Paul Strand, W. Eugene Smith, Edward Weston, and Louise Dahl-Wolfe. Changing exhibits in the main gallery display selected pieces from the collection, but if you'd like to see the work of a particular photographer in the archives, call to arrange an appointment. ✉ *1030 N. Olive Rd., north of 2nd St., University* 🕾 *520/621–7968* ⊕ *www.creativephotography. org* 🎟 *Free* ☉ *Weekdays 9–5, weekends noon–5.*

☾ ⑪ **Flandrau Science Center and Planetarium.** Attractions include a 16-inch public telescope; the impressive Star Theatre, where a multimedia show brings astronomy to life; an interactive meteor exhibit; and a Mineral Museum, which exhibits more than 2,000 rocks and gems, some quite rare. Bring a camera—special adapters allow you to take pictures through the telescopes. ⊠*Cherry Ave. and University Blvd., University* ☎*520/621–4515, 520/621–7827 recorded message* ⊕*www.flandrau.org* ⬚*Exhibits $2.50; planetarium shows $5.50; observatory free* ⊙*Exhibits Wed. 6 PM–9 PM, Thurs. and Fri. 9–3 and 6 PM–9 PM, Sat. 12–9, Sun. 12–5. Planetarium show times vary. Observatory Wed.–Sat. 7 PM–10 PM.*

⓯ **4th Avenue.** Students and counterculturists favor this ½-mi strip of 4th Avenue where vintage-clothing stores rub shoulders with ethnic eateries from Guatemalan to Greek. After dark, 4th Avenue bars pulse with live and recorded music. ⊠*Between University and 9th Sts.*

NEED A BREAK?

Just outside the west campus gate, University Boulevard is lined with student-oriented eateries. **Sinbad's** (⊠*810 E. University Blvd., University* ☎*520/623–4010*), nestled in the verdant Geronimo Plaza, serves falafel and other Middle-Eastern fare, and has a great patio. The Chinese and Thai fast food at **Pei Wei** (⊠*845 E. University Blvd., University* ☎*520/884–7413*) is flavorful, healthy, and affordable. Beer lovers should head to **Gentle Ben's** (⊠*865 E. University Blvd., University* ☎*520/624–4177*), a burger-and-brew pub that also makes a scrumptious veggie burger. The deck upstairs has a good view of the sunset.

ALSO WORTH SEEING

⓮ **Old Pueblo Trolley.** You can ride historic electric trolleys through the streets of Tucson along University Boulevard and 4th Avenue past shops and restaurants. The route passes restored historic buildings on part of the original 1898 streetcar track and terminates near the Arizona Historical Society. ⊠*360 E. 8th St., University* ☎*520/792–1802* ⊕*www.oldpueblotrolley.org* ⬚*Fri. and Sat. $1, Sun. 25¢* ⊙*Fri. 6 PM–10 PM, Sat. noon–midnight, Sun. noon–6.*

⓭ **University of Arizona Museum of Art.** This small museum houses a collection of European paintings from the Renaissance through the 17th century. A highlight is the Kress Collection's Retablo from Ciudad Rodrigo: 26 panels of an altarpiece made in 1488 by Fernando Gallego. ⊠*Fine Arts Complex, Bldg. 2, southeast corner of Speedway Blvd. and Park Ave., University* ☎*520/621–7567* ⊕*www.artmuseum.arizona. edu* ⬚*Free* ⊙*Tues.–Fri. 9–5, weekends noon–4.*

CENTRAL AND EAST TUCSON

Tucson expanded north and east from the university during the 1950s and '60s. The sights worth seeing in this mostly residential area include the Tucson Botanical Gardens, the small Reid Park Zoo, and the Fort Lowell Park and Museum. Colossal Cave Mountain Park and Pima Air and Space Museum are on the southeast outskirts.

■**TIP**➔**If it's warm, visit outdoor attractions such as the zoo or Tucson Botanical Gardens in the morning; note that Colossal Cave stays at a constant, cool temperature so it's a good option when it's hot.**

Numbers in the text correspond to numbers in the margin and on the Tucson Central & East and Catalina Foothills maps.

WHAT TO SEE

 20 Colossal Cave Mountain Park. This limestone grotto 20 mi east of Tucson (take Broadway Boulevard or 22nd Street East, to Colossal Cave Road) is the largest dry cavern in the world. Guides discuss the fascinating crystal formations and relate the many romantic tales surrounding the cave, including the

> ### BOTANICAL GARDEN OR DESERT MUSEUM?
>
> The Tucson Botanical Garden is a pretty, in-town garden for strolling, watching butterflies and birds, and getting ideas for planning your own garden. The Desert Museum is a world-class tourist destination, with brilliant exhibits of the exhibits of the flora, fauna, and minerals/geology of this region.

legend that an enormous sum of money stolen in a stagecoach robbery is hidden here. Forty-five-minute cave tours begin every 30 minutes and require a ½-mi walk and climbing 363 steps. The park includes a ranch area with trail rides ($27 per hour), a gemstone-sluicing area, a small museum, nature trails, a butterfly garden, a snack bar, and a gift shop. ⊠ *Colossal Cave Rd. at Old Spanish Trail Rd., Eastside* ☎ *520/647-7275* ⊕ *www.colossalcave.com* 💲 *Park $5 per car; cave tour $8.50 per person* ⊙ *Oct.–mid-Mar., Mon.–Sat. 9–5, Sun. 9–6; mid-Mar.–Sept., Mon.–Sat. 8–6, Sun. 8–7.*

18 Fort Lowell Park and Museum. Fertile soil and proximity to the Rillito River once enticed the Hohokam to construct a village on this site. Centuries later, a fort (in operation from 1873–91) was built here to protect the fledgling city of Tucson against the Apaches. The former commanding officer's quarters has artifacts from military life in territorial days. The park has a playground, ball fields, tennis courts, and a duck pond. ⊠ *2900 N. Craycroft Rd., Central* ☎ *520/885-3832* 💲 *museum $3; free first Sat. of every month* ⊙ *Wed.–Sat. 10–4.*

19 Pima Air and Space Museum. This huge facility ranks among the largest private collections of aircraft in the world. More than 200 airplanes are on display, including a presidential plane used by both John F. Kennedy and Lyndon B. Johnson, a full-scale replica of the Wright brothers' 1903 Wright Flyer, and a mock-up of the X-15, the world's fastest aircraft. World War II planes are particularly well-represented. Hour-long van tours of Aerospace Maintenance and Regeneration Center (AMARC)—affectionately called "The Boneyard"—at Davis-Monthan Air Force Base provide an eerie glimpse of hundreds of moth-balled aircraft lined up in rows on a vast tract of desert; you must reserve in advance for the tour. ⊠ *6000 E. Valencia Rd., I–10, Exit 267, South* ☎ *520/574-0462* ⊕ *www.pimaair.org* 💲 *$11.75; tram tour $5; AMARC tour $6* ⊙ *Daily 9–5, last admission at 4; AMARC tours weekdays only.*

17 Reid Park Zoo. This small but well-designed zoo won't tax the children's— or your—patience. There are plenty of shady places to sit, a wonderful gift shop, and a snack bar to rev you up when your energy flags. The

6

Colossal Cave
Mountain Park **20**

Fort Lowell
Park and
Museum **18**

Pima Air
and Space
Museum **19**

Reid Park
Zoo **17**

Tucson Botanical
Gardens **16**

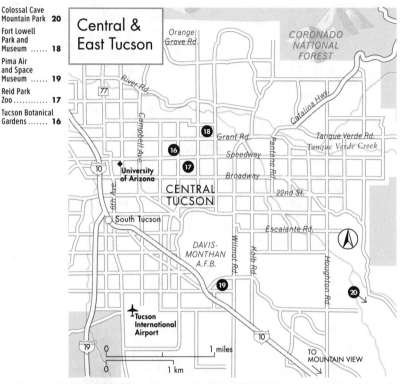

zoo's adorable newborns and the South American enclosure with its rain forest and exotic birds are popular. ■ **TIP→ If you're visiting in summer, go early in the day when the animals are active.** The park surrounding the zoo has playground structures and a lake where you can feed ducks and rent paddleboats. ✉*Reid Park, Randolph Way off 22nd St. between Alvernon Way and Country Club Rd., Central* ☎*520/791–3204* ⊕*www.tucsonzoo.org* ✉*$6* ☉*Daily 9–4.*

🔟 **Tucson Botanical Gardens.** The five acres are home to a variety of experiences: a tropical greenhouse; a sensory garden, where you can touch and smell the plants and listen to the abundant bird life; historical gardens that display the Mediterranean landscaping the property's original owners planted in the 1930s; a garden designed to attract birds; and a cactus garden. Other special gardens showcase wildflowers, Australian plants, and Native American crops and herbs. Call ahead to find out what's blooming. All paths are wheelchair accessible. ✉*2150 N. Alvernon Way, Central* ☎*520/326–9686* ⊕*www.tucsonbotanical.org* ✉*$5* ☉*Daily 8:30–4:30.*

De Grazia's
Gallery
in the Sun **22**

Mount
Lemmon **23**

Sabino
Canyon **21**

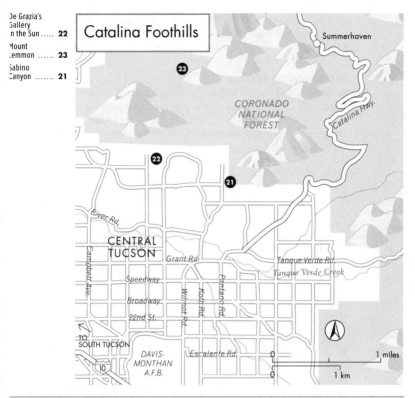

CATALINA FOOTHILLS (NORTH)

Considered by some to be the "Beverly Hills of Tucson," the Catalina Foothills area is home to posh resorts and upscale shopping. Because the neighborhood backs on the beautiful Santa Catalina mountains, it also has an abundance of hiking trails. If you want to venture farther into the mountains, head up to Mount Lemmon: it's time consuming (a one-hour drive each way), but the higher elevation and cooler temperatures make it an excellent midday destination in summer.

MAIN ATTRACTIONS

★ ㉑ **Sabino Canyon.** Year-round, but especially in summer, locals flock to Coronado National Forest to hike, picnic, and enjoy the waterfalls, streams, swimming holes, and shade trees. No cars are allowed, but a narrated tram ride (about 45 minutes round-trip) takes you up a WPA-built road to the top of the canyon; you can hop off and on at any of the nine stops or hike any of the numerous trails. There's also a shorter tram ride to adjacent Bear Canyon, where a much more rigorous but rewarding hike leads to the popular Seven Falls (it'll take about 1½ hours each way from the drop-off point, so carry plenty of water). If you're in Tucson near a full moon, take the special night tram and watch the desert come alive with nocturnal critters. ⊠*Sabino Canyon Rd. at Sunrise Dr., Foothills* ☎*520/749–2861 recorded tram infor-*

*mation, 520/749–8700 visitor center ⊕www.fs.fed.us/r3/coronado
⊠$5 per vehicle per day or $20 for an annual pass, includes Mount
Lemmon; tram $5; Bear Canyon tram $3 ⊙ Visitor center weekdays
8–4:30, weekends 8:30–4:30; call for tram schedules.*

ALSO WORTH SEEING

㉒ **De Grazia's Gallery in the Sun.** Arizonan artist Ted De Grazia, who
depicted Southwest Native American and Mexican life in a manner
some find kitschy and others adore, built this sprawling, spacious single-story museum with the assistance of Native American friends, using
only natural material from the surrounding desert. You can visit De
Grazia's workshop, former home, and grave. Although the original
works are not for sale, the museum's gift shop has a wide selection of
prints, ceramics, and books by and about the colorful artist. ⊠6300
N. Swan Rd., Foothills ☎520/299–9191 ⊕www.degrazia.org ⊠Free
⊙ Daily 10–4.

㉓ **Mount Lemmon.** Part of the Santa
Catalina range, Mount Lemmon—
named for Sara Lemmon, the first
woman to reach the peak of this
mountain, in 1881—is the southernmost ski slope in the continental
United States, but you don't have
to be a skier to enjoy it: it's a popular place for picnicking and there
are 150 mi of marked and well-
maintained trails for hiking. The
mountain's 9,157-foot elevation
brings relief from summer heat.

Mount Lemmon Highway twists
its way for 28 mi up the mountainside. Every 1,000-foot climb in
elevation is equivalent, in terms of

> ### WORD OF MOUTH
>
> "Another 'must do' if you're in
> the Tucson area is to drive up
> Mt. Lemmon. You'll start in the
> Sonoran Desert at the base and
> end up in the alpine climate at
> the summit. On the way up you
> pass through every climate zone
> that exists in the entire state of
> Arizona. It's like a mini tour of
> what the state has to offer. Great
> views all along the way up. Out
> of the desert and into the forest!
> Bring the cameras!"
>
> –peterb

climate, to traveling 300 mi north: you'll move from typical Sonoran
Desert plants in the foothills to vegetation similar to that found in
southern Canada at the top. Rock formations along the way look as
though they were carefully balanced against each other by sculptors
from another planet.

At milepost 18 of your ascent, on the left-hand side of the road, is
the Palisades Ranger Station of **Coronado National Forest** (☎520/749–
8700). Rangers have information on the mountain's campgrounds,
hiking trails, and picnic spots. It's open daily 8 to 4:30. Even if you
don't make it to the top of the mountain, you'll find stunning views of
Tucson at Windy Point, about halfway up. Look for a road on your
left between the Windy Point and San Pedro lookouts; it leads to Rose
Canyon Lake, a lovely reservoir.

Just before you reach the ski area, you'll pass through the tiny alpine-
style village of **Summerhaven**, which has some casual restaurants,
gift shops, and pleasant lodges. Though much of Summerhaven was

Tucson: City in the Foothills

Native Americans have lived along the waterways in this valley for thousands of years. During the 1500s, Spanish explorers arrived to find Pima Indians growing crops in the area. Father Eusebio Francisco Kino, a Jesuit missionary whose influence is still strongly felt throughout the region, first visited the area in 1687 and returned a few years later to build missions.

The name Tucson came from the Native American word *stjukshon* (pronounced *stook*-shahn), meaning "spring at the foot of a black mountain." (The springs at the foot of Sentinel Peak, made of black volcanic rock, are now dry.) The name was pronounced *tuk*-son by the Spanish explorers who built a wall around the city in 1776 to keep Native Americans from reclaiming it. At the time, this *presidio* (fortified city), called San Augustin del Tuguison, was the northernmost Spanish settlement in the area, and current-day Main Avenue is a quiet reminder of the former Camino Real ("royal road") that stretched from this tiny walled fort all the way to Mexico City.

Four flags have flown over Tucson—Spanish, Mexican, Confederate, and, finally, the Stars and Stripes. Tucson's allegiance changed in 1820 when Mexico declared independence from Spain, and again in 1853 when the Gadsden purchase made it part of the United States, though Arizona didn't become a state until 1912. In the 1850s the Butterfield stage line was extended to Tucson, bringing adventurers, a few settlers, and more than a handful of outlaws. The arrival of the railroad in 1880 marked another spurt of growth, as did the opening of the University of Arizona in 1891.

Tucson's 20th-century growth occurred after World War I, when veterans with damaged lungs sought the dry air and healing power of the sun, and again during World War II with the opening of Davis-Monthan Air Force Base and the rise of local aeronautical industries. It was also around this time that air-conditioning made the desert climate hospitable year-round.

destroyed by a forest fire in summer 2003, rebuilding is well underway. An excursion up the mountain can be capped off with breakfast, lunch, or a slice of home-made pie at **Mount Lemmon Café** (☎ *520/576–1234*), the first building on the left as you enter the village.

Mount Lemmon Highway ends at **Mount Lemmon Ski Valley** (☎ *520/576– 1321*). Skiing depends on natural conditions—there's no artificial snow, so call ahead. There are 16 runs, open daily in winter, ranging from beginner to advanced. Lift tickets cost $35 for an all-day pass and $30 for a half-day pass (starting at 1 PM). Equipment rentals and instruction are available. Off-season you can take a ride ($9) on the chairlift, which whisks you to the top of the slope—some 9,100 feet above sea level. Many ride the lift, then hike on one of several trails that crisscross the summit. There are some concessions at the ski lift.

■ **TIP→There are no gas stations on Mount Lemmon Highway, so gas up before you leave town and check the road conditions in winter.** To reach the highway, take Tanque Verde Road to Catalina Highway, which

The Desert's Fragile Giant

Easy to anthropomorphize because they have "arms," saguaros are thought to be the descendants of tropical trees that lost their leaves and became dormant during drought. *Carnegiea gigantea* (the saguaro's scientific name) grows nowhere else on Earth other than the Sonoran Basin, an area that includes southern Arizona and northern Mexico.

Tourists are often amazed to find that these odd-looking plants actually bloom each May or June. Each bloom opens only for a few evening hours after sunset. The next afternoon, the creamy-white chalice closes forever. An adult saguaro produces six or seven flowers a day for about a month. They are cross-pollinated by bees, Mexican white-winged doves, and brown bats.

Because the saguaro stores massive quantities of water (enough to conceivably last two years), it's often called the "cactus camel." New saguaros are born when the seeds of the flower take root, an arduous process. Late freezes and even high heat can kill a seedling in its first days. Once a seed is established, it grows up under the protection of a "nurse" tree, such as a paloverde. Fully grown, a saguaro can weigh as much as 7 tons.

The saguaro, like many other wild plants, is protected by Arizona law. Without an Arizona Department of Agriculture permit, it's illegal to move a saguaro or sell one from private property.

Some say the saguaro has its own means of protecting itself from would-be poachers or vandals: in the early 1980s a hunter fired a shotgun at a large saguaro near Phoenix. It collapsed onto him, killing him instantly!

becomes Mount Lemmon Highway as you head north. ⊠*Mount Lemmon Hwy., Northeast* ☎*520/576–1400 recorded snow report, 520/547–7510 winter road conditions* ⊡*$5 per vehicle per day or $20 for an annual pass, includes Sabino Canyon* ⊙*Daily, depending on snow in ski season.*

NORTHWEST TUCSON, THE WESTSIDE & THE SONORAN DESERT

Once a vast, open space dotted with horse ranches, Northwest Tucson is now a rapidly growing residential area encompassing the townships of Oro Valley and Marana. Families and retirees are moving here in droves, and the traffic congestion proves the point, but you'll also find the oases of Tohono Chul Park and Catalina State Park, which calm the senses.

If you're interested in the flora and fauna of the Sonoran Desert—as well as some of its appearances in the cinema—heed the same advice given the pioneers: go west. A good idea is to start the morning at Saguaro National Park and then head over to the Arizona–Sonora Desert Museum, where you can lunch at the Ironwood Terrace or the more upscale Ocotillo Café. How long you spend at Saguaro National Park depends on whether you choose a short walk to see petroglyphs at Signal Hill on the Loop Drive (an hour should suffice), or hike a lon-

Arizona-Sonora Desert Museum **25**

Mission San Xavier del Bac **27**

Old Tucson Studios **26**

Tohono Chul Park **24**

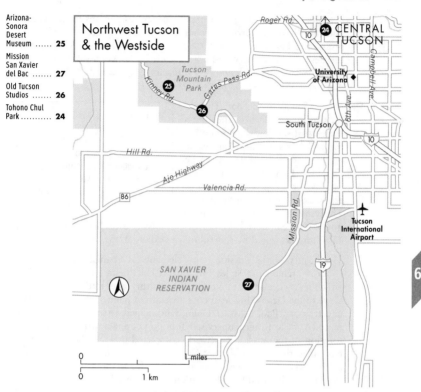

Northwest Tucson & the Westside

ger mountain trail, but leave yourself at least two hours for your visit at the Desert Museum. The hottest part of an afternoon can be spent ducking in and out of attractions at Old Tucson Studios or enjoying the indoor sanctuary of San Xavier mission, although the mission is also a good stop if you're heading out of town to Tubac, Tumacácori, and Nogales.

MAIN ATTRACTIONS

25 Arizona–Sonora Desert Museum. The name "museum" is a bit misleading since this delightful site is actually a beautifully planned zoo and botanical garden featuring the animals and plants of the Sonoran Desert. Hummingbirds, cactus wrens, rattlesnakes, scorpions, bighorn sheep, and prairie dogs all busy themselves in ingeniously designed habitats. An Earth Sciences Center has an artificial limestone cave and a hands-on meteor and mineral display. The coyote and javelina

WORD OF MOUTH

"We just had a half day in Tucson so we went to the Arizona-Sonora Desert Museum, and I have to say that I was a little apprehensive visiting because we are from Vegas and I'm not a big 'desert' fan as it is—but it was wonderful. First, the drive over the mountain was terrific, the saguaro cacti are beautiful! The desert museum was a delight, at almost every turn they had 'live interpretations' with animals, minerals, [and] plants."

—vegasnative

exhibits have "invisible" fencing that separates humans from animals, and the Riparian Corridor section affords great underwater views of otters and beavers. The gift shop carries books about Arizona and the desert, plus jewelry and crafts. ⊠*2021 N. Kinney Rd., Westside* ☎*520/883–2702* ⊕*www.desertmuseum.org* ⊠*$12* ⊙*Mar.–Sept., daily 7:30–5; Oct.–Feb., daily 8:30–5.*

㉗ **Mission San Xavier del Bac.** The old-
Fodor'sChoice est Catholic church in the United
★ States still serving the community for which it was built, San Xavier was founded in 1692 by Father Eusebio Francisco Kino, who established 22 missions in northern Mexico and southern Arizona. The current structure was made

> ### WORD OF MOUTH
>
> "[Mission San Xavier del Bac] is beautiful. And don't forget to get some Indian fry bread from the vendors in the parking lot—yum!"
> –Jill2

out of native materials by Franciscan missionaries between 1777 and 1797 and is owned by the Tohono O'odham tribe.

The beauty of the mission, with elements of Spanish, baroque, and Moorish architectural styles, is highlighted by the stark landscape against which it is set, inspiring an early-20th-century poet to dub it the White Dove of the Desert. Inside, there's a wealth of painted statues, carvings, and frescoes. Paul Schwartzbaum, who helped restore Michelangelo's masterwork in Rome, supervised Tohono O'odham artisans in the restoration of the mission's artwork, completed in 1997; Schwartzbaum has called the mission the Sistine Chapel of the United States. Mass is celebrated at 8:30 AM weekdays in the church and three times on Sunday morning. Call ahead for information about special celebrations.

Across the parking lot from the mission, San Xavier Plaza has a number of crafts shops selling the handiwork of the Tohono O'odham tribe, including jewelry, pottery, friendship bowls, and baskets with man-in-the-maze designs. ⊠*San Xavier Rd., 9 mi southwest of Tucson on I-19, South* ☎*520/294–2624* ⊕*www.sanxaviermission.org* ⊠*Free* ⊙*Church daily 8–5, gift shop daily 8:30–5.*

▮ **NEED A BREAK?**

For wonderful Indian fry bread—large, round pieces of dough taken fresh from the hot oil and served with sweet or savory toppings like honey, powdered sugar, beans, meats, or green chiles—stop in the **Wa:k Snack Shop** (☎*No phone*) at the back of San Xavier Plaza. You can also have breakfast or a lunch of Mexican food here, and if you're lucky, local dancers will be performing for one of the many tour groups that stop here.

㉔ **Tohono Chul Park.** A 48-acre retreat designed to promote the conservation of arid regions, Tohono Chul—the name means "desert corner" in the language of the Tohono O'odham—uses a demonstration garden, greenhouse, and geology wall to explain this unique desert area. Shady nooks, nature trails, a small art gallery, a great gift shop, and a tearoom can all be found at this peaceful spot. ⊠*7366 N. Paseo del Norte, Northwest* ☎*520/742–6455* ⊕*www.tohonochulpark.org* ⊠*$5* ⊙*Park daily 8 AM–sunset; buildings daily 9–5.*

Sagauro Flora & Fauna

The saguaro may be the centerpiece of Saguaro National Park, but more than 1,200 plant species, including 50 types of cactus, thrive in the park. Among the most common cacti here are the prickly pear, barrel cactus, and teddy bear cholla—named so because it appears cuddly, but rangers advise packing a comb to pull its barbed hooks from unwary fingers.

For many of the desert fauna, the saguaro functions as a high-rise hotel. Each spring, the Gila woodpecker and gilded flicker create holes in the cactus and then nest there. When they give up their temporary digs, elf owls, cactus wrens, sparrow hawks, and other avians move in, as do dangerous Africanized honeybees.

You're not likely to encounter the six species of rattlesnake and the Gila monster, a venomous lizard, that inhabit the park, but avoid sticking your hands or feet under rocks or into crevices. If you do get bitten, get to a clinic or hospital as soon as possible. Not all snakes pass on venom; 50% of the time, the bite is "dry" (non-poisonous).

6

OFF THE BEATEN PATH

Biosphere 2 Center. In the town of Oracle, about 30 minutes north of Tucson, this self-contained, closed ecosystem opened in 1991 as a facility to test nature technology and human interaction with it. The miniature world within Biosphere includes tropical rain forest, savanna, desert, thorn scrub, marsh, ocean, and agricultural areas, including almost 3,000 plant and animal species. A film and a large, rotating cutaway model in the visitor center explain the project, which included two "human missions" wherein scientists entered the ecosystem for extended periods of time—once for six months, once for 2 years. Guided walking tours, which last about two hours, take you inside some of the biomes, and observation areas let you peer in at the rest. A snack bar overlooks the Santa Catalina Mountains. ⊠ *AZ 77, Milepost 96.5, Oracle* ☎ *520/838–6200* ⊕ *www.bio2.com* ☜ *$19.95* ⊗ *Daily 9–4.*

ALSO WORTH SEEING

☺ **26** **Old Tucson Studios.** This film studio–cum–theme park, originally built for the 1940 motion picture *Arizona,* has been used to shoot countless movies, such as *Rio Bravo* (1959) and *The Quick and the Dead* (1994), and the TV shows *Gunsmoke, Bonanza,* and *Highway to Heaven.* Actors in Western garb perform and roam the streets talking to visitors. Youngsters enjoy the simulated gunfights, rides, stunt shows, and petting farm, while adults might appreciate the screenings of old Westerns and the little-bit-bawdy Grand Palace Hotel's Dance Hall Revue. There are plenty of places to chow down and to buy souvenirs. ⊠ *Tucson Mountain Park, 201 S. Kinney Rd., Westside* ☎ *520/883–0100* ⊕ *www.oldtucson.com* ☜ *$14.95* ⊗ *Daily 10–4.*

SAGUARO NATIONAL PARK

By Carrie
Miner

To reach the West Section of Saguaro National Park (Tucson Mountain District) from I–10, take exit 242 or exit 257, then Speedway Blvd. (the name will change to Gates Pass Rd.) west to Kinney Rd. and turn right. To reach the East Section of Sagauro (Rincon Mountain District) from I–10, take exit 257 or exit 275, then go east on Speedway Blvd. to Old Spanish Trail and turn right.

Standing sentinel in the desert, the towering saguaro is perhaps the most familiar emblem of the Southwest. Known for their height (often 50 feet) and arms reaching out in weird configurations, these slow-growing giants can take 15 years to grow a foot high and up to 75 years to grow their first arm. They are found only in the Sonoran Desert, and the largest concentration is in Saguaro National Park. In late spring (usually May), the succulent's top is covered with tiny white blooms—the Arizona state flower. The cacti are protected by state and federal laws, so don't disturb them.

Saguaro National Park preserves some of the densest stands of these massive cacti, which can live up to 200 years and weigh up to two tons. Today more than 90,000 acres include habitats stretching from the arid Sonoran Desert up to high mountain forests. The park is split into two sections, with Tucson sandwiched in the middle. Both districts are about a half-hour drive from central Tucson.

When should you go? Saguaro never gets crowded; however, most people visit in milder weather, December through April. December through February is cool and prone to gentle afternoon rain showers. The spring months from March through May offer bright, sunny days and desert wildflowers in bloom. Because of high temperatures, it's best to visit the park in the early morning or late afternoon from June through August. The intense heat puts off most hikers, at least at lower elevations, and lodging prices are much cheaper—rates at top resorts in Tucson drop by as much as 70%. The cooler temperatures in September, October, and November are perfect for hiking and camping throughout the park. ■ TIP➡ **The wildlife, from bobcats to jackrabbits, is most active in early morning and at dusk. In spring and summer lizards and snakes are out and about, but keep a low profile during the midday heat.** ✉ *Saguaro West: 2700 N. Kinney Rd., 2 mi north of Arizona–Sonora Desert Museum entrance; Saguaro East: 3693 S. Old Spanish Trail* ☎ *520/733–5158 Saguaro West, 520/733–5153 Saguaro East* ⊕ *nps. gov/sagu* 🎫 *$10 per vehicle or $5 per person on foot or bike, good for seven days. Annual passes $25* ☉ *Visitor centers daily 9–5, park roads daily 7 AM–sunset.*

SCENIC
DRIVES

Unless you're ready to lace up your hiking boots for a long desert hike, the best way to see Saguaro National Park is from the comfort of your car.

Bajada Loop Drive. This 6-mi drive winds through thick stands of saguaros and offers two picnic areas and a few short hikes, including one to a rock-art site. Although the road is unpaved and moderately bumpy,

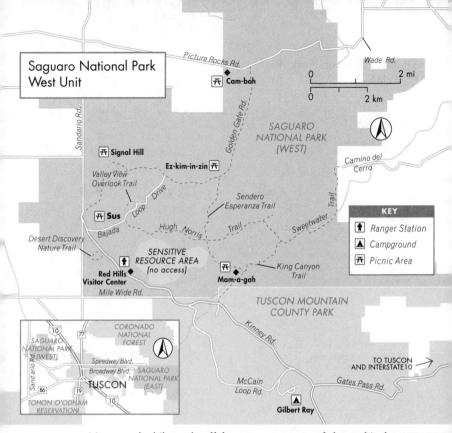

Saguaro National Park
West Unit

Picture Rocks Rd.

Wade Rd.

🏕 Cam-boh

0   2 mi

0   2 km

Sandario Rd.

Golden Gate Rd.

SAGUARO
NATIONAL PARK
(WEST)

🏕 Signal Hill

Ez-kim-in-zin 🏕

Camino del
Cerro

Valley View
Overlook Trail

Loop Drive

Sendero
Esperanza Trail

🏕 Sus

Bajada

Hugh Norris Trail

Sweetwater Trail

KEY

Desert Discovery
Nature Trail

SENSITIVE
RESOURCE AREA
(no access)

🏕 Mam-a-gah

King Canyon
Trail

🚹 Ranger Station

▲ Campground

🏕 Picnic Area

Red Hills
Visitor Center

Mile Wide Rd.

TUSCON MOUNTAIN
COUNTY PARK

CORONADO
NATIONAL
FOREST

10   77

SAGUARO
NATIONAL PARK
(WEST)

Sandario Rd.

Speedway Blvd.

Broadway Blvd.

TUSCON

86   19

10

SAGUARO
NATIONAL PARK
(EAST)

TOHON O'ODHAM
RESERVATION

Kinney Rd.

McCain
Loop Rd.

Gates Pass Rd.

TO TUSCON
AND INTERSTATE 10 →

▲
Gilbert Ray

it's a worthwhile trade-off for access to some of the park's densest desert growth. It's one way between Hugh Norris Trail and Golden Gate Road, so if you want to make the complete circuit, travel counter-clockwise. The road is susceptible to flash floods during the monsoon season, so check road conditions at the visitor center before proceed-ing. ✉*Saguaro West.*

★ **Cactus Forest Drive.** This paved 8-mi drive provides a great overview of all Saguaro has to offer. The one-way road, which circles clockwise, also has several turnouts that make it easy to stop and linger over the scenery or stop at one of two picnic areas or three easy nature trails. The road was repaved in 2006 and now offers more scenic pullouts, new roadside displays, and wider bicycle lanes. It's open from 7 AM to sunset daily. ✉*Saguaro East.*

WHAT TO SEE

Manning Camp. The summer home of Levi Manning, onetime Tucson mayor, was a popular gathering spot for the city's elite in the early 1900s. The cabin can be reached via one of several challenging high-country trails: Douglas Spring Trail to Cow Head Saddle Trail (12 mi), Turkey Creek Trail (7½ mi), and Tanque Verde Ridge Trail (15 4/10 mi). The cabin itself is not open for viewing. ✉*Douglas Spring Trail (6 mi) to Cow Head Saddle Trail (6 mi).*

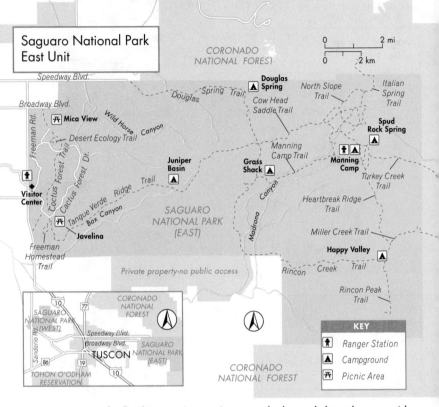

Saguaro National Park
East Unit

CORONADO NATIONAL FOREST

0   2 mi
0   2 km

Speedway Blvd.

Broadway Blvd.

Douglas Spring Trail

Douglas

Mica View

Wild Horse Canyon

Desert Ecology Trail

Cactus Forest Dr.

Cactus Forest Trail

Freeman Rd.

Visitor Center

Tanque Verde Ridge Trail

Box Canyon

Javelina

Freeman Homestead Trail

Juniper Basin

SAGUARO NATIONAL PARK (EAST)

Madrona Canyon

Douglas Spring

Cow Head Saddle Trail

North Slope Trail

Italian Spring Trail

Spud Rock Spring

Manning Camp Trail

Grass Shack

Manning Camp

Turkey Creek Trail

Heartbreak Ridge Trail

Miller Creek Trail

Happy Valley

Private property–no public access

Rincon Creek Trail

Rincon Peak Trail

CORONADO NATIONAL FOREST

SAGUARO NATIONAL PARK (WEST)

Speedway Blvd.

Broadway Blvd.

TUSCON

SAGUARO NATIONAL PARK (EAST)

Sandario Rd.

TOHON O'ODHAM RESERVATION

CORONADO NATIONAL FOREST

KEY	
↑	Ranger Station
▲	Campground
🌲	Picnic Area

Signal Hill. The most impressive petroglyphs, and the only ones with explanatory signs, are on the Bajada Loop Drive in Saguaro West. An easy 5-minute stroll from the signposted parking area takes you to one of the largest gatherings of rock carvings in the Southwest. You'll have a close-up view of the designs left by the Hohokam people between AD 900 and 1200, including large spirals some believe are astronomical markers. ⊠ *4½ mi north of visitor center on Bajada Loop Dr.*

VISITOR CENTERS

Neither center serves coffee; they do sell bottled water.

Red Hills Visitor Center. Take in gorgeous views of nearby mountains and the surrounding desert from the center's large windows and shaded outdoor terrace. A spacious gallery is filled with educational exhibits, and a lifelike display simulates the flora and fauna of the region. A 15-minute slide show, "Voices of a Desert," offers a poetic, Native American perspective on the saguaro. Park rangers and volunteers provide maps and suggest hikes to suit your interests. A nicely appointed gift shop and bookstore add to the experience. ⊠ *2700 N. Kinney Rd., Saguaro West* ☎ *520/733–5158* ⊙ *Daily 9–5.*

Saguaro East Visitor Center. Stop here to pick up free maps and printed materials on various aspects of the park, including maps of hiking trails and backcountry camping permits (Red Hills Visitor Center does not

Saguaro Planning

CLOSE UP

EAST OR WEST?

Saguaro West, also known as the Tucson Mountain District, is the smaller, more-visited section of the park. Here you'll find a Native American video orientation to saguaros at the visitor center, hiking trails, an ancient Hohokam petroglyph site at Signal Hill, and a scenic drive through the park's densest desert growth.

Saguaro East, also known as the Rincon Mountain District, is on the eastern side of Tucson in the Rincon Mountains, and encompasses 57,930 acres of designated wilderness, an easily accessible scenic loop drive, several easy and intermediate trails through the cactus forest, and opportunities for adventure and backcountry camping at six rustic campgrounds.

Also in the East part of the park is the Rincon Valley Area, a 4,011-acre expansion along the southern border of Saguaro's Rincon Mountain District with access to the area along Rincon Creek. The backcountry Saguaro Wilderness Area moves from desert scrublands at 3,000 feet to mixed conifer forests at 9,000 feet.

IN ONE DAY

Before setting off, choose which section of the park to visit and pack a lunch. Bring plenty of water—you can't depend on finding it in the park.

In the western section, start out by watching the 15-minute slide show at the **Red Hills Visitor Center**, then stroll along the ½-mi-long **Desert Discovery Trail.**

In the car, head north along Kinney Road, then turn right onto the graded dirt **Bajada Loop Drive.** Before long you'll soon see a turnoff for the **Hugh Norris Trail** on your right. Hike up and after about 45 minutes, you'll reach a perfect spot for a picnic. Hike back down and drive along the Bajada Loop Drive until you reach the turnoff for **Signal Hill.** From here, it's a short walk to the **Hohokam petroglyphs.**

Alternatively, in the eastern section, pick up a free map of the hiking trails at the **Saguaro East Visitor Center.** Drive south along the paved **Cactus Forest Drive** to the Javelina picnic area, where you'll see signs for the **Freeman Homestead Trail,** an easy 1-mi loop that winds through a stand of mesquite as interpretive signs describe early inhabitants in the Tucson basin. If you're reasonably fit you might want to tackle part of the **Tanque Verde Ridge Trail,** which affords excellent views of saguaro-studded hillsides.

Along the northern loop of the Cactus Forest Drive is **Cactus Forest Trail,** which branches off into several fairly level paths. You can easily spend the rest of the afternoon strolling among the saguaro.

■ TIP➔ Public restrooms are available at the visitor centers and at all picnic areas in both sections.

6

offer permits). Exhibits at the center are comprehensive, and a relief map of the park lays out the complexities of this protected landscape. A 15-minute "Home in the Desert" slide-show program gives the history of the region, and there is a short self-guided nature hike along the Cactus Garden Trail. A small, select variety of books and other gift items are sold here, too. ✉ *3693 S. Old Spanish Trail, Saguaro East* ☎ *520/733–5153* ⊙ *Daily 9–5.*

SPORTS & THE OUTDOORS

BICYCLING **Bajada Loop Drive.** This 6-mi dirt road, starting north of the Red Hills Visitor Center in Saguaro West, has "washboards" worn into the ground by seasonal drainage, which make biking a challenge. You'll share the bumpy route with cars, but most of it is one way, and the views of saguaros set against the mountains are stunning. ⊠ *Off Kinney Rd., 1½-mi from the Red Hills Visitor Center.*

Cactus Forest Drive. Expansive vistas of saguaro-covered hills in Saguaro East highlight this paved 8-mi loop road. Go slowly during the first few hundred yards because of an unexpectedly sharp curve. Snakes and javelinas traverse the roads. ⊠ *Saguaro East Visitor Center.*

WORD OF MOUTH

"Our first trip was to the eastern Saguaro National Park, which features magnificent mountain/desert scenery populated with gazillions of tall, branched Saguaro cactus, along with more kinds of colorful and oddly shaped cactus than we Easterners knew existed. It was a fascinating place, and we vastly enjoyed the slow 8-mile drive through. There are lots of trails, which younger people would do well to explore. We old folks were quite content to drive and occasionally get out to stroll around."

–ckwald

Cactus Forest Trail. Accessed from Cactus Forest Drive, the 2½-mi trail near Saguaro East Visitor Center is a sand, single track with varied terrain. It's good for both beginning and experienced mountain bikers who don't mind sharing the path with hikers and the occasional horse, to whom bikers must yield. You'll see plenty of wildlife and older, larger saguaro alongside palo verde and mesquite trees. ⊠ *1 mi south of Saguaro East Visitor Center on Cactus Forest Dr.*

BIRD-WATCHING To check out the more than 200 species of birds living or migrating through the park, begin by focusing your binoculars on the limbs of the saguaros, where many birds make their home. In general, early morning and early evening are the best times for sightings. In winter and spring, volunteer-led birding hikes begin at the visitor centers.

The finest areas to flock to in the Rincon Mountain District are the Desert Ecology Trail, where you may find rufous-winged sparrow, verdins, and Cooper's hawks along the washes, and the Javelina picnic area, where you will most likely spot canyon wrens and black-chinned sparrows. At the Tucson Mountain District, sit down on one of the visitor center benches and look for ash-throated flycatchers, Say's phoebes, curve-billed thrashers, and Gila woodpeckers. During the cooler months keep a lookout for the wintering neotropical migrants such as hummingbirds, swallows, orioles, and warblers.

HIKING The park has more than 100 mi of trails. The shorter hikes, such as the Desert Discovery and Desert Ecology trails are perfect for those looking to learn about the desert ecosystem without expending too much energy. Rattlesnakes are sometimes seen on trails; so are coyotes, javelinas, roadrunners, Gambel's quail, and desert spiny lizards. Hikers should keep their distance from all wildlife.

EASY **Cactus Forest Trail.** This 2½-mi one-way loop drive in the East district is open to pedestrians, bicyclists, and equestrians. It is an easy walk along a dirt path that passes historic lime kilns and a wide variety of Sonoran Desert vegetation. While walking this trail, keep in mind that it is the only off-road trail for bicyclists.

Cactus Garden Trail. This 100-yard paved trail in front of the Red Hills Visitor Center is wheelchair accessible and has resting benches and interpretive signs about common desert plants.

> ## THE TOHONO O'ODHAM
>
> The Tohono O'odham people, whose reservation near Tucson is second only in size to that of the Navajo, believe the saguaros were put on Earth to inspire humans with their stalwartness and dignity. They celebrate the harvest of the saguaro's sweet fruit every summer, and use the plant's woody skeleton, called saguaro ribs, to build fences and building supports.

♻ **Desert Discovery Trail.** Learn about plants and animals native to the region on this paved path in Saguaro West. The ½-mi loop is wheelchair accessible and has resting benches and ramadas (wooden shelters that supply shade for your table). ✉ *1 mi north of Red Hills Visitor Center.*

♻ **Desert Ecology Trail.** Exhibits on this ¼-mi loop near the Mica View picnic area explain how local plants and animals subsist on a limited supply of water. ✉ *2 mi north of Saguaro East Visitor Center.*

Freeman Homestead Trail. Learn a bit about the history of homesteading in the region on this 1-mi loop. Look for owls living in the cliffs above as you make your way through the lowland vegetation. ✉ *2 mi south of Saguaro East Visitor Center at Javelina picnic area.*

♻ **Signal Hill Trail.** This ¼-mi trail in Saguaro West is an easy, rewarding ascent to ancient petroglyphs carved a millennium ago by the Hohokam people. ✉ *4½ mi north of Red Hills Visitor Center on Bajada Loop Dr.*

MODERATE **Douglas Spring Trail.** This challenging 6-mi trail leads almost due east into the Rincon Mountains. After a half mile through a dense concentration of saguaros you reach the open desert. About 3 mi in is Bridal Wreath Falls, worth a slight detour in early spring when melting snow creates a larger cascade. Blackened tree trunks at the Douglas Spring Campground are one of the few traces of a huge fire that swept through the area in 1989. ✉ *Eastern end of Speedway Blvd.*

Fodor's Choice ★ **Hope Camp Trail.** Well worth the 5 6/10-mi round-trip trek, this Rincon Valley Area hike offers gorgeous views of the Tanque Verde Ridge and Rincon Peak. ✉ *From the Camino Loma Alto trailhead to Hope Camp.*

Sendero Esperanza Trail. You'll follow a sandy mine road for the first section of this 6-mi trail in Saguaro West, then ascend via a series of switchbacks to the top of a ridge where you'll cross the Hugh Norris Trail. Descending on the other side, you'll meet up with the King Canyon Trail. The Esperanza ("Hope") Trail is often rocky and sometimes steep, but rewards include ruins of the Gould Mine, dating back to 1907. ✉ *1½ mi east of the intersection of Bajada Loop Dr. and Golden Gate Rd.*

6

Sweetwater Trail. In Saguaro West, this one-way trail is the only footpath with access to Wasson Peak from the eastern side of the Tucson Mountains. The trailhead is located at the western end of El Camino del Cerro Road. After climbing 3 4/10 mi it ends at King Canyon Trail. Long and meandering, this little-used trail allows more privacy to enjoy the natural surroundings than some of the more frequently used trails.

Valley View Overlook Trail. On clear days you can spot the distinctive slope of Picacho Peak from this 1½-mi trail in Saguaro West. Even on an overcast day you'll be treated to splendid vistas of Avra Valley. ⊠ *3 mi north of Red Hills Visitor Center on Bajada Loop Dr.*

DIFFICULT
Fodor'sChoice
★

Hugh Norris Trail. This 10-mi trail through the Tucson Mountains is one of the most impressive in the Southwest. It's full of switchbacks and some sections are moderately steep, but at the top of 4,687-foot Wasson Peak you'll enjoy views of the saguaro forest spread across the *bajada* (the gently rolling hills at the base of taller mountains). ⊠ *2½ mi north of Red Hills Visitor Center on Bajada Loop Dr.*

King Canyon Trail. This 3½-mi trail is the shortest, but steepest, route to the top of Wasson Peak in Saguaro West. It meets the Hugh Norris Trail less than half a mile from the summit. The trail, which begins across from the Arizona–Sonora Desert Museum, is named after the Copper King Mine. It leads past many scars from the search for mineral wealth. Look for petroglyphs in this area. ⊠ *2 mi south of Red Hills Visitor Center.*

★ **Tanque Verde Ridge Trail.** Be rewarded with spectacular scenery on this 15 4/10-mi trail through desert scrub, oak, alligator juniper, and piñon pine at the 6,000-foot peak, where views of the surrounding mountain ranges from both sides of the ridge delight. ⊠ *2 mi south of Saguaro East Visitor Center at Javelina picnic area.*

HORSEBACK
RIDING

More than 100 mi of trails in the park are open to use by livestock (mules, donkeys, and horses); however, animals are prohibited from off-trail travel and require a special permit, which can be obtained in person at one of the visitor centers or by mail.

Junior Ranger Program. Offered several times in June, for 2–3 days at a time, a **camp** for kids 5–12 includes daily hikes and workshops on pottery and petroglyphs. In the **Junior Ranger Discovery program,** young visitors can pick up an activity pack and complete it within an hour or two. ⊠ *Saguaro East Visitor Center* ☎ *520/733–5153* ⊠ *Red Hills Visitor Center* ☎ *520/733–5158.*

Orientation Programs. Daily programs introduce you to the desert. You might find slide shows on bats, birds, or desert blooms; naturalist-led hikes; and, in the summer only, films. ⊠ *Saguaro East Visitor Center* ☎ *520/733–5153* ⊠ *Red Hills Visitor Center* ☎ *520/733–5158* ☜ *Free* ☉ *Daily.*

Ranger Talks. Hear about wildlife, geology, and archaeology. ⊠ *Saguaro East Visitor Center* ☎ *520/733–5153* ⊠ *Red Hills Visitor Center* ☎ *520/733–5158* ☜ *Free* ☉ *Nov.–mid-Apr.*

WHERE TO EAT

The majority of the best Mexican restaurants are concentrated in South Tucson and downtown. Up in the Foothills, at resorts along Sunrise Drive, upscale Southwestern cuisine flourishes at such destination restaurants as Janos at the Westin La Paloma, the Grill at Hacienda del Sol Resort, and the Ventana Room at Loews Ventana Canyon. Cheaper but no less tasty fare as varied as Chinese, Guatemalan, and Greek can be enjoyed on the west side of U of A's campus, along University Boulevard and 4th Avenue. Tucson also has good sushi, Indian, Italian, and Thai food at reasonable prices, scattered around town.

Although the city's selection of restaurants is impressive, Tucson doesn't offer much in the way of late-night dining. Most restaurants in town are shuttered by 10 PM; some spots that keep later hours are noted below.

DOWNTOWN TUCSON

AMERICAN

¢–$$ ✕ **Cup Café.** This charming spot off the lobby of Hotel Congress is at the epicenter of Tucson's hippest downtown scene, but it's also a down-home, friendly place. Try the Gunpowder (eggs, potatoes, chorizo, and cheese) for breakfast or the Queer Steer Burger (a veggie burger) for lunch. The Heartbreaker appetizer (Brie melted over artichoke hearts and apple slices on a baguette) complements such entrées as chicken satay or "Tornados" of Beef. Open until 11 PM, it becomes interestingly crowded in the evening with patrons from the Club Congress, the hotel nightclub. ⊠*Hotel Congress, 311 E. Congress St., Downtown* ☎*520/798–1618* ⊟*AE, D, MC, V.*

MEXICAN

$$ ✕ **Café Poca Cosa.** In what is arguably Tucson's most creative Mexican
Fodor'sChoice restaurant, the chef prepares recipes inspired by different regions of her
★   native country. The menu, which changes daily, might include chicken mole or pork *pibil* (made with a tangy Yucatán barbecue seasoning). Servings are plentiful, and each table gets a stack of warm corn tortillas and a bowl of beans to share. Order the daily Plato Poca Cosa, and the chef will select one beef, one chicken, and one vegetarian entrée for you to sample. The bold-color walls are hung with Latin American art. ⊠*110 E. Pennington St., Downtown* ☎*520/622–6400* ⊟*MC, V* ⊗*Closed Sun. and Mon.*

¢–$$ ✕ **El Charro Café.** Started by Monica Flin in 1922, El Charro still serves splendid versions of the Mexican-American staples Flin claims to have originated, most notably chimichangas and cheese crisps. The *carne seca* chimichanga, made with beef dried on the premises—on the roof—is delicious. ⊠*311 N. Court Ave., Downtown* ☎*520/622–1922* ⊟*AE, D, DC, MC, V.*

¢–$ ✕ **El Minuto Café.** Popular with local families and the business crowd at lunch, this bustling restaurant is in Tucson's Barrio Historico neighborhood and open until midnight Friday and Saturday and until 10 PM the

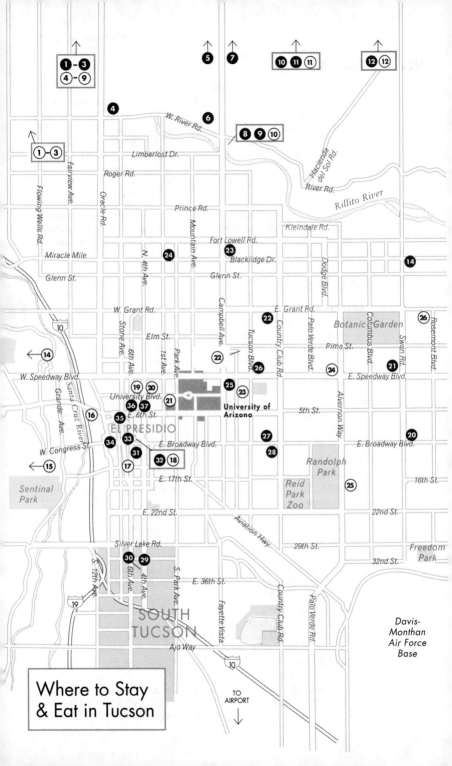

Where to Stay & Eat in Tucson

SOUTH TUCSON

EL PRESIDIO

University of Arizona

Botanic Garden

Randolph Park

Reid Park Zoo

Sentinal Park

Freedom Park

Davis-Monthan Air Force Base

Rillito River

Santa Cruz River

Streets and landmarks:

Fairview Ave.
Flowing Wells Rd.
Oracle Rd.
W. River Rd.
Limberlost Dr.
Roger Rd.
Prince Rd.
Mountain Ave.
N. 4th Ave.
Miracle Mile
Glenn St.
Fort Lowell Rd.
Blacklidge Dr.
Kleindale Rd.
Hacienda del Sol Rd.
River Rd.
Dodge Blvd.
Columbus Blvd.
Swan Rd.
Rosemont Blvd.
W. Grant Rd.
E. Grant Rd.
Stone Ave.
Elm St.
6th Ave.
1st Ave.
Park Ave.
Campbell Ave.
Tucson Blvd.
Country Club Rd.
Palo Verde Blvd.
Pima St.
W. Speedway Blvd.
E. Speedway Blvd.
Grande Ave.
University Blvd.
E. 6th St.
E. Broadway Blvd.
5th St.
Alvernon Way
W. Congress St.
E. 17th St.
16th St.
E. 22nd St.
22nd St.
Aviation Hwy.
29th St.
32nd St.
Silver Lake Rd.
S. 12th Ave.
4th Ave.
S. Park Ave.
E. 36th St.
Fayette Vista
Country Club Rd.
Palo Verde Rd.
Ajo Way

TO AIRPORT

KEY

① Hotels
❶ Restaurants

Restaurants ▼

Acacia **8**
Arizona Inn
Restaurant **14**
Athens **37**
B Line **36**
Bangkok Cafe **26**
Barrio **31**
Beyond Bread **23, 18**
Bistro Zin **6**
Café Poca Cosa **33**
Café Terra Cotta **11**
Cup Café **32**
El Charro Café **35**
El Minuto Café **34**
Elle **28**
The Gold Room **3**
Govinda **11**
The Grill at
Hacienda del Sol **12**
Janos **10**
Kingfisher Bar
and Grill **17**
Marlene's
Hungry Fox **20**
Mi Nidito **29**
Micha's **30**
Molina's Midway **21**
Montana Avenue **15**
New Delhi Palace:
Cuisine of India **19**
North **5**
Pinnacle Peak
Steakhouse **16**
Red Sky Cafe **14**
Sachiko Sushi **17**
Soleil **7**
Tohono Chul
Tea Room **1**
Ventana Room **13**
Vivace **9**
Wildflower Grill **2**
Zemam **27**
Zona 78 .... **4**

Hotels ▼

Adobe Rose Inn **23**
Arizona Inn **22**
Canyon Ranch **31**
Casa Tierra **14**
Catalina Park Inn **19**
Doubletree Hotel
at Reid Park **25**
Extended
StayAmerica **26**
Hacienda del Sol
Guest Ranch Resort **12**
Hilton Tucson
El Conquistador **9**
Hotel Congress **18**
Inn Suites Hotel
& Resort **16**
JW Marriott Starr
Pass Resort & Spa **15**
La Posada Lodge
and Casitas **4**
Lazy K Bar
Guest Ranch **3**
Loews Ventana
Canyon Resort **13**
Marriott TownePlace
Suites **5**
Miraval **7**
Omni Tucson National Golf
Resort & Spa **1**
Peppertrees
B&B Inn **21**
Quail's Vista
Bed and Breakfast **6**
Ramada Inn
Foothills **27**
The Royal Elizabeth
Bed and
Breakfast Inn **17**
The SunCatcher **28**
Tanque Verde
Ranch **29**
Tucson Hilton East **30**
Tucson Marriott
University Park **20**
Varsity Clubs
of America **24**
Westin La Paloma **11**
Westward Look
Resort **8**
White Stallion
Ranch **2**
Windmill Inn at
St. Philip's Plaza **10**

rest of the week. For more than 50 years, El Minuto has served *topopo* salads (a crispy tortilla shell heaped with beans, guacamole, and many other ingredients), huge burritos, and green-corn tamales (in season) made just right. The spicy *menudo* (tripe soup) is reputed to be a great hangover remedy. ✉ *354 S. Main Ave., Downtown* ☎ *520/882–4145* ⊟ *AE, D, DC, MC, V.*

> **DID YOU KNOW?**
>
> Tucson is also the birthplace of the *chimichanga* (Spanish for "whatchamacallit"), a flour tortilla filled with meat or cheese, rolled and deep-fried.

SOUTHWESTERN

$–$$$ ✕ **Barrio.** Lively at lunchtime, this trendy grill serves the most innovative cuisine in the downtown area. Try a "little plate" of black tiger shrimp rubbed with tamarind paste, or stuffed Anaheim chile in red bell-pepper cream. Entrées are as varied as the simple but delicious fish tacos and the linguine with chicken, dried papaya, and mango in a chipotle-chardonnay cream sauce. Save room for an elegant dessert of fresh berries drenched in crème anglaise or a chilled chocolate custard topped with caramel. ✉ *135 S. 6th Ave., Downtown* ☎ *520/629–0191* ⊟ *AE, D, DC, MC, V* ⊘ *Closed Mon. No lunch weekends.*

UNIVERSITY OF ARIZONA

AMERICAN

¢   ✕ **B Line.** In the heart of 4th Avenue's amalgam of antique clothing stores, pubs, and natural food grocers, this casual café in a converted 1920s bungalow attracts a mix of students, professors, downtown professionals, and artists with its simple but refined meals and desserts. Homemade biscuit sandwiches and excellent coffee start the day and the lunch–dinner menu features soups, salads, pastas, and burritos. ✉ *621 N. 4th Ave., University* ☎ *520/882–7575* ⊟ *MC, V.*

CONTINENTAL

$$$–$$$$ ✕ **Arizona Inn Restaurant.** Executive chef Odell Baskerville presides over the Arizona Inn, one of Tucson's most elegant restaurants. Dine on the patio overlooking the lush grounds, or enjoy the view from the dining room, which has Southwestern details from the 1930s. The culinary range is broad, from bouillabaisse to a vegetarian corn and butternut squash cannelloni. Locals also come for weekday power-breakfast meetings, Sunday brunch, or afternoon high tea in the library. ✉ *Arizona Inn, 2200 E. Elm St., University* ☎ *520/325–1541* ⊟ *AE, MC, V.*

GREEK

$–$$ ✕ **Athens.** The tranquil dining room in this Greek spot off 4th Avenue is furnished with lace curtains, white stucco walls, and potted plants. Enjoy classics like *kotopoulo stin pita* (grilled chicken breast with a yogurt-cucumber sauce on fresh pita), moussaka, or the *pastitsio* (a casserole made with pasta, meat, and béchamel). The house favorite is braised lamb shoulder in a light tomato sauce over pasta—call to reserve your order ahead of time. ⊠*500 N. 4th Ave., at 6th St., University* ☎*520/624–6886* ⊟*AE, D, DC, MC, V* ⊘*Closed Sun.*

CENTRAL TUCSON

AMERICAN

$–$$$ ✕ **Kingfisher Bar and Grill.** Kingfisher is a standout for American cuisine. The emphasis is on fresh seafood, but the kitchen does baby-back ribs and steak with equal success. Try the delicately battered fish-and-chips or the clam chowder on the late-night menu, served from 10 PM to midnight. Bright panels of turquoise and terra-cotta, black banquettes, and neon lighting make for a chic space. ⊠*2564 E. Grant Rd., Central* ☎*520/323–7739* ⊟*AE, D, DC, MC, V* ⊘*No lunch weekends.*

AMERICAN–CASUAL

¢ ✕ **Beyond Bread.** Twenty-seven varieties of bread are made at this bustling bakery, and highlights from the huge sandwich menu include Annie's Addiction (hummus, tomato, sprouts, red onion, and cucumber) and Brad's Beef (roast beef, provolone, onion, green chiles, and Russian dressing); soups and salads are equally scrumptious. Eat inside or on the patio, or order takeout, but be sure to splurge on one of the incredible desserts. ⊠*3026 N. Campbell Ave., Central* ☎*520/322–9965* ⊠*6260 E. Speedway Blvd., Eastside* ☎*520/747–7477* ⊟*AE, D, MC, V.*

¢ ✕ **Marlene's Hungry Fox.** Marlene's hungry customers have been coming here for good ol' fashioned breakfasts, served until 2 PM, since 1962. It's the home of the double yolk, meaning when you order one egg, you'll get two (and so on). You'll also get a real slice of Tucson life at this cheerful, unpretentious place decorated with cow and farm photos, and a spoon collection that lines the walls. ⊠*4637 E. Broadway Blvd., Central* ☎*520/326–2835* ⊟*AE, D, MC, V* ⊘*No dinner.*

ETHIOPIAN

¢–$ ✕ **Zemam.** It can be hard to get a table in this small eatery—except in summer, when the lack of air-conditioning presents a challenge. The sampler plate of any three items allows you to try dishes like *yesimir wat* (a spicy lentil dish) and *lega tibs* (a milder beef dish with a tomato sauce). Most of the food has a stewlike consistency, so don't come if you feel the need to crunch. Everything is served on a communal platter with *injera*, a spongy bread, and eaten with the hands. ⊠*2731 E. Broadway Blvd., Central* ☎*520/323–9928* ⌧*Reservations not accepted* ⊟*MC, V* ⓎⓎ*BYOB* ⊘*Closed Mon.*

ITALIAN

$–$$$ ✕ **Elle.** Italian, French, and Northern Californian cuisines influence Elle's menu. You can choose from pasta and risotto dishes, including squash ravioli with spinach, mushrooms, and sage butter, or try the grilled venison in roasted-garlic sauce with polenta. Servers provide expert assistance in selecting the perfect wine—from the nearly 90 vintages available (all from California, Oregon, and Washington), 45 can be ordered by the glass. The dining area is open and expansive. ⊠*3048 E. Broadway Blvd., Central* ☎*520/327–0500* ⊟*AE, DC, MC, V.*

★ **$-$$** ✕ **Zona 78.** Fresh food takes on a whole new meaning at this contemporary bistro emphasizing inventive pizzas, pastas, and salads. The casual interior's focal point is a huge stone oven, where the pies are fired with toppings like Australian blue cheese, kalamata olives, sausage, and even chicken with peanut sauce. Whole wheat crust is an option and for those avoiding carbs, there are baked salmon and chicken entrées. The housemade mozzarella is delectable, either on top of a pizza or in a salad with organic tomatoes. ⊠ *78 W. River Rd., Central* ☎ *520/888–7878* ▤ *AE, D, MC, V* ⊙ *No lunch Sun.*

MEXICAN

¢–$ ✕ **Molina's Midway.** Tucked into a side street just north of Speedway, this unassuming restaurant holds its own against any in South Tucson. Specialties include Sinchiladas (chicken or beef with chiles, cheese, and a cream sauce) and *carne asada* (chunks of mildly spiced steak) wrapped in soft corn or flour tortillas. Seating is plentiful and the service is friendly. ⊠ *1138 N. Belvedere, Central* ☎ *520/325–9957* ▤ *AE, D, MC, V* ⊙ *Closed Mon.*

SOUTHWESTERN

$$–$$$ ✕ **Red Sky Cafe.** Trained in Paris, chef-owner Steve Schultz returned to Tucson to create his own contemporary cuisine, a fusion of French, Californian, and Southwestern flavors; the result is well-prepared, exquisitely presented meals. For a starter, try the foie gras with a potato pancake. Main courses include soup or salad made with fresh (and often exotic) produce from the U of A's greenhouses. ⊠ *Plaza Palomino, 2910 N. Swan Rd., Central* ☎ *520/326–5454* ▤ *AE, MC, V* ⊙ *Closed Sun.*

THAI

¢–$ ✕ **Bangkok Cafe.** This is the best Thai food in town. You'll find all of your favorite dishes in this bright, spacious café, along with exceptionally pleasant service and reasonable prices. ⊠ *2511 E. Speedway Blvd., Central* ☎ *520/323–6555* ▤ *AE, MC, V* ⊙ *Closed Sun.*

VEGETARIAN

¢–$ ✕ **Govinda.** One of the few places in town with a strictly meatless menu, this Hare Krishna–run restaurant has reasonably priced all-you-can-eat lunch and dinner buffets, which include vegan options. Hot and cold dishes vary daily, but ingredients are consistently fresh, and the food is tasty if not spicy. Choose from three seating areas, including an outdoor patio with a koi pond and an aviary, where you can hear the calls of the resident peacocks. No alcohol is served or permitted. ⊠ *711 E. Blacklidge Dr., Central* ☎ *520/792–0630* ⌂ *Reservations not accepted* ▤ *MC, V* ⊙ *Closed Mon. No lunch Tues. No dinner Sun.*

EASTSIDE

AMERICAN

★ **$$–$$$** ✕ **Montana Avenue.** The newest sister restaurant to North, Bistro Zin, and Wildflower satisfies with upscale comfort food in a sophisticated setting, this one named for the chic dining district in L. A.'s Santa Monica. There's no view here, but floor-to-ceiling windows create a bright backdrop for nouvelle dishes like shrimp risotto with shiitake mushrooms and buttermilk chicken with chayote squash. Just for fun, toss the carb-counter aside and indulge in their sumptuous macaroni and cheese, grown-up style. ⊠*6390 E. Grant Rd., Eastside* ☎*520/298–2020* ⊟*AE, D, MC, V.*

INDIAN

$–$$ ✕ **New Delhi Palace: Cuisine of India.** Vegetarians, carnivores, and seafood lovers will all find something to enjoy at this savory Indian restaurant. The congenial staff is helpful in explaining the menu, which includes lots of tandoori dishes, curries, rice, and breads. The heat of each dish can be adjusted to individual preference by the chef. ⊠*6751 E. Broadway Blvd., Eastside* ☎*520/296–8585* ⊟*AE, MC, V.*

JAPANESE

$–$$ ✕ **Sachiko Sushi.** Perfectly prepared sushi, generous combinations of tempura and teriyaki, and friendly service greet you at what many locals consider the best Japanese restaurant in Tucson. Try a bowl of udon noodles, served in broth with assorted meat, seafood, or vegetables; it's a satisfying meal in itself. ⊠*1101 Wilmot Rd., Eastside* ☎*520/886–7000* ⊟*AE, DC, MC, V* ⊗*No lunch Sun.*

STEAK

☾ ¢–$$ ✕ **Pinnacle Peak Steakhouse.** Anybody caught eating newfangled foods like fish tacos here would probably be hanged from the rafters—along with the ties snipped from city slickers who overdressed. This cowboy steak house serves basic, not stellar, cowboy fare: mesquite-broiled steak, chicken, and grilled fish with salad and pinto beans. The restaurant is part of Trail Dust Town, a re-creation of a turn-of-the-20th-century town, complete with a working antique carousel and a narrow-gauge train. Gunfights are staged outside nightly at 7, 8, and 9. Expect a long wait on weekends. ⊠*6541 E. Tanque Verde Rd., Eastside* ☎*520/296–0911* ⌖*Reservations not accepted* ⊟*AE, D, DC, MC, V* ⊗*No lunch.*

CATALINA FOOTHILLS (NORTH)

AMERICAN

$$–$$$ ✕ **Bistro Zin.** French cooking meets American comfort food at this high-energy (and somewhat noisy) hip sister restaurant to Wildflower Grill, North, and Montana Avenue. Indulge in delicately flaky chicken potpie and french fries, a bistro steak, or scallops à l'orange. A hundred wines are available by the glass or "flight"—three tastes of the same type of wine from different vintners. Although lunch hums with the business crowd, at night it's a place to see and be seen. ⊠*1865 E. River Rd., Foothills* ☎*520/299–7799* ⊟*AE, D, DC, MC, V* ⊗*No lunch weekends.*

6

CONTINENTAL

★ **$$$$** ✕ **Ventana Room.** This formal restaurant is a triumph of dining elegance: muted colors, a fireplace, grand views of the city lights, and waiters who attend to every detail. The contemporary Continental menu contains such entrées as a mixed grill of game (venison, quail, and buffalo) with black barley and huckleberries, and potato-wrapped striped sea bass with spinach, tomato, and sweet-basil wine sauce. There's also a spa tasting menu for those watching fat and calories. ⊠*Loews Ventana Canyon Resort, 7000 N. Resort Dr., Foothills* ☎*520/299–2020 Ext. 5194* Jacket required ▭*AE, D, DC, MC, V* ⊘*No lunch.*

FRENCH

★ **$$–$$$** ✕ **Soleil.** Watch the sun set over the Tucson Mountains from either the outdoor terrace or the panoramic picture window inside—then gaze at the twinkling city lights below as you feast on contemporary French-influenced fare like caramelized sea scallops or filet mignon with sweet corn and shiitake mushrooms. A full vegetarian menu with vegan options also shines. The unique champagne bar is well stocked. After dinner, stroll by the fine art galleries in the imaginatively designed El Cortijo shopping complex. ⊠*El Cortijo, 3001 E. Skyline Dr., Foothills* ☎*520/299–3345* ▭*AE, D, MC, V* ⊘*Closed Mon.*

ITALIAN

$$–$$$ ✕ **Vivace.** A nouvelle Italian bistro in the lovely St. Philip's Plaza, Vivace has long been a favorite with Tucsonans. Wild mushrooms and goat cheese in puff pastry is hard to resist as a starter. For a lighter alternative to such entrées as a rich osso buco, try the fettuccine with grilled salmon. For dessert, the molten chocolate cake with spumoni is worth the 20 minutes it takes to create. Patio seating is especially inviting on warm evenings. ⊠*4310 N. Campbell Ave., Foothills* ☎*520/795–7221* ▭*AE, D, MC, V* ⊘*Closed Sun.*

★ **$–$$$** ✕ **North.** This trendy eatery in the upscale La Encantada Shopping Center sports an urban loft look with exposed pipe ceiling, white leather booths, dark concrete floors, and an open kitchen—and it draws crowds for its excellent thin-crust pizzas, pasta, fish, and steak. Alfresco dining on plush lounge furniture affords views of the city and quieter conversation; on most evenings, the expansive bar area inside buzzes with Tucson's young professionals. ⊠*2995 E. Skyline Dr., La Encantada, Foothills* ☎*520/299–1600* ▭*AE, D, MC, V.*

SOUTHWESTERN

★ **$$$–$$$$** ✕ **The Grill at Hacienda del Sol.** Tucked into the foothills and surrounded by flowering gardens, this special-occasion restaurant, a favorite among locals hosting out-of-town visitors, provides an alternative to the chile-laden dishes of most Southwestern nouvelle cuisine. Wild-mushroom bisque, pecan-grilled buffalo, and pan-seared sea bass are among the menu choices. Tapas (and most items on the full menu) can be enjoyed on the more casual outdoor patio, accented by live Flamenco guitar music. The lavish Sunday brunch buffet is worth a splurge. ⊠*Hacienda del Sol Guest Ranch Resort, 5601 N. Hacienda del Sol Rd., Foothills* ☎*520/529–3500* ▭*AE, DC, MC, V.*

$$$–$$$$
Fodor's Choice
★
✕ **Janos.** Chef Janos Wilder was one of the first to reinvent Southwestern cuisine, and the menu, wine list, and service place this restaurant among the finest in the West. The hillside location on the grounds of the Westin La Paloma is a stunning backdrop for such dishes as sweet and spicy glazed quail with butternut-squash cannelloni, salmon with a scallop mousse served on polenta, and venison loin with chile-lime paste and pecans. Have a drink or a more casual meal of Caribbean fare next door at J Bar, a lively and lower-priced venue for sampling Janos's innovative cuisine. ⊠ *Westin La Paloma, 3770 E. Sunrise Dr., Foothills* ☎ *520/615–6100* ⊟ *AE, DC, MC, V* ☾ *Closed Sun. No lunch.*

$$–$$$
✕ **Acacia.** One of Tucson's premier chefs, Albert Hall, has opened a restaurant in one of the area's most artistic settings. A glass waterfall sculpture by local artist Tom Philabaum graces one wall and bold red-and-blue glass plates and stemware seem to float atop the tables. Roasted plum tomato–and–basil soup, a recipe from Albert's mom, is a favorite starter. Creative dishes like wild salmon with a pecan honey-mustard glaze and wood-fired quail filled with pancetta, mozzarella, roasted tomatoes, and Oaxacan risotto are among the many tempting entrées. Weekend evenings bring live jazz to the patio, which overlooks pretty, flower-filled St. Philip's Plaza. ⊠ *4340 N. Campbell Ave., St. Philip's Plaza, Foothills* ☎ *520/232–0101* ⊟ *AE, D, MC, V.*

$–$$$
✕ **Café Terra Cotta.** Everything about this restaurant says Southwest—from the bright orange and purple walls, large windows, and exposed beams to the contemporary art—but especially the food. Specialties include tortilla soup, maple-leaf duck in a drunken cherry sauce, and creative pizzas with toppings like grilled shrimp and chiles or goat cheese and artichokes. This is the ultimate casual and lively yet classy place to dine in town. ⊠ *3500 E. Sunrise Dr., Foothills* ☎ *520/577–8100* ⊟ *AE, D, DC, MC, V.*

NORTHWEST TUCSON

AMERICAN

$$–$$$
✕ **Wildflower Grill.** A glass wall separates the bar from the dining area, where an open kitchen, high ceiling with painted clouds, and rose-color banquettes complete the light and airy effect. Wildflower Grill is well known for its creative American fare and stunning presentation, and the menu has compelling choices like warm Maine lobster salad; bow-tie pasta with grilled chicken, tomatoes, spinach, and pine nuts; and rack of lamb with a Dijon crust. The decadently huge desserts are equally top-notch. Request a banquette in the evening if you want quiet conversation, as the room can be noisy. ⊠ *7037 N. Oracle Rd., Northwest* ☎ *520/219–4230* ⊟ *AE, D, DC, MC, V* ☾ *No lunch Sun.*

SOUTHWESTERN

$$–$$$$
✕ **The Gold Room.** Every seat in this casually elegant and quiet dining room at the Westward Look Resort, high in the Catalina Foothills, has a spectacular view of the city below. The fare includes classics like sautéed halibut and roasted rack of lamb in truffle port sauce, as well as regional specialties such as mesquite-grilled buffalo sirloin.

6

✉ *Westward Look Resort, 245 E. Ina Rd., Northwest* ☎*520/297–1151* ⊟*AE, DC, MC, V.*

¢–$ ✗ **Tohono Chul Tea Room.** The food is fine, but what stands out here is the location—inside a wildlife sanctuary, surrounded by desert gardens. The Southwestern interior has Mexican tile, light wood, and a cobblestone patio. Dine outside to watch hummingbirds and butterflies. House favorites include tortilla soup with avocado, served with bread and scones baked on the premises, and grilled raspberry-chipotle chicken. Open daily 8 to 5, the Tea Room is popular for Sunday brunch—which can mean long waits in high season. ✉*Tohono Chul Park, 7366 N. Paseo del Norte, Northwest* ☎*520/797–1222* ⊟*AE, MC, V* ☉*No dinner.*

SOUTH TUCSON

MEXICAN

¢–$ ✗ **Mi Nidito.** A perennial favorite among locals (be prepared to wait
FodorsChoice awhile), Mi Nidito—"my little nest"—has also hosted its share of visit-
★ ing celebrities. Following President Clinton's lunch here, the rather hefty "Presidential Plate" (bean tostada, taco with barbecued meat, chile relleno, chicken enchilada, and beef tamale with rice and beans) was added to the menu. Top that off with the mango chimichangas for dessert, and you're talkin' executive privilege. ✉*1813 S. 4th Ave., South* ☎*520/622–5081* ⊟*AE, DC, MC, V* ☉*Closed Mon. and Tues.*

¢–$ ✗ **Micha's.** Family-owned for 24 years, this local institution is a nondescript Mexican diner serving some of the best Sonoran classics this side of the border. House specialties include *machaca* (shredded beef) enchiladas and chimichangas, and *cocido,* a hearty vegetable-beef soup. Homemade chorizo spices up breakfast, which is served daily. A second location now brings this great food close to the university. ✉*2908 S. 4th Ave., South* ☎*520/623–5307* ✉*1220 E. Prince Rd., University* ☎*520/293–0375* ⊟*AE, DC, MC, V* ☉*No dinner Mon.*

WHERE TO STAY

If you like being able to walk to sights, shops, and restaurants, plan on staying in the downtown, University, or Central Tucson neighborhood. The posh resorts in the Catalina Foothills and Northwest areas, while farther away from town, have many activities on-site, as well as some of the town's top-rated restaurants, and can arrange transportation to shopping and sights. Resorts here typically charge an additional daily resort fee for "use of facilities," such as pools, tennis courts, and exercise classes and equipment so be sure to ask what is included when you book a room.

Summer rates (late May–September) are up to 60% lower than those in the winter. Note that unless you book months in advance, you'll be hard-pressed to find a Tucson hotel room at any price the week before and during the huge gem and mineral show, which is usually held the first two weeks in February.

DOWNTOWN TUCSON

$$ ⊡ **The Royal Elizabeth Bed and Breakfast Inn.** Fans of Victoriana will adore this B&B built in 1878. The inn, in the Armory Park historic district, is beautifully furnished with period antiques and the six rooms are quite spacious. The two larger rooms have separate sitting areas with pull-out sofa beds. Gracious hosts Jeff and Charles take turns in the kitchen, preparing two-course breakfasts that might include chiles rellenos, a wild-mushroom frittata, or a fresh-fruit soufflé. ⊠204 S. Scott Ave., Downtown, 85701 ☎520/670–9022 ☐928/833–9974 ⊕www.royalelizabeth.com ⇋6 rooms ᗐIn-room: VCR, Wi-Fi. In-hotel: pool, no-smoking rooms ☐AE, D, MC, V ⏏BP.

$–$$ ⊡ **Inn Suites Hotel & Resort.** Just north of the El Presidio district of downtown, this hotel is next to I–10 but quiet nevertheless. The large, peach-and-green Southwestern-theme rooms, circa 1980, face an interior courtyard with a sparkling pool and palapas (thatched open gazebos). Free daily extras such as a breakfast buffet, newspaper, and happy-hour cocktails make this a haven in the center of the city. ⊠475 N. Granada Ave., Downtown, 85701 ☎520/622–3000 or 877/446–6589 ☐520/623–8922 ⊕www.innsuites.com ⇋265 rooms, 35 suites ᗐIn-room: refrigerator. In-hotel: restaurant, room service, bar, pool, no-smoking rooms ☐AE, D, DC, MC, V ⏏BP.

¢ ⊡ **Hotel Congress.** This hotel built in 1919 has been artfully restored
Fodor'sChoice to its original Western version of art deco. The gangster John Dillinger
★ was almost caught here in 1934 (apparently his luggage, filled with guns and ammo, was suspiciously heavy). Each room has a black-and-white tile bath and the original iron bed frames. The convenient location downtown means it can be noisy, so make sure you don't get a room over the popular Club Congress or you'll be up until the wee hours. A great place to stay for younger or more adventurous visitors, it's the center of Tucson's hippest scene. ⊠311 E. Congress St., Downtown, 85701 ☎520/622–8848 or 800/722–8848 ☐520/792–6366 ⊕www.hotelcongress.com ⇋40 rooms ᗐIn-room: no TV. In-hotel: restaurant, bar, no-smoking rooms, no elevator ☐AE, D, MC, V.

UNIVERSITY OF ARIZONA

$$$ ⊡ **Arizona Inn.** Although close to the university and many sights, the
Fodor'sChoice beautifully landscaped lawns and gardens of this 1930 inn seem far
★ from the hustle and bustle. The spacious rooms are spread over 14 acres in pink adobe-style casitas—most have private patios and some have fireplaces. The resort also has two luxurious two-story houses with their own heated pools and full hotel service. The main building has a library, a fine-dining restaurant, and a cocktail lounge where a jazz pianist plays. ⊠2200 E. Elm St., University, 85719 ☎520/325–1541 or 800/933–1093 ☐520/881–5830 ⊕www.arizonainn.com ⇋70 rooms, 16 suites, 3 casitas ᗐIn-room: ethernet. In-hotel: 2 restaurants, room service, bar, tennis courts, pool, gym, laundry service, no-smoking rooms ☐AE, DC, MC, V.

$$$ ⊡ **Tucson Marriott University Park.** With the University of Arizona less
★ than a block from the front door, the Marriott is an ideal place to stay

when visiting the campus. This clean, contemporary hotel has a lush atrium lobby area that can be enjoyed from the restaurant and bar, and the university shopping district's cafés, pubs, and stores are all within a short stroll. ⊠ *880 E. 2nd St., University, 85719* ☎ *520/792–4100 or 888/236–2427* ☏ *520/882–4100* ⊕ *www.marriott.com* ⇗ *234 rooms, 16 suites* ⚡ *In-room: refrigerator (some), ethernet. In-hotel: restaurant, room service, bar, pool, gym, laundry service, executive floor, no-smoking rooms* ☰ *AE, D, DC, MC, V.*

$$ 🏨 **Adobe Rose Inn.** This 1933 adobe home offers six rooms of varying sizes and amenities. Two have beehive fireplaces and stained-glass windows, two have kitchenettes, and one is an upstairs suite with its own balcony. In the historic Sam Hughes neighborhood just east of the university, the well-maintained inn is within easy walking distance of shops, restaurants, and two major bus lines. Breakfast dishes like Southwestern soufflés or blueberry pancakes, always served with fruit and muffins, are enjoyed in a dining room overlooking the bougainvillea-draped pool area. ⊠ *940 N. Olsen Ave., University, 85719* ☎ *520/318–4644 or 800/328–4122* ⊕ *www.aroseinn.com* ⇗ *6 rooms* ⚡ *In-room: Wi-Fi. In-hotel: pool, no kids under 10, no-smoking rooms, no elevator* ☰ *AE, D, MC, V* ⏘*BP.*

$$ 🏨 **Catalina Park Inn.** Classical music plays softly in the living room of this beautifully restored 1927 neoclassical house. The original art nouveau–tile work and a butler's pantry are among many charming architectural details and all rooms are spacious and quite private. You might be tempted to fill your suitcase with the papaya and lime scones that are part of breakfast. ⊠ *309 E. 1st St., University, 85705* ☎ *520/792–4541 or 800/792–4885* ⊕ *www.catalinaparkinn.com* ⇗ *6 rooms* ⚡ *In-room: Wi-Fi. In-hotel: no kids under 10, no-smoking rooms, no elevator* ☰ *AE, D, MC, V* ⏘*BP.*

★ $$ 🏨 **Peppertrees B&B Inn.** This restored 1905 Victorian just west of the U of A campus affords privacy along with B&B camaraderie. Two contemporary-style guesthouses at the rear of the tree-shaded main house have full kitchens, separate phone lines, private patios, and washers and dryers (for guesthouse guests only). The antique-filled main house (furnished with pieces from innkeeper Jill Light's family in England) has several guest rooms, as well as a separate one-bedroom apartment. Light prepares elaborate breakfasts, and dinner and room service are available on request. ⊠ *724 E. University Blvd., University, 85719* ☎ *520/622–7167 or 800/348–5763* ⊕ *www.peppertreesinn.com* ⇗ *3 rooms, 1 suite, 2 guesthouses* ⚡ *In-room: kitchen (some), Wi-Fi. In-hotel: no-smoking rooms, no elevator* ☰ *D, MC, V* ⏘*BP.*

CENTRAL TUCSON

$$–$$$ 🏨 **Doubletree Hotel at Reid Park.** The municipal golf course at Randolph Park hosts the LPGA tournament every year, and most of the participants stay across the street at this hotel and conference center. Reid Park (adjacent to Randolph Park) has a pleasant jogging trail and a zoo. This sprawling, contemporary hotel is also convenient to the airport, the center of town, and the El Con shopping mall. ⊠ *445 S. Alvernon Way,*

Central, 85711 ☎*520/881–4200 or 800/222–8733* 🖶*520/323–5225*
⊕*www.doubletree.com* 💬*295 rooms* ♿*In-room: ethernet. In-hotel:*
2 restaurants, room service, bar, tennis courts, pool, gym, laundry ser-
vice, no-smoking rooms ▤*AE, D, DC, MC, V* ⛺|*BP.*

$$ 🏨 **Varsity Clubs of America.** This sports-theme time-share facility also
doubles as a hotel, so it may have any or all of its suites available for
rental at any given time. Home to the Diamondbacks and the Rockies
teams during spring training, its handy location is surprisingly quiet.
One- and two-bedroom suites have whirlpool tubs and full kitchens,
but alternatives to cooking include the Stadium Sports Grill down-
stairs or any of the several restaurants within walking distance. There
are a billiard room, a putting green, and a cozy library with a fire-
place. ⊠*3855 E. Speedway Blvd., Central, 85716* ☎*520/318–3777 or*
888/594–2287 🖶*888/410–9770* ⊕*www.ilxresorts.com* 💬*59 suites*
♿*In-room: kitchen, Wi-Fi. In-hotel: restaurant, pool, gym, no-smoking*
rooms ▤*AE, D, MC, V.*

$ 🏨 **Extended StayAmerica.** If you're seeking convenience and value (and
don't mind a certain blandness), this modern chain property will suf-
fice. All rooms have kitchenettes, queen-size beds, and recliner chairs,
but don't expect a view or coffee in the lobby—Crossroads Shop-
ping Center, where there are restaurants, a Starbucks, a grocery store,
shops, and a cinema, is only two blocks away. ⊠*5050 E. Grant Rd.,*
Central, 85712 ☎*520/795–9510 or 800/398–7829* 🖶*520/795–9504*
⊕*www.extendedstayhotels.com* 💬*120 rooms* ♿*In-room: kitchen,*
refrigerator, Wi-Fi. In-hotel: laundry facilities, no-smoking rooms
▤*AE, D, MC, V.*

EASTSIDE

★ $$$$ 🏨 **Tanque Verde Ranch.** The most upscale of Tucson's guest ranches and
one of the oldest in the country, the Tanque Verde sits on 640 beau-
tiful acres in the Rincon Mountains next to Saguaro National Park
East. Rooms in one-story casitas have tasteful Western-style furnish-
ings, fireplaces, and picture-window views of the desert. Breakfast and
lunch buffets are huge, and barbecues add variety to the daily dinner
menu. Horseback excursions are offered for every skill level (lessons
are included in rates), and children can participate in daylong activity
programs, from riding to tennis to crafts, leaving parents to their lei-
sure. ⊠*14301 E. Speedway Blvd., Eastside, 85748* ☎*520/296–6275*
or 800/234–3833 🖶*520/721–9426* ⊕*www.tanqueverderanch.com*
💬*49 rooms, 23 suites, 2 casitas* ♿*In-room: no TV. In-hotel: tennis*
courts, pools, gym, bicycles, children's programs (ages 4–11), no-smok-
ing rooms ▤*AE, D, MC, V* ⛺|*FAP.*

$$–$$$ 🏨 **The SunCatcher.** The four rooms in this B&B are decorated in honor
of four groups who settled the Old West: Cowboys, Native Ameri-
cans, Spanish, and Oriental. Some have fireplaces and Jacuzzi tubs,
and can be reconfigured as suites for families. The spacious living room
has a sunken seating area facing a copper-hooded fireplace and a mes-
quite-wood bar where happy-hour snacks are served. It's a comfortable
retreat after a day of sightseeing or hiking (trailheads into Saguaro

National Park East are just down the road). ⊠*105 N. Avda. Javelina, Eastside, 85748* ☎*520/885–0883* ⊕*www.thesuncatcher.com* ☞*4 rooms* ♿*In-room: DVD, dial-up. In-hotel: pool, no-smoking rooms* ☰*AE, D, MC, V* ⦿*BP.*

$$ 🏨 **Tucson Hilton East.** This high-rise hotel and conference center is set back from a main road on the suburban east side of town. An airy atrium lobby takes advantage of the view of the Santa Catalina Mountains; better yet, push "6" in the glass elevator and ascend for spectacular vistas. Rooms are spacious and well tended but not particularly distinctive. ⊠*7600 E. Broadway Blvd., Eastside, 85710* ☎*520/721–5600 or 800/774–1500* ☒*520/721–5696* ⊕*www.tucsoneast.hilton. com* ☞*225 rooms, 8 suites* ♿*In-room: Wi-Fi. In-hotel: restaurant, bar, pool, gym, no-smoking rooms* ☰*AE, D, DC, MC, V.*

$–$$ 🏨 **Ramada Inn Foothills.** Families and business travelers stay in this Ramada on the northeast side of town, not really in the Foothills but fairly close to Sabino Canyon. An attractive stucco building with a Spanish tile roof and a fake bell tower, the hotel has serviceable, if generic, rooms and small suites. Complimentary beer, wine, and appetizers are served in the afternoon and free passes to a local health club are available. There is no restaurant on-site but many are nearby. ⊠*6944 E. Tanque Verde Rd., Eastside, 85715* ☎*520/886–9595 or 800/228–2828* ☒*520/721–8466* ⊕*www.ramadafoothillstucson.com* ☞*52 rooms, 61 suites* ♿*In-room: refrigerator, Wi-Fi. In-hotel: pool, laundry facilities, no-smoking rooms* ☰*AE, D, DC, MC, V* ⦿*CP.*

CATALINA FOOTHILLS (NORTH)

★ $$$$ 🏨 **Canyon Ranch.** The Canyon Ranch draws an international crowd of well-to-do health seekers to its superb spa facilities on 70 acres in the desert foothills. Two activity centers include an enormous spa complex and a Health and Healing Center, where dietitians, exercise physiologists, behavioral-health professionals, and medical staff attend to body and soul. Just about every type of physical activity is possible, from Pilates to guided hiking, and the food is plentiful and healthy. Rates include all meals, activities, taxes, and gratuities. There's a four-night minimum. ⊠*8600 E. Rockcliff Rd., Foothills, 85750* ☎*520/749–9000 or 800/742–9000* ☒*520/749–1646* ⊕*www.canyonranch.com* ☞*240 rooms* ♿*In-room: refrigerator, dial-up. In-hotel: restaurant, tennis courts, pools, gym, spa, laundry facilities, airport shuttle, no kids under 12, no-smoking rooms* ☰*AE, D, MC, V* ⦿*AI.*

$$$$ 🏨 **Loews Ventana Canyon Resort.** This is one of the most luxurious of the ★ big resorts, with dramatic stone architecture and an 80-foot waterfall cascading down the mountains. Rooms, facing either the Catalinas or the golf course and city, are modern and elegantly furnished in muted earth tones and light woods; each bathroom has a miniature TV and a double-wide tub. Dining options include everything from poolside snacks at Bill's Grill to fine Continental cuisine at the Ventana Room. The scenic Ventana Canyon trailhead is steps away, and there's a free shuttle to nearby Sabino Canyon. ⊠*7000 N. Resort Dr., Foothills, 85750* ☎*520/299–2020 or 800/234–5117* ☒*520/299–6832* ⊕*www.*

loewshotels.com 📞*384 rooms, 14 suites* ♿*In-room: refrigerator, ethernet. In-hotel: 4 restaurants, room service, bar, golf courses, tennis courts, pools, gym, spa, bicycles, public Wi-Fi, children's programs (ages 4–12), no-smoking rooms* ☰*AE, D, DC, MC, V.*

$$$$ 🏨 **Westin La Paloma.** Vying with the Hilton El Conquistador and Loews
★ Ventana for convention business, this sprawling resort offers views of the Santa Catalina Mountains above and the city below. It specializes in relaxation with an emphasis on fun: the golf, tennis, and spa facilities are top notch, and the huge pool complex has an impressively long water slide, as well as a swim-up bar and grill for those who can't bear to leave the water. On-site kids' programs, including weekly "dive-in movies," make for a vacation the whole family can enjoy. Janos, one of Tucson's top restaurants, is also here. ✉*3800 E. Sunrise Dr., Foothills, 85718* ☎*520/742–6000 or 888/625–5144* 📠*520/577–5878* 🌐*www. starwood.com* 📞*455 rooms, 32 suites* ♿*In-room: refrigerator, Wi-Fi. In-hotel: 4 restaurants, room service, bars, golf courses, tennis courts, pools, gym, spa, children's programs (ages 6 months–12 years), no-smoking rooms* ☰*AE, D, DC, MC, V.*

★ $$–$$$ 🏨 **Hacienda del Sol Guest Ranch Resort.** This 32-acre hideaway in the Santa Catalina foothills is part guest ranch, part resort, and entirely gracious. It's a charming and lower-price alternative to the larger resorts. Designed in classic Mexican hacienda style, this former finishing school for girls attracted stars like Clark Gable, Katharine Hepburn, and Spencer Tracy when it was converted to a guest ranch during World War II. Some of the one- and two-bedroom casitas have fireplaces and private porches, where you can watch the sun set over the Tucson Mountains. The superb Grill at Hacienda del Sol is part of the resort. ✉*5601 N. Hacienda del Sol Rd., Foothills, 85718* ☎*520/299–1501 or 800/728–6514* 📠*520/299–5554* 🌐*www.haciendadelsol.com* 📞*22 rooms, 8 suites* ♿*In-room: refrigerator, ethernet. In-hotel: restaurant, pool, no-smoking rooms* ☰*AE, D, MC, V.*

$$ 🏨 **Windmill Inn at St. Philip's Plaza.** This all-suites hotel is in a chic shopping plaza filled with glitzy boutiques, galleries, and good restaurants. Each 500-square-foot suite has a small sitting area, wet bar, two TVs, and three telephones (local calls are free). A few dollars extra will buy you a view of the pool and fountain rather than the parking lot. Complimentary coffee, muffins, juice, and a newspaper are delivered to your door; additional breakfast goodies are set up in the lobby. There are bicycles available for excursions along the nearby Rillito River, and free passes to a nearby gym are included in the rate. ✉*4250 N. Campbell Ave., Foothills, 85718* ☎*520/577–0007 or 800/547–4747* 📠*520/577–0045* 🌐*www.windmillinns.com* 📞*122 suites* ♿*In-room: refrigerator, Wi-Fi. In-hotel: pool, bicycles, laundry facilities, no-smoking rooms* ☰*AE, D, DC, MC, V* ❘⊙❘*BP.*

NORTHWEST TUCSON

$$$$ 🏨 **Hilton Tucson El Conquistador.** A huge copper mural of cowboys and cacti, and a wide view of the Santa Catalina Mountains grace the lobby of this golf and tennis resort. A friendly upscale property, it draws fami-

lies and conventioneers, some taking advantage of low summer rates for the excellent sports facilities, the spa, and the pool complex with a 140-foot waterslide. Rooms, either in private one-bedroom casitas or the main hotel building, are done in desert tones of taupe, sand, and gold, and more than half of them have kiva-style fireplaces. ☒*10000 N. Oracle Rd., Northwest, 85737* ☎*520/544–5000 or 800/325–3525* 🖷*520/544–1224* ⊕*www.hiltonelconquistador.com* ↩*328 rooms, 57 suites, 43 casitas* ♿*In-room: refrigerator, dial-up. In-hotel: 5 restaurants, bar, golf courses, tennis courts, pools, gym, spa, bicycles, children's programs (ages 4–12), no-smoking rooms* ☰*AE, D, DC, MC, V.*

$$$$ 🏨 **Lazy K Bar Guest Ranch.** Though new housing subdivisions are encroaching on this family-oriented guest ranch in the Tucson Mountains northwest of town, greenhorns can feel like they've escaped to a slower, simpler vacation here. Guest rooms are in eight casitas. Those in the older structures, made of Mexican stucco, have fireplaces and wood-beam ceilings; rooms in the newer, adobe-brick buildings are larger and more modern. In addition to horseback riding offered twice daily, you can enjoy cookouts, hayrides, and evening entertainment such as square dancing and cowboy roping tricks. There are also hammocks, a heated pool, and a hot tub to relax those post-equestrian muscles. ☒*8401 N. Scenic Dr., Northwest, 85743* ☎*520/744–3050 or 800/321–7018* 🖷*520/744–7628* ⊕*www.lazykbar.com* ↩*19 rooms, 4 suites* ♿*In-room: no phone, no TV. In-hotel: pool, airport shuttle, no-smoking rooms* ☰*AE, D, MC, V* ☉*Closed June–Aug.* ⦿*FAP.*

★ $$$$ 🏨 **Miraval.** Giving Canyon Ranch a run for its money, this New Age health spa 30 mi north of Tucson has a secluded desert setting and beautiful Southwestern rooms. Most of the spa services and wellness programs, based primarily on Eastern philosophies, help you get in touch with your inner self. Whether you prefer to be pampered with a hot stone massage or seaweed body mask, partake in fitness and nature activities, or just do yoga, it's all here. All gratuities and meals, including tasty buffets (with calories and fat content noted), are included. ☒*5000 E. Via Estancia Miraval, Catalina 85739* ☎*520/825–4000 or 800/825–4000* 🖷*520/825–5163* ⊕*www.miravalresort.com* ↩*106 rooms* ♿*In-room: safe, refrigerator, dial-up. In-hotel: 2 restaurants, bar, tennis courts, pools, gym, spa, bicycles, laundry facilities, laundry service, no-smoking rooms* ☰*AE, D, DC, MC, V* ⦿*FAP.*

$$$$ 🏨 **Omni Tucson National Golf Resort & Spa.** Perfect for couples with differing ideas on how to spend a vacation, Tucson National is both a premier golf resort (it hosts the Tucson Open) and a full-service European-style spa, where you can be coiffed, waxed, wrapped, and worked over to your heart's content. Most of the rooms, although not technically suites, are spacious with separate sitting areas. Some casitas have full kitchens and dining rooms. Although this resort is a little farther from central Tucson than others, it's still convenient to shopping and restaurants in the thriving Northwest area. ☒*2727 W. Club Dr., Northwest 85742* ☎*520/297–2271 or 800/528–4856* 🖷*520/297–7544* ⊕*www.omnihotels.com* ↩*143 rooms, 24 suites* ♿*In-room: refrigerator, dial-up (some), Wi-Fi (some). In-hotel: 3 restaurants, bars, golf courses, tennis courts, pools, gym, spa, concierge, no-smoking rooms* ☰*AE, D, DC, MC, V.*

CLOSE UP

Where the West Is Still Wild

If you think Tucson has gone the way of those sprawling suburban development like Phoenix to the north, well, you're partly right. Many of the wide-open spaces that inspired the lyrics of old cowboy songs have become housing tracts, golf courses, and shopping malls. But a sliver of the rugged and free-spirited ranching life that shaped the American West is alive and well on the outskirts of town, where urban cowboys and cowgirls come to fulfill their dreams at dude ranches, also called guest ranches.

Riding is the preferred activity on the ranch. Slow, fast, mountain, and all-day rides are offered, and some ranches allow you to help groom and feed the horses. As you ride up into Saguaro National Park or the Coronado National Forest, wranglers give sage advice on horsemanship and tell tales (some tall) of their most harrowing cattle drives. For those who don't saddle up, there are activities including birding and nature walks, mountain hikes, tennis, and swimming Afterwards, you can soak in the hot tub, get a massage, or laugh with new friends about the day's adventures over margaritas.

After a day of riding or hiking, or maybe just sitting outside with a book, guests find a warm welcome at happy hour, dinner, and around the campfire. Lodges are outfitted with comfortable couches, crackling fireplaces, board games, and Western saloon-type bars (one even has saddles for barstools). Ranch stays are popular for family vacations but the ranch experience also draws many single travelers who can easily find camaraderie in this setting.

Though accommodations are a bit more rustic than at resort hotels, there are arguably more comforts and the dude ranch experience eliminates many stresses often associated with more traditional vacations: Since all meals and activities are included, you have fewer decisions to make about structuring your day (will it be the mountain ride or team penning?), and no anxiety about choosing a restaurant or dealing with crowds.

Three ranches are in the Tucson area. The large and luxurious **Tanque Verde Ranch,** on the eastern edge of town, has two swimming pools (one indoor), a tennis pro, and lavish buffet meals. Children are separated from adults for rides and activities. The **White Stallion Ranch,** adjacent to Saguaro National Park's west unit, has challenging riding as well as massages and a fitness center. The owners live and work on this 3,000-acre cattle ranch, the setting for *High Chaparral.* The smaller and more rustic **Lazy K Bar Guest Ranch,** also in the Northwest, has hayrides and two hilltop banquet rooms for special events.

6

$$$$
Fodor'sChoice
★

☑ **White Stallion Ranch.** A 3,000-acre working cattle ranch run by the hospitable True family since 1965, this place is the real deal. You can ride up to four times daily, hike in the mountains, enjoy a hayride cookout, and compete in team cattle penning. Most rooms retain their original Western furniture, and newer deluxe rooms have whirlpool baths or fireplaces. A recently completed spa and fitness center bring even more comforts to this well-endowed but authentic setting. Rates include all meals, riding, and entertainment such as weekend rodeos, country line dancing, telescopic stargazing, and campfire sing-alongs. ✉*9251 W. Twin Peaks Rd., Northwest, 85743* ☎*520/297–0252 or 888/977–2624* 🖷*520/744–2786* ⊕*www.wsranch.com* ⥼*24 rooms, 17 suites* ♿*In-room: no phone, no TV. In-hotel: bar, tennis courts, pool, gym, airport shuttle* ▭*No credit cards* ☾*Closed June–Aug.* ⏴*FAP.*

$$$–$$$$ 🏨 **Westward Look Resort.** Originally the 1912 homestead of William and
★ Mary Watson, this laid-back lodging offers Southwestern character, attentive service, and all the amenities you expect at a major resort. The Watsons' original living room, with beautiful, dried ocotillo branches draped along the ceiling and antique furnishings, is now a comfortable lounge off the main lobby. The couple probably never envisioned anything like the Sonoran Spa, offering hot desert-stone massages and three-mud body masks. Spacious rooms have wrought-iron beds and Mission-style furniture. You can borrow a bike or take a stroll along the beautiful and well-marked nature trails. ✉*245 E. Ina Rd., Northwest, 85704* ☎*520/297–1151 or 800/722–2500* 🖷*520/297–9023* ⊕*www.westwardlook.com* ⥼*244 rooms* ♿*In-room: refrigerator, Wi-Fi. In-hotel: 2 restaurants, tennis courts, pools, gym, spa, bicycles, concierge, no-smoking rooms* ▭*AE, D, DC, MC, V.*

$$ 🏨 **Marriott TownePlace Suites.** With full kitchens in all of its studio, one-bedroom, and two-bedroom suites, this property is suitable for short or extended stays. In fact, the longer you stay, the lower your nightly rate. Its location is handy, yet the interior hallways and the way the buildings are set back from the road make for a quiet retreat. Some suites have a view of the neighboring golf course. ✉*405 W. Rudasill Rd., Northwest, 85704* ☎*520/292–9697 or 800/257–3000* 🖷*520/292–9884* ⊕*www.towneplacesuites.com* ⥼*77 suites* ♿*In-room: kitchen, dial-up. In-hotel: pool, laundry facilities, no-smoking rooms* ▭*AE, MC, V* ⏴*CP.*

$–$$ 🏨 **La Posada Lodge and Casitas.** This 1960s motor lodge has been reborn as a charming Santa Fe–style boutique hotel. Though most rooms in the three-story building have Saltillo-tile floors and hand-painted Mexican headboards, a few are whimsically decorated with blue-and-lime-green–checkered bedspreads and curtains, along with kitschy furniture and lava lamps, as a tribute to the hotel's past life. Upper-floor rooms have balconies with mountain and city views, and the one-story casitas have kitchenettes and patios. The restaurant, Miguel's ($$–$$$), is an upscale Latin-theme jewel, specializing in seafood. ✉*5900 N. Oracle Rd., Northwest, 85704* ☎*520/887–4800 or 800/810–2808* 🖷*520/293–7543* ⊕*www.laposadalodge.com* ⥼*72 rooms* ♿*In-room: kitchen (some), refrigerator, dial-up. In-hotel: restaurant, room service, bar, pool, gym, no-smoking rooms* ▭*AE, MC, V* ⏴*BP.*

¢–$ 🏨 **Quail's Vista Bed and Breakfast.** Innkeeper and former concierge Barbara Bauer and her husband, Richard, can direct you to all the best things to see and do in Tucson; some activities, like bird-watching or soaking in a hot tub that faces the dramatic Santa Catalina Mountains, can be done right in the inn's backyard. Inside, peeled-spruce columns support the beamed ceiling and rounded walls of this adobe home. Fiesta dinnerware, Native American pottery, and bright Mexican blankets decorate the common area, which has cozy nooks for reading or watching the wildlife out the windows. ✉826 E. Palisades Rd., Northwest, 85737 ☎520/297–5980 ⊕www.quails-vista-bb.com ➪3 rooms, 1 with bath △In-room: no TV (some), Wi-Fi. In-hotel: laundry facilities, no-smoking rooms ⊟No credit cards ⊘Closed May–Sept. ⊠CP.

WEST OF TUCSON

$$$–$$$$ ⊡ **JW Marriott Starr Pass Resort & Spa.** Set amid saguaro forests and mesquite groves in the Tucson Mountains (yet only 15 minutes to downtown), the city's newest—and largest—resort opened in early 2005. Massive sun-bleached stone walls blend rather than compete with the natural surroundings, and there are stunning views from the interior dining areas and lounges. Outside terraces, with chairs and sofas clustered around kiva fireplaces, overlook the pools, golf course, and desert valley. Complimentary tequila shots, along with a dramatic recitation of the story of Pancho Villa, liven up the bar during happy hour. Resort amenities include an on-site Starbucks. ✉3800 W. Starr Pass Blvd., Westside, 85701 ☎520/792–3500 ⊟520/792–3351 ⊕www.starrpassmarriott. com ➪538 rooms, 37 suites △In-room: refrigerator, ethernet. In-hotel: 4 restaurants, room service, bar, golf courses, pools, gym, spa, concierge, no-smoking rooms ⊟AE, D, MC, V.

$$ ⊡ **Casa Tierra.** For a real desert experience, head to this B&B on 5 acres
Fodor'sChoice   near the Desert Museum and Saguaro National Park West. The last
★   1½ mi are on a dirt road. All rooms have private patio entrances and look out onto a lovely central courtyard. The Southwestern-style furnishings include Mexican *equipales* (chairs with pigskin seats) and tile floors. A full vegetarian breakfast served on fine china is included, and there's a media room in case you need a break from the quiet. There's a minimum stay of two nights. ✉11155 W. Calle Pima, Westside, 85743 ☎520/578–3058 or 866/254–0006 ⊟520/578–8445 ⊕www. casatierratucson.com ➪3 rooms, 1 suite △In-room: refrigerator, no TV. In-hotel: gym, no-smoking rooms ⊟AE, MC, V ⊘Closed mid-June–mid-Aug. ⊠BP.

NIGHTLIFE & THE ARTS

THE ARTS

For a city of its size, Tucson is abuzz with cultural activity. It's one of only 14 cities in the United States with a symphony as well as opera, theater, and ballet companies. Wintertime, when Tucson's population swells with vacationers, is the high season, but the arts are alive and well year-round. The low cost of Tucson's cultural events comes as a pleasant surprise to those accustomed to paying East or West Coast prices: symphony tickets are as little as $10 for some performances, and touring Broadway musicals can often be seen for $24. Parking is plentiful and frequently free.

The free *Tucson Weekly* (⊕www.tucsonweekly.com) and the "Caliente" section of the *Arizona Daily Star* (⊕www.azstarnet.com) both hit the stands on Thursday and have listings of what's going on in town.

Much of the city's cultural activity takes place at or near the **Tucson Convention Center** (⊠*260 S. Church St., Downtown* ☎*520/791–4101, 520/791–4266 box office* ⊕*www.tucsonconventioncenter.org*), which includes the Music Hall and the Leo Rich Theater. Dance, music, and other kinds of performances take place at the University of Arizona's **Centennial Hall** (⊠*1020 E. University Blvd., University* ☎*520/621–3341* ⊕*www.uapresents.org*).

One of Tucson's hottest rock-music venues, the **Rialto Theatre** (⊠*318 E. Congress St., Downtown* ☎*520/798–3333* ⊕*www.rialtotheatre.com*), was once a silent-movie theater but now reverberates with the sounds of jazz, folk, and world-music concerts, although the emphasis is on hard rock. The Rialto hosts dance and dramatic productions as well.

Each season brings visiting opera, theater, and dance companies to Tucson. Tickets to many events can be purchased through **Ticketmaster** (☎*520/321–1000* ⊕*www.ticketmaster.com* ⊠*Robinsons-May, El Con Mall, 3435 E. Broadway Blvd., Central* ☎*520/795–3950* ⊠*Robinsons-May, Tucson Mall, 4470 N. Oracle Rd., Central* ☎*520/292–0345*).

DANCE

Tucson shares its professional-ballet company, **Ballet Arizona** (☎*888/322–5538* ⊕*www.balletaz.org*), with Phoenix. Performances, from classical to contemporary, are held at the Music Hall in the Tucson Convention Center. The city's most established modern dance company, **Orts Theatre of Dance** (⊠*930 N. Stone Ave., Downtown* ☎*520/624–3799* ⊕*www. orts.org*), incorporates trapeze flying into their dances. Outdoor and indoor performances are staged throughout the year.

MUSIC

A Wednesday-night chamber-music series is hosted by the **Arizona Friends of Chamber Music** (☎*520/577–3769* ⊕*arizonachambermusic. org*) at the Leo Rich Theater in the Tucson Convention Center from October through April. They also have a music festival the first week of March. The **Arizona Opera Company** (☎*520/293–4336* ⊕*www.azopera. com*), based in Tucson, puts on five major productions each year at the Tucson Convention Center's Music Hall. The **Arizona Symphonic Winds** (⊠*Tanque Verde and Sabino Canyon Rds., Northeast* ⊕*www.azsym winds.org*) has a winter and a spring–summer schedule of performances. Many of the spring–summer performances are in Morris T. Udall Park. Performances are usually at 7 PM, but you need to arrive at least an hour early. From late February through late June, the **Tucson Pops Orchestra** (⊠*Lake Shore La. off 22nd St. between Alvernon Way and Country Club Rd., Central* ⊕*www.tucsonpops.org*) gives free concerts each Saturday evening at the De Meester Outdoor Performance Center in Reid Park. Arrive about an hour before the music starts (usually at 7 PM) to stake your claim on a viewing spot.

The **Tucson Symphony Orchestra** (⊠*443 S. Stone Ave., Downtown* ☎*520/882–8585 box office, 520/792–9155 main office* ⊕*www.tucson*

symphony.org), part of Tucson's cultural scene since 1929, holds concerts in the Music Hall in the Tucson Convention Center and at sites in the Foothills and the Northwest as well.

Tucson's small but vibrant jazz scene encompasses everything from afternoon jam sessions in the park to Sunday jazz brunches at resorts in the Foothills. Call the **Tucson Jazz Society Hot Line** (☎*520/903–1265*) for information.

POETRY

The first weekend in April brings the **Tucson Poetry Festival** (☎*520/620– 2045* ⊕*www.tucsonpoetryfestival.org*) and its four days of readings and related events, including workshops, panel discussions, and a poetry slam. Such internationally acclaimed poets as Jorie Graham and Sherman Alexie have participated.

The **University of Arizona Poetry Center** (✉*1600 E. 1st St., University* ☎*520/626–3765* ⊕*www.poetrycenter.arizona.edu*) runs a free series open to the public. Check during fall and spring semesters for info on scheduled readings.

THEATER

Arizona's state theater, the **Arizona Theatre Company** (✉*Temple of Music and Art, 330 S. Scott Ave., Downtown* ☎*520/622–2823 box office, 520/884–8210 company office* ⊕*www.aztheatreco.org*), performs classical pieces, contemporary drama, and musical comedy at the historic Temple of Music and Art from September through May. It's worth coming just to see the beautifully restored historic Spanish colonial–Moorish-style theater; ■TIP➜**dinner at the adjoining Temple Café is a tasty prelude.**

The University of Arizona's **Arizona Repertory Theatre** (✉*Speedway Blvd. and Olive St., University* ☎*520/621–1162* ⊕*www.uatheatre.org*) has performances during the academic year. **Borderlands Theater** (✉*40 W. Broadway, Downtown* ☎*520/882–7406*) presents new plays about Southwest border issues—often multicultural and bilingual—at venues throughout Tucson, usually from late June through April. Children of all ages love the clever melodramas at the **Gaslight Theatre** (✉*7010 E. Broadway Blvd., Eastside* ☎*520/886–9428 box office*), where hissing at the villain and cheering the hero are part of the audience's duty. **Invisible Theatre** (✉*1400 N. 1st Ave., Central* ☎*520/882–9721*) presents contemporary plays and musicals.

NIGHTLIFE

BARS & CLUBS

In addition to the places listed below, most of the major resorts have late spots for drinks or dancing. The Westward Look Resort's Lookout Bar, with its expansive view and classic rock band on Friday and Saturday nights, is a popular spot for dancing. The bars at Westin La Paloma, Hacienda del Sol, and Loews Ventana have live acoustic music on weekends.

BLUES & JAZZ   **Boondocks** (⊠ *3306 N. 1st Ave., Central* ☎ *520/690–0991*) is the unofficial home of the Blues Heritage Foundation, hosting local and touring singer-songwriters. A jazz combo plays Wednesday–Saturday nights on the lovely patio of **Acacia** (⊠ *4340 N. Campbell Ave., St. Philip's Plaza, Central* ☎ *520/232–0101*). **Old Pueblo Grille** (⊠ *60 N. Alvernon Way, Central* ☎ *520/326–6000*) has live jazz on Sunday nights. **Ric's Café** (⊠ *5605 E. River Rd., Northeast* ☎ *520/577–7272*) features jazz musicians in the courtyard on Friday and Saturday nights.

COUNTRY &   An excellent house band gets the crowd two-stepping on Tuesday,
WESTERN   Thursday, Friday, and Saturday nights at the **Maverick** (⊠ *6622 E. Tanque Verde Rd., Eastside* ☎ *520/298–0430*).

GAY & LESBIAN   **Ain't Nobody's Bizness** (⊠ *2900 E. Broadway Blvd., Central* ☎ *520/318–*
BARS   *4838*) is the most popular lesbian bar in town. **IBT's (It's 'Bout Time)** (⊠ *616 N. 4th Ave., University* ☎ *520/882–3053*) is Tucson's most popular gay men's bar, with a patio, rock and disco DJ music, and Sunday-night drag shows. Expect long lines on weekends.

ROCK & MORE   **Berky's** (⊠ *5769 E. Speedway Blvd., Central* ☎ *520/296–1981*) has live R&B and rock and roll every night, though mostly cover songs rather than original music. The **Cactus Moon Café** (⊠ *5470 E. Broadway Blvd., Central* ☎ *520/748–0049*), catering to a mostly yuppie crowd, offers a standard mix of Top 40, hip-hop, and modern country, often with free appetizer buffets during happy hour. The **Chicago Bar** (⊠ *5954 E. Speedway Blvd., Central* ☎ *520/748–8169*) is a good place to catch blues, reggae, and rock.

★   **Club Congress** (⊠ *Hotel Congress, 311 E. Congress St., Downtown* ☎ *520/622–8848*) is the main Friday venue for cutting-edge rock bands, with a mixed-bag crowd of alternative rockers, international travelers, and college kids. Saturday brings a more outrageous crowd dancing to an electronic beat. **El Parador** (⊠ *2744 E. Broadway, Central* ☎ *520/881–2808*) has a live salsa band Friday and Saturday nights, with dance lessons at 10 PM.

★   The **Nimbus Brewing Company** (⊠ *3850 E. 44th St., Southeast* ☎ *520/745–9175*) is the place for acoustic blues, folk, and bluegrass, not to mention good, cheap food and microbrew beer.

Plush (⊠ *340 E. 6th St., University* ☎ *520/798–1298*) hosts bands like Camp Courageous and Greyhound Soul, as well as local performers with a loyal following. You can go totally retro at the **Shelter** (⊠ *4155 E. Grant Rd., Central* ☎ *520/326–1345*), a former bomb shelter decked out in plastic 1960s kitsch, lava lamps, and JFK memorabilia, which plays Elvis videos and music by the likes of Burt Bacharach and Martin Denny.

CASINOS

After a long struggle with the state of Arizona, two Native American tribes operate casinos on their Tucson-area reservations west of the airport. They are quite unlike their distant and much grander cousins in Las Vegas and Atlantic City. Don't expect much glamour, ersatz or otherwise: these casinos are more like glorified video arcades, though you can lose money much faster. You'll be greeted by a wall of cigarette smoke (the reservation is exempt from the city's antismoking laws) and the wail of slot machines, video poker, blackjack, roulette, and craps machines. The only "live" gaming is keno, bingo, blackjack, and certain types of poker. No one under age 21 is permitted.

The Pascua Yaqui tribe's **Casino of the Sun** (✉7406 S. Camino de Oeste, off W. Valencia Rd. about 5 mi west of I-19, South ☎520/883–1700 or 800/344–9435 ⊕www.casinosun.com) has slot and video-gambling machines, high-stakes bingo, and live poker. A few miles farther west is their newer, larger facility, **Casino del Sol** (✉5655 W. Valencia, Southwest ☎520/883–1700 or 800/344–9435 ⊕www.casinodelsol.com), with live poker and blackjack, bingo, slots, and an above-average Italian restaurant. An adjacent 4,600-seat outdoor amphitheater books entertainers like Bob Dylan and James Taylor. Free shuttle buses operate from points all over Tucson; call for a schedule. The Tohono O'odham tribe operates the **Desert Diamond Casinos** (✉7350 S. Old Nogales Hwy., 1 mi south of Valencia, just west of the airport, South ✉I-19 at Pima Mine Rd. ☎520/294–7777 or 866/332–9467 ⊕www.desertdiamondcasino. com), which has an indoor concert venue, one-arm bandits, and video poker in addition to live keno, bingo, and Stud High, Texas Hold'em, Omaha, and Stud Lo poker.

SPORTS & THE OUTDOORS

BALLOONING

Three companies in Tucson offer hot-air-balloon flights from September through May, flown by FAA-certified pilots. Passengers toast with champagne on tours by **Balloon America** (✆Box 31255, Tucson 85751 ☎520/299–7744 ⊕www.balloonrideusa.com). Tours depart from the east side of Tucson. **Fleur de Tucson Balloon Tours** (✆4635 N. Caida Pl., Tucson 85718 ☎520/529–1025 ⊕www.fleurdetucson.net) has two flight options: over the Tucson Mountains and Sagauro National Park West, or over the Avra Valley.

BICYCLING

Tucson, ranked among America's top five bicycling cities by *Bicycling* magazine, has well-maintained bikeways, routes, lanes, and paths all over the city. Scenic-loop roads in both sections of Saguaro National Park offer rewarding rides for all levels of cyclists. Most bike stores in Tucson carry the monthly newsletter of the Tucson chapter of **GABA** (*[Greater Arizona Bicycling Association]* ✆Box 43273, Tucson 85733 ⊕www.bikegaba.org), which lists rated group rides. You can pick up a map of Tucson-area bike routes at the **Pima Association of Governments** (✉177 N. Church St., Suite 405, Downtown ☎520/792–1093).

Mountain bikes, comfort bikes, and road bikes can be rented by the day or week at **Fair Wheel Bikes** (✉1110 E. 6th St., University ☎520/884–9018). **Tucson Bicycles** (✉4743 E. Sunrise Dr., Foothills ☎520/577–7374) rents a selection of road and mountain bikes and organizes group rides of varying difficulty.

BIRD-WATCHING

The naturalist and illustrator Roger Tory Peterson (1908–96) considered Tucson one of the country's top birding spots, and avid "life listers"—birders who keep a list of all the birds they've sighted and identified—soon see why. In the early morning and early evening, Sabino Canyon is alive with cactus and canyon wrens, hawks, and quail. Spring and summer, when species of migrants come in from Mexico, are great hummingbird seasons. In the nearby Santa Rita Mountains and Madera Canyon, you can see elegant trogons nesting in early spring. The area also supports species usually found only in higher elevations. You can get the latest word on the bird on the 24-hour line at the **Tucson Audubon Society** (☎520/798–1005 ⊕*www. tucsonaudubon.org*); sightings of rare or interesting birds in the area are recorded regularly.

The society's **Audubon Nature Shop** (⊠*300 E. University Blvd., Suite 120, University* ☎*520/629–0510*) carries field guides, bird feeders, binoculars, and natural-history books. The **Wild Bird Store** (⊠*3526 E. Grant Rd., Central* ☎*520/322–9466*) is an excellent resource for bird-watching books, maps, and trail guides.

GOLF

For a detailed listing of the state's courses, contact the **Arizona Golf Association** (⊠*7226 N. 16th St., Phoenix 85020* ☎*602/944–3035 or 800/458–8484* ⊕*www.azgolf.org*). The **Golf Stop Inc.** (⊠*1830 S. Alvernon Way, South* ☎*520/790–0941*), a shop owned and run by two LPGA pros, can fit you with custom clubs, repair your old irons, or give you lessons. If you're planning to stay a week or more, **Tucson's Resort Golf Card** (☎*520/886–8800*), offering discounts at 13 of the area's best courses, is a good deal. Tee off after 1 PM at many of these courses, and you can shave off nearly half the green fees. Some courses also have slightly lower fees Monday through Thursday.

MUNICIPAL COURSES One of Tucson's best-kept secrets is that the city's five low-price, municipal courses are maintained to standards usually found only at the best country clubs. To reserve a tee time at one of the city's courses, call the **Tucson Parks and Recreation Department** (☎*520/791–4653 general golf information, 520/791–4336 automated tee-time reservations* ⊕*www. tucsoncitygolf.com*)at least a week in advance.

Dell Urich Golf Course (⊠*600 S. Alvernon Way, Central* ☎*520/791–4161*), adjacent to Randolph and formerly known as Randolph South, is a par-70, 18-hole course with tall trees and dramatic elevation changes ($39 to walk, $49 with a cart).

El Rio Golf Course (⊠*1400 W. Speedway Blvd., Westside* ☎*520/791–4229*) has 18 holes of tight fairways, small greens, and two lakes on fairly flat terrain ($34 to walk, $44 with a cart).

Fred Enke Golf Course (⊠*8251 E. Irvington, Eastside* ☎*520/791–2539*) is a hilly, semi-arid (less grass and more native vegetation) 18-hole course ($34 to walk, $44 with a cart). It's southeast of town.

FodorśChoice ★ **Randolph Park Golf Course–North Course** (⊠*600 S. Alvernon Way, Central* ☎*520/791–4161*), a long, scenic 18-hole course that has hosted the LPGA Tour for many years, is the flagship of Tucson's municipal courses ($39 to walk, $49 with a cart).

Silverbell Golf Course (✉ *3600 N. Silverbell Rd., Northwest* ☎ *520/791–5235*), with spacious fairways and ample greens, has an 18-hole layout along the Santa Cruz River ($30 to walk, $40 with a cart).

Arizona National Golf Club (✉ *9777 E. Sabino Greens Dr., Eastside* ☎ *520/749–3636* ⊕ *www.arizonanationalgolfclub.com*) is a gorgeous 18-hole, par-71 course ($165).

Dorado Golf Course (✉ *6601 E. Speedway Blvd., Eastside* ☎ *520/885–6751*) has an 18-hole executive course good for those who want to play just a few short rounds ($20 to walk, $29 with a cart).

Esplendor Resort & Country Club (✉ *1069 Camino Carampi, Rio Rico* ☎ *800/288–4746* ⊕ *www.esplendor-resort.com*), south of Tucson, near Nogales, was designed by Robert Trent Jones, Sr. This 18-hole course is one of Arizona's lesser-known gems ($65).

San Ignacio Golf Club (✉ *4201 S. Camino del Sol, Green Valley* ☎ *520/648–3468* ⊕ *www.irigolfgroup.com*) was designed by Arthur Hills and is a challenging 18-hole desert course ($65).

Tubac Golf Resort (✉ *1 Otero Rd., Tubac* ☎ *520/398–2021* ⊕ *www.tubacgolfresort.com*), an 18-hole course 45 minutes south of Tucson, will look familiar to you if you've seen the movie *Tin Cup* ($89).

RESORT COURSES Avid golfers check into one of Tucson's many tony resorts and head straight for the links. The resort courses listed below are open to the public but resort guests pay slightly lower greens fees. Those who don't mind getting up early to beat the heat will find some excellent golf packages at these places in the summer.

Hilton Tucson El Conquistador (✉ *10000 N. Oracle Rd., Northwest* ☎ *520/544–5000* ⊕ *www.hiltonelconquistador.com*) has 45 holes of golf in the Santa Catalina foothills with panoramic views of the city ($120).

Fodor's Choice ★ **Lodge at Ventana Canyon** (✉ *6200 N. Clubhouse La., Northeast* ☎ *520/577–1400 or 800/828–5701*) has two 18-hole Tom Fazio–designed courses ($209). Their signature hole, No. 3 on the mountain course, is a favorite of golf photographers. Guests staying up the road at Loews Ventana Resort also have privileges here.

★ **Omni Tucson National Golf Resort** (✉ *2727 W. Club Dr., Northwest* ☎ *520/575–7540* ⊕ *www.tucsonnational.com*), cohost of an annual PGA winter open, offers 27 holes and beautiful, long par 4s. The resort's orange and gold courses were designed by Robert Van Hagge and Bruce Devlin ($180).

Starr Pass Golf Resort (✉ *3645 W. Starr Pass Blvd., Westside* ☎ *520/670–0400* ⊕ *www.starrpasstucson.com*), with 18 magnificent holes in the Tucson Mountains, was developed as a Tournament Player's Course. Managed by Arnold Palmer, Starr Pass has become a favorite of visiting pros; playing its No. 15 signature hole has been likened to threading a moving needle ($185). Guests at the JW Marriott Starr Pass Resort also have privileges here.

Westin La Paloma (✉ *3800 E. Sunrise Dr., Foothills,* ☎ *520/742–6000* ⊕ *www.westinlapalomaresort.com*), in the Tucson foothills, is rated among the top resort courses by *Golf Digest*. The 27-hole layout was designed by Jack Nicklaus ($185).

HIKING

For hiking inside Tucson city limits, you can test your skills climbing trails up Sentinel Peak ("A" Mountain), but there are also hundreds of other trails in the immediate Tucson area. The Santa Catalina Mountains, Sabino Canyon, and Saguaro National Park East and West beckon hikers with waterfalls, birds, critters, and huge saguaro cacti. For hiking trails in Saguaro, *see Saguaro National Park in* this chapter.

Catalina State Park (⊠*11570 N. Oracle Rd., Northwest* ☎*520/628–5798* ⊕*www.pr.state.az.us*) is crisscrossed by hiking trails. One of them, the relatively easy, two-hour (5.5-mi round-trip) Romero Canyon Trail, leads to Romero Pools, a series of natural *tinajas,* or stone "jars," filled with water much of the year. The trailhead is on the park's entrance road, past the restrooms on the right side.

★ The Bear Canyon Trail in **Sabino Canyon** (⊠*Sabino Canyon Rd. at Sunrise Dr., Foothills* ☎*520/749–8700* ⊕*www.fs.fed.us/r3/coronado*), also known as Seven Falls Trail, is a three-hour, 7.8-mi round-trip that is moderately easy and fun, crisscrossing the stream several times on the way up the canyon. Kids enjoy the boulder-hopping and all are rewarded with pools and waterfalls as well as views at the top. The trailhead can be reached from the parking area by either taking a five-minute Bear Canyon Tram ride or walking the 1.8-mi tram route.

The local chapter of the **Sierra Club** (⊠*738 N. 5th Ave., University,* ☎*520/620–6401*) welcomes out-of-towners on weekend hikes. The **Southern Arizona Hiking Club** (☎*520/751–4513* ⊕*www.sahcinfo.org*) leads weekend hikes of varying difficulty. For hiking on your own, a good source is **Summit Hut** (⊠*5045 E. Speedway Blvd., Central* ☎*520/325–1554*), which has a collection of hiking reference materials and a friendly staff who will help you plan your trip. Packs, tents, bags, and climbing shoes can be rented here.

HORSEBACK RIDING

Colossal Cave Stables (⊠*16600 Colossal Cave Rd., Eastside* ☎*520/647–3450*) takes riders into Saguaro National Park East on one-hour or longer trail rides. Wranglers at **Corcoraque Ranch** (⊠*Mile Wide Rd., Westside* ☎*520/682–8594*) lead riders through their working cattle ranch into Saguaro National Park's west district. **Pantano Riding Stables** (⊠*4450 South Houghton Rd.East Side* ☎*520/298–8980* ⊕*http:// horsingaroundarizona.com/*) is a reliable operator offering one- and two-hour rides. **Pusch Ridge Stables** (⊠*13700 N. Oracle Rd., Northwest* ☎*520/825–1664*), adjacent to Catalina State Park, can serve up a cowboy-style breakfast on your trail ride; gentle children's horse walks, one-hour, and overnight rides are available.

RODEO

In the last week of February, Tucson hosts **Fiesta de Los Vaqueros,** the largest annual winter rodeo in the United States, a five-day extravaganza with more than 600 events and a crowd of more than 44,000 spectators a day at the **Tucson Rodeo Grounds** (✉ *4823 S. 6th Ave., South* ☎ *520/294–8896* ⊕ *www.tucsonrodeo.com*). The rodeo kicks off with a 2-mi parade of horseback riders (Western and fancy-dress Mexican *charro*), wagons, stagecoaches, and horse-drawn floats; it's touted as the largest nonmotorized parade in the world. Local schoolkids especially love the celebration—they get a two-day holiday from school. Daily seats at the rodeo vary from $8 to $14.

SHOPPING

Much of Tucson's retail activity is focused around malls, but shops with more character and some unique wares can be found in the city's open plazas: St. Philip's Plaza (River Road and Campbell Avenue), Plaza Palomino (Swan and Fort Lowell roads), Casas Adobes Plaza (Oracle and Ina roads), and La Encantada (Skyline Drive and Campbell Avenue).

The 4th Avenue neighborhood near the University of Arizona— especially 4th Avenue between 2nd and 9th streets—is fertile ground for unusual items in the artsy boutiques, galleries, and secondhand-clothing stores. Be forewarned though: you may experience aggressive panhandling here.

Hard-core bargain hunters usually head south to the Mexican border town of Nogales *(*⇨ *Southern Arizona chapter)* for jewelry, liquor, home furnishings, and leather goods. For in-town deals, the outlet stores at the Foothills Mall in northwest Tucson score high marks.

6

MALLS & SHOPPING CENTERS

★ **Casa Adobes Plaza** (✉ *Oracle and Ina Rds., southwest corner, Northwest* ⊕ *www.casasadobesplaza.com*) originally served the ranchers and orange grove owners in this once remote part of town, now the city's fastest-growing area. It's an outdoor, Mediterranean-style shopping center with a grocery store, the superb Wildflower Grill, a gelato shop, a bagelry, Starbucks, and diverse boutiques and gift shops.

Foothills Mall (✉ *7401 N. La Cholla Blvd. at Ina Rd., Northwest* ☎ *520/742–7191* ⊕ *www.shopfoothillsmall.com*) has a Barnes & Noble Superstore, a Saks Fifth Avenue outlet store, and many other outlets including Samsonite, Nike, and Adidas. A 16-screen cineplex, video arcade, and several restaurants round out the place.

Historic Broadway Village (✉ *Country Club Rd. and Broadway Blvd., Central*), Tucson's first shopping center, was built in 1939. Although small by today's standards, this outdoor complex and neighboring strip of shops houses interesting boutiques such as Zocalo for colonial Mexican furniture, Yikes! for fabulous off-the-wall toys, and Picante for Mexican clothing and crafts.

La Encantada (✉ *Skyline Dr. and Campbell Ave., Foothills* ☎ *520/299–3566*), the newest outdoor mall, has close to 50 stores (and four restaurants) decidedly aimed at affluent consumers. North, a nouvelle Italian bistro, is here, as well as trendy tenants Crate & Barrel and Pottery Barn, plus a huge gourmet grocery that also serves casual meals.

The Lost Barrio (⊠*Park Ave. and 12th St., south of Broadway, Central* ☎*No phone*) is a cluster of 10 shops in an old warehouse district; Southwestern and ethnic art, furniture, and funky gifts (both antique and modern) are specialties.

Old Town Artisans Complex (⊠*186 N. Meyer Ave., Downtown* ☎*520/623–6024*), across from the Tucson Museum of Art, has a large selection of Southwestern wares, including Native American jewelry, baskets, Mexican handicrafts, pottery, and textiles.

Park Place (⊠*5870 E. Broadway Blvd., Eastside* ☎*520/747–7575*) is a busy enclosed mall with an extensive food court, a 20-screen cineplex, and more than 120 stores, including Macy's and Borders.

Plaza Palomino (⊠*2980 N. Swan Rd., at Fort Lowell Rd., Central* ☎*520/795–1177*), an outdoor mall, has unique shops, galleries, and clothing boutiques. On Saturday, you can sample locally grown produce, baked goods, salsas, and tamales at the farmers' market. The Red Sky Cafe is also here.

St. Philip's Plaza (⊠*4280 N. Campbell Ave., at River Rd., Foothills* ☎*520/886–7485*) has more than a dozen chic boutiques arranged around a series of Spanish-style outdoor patios. The restaurants Vivace and Acacia are located here, too.

Tucson Mall (⊠*4500 N. Oracle Rd., at Wetmore Rd., Central* ☎*520/293–7330*), an indoor mall on the Westside, has Dillard's, Macy's, Mervyn's, JCPenney, and more than 200 specialty shops. For tasteful Southwestern-style T-shirts, belts, jewelry, and prickly pear candies, check out the shops on "Arizona Avenue," a section of the first floor that's devoted to regional items.

SPECIALTY SHOPS

ART GALLERIES   If you're seeking work by regional artists, you might want to drive down to Tubac, a community 45 mi south of Tucson *(⇨ Sidetrips Near Tucson). Art Life in Southern Arizona* (☎*520/797–1271* ⊕*artlifearizona. com*), published annually, lists galleries and artists statewide.

Dinnerware Contemporary Arts (⊠*210 N. 4th Ave., Downtown* ☎*520/792–4503*), a nonprofit, membership gallery, focuses on artists of Southern Arizona in various media, including painting, sculpture, digital art, and furniture.

Etherton Gallery (⊠*135 S. 6th Ave., Downtown* ☎*520/624–7370*) specializes in photography but also represents artists in other media.

Gallery Row at El Cortijo (⊠*3001 E. Skyline Dr., Foothills* ☎*520/298–0390*) is a complex of nine galleries that collectively represent regional and national artists working in all media, including Native American, Western, and contemporary painting, crafts, and jewelry. The highly regarded **Rosequist Galleries** (☎*520/577–8107*) is the oldest in town.

Obsidian Gallery (⊠*St. Philip's Plaza, 4340 N. Campbell Ave., Suite 90, Central* ☎*520/577–3598*) has exquisite glass, ceramic, and jewelry pieces.

Philabaum Contemporary Glass (⊠*St. Philip's Plaza, 4280 N. Campbell Ave., Suite 105, Foothills* ☎520/299–1939) sells magnificent hand-blown vases, artwork, table settings, and jewelry.

BOOKS The major chains like Barnes & Nobles, Borders, and Waldenbooks are all represented in Tucson, but there are also some good independents.

Antigone (⊠*411 N. 4th Ave., University* ☎520/792–3715) specializes in books by and about women and also sells creative feminist cards and T-shirts.

Barnes & Noble (⊠*5130 E. Broadway Blvd., Eastside* ☎520/512–1166 ⊠*Foothills Mall, 7325 N. La Cholla Blvd., Northwest* ☎520/742–6402) is capacious but comfortable, with a well-stocked children's section and bustling café.

★ **Bookman's** (⊠*1930 E. Grant Rd., Central* ☎520/325–5767 ⊠*3733 W. Ina Rd., Northwest* ☎520/579–0303 ⊠*6230 E. Speedway Blvd., Eastside* ☎520/748–9555) carries an eclectic selection of used and new books, music, magazines, and software in three spacious locations.

Book Stop (⊠*2504 N. Campbell Ave., Central* ☎520/326–6661) is a wonderful browsing place for used and out-of-print books.

Borders Books and Music (⊠*Park Place Mall, 5870 E. Broadway Blvd., Eastside* ☎520/584–0111 ⊠*4235 N. Oracle Rd., Northwest* ☎520/292–1331) has a vast selection of books, music, and DVDs.

Clues Unlimited (⊠*Historic Broadway Village, 3000 E. Broadway Blvd., Central* ☎520/326–8533) specializes in mysteries.

Crescent Tobacco and Newsstand (⊠*200 E. Congress St., Downtown* ☎520/622–1559 ⊠*7037 E. Tanque Verde Rd., Northeast* ☎520/296–3102) carries hundreds of daily newspapers and magazines from around the world, not to mention imported cigars and cigarettes.

Tucson's Map and Flag Center (⊠*3239 N. 1st Ave., Central* ☎520/887–4234) is the place to pick up your topographical maps and specialty guides to Arizona.

Waldenbooks (⊠*Tucson Mall, 4500 N. Oracle Rd., Central* ☎520/293–6799) is handy if you need to take a break from souvenir shopping at the mall.

CACTI **B&B Cactus Farm** (⊠*11550 E. Speedway Blvd., Eastside* ☎520/721–4687), which you'll pass en route to Saguaro National Park East, has a huge selection of cacti and succulents. They ship anywhere in the country.

★ **Native Seeds/Search** (⊠*526 N. 4th Ave., University* ☎520/622–5561), dedicated to preserving native crops and traditional farming methods, sells 350 kinds of seeds as well as Native American crafts.

JEWELRY **Abbott Taylor** (⊠*6383 E. Grant Rd., Eastside* ☎520/745–5080) creates custom designs in diamonds and other precious stones.

Beth Friedman (⊠*Joesler Village, 1865 E. River Rd., Suite 121, Foothills* ☎520/577–6858) sells unsurpassed designs in silver and semiprecious stones. The store also carries an eclectic selection of ladies' apparel, fine art, and home furnishings.

Patania's Originals (⊠*3000 E. Broadway Blvd., Central* ☎*520/795–0086*) is one of the best-known jewelers in the Southwest. The Patania family has been creating unique designs in silver, gold, and platinum here and in Santa Fe for three generations. The shop is 1 mi east of the El Con mall.

Turquoise Door (⊠*St. Philip's Plaza, 4340 N. Campbell Ave., Foothills* ☎*520/299–7787*) creates innovative jewelry that amounts to a modern take on classic Southwestern designs.

Antigua de Mexico (⊠*3235 W. Orange Grove Rd., Northwest* ☎*520/742–7114*) sells well-made furniture and crafts that you are not likely to find elsewhere in town.

Del Sol (⊠*435 N. 4th Ave., University* ☎*520/628–8765*) specializes in Mexican folk art, jewelry, and Southwest-style clothing.

NATIVE
AMERICAN
ARTS & CRAFTS
San Xavier Plaza, across from San Xavier mission and also part of the Tohono O'odham reservation, is a good place to find vendors and stores selling the work of this and other area tribes. Other shops are listed below.

Bahti Indian Arts (⊠*St. Philip's Plaza, 4300 N. Campbell Ave., Foothills* ☎*520/577–0290*) is owned and run by Mark Bahti, whose father, Tom, literally wrote the book on Native American art, including an early definitive work on katsinas. The store sells high-quality jewelry, pottery, rugs, art, and more.

Grey Dog Trading Company (⊠*Plaza Palomino, 2970 N. Swan Rd., Central* ☎*520/881–6888*) has an ample selection of jewelry, katsinas, weaving, pottery, and Zuni fetishes.

Kaibab Courtyard Shops (⊠*2837 N. Campbell Ave., Central* ☎*520/795–6905*) sells traditional Native American arts, along with Mexican imports and Nambé dinnerware.

Silverbell Trading (⊠*Casas Adobes Plaza, 7007 N. Oracle Rd., Northwest* ☎*520/797–6852*) carries the work of local and regional artists.

WESTERN
WEAR
Tucsonans who wear Western gear keep it simple for the most part— jeans, a Western shirt, maybe boots. This ain't Santa Fe.

Arizona Hatters (⊠*3600 N. 1st Ave., Central* ☎*520/292–1320*) can fit you for that Stetson you've always wanted.

Corral Western Wear (⊠*4525 E. Broadway Blvd., Eastside* ☎*520/322–6001*) sells shirts, hats, belts, jewelry, and boots, catering to both urban and authentic cowboys and cowgirls.

Stewart Boot Manufacturing (⊠*30 W. 28th St., South* ☎*520/622–2706*) has been making handmade leather boots since the 1940s.

Western Warehouse (⊠*3719 N. Oracle Rd., Northwest* ☎*520/293–1808* ⊠*6701 E. Broadway Blvd., Eastside* ☎*520/885–4385*) is the place if you want to go where native Tucsonans shop for their everyday Western duds.

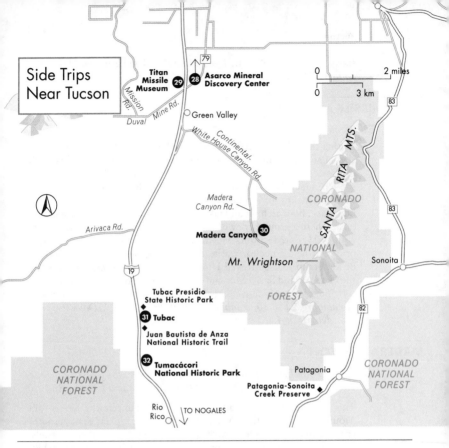

Titan
Missile **29** **28** Asarco Mineral
Museum Discovery Center

79

Mission Mine Rd.

Duval

Green Valley

Continental-
White House Canyon Rd.

Madera
Canyon Rd.

Arivaca Rd.

Madera Canyon **30**

Mt. Wrightson

19

Tubac Presidio
State Historic Park

31 Tubac

Juan Bautista de Anza
National Historic Trail

32 Tumacácori
National Historic Park

Rio
Rico

TO NOGALES

SANTA RITA MTS.

CORONADO

NATIONAL

FOREST

Sonoita

Patagonia

Patagonia-Sonoita
Creek Preserve

CORONADO
NATIONAL
FOREST

CORONADO
NATIONAL
FOREST

0   2 miles

0   3 km

83

83

82

SIDE TRIPS NEAR TUCSON

Interstate 19 heads south from Tucson to Tubac, carrying with it history buffs, bird-watchers, hikers, art enthusiasts, duffers, and shoppers.
The road roughly follows the Camino Real (King's Road), which the
conquistadors and missionaries traveled from Mexico up to what was
once the northernmost portion of New Spain.

THE ASARCO MINERAL DISCOVERY CENTER

28 *15 mi south of Tucson off I–19.*

Operated by the American Smelting and Refining Co. (ASARCO), this
facility is designed to elucidate the importance of mining to everyday
life. Exhibits include a walk-through model of an ore crusher, video
stations that explain refining processes, and a film on extraction of
minerals from the earth. The big draw, though, is the yawning open pit
of the Mission Mine, some 2 mi long and 1¾ mi wide because so much
earth has to be torn up to extract the 1% that is copper. It's impressive, but doesn't bolster the case the center tries to make about how
environmentally conscious mining has become. Tours of the pit, which
take about one hour, leave the center on the half hour; the last one

starts at 3:30. ⌧*1421 W. Pima Mine Rd.* ⊕*www.mineraldiscovery. com* ☎*520/625–0879* ⌧*$6* ⊙*Tues.–Sat. 9–5.*

TITAN MISSILE MUSEUM

㉙ *25 mi south of Tucson, off I–19.*

During the cold war, Tucson was ringed by 18 of the 54 Titan II missiles that existed in the United States. After the SALT II treaty with the Soviet Union was signed in 1979, this was the only missile-launch site left intact. Now a National Historic Landmark, the Titan Missile Museum makes for a sobering visit. Guided tours, running every half hour, last about an hour and take you down 55 steps into the command post, where a ground crew of four lived and waited. Among the sights is the 103-foot, 165-ton, two-stage liquid-fuel rocket. Now empty, it originally held a nuclear warhead with 214 times the explosive power of the bomb that destroyed Hiroshima. This museum is operated by the Pima Air and Space Museum and combination tickets are available. ⌧*1580 W. Duval Mine Rd., I–19, Exit 69* ☎*520/625–7736* ⊕*www. pimaair.org* ⌧*$8.50; combination with PASM $18* ⊙*Daily 9–5; last tour departs at 4.*

MADERA CANYON

㉚ *61½ mi southeast of Tucson; Exit 63 off I–19, then east on White House Canyon Rd. for 12½ mi (it turns into Madera Canyon Rd.)*

This is where the Coronado National Forest meets the Santa Rita Mountains—among them Mount Wrightson, the highest peak in southern Arizona, at 9,453 feet. With approximately 200 mi of scenic trails, the Madera Canyon recreation area is a favorite destination for hikers. Higher elevations and thick pine cover make it especially popular with Tucsonans looking to escape the summer heat. Trails vary from a steep trek up Mount Baldy to a paved, wheelchair-accessible path. Birders flock here year-round; about 400 avian species have been spotted in the area. The small, volunteer-run visitor center is open only on weekends. ⌧*Madera Canyon Rd., Madera Canyon* ☎*520/281–2296 Nogales Ranger District office* ⊕*www.fs.fed.us/r3/coronado* ⌧*Donation requested* ⊙*Daily.*

TUBAC

★ **㉛** *45 mi south of Tucson at Exit 40 off I–19.*

Established in 1726, Tubac is the site of the first European settlement in Arizona. A year after the Pima Indian uprising in 1751, a military garrison was established here to protect Spanish settlers, missionaries, and peaceful Native American converts of the nearby Tumacácori Mission. It was from here that Juan Bautista de Anza led 240 colonists across the desert—the expedition resulted in the founding of San Francisco in 1776. In 1860 Tubac was the largest town in Arizona. Today, the quiet little town is a popular art colony. More than 80 shops sell such crafts as carved wooden furniture, hand-thrown pottery, delicately painted tiles, and silk-screen fabrics (many shops are closed on Monday). You can also find Mexican pottery and trinkets without having to cross the border. The annual **Tubac Festival of the Arts** has been held in February for more than 30 years.

There's an archaeological display of portions of the original 1752 fort at the **Tubac Presidio State Historic Park and Museum** in the center of town. In addition to the visitor center and the adjoining museum, which has detailed exhibits on the history of the early colony, the park includes Tubac's 1885 schoolhouse. ⊠*Presidio Dr.* ☎*520/398–2252* ⊕*www. pr.state.az.us* ☞*$3* ☉*Daily 8–5.*

WHERE TO STAY & EAT

¢ ✕ **Tubac Deli & Coffee Co.** Smack in the middle of Tubac village, this pleasant little eatery serves generous sandwiches, pizza, salads, and soups—as well as cappuccinos and pastries—every day until 8 PM. ⊠*6 Plaza Rd.* ☎*520/398-3330* ▤*No credit cards.*

> ### WORD OF MOUTH
>
> "Tubac is one of our very favorite places and I would definitely recommend staying there…That area is gorgeous."
>
> –desertduds

$$ ✕▦ **Amado Territory Inn and Café.** Although this quiet, friendly B&B is directly off the highway frontage road, it feels worlds away. The inn resembles a late-19th-century ranch house, but its soaring ceiling and contemporary Southwestern art make the interior distinctly modern. Rooms are furnished with handcrafted Mexican pieces, and some have a view of the garden and the Santa Rita Mountains. Breakfast is included (try the huevos rancheros); next door, the Amado Café serves savory Greek-style pasta, chicken, and fish specialties for lunch and dinner. ⊠*3001 E. Frontage Rd., off Exit 48 of I–19* ✒*Box 81, Amado 85645* ☎*520/398–8684 or 888/398–8684* ▤*520/398–8186* ⊕*www.amado-territory-inn.com* ☞*9 rooms, 2 suites* ☖*In-room: Wi-Fi, no phone, no TV. In-hotel: restaurant, no-smoking rooms* ▤*MC, V* ⏝*BP* ☉*Café closed Mon., no dinner Sun.*

$$ ▦ **Tubac Country Inn.** Down the lane from the shops and eateries of Tubac village is this charming two-story inn. Tastefully decorated in contemporary Southwest style, all rooms and suites have kitchenettes, and the common outdoor space is a tranquil desert flower garden with willow chairs and a Mexican fireplace. Each morning a breakfast basket of muffins, cheeses, fruits, and juice is brought to your door. ⊠*13 Burruel St., Tubac 85646* ☎*520/398–3178* ▤*520/398–3178* ⊕*www.tubaccountryinn.com* ☞*3 rooms, 2 suites* ☖*In-room: no phone, kitchen, refrigerator, Wi-Fi. In-hotel: no-smoking rooms* ▤*AE, D, MC, V* ⏝*BP.*

EN ROUTE You can tread the same road as the conquistadors: the first 4½ mi of the **Juan Bautista de Anza National Historic Trail** (⊕*www.nps.gov/juba*) from Tumacácori to Tubac were dedicated in 1992. You'll have to cross the Santa Cruz River (which is usually low) three times to complete the hike, and the path is rather sandy, but it's a pleasant journey along the tree-shaded banks of the river.

TUMACÁCORI NATIONAL HISTORIC PARK

㉜ *3 mi south of Tubac, Exit 29 off I–19.*

The site where Tumacácori National Historic Park now stands was visited by missionary Father Eusebio Francisco Kino in 1691, but the Jesuits didn't build a church here until 1751. You can still see some ruins of this simple structure, but the main attraction is the mission of San José de Tumacácori, built by the Franciscans around 1799–1803. A combination of circumstances—Apache attacks, a bad winter, and Mexico's withdrawal of funds and priests—caused the remaining inhabitants to flee in 1848. Persistent rumors of wealth left behind by both the Franciscans and the Jesuits led treasure seekers to pillage the site; it still bears those scars. The site was finally protected in 1908, when it became a national monument.

Information about the mission and the Anza trail is available at the visitor center, and guided tours are offered daily (more in winter than in summer). A small museum displays some of the mission's artifacts, and sometimes fresh tortillas are made on a wood-fire stove in the courtyard. In addition to a Christmas Eve celebration, costumed historical high masses are held at Tumacácori in spring and fall. An annual fiesta the first weekend of December has arts and crafts and food booths. ⊠*I–19, Exit 29, Tumacácori* ☎*520/398–2341* ⊕*www.nps.gov/tuma* ☞*$3* ☉*Daily 8–5.*

WHERE TO STAY

$$ 🏨 **Esplendor Resort.** This hotel and conference center has a historic, rather than hokey, Western feel, with a working blacksmith on-site and an elongated bar reminiscent of a Tombstone saloon. Some rooms continue the theme with cowhide headboards, tepee bed canopies, or whimsical bordello furnishings. Horseback riding is a popular activity here, but most guests come for the excellent golf course, the splendid views, and the isolation. Nogales, Mexico, is a short drive south. ⊠*1069 Camino Caralampi, off I–19 at Rio Rico Rd. (Exit 17), Rio Rico 85648* ☎*520/281–1901 or 800/288–4746* 🖷*520/281–7132* ⊕*www.esplendor-resort.com* ➾*166 rooms, 14 suites* ♿*In-room: refrigerator, Wi-Fi. In-hotel: restaurant, bar, golf course, tennis courts, pool, gym, laundry service, no-smoking rooms* ▤*AE, D, MC, V.*

TUCSON ESSENTIALS

To research prices, get advice from other travelers, and book travel arrangements, visit ⊕*www.fodors.com.*

TRANSPORTATION

BY AIR

Tucson International Airport is 8½ mi south of downtown, west of I–10 off the Valencia exit.

Many hotels provide courtesy airport shuttle service; inquire when making reservations.

Arizona Stagecoach carries groups and individuals between the airport and all parts of Tucson and Green Valley, for $9 to $38, depending on the location. If you're traveling light and aren't in a hurry, you can take a city Sun Tran bus to central Tucson. Bus 11, which leaves every half hour from a stop at the left of the lower level as you come out of the terminal, goes north on Alvernon Way, and you can transfer to most of the east–west bus lines from this main north–south road; ask the bus driver which one would take you closest to the location you need. You can also transfer to several lines from Bus 6, which leaves less frequently from the same airport location and heads to the Roy Laos center at the south of town.

Contacts Arizona Stagecoach (☏520/889–1000). **Sun Tran** (☏520/792–9222). **Tucson International Airport (TUS)** (☏520/573–8000 ⊕www.tucsonairport.org).

BY BUS

Within the city limits, public transportation, which is geared primarily to commuters, is available through Sun Tran, Tucson's bus system. On weekdays, bus service starts around 5 AM; some lines operate until 10 PM, but most go only until 7 or 8 PM, and weekend service is limited. A one-way ride costs $1; transfers are free, but be sure to request them when you pay your fare, for which exact change is required. An all-day pass costs $2. Those with valid Medicare cards can ride for 40¢. Call for information on Sun Tran bus routes.

Buses to Los Angeles, El Paso, Phoenix, Flagstaff, Douglas, and Nogales (Arizona) depart and arrive regularly from Tucson's Greyhound Lines terminal. For travel to Phoenix, Arizona Shuttle Service, Inc., runs express service from three locations in Tucson every hour on the hour, 4 AM to 9 PM every day; the trip takes about 2¼ hours. One-way fare is $24. Call 24 hours in advance for reservations.

Information Arizona Shuttle Service, Inc. (☏520/795–6771). **Greyhound Lines terminal** (✉2 S. 4th Ave., at E. Broadway Blvd., Downtown ☏520/792–3475 or 800/229–9424 ⊕www.greyhound.com). **Sun Tran** (☏520/792–9222).

BY CAR

You'll need a car to get around Tucson and the surrounding area and it makes sense to rent at the airport; all the major car-rental agencies are represented. Driving time from the airport to the center of town varies, but it's usually less than a half hour; add 15 minutes to any destination during rush hours (7:30 AM–9 AM and 4:30 PM–6 PM). Parking is not a problem in most parts of town, except near the university, where there are several pay lots.

If you haven't rented a car at the Tucson International Airport, or if you want to save the 10% "airport concession fee" the airport imposes on renters there, several car-rental agencies have pick-up and drop-off locations in the central, northwest, and east areas of town. Carefree Rent-a-Car, a local company, rents reliable used cars at good rates. If you think you might be interested in driving farther into Mexico than Nogales (where you can park on the U.S. side of the border), check in advance to make sure that the rental company will allow this and that you are covered on your rental-insurance policy: many rental-insurance agreements do not cover accidents or thefts that occur outside the United States.

From Phoenix, 111 mi northwest, I–10 east is the road that will take you to Tucson. Also a major north–south traffic artery along the west side of town, I–10 has well-marked exits all along the route. At Casa Grande, 70 mi north of Tucson, I–8 connects with I–10, bringing travelers into the area from Yuma and San Diego. From Nogales, 63 mi south on the Mexican border, take I–19 into Tucson.

Information Carefree Rent-a-Car (☎ *520/790–2655*).

BY TAXI

Taxi rates vary widely since they're unregulated in Arizona. It's always wise to inquire about the cost of a trip before getting into a cab. It should be about $24 from the airport to central Tucson. Two of the more reliable Tucson cab companies are Allstate Taxi and Yellow Cab, which also operates Fiesta Taxi, whose drivers speak English and Spanish.

Information Allstate Taxi (☎ *520/798–1111*). **Fiesta Taxi** (☎ *520/622–7777*). **Yellow Cab** (☎ *520/624–6611*).

BY TRAIN

Amtrak serves the city with westbound and eastbound trains six times a week.

Information Amtrak (✉ *400 E. Toole Ave., Downtown* ☎ *520/623–4442 or 800/872–7245* ⊕ *www.amtrak.com*).

CONTACTS & RESOURCES

EMERGENCIES

Hospitals Columbia Northwest Medical Center (✉ *6200 N. La Cholla Blvd., Northwest* ☎ *520/742–9000*). **St. Joseph's Hospital** (✉ *350 N. Wilmot Rd., East-side* ☎ *520/873–3000*). **Tucson Medical Center** (✉ *5301 E. Grant Rd., Central* ☎ *520/327–5461*). **University Medical Center** (✉ *1501 N. Campbell Ave., University* ☎ *520/694–0111*); a teaching hospital with a first-rate trauma center.

INTERNET

INTERNET CAFÉS   It's not hard to find Internet access in Tucson; most hotels have it, but if you're out and about, there are Internet cafés around town as well, especially around the university.

For travelers who left home without their computer, Coffee Exchange rents computers for $3 per hour and includes dial-up Internet service. The Epic Café has free Wi-Fi if you have a laptop.

Coffee Exchange (✉ *2443 N. Campbell Ave., University* ☎ *520/327–6783* ⊕ *www.coffeexchange.com*). **Epic Café** (✉ *745 N. 4th Ave., University* ☎ *520/624–6844*).

TOUR OPTIONS

ADVENTURE & ECOTOURS
Sunshine Jeep Tours and Trail Dust Adventures arrange trips into the Sonoran Desert outside Tucson in open-air, four-wheel-drive vehicles. Baja's Frontier Tours explores the natural history of Tucson and the surrounding area.

BIRDING TOURS
Several companies offer birding tours in the Tucson area. Borderland Tours leads bird-watching tours in Arizona and all over the world. Wings, a Tucson-based company, leads ornithological expeditions locally and worldwide.

MISSION TOURS
In the spring and fall, those interested in visiting the area's historic missions can contact Kino Mission Tours, which has professional historians and bilingual guides on staff.

ORIENTATION TOURS
Great Western Tours takes individuals and groups to such popular sights as Old Tucson, Sabino Canyon, and the Arizona–Sonora Desert Museum; in-depth tours of the city and its neighborhoods are also available. Tour operators are on limited schedules (or close altogether) in summer.

WALKING TOURS
The friendly, knowledgeable docents of the Arizona Historical Society conduct walking tours of the downtown historic districts (departing from the Sosa-Carillo-Fremont House) every Saturday at 10 from November through mid-April, for $10.

Contacts **Arizona Historical Society** (☎ *520/622–0956*). **Baja's Frontier Tours** (☎ *520/887–2340 or 888/297–2508* ⊕ *www.bajasfrontiertours.com*). **Borderland Tours** (✉ *2550 W. Calle Padilla, Northwest, Tucson 85745* ☎ *520/882–7650 or 800/525–7753* ⊕ *www.borderland-tours.com*). **Great Western Tours** (☎ *520/572–1660* ⊕ *www.gwtours.net*). **Kino Mission Tours** (☎ *520/628–1269*). **Sunshine Jeep Tours** (☎ *520/742–1943* ⊕ *www.sunshinejeeptours.com*). **Trail Dust Adventures** (☎ *520/747–0323* ⊕ *www.traildustadventures.com*). **Wings** (✉ *1643 N. Alvernon Way, Suite 105, Central, Tucson 85712* ☎ *520/320–9868* ⊕ *www.wingsbirds.com*).

VISITOR INFORMATION

Contacts **Metropolitan Tucson Convention and Visitors Bureau** (☎ *520/624–1817 or 800/638–8350* ⊕ *www.visittucson.org*).

Southern Arizona

Cowboy gravestone in historic Boot Hill Graveyard. Tombstone, America's gunfight capital.

HERE
LIES
Lester Moore
FOUR SLUGS
FROM A 44
NO LES
NO MORE

WORD OF MOUTH

"We spent a week in Tucson and drove to Bisbee and Tombstone for a day...one of those times where the drive was as much a pleasure as the destination. We toured the mine, ate at the Bisbee Grille and walked around, then drove back to Tombstone...It's very touristy but that's OK. (Get it, OK, like corral.) I bought a nice pair of Navajo earrings at the Cochise Trading Post; seemed like the best place for quality and value."

—elizabeth_reed

WELCOME TO SOUTHERN ARIZONA

Chiricahua hiker

TOP REASONS TO GO

★ **Tour Kartchner Caverns:** The underground world of a living, "wet" cave system is a rare and wonderful sensory experience. You'll see a multicolor limestone kingdom and probably feel "cave kiss" droplets grace your head; just *don't touch anything.*

★ **Hike in the Chiricahuas:** Stunning "upside-down" rock formations, flourishing wildlife, and relatively easy trails make for great hiking in this unspoiled region. The 3.4-mi Echo Canyon Loop Trail is a winner.

★ **Explore Bisbee:** Board the Queen Mine Train and venture into the life of a copper miner at the turn of the last century. Afterward, check out the narrow, hilly town's Victorian houses and thriving shops.

★ **Bargain hunt in Nogales, Mexico:** Shop for glassware, silver, leather, and pottery—and bargain for 30% to 50% off the marked price. Park on the Arizona side and walk across the border to enjoy a different culture and spicy Sonoranstyle Mexican food.

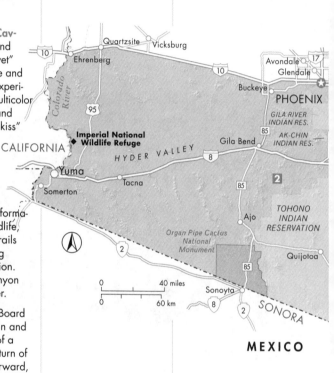

Organ-Pipe cactus

1 Southeast Arizona. Old West history, colorful limestone caverns, bizarre hoodoo formations, sweeping "Sky Islands," Arizona's wine country, rolling grasslands, a world-renowned birding paradise, and rustic ranch retreats create a perfect mix of historical adventure and outdoor recreation.

Bisbee

GETTING ORIENTED

Southern Arizona ranges from the searing deserts surrounding Organ Pipe Cactus National Monument and the town of Yuma in the southwest to the soaring "Sky Islands" and rolling grasslands in the southeast. Towns are few and far between in the southwestern corner of the state where the desert and dry climate rule. In stark contrast, the varied terrain in the southeastern region ranges from pine-forested mountains and cool canyons to desert grasslands and winding river valleys. A complex network of highways links the many communities situated in this part of the state, where the next town or attraction is just over the hill, making the decision on which way you want to go next the hardest part of traveling.

7

Map labels:

Scottsdale
Tempe
Mesa
Chandler
10
Casa Grande
Coolidge
Eloy
79
Catalina
10
Saguaro National Monument West
Oro Valley
Tucson
Saguaro National Monument East
Willcox
191
10
Sells 86
SAN XAVIER INDIAN RES.
South Tucson
Benson
Kit Peak National Observatory
Green Valley
Kartchner Caverns State Park
1
Chiricahua National Monument
286
19
Tombstone
Sasabe
Patagonia
82 Huachuca City
80
McNeal 80
Nogales
Coronado Nat'l Mon.
Sierra Vista
Bisbee
Douglas
Nogales
Agua Prieta 2
15
2
17
NEW MEXICO

2 Southwest Arizona.
The historical Yuma Territorial Prison, Yuma Crossing Historic Park, national wildlife refuges, Colorado River recreation, and Organ Pipe Cactus National Monument keep visitors busy in this remote desert region.

SOUTHERN ARIZONA PLANNER

Getting Here & Around

Tucson is the major starting point for exploring the southeast corner of the state but those arriving by air can also land in Sierra Vista, which makes a convenient hub for travels to Bisbee and Tombstone to the east, Benson and Kartchner Caverns to the north, Sonoita and Patagonia to the west, and Nogales to the south. Yuma's remote location on the California-Arizona border makes it a destination in itself, and while it can be reached by a lengthy drive from Tucson, it's most easily accessed through Yuma International Airport.

The best way to explore southeastern Arizona is on a leisurely road trip. The intimate network of highways in the San Pedro Valley provides looping access to the many scenic vistas and Old West communities, which makes the drive an integral part of the adventure. In stark contrast, a drive through the southwestern portion of the state is filled with long stretches of desert broken infrequently with tiny towns and intermittent gas stations. If you're heading west, pack a lunch, a few games, and plenty of music for entertainment along the way.

Making the Most of Your Time

The diverse geography of the region and the driving distances between sights require that you strategize when planning your trip. With Tucson as a starting point, the rolling hills and grasslands of Sonoita and Patagonia are little more than an hour away, as are the underground marvels in Kartchner Caverns (to the southeast) and the starry skies above Kitt Peak Observatory (to the southwest). You can explore the Old West of Tombstone, Bisbee, and the surrounding ghost towns in one day, or more leisurely in two. If you're heading to the cactus-studded hillsides at Organ Pipe Cactus National Monument, leave yourself at least a full day to explore the monument and the nearby town of Ajo. A trek through the stunning Chiricahua rock formations calls for an overnight stay, since the area is a 2½-hour drive southeast of Tucson.

What to Do and Where to Do It

Recreation in Cochise County centers on historic and natural treasures. History buffs can walk the streets of the Old West in Tombstone, revisit the infamous shootout at the OK Corral, and peek into the "birdcages" of a historic brothel. For a look at the mineral wealth that built Bisbee, take a tour of the Copper Queen Mine and visit the historic sights in this two-canyon town. Natural beauty and some of the best birding in the world draw flocks of visitors to southeastern Arizona's "Sky Islands," Coronado National Forest, and Chiricahua National Monument. Military might takes center stage at the remote ruins found at the Fort Bowie National Historic Site and at the active outpost of historic Fort Huachuca. However, in the southwestern portion of the state the major sights are few and far between. Organ Pipe Cactus National Monument is worth the trip if you have a day to spare. If you're out this way, you may also want to visit the revitalized downtown district and historic highlights in Yuma.

When to Go

As you might expect, the desert areas are popular in winter and the cooler mountain areas are more heavily visited in summer. Southern Arizona has developed seasonal travel, causing area hotels to adopt high-season (winter and spring) and low-season (summer and early fall) prices. In general, however, prices tend to be lower here than in the north. If you're seeking outdoor adventure, spring and fall are the best times to visit this part of the state. The region is in full bloom by late March and early April, and spring and fall are the peak of birding season.

Local Food & Lodging

There are plenty of chain hotels and major motels found throughout the southern region of Arizona, but why settle for boring basics in this beautiful and historic corner of the state? For the best experience, seek out an old-fashioned room in a historic hotel, a rustic casita at a working cattle ranch, or a spacious suite in a stunning bed-and-breakfast. There are a few scattered dude ranches found in the sweeping grasslands to the south, but not nearly as many as you'll find closer to metropolitan Tucson. It's usually not hard to find a room any time of the year, but keep in mind that prices tend to go up in high season (winter and spring) and down in low season (summer through early fall).

In southern Arizona, cowboy fare is more common than haute cuisine. There are exceptions to the rule, though, especially in the wine-growing area of Sonoita and in the trendy town of Bisbee, both popular for weekend outings from Tucson. And, as one would expect, Mexican food dominates the menus on both sides of the border.

Festivals to Plan a Trip Around

For the best of the West, October is the month for travel to southeastern Arizona.

The Rex Allen Days, the first weekend in October, in Willcox, are a wickedly fun event featuring a rodeo and Western music and dance.

Helldorado Days are the third weekend of October, in Tombstone: history comes alive with gunfights in the streets, a parade, and an 1880s fashion show.

The Cochise Cowboy Poetry and Music Gathering, in early February in Sierra Vista, showcases Western culture, history and folklore.

Wings Over Willcox, in mid-January, is a birding extravaganza highlighted by the morning flights of thousands of wintering sandhill cranes lifting off from the Willcox Playa.

What It Costs

	¢	$	$$	$$$	$$$$
Restaurants	under $8	$8–$12	$13–$20	$21–$30	over $30
Hotels	under $70	$70–$120	$121–$175	$176–$250	over $250

Restaurant prices are per person for a main course at dinner. Hotel prices are for a standard double in high season, excluding taxes and service charges.

Updated by
Carrie Miner

SOUTHERN ARIZONA CAN DO LITTLE to escape its cliché-ridden image as a landscape of cow skulls, tumbleweed, dried-up riverbeds, and mother lodes—but it doesn't need to. The area that evokes such American dime-novel notions as Indian wars, vast land grants, and savage shoot-'em-ups is not simply another part of the Wild West drunk on romanticized images of its former self; local farmers and ranchers here evoke the self-sufficiency and ruggedness of their pioneer ancestors and revel in the area's rowdy past. Abandoned mining towns and sleepy Western hamlets dot a lonely landscape of rugged rock formations, deep pine forests, dense mountain ranges, and scrubby grasslands.

South of Sierra Vista, just above the Mexican border, a stone marker commemorates the spot where the first Europeans set foot in what is now the United States. In 1540, 80 years before the pilgrims landed at Plymouth Rock, Spanish conquistador Don Francisco Vásquez de Coronado led one of Spain's largest expeditions from Mexico along the fertile San Pedro River valley, where the little towns of Benson and St. David are found today. They had come north to seek the legendary Seven Cities of Cíbola, where Native American pueblos were rumored to have doors of polished turquoise and streets of solid gold. The wealth of the region, however, lay in its rich veins of copper and silver, not tapped until more than 300 years after the Spanish marched on in disappointment. Once word of this cache spread, these parts of the West quickly became much wilder: fortune seekers who rushed to the region came face-to-face with the Chiricahua Apaches, led by Cochise and Geronimo, while Indian warriors battled encroaching settlers and the U.S. Cavalry sent to protect them.

Although the search for mineral booty in southeastern Arizona is more notorious, the western side of the state wasn't untouched by the rage to plunder. The leaching plant built by the New Cornelia Copper Company in 1917 transformed the sleepy desert community of Ajo into one of the most important mining districts in the state. Interest in going for the gold in California gave rise to the town of Yuma: the Colorado River had to be crossed to get to the West Coast, and Fort Yuma was established in part to protect the Anglo ferry business at a good fording point of the river from Indian competitors. The Yuma tribe lost that battle, but another group of Native Americans, the Tohono O'odham, fared better in this part of the state. Known for a long time as the Papago—or "bean eaters"—they were deeded a large portion of their ancestral homeland by the U.S. Bureau of Indian Affairs.

SOUTHEAST ARIZONA

From the rugged mountain forests to the desert grasslands of Sierra Vista, the southeast corner of Arizona is one of the state's most scenic regions. Much of this area is part of Cochise County, named in 1881 in honor of the chief of the Chiricahua Apache. Cochise waged war against troops and settlers for 11 years, and was respected by Indian and non-Indian alike for his integrity and leadership. Today Cochise County is dotted with small towns, many of them smaller—and

BIRDS OF A FEATHER

Southern Arizona is one of the best areas for bird-watching in the United States; nearly 500 species have been spotted here. To the east, birders flock to the Patagonia-Sonoita Creek and Ramsey Canyon preserves, the San Pedro Riparian National Conservation Area, the ponds and dry lake beds south of Willcox, and the Portal-Cave Creek area in the Chiricahua Mountains near the New Mexico border. To the west, the Buenos Aires and Imperial national wildlife refuges are among the many places famed for their abundance of avian visitors. All and all, more than a quarter of the birds found in North America nest in the rich habitats provided by the secluded canyons and diverse microclimates of southern Arizona's "Sky Islands." Some of the most coveted avian species spotted in this birder's paradise include painted redstarts, elegant trogons, violet-crowned hummingbirds,

northern goshawk and sulphur-bellied flycatchers.

Nearby, Sierra Vista holds the birding claim to fame as the "Hummingbird Capital of the United States." The proliferation of the colorful, winged wonders (14 species in all) is the focus of the Southwest Wings Birding and Nature Festival, held in August. It's even possible to get up close and personal with these tiny birds by participating with Nature Conservancy researchers in weighing and banding the colorful critters. For more information on birding sites in the area, send for a Southeastern Arizona Birding Trail Guide from the Southeastern Arizona Birding Observatory (☎ 520/432–1388 ⊕ www.sabo. org) or pick up a copy at the Tucson Audubon Nature Shop (✉ 300 E. University Blvd., #120 ☎ 520/629–0510 ⊕ www.tucsonaudubon.org).

tamer—than they were in their heyday. Cochise County encompasses six, and part of the seventh, of the 12 mountain ranges that compose the 1.7-million-acre Coronado National Forest.

In the valleys between southeastern Arizona's jagged mountain ranges you'll discover the 19th-century charm of Bisbee—Queen of the Copper Camps. You can explore the eerie hoodoos and spires of Chiricahua National Monument and walk in the footsteps of the legendary Apaches, who valiantly stood against the U.S. Army until Geronimo's final surrender in 1886. This is also where you can travel through the grassy plains surrounding Sonoita and Elgin—the heart of Arizona's wine country.

A trip to this historically and ecologically important corner of the state will also take you to Fort Huachuca, the oldest continuously operating military installation in the Southwest; to southeastern Arizona's "sky islands," the lush microclimates in the Huachuca and Chiricahua Mountains where jaguars roam and migratory tropical birds flit through the canopy; and to historic mining and military towns, the tenacious survivors of the Old West—including Bisbee, Sierra Vista, and Tombstone.

TOMBSTONE

❶ *28 mi northeast of Sierra Vista via AZ 90, 24 mi south of Benson via AZ 80.*

When prospector Ed Schieffelin headed out in 1877 to seek his fortune along the arid washes of San Pedro Valley, a patrolling soldier warned that all he'd find was his tombstone. Against all odds, his luck held out: he evaded bands of hostile Apaches, braved the harsh desert terrain, and eventually stumbled across a ledge of silver ore. The town of Tombstone was named after the soldier's offhand comment.

The rich silver lodes from the area's mines attracted a wide mix of fortune seekers ranging from prospectors to prostitutes and gamblers to gunmen. But as the riches continued to pour in, wealthy citizens began importing the best entertainment and culture that silver could purchase. Even though saloons and gambling halls made up two out of every three businesses on Allen Street, the town also claimed the Cochise County seat, a cultural center, and fancy French restaurants. By the early 1880s, the notorious boomtown was touted as the most cultivated city west of the Mississippi.

In 1881, a shootout between the Earp brothers and the Clanton gang ended with three of the "cowboys" (Billy Clanton and Tom and Frank McLaury) dead and two of the Earps (Virgil and Morgan) and Doc Holliday wounded. The infamous "Gunfight at the OK Corral" and the ensuing feud between the Earp brothers and the Clanton gang firmly cemented Tombstone's place in the Wild West—even though the actual course of events is still debated by historians.

All in all, Tombstone's heyday only lasted a decade, but the colorful characters attached to the town's history live on—immortalized on the silver screen in such famous flicks as *Gunfight at the O.K. Corral, Tombstone,* and *Wyatt Earp.* The town's tourist industry parallels Hollywood hype. As a result, the main drag on Allen Street looks and feels like a movie set complete with gunning desperados, satin-bedecked saloon girls, and leather-clad cowboys. Today, the "Town Too Tough to Die" attracts a kitschy mix of rough-and-tumble bikers, European socialites, and pulp fiction thrill–seekers looking to walk the boardwalks of Tombstone's infamous past.

Start your tour of this tiny town at **Tombstone Visitor Center** (✉*4th and Allen Sts.* ☎*520/457-3929* ⊕*www.tombstone.org*). There's a self-guided walking tour, but the best way to get the lay of the land is to take the 15-minute **stagecoach ride** ($10, $5 for kids) around downtown. Drivers relate a condensed version of Tombstone's notorious past. You'll also pass the Tombstone Courthouse and travel down

CLOSE UP

The Legend of Wyatt Earp

Popularized in dime novels and on the silver screen, the legend of Wyatt Earp follows the American tradition of the tall tale. This larger-than-life hero of the Wild West is cloaked with romance and derring-do. Stripped of the glamour, though, Earp emerges as a man with a checkered past who switched from fugitive to lawman several times over his long life.

Born in 1848, Wyatt Berry Stapp Earp earned renown as the assistant city marshal of Dodge City. Wyatt and his brothers James, Virgil, and Morgan moved to Tombstone with their wives in 1879 and it was here that they, along with Wyatt's friend Doc Holliday, made their mark in history. Wyatt ran a gambling concession at the Oriental Saloon, and Virgil became the city marshal of Tombstone. When trouble began to brew with the Clanton gang, Virgil recruited Wyatt and Morgan as deputy policemen. The escalating animosity between the "cowboys" and the Earps peaked on October 26, 1881, at the OK Corral—a 30-second gunfight that left three of the Clanton gang dead and Morgan and Virgil wounded. Doc Holliday was creased, but Wyatt walked away from the fight uninjured. And then the real trouble for the Earps began.

In December, Virgil was shot and crippled by unknown assailants and on March 18, 1882, Morgan was shot to death in a pool hall. In retribution, Wyatt went on a bloody vendetta. After the smoke had settled, the remaining "cowboys" were dead and Wyatt had left Tombstone for good. He made the rounds of mining camps in the West and up into Alaska, then settled in California. He died on January 13, 1929. His legend lives on in recent movies such as *Tombstone* and *Wyatt Earp*.

Toughnut Street, once called Rotten Row—because of the lawyers that lived there.

Boot Hill Graveyard, where the victims of the OK Corral shoot-out are buried, is on the northwest corner of town, facing U.S. 80. Chinese names in one section of the "bone orchard" bear testament to the laundry and restaurant workers who came from San Francisco during the height of Tombstone's mining fever. One of the more amusing epitaphs at the cemetery, however, is engraved on the headstone of Wells Fargo agent Lester Moore; it poetically lists the cause of his untimely demise: "Here lies Lester Moore, four slugs from a .44, no less, no more." If you're put off by the commercialism of the place—you enter through a gift shop that sells novelty items in the shape of tombstones—remember that Tombstone itself is the result of crass acquisition. ⊠ *U. S. 80* ☎ *520/457–3300* ☐ *Free* ⊙ *Daily 9–5.*

For an introduction to the town's—and the area's—past, visit the **Tombstone Courthouse State Historic Park.** This redbrick 1882 county courthouse offers exhibits on the area's mining and ranching history and pioneer lifestyles; you can also see the restored 1904 courtroom and district attorney's office. The two-story building housed the Cochise County jail, a courtroom, and public offices until the county seat was moved to Bisbee in 1929. The stately building became the corner-

Southeast Arizona

CORONADO NATIONAL FOREST
CORONADO NATIONAL FOREST
CORONADO NATIONAL FOREST
CORONADO NATIONAL FOREST

0   20 miles
0   30 km

Bowie

8 Willcox

San Simon

Cochise

7 Fort Bowie National Historical Site

Dragoon

TO TUCSON

Vail

Benson 10

Sunsites

Chiricahua National Monument 6

9 Texas Canyon

Pearce

Sunizona

Portal

Kartchner Caverns State Park 11

Gleeson

CORONADO NATIONAL FOREST

Fairbank

1 Tombstone

Elfrida

SAN PEDRO RIPARIAN NAT'L CONSERVATION AREA

3 Sonoita

Elgin

McNeal

4 Patagonia

Sierra Vista 5

Nicksville

Bisbee 2

Pirtleville

CORONADO NATIONAL FOREST

Lavender Pit

Douglas

Palominas

NEW MEXICO

DOS CABEZAS MTS.
DRAGOON MTS.
SWISSHELM MTS.
PEDREGOSA MTS.

MEXICO

stone of Tombstone's historic preservation efforts in the 1950s and was Arizona's first operational state park. Today, you can relax with an outdoor lunch at the park's tree-shaded picnic tables. ⊠ *219 E. Toughnut St., at 3rd St.* ☎ *520/457–3311* ⊕ *www.pr.state.az.us* ✉ *$4* ⊙ *Daily 8–5.*

Originally a boarding house for the Vizina Mining Company and later a popular hotel, the **Rose Tree Inn Museum** has 1880s period rooms. Covering more than 8,600 square feet, the Lady Banksia rose tree, planted by a homesick bride in 1885, is reported to be the largest of its kind in the world. The best time to see the tree is in April when its tiny white roses bloom. Romantics can purchase a healthy clipping from the tree ($10.95 plus tax) to plant in their own yard. The museum might not look like much from the outside, but the collectibles and tree make this one of the best places to visit in town. ⊠ *116 S. 4th St., at Toughnut St.* ☎ *520/457–3326* ✉ *$3* ⊙ *Daily 9–5.*

Vincent Price narrates the dramatic version of the town's past in the **Historama**—a 26-minute multimedia presentation. At the adjoining **OK Corral**, a recorded voice-over details the town's famous shootout, while life-size figures of the gunfight's participants stand poised to shoot. A reenactment of the gunfight at the OK Corral is held daily at 2 PM. Photographer C. S. Fly, whose studio was next door to the corral, didn't record this bit of history, but Geronimo and his pursuers were among the historic figures he did capture with his camera. Many of his fascinating Old West images may be viewed at the **Fly Exhibition Gallery.** ⊠*Allen St. between 3rd and 4th Sts.* ☎*520/457-3456* ⊕*www.ok-corral.com* ⊠*Historama, OK Corral, and Fly Exhibition Gallery $5.50, gunfight $2* ⊙*Daily 9–5; Historama shows on the half hr 9:30–4:30.*

You can see the original printing presses for the town's newspaper at the **Tombstone Epitaph Museum** (⊠*9 S. 5th St.* ☎*520/457-2211* ⊠*Free* ⊙*Daily 9:30–5*). The newspaper was founded in 1880 by John P. Clum and is still publishing today. You can purchase one of the newspaper's special editions—*The Life and Times of Wyatt Earp, The Life and Times of Doc Holliday,* or *Tombstone's Pioneering Prostitutes.*

A Tombstone institution, known as the wildest, wickedest night spot between Basin Street and the Barbary Coast, the **Bird Cage Theater** is a former music hall where Enrico Caruso, Sarah Bernhardt, and Lillian Russell—among others—performed. It was also the site of the longest continuous poker game recorded: the game started when the Bird Cage opened in 1881 and lasted eight years, five months, and three days. Some of the better-known players included Diamond Jim Brady, Adolphus Busch (of brewery fame), and William Randolph Hearst's father. The cards were dealt round the clock; players had to give a 20-minute notice when they were planning to vacate their seats, because there was always a waiting list of at least 10 people ready to shell out $1,000 (the equivalent of about $30,000 today) to get in. In all, some $10 million changed hands.

When the mines closed in 1889, the Bird Cage was abandoned but the building has remained in the hands of the same family, who threw nothing out. You can walk on the stage visited by some of the top traveling performers of the time, see the faro table once touched by the legendary gambler Doc Holliday, and pass by the hearse that carried Tombstone's deceased to Boot Hill. The basement, which served as an upscale bordello and gambling hall, still has all the original furnishings and fixtures intact, and you can see the personal belongings left behind by the ladies of the night when the mines closed and they, and their clients, headed for California. The $22 family special admission admits two parents and all children under the age of 18. ⊠*308 E. Allen St., at 6th St.* ☎*520/457-3421* ⊠*$8* ⊙*Daily 8–6.*

Aficionados of the Old West have most likely seen the photograph of Billy Clanton in his coffin, which was taken after his demise at the infamous gunfight at the OK Corral. But Steve Elliott, owner of the **Tombstone Western Heritage Museum,** offers another glimpse of this cowboy—one with his eyes wide open. The 5"x7" black-and-white photograph, taken by C. S. Fly in the 1880s, shows the Clantons, the McLaury brothers, and Billy Claiborne all saddled up and ready to ride. According to Elliott, it is the only known photograph of Billy Clanton taken while he was still among the living. Other relics of the Old West at the museum include 1880s dentist tools, clay poker chips, historic photographs, vintage firearms, and a stagecoach strongbox. ✉*515 Fremont St., at 6th St.* ☎*520/457–3800* ✍*$5* ◷*Mon.–Sat. 9–6, Sun. 12:30–6.*

WHERE TO STAY & EAT

$–$$ ✕**Lamplight Room.** The 1880s might have been a rough-and-tumble time for residents of Tombstone, but elegance found its way into the mining town—something reflected in its dining establishments. If you have the hankering to try some of the most elegant fare in town, dine at the Tombstone Boarding House Bed and Breakfast's Lamplight Room. The restaurant, decked out in Victorian finery, serves up period recipes and a complete Mexican menu every night. Wyatt Earp and Doc Holliday would feel right at home. ✉*108 N. 4th St.* ☎*520/457–3716 or 877/225–1319* ☰*AE, D, MC, V.*

¢–$$ ✕**Nellie Cashman's.** In 1882, a generous Tombstone pioneer opened a boarding house and restaurant catering to hardrock miners. Named the "Angel of the Mining Camp," this kind-hearted entrepreneur was as well known for her hearty meals as for her good deeds. Today, her spirit lives on at Nellie Cashman's—an 1880s-style restaurant decked out with cheery mismatched tablecloths and historical photographs. This homey favorite serves basic American food including biscuits and gravy, chicken-fried steak, and hefty hamburgers. The strawberry-rhubarb pie is worth the trip alone. ✉*117 5th St.* ☎*520/457–2212* ☰*AE, D, MC, V.*

$–$$ 🖼**Curly Bill's Bed & Breakfast.** Though named for one of the baddest outlaws in Tombstone Territory, this B&B is quite serene. Five blocks from Allen Street, the hacienda has views of the Dragoon Mountains from the sun porch and hot tub. Two rooms furnished with Victorian antiques share a bath, and two larger rooms with fireplaces have private baths. Hosts Curly and Sally, both historians, can inform and advise you about Tombstone highlights. ✉*210 N. 9th St., 85638* ☎*520/457–3858* ⊕*www.curlybillsbandb.com* ➥*4 rooms, 2 with shared bath* ⟠*In-room: VCR (some), no TV (some). In-hotel: no-smoking rooms, no elevator* ☰*MC, V* ⊚*BP.*

$ 🖼**Holiday Inn Express.** Nestled into a hill just outside of town, this newer two-story property offsets basic rooms with spectacular views of the mountains and desert valley. The rooms are Western-theme, of course, and every night an old Western movie is screened in the dining room (with free popcorn). ✉*1001 N. Highway 80, 85638* ☎*520/457–9507 or 888/465–4329* 📠*520/457–9506* ⊕*www.hitombstone.com* ➥*60 rooms, 7 suites* ⟠*In-room: refrigerator (some), ethernet. In-hotel: pool, laundry facilities, no-smoking rooms, no elevator* ☰*AE, D, MC, V* ⊚*CP.*

★ $ 🖼**Tombstone Boarding House Bed & Breakfast.** This friendly B&B is actually two meticulously restored 1880s adobes that sit side by side: guests sleep in one house and go next door for a hearty country breakfast. The spotless rooms, all with private entrances, have period furnishings collected from around Cochise County. Even if you don't stay here, the Lamplight Room restaurant is worth a visit. ✉*108 N. 4th St.* ✉*Box 906, 85638* ☎*520/457–3716 or 877/225–1319* ⊕*www.tombstoneboardinghouse.com* ➥*6 rooms* ⟠*In-room: no phone, no*

TV. In-hotel: restaurant, no-smoking rooms, no elevator, some pets allowed ⊟*AE, D, MC, V* ⊙❙*BP.*

NIGHTLIFE

★ If you're looking to wet your whistle, stop by the **Crystal Palace** (⊠*420 E. Allen St., at 5th St.* ☎*520/457–3611*), where a beautiful mirrored mahogany bar, wrought-iron chandeliers, and tinwork ceilings date back to Tombstone's heyday. Locals come here on weekends to dance to live country-and-western music. Another hopping bar on Allen Street is **Big Nose Kate's Saloon** (⊠*Allen St. between 4th and 5th Sts.* ☎*520/457–3107* ⊕*www.bignosekate.com*). Occasionally an acoustic concert livens things up even more at this popular pub, once part of the original Grand Hotel built in 1881. Saloon girls encourage visitors to get into the 1880s spirit by dressing up in red-feather boas and dusters.

SHOPPING

Several curio shops and old-time photo emporiums await in the kitschy collection of stores lining Allen Street. Given the town's bloody history, it's not surprising that guns aren't permitted in most of the establish-
★ ments, but it's worth visiting **G. F. Spangenberg Pioneer Gun Shop** (⊠*17 S. 4th St., at Allen St.* ☎*520/457–3227*), which opened in 1880. Wyatt Earp, Virgil Earp, Doc Holliday, the Clantons, and the McLowrys all purchased weapons at this shop, which still sells period firearms. Get into the spirit of the Old West by renting or purchasing 1880s-style costumes at the **Oriental Saloon** (⊠*500 E. Allen St., at 5th St.* ☎*520/457–3922*), which originally opened in 1880 and was touted as one of the fanciest bars in town. **Silver Hills Trading Co** (⊠*504 E. Allen St.* ☎*520/457–3335*) offers everything from Native American jewelry to Southwestern souvenirs. Well-stocked **Tombstone Old West Books** (⊠*401 E. Allen St.* ☎*520/457–2252*) has a wide selection of books about Cochise County and the Old West.

BISBEE

★ ❷ *24 mi south of Tombstone.*

Like Tombstone, Bisbee was a mining boomtown, but its wealth was in copper, not silver, and its success was much longer lived. The gnarled Mule Mountains aren't as impressive as some of the other mountain ranges in southern Arizona, but their rocky canyons concealed one of the richest mineral sites in the world.

Jack Dunn, a scout with Company C from Fort Huachuca chasing hostile Apaches in the area, first discovered an outcropping of rich ore

> ### WORD OF MOUTH
>
> "I loved Bisbee…it is so quaint and charming…surrounded by beautiful hills and mountains… the Copper Queen Hotel is in the center of town and it dates back to the turn of the century…there's a Southeastern Arizona Bird Observatory based in Bisbee…my kids loved the Bisbee Mining and Historical Museum…you can actually go for a ride in a mine…Bisbee gets my vote."
>
> –Merilee

7

here in 1877. By 1900 more than 20,000 people lived in the crowded canyons around the Bisbee mines. Phelps Dodge purchased all of the major mines by the time the Great Depression rolled around and mining continued until 1975, when the mines were closed for good. In less than 100 years of mining, the area surrounding Bisbee yielded more than 6.1 billion dollars of mineral wealth.

Once known as the Queen of the Copper Camps, Bisbee is no longer one of the biggest cities between New Orleans and San Francisco. It was rediscovered in the early 1980s by burned-out city dwellers and revived as a kind of Woodstock West. The population is a mix of retired miners and their families, aging hippie jewelry makers, and enterprising restaurateurs and boutique owners from all over the country.

If you want to head straight into town from U.S. 80, get off at the Brewery Gulch interchange. You can park and cross under the highway, taking Main, Commerce, or Brewery Gulch Street, all of which meet here.

Bisbee Visitors Center. This is a good place to start your visit of this historic mining town. It offers up-to-date information on attractions, dining, lodging, and special events. ⊠ *2 Copper Queen Plaza* ☎ *520/432–3554 or 866/224–7233* ⊕ *www.discoverbisbee.com.*

About ¼ mi after AZ 80 intersects with AZ 92, you can pull off the highway into a gravel parking lot, where a short, typewritten history of the **Lavender Pit Mine** (⊠ *AZ 80)* is attached to the hurricane fence surrounding the area (Bisbee isn't big on formal exhibits). The hole left by the copper miners is huge, with piles of lavender-hue "tailings," or waste, creating mountains around it. Arizona's largest pit mine yielded some 94 million tons of copper ore before mining activity came to a halt.

☚ For a lesson in mining history, take the **Copper Queen Mine Underground Tour.** The mine is less than ½ mi to the east of the Lavender Pit, across AZ 80 from downtown at the Brewery Gulch interchange. Tours are led by Bisbee's retired copper miners, who are wont to embellish their spiel with tales from their mining days.

The 75-minute tours (you can't enter the mine at any other time) go into the shaft via a small open train, like those the miners rode when the mine was active. Before you climb aboard, you're outfitted in miner's garb—a yellow slicker and a hard hat with a light that runs off a battery pack. You may want to wear a sweater or light coat under your slicker because temperatures inside are cool. You'll travel thousands of feet into the mine, up a grade of 30 feet (not down, as many visitors expect). Those who are a bit claustrophobic might instead consider taking one of the van tours of the surface mines and historic district that depart from the building at the same times as the mine tours (excluding 9 AM). Reservations are suggested. ⊠ *478 N. Dart Rd.* ☎ *520/432–2071 or 866/432–2071* ⊕ *www.queenminetour.com* ✉ *Mine tour $12, van tour $10* ☉ *Tours daily at 9, 10:30, noon, 2, and 3:30.*

★ The **Bisbee Mining and Historical Museum** is in a redbrick structure built in 1897 to serve as the Copper Queen Consolidated Mining Offices. The rooms today are filled with exhibits, photographs, and artifacts that offer a glimpse into the everyday life of Bisbee's early mining community. Even though the exhibit "Bisbee: Urban Outpost on the Frontier" paints a flattering portrait of this Shady Lady's early years and the funky gift store gets in the groove with feathered ladies hats and locally written books, most visitors will spend less than an hour taking in this dusty little museum. This was the first rural museum in the United States to become a member of the Smithsonian Institution Affiliations Program. ⊠*5 Copper Queen Plaza* ☎*520/432–7071* ⊕*www. bisbeemuseum.org* ⊇*$7.50* ⊙*Daily 10–4.*

The **Copper Queen Hotel** (⊠*11 Howell Ave.*), built a century ago and still in operation *(⇨ Where to Stay & Eat)*, is behind the Mining and Historical Museum. It has housed the famous as well as the infamous: General John "Black Jack" Pershing, John Wayne, Theodore Roosevelt, and mining executives from all over the world made this their home away from home. The hotel also hosts three resident ghosts. Take a minute to look through the ghost journal at the front desk where guests have described their haunted encounters.

Brewery Gulch, a short street running north–south, is adjacent to the Copper Queen Hotel. In the old days, the brewery housed here allowed the dregs of the beer that was being brewed to flow down the street and into the gutter.

Bisbee's **Main Street** is alive and retailing. This hilly commercial thoroughfare is lined with appealing art galleries, antiques stores, crafts shops, boutiques, and restaurants—many in well-preserved turn-of-the-20th-century brick buildings.

Tom Mosier, a native of Bisbee, gives the **Lavender Jeep Tours** (⊠*45 Gila Dr.* ☎*520/432–5369*) for $25 to $49. He regales locals and visitors with tales of the town and its buildings.

WHERE TO STAY & EAT

★ $$–$$$ ✕**Café Roka.** This is the deserved darling of the hip Bisbee crowd. The constantly changing northern Italian–style evening menu is not extensive, but whatever you order—gulf shrimp tossed with lobster ravioli, roasted quail, New Zealand rack of lamb—will be wonderful. Portions are generous, and entrées include soup, salad, and sorbet. Exposed-brick walls and soft lighting form the backdrop for original artwork, and the 1875 bar hearkens to Bisbee's glory days. There's live jazz on Friday nights. ⊠*35 Main St.* ☎*520/432–5153* ▭*AE, MC, V* ⊙*Closed Sun.–Wed. No lunch.*

$–$$ ✕**The Bisbee Grille.** You might not expect diversity at a place with a reputation for having the best burger in town, but this restaurant delivers with salads, sandwiches, fajitas, pasta, salmon, steaks, and ribs. The dining room, built to resemble an old train depot, fills up fast on the weekends. ⊠*#2 Copper Queen Plaza* ☎*520/432–6788* ▭*AE, D, MC, V.*

$–$$$ 🏨 **Canyon Rose Suites.** Steps from the heart of downtown, this all-suites
★ B&B is in the 1905 Allen Block Building, formerly a furniture store
and miners' rooming house. Upstairs are six spacious units, all with
hardwood floors, 10-foot ceilings, and fully equipped kitchens. Local
art (for sale) adorns the walls. ⊠*27 Subway St.* ⌂*Box 1915, 85603*
☎*520/432–5098 or 866/296–7673* ⊕*www.canyonrose.com* ⇌*6
suites* ♿*In-room: kitchen, VCR. In-hotel: laundry facilities; no eleva-
tor* ⊟*AE, MC, V.*

$–$$ 🏨 **Copper Queen Hotel.** Built by the Copper Queen Mining Company
when Bisbee was the biggest copper-mining town in the world, this
hotel has been operating since 1902. Some rooms are small or oddly
laid out, and walls are thin, but all have a Victorian charm. You might
want to request room 211, where John Wayne once stayed; room 315,
which is said to be inhabited by the ghost of former employee Julia
Lowell; or room 406, which was once occupied by President Teddy
Roosevelt. Not all visitors experience haunted happenings. A previous
guest in the Teddy Roosevelt room wrote, "Teddy did not show up, nor
any of his dead friends." Another visitor noted: "The scariest thing I
saw was my mom without her makeup in the morning." ⊠*11 Howell Ave.* ⌂*Drawer CQ, 85603* ☎*520/432–2216* 🖶*520/432–3819*
⊕*www.copperqueen.com* ⇌*48 rooms* ♿*In-hotel: restaurant, bar,
pool* ⊟*AE, MC, V.*

¢–$$ 🏨 **School House Inn Bed & Breakfast.** You might flash back to your class-
Fodor'sChoice room days at this B&B, a schoolhouse built in 1918 at the height
★ of Bisbee's mining days. Perched on the side of a hill, the two-story
brick building has a pleasant outdoor patio shaded by an oak tree. The
inn's rooms all have a theme—history, music, library, reading, arith-
metic, art, geography, and the principal's office—reflected in the decor.
The upstairs deck and a comfy TV room are places to lounge after a
day's adventures. ⊠*818 Tombstone Canyon Rd.* ⌂*Box 32, 85603*
☎*800/537–4333* 🖶*520/432–2996* ⊕*www.schoolhouseinnbb.com*
⇌*6 rooms, 3 suites* ♿*In-room: no a/c, no phone, no TV, Wi-Fi. In-
hotel: no kids under 14, no-smoking rooms, no elevator* ⊟*AE, D,
MC, V* ⟊*BP.*

¢–$$ 🏨 **Shady Dell Vintage Trailer Park.** For a blast to the past, stay in one of
Fodor'sChoice the funky, vintage aluminum trailers at this trailer park off the beaten
★ path. Choices include a 1952, 10-foot homemade unit and a 1951, 33-
foot Royal Mansion. The entire collection is decked out 1950s style
including vintage magazines, books, and vinyl records. Some have private bathrooms but none have private showers; the park restrooms are
clean, with hot showers. Dot's Diner, on-site, serves burgers, fries, and
milk shakes. ⊠*1 Old Douglas Rd., 85603* ☎*520/432–3567* ⊕*www.
theshadydell.com* ⇌*11 trailers* ♿*In-room: no a/c, no phone, kitchen,
no TV. In-hotel: restaurant, laundry facilities, no kids under 10, no-
smoking rooms* ⊟*MC, V.*

NIGHTLIFE

Once known for shady ladies and saloons, Brewery Gulch retains a
few shadows of its rowdy past. Established in 1902, **St. Elmo Bar** (⊠*36
Brewery Gulch* ☎*520/432–5578*) is decorated with an assortment of
the past and present—a 1922 official map of Cochise County hangs

next to a neon beer sign. The jukebox plays during the week but on weekends Buzz and the Soul Senders rock the house with rhythm and blues. **The Stock Exchange Bar** (⊠*15 Brewery Gulch* ☎*520/432–5240*), in the historic Muheim building, has shuffleboard, a pool table, and off-track betting. The 1914 stock board still hangs on the wall. **Hot Licks Barbeque and Blues Saloon** (⊠*37 OK St.* ☎*520/432–7200* ⊕*www. hotlicksbbq.com*) offers more than 70 imported and micro-brewed beers as well as a nice selection of single malt scotches and tequilas. Local and national blues acts jazz up the joint on the weekends.

SHOPPING

★ Artist studios, galleries, and boutiques in historic buildings line Main Street, which runs though Tombstone Canyon. **55 Main Gallery** (⊠*55 Main St.* ☎*520/432–4694*) is just one of many art galleries selling contemporary work along the main drag. **Belleza Fine Arts Gallery** (⊠*29 Main St.* ☎*520/432–5877* ⊕*www.bellezagallery.org*) is owned and operated by Bisbee's Women's Transition Project, which aids homeless women and their children. This unusual gallery features the artwork of local and national artists as well as Adirondack chairs and birdhouses made by women receiving assistance from the program. The gallery's 50% commission goes directly into funding the Transition project. A trip to Bisbee wouldn't be complete without a stop at **The Killer Bee Guy** (⊠*15 Main St.* ☎*520/432–2938 or 877/227–9338* ⊕*www. killerbeeguy.com*). Beekeeper Reed Booth has appeared on the Discovery Channel and the Food Network; you can sample his honey butters and mustards and pick up some killer honey recipes. Nationally renowned **Optimo Custom Panama Hatworks** (⊠*47 Main St.* ☎*520/432–4544 or 888/346–3428* ⊕*www.optimohatworks.com*) ispopular for its custom, hand-woven Panama hats. It also sells works of beaver, cashmere, hare, and rabbit felt.

7

SONOITA

❸ *34 mi southeast of Tucson on I–10 to AZ 83, 57 mi west of Tombstone on AZ82.*

The grasslands surrounding modern-day Sonoita captured the attention of early Spanish explorers, including Father Eusebio Francisco Kino, who mapped and claimed the area in 1701. The Tuscan-like beauty of the rolling, often green hills framed by jutting mountain ranges has been noticed by Hollywood filmmakers. As you drive along AZ 83 and AZ 82 you might recognize the scenery from movies filmed here, including *Oklahoma* and *Tin Cup*.

Today, this region is known for its vineyards and wineries as well as for its ranching history. Sonoita, at the junction of AZ 83 and AZ 82, offers several restaurants and upscale B&Bs, but it's the nearby wineries that draw the crowds. There are several events at the wineries, including the Blessing of the Vines in the spring and the Harvest Festivals in fall. Summer is also a good time to visit, when you can sample some of Arizona's vintages and chat with a wine master or local vintner.

GRAPE ESCAPE

"Arizona wine country" may sound odd, but the soil and climate in the Santa Cruz Valley southeast of Tucson are ideal for growing grapes. Wine grapes first took root in the region 400 years ago, when the Spanish missionaries planted the first vines of "mission" grapes for the production of sacramental wine. But it wasn't until the 1970s that the first commercial vinifera grapes were planted in the region as part of an agricultural experiment.

Connoisseurs have debated the merits of the wines produced in this area since 1974, but if you want to decide for yourself, tour some of the region's wineries. **Callaghan Vineyards**, the **Village of Elgin Winery**, and **Sonoita Vineyards** all have something to tantalize the tastebuds. See the listings in this chapter for contact info.

To explore the wineries of southern Arizona, head south on AZ 83 from Sonoita and then east on Elgin Road. Most of the growers are in and around the tiny village of Elgin, 9 mi southeast of Sonoita. The best times to visit the vineyards are in the summer and early fall. To plot your course through Arizona's wine country, check out the Arizona Wines Adventure Trail Map (⊕ *http://arizonawine.org*).

Fodor's Choice **Callaghan Vineyards** (⊠ *336 Elgin Rd., Elgin* ☎ *520/455–5322* ⊕ *www.*
★ *callaghanvineyards.com*), open Friday through Sunday, 11 to 3, produces the best wine in Arizona. Its Buena Suerte ("good luck" in Spanish) Cuvée is a favorite, and its 1996 fumé blanc was named as one of the top wines in the U.S. by the *Wall Street Journal*.

In Elgin, stop for tastings daily from 10 to 5 at **Village of Elgin Winery** (⊠ *The Elgin Complex, Upper Elgin Rd., Elgin* ☎ *520/455–9309* ⊕ *www.elginwines.com*), one of the largest producers of wines in the state and the home to Tombstone Red, which the winemaker claims is "great with scorpion, tarantula, and rattlesnake meat."

Sonoita Vineyards (⊠ *Canelo Rd., 3 mi south of town, Elgin* ☎ *520/455–5893* ⊕ *www.sonoitavineyards.com*), known for its high-quality reds, offers tours and tastings daily 10 to 4. Originally planted in the early 1970s as an experiment by Dr. Gordon Dutt, former agriculture professor at the University of Arizona, this was the first commercial vineyard in Arizona.

WHERE TO STAY & EAT

¢–$$$$ ╳ **Steak Out Restaurant & Saloon.** A frontier-style design and a weathered-wood exterior help to create the mood at this Western restaurant and bar known for its tasty margaritas and live country music played on weekend evenings. Built and owned by the family that operates the Sonoita Inn next door, the restaurant serves cowboy fare: mesquite-grilled steaks, ribs, chicken, and fish. ⊠ *3235 AZ 82* ☎ *520/455–5205* ▭ *AE, D, DC, MC, V* ⊗ *No lunch weekdays*.

★ ¢–$$ ✕**Café Sonoita.** Like Sonoita itself, the Café Sonoita combines city sophistication with small-town charm. A local favorite, the restaurant also draws day-trippers from Tucson and tourists from afar. The dinner menu, which changes daily, incorporates locally grown produce and local wines. Specialties include prickly-pear barbecue ribs, buffalo burgers, and the tequila shrimp chile relleno. Save room for the homemade pies, cheesecakes, and brownies. ✉*3280 AZ 82* ☎*520/455–5278* ▤*MC, V* ⊘*Closed Sun.–Tues.*

$$ ▥**Rainbow's End.** An old ranch manager's house on a horse farm overlooking the Sonoita countryside is now a B&B furnished in period antiques. Four bedrooms, each with a modern bathroom, share a great room with fireplace and a big kitchen, where guests can assemble their own Continental breakfast and organic snacks (supplied by the hosts, who live just down the hill). ✉*3088 AZ 83* ✎*Box 717, 85637* ☎*520/455–0202* ☐*520/455–0303* ⊕*www.rainbowsendbandb.com* ⤺*4 rooms* ⚹*In-room: no TV. In-hotel: restaurant, no-smoking rooms, some pets allowed, no elevator* ▤*AE, D, MC, V* ▯⧁*CP.*

$–$$ ▥**Sonoita Inn.** The owner of the Sonoita also owned the Triple Crown–winning racehorse Secretariat, and the walls of the inn celebrate the horse's career with photos, racing programs, and press clippings. Hardwood floors, colorful woven rugs, and retro-cowboy bedspreads distinguish the spacious rooms, some of which have views of the Santa Rita mountains. The inn is near the intersection of AZ 82 and AZ 83 and is adjacent to the Steak Out Restaurant & Saloon. ✉*3243 AZ 82* ✎*Box 99, 85637* ☎*520/455–5935 or 800/696–1006* ☐*520/455–5069* ⊕*www.sonoitainn.com* ⤺*18 rooms* ⚹*In-room: VCR. In-hotel: some pets allowed, no elevator* ▤*AE, D, MC, V* ▯⧁*CP.*

PATAGONIA

❹ *12 mi southwest of Sonoita via AZ 82.*

Served by a spur of the Atchison, Topeka & Santa Fe Railroad, Patagonia was a shipping center for cattle and ore. The town declined after the railroad departed in 1962, and the old depot is now the town hall. Today, with the migration of artists here in recent years, art galleries and boutiques coexist with real Western saloons in this tiny, tree-lined village in the Patagonia Mountains. The surrounding region is a prime birding destination with more than 275 species of birds found around Sonoita Creek.

The **Patagonia Visitors Center** (✉*317 McKeown Ave.* ☎*520/394–0060 or 888/794–0060* ⊕*www.patagoniaaz.com*) is a good first stop for an overview.

Mariposa Books & More (✉*317 McKeown Ave.* ☎*520/394–9186*) shares quarters with the visitor center and has a nice selection of new and used books with topics ranging from cooking to regional history.

Creative Spirit Artists Co-op (✉*317 McKeown Ave.* ☎*520/394–9186*) features jewelry, paintings, photography, quilts, and pottery of more than 60 local artists.

At the Nature Conservancy's **Patagonia–Sonoita Creek Preserve,** 1,350 acres of cottonwood-willow riparian habitat are protected along the Patagonia–Sonoita Creek watershed. More than 275 bird species have been sighted here, along with white-tailed deer, javelina, coatimundi (raccoon-like animals native to the region), desert tortoise, and snakes. There's a self-guided nature trail; guided walks are given every Saturday at 9 AM along 2 mi of loop trails. Three concrete structures near an elevated berm of the Railroad Trail serve as reminders of the land's former life as a truck farm. To reach the preserve from Patagonia, make a right on 4th Avenue; at the stop sign, turn left onto Blue Haven Road. This paved road soon becomes dirt and leads to the preserve in about 1¼ mi. The admission fee is good for seven days. ⊠ *150 Blue Haven Rd.* ☎ *520/394–2400* ⊕ *www.nature.org* ⊇ *$5* ⊗ *Apr.–Sept., Wed.–Sun. 6:30–4; Oct.–Mar., Wed.–Sun. 7:30–4.*

ⓒ Eleven miles south of town, **Patagonia Lake State Park** is the spot for water sports, picnicking, and camping. Formed by the damming of Sonoita Creek, the 265-acre reservoir lures anglers with its largemouth bass, crappie, bluegill, and catfish; it's stocked with rainbow trout in the wintertime. You can rent rowboats, paddleboats, canoes, and camping and fishing gear at the marina. Most swimmers head for Boulder Beach. The entrance fee is good for both Patagonia Lake State Park and for the Sonoita Creek State Natural Area. ⊠ *400 Lake Patagonia Rd.* ☎ *520/287–6965* ⊕ *www.pr.state.az.us* ⊇ *$7 per vehicle* ⊗ *Visitor center daily 9–4:30, gates closed 10 PM–4 AM.*

Arizona State Parks has designated almost 5,000 acres surrounding Patagonia Lake as **Sonoita Creek State Natural Area.** This project, funded by the Arizona State Parks Heritage Fund (lottery monies) and the State Lake Improvement Fund, offers environmental educational programs and university-level research opportunities. The riparian area is home to giant cottonwoods, willows, sycamores, and mesquites; nesting black hawks; and endangered species. Rangers offer guided birding tours (for an additional small fee) every Tuesday, Saturday, and Sunday at 9, 10:15, and 11:30 AM. The entrance fee is good for both Patagonia Lake State Park and for the Sonoita Creek State Natural Area. ⊠ *AZ 82, 5 mi south of town* ☎ *520/287–2791 or 800/285–3703* ⊕ *www. pr.state.az.us* ⊇ *$7 per vehicle.*

WHERE TO STAY & EAT

$ ✕ **Wagon Wheel Saloon.** The Wagon Wheel's restaurant, serving ribs, steaks, and burgers, is a more recent development, but the cowboy bar, with its neon beer signs and mounted moose head, has been around since the early 1900s. This is where every Stetson-wearing ranch hand in the area comes to listen to the country jukebox and down a longneck, maybe accompanied by some jalapeño poppers. ⊠ *400 W. Naugle Ave.* ☎ *520/394–2433* ⊟ *MC, V.*

★ ¢–$$ ✕ **Velvet Elvis Pizza Co.** There aren't too many places where you can enjoy a pizza heaped with organic veggies, a crisp salad of organic greens tossed with homemade dressing, freshly pressed juice (try the beet, apple, and lime juice concoction), organic wine, and microbrewed or imported beer while surrounded by images of Elvis *and* the Virgin

Mary. Owner Cecilia San Miguel uses a 1930s dough recipe for the restaurant's delightful crust, and you can pick up some pizza sauce in the gift shop if you want to try your hand at pizza-making at home. They also have fabulous fruit pies. ⊠*292 Naugle Ave.* ☎*520/394–2102* ⊟*MC, V* ⊗*Closed Mon.–Wed.*

¢–$ ✕**Gathering Grounds.** This colorful café and espresso bar, which also doubles as an art gallery featuring local artists, serves healthful breakfasts and imaginative soups, salads, and sandwiches through the late afternoon. ⊠*319 McKeown Ave.* ☎*520/394–2097* ⊟*MC, V.*

⟳ $$$$ ⬚**Circle Z Ranch.** Rimmed by giant sycamore, ash, and cottonwood trees and surrounded by the Patagonia–Sonoita Creek Preserve, this guest ranch served as a setting in the movie *Red River* and in several episodes of *Gunsmoke*. Rooms in the adobe-style buildings have hardwood floors and area rugs, king-size or twin beds, and antique Monterey pine chests. Riders from beginner through advanced can be accommodated on adventurous, scenic trails. All meals, riding, and amenities are included. Minimum stay is three days. ⊠*AZ 82, 4 mi southwest of town* ⬚*Box 194, 85624* ☎*520/394–2525 or 888/854–2525* ⊕*www.circlez.com* ⊷*24 rooms* ⬚*In-room: no a/c, no phone, no TV. In-hotel: restaurant, tennis court, pool, no-smoking rooms, no elevator* ⊟*MC, V* ⊗*Closed mid-May–Oct.* ⬚*AI.*

★ $ ⬚**Duquesne House Bed & Breakfast/Gallery.** Built as a miners' boarding house at the turn of the 20th century, this adobe home has rooms painted in pastel Southwest colors, lovingly and whimsically detailed by a local artist, and decorated with Mexican folk art. Breakfast is served in your room or in the Santa Fe–style great room. A tiered backyard garden with hammocks adds to the tranquility. ⊠*357 Duquesne Ave.* ⬚*Box 772, 85624* ☎*520/394–2732* ⊷*4 suites* ⬚*In-room: no TV (some), Wi-Fi. In-hotel: no elevator* ⊟*No credit cards* ⬚*BP.*

$ ⬚**Stage Stop Inn.** Old territorial appearance notwithstanding, the building isn't historic and the rooms are standard motel issue, but this is a decent place to lay your head. The center-of-town location is prime and the price is right. ⊠*303 W. McKeown Ave.* ⬚*Box 777, 85624* ☎*520/394–2211 or 800/923–2211* ⬚*520/394–2212* ⊷*43 rooms* ⬚*In-room: kitchen (some). In-hotel: restaurant, bar, pool, some pets allowed, no elevator* ⊟*AE, D, MC, V.*

NIGHTLIFE

If you're looking for some weekend rock 'n' roll fun in this sleepy section of the state, stop by **La Mision de San Miguel** (⊠*335 McKeown Ave.* ☎*520/394–0123* ⊕*www.lamisionpatagonia.com* ⊗*Closed Sun.–Tues.*). Inside a replica of a Spanish Colonial church, this tongue-in-cheek venue offers a smoke-free environment, a diverse mix of live country, bluegrass, flamenco, acoustic, and rockabilly music, and dancing into the wee hours.

SHOPPING

Patagonia is quickly turning into a shopping destination in its own right. Unlike the trendy shops in nearby Tubac, the stores here have reasonable prices in addition to small-town charm. Some of the artist spaces are open only by appointment. **Global Arts Gallery** (⊠*315*

McKeown Ave. ☎*520/394–0077*) showcases everything from local art and antiques to Native American jewelry, Middle Eastern rugs, and exotic musical instruments. At **High Spirits, Inc** (✉*714 Red Rock Ave.* ☎*520/394–2900 or 800/394–1523* ⊕*www.highspirits.com*), you can pick up Odell Borg Native American flutes. Shirley and Bill Ambrose sell decorative gourds and horseshoe art at their studio **Lil' Bit of Everything** (✉*567 Harshaw Rd.* ☎*520/394–2923*), by appointment only. **Painted House Studio** (✉*355 McKeown Ave.* ☎*520/394–2740*) has an intriguing collection of hand-painted pieces including chairs, hutches, bowls, pillows, and birdhouses. The studio is open by appointment. The **Shooting Star Pottery** (✉*370 Smelter Ave.* ☎*520/394–2752*) displays clay pieces created by the village potter Martha Kelly by appointment only—or you can check out the mosaics Kelly and her students completed at the Patagonia Community Arts Center just off Highway 82.

SIERRA VISTA

❺ *42 mi southeast of Patagonia via AZ 82 to AZ 90.*

A characterless military town on the outskirts of Fort Huachuca, Sierra Vista is nonetheless a good base from which to explore the more scenic areas that surround it—and at 4,620 feet above sea level, the whole area has a year-round temperate climate. There are a few fast-food and chain restaurants for your basic dining needs, and more than 1,100 rooms in area hotels, motels, and B&Bs offer shelter for the night.

Fort Huachuca, headquarters of the army's Global Information Systems Command, is the last of the great Western forts still in operation. It dates back to 1877, when the Buffalo Soldiers (yes, Bob Marley fans—*those* Buffalo Soldiers), the first all-black regiment in the U.S. forces, came to aid settlers battling invaders from Mexico, Indian tribes reluctant to give up their homelands, and assorted American desperadoes on the lam from the law back East.

Three miles from the fort's main gate are the **Fort Huachuca museums.** The late-19th-century bachelor officers' quarters and the annex across the street provide a record of military life on the frontier. More often than not, you'll be sharing space with new cadets learning about the history of this far-flung outpost. Motion sensors activate odd little sound bites to the multimedia experience. Another half block south, the **U.S. Army Intelligence Museum** focuses on American intelligence operations from the Apache Scouts through Desert Storm. Code machines, code books, decoding devices, and other intelligence gathering equipment are on display. Enter the main gate of Fort Huachuca on AZ 90, west of Sierra Vista. You need a driver's license, vehicle registration, and proof of insurance to get on base. ✉*Grierson St., off AZ 90, west of Sierra Vista, Fort Huachuca* ☎*520/533–5736* ⊕*huachuca-www. army.mil* 🖾*Free* ☉ *Weekdays 9–4, weekends 1–4.*

☾ Those driving to **Coronado National Memorial,** dedicated to Francisco Vásquez de Coronado, will see many of the same stunning vistas of Arizona and Mexico the conquistador saw when he trod this route in 1540 seeking the mythical Seven Cities of Cíbola. It's a little more than 3 mi via a dirt road from the visitor center to Montezuma Pass, and another ½ mi on foot to the top of the nearly 7,000-foot Coronado Peak, where the views are best. Other trails include Joe's Canyon Trail, a steep 3-mi route (one-way) down to the visitor center, and Miller Peak Trail, 12 mi round-trip to the highest point in the Huachuca Mountains (Miller Peak is 9,466 feet). Kids ages 5 to 12 can participate in the memorial's Junior Ranger program, explore Coronado Cave, and dress up in replica Spanish armor or missionary robes. The turnoff for the monument is 16 mi south of Sierra Vista on AZ 92; the visitor center is 5 mi. ⊠*4101 E. Montezuma Canyon Rd., Hereford* ☎*520/366–5515* ⊕*www.nps.gov/coro* ✉*Free* ☉ *Visitor center daily 9–5.*

Fodor'sChoice
★ **Ramsey Canyon Preserve,** managed by the Nature Conservancy, marks the convergence of two mountain and desert systems: this spot is the northernmost limit of the Sierra Madre and the southernmost limit of the Rockies, and it's at the edge of the Chihuahuan and Sonoran deserts. Visitors to this world-famous bird-watching hot spot train their binoculars skyward hoping to catch a glimpse of some of the preserve's most notable inhabitants. Painted redstarts nest, and 14 magnificent species of hummingbirds congregate here from spring through autumn—the jewels of this pristine habitat. Even for nonbirders, the beauty of the canyon makes this a destination in its own right. The rare stream-fed, sycamore-maple riparian corridor provides a lush contrast to the desert highlands at the base of the mountains. Guided hikes begin at 9 AM Tuesday, Thursday, and Saturday from March through October. Stop at the visitor center for maps and books on the area's natural history, flora, and fauna. To get here, take AZ 92 south from Sierra Vista for 6 mi, turn right on Ramsey Canyon Road, and then go 4 mi to the preserve entrance. Admission is good for seven days. ⊠*27 Ramsey Canyon Rd., Hereford* ☎*520/378–2785* ⊕*www.nature.org* ✉*$5, free 1st Sat. of the month* ☉ *Mar.–Oct., daily 8–5; Nov.–Feb., daily 9–4.*

OFF THE BEATEN PATH
San Pedro Riparian National Conservation Area. The San Pedro River, partially rerouted underground by an 1887 earthquake, may not look like much, but it sustains an impressive array of flora and fauna. To maintain this fragile creek-side ecosystem, 56,000 acres along the river were designated a protected riparian area in 1988. More than 350 species of birds come here, as well as 82 mammal species and 45 reptiles and amphibians. Forty thousand years ago, this was the domain of woolly mammoths and mastodons: many of the huge skeletons in Washington's Smithsonian Institute and New York's Museum of Natural History came from the massive fossil pits in the area. As evidenced by a number of small, unexcavated ruins, the migratory Indian tribes who passed through centuries later also found this valley hospitable, in part because of its many useful plants. Information, guided tours, books, and gifts are available from the volunteer staff at San Pedro House, a visitor center operated by Friends of the San Pedro River. ⊠*San Pedro House, 9800 AZ 90* ☎*520/508–4445, 520/439–6400*

Sierra Vista BLM Office ⊕*www.az.blm.gov* ✉*Free* ⊙*Visitor center daily 9:30–4:30, conservation area daily sunrise–sunset.*

WHERE TO STAY & EAT

$–$$$$ ✕**The Outside Inn.** Crisp white tablecloths, lace curtains, and glimmering candlelight all add to the romance of the Outside Inn, a favorite special-occasion dining destination with birders and locals alike. The prices may seem high, until you sample the delicious dinners. Delicacies include crumb-crusted lamb, prime rib, and blackened mahimahi. ✉*4907 S. AZ 92* ☎*520/378–4645* ▭*AE, MC, V* ⊙*Closed Sun. No lunch Sat.*

$$ ▦**Casa de San Pedro.** Bird-watchers are drawn to this contemporary hacienda-style B&B abutting the San Pedro Riparian National Conservation Area, and the hosts do everything they can to accommodate them. Hiking trails pass behind the property, and guided birding tours can be arranged. Each of the bright and modern rooms has handcrafted wooden furnishings from northern Mexico. A labyrinth for meditation and butterfly gardens surround the house. ✉*8933 S. Yell La., Hereford 85615* ☎*520/366–1300 or 888/257–2050* ▤*520/366–0701* ⊕*www.bedandbirds.com* ⇆*10 rooms* ⌂*In-room: no phone, no TV, Wi-Fi. In-hotel: pool, laundry facilities, no kids under 12, no elevator* ▭*AE, D, MC, V* ℉BP.

★ $$ ▦**Ramsey Canyon Inn Bed & Breakfast.** The Ramsey Canyon Preserve is a bird haven, and the nearby Ramsey Canyon Inn is a bird-watcher's delight. Antique furnishings and original watercolors of hummingbirds adorn the inn's rooms and apartment suites. The innkeepers serve a rotating menu of breakfast treats, such as French toast stuffed with cream cheese and nuts, as well as homemade pie in the afternoon. Reserve rooms in advance during the busy spring season. Birders have only to step out the front door to view the winged jewels of this internationally renowned birding destination. ✉*29 Ramsey Canyon Rd., Hereford 85615* ☎*520/378–3010* ▤*520/378–0487* ⊕*www.ramseycanyoninn.com* ⇆*6 rooms, 3 suites* ⌂*In-room: no a/c (some), no phone (some), kitchen (some), no TV. In-hotel: no-smoking rooms, no elevator, no children under 16* ▭*D, MC, V* ℉BP.

$ ▦**Windemere Hotel & Conference Center.** This hotel complex, across from the area's shopping mall, is on AZ 92 in what used to be the eastern outskirts of Sierra Vista but is now a rapidly growing commercial corridor. Despite the development, it's not uncommon to see roadrunners dashing about the hotel grounds. The three-story hotel has large, comfortable rooms, most with sweeping views of the Huachuca Mountains. Rates include evening cocktails. ✉*2047 S. AZ 92, 85635* ☎*520/459–5900 or 800/825–4656* ▤*520/458–1347* ⊕*www.windemerehotel.com* ⇆*149 rooms, 3 suites* ⌂*In-room: refrigerator, Wi-Fi. In-hotel: restaurant, bar, pool, laundry facilities, laundry service, no-smoking rooms, some pets allowed* ▭*AE, D, DC, MC, V* ℉BP.

CHIRICAHUA NATIONAL MONUMENT

6 58 *mi northeast of Douglas on U.S.*
Fodor'sChoice *191 to AZ 181; 36 mi southeast*
★ *of Willcox.*

Vast fields of desert grass are suddenly transformed into a landscape of forest, mountains, and striking rock formations as you enter the 12,000-acre Chiricahua National Monument. The Chiricahua Apache—who lived in the mountains for centuries and, led by Cochise and Geronimo, tried for 25 years to prevent white pioneers from settling here—dubbed it the Land of the Standing-Up Rocks. Enormous outcroppings of volcanic rock have been worn by erosion and fractured by uplift into strange pinnacles and spires. Because of the particular balance of sunshine and rain in the area, in April and May visitors will see brown, yellow, and red leaves coexisting with new green foliage. Summer in Chiricahua National Monument is exceptionally wet: from July through September there are thunderstorms nearly every afternoon. Few other areas in the United States have such varied plant, bird, and animal life. Deer, coatimundi, peccaries, and lizards live among the aspen, ponderosa pine, Douglas fir, oak, and cypress trees—to name just a few. Well worth the driving distance, this is an excellent area for bird-watchers, and hikers have more than 17 mi of scenic trails. The admission fee is good for seven days. Some of the most beautiful and untouched camping areas in Arizona are nearby, in the Chiricahua Mountains. ☒*AZ 181, 36 mi southeast of Willcox* ☎*520/824–3560* ⊕*www.nps.gov/chir* ☒*$5* ☉ *Visitor center daily 8–4:30.*

> **WORD OF MOUTH**
>
> "I think our biggest thrill came on the day we traveled to the Chiricahua National Monument, a stunningly beautiful mountain landscape that we reached after a mind-numbing couple of hours driving through desert grasslands. It rises up dramatically from the valley floor to over 9,000 feet, cresting in a series of uneven, volcanic looking peaks. As you drive up and into them you discover areas of spectacular pinnacles, columns, spires and precariously balanced boulders that are simply breathtakingly beautiful."
>
> –ckwald

7

WHERE TO STAY

$$$–$$$$ 🏠 **Sunglow Guest Ranch.** Named after the ghost town of Sunglow, this ranch consists of nine casitas decked out in Southwestern style with fireplaces. Breakfast and dinner are served in a cozy dining room with a wraparound porch. You can borrow mountain bikes to explore the trails in the Coronado National Forest, which borders the property on three sides. Birding and hiking are popular, and "star parties" attract astronomers, as this remote region offers some of the blackest skies around and perfect conditions for stargazing. Additional attractions include writing workshops and yoga retreats. ☒*14066 S. Sunglow Rd.* ⌂*Pearce 85625* ☎*520/824–3334 or 866/786–4569* 🖶*520/824–3176* ⊕*www.sunglowranch.com* ⇌*4 1-room casitas, 4 2-room casitas, 1 2-bedroom casita* ⌂*In-room: no phone, refrigerator, no TV. In-hotel: restaurant, bicycles, no-smoking rooms, no elevator, some pets allowed* ▤*AE, D, DC, MC, V* ⍾*MAP* ☉ *Closed July and Aug.*

No Bullet Shall Pass

The fearless Apache war shaman Geronimo, known among his people as "one who yawns," fought to the very last in the Apache Wars. His surrender to General Nelson Miles on September 5, 1886, marked the end of the Indian Wars in the West. Geronimo's fleetness in evading the massed troops of the U.S. Army and his legendary immunity to bullets made him the darling of sensationalistic journalists, and he became the most famous outlaw in America.

When the combined forces of the U.S. Army and Mexican troops failed to rout the powerful shaman from his territory straddling Arizona and Mexico, General Miles sent his officer Lieutenant Gatewood and relatives of Geronimo's renegade band of warriors to persuade Geronimo to parley with Miles near the mouth of Skeleton Canyon, at the edge of the Peloncillo Mountains. After several days of talks, Geronimo and his warriors agreed to the presented treaty and surrendered their arms.

Geronimo related the scene years later: "We stood between his troopers and my warriors. We placed a large stone on the blanket before us. Our treaty was made by this stone, as it was to last until the stone should crumble to dust; so we made the treaty, and bound each other with an oath." However, the political promises quickly unraveled, and the most feared of Apache medicine men spent the next 23 years in exile as a prisoner of war. He died on February 17, 1909, never having returned to his beloved homeland, and was buried in the Apache cemetery in Fort Sill, Oklahoma.

In 1934, a stone monument was built on State Route 80 in Apache, Arizona, as a reminder of Geronimo's surrender in 1886. The 16-foot-tall monument lies 10 mi northwest of the actual surrender site in Skeleton Canyon, where an unobtrusive sign and a pile of rocks marks the place where the last stone was cast.

$$$ **Grapevine Canyon Ranch.** Nestled deep in the Dragoon Mountains'
★ Grapevine Canyon, this historic cattle ranch spurs the imagination with hair-raising tales of marauding Apache Indians and pioneering homesteaders. This natural stronghold once used by Chiricahua Indians led by Geronimo and Cochise is tamer these days, but the striking high desert terrain and scattered cienegas still provide enticing opportunities for adventurous exploration. Adjacent is a working cattle ranch, where visitors get the chance to watch—and, in some cases, participate in—day-to-day cowboy activities. Riders of all levels of experience are welcome, and hiking trails crisscross this quintessentially Western terrain. Rooms are decorated in a mix of country and Southwestern-style furnishings—and all have spacious decks and porches. Rates include meals and all activities. There's a three-night minimum. ⊠ *Highland Rd.* ⊕ *Box 302, Pearce 85625* ☎ *520/826–3185 or 800/245–9202* 🖨 *520/826–3636* ⊕ *www.gcranch.com* ⛵ *12 rooms* ⚲ *In-room: no phone, refrigerator, no TV. In-hotel: pool, laundry facilities, no kids under 12, no elevator* ⊟ *D, MC, V* ⊘ *FAP.*

$ **Portal Peak Lodge.** This barracks-style structure, just east of Chiricahua National Monument near the New Mexico border, is notable less for its rooms (clean and pleasant but nondescript) than for its winged visitors: the elegant trogon, 14 types of hummingbird, and 10 species of owl are among the 330 varieties of birds that flock to nearby Cave Creek Canyon. Decks outside each room provide a good vantage point. ⊠*1215 Main St.* ☎*Box 364, Portal 85632* 📞*520/558–2223* 🖨*520/558–2473* 🌐*www.portalpeaklodge.com* 🛏*16 rooms* �'*In-room: no phone. In-hotel: restaurant, shop, no-smoking rooms, no elevator* 🚫*AE, D, MC, V.*

FORT BOWIE NATIONAL HISTORICAL SITE

❼ *8 mi northwest of Chiricahua National Monument. Take AZ 186 east from Chiricahua National Monument; 5 mi north of junction with AZ 181, signs direct you to road leading to fort.*

It's a bit of an outing to the site of Arizona's last battle between Native Americans and U.S. troops in the Dos Cabezas (Two-Headed) Mountains, but history buffs will find it an interesting diversion with the added benefit of high desert scenic beauty. Once a focal point for military operations—the fort was built here because Apache Pass was an important travel route for Native Americans and wagon trains—it now serves as a reminder of the brutal clashes between the two cultures.

Upon entering the site, you'll drive down a winding gravel road to a parking lot where a challenging trail leads 1½ mi to the historic site. The fort itself is virtually in ruins, but there's a small ranger-staffed visitor center with historical displays, restrooms, and books for sale.

Points of interest along the trail, indicated by historic markers, include the remnants of an Apache wickiup (hut), the fort cemetery, Apache Springs (their water source), and the **Butterfield stage stop,** a crucial link in the journey from east to west in the mid-19th century that happened to be in the heart of Chiricahua Apache land. Chief Cochise and the stagecoach operators ignored one another until sometime in 1861, when hostilities broke out between U.S. Cavalry troops and the Apache. After an ambush by the chief's warriors at Apache Pass in 1862, U.S. troops decided a fort was needed in the area, and Fort Bowie was built within weeks. There were skirmishes for the next 10 years, followed by a peaceful decade. Renewed fighting broke out in 1881. Geronimo, the new leader of the Indian warriors, finally surrendered in 1886. ⊠*3203 S. Old Fort Bowie Rd., Apache Pass Rd., 26 mi southeast of Willcox, 85605* 📞*520/847–2500* 🌐*www.nps.gov/fobo* 🎟*Free* 🕐*Daily 8–4:30.*

WILLCOX

❽ *26 mi northwest of Fort Bowie National Historical Site on AZ 186.*

The small town of Willcox, in the heart of Arizona ranching country, began in the late 1870s as a railroad construction camp called Maley. When the Southern Pacific Railroad line arrived in 1880, the town was renamed in honor of the highly regarded Fort Bowie commander, General Orlando B. Willcox. Once a major shipping center for cattle ranchers and mining companies, the town has preserved its rustic charm; the downtown area looks like an Old West movie set. An elevation of 4,167 feet means moderate summers and chilly winters, ideal for growing apples, and apple pie fans from as far away as Phoenix make pilgrimages to sample the harvest.

Don't miss the mile-high apple pies and hand-pressed cider at **Stout's Cider Mill** (⊠ *1510 N. Circle I Rd.* ☎ *520/384–3696*). Pick your own apples from late August to mid-September.

If you visit in winter, you can see some of the more than 10,000 sandhill cranes that roost at the **Willcox Playa,** a 37,000-acre area resembling a dry lake bed 12 mi south of Willcox. They migrate in late fall and head north to nesting sites in February, and bird-watchers migrate to Willcox the third week in January for the annual Wings over Willcox bird-watching event held in their honor.

Outside Willcox is the headquarters for the **Muleshoe Ranch Cooperative Management Area** (⊠ *6502 N. Muleshoe Ranch Rd.* ☎ *520/507–5229* ⊕ *www.nature.org* ☉ *Mar.–Apr., daily 8–5; June–Aug, weekends 8–5; Sept.–Feb. and May, Thurs.–Mon. 8–5*), nearly 50,000 acres of riparian desert land in the foothills of the Galiuro Mountains that are jointly owned and managed by the Nature Conservancy, the U.S. Forest Service, and the U.S. Bureau of Land Management. It's a 30-mi drive on a dirt road to the ranch—it takes about an hour—but the scenery, wildlife, and hiking are worth the bumps. The varied terrain of mesquite bosques, desert grasslands, and rocky canyons are home to a diverse array of wildlife, including desert tortoise, javelina, mule deer, hognose skunk, Montezuma quail, and great horned owl. You might also catch a glimpse of roaming bands of coatimundi—unusual looking omnivores resembling land-bound monkeys. Backcountry hiking and mountain-biking trips can be arranged by the ranch, and overnight accommodations are available. Guided 1-mi nature hikes are held on Saturdays at 8 AM from September through May. To reach the ranch, take Exit 340 off I–10, turn right on Bisbee Avenue and continue to Airport Road, turn right again, and after 15 mi take the right fork at a junction just past a group of mailboxes and continue to the end of the road.

☾ The **Rex Allen Arizona Cowboy Museum,** in Willcox's historic district, is a tribute to Willcox's most famous native son, cowboy singer Rex Allen. He starred in several rather average cowboy movies during the 1940s and '50s for Republic Pictures, but he's probably most famous as the friendly voice that narrated Walt Disney nature films of the 1960s. Check out the glittery suits the star wore on tour—they'd do Liberace proud. If you're visiting this museum as a family, you can all get in for the special family rate of $5. ⊠ *150 N. Railroad Ave.* ☎ *520/384–4583 or 877/234–4111* ⊕ *www.rexallenmuseum.org* ☞ *$2* ☉ *Daily 10–4.*

Learn about the fierce Chiricahua Apaches and the fearless leaders Cochise and Geronimo at the **Chiricahua Regional Museum and Research Center,** located in downtown Willcox. Other interesting tidbits about the area can be found in displays featuring the U.S. Cavalry, a nice collection of rocks and minerals, and relics of the famed Butterfield Overland Stage Route. One oddity the museum points out is that the memoirs of Civil War general Orlando Willcox, for whom the town was named, don't even mention a visit to Arizona. ✉ *127 E. Maley St.* ☎ *520/384–3971* 💲 *$2* ⊘ *Mon.–Sat. 10–4.*

WHERE TO STAY & EAT

$–$$$ ✕**Desert Rose Café.** Enjoy breakfast, lunch, dinner, or the Sunday buffet with the locals at this family-owned, family-friendly restaurant in Willcox. The food is as down-home as the atmosphere—mostly burgers, chicken, steak, and seafood standards—so it's just the place to go when you want a meal that's predictable, unpretentious, and tasty. ✉ *706 S. Haskell Ave.* ☎ *520/384–0514* ▤ *AE, MC, V.*

¢–$ ✕**Salsa Fiesta Mexican Restaurant.** You can't miss the bright neon lights of this little restaurant, just south of I–10 at Exit 340 in Willcox. The interior is cheerful and clean, with tables, chairs, and walls painted in a spicy medley of hot pink, purple, turquoise, green, and orange. The menu consists of Mexican standards, and the salsa bar runs the gamut from mild to super-hot. There is a modest selection of domestic and Mexican beers, and takeout is available. ✉ *1201 W. Rex Allen Dr.* ☎ *520/384–4233* ▤ *AE, D, MC, V* ⊘ *Closed Tues.*

$–$$ ▥**Muleshoe Ranch.** This turn-of-the-20th-century ranch is run by the Arizona chapter of the Nature Conservancy. Five casitas with kitchens sit in the pristine grassland foothills of the Galiuro Mountains, four around a courtyard hacienda-style. The fifth, a stone cabin set off by itself for more privacy, is the only unit open to families with children. The ranch has a visitor center, 22 mi of hiking trails, a guided, ¾-mi nature walk on Saturday at 9 AM, and private natural hot springs. There's a two-night minimum from September to May, and a three-night minimum on holiday weekends. ✉ *6502 N. Muleshoe Ranch Rd.* 🖃 *R.R. 1, Box 1542, 85643* ☎ *520/507–5229* ⊕ *www.muleshoelodging. org* ✑ *5 units* ⚅ *In-room: no a/c (some), no phone, kitchen, no TV* ▤ *AE, D, MC, V* ⊘ *Closed June–Aug.*

TEXAS CANYON

❾ *16 mi west of Willcox off I–10.*

Fodor's Choice ★   A dramatic change of scenery along I–10 will signal that you're entering Texas Canyon. The rock formations here are exceptional—huge boulders appear to be delicately balanced against each other.

Texas Canyon is the home of the **Amerind Foundation** (a contraction of "American" and "Indian"), founded by amateur archaeologist William Fulton in 1937 to foster understanding about Native American cultures. The research facility and museum are housed in a Spanish colonial revival–style structure designed by noted Tucson architect H. M. Starkweather. The museum's rotating displays of archaeological materials, crafts, and photographs give an overview of Native American cultures of the Southwest and Mexico. The adjacent Fulton–Hayden Memorial Art Gallery displays an assortment of art collected by William Fulton. Permanent exhibits include the work of O'odham women potters, an exquisite collection of Hopi katsina dolls, prized paintings by acclaimed Hopi artists, Pueblo pottery ranging from prehistoric pieces to modern ceramics, and archaeological exhibits on the Indian cultures of the prehistoric Southwest. The museum's gift shop has a superlative selection of Native American art, crafts, and jewelry. ⊠ *2100 N. Amerind Rd., 1 mi southeast of I–10, Exit 318, Dragoon* ☎ *520/586–3666* ⊕ *www.amerind.org* ⊠ *$5* ⊙ *Tues.–Sun. 10–4.*

WHERE TO STAY

$$–$$$ 🛏 **Triangle T Guest Ranch.** Enjoy the romance of the Old West at this historic ranch, situated on 160 acres of prime real estate in Texas Canyon. While the cozy casitas offer Western charm, the big draw to this rustic ranch is the immediate access to the startling and stunning rock formations found in the canyon. Hiking and horseback riding top the list of activities in the area, but the convenient location also makes this a great base for exploring the region. ⊠ *Dragoon Rd., at Exit 318 off I–10* 📪 *Box 218, 85609* ☎ *520/586–7533 or 866/586–7533* ⊕ *www.triangletguestranch.com* 🛏 *11 casitas* 🛏 *In room: no phone, no TV, kitchen (some). In-hotel: restaurant, pool, bicycles, bar, some pets allowed, no-smoking rooms, no elevator* ⊟ *MC, V.*

BENSON

🔟   *12 mi west of Texas Canyon and 50 mi east of Tucson via I–10.*

Back in its historic heyday as a Butterfield stagecoach station, and later as the hub of the Southern Pacific Railroad, Benson was just a place to stop on the way to somewhere else. That started to change with the 1974 discovery of a pristine cave beneath the Whetstone Mountains west of Benson, culminating 25 years later with the opening of Kartchner Caverns State Park, one of the most remarkable living cave systems in the world.

Though the city is undergoing dramatic changes, you can see the story of Benson's past at the little **San Pedro Valley Arts and Historical Society Museum** (⊠ *S. San Pedro Ave. at E. 5th St.* ☎ *520/586–3070*), a free museum that is closed in August. Exhibits include a re-creation of an old-fashioned grocery store and railroad paraphernalia.

As you pass Benson on I–10, watch for Ocotillo Avenue, Exit 304. Take a left and drive about 2¼ mi, where a mailbox with a backward SW signals
Fodor's Choice   that you've come to the turnoff for **Singing Wind Bookshop.** Make a right
★   at the mailbox and drive ¼ mi until you see a green gate. Let yourself in, close the gate, and go another ¼ mi to the shop. If you don't see Winifred Bundy, who also runs the ranch, ring the gong out front. She knows just about every regional author around, so this unique bookshop-on-a-ranch has signed copies of books on just about any Southwestern topic. This chatty bibliophile also frequently shares her love of the area with visitors, throwing in choice tidbits about obscure sights and her literary friends' favorite haunts. She doesn't take credit cards, though. ⊠ *700 W. Singing Wind Rd.* ☎ *520/586–2425* ⊙ *Daily 9–5.*

WHERE TO STAY & EAT

$–$$$ ✕**Chute-Out Steakhouse & Saloon.** Don't be deceived by the unassuming exterior of this stucco steak house a block from Benson's main street. Once inside this warm and welcoming place, you'll understand why it's so popular. The food is excellent, and the service is efficient and friendly. Mesquite-grilled steaks, ribs, chicken, and seafood, fresh-baked breads and desserts, and salads (the house dressing is superb) make this spot well worth the visit. ⊠*161 S. Huachuca St.* ☎*520/586–7297* ▭*AE, D, MC, V* ⊘*No lunch.*

$–$$ ✕**Galleano's.** The kitchen at this upscale roadhouse, a local favorite, turns out traditional diner fare—including great burgers and fries—as well as pastas and salads. There's a big salad bar, too—unusual in these parts. ⊠*601 W. 4th St.* ☎*520/586–3523* ▭*AE, MC, V* ⊘*No dinner Sun.*

¢–$$ ✕**Horseshoe Steakhouse & Cantina.** For a good green-chile burrito, stop at this eclectic eatery, which has graced Benson's main street for more than 60 years. You'll know you're in cowboy country when you see the neon horseshoe on the ceiling, the macramés of local cattle brands, and the jukebox with its selection of country-and-western ballads. ⊠*154 E. 4th St.* ☎*520/586–3303* ▭*AE, D, MC, V.*

¢ ✕**Ruiz's Mexican Food & Cantina.** In this part of the world, the name
Fodor's Choice is pronounced "Reese." This tiny spot on the main drag has been in
★ operation since 1959, serving a daily stream of customers, morning to night, hungry for green-corn tamales, chiles rellenos, *topopo* (deep-fried tortilla) salads, and other specialties. The hand-made Sonoran-style dishes all originate from the owner's family recipes, giving the food a truly authentic flair rarely found on this side of the border. The adjoining bar serves beer, wine, and cocktails. ⊠*687 W. 4th St.* ☎*520/586–2707* ▭*MC, V.*

♻ ★ $–$$ ☷**Astronomers Inn.** You don't have to be an astronomer to enjoy this hilltop lodging on the grounds of the private Vega-Bray Observatory, but eight powerful telescopes are available for your universe-viewing pleasure. The B&B reflects the owners' delight in science: the comfortable rooms have such gadgets as lamps that simulate lightning and decorations (visible in black light) that resemble constellations painted on the ceiling. A special section in the science room is dedicated to kids. Astronomers travel from Tucson to the observatory on clear evenings to lead an evening of observation and science classes. The inn also provides a classroom complete with computers and hands-on science projects, a 2-mi nature trail, and two ponds for relaxed boating. ⊠*1311 Astronomers Rd., 2 mi southeast of I–10, Exit 306* ☎*520/586–7906* ☒*520/586–1123* ⊕*www.astronomersinn.com* ➦*5 rooms* △*In-room: kitchen (some), Wi-Fi. In-hotel: no-smoking rooms, no elevator* ▭*D, MC, V* ⦿*BP.*

$–$$ ☷**Holiday Inn Express.** The closest lodging to Kartchner Caverns State Park, this motel sits just off I–10 at the "Kartchner Corridor," a few miles west of Benson. It has the comfort and amenities you'd expect but with a Southwestern elegance rarely found in chain motels around the area. Rooms have coffeemakers and hair dryers, and a Continental breakfast is included. ⊠*630 S. Village Loop* ✉*Box 2252, 85602*

7

☎520/586–8800 or 888/263–2283 🖷520/586–1370 ⊕www.hiex-
press.com/bensonaz ➷62 rooms ⚭In-room: refrigerator, Wi-Fi. In-
hotel: pool, gym, laundry facilities ▭AE, D, DC, MC, V ⦿CP.

KARTCHNER CAVERNS STATE PARK

⓫ *9 mi south of Benson on AZ 90.*

Fodor's Choice
★

The publicity that surrounded the official opening of the Kartchner Caverns in November 1999 was in marked contrast to the secrecy that shrouded their discovery 25 years earlier and concealed their existence for 14 years. The two young men who stumbled into what is now considered one of the most spectacular cave systems anywhere played a fundamental role in its protection and eventual development. Great precautions have been taken to protect the wet-cave system—which comprises 13,000 feet of passages and two chambers as long as football fields—from damage by light and dryness.

WORD OF MOUTH

"If you haven't been to Kartchner Caverns, just outside of Tucson, it's awesome!… If you want to see Kartchner, you'll need to either pre-book or take a chance on the 100 or so tickets they reserve for first come, first served each day. It is well worth the wait. It's a living cave and they've gone to great lengths to preserve it that way while allowing those of us who don't like crawling through tiny spaces to see it."

–casugi

The Discovery Center introduces visitors to the cave and its formations, and hour-long guided tours take small groups into the upper cave. Spectacular formations include the longest soda straw stalactite in the United States at 21 feet and 2 inches. The Big Room is viewed on a separate tour: it holds the world's most extensive formation of brushite moonmilk, the first reported occurrence of turnip shields, and the first noted occurrence of birdsnest needle formations. Other funky and fabulous formations include brilliant red flowstone, rippling multi-hued stalactites, delicate white helictites, translucent orange bacon, and expansive mud flats. It's also the nursery roost for female cave myotis bats from April through September, during which time the lower cave is closed in an effort to foster the cave's unique ecosystem. Kartchner Caverns is a wet, "live" cave, meaning that water still rises up from the surface to increase the multicolored calcium carbonate formations already visible.

The total cavern size is 2 2/5 mi long, but the explored areas cover only 1,600 feet by 1,100 feet. The average relative humidity inside is 99%, so visitors are often graced with "cave kisses," water droplets from above. Because the climate outside the caves is so dry, it is estimated that if air got inside, it could deplete the moisture in only a few days, halting the growth of the speleothems that decorate its walls. To prevent this, there are 22 environmental monitoring stations that measure air and soil temperature, relative humidity, evaporation rates, air trace gases, and airflow inside the caverns. Tour reservations are required and should be made several months in advance; hiking trails, picnic areas, and campsites are available on the park's 550 acres. If you're here and didn't make a reservation, you may be in luck: the park reserves 100 walk-up tickets, available on a first-come, first-served basis, for the Rotunda/Throne Room tour. ✉ *AZ 90, 9 mi south of Exit 302 off I–10* ☎ *520/586–4100 information, 520/586–2283 tour reservations* ⊕ *www.pr.state.az.us* ✉ *$5 per vehicle up to 4 people, $1 each additional person; Rotunda/Throne Room tours $18.95, Big Room tours $22.95* ⊘ *Daily 7:30–6, cave tours, by reservation, daily 8:40–4:40.*

SOUTHWEST ARIZONA

The turbulent history of the West is writ large in this now-sleepy part of Arizona. It's home to the Tohono O'odham Indian Reservation (the largest in the country after the Navajo Nation's) and towns such as Ajo, created—and almost undone—by the copper-mining industry, and Nogales, a vital entry point on the U.S.–Mexico border. Yuma, abutting the California border, was a major crossing point of the Colorado River as far back as the time of the conquistadors.

These days, people mostly travel *through* Sells, Ajo, and Yuma en route to the closest beaches: during the school year, especially on warm weekends and semester breaks, the 130-mi route from Tucson to Ajo is busy with traffic headed southwest to Puerto Penasco (Rocky Point), Mexico, the closest outlet to the sea for Arizonans. All summer long, I–8 takes heat-weary Tucsonans and Phoenicians to San Diego, California, and Yuma is the mid-point.

Natural attractions are a lure in this starkly scenic region: Organ Pipe Cactus National Monument provides trails for desert hikers, and Buenos Aires and Imperial wildlife refuges—homes to many unusual species—are important destinations for birders and other nature watchers. Much of the time, however, your only companions will be the low-lying scrub and cactus and the mesquite, ironwood, and paloverde trees.

NOGALES

⑫ *15 mi south of Tumacácori, 63 mi south of Tucson on I–19 at the Mexican border.*

Nogales, named for the walnut trees that grew along the river here, is actually two towns: the somewhat bland, industrial American city and the smaller Mexican town over the border. The American side was once a focal point for cattle shipping between Sonora and the United States. Today, Nogales reaps the benefits of NAFTA, with warehouses and trucking firms dedicated to the distribution of Mexican produce, making it one of the world's busiest produce ports. The American side depends on the health of the peso and the shoppers who cross the border from Mexico to buy American goods that they can't get in their country. The Mexican side has grown with the economic success

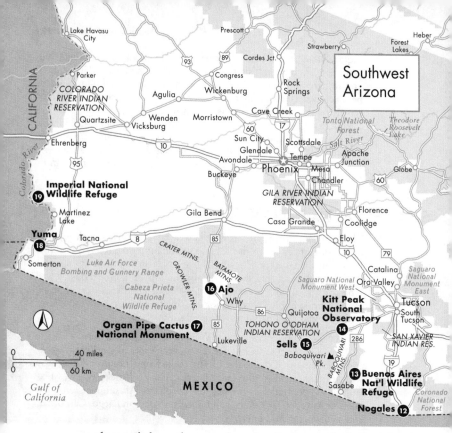

Southwest Arizona

of *maquiladoras,* factories that manufacture goods destined for the United States. There's a great deal of commerce between the two sides of Nogales.

Some of this trade is in narcotics and undocumented workers, giving this border town a more edgy quality than its American counterpart. Bustling Nogales, Mexico can become fairly rowdy on weekend evenings, when underage Tucsonans head south of the border to drink. It has some good restaurants, however, and fine-quality crafts in addition to the usual souvenirs—and tourists as well as locals from Tucson and Phoenix enjoy a day trip of shopping and dining on the Mexico side.

■TIP→ **To make calls to Mexico use the prefix 011 along with the country code of 52.** Security on the American side of the border is very tight; don't even think about taking a firearm near the border. You'll also do better not to drive your car into Mexico: not only is there a very real possibility it may be stolen, but you'll face significant delays because of the thorough search you and your vehicle will receive upon returning. This hassle is unnecessary, though, because you can cover Nogales in a day trip, and most of the good shopping is within easy walking distance of the border crossing. Park on the Arizona side, either on the street or, better yet, in one of many guarded lots that cost about $8 for the day (use restrooms on the U.S. side before you cross). Keep in mind that as of January 1, 2008, all travelers must have a passport or other accepted secure document to enter or reenter the United States.

■**TIP→ Don't bother trading your dollars for pesos. Merchants prefer dollars and always have change on hand. Be prepared for aggressive selling tactics and sometimes-disorienting hubbub, but locals are always glad to point you in the right direction, and almost all speak some English.**

WHERE TO STAY & EAT

★ $–$$$ ✕**La Roca.** East of the railroad tracks and off the beaten tourist path, La Roca is a favorite of Tucsonans. It isn't difficult to find, just look for the towering black sign to the east of the border entrance. The setting—a series of tiled rooms and courtyards in a stately old stone house, with a balcony overlooking a charming patio—is lovely. Try the *carne tampiqueña,* an assortment of grilled meats that comes with chiles rellenos and an enchilada. Chicken mole is also a favorite. ⊠*Calle Elias 91, Nogales, Mexico* ☎*631/312–0891* ⊟*MC, V.*

$–$$ ✕**Elvira.** The free shot of tequila that comes with each meal will whet your appetite for Elvira's reliable fish dishes, chicken mole, and chiles rellenos. Tequila lovers can sample more than one hundred different tequilas at the bar. This large, friendly restaurant (divided into intimate dining areas) is at the foot of Avenida Obregón just south of the border and popular with those who visit Nogales often. ⊠*Avda. Obregón 1, Nogales, Mexico* ☎*631/312–4773* ⊟*MC, V.*

¢–$$ ✕**Zula's.** Standard, old-fashioned border restaurant fare is served with Greek flair on the Arizona side of the border, with Sonoran food (tortillas, cheese, refried beans) alongside gyros and American selections such as burgers, steaks, and seafood entrées. It's not as glitzy as the south-of-the-border places, but the food is just as tasty. ⊠*982 N. Grand Ave., Nogales* ☎*520/287–2892* ⊟*MC, V.*

$–$$$ ⊡**Holiday Inn Express Nogales.** Although this chain hotel caters predominantly to business travelers, it suits the casual visitor as well. Spacious rooms, decked out with cushiony wing chairs and cushy beds, make this a favorite place to stay near the border. Best of all, the comfortable hotel is cleaner than its local counterparts and offers added security and a friendly staff. ⊠*850 W. Shell Rd., I–19 and Mariposa Rd.* ☎*520/281–0123 or 877/270–6397* ☏*520/281–2005* ⊕*www.hiexpress.com* ⇨*99 rooms, 10 suites* ₺*In-room: Wi-Fi, VCR, refrigerator. In-hotel: pool, gym, laundry facilities, no-smoking rooms* ⊟*AE, D, DC, MC, V.*

¢ ⊡**Americana Motor Hotel.** A serviceable place that has seen better days, the Americana has large, Aztec-style stone sculptures scattered around the grounds. Decorated in a Southwest motif, rooms are comfortable

7

Snap "Shot" of Tequila

Agave, the plant from which fine tequila is made, flourishes in southern Arizona. Many people think the agave is a cactus, but it's actually a succulent, closely related to the lily and amaryllis. Only blue agave—just one of 136 species—is used to make true tequila, but other species are used to make mezcal, the more generic type of liquor. Tequila is a specific type of mezcal, just as bourbon or scotch are specific types of whiskey. Many of the cheap brands are actually *mixtos*, which means they aren't 100% agave; true tequila isn't cheap, and you can pay more than $50 per bottle for a premium brand.

Across the border in Mexico, there are more than 50 tequila producers, so it's understandable that tequila is a popular drink in Arizona. In fact, more tequila is consumed in the United States than anywhere else, including Mexico. The heart of the tequila-making region is Tequila itself, 30 mi west of Guadalajara, in the state of Jalisco. The hills around the town are responsible for its name, "tel" meaning "hill," and "quilla," a kind of lava around the dead volcanoes in the area.

To produce tequila, the bulb of the blue agave plant is harvested (it may weigh up to 150 pounds), heated to break down the sugars, and fermented. The best brands, Herradura and El Tesoro, are fermented with wild yeasts that add distinctive flavors to the final product. The fermented tequila is then placed into pot stills, where it is double-distilled to 90 proof or higher. Bottles designated "añejo" have been aged for a minimum of a year in oak barrels—these tequilas are the most expensive.

but worn. The restaurant and lounge are casual places to eat American food. ⊠ *639 N. Grand Ave., 85621* ☎ *520/287–7211 or 800/874–8079* ⟿ *97 rooms* ⌂ *In-hotel: restaurant, bar, pool, no elevator* ☰ *AE, MC, V.*

¢ ⊡ **El Dorado Motel.** This typical motel offers casual, unpretentious border flavor. The small-town service, although friendly, is not particularly quick. ⊠ *884 N. Grand Ave., 85621* ☎ *520/287–4611* ⎙ *520/287–0101* ⟿ *100 rooms* ⌂ *In-hotel: pool, no elevator* ☰ *AE, D, MC, V.*

SHOPPING

The main shopping area is on the Mexican side, on Avenida Obregón, which begins a few blocks west (to your right) of the border entrance and runs north–south; just follow the crowds. You'll find handicrafts, furnishings, and jewelry here, but if you go off on some of the side streets, you might come across more interesting finds at better prices. Except at shops that indicate otherwise, bargaining is not only acceptable but expected. Playing this customary game can save you, on average, 50%, so don't be shy. The shops listed below tend to have fixed prices, so either buy here if you don't want to bargain at all, or note their prices and see if you can do better elsewhere.

Casa Bonita (⊠ *Avda. Obregón 134, Nogales, Mexico* ☎ *631/312–3059*) carries jewelry, tinwork mirrors, carved wooden chests, and household items. **El Sarape** (⊠ *Avda. Obregón 161, Nogales, Mexico* ☎ *631/312–0309*) specializes in sterling silver jewelry from Taxco and women's designer clothing. **Maya de México** (⊠ *Avda. Obregón 150, Nogales, Mexico* ☎ *No phone*) is the place to come for smaller folk-art items, including Day of the Dead displays, blue glass, painted dishes, and clothing.

BUENOS AIRES NATIONAL WILDLIFE REFUGE

⑬ *66 mi southwest of Tucson; from Tucson, take AZ 86 west 22 mi to AZ 286; go south 40 mi to Milepost 8, and it's another 3 mi east to the preserve headquarters.*

This remote nature preserve, in the Altar Valley and encircled by seven mountain ranges, is the only place in the United States where the Sonoran–savanna grasslands that once spread over the entire region can still be seen. The fragile ecosystem was almost completely destroyed by overgrazing, and a program to restore native grasses is currently in progress. In 1985 the U.S. Fish and Wildlife Service purchased the Buenos Aires Ranch—now headquarters for the 115,000-acre preserve—to establish a reintroduction program for the endangered masked bobwhite quail. Bird-watchers consider Buenos Aires unique because it is the only place in the United States where they can see a "grand slam" (four species) of quail: Montezuma quail, Gambel's quail, scaled quail, and masked bobwhite. If it rains, the 100-acre Aguirre Lake, 1½ mi north of the headquarters, attracts wading birds, shorebirds, and waterfowl—in all, more than 320 avian species have been spotted here. They share the turf with deer, antelope, coatimundi, badgers, bobcats, and mountain lions. Touring options include a 10-mi auto tour through the area, nature trails, a boardwalk through the marshes at Arivaca Cienega, and, by reservation only, weekend guided tours. ⊠ *AZ 286, Box 109, Sasabe 85633* ☎ *520/823–4251* 🖶 *520/823–4247* ⊕ *http://refuges.fws.gov* ✉ *Free* ☉ *Refuge headquarters and visitor center daily 7:30–4.*

WHERE TO STAY

$$$$ 🏨 **Rancho de la Osa.** This ranch, set on 250 eucalyptus-shaded acres near the Mexican border and Buenos Aires preserve, was built in 1889, and two adobe structures were added in the 1920s to accommodate guests. The rooms have modern plumbing and fixtures, wood-burning fireplaces, and porches with Adirondack chairs. Bread baked on the premises, salads made with ingredients grown in the garden, and water drawn from the well all contribute to the back-to-basics serenity. Rates include all meals and horseback riding, and guests are expected to dress for dinner. ⊠ *AZ 286* 🖂 *Box 1, Sasabe 85633* ☎ *520/823–4257 or 800/872–6240* 🖶 *520/823–4238* ⊕ *www.ranchodelaosa.com* 📞 *19 rooms* ♿ *In-room: no TV. In-hotel: restaurant, bar, pool, bicycles, public Internet, no kids under 6, no-smoking rooms, no elevator* ⊟ *MC, V* ⦿ *FAP.*

KITT PEAK NATIONAL OBSERVATORY

⑭ *56 mi southwest of Tucson; to reach Kitt Peak from Tucson, take I–10 to I–19 south, and then AZ 86. After 44 mi on AZ 86, turn left at AZ 386 junction and follow winding mountain road 12 mi up to observatory. In inclement weather, contact the highway department to confirm that the road is open.*

Funded by the National Science Foundation and managed by a group of more than 20 universities, Kitt Peak National Observatory is part of the Tohono O'odham Reservation. After much discussion back in the late 1950s, tribal leaders agreed to share a small section of their 4,400 square mi with the observatory's telescopes. Among these is the McMath, the world's largest solar telescope, which uses piped-in liquid coolant. From the visitors' gallery you can see into the telescope's light-path tunnel, which goes down hundreds of feet into the mountain. Kitt Peak scientists use these high-power telescopes to conduct vital solar research and observe distant galaxies.

The visitor center has exhibits on astronomy, information about the telescopes, and hour-long guided tours ($3.50 per person) that depart daily at 10, 11:30, and 1:30. Complimentary brochures enable you to take self-guided tours of the grounds, and there's a picnic area about 1½ mi below the observatory. The observatory buildings have vending machines, but there are no restaurants or gas stations within 20 mi of Kitt Peak. The observatory offers a nightly observing program ($39 per person) except from July 15 to September 1; reservations are necessary. ⊠ *AZ 386, Pan Tak* ☎ *520/318–8726, 520/318–7200 recorded message* ⊕ *www.noao.edu/kpno* 💲 *$2 suggested donation* ☉ *Visitor center daily 9–3:45.*

SELLS

⑮ *32 mi southwest of Kitt Peak via AZ 386 to AZ 86.*

The Tohono O'odham Reservation, the second-largest in the United States, covers 4,400 square mi between Tucson and Ajo, stretching south to the Mexican border and north almost to the city of Casa Grande. To the south of Kitt Peak, the 7,730-foot Baboquivari Peak is considered sacred by the Tohono O'odham as the home of their deity, I'itoi ("elder brother"). Less than halfway between Tucson and Ajo, Sells—the tribal capital of the Tohono O'odham—is a good place to stop for gas or a soft drink. Much of the time there's little to see or do in Sells, but in winter an annual rodeo and fair attract thousands of visitors.

If you want something more substantial than a snack, head for the Sells Shopping Center, where the good-size market **Basha's Deli & Bakery** (⊠ *Topawa Rd.* ☎ *520/383–2546*) can supply all the makings for a picnic.

For traditional Indian and Mexican food like fry bread, tacos, and chili, try the **Papago Cafe** (⊠*AZ 86, near Chevron Station* ☎*520/383–3510*).

AJO

🔟 *90 mi northwest of Sells.*

"Ajo" (pronounced *ah*-ho) is Spanish for garlic, and some say the town got its name from the wild garlic that grows in the area. Others claim the word is a bastardization of the Indian word *au-auho,* referring to red paint derived from a local pigment.

For many years Ajo, like Bisbee, was a thriving Phelps Dodge Company town. Copper mining had been attempted in the area in the late 19th century, but it wasn't until the 1911 arrival of the Calumet & Arizona Mining Company that the region began to be developed profitably. Calumet and Phelps Dodge merged in 1935, and the huge pit mine produced millions of tons of copper until it closed in 1985. Nowadays, Ajo is pretty sleepy; the town's population of 4,000 has a median age of 51, and most visitors are on their way to or from Rocky Point, Mexico.

At the center of town is a sparkling white Spanish-style plaza. The shops and restaurants that line the plaza's covered arcade today are rather modest. Unlike Bisbee, Ajo hasn't yet drawn an artistic crowd—or the upscale boutiques and eateries that tend to follow. Chain stores and fast-food haven't made a bee line here either—you'll find only one Dairy Queen and a Pizza Hut in this remote desert hamlet.

You get an expansive view of Ajo's ugly gash of an open-pit mine, almost 2 mi wide, from the **New Cornelia Open Pit Mine Lookout Point.** Some of the abandoned equipment remains in the pit, and mining operations are diagrammed at the visitors' shelter, where there's a 30-minute film about mining. ⊠*Indian Village Rd.* ☎*520/387–7742* 🎟*Free* 🕙*Call for hrs.*

The **Ajo Historical Society Museum** has collected a mélange of articles related to Ajo's past from local townspeople. The displays are rather disorganized, but the historical photographs and artifacts are interesting, and the museum is inside the territorial-style St. Catherine's Indian Mission, built around 1942. ⊠*160 Mission St.* ☎*520/387–7105* 🎟*Donations requested* 🕙*Mon.–Sat. 10–4, Sun. noon–4.*

The 860,000-acre **Cabeza Prieta National Wildlife Refuge,** about 10 minutes from Ajo, was established in 1939 as a preserve for endangered bighorn sheep and other Sonoran Desert wildlife. A permit is required to enter, and only those with four-wheel-drive vehicles, needed to traverse the rugged terrain, can obtain one from the refuge's office. ⊠*1611 N. 2nd Ave., Ajo 85321* ☎*520/387–6483* ⊕*http://refuges.fws.gov* 🎟*Free* 🕙*Office weekdays 7:30–4:30, refuge daily dawn–dusk.*

7

WHERE TO STAY & EAT

¢–$ ✕**Señor Sancho.** Just about everybody in Ajo comes to this unprepossessing roadhouse at the north end of town for generous portions of Mexican food, well prepared and very reasonably priced. This friendly spot has light-wood booths and colorful murals with a Mexican motif. All the standard favorites are on the menu—hearty combination platters, tacos, enchiladas, chiles rellenos, flautas, and good chicken mole. ⊠ *663 N. 2nd Ave.* ☏ *520/387–6226* ▤ *MC, V.*

$ ▥**Guest House Inn Bed & Breakfast.** Built in 1925 to accommodate visiting Phelps Dodge VIPs, this lodging is a favorite for birders: guests can head out early to nearby Organ Pipe National Monument or just sit on the patio and watch the quail, cactus wrens, and other warblers that fly in to visit. Rooms are furnished in various Southwestern styles, from light Santa Fe to rich Spanish colonial. A full breakfast is served. ⊠ *700 Guest House Rd., 85321* ☏ *520/387–6133* ⊕ *www.guesthouseinn.biz* ↻ *4 rooms* △ *In-room: no phone, refrigerator, no TV, Wi-Fi. In-hotel: no-smoking rooms, no elevator* ▤ *DC, MC, V* ¶○¶*BP.*

ORGAN PIPE CACTUS NATIONAL MONUMENT

⓱ *32 mi southwest of Ajo; from Ajo, backtrack to Why and take AZ 85 south for 22 mi to reach the visitor center.*

Organ Pipe Cactus National Monument, abutting Cabeza Prieta National Wildlife Refuge but much more accessible to visitors, is the largest habitat north of the border for organ-pipe cacti. These multi-armed cousins of the saguaro are fairly common in Mexico but rare in the United States. Because they tend to grow on south-facing slopes, you won't be able to see many of them unless you take one of the two scenic loop drives: the 21-mi **Ajo Mountain Drive** or the 53-mi **Puerto Blanco Drive,** both on winding, graded one-way dirt roads.

■**TIP**→ **Be aware that Organ Pipe has become an illegal border crossing hot spot. Migrant workers and drug traffickers cross from Mexico under cover of darkness. At this writing Puerto Blanco Drive was closed to the public. A two-way road that only travels 5 of the 53 mi on Puerto Blanco Drive is open, but the rest of the road will remain closed due to continuing concerns over its proximity to the U.S.–Mexico border. Even so, park officials emphasize that tourists have only occasionally been the victims of isolated property crimes—primarily theft of personal items from parked cars. Visitors are advised by rangers to keep valuables locked and out of plain view and not to initiate contact with groups of strangers whom they may encounter on hiking trails.**

A campground at the monument has 208 RV (no hookups) and tent sites. Facilities include a dump station, flush toilets, grills, and picnic tables. ⊠ *AZ 85* ☏ *520/387–6849* ⊕ *www.nps.gov/orpi* ▣ *$8 per vehicle* ⊙ *Visitor center daily 8–5.*

YUMA

18 *170 mi northwest of Ajo.*

Today, many people think of Yuma as a convenient stop between Phoenix or Tucson and San Diego—and this was equally true in the relatively recent past. It's difficult to imagine the lower Colorado River, now dammed and bridged, as either a barrier or a means of transportation, but until the early part of the 20th century, this section of the great waterway was a force to contend with. Records show that since at least 1540 the Spanish were using Yuma (then the site of a Quechan Indian village) as a ford across a relatively shallow juncture of the Colorado.

Three centuries later, the advent of the shallow-draft steamboat made the settlement a point of entry for fortune seekers heading through the Gulf of California to mining sites in eastern Arizona. Fort Yuma was established in 1850 to guard against Indian attacks, and by 1873 the town was a county seat, a U.S. port of entry, and an army depot.

The steamboat shipping business, undermined by the completion of the Southern Pacific Railroad line in 1877, was finished off by the building of Laguna Dam in 1909. In World War II, Yuma Proving Ground was used to train bomber pilots, and General Patton readied some of his desert war forces for battle at classified areas near the city. Many who served here during the war returned to Yuma to retire, and the city's economy now relies largely on tourism. The population swells during the winter months with retirees from cold climates who park their homes on wheels at one of the many RV communities on the outskirts of town. One fact may shed some light on why: according to National Weather Service statistics, Yuma is the sunniest city in the United States.

Most of the interesting sights in Yuma are at the north end of town.

Stop in at the **Yuma Convention and Visitors Bureau** (✉ *377 S. Main St.* ☎ *928/783–0071 or 800/293–0071* ⊕ *www.visityuma.com*) and pick up a walking-tour guide to the historic downtown area.

The adobe-style **Sanguinetti House Museum,** run by the Arizona Historical Society, was built around 1870 by merchant E. F. Sanguinetti; it exhibits artifacts from Yuma's territorial days and details the military presence in the area. If you're dining at The Garden Café this makes for an interesting stop, but it's not worth a visit on its own, especially if you plan on visiting the more popular Yuma Crossing State Historic Park. ✉ *240 S. Madison Ave.* ☎ *928/782–1841* 🏷 *$3* 🕐 *Tues.–Sat. 10–4.*

The mess hall of Fort Yuma, which is on the California side of the Colorado River and was later used as a school for Native American children, now serves as the small **Fort Yuma Quechan Indian Museum.** Historical photographs, archaeological items, and Quechan arts and crafts are on display. ⊠*CA 24* ☎*760/572–0661* 💲*$1* ⊙*Daily 8–noon and 1–5.*

On the other side of the river from Fort Yuma, the Civil War–period quartermaster depot resupplied army posts to the north and east and served as a distribution point for steamboat freight headed overland to Arizona forts. The 1853 home of riverboat captain G. A. Johnson is the depot's earliest building and the centerpiece of the **Yuma Crossing State Historic Park.** The residence also served as a weather bureau and home for customs agents, among other functions, and the guided tour through the house provides a complete history. The Transportation Museum has stagecoaches, Wells Fargo wagons, and antique surreys, as well as more "modern" modes of transportation like the 1931 Model A pickup. You can also visit a re-creation of the Commanding Officer's Quarters, complete with period furnishings. ⊠*201 N. 4th Ave., between 1st St. and Colorado River Bridge* ☎*928/329–0471* ⊕*www.pr.state.az.us* 💲*$3* ⊙*Daily 9–5.*

The most notorious tourist sight in town, **Yuma Territorial Prison,** now an Arizona state historic park, was built for the most part by the convicts who were incarcerated here from 1876 until 1909, when the prison outgrew its location. The hilly site on the Colorado River, chosen for security purposes, precluded further expansion.

Visitors gazing today at the tiny cells that held six inmates each, often in 115°F heat, are likely to be appalled, but the prison—dubbed the Country Club of the Colorado by locals—was considered a model of enlightenment by turn-of-the-20th-century standards: in an era when beatings were common, the only punishments meted out here were solitary confinement and assignment to a dark cell. The complex housed a hospital as well as Yuma's only public library, where the 25¢ that visitors paid for a prison tour financed the acquisition of new books.

The 3,069 prisoners who served time at what was then the territory's only prison included men and women from 21 different countries. They came from all social classes and were sent up for everything from armed robbery and murder to polygamy. R. L. McDonald, incarcerated for forgery, had been the superintendent of the Phoenix public school system. Chosen as the prison bookkeeper, he absconded with $130 of the inmates' money when he left.

The mess hall opened as a museum in 1940, and the entire prison complex was designated a state historic park in 1961. ⊠*1 Prison Hill Rd., near Exit 1 off I–8* ☎*928/783–4771* ⊕*www.pr.state.az.us* 💲*$4* ⊙*Daily 8–5.*

WHERE TO STAY & EAT

★ **$–$$$** ✕**River City Grill.** This hip downtown restaurant is a favorite dining spot for locals and visitors. It gets a bit loud on weekend nights, but the camaraderie of diners is well worth it. Owners Nan and Tony Bain dish out a melody of flavors drawing on Mediterranean, Pacific Rim, Indian, and Caribbean influences. For starters you can sample everything from Vietnamese spring rolls to curried mussels. Entrées include delicacies like grilled wild salmon, rack of lamb, and such vegetarian dishes as ricotta-and-spinach ravioli. ⊠*600 W. 3rd St.* ☎*928/782–7988* ⊟*AE, D, DC, MC, V* ⊗*No lunch weekends.*

$–$$ ✕**Chretin's Mexican Food.** A Yuma institution, Chretin's opened as a dance hall in the 1930s before it became one of the first Mexican restaurants in town in 1946. Don't be put off by the nondescript exterior or the entryway, which leads back past the kitchen and cashier's stand into three large dining areas. The food is all made on the premises, right down to the chips and tortillas. Try anything that features *machaca* (shredded spiced beef or chicken). ⊠*485 S. 15th Ave.* ☎*928/782–1291* ⊟*D, MC, V* ⊗*Closed Sun.*

$–$$ ✕**The Garden Café.** After a visit to the Sanguinetti House Museum, this adjoining café is a good place to stop for breakfast or lunch. This charming dining spot features lush gardens and aviaries on the outdoor patio, historical photos on the walls, and a menu of homemade salads, soups, and sandwiches. Favorites include the quiche, served with homemade fruit bread, and the tortilla soup. Sunday brunch—complete with carne asada, tortillas, potatoes, scrambled eggs, a layered ham and egg strata, breakfast meats, fruit, and dessert—is one of the best times to visit. ⊠*248 S. Madison Ave.* ☎*928/783–1491* ⊟*AE, MC, V* ⊗*Closed Mon.*

★ ¢–$ ✕**Lutes Casino.** Almost always packed with locals at lunchtime, this large, funky restaurant and bar claims to be the oldest pool hall and domino parlor in Arizona. It's a great place for a burger and a brew. If you can't choose between a cheeseburger and a hot dog, have both. The "Especial" combines these two American favorites and adds a generous dollop of Lutes' "special sauce." ⊠*221 S. Main St.* ☎*928/782–2192* ⊟*No credit cards.*

☺ $$$ ▦**Shilo Inn.** The full kitchens offered in the suites make this an excellent place for families to stay. Rooms are spacious and most have views of the courtyard and pool. A full breakfast is included in the rates and served in the restaurant. ⊠*1550 S. Castle Dome Rd., 85365* ☎*928/782–9511 or 800/222–2244* ⊟*928/783–1538* ⊕*www.shiloinns.com* ⊷*131 rooms, 15 suites* ♿*In-room: refrigerator. In-hotel: restaurant, bar, pool, gym, some pets allowed* ⊟*AE, D, DC, MC, V* ⋈*BP.*

$$–$$$ ▦**Clarion Suites.** One wing of this sprawling hotel surrounds a well-manicured courtyard with a fountain and several orange trees; another faces the pool and Cabana Club, where the complimentary Continental breakfast and happy-hour drinks are served. This is an all-suites property, and each accommodation has a coffeemaker and a separate sitting area with a desk. ⊠*2600 S. 4th Ave., 85364* ☎*928/726–4830 or 800/333–3333* ⊟*928/341–1152* ⊕*www.choicehotels.com* ⊷*164 suites* ♿*In-room: refrigerator. In-hotel: bar, pool, laundry facilities, airport shuttle* ⊟*AE, D, DC, MC, V* ⋈*CP.*

$–$$ ▦**Best Western Coronado Motor Hotel.** This Spanish tile–roofed motor hotel, convenient to the freeway and downtown, was built in 1938. Bob Hope used to stay here during World War II, when he entertained the gunnery troops training in Yuma. Yuma Landing Restaurant & Lounge is on-site with an impressive collection of historical photos. ⊠*233*

4th Ave., 85364 ☎*928/783–4453 or 800/528–1234* 🖷*928/782–7487*
⊕*www.bestwestern.com* ➴*86 rooms* ⅃*In-room: refrigerator, VCR,*
dial-up. In-hotel: restaurant, bar, pool, laundry facilities, no elevator
🖃*AE, D, DC, MC, V* 🍴*BP.*

SHOPPING
Art studios, antiques shops, and specialty boutiques have taken advantage of downtown Yuma's facelift. **Colorado River Pottery** (✉*67 W. 2nd
St.* ☎*928/343–0413*) features hand-crafted bowls, vases, and dishes.
Kirstin's (✉*261 S. Main St.* ☎*928/783–6180*) is a specialty store filled
with Southwestern and Mexican art and furniture. **Prickly Pear** (✉*324
S. Main St.* ☎*928/343–0390*) is packed with an assortment of gourmet sauces, turquoise jewelry, imported dishes, hand-carved furniture,
and wall art.

IMPERIAL NATIONAL WILDLIFE REFUGE

☙ ❶⑨ *40 mi north of Yuma; from Yuma, take U.S. 95 north past the Proving
Ground and follow the signs to the refuge.*

A guided tour is the best way to visit the 25,765-acre Imperial National
Wildlife Refuge, created by backwaters formed when the Imperial Dam
was built. Something of an anomaly, the refuge is home both to species
indigenous to marshy rivers and to creatures that inhabit the adjacent
Sonoran Desert—desert tortoises, coyotes, bobcats, and bighorn sheep.
Mostly, though, this is a major bird habitat. Thousands of waterfowl
and shorebirds live here year-round, and migrating flocks of swallows
pass through in spring and fall. During those seasons, expect to see
everything from pelicans and cormorants to Canada geese, snowy
egrets, and some rarer species. Canoes can be rented at Martinez Lake
Marina, 3½ mi southeast of the refuge headquarters. It's best to visit
from mid-October through May, when it's cooler and the ever-present
mosquitoes are least active. Kids especially enjoy the 1.3-mi Painted
Desert Nature Trail, which winds through the different levels of the
Sonoran Desert. From an observation tower at the visitor center you
can see the river, as well as the fields being planted with rye and millet, on which the migrating birds like to feed. ✉*Martinez Lake Rd.,
Box 72217 Martinez Lake 85365* ☎*928/783–3371* 🖷*928/783–0652*
⊕*http://refuges.fws.gov* 🎫*Free* 🕐*Visitor center mid-Apr.–mid-Oct.,
weekdays 7:30–4; mid-Oct.–mid-Apr., weekdays 7:30–4, weekends
9–4.*

SOUTHERN ARIZONA ESSENTIALS

To research prices, get advice from other travelers, and book travel arrangements, visit ⊕www.fodors.com.

TRANSPORTATION

BY AIR

Great Lakes Airlines flies direct from Phoenix to Sierra Vista. America West Express has direct flights to Yuma from Phoenix. Sky West, a United subsidiary, flies nonstop from Los Angeles to Yuma.

Contacts America West Express (☎800/235–9292 ⊕www.americawest.com). **Great Lakes Airlines** (☎800/554–5111 ⊕www.greatlakesav.com). **Sierra Vista Municipal Airport/Fort Huachuca** (✉2100 Airport Ave. ☎520/458–5775 ⊕www.ci.sierra-vista.az.us/Airport/index.htm). **Sky West** (☎435/634–3000 ⊕www.skywest.com). **Yuma International Airport (YUM)** (☎928/726–5882 ⊕www.yumainternationalairport.com).

BY BUS

Greyhound Lines has service from Tucson to the stations in Benson, Willcox, and Yuma. Ajo Transportation offers regular shuttle van service from Tucson to Ajo.

Contacts Ajo Transportation (☎520/387–6467 or 800/942–1981). **Greyhound Lines** (☎800/454–2487 ⊕www.greyhound.com ✉McDonalds, 618 S. VLG Loop Hwy. 90, Benson ☎No phone ✉Oasis Arcade, 100 N. Arizona St., Willcox ☎520/384–2183 ✉170 E. 17th Pl., Yuma ☎928/783–4403).

BY CAR

A car is essential in southern Arizona. The best plan is to fly into Tucson, which is the hub of the area, or Phoenix, which has the most flights, and pick up a car at the airport.

You can rent a car from several national companies at Yuma International Airport; Sierra Vista has an Enterprise branch. Most agencies allow you to take your rental into Mexico only if you buy their Mexican insurance packages. Be aware that road conditions in Mexico can be poor and that signs are in Spanish.

To get to southeastern Arizona from Tucson, take I–10 east. AZ 90 is the turnoff for Kartchner Caverns. When you get to Benson, take AZ 80 south to reach Tombstone, Bisbee, and Douglas. If you want to go to Sonoita and Patagonia, or just take a pretty drive, turn off I–10 earlier, at the exit for AZ 83 south; you'll come to Sonoita, where this road intersects AZ 82. From here you can either continue south to Sierra Vista, head southwest on AZ 82 to Patagonia, or head east to Tombstone.

If you're driving to Southwestern Arizona, Ajo lies on AZ 85 (north–south) and Yuma is at the junction of I–8 and U.S. 95. For a scenic route to Ajo from Tucson (126 mi), take AZ 86 west to Why and turn north on AZ 85. Yuma is 170 mi from San Diego on I–8, and it is 300 mi from Las Vegas on U.S. 95.

BY TAXI

Benson Taxi offers transport services in the Benson area. In Sierra Vista, ABC Cab Co. provides both local and regional transport. Yuma City Cab has the best taxi service in Yuma.

Contacts ABC Cab Co. (✉ *Sierra Vista* ☎ *520/458–8429*). **Benson Taxi** (✉ *Benson* ☎ *520/586–1294*). **Yuma City Cab** (✉ *Yuma* ☎ *928/782–4444*).

BY TRAIN

Amtrak trains run three times a week from Tucson east to the Benson depot and west to Yuma. Both stations are unstaffed with Amtrak personnel; however, the Benson Visitor Center is in the train depot.

Contacts Benson train station (✉ *4th St. at San Pedro Ave., Benson*). **Yuma train station** (✉ *281 Gila St., Yuma*).

CONTACTS & RESOURCES

BANKS AND EXCHANGING SERVICES

Even though most shops and restaurants in Mexican border towns prefer U.S. dollars to Mexican pesos, travelers can exchange currency at local banks. Another option is to withdraw pesos from ATM machines on the Mexican side of the border. Peso bills are issued in denominations of 20, 50, 100, 200, and 500. Before paying in pesos, be sure to check on the current exchange rate.

EMERGENCIES

In the U.S., call 911 for fire or police emergencies, or for an ambulance. If you're in Mexico, call 060.

There are local hospitals in many of the larger cities of southern Arizona, and many of the chain drugstores have locations in the area.

Benson Hospital in Benson, Copper Queen Community Hospital in Bisbee, Holy Cross Hospital in Nogales, Northern Cochise Community Hospital in Willcox, Sierra Vista Regional Health Center in Sierra Vista, and Yuma Regional Medical Center in Yuma all offer 24-hour emergency medical care.

Contacts Benson Hospital (✉ *450 S. Ocotillo St., Benson* ☎ *520/586–2261* ⊕ *www.bensonhospital.org*). **Carondelet Health Network/Holy Cross Hospital** (✉ *1171 W. Target Range Rd., Nogales* ☎ *520/285–3000* ⊕ *www.Carondelet.org*). **Copper Queen Community Hospital** (✉ *101 Cole St., Bisbee* ☎ *520/432–5383* ⊕ *www.cqch.org*). **Desert Senita Community Health Center** (✉ *410 Malacate St., Ajo* ☎ *520/387–5651* ⊕ *www.ajochc.org*). **Northern Cochise Community Hospital** (✉ *901 W. Rex Allen Dr., Willcox* ☎ *520/384–3541 or 800/696–3541* ⊕ *www.ncch. com*). **Sierra Vista Regional Health Center** (✉ *300 El Camino Real, Sierra Vista* ☎ *520/458–4641 or 800/880–0088* ⊕ *www.svrhc.org*). **Yuma Regional Medical Center** (✉ *2400 S. Ave. A, Yuma* ☎ *928/344–2000* ⊕ *www.yumaregional.org*).

SPORTS & THE OUTDOORS

HIKING Douglas Ranger District and the Sierra Vista Ranger Station of the National Forest Service can give you information about hiking in the Coronado National Forest, which covers most of the mountain ranges in southeastern Arizona. The Bureau of Land Management Yuma Field Office can give you details about outdoor recreational activities in that area.

Contacts **Bureau of Land Management Yuma Field Office** (⊠ *2555 E. Gila Ridge Rd., Yuma 85365* ☎ *928/317–3200* ⊕ *www.blm.gov/az*). **Coronado National Forest** (*Douglas Ranger District* ⊠ *1192 W. Saddleview Rd., Douglas* ☎ *520/364–3468* ⊕ *www.fs.fed.us/r3/coronado Sierra Vista Ranger Station* ⊠ *5990 S. AZ 92, Hereford 85615* ☎ *520/378–0311* ⊕ *www.fs.fed.us/r3/coronado*).

INTERNET, MAIL & SHIPPING

The U.S. Postal Service has post office locations throughout southern Arizona. For additional express services, FedEx has offices in Nogales, Sierra Vista, and Yuma. UPS Stores can be found in Sierra Vista and Yuma.

Mail and Shipping **Fed Ex** (⊕ *www.fedex.com*). **The UPS Store** (⊕ *www.theupssstore.com*). **U.S. Post Office** (☎ *800/275–8777* ⊕ *www.usps.com*).

TOUR OPTIONS

BIRD-WATCHING TOURS The Southeastern Arizona Bird Observatory is a nonprofit organization that offers guided tours, educational programs, and informational materials for bird-watchers visiting, or living in, Arizona. As an aid to birders, SABO offers a map of the best bird-watching sites along the Southeastern Arizona Birding Trail, which was created in collaboration with several private and public organizations. Write to the SABO or go on their Web site for a copy of the map. High Lonesome Ecotours offers birding tours with lodging.

BOAT TOURS You can take a boat ride up the Colorado with Yuma River Tours. You can book 12- to 45-person jet-boat excursions through Smokey Knowlton, who has been exploring the area for more than 35 years.

GUIDED TOURS Southern Arizona Adventures offers ecotours, hiking, backpacking, mountain biking, and historical/cultural expeditions from its base in Bisbee. Lavender Jeep Tours takes visitors on guided tours through the back streets of Bisbee and into the mineral-rich Mule Mountains.

Contacts **High Lonesome Ecotours** (⊠ *570 S. Little Bear Trail, Sierra Vista* ☎ *520/458–9446 or 800/743–2668* ⊕ *www.hilonesome.com*). **Lavender Jeep Tours** (⊠ *45 Gila Dr., Bisbee* ☎ *520/432–5369*). **Southern Arizona Adventures** (⊠ *22 Main St., Bisbee* ☎ *520/432–9058 or 800/319–7377* ⊕ *www.arizonatour.com*). **Southeastern Arizona Bird Observatory** (☏ *Box 5521, Bisbee 85603* ☎ *520/432–1388* ⊕ *www.sabo.org*). **Yuma River Tours** (⊠ *1920 Arizona Ave., Yuma 85364* ☎ *928/783–4400* ⊕ *www.yumarivertours.com*).

VISITOR INFORMATION

In Southeastern Arizona **Benson Railroad Depot and Visitor Center** (⊠ *249 E. 4th St., Benson 85602* ☎ *520/586–4293* ⊕ *www.bensonvisitorcenter.com* ☺ *Mon.–Sat. 9–5*). **Bisbee Visitor Center** (⊠ *#2 Copper Queen Plaza, Bisbee 85603*

🖾 520/432–3554 or 866-2BISBEE ⊕ www.discoverbisbee.com ⊙ Weekdays 9–5, weekends 10–4). **City of Tombstone Visitor Center** (✉ 104 S. 4th St., at Allen St. Tombstone 85638 🖾 520/457–3929 or 888/457–3929 ⊕ www.cityoftombstone.com ⊙ Daily 9–5). **Patagonia Area Business Association Tourist Information Center** (✉ 307 McKeown Ave., Patagonia 85624 🖾 520/394–0060 or 888/794–0060 ⊕ www.patagoniaaz.com ⊙ Mon.–Sat. 10–5, Sun. 10–4). **Sierra Vista Convention and Visitors Bureau** (✉ 3020 E. Tacoma St., Sierra Vista 85635 🖾 520/458–6940 or 800/288–3861 ⊕ www.visitsierravista.com ⊙ Weekdays 8–5, Sat. 9–4). **Willcox Chamber of Commerce & Agriculture** (✉ 1500 N. Circle I Rd., Willcox 85643 🖾 520/384–2272 or 800/200–2272 ⊕ www.willcoxchamber.com ⊙ Weekdays 8–5, Sat. 9–4, Sun. 9–1).

In Southwestern Arizona **Ajo Chamber of Commerce** (✉ 400 Taladro St., Ajo 85321 🖾 520/387–7742 ⊙ Weekdays 9–4:30). **Nogales-Santa Cruz County Chamber of Commerce Visitor Center** (✉ 123 W. Kino Park Way, Nogales 85621 🖾 520/287–3685 ⊕ www.nogaleschamber.com ⊙ Weekdays 9–4). **Yuma Convention and Visitors Bureau** (✉ 377 S. Main St., Yuma 85364 🖾 928/783–0071 or 800/293–0071 ⊕ www.visityuma.com ⊙ Weekdays 9–5, Sat. 9–4).

Northwest Arizona & Southeast Nevada

Route 66 sign Williams Arizona

WORD OF MOUTH

"I think Oatman is my favorite Route 66 stop. Make sure you are there in late afternoon for the gunfight on the main street. Take carrots for the burros."

—utahtea

WELCOME TO NORTHWEST ARIZONA & SOUTHEAST NEVADA

Colorado River below Hoover Dam on border of Arizona

TOP REASONS TO GO

★ **Get Wet:** Boating, fishing, and water adventure top the list of favorite activities on the cool Colorado River and the adjoining lakes of Havasu, Mohave, and Mead.

★ **My Fair Lady:** Experience a slice of England while passing under London Bridge in Lake Havasu City.

★ **Road Warriors:** Get your kicks on Route 66 and cruise the longest remaining stretch of the Mother Road from Seligman to Kingman.

★ **Take a Walk on the Wild Side:** For Vegas-style gambling and glitz spend some quality play time in the twin cities of Laughlin, Nevada and Bullhead City, Arizona.

★ **Hike Hualapai:** Take a break from the desert and climb the cool climes of Hualapai Mountain Park—the highest point in western Arizona.

1 Northwest Arizona.
Wide open spaces, colorful desert vistas, funky little ghost towns, the open road on Route 66, and gleaming aquamarine waterways offer a wide variety of recreational pastimes.

2 Southeast Nevada.
Laughlin attracts laid-back gamblers and elite entertainers looking for all of the glitz and glamour of Las Vegas without the high prices and large crowds.

Boaters flock to Lake Havasu

GETTING ORIENTED

In the far northwestern corner of Arizona, Kingman is a good base for the wide range of activities found in the Arizona communities of Lake Havasu City and Bullhead City as well as Laughlin, Nevada. Kingman is the largest city out in this neck of the woods and acts as the Mohave County seat. The Colorado River flows out of the Grand Canyon to the north and then sweeps directly south, serving as the western border of the state of Arizona and supplying the lifeblood to the otherwise desolate desert region. Created from dams on the mighty Colorado River, the lakes Mead, Mohave, and Havasu provide a common link in the tri-state area by offering some of the best water recreation around.

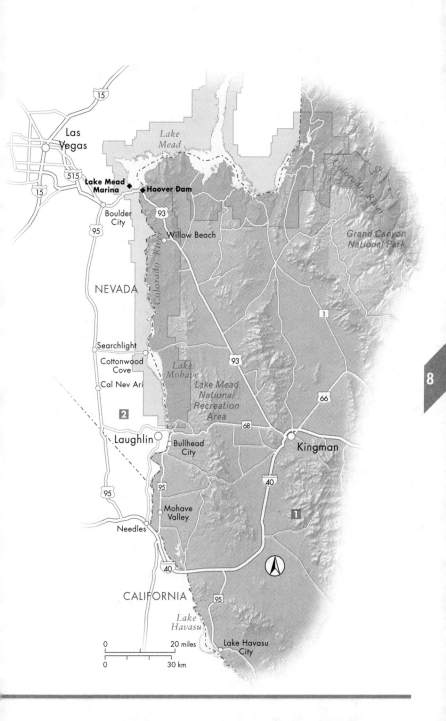

NORTHWEST ARIZONA & SOUTHEAST NEVADA PLANNER

Getting Here and Around

Kingman, Lake Havasu City, and Laughlin are accessible by air but most visitors drive to this corner of the state—after all, the road to Kingman is the longest remaining stretch of Route 66. At first glance, the countryside seems stark and remote, but there are many surprises along the way, including the strange-looking Joshua tree, the defining plant of the Mojave Desert.

The long stretches of open highway here lend themselves to leisurely drives and relaxed schedules and the trip down Historic Route 66 takes visitors on a nostalgic ride through the past, where the journey is as enjoyable as the destination. There are no traffic jams and navigation is as easy as travel in a one-stoplight town.

Most visitors explore the region by car, but you can get a different perspective by boat: Arizona has more than 1,000 mi of shoreline. Keep in mind that Lake Mead is at its lowest water level in more than 40 years, leaving dangerous reefs lurking just below the surface in some spots. To fish on lakes Mead and Mojave, anglers must have a valid fishing license.

Making the Most of Your Time

Kingman is an ideal base for exploring Lake Mead National Recreation Area, the ghost towns of Oatman and Chloride, and the forested climes of Hualapai Mountain Park. You'll need at least a day to enjoy water sports on Lake Mead, whereas an hour or two is enough to explore the funky little towns of Oatman and Chloride. Even though Lake Havasu is only an hour away from Kingman, visitors heading down to those sandy shores can get the most out of their trip by staying at one of the local resorts. Water activities dominate the scene here, but if you have an extra hour or two consider a side trip to London Bridge, a birding expedition at Havasu National Wildlife Refuge, or a foray into the quaint shops in English Village. If gambling is on your list of things to do, you can take a quick jaunt across the Colorado River to Laughlin, where you can easily spend hours or days reveling in the glitz and glitter.

What to Do and Where to Do It

Three of North America's Deserts—the Mohave, Sonoran, and Chihuahuan—converge along the sinuous shores of the mighty Colorado River as it winds along Arizona's western border into Mexico. With more than 1,000 mi of shoreline and three large reservoirs—Lake Mead, Lake Mohave, and Lake Havasu—Arizona's west coast offers warm weather and cool waters perfect for a wide array of year-round water sports including boating, kayaking, water-skiing, sailing, and fishing. Laughlin, Bullhead City, and Lake Havasu City all offer waterfront digs, while houseboat accommodations on the region's large reservoirs take lakefront living to a new level.

For the best canoeing and kayaking, head to Topock Gorge on the Colorado River. Lake Havasu has the best swimming beaches and sailing. Fishermen looking to hook the big one will want to launch a boat on Lake Mead or Lake Mohave, both of which offer excellent year-round fishing.

Festivals to Plan Your Trip Around

July 4: The yearly Solar Egg Frying Contest, in Oatman takes place at high noon. Accompanying the cook-off are Old West gun fights and other entertainment and food.

October: The Andy Devine Days festival honors the film and television actor with a parade and rodeo.

Also in October is the weeklong London Bridge Days, which includes a Renaissance festival, a parade, and British-theme contests in Lake Havasu City.

Local Food and Lodging

Motel chains make up the most abundant and affordable lodging options in the major communities of Kingman, Lake Havasu City, and Bullhead City, and a few historic hotels break up the modern mix. The swanky resorts at Lake Havasu City and the glittery casino attractions in Laughlin provide upscale rooms for visitors seeking more refined relaxation. Staying in a houseboat on Lake Havasu or Lake Mead puts a decidedly different twist on water recreation. Best of all, these floating rooms with a view can be maneuvered into countless coves and inlets, allowing for peaceful solitude rarely found on the busy beaches and popular waterways.

Dining in this remote corner of the state is generally as casual as the lodging options. You're more likely to find a 1950s diner, a taqueria, or a family-owned café than a five-star dining establishment. For the most part you'll find home-cooked American favorites and "South of the Border" specialties. For the best in fine dining, head across the Colorado River to the casinos in Laughlin, Nevada, where you'll find a sophisticated medley of gourmet restaurants serving everything from seafood to steaks.

When to Go

Unlike many destinations, the communities in northwestern Arizona don't have distinct high and low seasons. The arid climate and clear winter skies attract "snowbirds," retirees flocking south to escape the harsh northern climes. On the flip side, the hot, sunny summer months attract sports enthusiasts looking to cavort in the cool, blue waterways—despite searing temperatures topping out in the 120s°F.

Lake Havasu City plays host to hordes of college revelers during Spring Break in March and Kingman fills up fast during the annual Route 66 Fun Run in May. Things simmer down a bit during the spring and fall months—but not much! Overall, expect crowded weekends during the busy summer months and sold-out rooms during

8

What It Costs

	¢	$	$$	$$$	$$$$
Restaurants	Under $8	$8–$12	$13–$20	$21–$30	over $30
Hotels	Under $70	$70–$120	$121–$175	$176–$250	over $250

Restaurant prices are per person for a main course at dinner. Hotel prices are for a standard double in high season, excluding taxes and service charges.

Updated by
Carrie Miner

NORTHWESTERN ARIZONA AND SOUTHEASTERN NEVADA comprise a unique blend of deserts, mountains, and 1,000 mi of shoreline. From its highest elevation, Hualapai Peak at 8,417 feet, to its lowest along the Colorado River at approximately 630 feet, this wide-open region of the Southwest offers a diverse topography ranging from aspen- and pine-covered glades to the austere and soft-spoken grandeur of the Mojave Desert. Despite the superficial aridity of much of the landscape, the region bubbles with an abundance of springs and artesian wells. Without these water sources seeping from the rocks and sand, northwestern Arizona and southeastern Nevada would never have developed into the major crossroad it is today.

The defining feature of the region is the Colorado River. Since the late Pleistocene epoch when Paleo-Indians first set foot in the river that was once described as "too thick to drink and too thin to plow," the Colorado has been a blessing and a barrier. Prehistoric traders from the Pacific Coast crossed the river at Willow Beach on their way to trade shells for pelts with the Hopi Indians and other Pueblo tribes farther east. When gold was discovered in California in 1848, entrepreneurs built ferries up and down the river to accommodate the miners drawn to the area by what Cortez called "a disease of the heart for which the only cure is gold." Prosperity followed, particularly for Kingman.

Every spring the snowmelt of the Rocky Mountain watershed of the Colorado River rushed through high basaltic canyons like water through a garden hose and washed away crops and livestock. Harnessing such a powerful river required no ordinary dam. In 1935, notched into the steep and narrow confines of Black Canyon on the border separating Arizona and Nevada, 727-foot high Hoover Dam took control of the Colorado River and turned its power into electricity and its floodwaters into the largest man-made reservoir in the world: Lake Mead.

Today, interstate commerce brings hundreds of thousands of vehicles through northwestern Arizona and southeastern Nevada every day. For many who view the area through the glass of their air-conditioned vehicles, the landscape is a daunting vision of opaque and distant mountains shimmering in the heat rising from the sun-baked pavement. But for those who pull over and step into the clean open air, northwestern Arizona and southeastern Nevada offer an enchanting blend of past and present, earth and sky, river and wind.

EXPLORING NORTHWEST ARIZONA & SOUTHEAST NEVADA

Western Arizona is a wedge of paradise for any outdoors enthusiast. The Colorado River, and the lakes that take shape along it like blue beads on a brown string, provides 1,000 mi of opportunities for fishing and water sports of all kinds. The valleys and mountains offer the curious traveler a topography replete with reasons for exploration and discovery. The three major communities of the area are Kingman, Bullhead City, and Lake Havasu City. Interstate 40, Historic Route 66, and U.S. 93 intersect in Kingman, which is also the seat of Mohave County. Bullhead City is on the Colorado River across from Laughlin,

Northwest Arizona

Nevada, and Lake Havasu City is farther south on the river and home to the famous London Bridge. Just across the Colorado River, Boulder City and Laughlin seem to have more in common with Arizona than Nevada—especially considering their close proximity and interconnected communities. It bears repeating that driving in the desert requires extra preparation. Make certain you are well stocked with radiator coolant, and be sure to carry plenty of water, a spare tire, a jack, and emergency supplies.

NORTHWEST ARIZONA

Towns like Kingman hark back to the glory days of the old Route 66, and the ghost towns of Chloride and Oatman bear testament to the mining madness that once reigned in the region. Water-sports fans, or those who just want to laze on a houseboat, will enjoy Lake Havasu, where you'll find the misplaced English icon London Bridge.

A Short History of Old Route 66

In 1938 the 2,400 mi of roadway connecting Chicago and Los Angeles was declared "continuously paved." U.S. Route 66 was transformed from a hodge-podge string of local roads—most of them dirt in summer and mud in winter—connecting one isolated small town to another, into an "all-weather" highway that would enable commerce and the military to travel the route. And just as the road crews changed the landscape to accommodate the roadbed, Route 66 changed the social landscape as communities adapted to the new road.

The needs of the traveler were met by the new ideas of the gas station, the diner, and the motel—and nostalgic glimpses of those icons and that culture can still be found. In Seligman, for example, you can stop at Delgadillo's Snow Cap Drive-in for a "small soda" and a chance to admire vintage automobiles. If you take Exit 139 from I-40, 5 mi west of Ash Fork, you'll find yourself at the beginning of the longest remaining continuous stretch of Route 66. It will take you almost 160 mi through Seligman, Peach Springs, Truxton, Valentine, Hackberry, Kingman, and Oatman, and on to the Colorado River near Topock.

KINGMAN

① *188 mi northwest of Phoenix, 149 mi west of Flagstaff via I–40.*

The highway past Kingman may seem desolate, but the mountains that surround the area offer outdoor activities in abundance, especially along the Colorado River. Water sports play a big part in the area's recreation because about 1,000 mi of freshwater shoreline lie within the county along the Colorado River and around lakes Havasu, Mohave, and Mead—all of which are within a one-hour drive of this major stopping point for fishing and boating aficionados. And for those interested in the region's mineral wealth, the nearby "ghost" towns of Chloride and Oatman offer a glimpse of the Old West.

The **Powerhouse Tourist Information and Visitor Center** (✉ *120 W. Andy Devine Ave.* ☎ *928/753–6106* ⊕ *www.kingmantourism.org*) has T-shirts and the usual brochures to acquaint you with local attractions.

The **Historic Route 66 Museum** in the Powerhouse Visitor Center provides a nostalgic look at the evolution of the famous route that started as a footpath followed by prehistoric Indians and evolved into a length of pavement that reached from Chicago, Illinois, to Santa Monica, California. The first weekend of May each year, the Historic Route 66 Association of Arizona holds the three-day Route 66 Fun Run (⊕ www.azrt66.com), a 40-mi drive along the longest remaining section of the "Mother Road." Admission to the Historic Route 66 Museum also includes a visit to the Mohave Museum of History and Arts. ✉ *120 W. Andy Devine Ave.* ☎ *928/753–9889* ⊕ *www. kingmantourism.org/route66museum* ⊑ *$4* ⊙ *Mar.–Nov., daily 9–6; Dec.–Feb., daily 9–5.*

History buffs will enjoy a visit to the **Bonelli House** (✉ *430 E. Spring St.* ☎ *928/753–1413* ✉ *Donation* ☾ *Weekdays 11–3*), an excellent example of Anglo-Territorial architecture featuring a facade of light gray quarried stone and white-washed wood accents, a very popular style in the early 1900s. It is one of 62 buildings in the Kingman business district listed on the National Register of Historic Places and contains period pieces including a large wall clock that was once the only clock in Kingman.

The **Mohave Museum of History and Arts** includes an Andy Devine Room with memorabilia from Devine's Hollywood years and, incongruously, a portrait collection of every president and first lady. The museum has an exceptional library collection of research materials related to the region. There's also an exhibit of carved Kingman turquoise, displays on Native American art and artifacts, and a diorama depicting the mid-19th-century expedition of Lt. Edward Beale, who led his camel-cavalry unit to the area in search of a wagon road along the 35th parallel. You can follow the White Cliffs Trail from downtown to see the deep ruts cut into the desert floor by the wagons that came to Kingman after Beale's time. ✉ *400 W. Beale St.* ☎ *928/753–3195* ⊕ *www.ctaz.com/~mocohist/museum/index.htm* ✉ *$4 includes admission to Historic Route 66 Museum* ☾ *Weekdays 9–5, weekends 1–5.*

> **HOW DEVINE**
>
> Andy Devine (1905–77) is Kingman's most famous citizen. Born in Flagstaff, his family moved to Kingman when he was a year old. The raspy-voiced Western character actor appeared in more than 400 films, most notably as the comic cowboy sidekick "Cookie" to Roy Rogers in 10 films. He also played "the Cheerful Soldier" in *The Red Badge of Courage* and was in several John Wayne flicks, including *The Man Who Shot Liberty Valance* (he played the hapless sheriff Linc Appleyard), *Stagecoach,* and *Island in the Sky.*

Fodor's Choice
★

You haven't truly hiked in northwestern Arizona until you've hiked in **Hualapai Mountain Park** (✉ *6250 Hualapai Mountain Rd.* ☎ *928/757– 3859, 877/757–0915 for cabin reservations*). A 15-mi drive from town up Hualapai Mountain Road leads to the park's more than 2,300 wooded acres, with 10 mi of hiking trails, picnic areas, rustic cabins, and RV and tenting areas. There are dozens of fine trails, but the trail system in the higher elevations of the park offers a striking variety of plant life such as prickly pear cactus and Arizona walnut. Abundant species of birds and mammals such as the piñon jay and the Abert squirrel live here, and pristine stands of unmarred aspen mark the higher elevations. Any of the trails can be hiked in about three hours. If you can only visit one place and do one thing in northwestern Arizona, hiking in Hualapai Mountain Park should be it. A $5 per day use fee has been implemented to help defray the costs of maintaining the park.

OFF THE BEATEN PATH

Chloride. The ghost town of Chloride, Arizona's oldest silver mining camp, takes its name from a type of silver ore mined here. During its heyday, from 1900 to 1920, some 75 mines operated in the area: silver, gold, lead, zinc, molybdenum, and even turquoise were mined here. About 500 folks live in Chloride today; there are three cafés, two saloons, a grocery store, a B&B, and two RV parks. Some of the residents are artists and craftspeople who have small studios and shops in the historic buildings. Sights include the old jail, Chloride Baptist Church, Silverbelle Playhouse, and the Jim Fritz Museum. Western artist Roy Purcell painted the large murals on the rocks on the edge of town—10 feet high and almost 30 feet across, they depict a goddess figure, intertwined snakes, and eastern and Native American symbols. The marked turnoff for Chloride is about 12 mi north of Kingman on U.S. 93.

★ **Grand Canyon West Ranch.** This guest and working cattle ranch is a slice of the Old West. Once the home of Tap Duncan (a member of the Hole-in-the-Wall Gang), the ranch now offers rustic cabins, home-cooked meals, horseback riding, and a stagecoach excursion. Take U.S. 93 north from Kingman 25 mi and turn right onto Pearce Ferry Road. Follow the paved road for 27 mi, then turn right onto the unpaved Diamond Bar Road. The Grand Canyon West Ranch is 7 mi farther on the right side of the road. Reservations are required. ⊠ *3785 E. Diamond Bar Ranch Rd., Meadview 86444* ☎ *702/736–8787 or 800/359–8727* ⊕ *www.grandcanyonwestranch.com.*

☾ **Grand Canyon Caverns and Inn.** Nestled among rolling, juniper-covered hills 60 mi east of Kingman on Historic Route 66, the Grand Canyon Caverns and Inn have been a diversion for travelers for decades. Daily tours begin on the hour with an elevator descent to the main floor of the caverns, 210 feet below ground. These caves were formed in the limestone bed of a sea that covered northern Arizona more than 37 million years ago. The caverns are considered a dry cave, one that no longer grows, but their full extent is still unknown. The ¾-mi walking tour takes 45 minutes. In the rodeo arena behind the 48-room hotel, area cowboys often hold calf-roping competitions that are a hoot to watch, and free to boot. ⊠ *Rte. 66* ☎ *928/422–3223 or 422–4565* ⊕ *www.gccaverns.com* ⊠ *$12.95* ⊙ *Mar.–Oct., daily 8–6; Nov.–Feb., daily 10–5.*

SPORTS & THE OUTDOORS

HIKING   The **Hayden Peak Trail** is a branch of a 10-mi trail system within Hualapai Mountain Park. The hike begins at location No. 4, elevation 6,750 feet, shown on the trail-system map available at the ranger station. Markers along the trail coincide with the map. This is a strenuous, 5½-mi round-trip hike, and a hiking stick is a valuable companion. Benches and storm shelters dot the trail. Along the way you climb through a narrow and shallow canyon that botanists call an Interior Riparian Deciduous Forest. A forest fire scorched this part of the mountains more than 50 years ago, and today that scar has been replaced with pristine aspens, their thick, unmarred trunks white as parchment. The ground is covered with ungrazed grasses and soft foliage called deer's ears. At the end of the trail, elevation 8,050 feet, 200 feet below the summit of Hayden Peak, there's a bench with a view to the west that includes the gleaming surface of the Colorado River, some 60 mi away.

WHERE TO STAY & EAT

$$$–$$$$ ✕ **Hubb's Bistro.** The bustling eatery in the Brunswick Hotel caters to most tastes and does a wonderful job with everything from steaks to seafood. Menu favorites include salted pork loin, barbecue ribs, and lobster tail. An extensive wine list and multinational beer selections add to the flavor-filled experience. ⊠*315 E. Andy Devine Ave.* ☎*928/718–1800* ☰*AE, D, MC, V* ⊗*Closed Sun.*

$–$$ ✕ **Mr. D'z Route 66 Diner.** This popular hot spot serves up road food with a 1950s flair for breakfast, lunch, and dinner. Expect low prices and large servings of your favorite burgers and milkshakes. ⊠*105 E. Route 66* ☎*928/718–0066* ☰*AE, MC, V.*

$ ✕ **El Palacio of Kingman Mexican Restaurant.** Out of the way but worth the effort, this casual restaurant with a Mexican motif is at the north end of town, near the intersection of Bank Street and Northern Avenue. It's a local gem and serves Mexican and American cuisine, seafood—and what many believe are the best chiles rellenos in the county. ⊠*401 E. Andy Devine Ave.* ☎*928/718–0018* ☰*AE, D, MC, V.*

¢–$$ ☷ **Brunswick Hotel.** This hotel opened its doors in 1909 and was the first three-story building in town. Rooms have antique furnishings and the early 1900s ambience is coupled with courtesy and today's amenities. Budget-minded guests can save a few dollars by staying in the hotel's Cowboy and Cowgirl rooms, which share a bathroom. ⊠*315 E. Andy Devine Ave., 86401* ☎*928/718–1800* ⊕*www.hotel-brunswick.com* ⇗*18 rooms, 9 with shared bath, 6 suites* ⚐*In-room: no TV (some). In-hotel: restaurant, bar, public Internet, no-smoking rooms* ☰*AE, D, MC, V* ⦿*CP.*

$ ☷ **Best Western–Kings Inn.** Conveniently located at the intersection of I-40 and Highway 93, this hotel's clean, spacious rooms are a great base for exploring nearby Laughlin, Lake Mead, the ghost towns of Chloride and Oatman, and Hualapai Mountain Park. The mini-suites offer comfy beds and a sitting area. Several restaurants are within walking distance. ⊠*2930 E. Andy Devine Ave., 86401* ☎*928/753–6101 or 800/750–6101* ⇗*101 rooms* ⚐*In-room: refrigerator, dial-up. In-hotel: pool, no-smoking rooms, no elevator* ☰*AE, D, DC, MC, V* ⦿*CP.*

EN ROUTE A worthwhile stop on your way from Kingman to Lake Havasu, the ghost town of **Oatman** is reached via old Route 66. It's a straight shot across the Mojave Desert valley for a while, but then the road narrows and winds precipitously for about 15 mi through the Black Mountains. This road is public, but beyond a narrow shoulder, the land is privately owned and heavily patrolled by private security thanks to still-active gold mines throughout these low but rugged hills.

Oatman's main street is right out of the Old West; scenes from a number of films, including *How the West Was Won,* were shot here. It still has a remote, old-time feel: many of the natives carry side arms, and they're not acting. You can wander into one of the three saloons or visit the **Oatman Hotel,** where Clark Gable and Carole Lombard honeymooned in 1939 after they were secretly married in Kingman. The burros that often come in from nearby hills and meander down the street, however, are the town's real draw. A couple of stores sell hay to folks who want to feed these "wild" beasts, which at last count numbered about a dozen and which leave plenty of evidence of their visits in the form of "road apples"—so watch your step. For information about the town and its attractions, contact the **Oatman Chamber of Commerce** (🕾928/768–6222 ⊕www.oatmangoldroad.com).

Two miles east of Oatman is the **Gold Road Mine,** an active operation that dates back to 1900. A one-hour tour goes underground for a demonstration of drilling equipment and a visit to the "Glory Hole," where the vein structures in the rock are highlighted with a black light to show the gold. ⊠AZ 66 🕾928/768–1600 ⊕www.goldroadmine.com 🖃$12 ☉Daily 10–5.

SHOPPING

Several curio shops and eclectic boutiques line the length of Main Street. Get in the spirit of the Old West with the leather jackets, Western gun holsters, and moccasins offered at **The Leather Shop of Oatman** (⊠162 Main St. 🕾928/768–3833). Browse through a nice selection of Indian jewelry and Southwestern art at **The Ore House** (⊠194 Main St. 🕾928/768–3839). **Main Street Emporium** (⊠150 S. Main St. 🕾928/788–3298) offers a wide array of hand-crafted items including Western-theme wall art, hand-woven blankets, and cholla cactus candles.

SPORTS & THE OUTDOORS

BACKCOUNTRY EXPLORATION **Oatman Stables** (⊠AZ Rte. 66, Oatman 🕾928/768–3257 ⊕www.oatmanstables.com) has several tour packages. One- and two-hour trail rides follow old military and prospecting trails. Other options include a sunset steak ride and a cattle drive. Rates are $25 for one-hour rides and $45 for two-hour rides.

LAKE HAVASU CITY

❷ *60 mi southwest of Kingman.*

Remember the old nursery rhyme "London Bridge Is Falling Down"? Well, it was. In 1968, after about 150 years of constant use, the 294-foot-long landmark was sinking into the Thames. When Lake Havasu City founder, Robert McCullough, heard about this predicament, he actually set about buying **London Bridge,** having it disassembled, shipped ★ 10,000 mi to northwestern Arizona, and rebuilt, stone by stone. The bridge was reconstructed on mounds of sand and took three years to complete. When it was finished, a mile-long channel was dredged under the bridge and water was diverted from Lake Havasu through the Bridgewater Channel. Today, the entire city is centered on this unusual attraction.

If there's an Arizona Riviera, this is it. Lake Havasu has more than 45 mi of lake shoreline, and the area gets less than 4 inches of rain annually, which means it's almost always sunny. Spring, winter, and fall are the best times to visit; in summer, temperatures often exceed 100°F. You can rent everything from water skis to Jet Skis, small fishing boats to large houseboats. The lake area has no fewer than 13 RV parks and campgrounds, about 125 boat-in campsites, and hundreds of hotel and motel rooms for additional creature comforts. There are golf and tennis facilities, as well as fishing guides who'll help you find, and catch, the big ones.

Lean about the purchase and reconstruction of London Bridge at the exhibit showcased at the **Lake Havasu City Visitor Center** (⊠ *420 English Village* ☎ *928/855–5655* ⊕ *www.golakehavasu.com*), which is also a great place to pick up brochures and other information on area attractions.

The **Lake Havasu Museum of History** takes an in-depth look at the history of the region with exhibits on the Chemehuevi Indians, London Bridge, Parker Dam, the mining industry, and historic steamboat operation. ⊠ *320 London Bridge Rd.* ☎ *928/854–4938* ⊕ *www.havasumuseum. com* 🖾 *$2* ⊙ *Tues.–Sat. 1–4.*

★ The **Havasu National Wildlife Refuge** (⊠ *Off I–40 south of Needles, CA* ☎ *760/326–3853* ⊕ *southwest.fws.gov*), between Needles and Lake Havasu City, is a 44,371-acre refuge for wintering Canada geese and other waterfowl, such as the snowy egret and the great blue heron.

The largest surviving cottonwood-willow woodland in the region is part of the **Bill Williams River National Wildlife Refuge** (⊠ *AZ 95, 23 mi south of Lake Havasu City* ☎ *928/667–4144*). To reach the 6,000-acre refuge, travel south on AZ 95; the entrance is between mileposts 160 and 161.

OFF THE BEATEN PATH

'Ahakhav Tribal Preserve. The 2,500-acre preserve is on the Colorado Indian Tribes Reservation and is a top spot in the area for bird-watching and hiking. There are several campgrounds, parks, and recreation areas along the Colorado River. Some 350 species of migratory and native birds live around the region or visit on their annual migrations. The best bird-watching is along the shoreline of the backwater area branching off the Colorado River. The 3-mi hiking trail has exercise stations along the way, and a trail extension will lead you to the tribal historical museum and gift shop. From AZ 95 in Parker, which is at the southern end of Lake Havasu, head west on Mohave Road for about 2 mi. When you reach the PARKER INDIAN RODEO ASSOCIATION sign, continue ½ mi farther and turn left at the TRIBAL PRESERVE sign at Rodeo Drive. ⊠ *25401 Rodeo Dr., Parker* ☎ *928/669– 2664* 🖷 *928/669–8024.*

SPORTS & THE OUTDOORS

GOLF The semi-private **London Bridge Golf Club** (⊠ *2400 Clubhouse Dr., Lake Havasu City* ☎ *928/855–2719*) has two regulation 18-hole courses. Green fees are $65 for the East course and $75 for the West course. The West course is championship caliber.

BACKCOUNTRY EXPLORATION **Outback Off-Road Adventures** (⊠ *403 English Village, Lake Havasu City* ☎ *928/680–6151* ⊕ *www.outbackadventures.us*) has several tour packages, including traveling in a six-wheel-drive Pinzguaer through the Sonoran Desert and Mohave Mountains. Rates range from $65 to $85 for adults and $50 to $65 for children.

WATER
SPORTS

When construction of Parker Dam was completed in 1938, the reservoir it created to supply water to southern California and Arizona became Lake Havasu. The lake is a 45-mi-long playground for water sports of all kinds. Whether it's waterskiing, jet skiing, power boating, houseboating, swimming, fishing, or you name it, if water is required, it's happening on Lake Havasu.

Lake Havasu State Park (⊠*699 London Bridge Rd.* ☎*928/855–2784* ⊕*www.pr.state.az.us*) is near the London Bridge. With four boat ramps and 42 campsites, it's an extremely popular spot in summer. On the eastern shore of the lake 15 mi south of Lake Havasu City is **Cattail Cove State Park** (⊠*AZ 95, 15 mi south of Lake Havasu* ☎*928/855–1223* ⊕*www.pr.state.az.us*). There are 62 campsites with access to electricity and water, and public restrooms with showers. Both parks charge $9 per vehicle for entry and are open from sunrise to 10.

If you have a boat, you have more options: You can find a quiet, secluded cove or beach to swim or fishing. If you have a need for speed, you can plane up and down the lake with or without a skier in tow.

If you don't have the equipment or the vessel necessary to enjoy your water sport, they're available for rent from a number of reputable merchants. You can rent everything from Jet Skis to pontoon boats, by the day or by the week, at **Sand Point Marina and RV Park** (⊠*17952 S. Sand Point Resort Rd.* ☎*928/855–0549* ⊕*www.sandpointresort. com*). **Arizona Water Sports** (⊠*655 Kiowa Ave.* ☎*800/393–5558* ⊕*www.arizonawatersports.com*) rents Jet Skis, jet boats, ski boats, and pontoon boats.

WHERE TO STAY & EAT
Many tourists make this stop a day trip on their way to Laughlin or Las Vegas, but there are plenty of accommodations if you want to stay the night.

★ $-$$$ ✕ **Shugrue's.** If you've dined at the Sedona branch of this restaurant, you know what to expect here. Shugrue's features hand-cut steaks, very fresh seafood, salads, and other well-prepared American fare. The baked desserts are worth saving room for. Most tables have good bridge views. ⊠*1425 McCulloch Blvd.* ☎*928/453–1400* ▭*AE, MC, V.*

$-$$ ✕ **Barley Brothers Brewery and Grill.** In the Island Mall adjacent to the English Village and the London Bridge, Barley Brothers offers casual dining and a microbrewery specializing in hefeweizen and a variety of ales. ⊠*1425 McCulloch Blvd.* ☎*928/505–7837* ⊕*www.barleybrothers. com* ▭*AE, D, MC, V.*

$-$$ ✕ **Juicy's River Café.** This is a favorite hangout for the local folks who know good food when they taste it. The Sunday breakfast is especially popular. The cozy restaurant is small and fills up fast, especially for breakfast. The varied menu includes corned beef and cabbage, smoked prime rib, meat loaf, pot roast and vegetables, and homemade soups and desserts. ⊠*25 N. Acoma Blvd.* ☎*928/855–8429* ▭*D, MC, V.*

¢ ✕ **Chico's Tacos.** The grill is always hopping at this Mexican fast-food joint, which specializes in grilled fish, chicken, and carne asada. The menu features such Mexican standards as tacos, enchiladas, flautas, burritos, and fajitas. Best of all, the six different salsas at the salsa bar add a bit of spice to the mix. ⊠*1641 McCulloch Blvd.* ☎*928/680–7010* ▤*D, MC, V.*

★ $$$ 🏨**London Bridge Resort.** If you want to be close to the bridge, this hotel is a dependable choice. The decor is a strange mix of Tudor and Southwestern; other than that, studios are standard motel rooms with kitchenettes. The restaurant Martini Bay serves tapas and delectable main dishes like crab cakes, mussels, teriyaki salmon, and gold shrimp crouda (a shrimp "tower" with avocado and salsa). After dinner, you can stretch the night out at Kokomo Havasu, a 10,000-square-foot nightclub featuring multiple dance floors, 21 bars, and an outdoor swimming pool. ⊠*1477 Queen's Bay, 86403* ☎*928/855–0888 or 800/624–7939* 📠*928/855–9209* ⊕*www.londonbridgeresort.com* 🛏*4 studios, 72 1-bedroom condos, 46 2-bedroom condos* ♿*In-room: kitchen (some). In-hotel: restaurant, pools, bars, beachfront, no-smoking rooms* ▤*AE, D, MC, V.*

$ 🏨**Havasu Springs Resort.** On a low peninsula reaching into Lake Havasu, the four hotels of this resort maximize your options. In addition to standard hotel rooms, the resort also offers suites and apartments. ⊠*2581 AZ 95, Parker 85344* ☎*928/667–3361* 📠*928/667–1098* ⊕*www.havasusprings.com* 🛏*38 rooms, 4 suites, 3 apartments* ♿*In-hotel: restaurant, bar, beachfront, watersports, golf course, tennis courts, no elevator* ▤*AE, D, MC, V.*

HOUSEBOATS **Club Nautical Houseboats.** What houseboats lack in speed and maneuverability, they make up for in comfort and shade. The houseboats offered by Club Nautical are some of the most luxurious boats on the lake and the crew makes certain that boaters get the best instruction and tips for their travel into cool blue waters. ⊠*1000 McCulloch Blvd.* ☎*800/843–9218* ⊕*www.lakehavasuhouseboatrental.com.*

SOUTHEAST NEVADA

Laughlin, Nevada and Bullhead City, Arizona are separated by a unique state line: the Colorado River. It's an interesting juxtaposition of cities, with the casino lights of Laughlin sparkling across the river from Bullhead City. Sixty miles upstream, just southeast of Las Vegas, Boulder City is prim, languid, and full of historic neighborhoods, small businesses, parks, greenbelts—and not a single casino. Over the hill from town, enormous Hoover Dam blocks the Colorado River as it enters Black Canyon. Backed up behind the dam is incongruous, deep-blue Lake Mead, the focal point of water-based recreation for southern Nevada and northwestern Arizona and the major water supplier to seven southwestern states. The lake is ringed by miles of rugged desert country.

Less than ½ mi downstream from the Hoover Dam and Lake Mead work continues on another engineering marvel—a bridge that will span the river canyon and link northwestern Arizona to southeastern Nevada, dramatically reducing traffic across Hoover Dam. It's set for completion in 2008.

Southeast
Nevada

BULLHEAD CITY, ARIZONA & LAUGHLIN, NEVADA

③ *35 mi northwest of Kingman.*

AZ 68, the highway from Kingman to Bullhead City and Laughlin, Nevada, crosses the Sacramento Valley and climbs over the Black Mountains through Union Pass, coming down the other side to the Colorado River valley. At night, across the river from Bullhead City, the lights of Laughlin glitter. Bullhead City has its small-town charms, but the lights of Laughlin are difficult to ignore. And while crowds flock to Las Vegas for all of its glitz and glamour, many prefer the more laid-back approach in Laughlin. Lodging and dining are considerably cheaper here than on the strip in Sin City. And in addition to a long lineup of Las Vegas–style shows, Laughlin's Colorado River access offers wet and wild entertainment from the waterfront casino hotels lining the cool blue waterway.

Laughlin's founder, Don Laughlin, bought an eight-room motel here in 1966 and basically built the town from scratch. By the early 1980s Laughlin's Riverside Hotel-Casino was drawing gamblers and river rats from northwestern Arizona, southeastern California, and even southern Nevada, and his success attracted other casino operators. Today Laughlin is Nevada's third major resort area, attracting more than 5

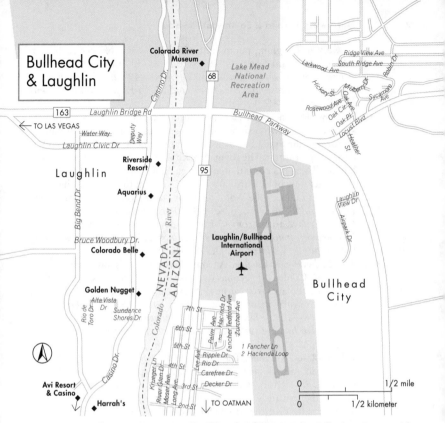

Bullhead City & Laughlin

Colorado River Museum

Lake Mead National Recreation Area

68

163 Laughlin Bridge Rd

← TO LAS VEGAS

Bullhead Parkway

Larkwood Ave
Ridge View Ave
South Ridge Ave
Robin Dr
Hickory St
Rosewood Ave
Mulberry St
Oak Cir.
Sycamore Ave
Oak Pl.
Oak Blvd
Locust Blvd
Locust Heather St

Water Way
Laughlin Civic Dr.
Deputy Way

Laughlin

Riverside Resort

95

Aquarius

Big Bend Dr.

Bruce Woodbury Dr.

Colorado Belle

Colorado River

NEVADA
ARIZONA

Laughlin/Bullhead International Airport

Laughlin View Dr
Airpark Dr.

Golden Nugget
Alta Vista Dr.
Rio de Toro Dr.
Sundance Shores Dr

7th St.
6th St.
5th St.
4th St.
3rd St.
2nd St.

Hacienda Dr.
Fancher Tedford Ave
Zurcher Ave

Palm Ave.

Krueger Ln.
River Glen Dr.
Moser Ave.
Long Ave.
Lee Ave.

Ripple Dr.
Rio Dr.
Carefree Dr.
Decker Dr.

1 Fancher Ln
2 Hacienda Loop

Bullhead City

Casino Dr.

Avi Resort & Casino

Harrah's

TO OATMAN

0   1/2 mile
0   1/2 kilometer

million visitors annually. The city fills up, especially in winter, with retired travelers who spend at least part of the winter in Arizona, and with a younger resort-loving crowd. The big picture windows overlooking the Colorado River lend a bright, airy, and open feeling unique to Laughlin casinos. Take a stroll along the river walk, then make the return trip by water taxi ($3 round-trip; $2 one-way). Boating, Jet Skis, and plain old wading are other options for enjoying the water.

★ Across the Laughlin Bridge, ¼ mi to the north, the **Colorado River Historical Museum** displays the rich past of the region where Nevada, Arizona, and California converge. There are artifacts from the Mojave Indian Tribe, models and photographs of steamboats that once plied the river, rock and fossil specimens, and the first telephone switchboard used in neighboring Bullhead City. ⊠*2201 AZ 68* ☎*928/754–3399* ⊕*www. bullheadcity.com/tourism/hismuseum.asp* ⊠*$2* ☉*Sept.–June, Tues.– Sat. 10–4, Sun. 1–4.*

WHERE TO STAY & EAT

¢–$$$ ╳🏨 **Colorado Belle.** This is a Nevada anomaly—a riverboat casino that's actually on a river. The 608-foot replica of a Mississippi paddle wheeler has nautical-theme rooms with views of the Colorado River. Non-smoking gamblers will appreciate the smoke-free section in the slot machine area. The **Boiler Room Brew Pub** ($), the only microbrewery in Laughlin, pumps out 155,000 gallons of beer each year. ⊠*2100 S. Casino Dr., 89029* ☎*702/298–4000 or 866/352–3553* ⊕*www.coloradobelle.com* ➪*1,119 rooms, 49 suites* ⌂*In-hotel: 6 restaurants, pools, laundry service, public Wi-Fi, no-smoking rooms* ⊟*AE, D, DC, MC, V.*

★ ¢–$$ ✕⛁**Harrah's.** This is the classiest joint in Laughlin, and it has a private sand beach and two casinos (one is no-smoking). Big-name entertainers perform in the Fiesta Showroom and at the 3,000-seat Rio Vista Outdoor Amphitheater. **The Range Steakhouse** ($$–$$$) serves Continental fare. There is a cocktail lounge in each of the casinos and another at the adults-only pool. Card fans might also want to check out the poker player's paradise at the World Series of Poker store. ⊠*2900 S. Casino Dr., Laughlin 89029* ☎*702/298–4600 or 800/427–7247* 🖷*702/298–6802* ⊕*www.harrahs.com* ➪*1,561 rooms* ⌂*In-room: dial-up (some). In-hotel: 5 restaurants, bars, pools, gym, spa, beachfront, no-smoking rooms, public Wi-Fi* ⊟*AE, D, DC, MC, V.*

¢–$ ✕⛁**Golden Nugget Laughlin.** A tropical atrium in this miniversion of the Las Vegas Golden Nugget has two cascading waterfalls and more than 300 types of plants from around the world. **Joe's Crab Shack** ($$–$$$) offers the only riverfront dining in town. ⊠*2300 S. Casino Dr., 89029* ☎*702/298–7111 or 800/950–7700* ⊕*www.goldennugget.com* ➪*300 rooms* ⌂*In-hotel: 4 restaurants, bar, pool, no-smoking rooms* ⊟*AE, DC, MC, V.*

¢ ✕⛁**Avi Resort & Casino.** The only tribally owned casino in Nevada is run by the Fort Mojave Tribe. The 25,000-square-foot casino houses nearly 1,000 slot and video-poker machines. The biggest draw, however, is the private white-sand beach where you can lounge or rent a watercraft. Visit the **Moonshadow Grille** ($$–$$$), preferably for their Sunday champagne brunch. ⊠*10000 Aha Macav Pkwy., Laughlin 89029* ☎*702/535–5555 or 800/284–2946* ⊕*www.avicasino.com* ➪*455 rooms, 29 spa suites* ⌂*In-hotel: 5 restaurants, bar, golf course, pool, gym, spa, beachfront, children's programs (ages 6 wks–12 yrs), no-smoking rooms, public Internet* ⊟*AE, D, DC, MC, V.*

★ ¢ ✕⛁**Riverside Resort.** Town founder Don Laughlin still runs this joint himself. Check out the Loser's Lounge, with its graphic homage to famous losers, such as the *Hindenburg,* the *Titanic,* and the like. And don't pass up Don's two free classic-car showrooms with more than 80 rods, roadsters, and tin lizzies. The **Gourmet Room** restaurant ($$$–$$$$) serves Continental and American cuisine. ⊠*1650 S. Casino Dr., Laughlin 89029* ☎*702/298–2535 or 800/227–3849* 🖷*702/298–2614* ⊕*www.riversideresort.com* ➪*1,400 rooms* ⌂*In-hotel: 6 restaurants, bar, pools, children's programs (ages 3 months–12 yrs), no-smoking rooms, public Wi-Fi* ⊟*AE, D, DC, MC, V.*

¢ ⛁**Aquarius.** The Flamingo Laughlin was re-named in late 2006 after an ownership change. Along with the new moniker, Aquarius boasts a fully renovated guest lobby and casino, featuring 1,500 slot and video-poker machines, a poker room, and a sports book. The 3,000-seat outdoor amphitheater, on the bank of the Colorado River, hosts big-name entertainers. ⊠*1900 S. Casino Dr., 89029* ☎*702/298–5111 or 800/352–6464* ⊕*www.flamingolaughlin.com* ➪*1,907 rooms, 82* *suites* ♿ *In-hotel: 6 restaurants, bars, tennis courts, pool, gym, no-smoking rooms* ▤ *AE, D, DC, MC, V.*

BOULDER CITY, NEVADA

④ *76 mi northwest of Kingman.*

In the early 1930s Boulder City was built by the federal government to house 5,000 construction workers on the Hoover Dam project. A strict moral code was enforced to ensure timely completion of the dam, and to this day, the model city is the only community in Nevada in which gambling is illegal. (Note that the two casinos at either end of Boulder City are just outside the city limits.) After the dam was completed, the town shrank but was kept alive by the management and maintenance crews of the dam and Lake Mead. Today it's a vibrant little Southwestern town; although it's not much of a destination in its own right, many travelers stop to try their luck at the casinos just outside town.

Built in 1933, the **Boulder Dam Hotel** (✉ *1305 Arizona St.* ☎ *702/293–3510*) was a favorite getaway for notables, including the man who became Pope Pius XII and actors Will Rogers, Bette Davis, and Shirley Temple. The **Boulder City/Hoover Dam Museum** (☎ *702/294–1988* ⊕ *www.bcmha.org* ☑ *$2* ⊙ *Mon.–Sat. 10–5, Sun. noon–5*), which preserves and displays artifacts relating to the workers and construction of Boulder City and Hoover Dam, occupies the second floor of the Boulder Dam Hotel. The **Boulder City Chamber of Commerce** (✉ *465 Nevada Way* ☎ *702/293–2034* ⊕ *www.bouldercitychamber.com* ⊙ *weekdays 9–5*) is a good place to gather information on the history of Hoover Dam and other historic sights around town.

HOOVER DAM

⑤ *67 mi northwest of Kingman via U.S. 93.*

Fodor'sChoice
★

Humanity's ability to reshape the natural world—for good or ill, depending on your viewpoint—is powerfully evident in the Hoover Dam. Completed in 1935, the dam is 726 feet high (the equivalent of a 70-story building) and 660 feet thick at the base (more than the length of two football fields). Its construction required 4.4 million cubic yards of concrete, enough to build a two-lane highway from San Francisco to New York. Originally referred to as Boulder Dam, the structure was later officially named Hoover Dam in recognition of President Herbert Hoover's role in the project. Look for artist Oskar Hansen's plaza sculptures, which include the 30-foot-tall *Winged Figures of the Republic*. Many people walk right over Hansen's most intriguing work: the plaza's terrazzo floor, inlaid with a celestial map.

The **Discovery Tour** allows you to see the power plant generators and other features. Guide staffers give talks every 15 minutes at each stopping point from 9 to 5:15 (early tours are less crowded). Cameras, pagers, tote bags, and cell phones are subject to X-ray screening. More

8

than a million people take this tour annually. January and February are the slowest months.

The top of the dam is open to pedestrians during daylight hours only; approved vehicles can cross the dam 24/7. Note: all specified hours are Pacific time. ⊠ *U.S. 93 east of Boulder City* ☎*702/494–2517; Security, road, and Hoover Dam crossing information: 888/248–1259* 🖷*702/494–2587* ⊕*www.usbr.gov/ lc/hooverdam* 🖃*Discovery Tour $11, parking $7* ☉*Daily 9–6.*

SPORTS & THE OUTDOORS

WATER SPORTS   The clear, cold water released by Hoover Dam from Lake Mead makes this leg of the Colorado River a pristine place to set off on a smoothwater rafting tour. The launch site lies in a sensitive security zone, which can only be accessed by permitted outfitters.

Black Canyon River Adventures (⊠*Hacienda Resort* ☎*702/294–1414* ⊕*www.blackcanyonadventures.com*) offers 3-hour float trips once a day. Rates are $82.95 and include a box lunch. For a more hands-on approach, try a guided kayak trip through Black Canyon with **Boulder City Outfitters** (⊠*1631 Industrial Rd.* ☎*702/293–1190 or 800/748– 3702* ⊕*www.bouldercityoutfitters.com*). Rates are $150 per person with a two-person minimum.

LAKE MEAD

❻ *67 mi northwest of Kingman on U.S. 93.*

Lake Mead, which is actually the Colorado River backed up behind the Hoover Dam, is the nation's largest man-made reservoir: it covers 229 square mi, is 110 mi long, and has an irregular shoreline that extends for 550 mi. You can get information about the lake's history, ecology, recreational opportunities, and the accommodations available along its shore at the **Alan Bible Visitors Center** (☎*702/293–8990* ☉*Daily 8:30–4:30*). People come to Lake Mead to swim: **Boulder Beach** on the Nevada side of the lake is the closest swimming beach to Arizona and only about a mile from the visitor center.

Angling and houseboating are favorite pastimes; marinas strung along the Nevada shore rent houseboats, personal watercraft, and ski boats. The lake is regularly stocked with a half-million rainbow trout, and at least a million fish are harvested every year. You can fish here 24 hours a day, year-round (except for posted closings). If you plan to catch and keep trout, be mindful that a trout stamp is required. Divers can explore the murk beneath, including the usually submerged foundations of St. Thomas, a farming community that was inundated in 1938. Other activities abound, including waterskiing, sailboarding, and snorkeling.

⊕www.nps.gov/lame ⊠*$5 per vehicle, good for 5 days; lake use fees $10 first vessel, $5 additional vessel, good for 5 days.*

SPORTS & THE OUTDOORS

BOATING Rental options include houseboats, patio boats, fishing boats, and ski boats—pick up a list of marinas at the Alan Bible Visitors Center.

Powerboats as well as houseboats are available at **Callville Bay Resort and Marina** (⊠*Callville Bay* ☎*702/565–8958 or 800/255–5561*). **Echo Bay Resort** (⊠*Echo Bay* ☎*702/394–4000 or 800/752–9669*) is a popular choice for Lake Mead houseboat rentals; the company also rents ski boats, fishing boats, and other personal watercraft. **Lake Mead Marina** (⊠*Boulder Beach, Boulder City* ☎*702/293–3484*) has boat rentals, a beach, camping facilities, a gift shop, and a floating restaurant.

CRUISES **Lake Mead Cruises** (⊠*Lake Mead Marina, near Boulder Beach, Boulder City* ☎*702/293–6180* ⊕*www.lakemeadcruises.com*) offers 1½-hour cruises of the Hoover Dam area on the 300-passenger *Desert Princess*. Also offered are breakfast-buffet cruises and early dinner and dinner-dance cruises. **Gray Line Tours** (☎*702/384–1234 or 800/634–6579* ⊕*www.pcap.com/grayline.htm*) has several sightseeing options.

WHERE TO STAY

¢–$$ ▦ **Temple Bar Resort.** This motel right on the Arizona shore of the lake is a good choice if you want a quiet room; the hotel's remote location ensures peace. The rooms are basic and all come with double beds. Rooms with lake views are definitely worth the upgrade. The fishing cabins are even more rustic, with shared, unattached bathroom facilities. The restaurant, which serves typical American fare, has outdoor seating overlooking the water. ⊠*Temple Bar, AZ 86643* ☎*928/767–3211 or 800/752–9669* ⇥*18 rooms, 4 cabins* ⌂*In-room: no TV, no phone. In-hotel: restaurant, beachfront, no elevator* ▭*AE, D, MC, V.*

¢ ▦ **Hacienda Resort.** Just outside city limits, this large, Vegas-style casino eludes the Boulder City ban on gambling. It has seven restaurants, live entertainment, and more than 800 slot machines. The rooms are basic; suites are slightly more stylish. Ask for a lake view upgrade, which livens up the otherwise unassuming surroundings. ⊠*U.S. 93, Boulder City, NV 89005* ☎*702/293–5000 or 800/245–6380* ⊕*www.haciendaonline. com* ⇥*375 rooms* ⌂*In-hotel: 7 restaurants* ▭*AE, D, MC, V.*

HOUSEBOATS **Seven Crown Resorts.** The beauty of renting a houseboat is that you can cruise down the lake and park where you please for as long as you like. It's an increasingly popular vacation option, especially for large groups. Seven Crown Resorts is a good resource for rentals. The boats come equipped with full kitchens and some have air-conditioning; they can sleep from 6 to 13 people. The minimum rental is three days, two nights; you get the best rates on a one-week rental. ☎*800/752–9669 or 928/767–3211* ⊕*www.sevencrown.com* ▭*AE, D, MC, V.*

8

NORTHWEST ARIZONA & SOUTHEAST NEVADA ESSENTIALS

To research prices, get advice from other travelers, and book travel arrangements, visit ⊕ www.fodors.com.

TRANSPORTATION

BY AIR

Great Lakes Airlines has daily flights between Kingman and Phoenix; America West Express flies daily between Lake Havasu City and Phoenix. Sun Country flies to Laughlin/Bullhead City from 50 cities in 18 states, including Seattle, Portland, Denver, Minneapolis/St. Paul, San Francisco, Phoenix, and Dallas/Fort Worth. Westwind Aviation, Inc. flies from Deer Valley (a suburb of Phoenix) to Bullhead City. Several hotel-casinos also sponsor charter flights.

Contacts America West Express (☎ 800/235-9292 ⊕ www.usairways.com). **Great Lakes Airlines** (☎ 800/554-5111 ⊕ www.greatlakesav.com). **Sun Country Airlines** (☎ 800/359-6786 ⊕ www.suncountry.com). **Kingman Airport** (☎ 928/757-5444). **Lake Havasu City Municipal Airport** (☎ 928/764-3330). **Laughlin/Bullhead International Airport** (☎ 928/754-2134). **Westwind Aviation, Inc.** (☎ 480/991-5557 or 866/887-5969 ⊕ www.westwindaviation.com).

BY BUS

Greyhound serves Kingman, Lake Havasu City, and Bullhead City. The Bullhead City bus stops at the Airport Chevron at 600 AZ 95. To get to Laughlin, Nevada, walk to the boat dock across the highway and take a free ride to a Nevada hotel river landing. Tri State Shuttle Service offers regular service from Bullhead City to Kingman and Lake Havasu.

Contacts Greyhound (☎ 800/231-2222 ⊕ www.greyhound.com). **Tri State Shuttle** (☎ 928/704-9000 ⊕ www.tristatesupershuttle.com).

BY CAR

The best way to get your "kicks on Route 66" is to travel by automobile. This holds true for travel throughout northwestern Arizona. Historic Route 66 crosses east–west and lies north of I–40, which also crosses the region. U.S. 93 is the main route for north–south travel. All of these roads are in excellent condition. On I–40 high winds occasionally raise enough blowing dust to restrict visibility. In winter, ice may be present on the stretch of I–40 between Kingman and Seligman, as well as on sections of Route 66. When signage warns of ice ahead, heed the warnings and slow down. Most of the county roads are improved dirt roads, but washboard sections may surprise you, so take your time and drive no faster than prudence dictates. Roll down the windows and enjoy the scent of desert air.

Fuel up while you're in this part of Arizona—all grades of gasoline can be as much as 30¢ to 50¢ per gallon less in Kingman and Bullhead City than in Laughlin. National car rental outfits have outposts in Kingman, Bullhead City, and Lake Havasu City.

Contacts **Anderson Toyota** (✉ *Kingman* ☎ *928/757–1228*). **Martin Swanty Rentals** (✉ *Kingman* ☎ *928/753–5151*).

BY TAXI

Kingman Taxi and Yellow Taxi offer transport services in the Kingman area. For transportation in Boulder City call Deluxe Taxicab Service. In Lake Havasu City call Arizona Road-runner Shuttle for local and regional transportation.

Contacts **Arizona Road-runner Shuttle** (✉ *Lake Havasu City* ☎ *928/854–9333*). **Deluxe Taxicab Service** (✉ *Henderson* ☎ *702/568–7700*). **Kingman Taxi** (✉ *Kingman* ☎ *928/753–1222*). **Yellow Taxi** (✉ *Kingman* ☎ *928/753–4444 or 928/718–9000*).

BY TRAIN

Amtrak's *Southwest Chief* stops in Kingman and in Needles, California, which is 25 mi south of Bullhead City/Laughlin. An Amtrak Thruway bus shuttles passengers to the Ramada Express in Laughlin.

Contacts **Amtrak-Kingman** (☎ *800/872–7245* ⊕ *www.amtrak.com*).

CONTACTS & RESOURCES

EMERGENCIES

In the U.S., call 911 for fire or police emergencies, or for an ambulance.

There are local hospitals in most of the larger cities of northwest Arizona and southeast Nevada, and many of the chain drugstores have locations in the area.

The Havasu Regional Medical City, Kingman Regional Medical Center, Valley View Medical Center, and Western Arizona Regional Medical Center provide 24-hour emergency medical care. The Walgreens pharmacies in Bullhead City and Lake Havasu City and CVS in Bullhead City are also open 24 hours a day.

Contacts **Boulder City Hospital** (✉ *901 Adams Blvd., Boulder City* ☎ *702/293–4111* ⊕ *www.bouldercityhospital.org*). **CVS** (✉ *2350 Miracle Mile, Bullhead City* ☎ *928/758–2212*). **Havasu Regional Medical Center** (✉ *101 Civic Center La., Lake Havasu City* ☎ *928/855–8185* ⊕ *www.havasuregional.com*). **Kingman Regional Medical Center** (✉ *3269 Stockton Hill Rd., Kingman* ☎ *928/757–2101 or 877/757–2101* ⊕ *www.azkrmc.com*). **Valley View Medical Center** (✉ *5330 S. Hwy. 95, Bullhead City* ☎ *928/788–CARE* ⊕ *www.valleyviewmedicalcenter.net*). **Walgreens** (✉ *2360 Highway 95, Bullhead City* ☎ *928/763–6777* ✉ *25 Lake Havasu Ave. S, Lake Havasu City* ☎ *928/453–2808* ⊕ *www.walgreens.com*). **Western Arizona Regional Medical Center** (✉ *2735 Silver Creek Rd., Bullhead City* ☎ *928/763–2273* ⊕ *www.warmc.com*).

SPORTS & THE OUTDOORS

HIKING The Bureau of Land Management Kingman Field Office and Lake Havasu Field Office can give you details about outdoor recreational activities in the northwestern corner of Arizona.

Contacts **Bureau of Land Management Kingman Field Office** (⊠ *2475 Beverly Ave., Kingman 86401* ☏ *928/718–3700* ⊕ *www.blm.gov/az*). **Bureau of Land Management Lake Havasu Field Office** (⊠ *2610 Sweetwater Ave., Lake Havasu City 86406* ☏ *928/505–1200* ⊕ *www.blm.gov/az*). **Bureau of Land Management Las Vegas Field Office** (⊠ *4701 North Torrey Pines Rd., Las Vegas 89130* ☏ *702/515–5000* ⊕ *www.nv.blm.gov/vegas*).

INTERNET, MAIL & SHIPPING

The U.S. Postal Service has post office locations throughout northwest Arizona and southeast Nevada. For additional express services, FedEx has offices in Lake Havasu City and Henderson. UPS Stores can be found in Kingman and Bullhead City.

TOURS

BOATING & RAFTING TOURS There is no white water on the Colorado River below Hoover Dam. Instead, the river and its lakes offer you many opportunities to explore the gorges and marshes that line the shores. If you prefer to do it yourself, look into the canoe and kayak rentals available on lakes Mead, Mohave, and Havasu. Raft adventures will take you through the Topock Gorge near Lake Havasu, or you can take a trip upriver from Willow Beach 12 mi to the base of Hoover Dam. Along the way, chances are good you'll see bighorn sheep moving along the steep basaltic cliffs. Expect to spend $35 to $40 for half a day, and twice that for a full-day adventure.

Contacts **Black Canyon Adventures** (☏ *800/455–3490* ⊕ *www.blackcanyon adventures.com*). **Desert River Outfitters** (☏ *888/529–2533* ⊕ *www.desertriver outfitters.com*). **Western Arizona Canoe & Kayak Outfitter** (☏ *928/715–6414 or 888/881–5038* ⊕ *www.azwacko.com*).

VISITOR INFORMATION

Contacts **Boulder City Chamber of Commerce** (⊠ *465 Nevada Way, Boulder City* ☏ *702/293–2034* ⊕ *www.bouldercitychamber.com*). **Bullhead City Area Chamber of Commerce** (⊠ *1251 Hwy. 95, Bullhead City* ☏ *928/754–4121* ⊕ *www.bullhead chamber.com*). **Kingman Visitors Bureau** (⊠ *120 W. Andy Devine Ave., Kingman* ☏ *928/753–6106 or 866/427–7866* ⊕ *www.kingmantourism.org*). **Lake Havasu Tourism Bureau** (⊠ *314 London Bridge Rd., Lake Havasu City* ☏ *928/453–3444 or 800/242–8278* ⊕ *www.golakehavasu.com*). **Laughlin Chamber of Commerce** (⊠ *1585 Casino Dr., Laughlin* ☏ *702/298–2214 or 800/227–5245* 🖷 *702/298–5708* ⊕ *www.laughlinchamber.com*). **Laughlin Visitors Bureau** (⊠ *1555 S. Casino Dr., Laughlin* ☏ *702/298–3321 or 800/452–8445* ⊕ *www.visitlaughlin.com*).

UNDERSTANDING ARIZONA

Arizona at a Glance

ARIZONA AT A GLANCE

FAST FACTS

Nickname: Grand Canyon State
Capital: Phoenix
Motto: Ditat Deus (God enriches)
State song: *Arizona*
State bird: Cactus Wren
State flower: Saguaro cactus blossom (carnegiea gigantea)
State tree: Palo verde (cercidium)
Administrative divisions: 15 counties
Entered the Union: February 14, 1912 (48th state)
Population: 5.8 million
Population density: 46.9 people per square mi
Median age: 34.2
Infant mortality rate: 6.9 deaths per 1,000 births
Literacy: 18% had trouble with basic reading. Twenty-six percent spoke a language other than English at home, usually Spanish. Forty percent reported that they did not speak English "very well."
Ethnic groups: White 62%; Latino 27%; Native American 4%; African American 3%; Asian 2%; other 2%
Religion: Unaffiliated 60%; Catholic 19%; Christian 12%; Mormon 5%; Jewish 2%; other 2%

Come to this land of sunshine
To this land where life is young.
Where the wide, wide world is
waiting,
The songs that will now be sung.

—opening lines of state song,
Arizona, by Margaret Rowe Clifford

GEOGRAPHY & ENVIRONMENT

Land area: 113,909 square mi
Terrain: Desert, with rocky mountains stretching across the southern area of the state. Along the Mogollon Rim that reaches in a crescent across the eastern third of the state, stands the largest ponderosa-pine forest in the world. The White Mountains of eastern Arizona receive over 150 inches of snow annually and the run-off provides much of the water that enables the desert communities to survive. Erosion by rivers has formed much of the state's geography, including the Grand Canyon and the Painted Desert
Highest point: Humphreys Peak, 12,655 feet
Natural resources: Cement, copper (Arizona leads the nation in production), gravel, molybdenum, pine and fir forests, sand
Natural hazards: Drought, earthquakes, floods, severe storms, wildfires
Environmental issues: Especially around Phoenix, air quality is bad enough that year-round monitoring is done for ground-level ozone pollution, carbon monoxide, and particulate matter; concern over how logging should be done in Arizona's pine forests; soil erosion from overgrazing, industrial development, urbanization, and poor farming practices; most of the state suffers from limited natural freshwater resources

Desert rains are usually so definitely
demarked that the story of the
man who washed his hands in the
edge of an Arizona thunder shower
without wetting his cuffs seems
almost credible.

—Arizona: A State Guide
(The WPA Guide to Arizona)

ECONOMY

GSP: $160.6 billion
Per-capita income: $33,704
Unemployment: 4.5%
Work force: 2.7 million; financial/management 21%; trade, transportation, and utilities 19%; government 18%; educational and health services 11%; leisure/hospitality 10%; construction 8%; manufacturing 7%; other 4%; publishing/telecom 2%
Major industries: Cattle, dairy goods, manufacturing, electronics, printing and publishing, processed foods, aerospace, transportation, high-tech research and development, communications, construction, tourism, military
Agricultural products: Broccoli, cattle, cauliflowers, cotton, dairy goods, lettuce, sorghum
Exports: $10.7 billion
Major export products: Electronic and electric equipment, fabricated metal products, industrial machinery and computers, scientific and measuring instruments, transportation equipment

The great pines stand at a considerable distance from each other. Each tree grows alone, murmurs alone, thinks alone. They do not intrude upon each other. The Navajos are not much in the habit of giving or of asking help. Their language is not a communicative one, and they never attempt an interchange of personality in speech. Over their forests there is the same inexorable reserve. Each tree has its exalted power to bear.

—Willa Cather (1873–1947), U.S. novelist, describing Navajo pine forests in northern Arizona.

DID YOU KNOW?

■ Yuma, Arizona, holds the world record for most sunshine. It gets an average of 4,055 hours, or more than 90%, of the 4,456 hours of sunshine possible in a year.

■ The Arizona or "Apache" Trout can only be found in the White Mountains of Arizona.

■ One of Arizona's most plentiful natural resources is molybdenum, an element linked with copper production. Molybdenum is used to make steel, as well as electrodes and catalysts.

■ During daylight saving time, it's possible to drive in and out of time zones in Arizona in less than an hour. While the rest of the state sticks to Mountain Standard Time year-round, the state's Navajo Nation observes daylight saving, but the Hopi Reservation inside the Navajo goes along with the rest of Arizona.

■ César Chávez, who organized agricultural laborers across America, was born near Yuma, Arizona.

■ In 1930, Pluto was discovered by Clyde Tombaugh at Lowell Observatory in Flagstaff.

■ The Central Arizona Project Canal is 336 mi long and annually brings 1.5 million gallons of Colorado River water from Lake Havasu City, through the Phoenix metropolitan area, to Tucson.

■ The Hohokam, Arizona's earliest known inhabitants, were good at something crucial to Arizona today: irrigation. They built canals more than 10 mi long that channeled water to fields in the southern part of the state in about AD 300.

■ More than 10% of the nation's Native Americans live in Arizona.

Arizona
Essentials

There are planners and there are those who, excuse the pun, fly by the seat of their pants. We happily place ourselves among the planners. Our writers and editors try to anticipate all the issues you may face before and during any journey, and then they do their research. This section is the product of their efforts. Use it to get excited about your trip to Arizona, to inform your travel planning, or to guide you on the road should the seat of your pants start to feel threadbare.

GETTING STARTED

We're really proud of our Web site: Fodors.com is a great place to begin any journey. Scan Travel Wire for suggested itineraries, travel deals, restaurant and hotel openings, and other up-to-the-minute info. Check out Booking to research prices and book plane tickets, hotel rooms, rental cars, and vacation packages. Head to Talk for on-the-ground pointers from travelers who frequent our message boards. You can also link to loads of other travel-related resources.

▌ RESOURCES

ONLINE TRAVEL TOOLS

For more specific information on Arizona, visit the following Web sites.

ALL ABOUT ARIZONA

Information of particular interest to outdoorsy types can be found on the Web site for **Arizona State Parks** (⊕*www.azstateparks.com*), which has links to the many beautiful state-operated reserves throughout Arizona. The site for the **National Park Service** (⊕*www.nps.gov*) has links to the several national parks in Arizona. Of course, the Grand Canyon is the most famous of Arizona's parks, and you can find out much more about the park at **The Canyon** (⊕*www.thecanyon.com*). The **Great Outdoor Recreation Page** (⊕*www.gorp.com*) is another font of information for hikers, skiers, and the like.

There are a handful of excellent general-interest sites related to travel in Arizona. A very good bet is the *Arizona Republic*-sponsored **AzCentral.com** (⊕*www.azcentral.com*), which provides news, reviews, and travel information on the entire state, with a particular emphasis on Phoenix. Alternative newsweeklies are another helpful resource, among them the *Phoenix New Times* (⊕*www.phoenixnewtimes.com*). For the southern

part of the state, look for *Tucson Weekly* (⊕*www.tucsonweekly.com*).

Safety Transportation Security Administration (TSA; ⊕www.tsa.gov)

Time Zones Timeanddate.com (⊕www.timeanddate.com/worldclock) can help you figure out the correct time anywhere.

Weather Accuweather.com (⊕www.accuweather.com) is an independent weather-forecasting service with good coverage of hurricanes. **Weather.com** (⊕www.weather.com) is the Web site for the Weather Channel.

WORD OF MOUTH

After your trip, be sure to rate the places you visited and share your experiences and travel tips with us and other Fodorites in Travel Ratings and Talk on www.fodors.com.

Other Resources CIA World Factbook (⊕www.odci.gov/cia/publications/factbook/index.html) has profiles of every country in the world. It's a good source if you need some quick facts and figures.

▌ VISITOR INFORMATION

For local tourism information, see Visitor Information in the Essentials section at the end of each chapter.

Tourist Information Arizona Office of Tourism (☎602/364–3700 or 866/275–5816 ⊕www.arizonaguide.com).

Native American Resources Arizona Commission of Indian Affairs (☎602/542–3123 ⊕www.indianaffairs.state.az.us). **Gila River Indian Community** (☎520/562–9500 ⊕www.gric.nsn.us). **Inter Tribal Council of Arizona: Hopi Tribe** (☎928/734–3000 ⊕www.itcaonline.com/tribes_hopi.html). **Navajo Nation Tourism Office** (☎928/871–6436 ⊕www.discovernavajo.com). **Salt River Pima-Maricopa Indian Community**

(☎480/850–8000 ⊕www.saltriver.
pima-maricopa.nsn.us). **Tohono O'odham
Nation** (☎520/383–2028 ⊕www.itcaonline.
com/tribes_tohono.html). **White Mountain Apache Nation** (☎928/338–4346 or
877/338–9628 ⊕www.wmat.nsn.us).

▌THINGS TO CONSIDER

GEAR

Pack casual clothing and resort wear for a
trip to Arizona. Stay cool in cotton fabrics
and light colors. T-shirts, polo shirts, sun-
dresses, and lightweight shorts, trousers,
skirts, and blouses are useful year-round
in the southwest. Bring sun hats, swim-
suits, sandals, and sunscreen—mandatory
warm-weather items. Bring a sweater and
a warm jacket in winter, necessary during
December and January throughout the
state, particularly in the high country—
anywhere around Flagstaff and in the
White Mountains. And don't forget jeans
and sneakers or sturdy walking shoes;
they're important throughout the year.

SHIPPING SPORTING EQUIPMENT

Arizona is a wonderful destination for all
kinds of equipment-intensive sports, from
skiing to cycling to golfing. If you're driving here, lugging your gear isn't much of
a hassle. But travelers arriving by plane
may find hauling bags of clubs, mountain bikes, and skis a bit daunting. Sports
Express specializes in shipping gear. The
service isn't cheap, but it is highly reliable
and convenient.

Contacts Sports Express (☎800/357–4174
⊕www.sportsexpress.com).

BOOKING YOUR TRIP

Unless your cousin is a travel agent, you're probably among the millions of people who make most of their travel arrangements online.

But have you ever wondered just what the differences are between an online travel agent (a Web site through which you make reservations instead of going directly to the airline, hotel, or car-rental company), a discounter (a firm that does a high volume of business with a hotel chain or airline and accordingly gets good prices), a wholesaler (one that makes cheap reservations in bulk and then re-sells them to people like you), and an aggregator (one that compares all the offerings so you don't have to)?

Is it truly better to book directly on an airline or hotel Web site? And when does a real live travel agent come in handy?

▌ ONLINE

You really have to shop around. A travel wholesaler such as Hotels.com or Hotel-Club.net can be a source of good rates, as can discounters such as Hotwire or Price-line, particularly if you can bid for your hotel room or airfare. Indeed, such sites sometimes have deals that are unavailable elsewhere. They do, however, tend to work only with hotel chains (which makes them just plain useless for getting hotel reservations outside of major cities) or big airlines (so that often leaves out upstarts like jetBlue and some foreign carriers like Air India).

Also, with discounters and wholesalers you must generally prepay, and everything is nonrefundable. And before you fork over the dough, be sure to check the terms and conditions, so you know what a given company will do for you if there's a problem and what you'll have to deal with on your own.

■ TIP→ To be absolutely sure everything was processed correctly, confirm reservations made through online travel agents, discounters, and wholesalers directly with your hotel before leaving home.

Booking engines like Expedia, Travelocity, and Orbitz are actually travel agents, albeit high-volume, online ones. And airline travel packagers like American Airlines Vacations and Virgin Vacations—well, they're travel agents, too. But they may still not work with all the world's hotels.

An aggregator site will search many sites and pull the best prices for airfares, hotels, and rental cars from them. Most aggregators compare the major travel-booking sites such as Expedia, Travelocity, and Orbitz; some also look at airline Web sites, though rarely the sites of smaller budget airlines. Some aggregators also compare other travel products, including complex packages—a good thing, as you can sometimes get the best overall deal by booking an air-and-hotel package.

▌ WITH A TRAVEL AGENT

If you use an agent—brick-and-mortar or virtual—you'll pay a fee for the service. And know that the service you get from some online agents isn't comprehensive. For example, Expedia and Travelocity don't search for prices on budget airlines like jetBlue, Southwest, or small foreign carriers. That said, some agents (online or not) *do* have access to fares that are difficult to find otherwise, and the savings can more than make up for any surcharge.

A knowledgeable brick-and-mortar travel agent can be a godsend if you're booking a cruise, a package trip that's not available to you directly, an air pass, or a complicated itinerary including several overseas flights. What's more, travel agents that specialize in a destination may have exclusive access to certain deals and insider information on things such as charter flights. Agents who specialize in types of travelers (senior citizens, gays and lesbians, naturists) or types of trips (cruises, luxury travel, safaris) can also be invaluable.

■ TIP→ Remember that Expedia, Travelocity, and Orbitz are travel agents, not just booking engines. To resolve any problems with a reservation made through these companies, contact them first.

Because Arizona has a well-developed tourism industry and its top destinations—the Grand Canyon, Sedona, Phoenix, Tucson—are geared toward attracting travelers, it's extremely easy to book rooms, golf outings, and package vacations yourself. For this reason, it's quite easy to forego a travel agent when planning a trip to Arizona. But if you're short on time, or if you aren't so savvy with the Internet, travel agents can more easily search among the many packages and deals available out there.

Agent Resources American Society of Travel Agents (☎703/739–2782 ⊕www. travelsense.org).

■ ACCOMMODATIONS

Arizona's hotels and motels run the gamut from world-class resorts to budget chains and from historic inns, bed-and-breakfasts, and mountain lodges to dude ranches, campgrounds, and RV parks. Make reservations well in advance for the high season—winter in the desert and summer in the high country. A few areas, such as Sedona and the Grand Canyon's South Rim, stay relatively busy year-round, so book as soon as you can. Tremendous bargains can be found off-season, especially in the Phoenix and Tucson areas during the summer, when even the most exclusive establishments can cut their rates by half or more.

Phoenix and Tucson have the greatest variety of accommodations in the state. Lodgings in Sedona and in some of the smaller, more exclusive desert communities can be pricey, but there are inexpensive chains in or near just about every resort-oriented destination. That said, even the budget chains in these areas can have rates in the upper double-digits. The Grand Canyon area is particularly pricey, but camping, cabins, and dorm-style resorts on or near the national park grounds offer lower rates. If you plan to stay at the Grand Canyon, make lodging reservations far in advance. You might have a more relaxing visit, and find better prices, in one of the gateway cities: Tusayan, Williams, and Flagstaff to the south, and Jacob Lake, Fredonia, and Kanab, Utah, to the north.

The lodgings we list are the cream of the crop in each price category. We always list the facilities that are available, but we don't specify whether they cost extra; when pricing accommodations, always ask what's included and what costs extra. Properties are assigned price categories based on the range from their least-expensive standard double room at high season (excluding holidays) to the most expensive. Properties marked ✕▣ are lodging establishments whose restaurants warrant a special trip. A price chart appears at the start of each chapter.

Most hotels and other lodgings require your credit-card details before they will confirm your reservation. If you don't feel comfortable e-mailing this information, ask if you can fax it (some places even prefer faxes). However you book, get confirmation in writing and have a copy handy when you check in.

Be sure you understand the hotel's cancellation policy. Some places allow you to cancel without any kind of penalty—even if you prepaid to secure a discounted rate—if you cancel at least 24 hours in advance. Others require you to cancel a week in advance or penalize you the cost

Online Booking Resources

AGGREGATORS		
Kayak	www.kayak.com	also looks at cruises and vacation packages.
Mobissimo	www.mobissimo.com	
Qixo	www.qixo.com	also compares cruises, vacation packages, and even travel insurance.
Sidestep	www.sidestep.com	also compares vacation packages and lists travel deals.
Travelgrove	www.travelgrove.com	also compares cruises and packages.
BOOKING ENGINES		
Cheap Tickets	www.cheaptickets.com	a discounter.
Expedia	www.expedia.com	a large online agency that charges a booking fee for airline tickets.
Hotwire	www.hotwire.com	a discounter.
lastminute.com	www.lastminute.com	specializes in last-minute travel; the main site is for the U.K., but it has a link to a U.S. site.
Luxury Link	www.luxurylink.com	has auctions (surprisingly good deals) as well as offers on the high-end side of travel.
Onetravel.com	www.onetravel.com	a discounter for hotels, car rentals, airfares, and packages.
Orbitz	www.orbitz.com	charges a booking fee for airline tickets, but gives a clear breakdown of fees and taxes before you book.
Priceline.com	www.priceline.com	a discounter that also allows bidding.
Travel.com	www.travel.com	allows you to compare its rates with those of other booking engines.
Travelocity	www.travelocity.com	charges a booking fee for airline tickets, but promises good problem resolution.
ONLINE ACCOMMODATIONS		
Hotelbook.com	www.hotelbook.com	focuses on independent hotels worldwide.
Hotel Club	www.hotelclub.net	good for major cities worldwide.
Hotels.com	www.hotels.com	a big Expedia-owned wholesaler that offers rooms in hotels all over the world.
Quikbook	www.quikbook.com	offers "pay when you stay" reservations that let you settle your bill at check out, not when you book.
OTHER RESOURCES		
Bidding For Travel	www.biddingfortravel.com	a good place to figure out what you can get and for how much before you start bidding on, say, Priceline.

of one night. Small inns and B&Bs are most likely to require you to cancel far in advance. Most hotels allow children under a certain age to stay in their parents' room at no extra charge, but others charge for them as extra adults; find out the cutoff age for discounts.

■TIP→ Assume that hotels operate on the **European Plan (EP, no meals)** unless we specify that they use the **Breakfast Plan (BP, with full breakfast)**, **Continental Plan (CP, Continental breakfast)**, **Full American Plan (FAP, all meals)**, **Modified American Plan (MAP, breakfast and dinner)** or are **all-inclusive (AI, all meals and most activities)**.

BED & BREAKFASTS

Arizona's one of the better destinations in the country when it comes to B&Bs. You'll find luxurious Spanish Colonial–style compounds in the more upscale destinations, such as Tucson, Sedona, and Prescott, as well as less fancy lodges virtually everywhere. Check with the Arizona Association of Bed and Breakfast Inns for details on its many members throughout the state. The Arizona Trails Reservation Service also has an extensive list of B&Bs and other lodgings and can also help with vacation packages, guided tours, and golf vacations. Mi Casa Su Casa offers properties in a range of styles, from adobe haciendas in areas like Sedona and Tucson to pine cabins in the White Mountains.

Reservation Services Arizona Association of Bed and Breakfast Inns (☎928/778–0442 ⊕www.arizona-bed-breakfast.com). **Arizona Trails Reservation Service** (☎480/837–4284 or 888/799–4284 ⊕www.arizonatrails.com). **Bed & Breakfast.com** (☎512/322–2710 or 800/462–2632 ⊕www.bedandbreakfast.com) also sends out an online newsletter. **Bed & Breakfast Inns Online** (☎615/868–1946 or 800/215–7365 ⊕www.bbonline.com). **BnB Finder.com** (☎212/432–7693 or 888/547–8226 ⊕www.bnbfinder.com). **Mi Casa Su Casa** (☎480/990–0682 or 800/456–0682 ⊕www.azres.com).

10 WAYS TO SAVE

1. Join "frequent guest" programs. You may get preferential treatment in room choice and/or upgrades in your favorite chains.

2. Call direct. You can sometimes get a better price if you call a hotel's local toll-free number (if available) rather than a central reservations number.

3. Check online. Check hotel Web sites, as not all chains are represented on all travel sites.

4. Look for specials. Always inquire about packages and corporate rates.

5. Look for price guarantees. For overseas trips, look for guaranteed rates. With your rate locked in you won't pay more, even if the price goes up in the local currency.

6. Look for weekend deals at business hotels. High-end chains catering to business travelers are often busy only on weekdays; to fill rooms they often drop rates dramatically on weekends.

7. Ask about taxes. Verify whether local hotel taxes are included in quoted rates. They can be significant.

8. Read the fine print. Watch for add-ons like resort fees, and "convenience" fees for things like unlimited local phone service you won't use.

9. Know when to go. If your destination's high season is December through April and you're trying to book, say, in late April, you might save money by changing your dates by a week or two. Ask when rates go down: if your dates straddle peak and nonpeak seasons, a property may still charge peak-season rates for the entire stay.

10. Weigh your options (we can't say this enough). Weigh transportation times and costs against the savings of staying in a hotel that's cheaper because it's out of the way.

DUDE-GUEST RANCHES

Guest ranches afford visitors a close encounter with down-home cooking, activities, and culture. Most of the properties are situated around Tucson and Wickenburg, northwest of Phoenix. Some are resort-style compounds where guests are pampered, whereas smaller, family-run ranches expect *everyone* to join in the chores. Horseback riding and other outdoor recreational activities are emphasized. Many dude ranches are closed in summer. The Arizona Dude Ranch Association provides names and addresses of member ranches and their facilities and policies.

Information **The Arizona Dude Ranch Association** (☎No phone ⊕www.azdra.com).

HOSTELS

Hostels offer bare-bones lodging at low, low prices—often in shared dorm rooms with shared baths—to people of all ages, though the primary market is young travelers, especially students. Most hostels serve breakfast; dinner and/or shared cooking facilities may also be available. In some hostels you aren't allowed to be in your room during the day, and there may be a curfew at night. Nevertheless, hostels provide a sense of community, with public rooms where travelers often gather to share stories. Many hostels are affiliated with Hostelling International (HI), an umbrella group of hostel associations with some 4,500 member properties in more than 70 countries. Other hostels are completely independent and may be nothing more than a really cheap hotel.

Membership in any HI association, open to travelers of all ages, allows you to stay in HI-affiliated hostels at member rates. One-year membership is about $28 for adults; hostels charge about $10–$30 per night. Members have priority if the hostel is full; they're also eligible for discounts around the world, even on rail and bus travel in some countries.

Arizona has just one Hostelling International property: Metcalf House in downtown Phoenix. It is well-regarded but, as hostels tend to be, quite basic.

Information **Hostelling International—USA** (☎301/495–1240 ⊕www.hiusa.org). **Hostelling International Phoenix–Metcalf House** (☎602/254–9803 ⊕http://home.earthlink.net/~phxhostel).

■ AIRLINE TICKETS

Most domestic airline tickets are electronic; international tickets may be either electronic or paper. With an e-ticket the only thing you receive is an e-mailed receipt citing your itinerary and reservation and ticket numbers.

The greatest advantage of an e-ticket is that if you lose your receipt, you can simply print out another copy or ask the airline to do it for you at check-in. You usually pay a surcharge (up to $50) to get a paper ticket, if you can get one at all.

The sole advantage of a paper ticket is that it may be easier to endorse over to another airline if your flight is canceled and the airline with which you booked can't accommodate you on another flight.

■TIP➔ Discount air passes that let you travel economically in a country or region must often be purchased before you leave home. In some cases you can only get them through a travel agent.

▌ RENTAL CARS

When you reserve a car, ask about cancellation penalties, taxes, drop-off charges (if you're planning to pick up the car in one city and leave it in another), and surcharges (for being under or over a certain age, for additional drivers, or for driving across state or country borders or beyond a specific distance from your point of rental). All these things can add substantially to your costs. Request car seats and extras such as GPS when you book.

Rates are sometimes—but not always—better if you book in advance or reserve through a rental agency's Web site. There are other reasons to book ahead, though: for popular destinations, during busy times of the year, or to ensure that you get certain types of cars (vans, SUVs, exotic sports cars).

▌TIP➔ **Make sure that a confirmed reservation guarantees you a car. Agencies sometimes overbook, particularly for busy weekends and holiday periods.**

Rates in Phoenix typically begin around $25 a day or $150 a week for an economy car with air-conditioning, automatic transmission, and unlimited mileage. This doesn't include taxes and fees on car rentals, which can range from about 15% to 50%, depending on pickup location. The base tax rate at Sky Harbor Airport is about 30%. When you add the daily fees (which are about $5 a day), taxes and fees can add up to almost half the cost of the car rental. You may be able to save by taking a cab to a retail location nearby to avoid the airport tax and additional daily fees. Taxes outside of the airport are typically around 25% or less.

Rates in Phoenix may be higher during the winter, which is considered high tourist season. Check the Internet or local papers for discounts and deals. Local rental agencies also frequently offer lower rates.

10 WAYS TO SAVE ✈

1. Nonrefundable is best. If saving money is more important than flexibility, then nonrefundable tickets work. Just remember that you'll pay dearly (as much as $100) if you change your plans.

2. Comparison shop. Web sites and travel agents can have different arrangements with the airlines and offer different prices for exactly the same flights.

3. Beware those prices. Many airline Web sites—and most ads—show prices *without* taxes and surcharges.

4. Stay loyal. Stick with one or two frequent-flier programs. You'll rack up free trips and other perks faster. On some airlines these include a special reservations number, early boarding, access to upgrades, and roomier, economy-class seating.

5. Watch those ticketing fees. Surcharges are usually added when you buy your ticket anywhere but on an airline Web site. (That includes by phone—even if you call the airline directly—and paper tickets regardless of how you book.)

6. Check early and often. Start looking for cheap fares up to a year in advance. Keep looking till you find a price you like.

7. Don't work alone. Some Web sites have tracking features that will e-mail you immediately when good deals are posted.

8. Jump on the good deals. Waiting even a few minutes might mean paying more.

9. Be flexible. Look for departures on Tuesday, Wednesday, and Thursday, typically the cheapest days to travel. And check on prices for departures at different times and to and from alternative airports.

10. Weigh your options. What you get can be as important as what you save. A cheaper flight might have a long layover, or it might land at a secondary airport, where your ground transportation costs might be higher.

Car Rental Resources

AUTOMOBILE ASSOCIATIONS		
American Automobile Association	315/797–5000	www.aaa.com; most contact with the organization is through state and regional members
National Automobile Club	650/294–7000	www.thenac.com; membership open to CA residents only
LOCAL AGENCIES		
ABC Rent-A-Car	800/773–6814	www.abc-rentacar.com
Arizona Auto Rental	520/624–4548	
Fox Rent A Car	800/225–4369	www.foxrentacar.com
MAJOR AGENCIES		
Alamo	800/462–5266	www.alamo.com
Avis	800/331–1084	www.avis.com
Budget	800/472–3325	www.budget.com
Hertz	800/654–3131	www.hertz.com
National Car Rental	800/227–7368	www.nationalcar.com

In Arizona most agencies won't rent to you if you're under the age of 21, and several major agencies will not rent to anyone under 25.

CAR-RENTAL INSURANCE

Everyone who rents a car wonders whether the insurance the rental companies offer is worth it. No one—including us—has a simple answer. It depends on how much regular insurance you have, how comfortable you are with risk, and whether money is an issue.

If you own a car and carry comprehensive car insurance for both collision and liability, your personal auto insurance will probably cover a rental, but read your policy's fine print to be sure. If you don't have auto insurance, then you should probably buy the collision- or loss-damage waiver (CDW or LDW) from the rental company. This eliminates your liability for damage to the car.

Some credit cards offer CDW coverage, but it's usually supplemental to your own insurance and rarely covers SUVs, minivans, luxury models, and the like.

If your coverage is secondary, you may still be liable for loss-of-use costs from the car-rental company (again, read the fine print). But no credit-card insurance is valid unless you use that card for *all* transactions, from reserving to paying the final bill.

■ TIP➡ Diners Club offers primary CDW coverage on all rentals reserved and paid for with the card. This means that Diners Club's company—not your own car insurance—pays in case of an accident. It *doesn't* mean that your car-insurance company won't raise your rates once it discovers you had an accident.

You may also be offered supplemental liability coverage; the car-rental company is required to carry a minimal level of liability coverage insuring all renters, but it's rarely enough to cover claims in a really serious accident if you're at fault. Your own auto-insurance policy will protect you if you own a car; if you don't, you have to decide whether you are willing to take the risk.

U.S. rental companies sell CDWs and LDWs for about $15 to $25 a day; supplemental liability is usually more than $10 a day. The car-rental company may offer you all sorts of other policies, but they're rarely worth the cost. Personal accident insurance, which is basic hospitalization coverage, is an especially egregious rip-off if you already have health insurance.

■ TIP→ You can decline the insurance from the rental company and purchase it through a third-party provider such as Travel Guard (www.travelguard.com)—$9 per day for $35,000 of coverage. That's sometimes just under half the price of the CDW offered by some car-rental companies.

In Arizona the car-rental agency's insurance is primary; therefore, the company must pay for damage to third parties up to a preset legal limit, beyond which your own liability insurance kicks in.

■ VACATION PACKAGES

Packages *are not* guided excursions. Packages combine airfare, accommodations, and perhaps a rental car or other extras (theater tickets, guided excursions, boat trips, reserved entry to popular museums, transit passes), but they let you do your own thing. During busy periods packages may be your only option, as flights and rooms may be sold out otherwise.

Packages will definitely save you time. They can also save you money, particularly in peak seasons, but—and this is a really big "but"—you should price each part of the package separately to be sure. And be aware that prices advertised on Web sites and in newspapers rarely include service charges or taxes, which can up your costs by hundreds of dollars.

■ TIP→ Some packages and cruises are sold only through travel agents. Don't always assume that you can get the best deal by booking everything yourself.

10 WAYS TO SAVE

1. Beware of cheap rates. Those great rates aren't so great when you add in taxes, surcharges, and insurance. Such extras can double or triple the initial quote.

2. Rent weekly. Weekly rates are usually better than daily ones. Even if you only want to rent for five or six days, ask for the weekly rate; it may very well be cheaper than the daily rate for that period of time.

3. Don't forget the locals. Price local companies as well as the majors.

4. Airport rentals can cost more. Airports often add surcharges, which you can sometimes avoid by renting from an agency whose office is just off airport property.

5. Wholesalers can help. Investigate wholesalers, which don't own fleets but rent in bulk from firms that do, and which frequently offer better rates (note that you must usually pay for such rentals before leaving home).

6. Look for rate guarantees. With your rate locked in, you won't pay more, even if the price goes up in the local currency.

7. Fill up farther away. Avoid hefty refueling fees by filling the tank at a station well away from where you plan to turn in the car.

8. Pump it yourself. Don't buy the tank of gas that's in the car when you rent it unless you plan to do a lot of driving.

9. Get all your discounts. Find out whether a credit card you carry or organization or frequent-renter program to which you belong has a discount program. And confirm that such discounts really are a deal. You can often do better with special weekend or weekly rates offered by a rental agency.

10. Check out packages. Adding a car rental onto your air/hotel vacation package may be cheaper than renting a car separately.

Each year consumers are stranded or lose their money when packagers—even large ones with excellent reputations—go out of business. How can you protect yourself?

First, always pay with a credit card; if you have a problem, your credit-card company may help you resolve it. Second, buy trip insurance that covers default. Third, choose a company that belongs to the United States Tour Operators Association, whose members must set aside funds to cover defaults. Finally, choose a company that also participates in the Tour Operator Program of the American Society of Travel Agents (ASTA), which will act as mediator in any disputes. You can check a tour operator's reputation among travelers by posting an inquiry on one of the Fodors.com forums.

Package tours are relatively popular in Arizona because they often offer great values on airline tickets, hotel rates, and sometimes even car rental. You can find packages that include golfing green fees, admission to national parks, and other perks. Also, it's nice having your airport transfers arranged for you. If you're visiting Arizona on a tight budget, this can be a great way to save money on lodgings. On the other hand, this is an easy state to navigate on your own, and the logistics of purchasing separate airfare, hotels, car rentals, activity fees, and attraction admissions are not especially daunting if you're even a modestly seasoned traveler. You may be able to find nearly comparable deals on your own, giving yourself more control over your trip.

Organizations American Society of Travel Agents (ASTA ☎703/739–2782 or 800/965–2782 ⊕www.astanet.com). **United States Tour Operators Association** (USTOA ☎212/599–6599 ⊕www.ustoa.com).

PACKAGE TOURS
Air/Hotel/Car **America West Vacations** (☎800/356–6611 ⊕www.americawest vacations.com). **Delta Vacations** (☎800/872–

7786 ⊕www.deltavacations.com). **Southwest Airlines Vacations** (☎800/243–8372 ⊕www.swavacations.com). **United Vacations** (☎800/328–6877 ⊕www.unitedvacations. com). **US Airways Vacations** (☎800/455–0123 ⊕www.usairwaysvacations.com).

Custom Packages **Amtrak Vacations** (☎800/321–8684 ⊕www.amtrak.com/ savings/amtrakvacations.html).

▌GUIDED TOURS

Guided tours are a good option when you don't want to do it all yourself. You travel along with a group (sometimes large, sometimes small), stay in prebooked hotels, eat with your fellow travelers (the cost of meals sometimes included in the price of your tour, sometimes not), and follow a schedule.

But not all guided tours are an if-it's-Tuesday-this-must-be-Belgium experience. A knowledgeable guide can take you places that you might never discover on your own, and you may be pushed to see more than you would have otherwise. Tours aren't for everyone, but they can be just the thing for trips to places where making travel arrangements is difficult or time-consuming (particularly when you don't speak the language).

Whenever you book a guided tour, find out what's included and what isn't. A "land-only" tour includes all travel (usually by bus) in the destination, but not necessarily your flights to and from. Also, in most cases prices in tour brochures don't include fees and taxes. Remember that you're expected to tip your guide (in cash) at the end of the tour.

SPECIAL-INTEREST TOURS
ARCHAEOLOGY
The Archaeological Conservancy offers a number of tours covering significant sites around the country, including a 10-day trip through Arizona called Master Potters of the Southern Deserts. Based in southwestern Colorado, Crow Canyon Archae-

ological Center has three different trips that touch on portions of Arizona: Four Corners, Hiking in Carrizo Mountain Country, and Rock Art in Arizona. Utah's Southwest Ed-Ventures can work with you to customize your own trip through Arizona's Hopi and Navajo regions.

Contacts Archaeological Conservancy (☎505/266-1540 ⊕www.american archaeology.org). **Crow Canyon Archaeological Center** (☎970/565-8975 or 800/422-8975 ⊕www.crowcanyon.org). **Southwest Ed-Ventures** (☎435/587-2156 or 800/525-4456 ⊕www.sw-adventures.org).

BIKING
A number of companies offer extensive bike tours that cover parts of the Southwest. Backroads organizes a nine-day Utah and northern Arizona national parks journey. Scottsdale-based AOA Adventures offers a variety of bike trips throughout the state. Timberline Adventure has biking tours of Arizona's White Mountains.

■TIP→ Most airlines accommodate bikes as luggage, provided they're dismantled and boxed.

Contacts AOA Adventures (☎480/945-2881 or 866/455-1601 ⊕www.aoa-adventures.com). **Backroads** (☎510/527-1555 or 800/462-2848 ⊕www.backroads.com). **Timberline Adventures** (☎303/368-4418 or 800/417-2453 ⊕www.timbertours.com).

GOLF
Golfpac organizes golf vacations all over the world, with Phoenix, Scottsdale, and Tucson among its most popular destinations.

Contacts Golfpac (☎888/848-8941 ⊕www.golfpactravel.com).

HIKING
Scottsdale-based AOA Adventures offers multiday hiking and biking tours through some of the state's most dramatic scenery, from the Grand Canyon to Havasupai.

Contacts AOA Adventures (☎480/945-2881 or 866/455-1601 ⊕www.aoa-adventures.com).

NATIVE AMERICAN HISTORY
Journeys into American Indian Territory offers a wide range of tours that cover Arizona's indigenous communities.

Contacts Journeys into American Indian Territory (☎631/878-8655 or 800/458-2632 ⊕www.indianjourneys.com).

NATURAL HISTORY
Consider booking a trip through Smithsonian Journeys if you're keen on experiencing the Grand Canyon with knowledgeable guides. Victor Emanuel Nature Tours is another excellent tour operator, offering four different tours that emphasize bird-watching. Off the Beaten Path has a variety of tours in Arizona and the southwest.

Contacts Off the Beaten Path (☎406/586-1311 or 800/445-2995 ⊕www.offthebeatenpath.com). **Smithsonian Journeys** (☎202/357-4700 or 877/338-8687 ⊕www.smithsonianjourneys.org). **Victor Emanuel Nature Tours** (☎512/328-5221 or 800/328-8368 ⊕www.ventbird.com).

RIVER RAFTING
Rafting on the Colorado River through the Grand Canyon is a once-in-a-lifetime experience for many who try it. Numerous reliable companies offer rafting tours through the canyon, including Action Whitewater Adventures, Grand Canyon Dories, OARS, and World Wide River Expeditions.

Contacts Action Whitewater Adventures (☎801/375-4111 or 800/453-1482 ⊕www.riverguide.com). **Grand Canyon Dories** (☎800/346-6277 ⊕www.grandcanyondories.com). **OARS** (☎209/736-4677 or 800/346-6277 ⊕www.oars.com). **World Wide River Expeditions** (☎435/259-7515 or 800/231-2769 ⊕www.worldwideriver.com).

TRANSPORTATION

Most visitors to Arizona either arrive by car via one of the main east–west interstates, I–40 or I–10/I–8, or they fly into the state's major airport in Phoenix. (Smaller numbers fly into Tucson.) Even visitors who fly in tend to rent cars; public transportation is limited and limiting, and this vast state is ideally suited to car touring. The state's highways are generally well-maintained and have high speed limits (up to 75 mph on some interstates), so traveling even significant distances by car isn't a great challenge.

▌BY AIR

Despite its high passenger volume, long lines at the check-in counters and security checkpoints at Phoenix Sky Harbor are usually not a problem, although during busy periods (spring break, holiday weekends, and so on) you should anticipate long waits and arrive at the airport 30 to 60 minutes earlier than you would otherwise. Because Phoenix is the hub for Southwest and USAirways, it has direct flights to most major U.S. cities and a number of international destinations. Sample flying times from major cities are: one hour from Los Angeles, three hours from Chicago, and five hours from New York City.

▌TIP➜ If you travel frequently, look into the TSA's Registered Traveler program. The program, which is still being tested in several U.S. airports, is designed to cut down on gridlock at security checkpoints by allowing prescreened travelers to pass quickly through kiosks that scan an iris and/or a fingerprint. How sci-fi is that?

Airlines & Airports Airline and Airport Links.com (⊕ www.airlineandairportlinks.com) has links to many of the world's airlines and airports.

Airline Security Issues Transportation Security Administration (⊕ www.tsa.gov) has answers for almost every question that might come up.

AIRPORTS

Major gateways to Arizona include Phoenix Sky Harbor International (PHX), about 3 mi southeast of Phoenix city center, and Tucson International Air Terminal (TUS), about 8½ mi south of the central business area.

Phoenix Sky Harbor International Airport is the fifth-busiest airport in the world for takeoffs and landings but rarely suffers from congestion or lengthy lines. Its spacious, modern terminals are easily navigable, with plenty of dining options as well as free Wi-Fi. Sky Harbor's three passenger terminals are connected by inter-terminal buses that run regularly throughout the day.

Tucson International Airport has one terminal that has restaurants and free Wi-Fi. Although it services far fewer passengers per day than Sky Harbor, it does offer nonstop flights to a number of major metropolitan areas around the country, especially cites in the West and Midwest.

▌TIP➜ Long layovers don't have to be only about sitting around or shopping. These days they can be about burning off vacation calories. Check out www.airportgyms.com for lists of health clubs that are in or near many U.S. and Canadian airports.

Airport Information Phoenix Sky Harbor International (☎ 602/273–3300 ⊕ www. phxskyharbor.com). Tucson International Airport (☎ 520/573–8100 ⊕ www. tucsonairport.org).

FLIGHTS

Phoenix is a hub for Southwest Airlines and US Airways. These carriers offer the most direct flights in and out of Phoenix. Most of the nation's other major airlines also fly into Phoenix and have a few flights into Tucson as well.

Among the smaller airlines, ATA flies between Phoenix and New York, Washington, and Hawaii. Frontier connects Phoenix with Denver. Midwest Express connects Phoenix and Milwaukee. JetBlue has service from Phoenix to Boston and New York, and from Tucson to New York. Sun Country Airlines flies from Phoenix to Minneapolis.

Flying time to Phoenix or Tucson is 5½ hours from New York, 3½ hours from Chicago, 1¼ hours from Los Angeles, and 11 hours from London.

Within Arizona, US Airways Express/ Mesa Airlines (part of US Airways) flies from Phoenix to Flagstaff, Lake Havasu, and Yuma. Great Lakes Airlines flies from Phoenix to Page, Kingman, Prescott, and Show Low. Scenic Airlines flies from Las Vegas to the Grand Canyon.

Airline Contacts Alaska Airlines (☎800/252–7522 or 206/433–3100 ⊕www.alaskaair.com). **American Airlines** (☎800/433–7300 ⊕www.aa.com). **ATA** (☎800/435–9282 or 317/282–8308 ⊕www.ata.com). **Continental Airlines** (☎800/523–3273 for U.S. and Mexico reservations, 800/231–0856 for international reservations ⊕www.continental.com). **Delta Airlines** (☎800/221–1212 for U.S. reservations, 800/241–4141 for international reservations ⊕www.delta.com). **jetBlue** (☎800/538–2583 ⊕www.jetblue.com). **Northwest Airlines** (☎800/225–2525 ⊕www.nwa.com). **Southwest Airlines** (☎800/435–9792 ⊕www.southwest.com). **United Airlines** (☎800/864–8331 for U.S. reservations, 800/538–2929 for international reservations ⊕www.united.com). **USAirways** (☎800/428–4322 for U.S. and Canada reservations, 800/622–1015 for international reservations ⊕www.usairways.com).

Smaller Airlines AeroMexico (☎800/800–9999 ⊕www.aeromexico.com). **Frontier Airlines** (☎800/432–1359 ⊕www.frontierairlines.com). **Great Lakes Airlines** (☎800/554–5111 ⊕www.greatlakesav.com). **Midwest Express** (☎800/452–2022 ⊕www.midwestexpress.com). **Scenic Airlines** (☎800/634–6801 ⊕www.scenic.com). **Sun Country Airlines** (☎800/359–6786 ⊕www.suncountry.com).

▌ BY BUS

It's neither the most glamorous nor the quickest way to travel, but Greyhound serves many Arizona destinations (Benson, Flagstaff, Kingman, Phoenix, Tucson, and Yuma among them) from most parts of the United States. The most popular route is the Los Angeles to Phoenix run, which is offered several times daily and takes 7 to 8½ hours; the fare is about $45 each way. Las Vegas to Phoenix is another popular route—this ride takes 9 to 12 hours and costs about $55 each way.

Bus Information Greyhound Lines (☎800/231–2222 ⊕www.greyhound.com).

▌ BY CAR

A car is a necessity in Arizona, as even bigger cities are challenging to get around using public transportation. Distances are considerable, but you can make excellent time on long stretches of interstate and other four-lane highways with speed limits of up to 75 mph. In cities, freeway limits are between 55 mph and 65 mph. If you wander off major thoroughfares, slow down. Speed limits here generally are only 55 mph, and for good reason. Many roadways have no shoulders; on many twisting and turning mountain roads speed limits dip to 25 mph. For the most part, the scenery you'll take in while driving makes it worth it.

At some point you will probably pass through one or more of the state's 23 Indian reservations. Roads and other areas within reservation boundaries are under the jurisdiction of reservation police and governed by separate rules and regulations. Observe all signs and respect Native Americans' privacy. Be careful not to hit any animals, which often wan-

FLYING 101

Flying may not be as carefree as it once was, but there are some things you can do to make your trip smoother.

Minimize the time spent standing in line. Buy an e-ticket, check in at an electronic kiosk, or—even better—check in on your airline's Web site before leaving home. Pack light and limit carry-on items to only the essentials.

Arrive when you need to. Research your airline's policy. It's usually at least an hour before domestic flights and two to three hours before international flights. But airlines at some busy airports have more stringent requirements. Check the TSA Web site for estimated security waiting times at major airports.

Get to the gate. If you aren't at the gate at least 10 minutes before your flight is scheduled to take off (sometimes earlier), you won't be allowed to board.

Double-check your flight times. Do this especially if you reserved far in advance. Schedules change, and alerts may not reach you.

Don't go hungry. Ask whether your airline offers anything to eat; even when it does, be prepared to pay.

Get the seat you want. Often, you can pick a seat when you buy your ticket on an airline Web site. But it's not guaranteed; the airline could change the plane after you book, so double-check. You can also select a seat if you check in electronically. Avoid seats on the aisle directly across from the lavatories. Frequent fliers say those are even worse than back-row seats that don't recline.

Got kids? Get info. Ask the airline about its children's menus, activities, and fares. Sometimes infants and toddlers fly free if they sit on a parent's lap, and older children fly for half price in their own seats. Also inquire about policies involving car seats; having one may limit seating options. Also ask about seat-belt extenders for car seats. And note that you can't count on a flight attendant to produce an extender; you may have to ask for one when you board.

Check your scheduling. Don't buy a ticket if there's less than an hour between connecting flights. Although schedules are padded, if anything goes wrong you might miss your connection. If you're traveling to an important function, depart a day early.

Bring paper. Even when using an e-ticket, always carry a hard copy of your receipt; you may need it to get your boarding pass, which most airports require to get past security.

Complain at the airport. If your baggage goes astray or your flight goes awry, complain before leaving the airport. Most carriers require this.

Beware of overbooked flights. If a flight is oversold, the gate agent will usually ask for volunteers and offer some sort of compensation for taking a different flight. If you're bumped from a flight *involuntarily*, the airline must give you some kind of compensation if an alternate flight can't be found within one hour.

Know your rights. If your flight is delayed because of something within the airline's control (bad weather doesn't count), the airline must get you to your destination on the same day, even if they have to book you on another airline and in an upgraded class. Read the Contract of Carriage, which is usually buried on the airline's Web site.

Be prepared. The Boy Scout motto is especially important if you're traveling during a stormy season. To quickly adjust your plans, program a few numbers into your cell: your airline, an airport hotel or two, your destination hotel, your car service, and/or your travel agent.

der onto the roads; the penalties can be very high.

Note that in Phoenix certain lanes on interstates are restricted to carpools and multi-occupant vehicles. Seat belts are required at all times. Tickets can be given for failing to comply. Driving with a blood-alcohol level higher than 0.08 will result in arrest and seizure of your driver's license. Fines are severe. Radar detectors are legal in Arizona, as is driving while using handheld phones.

Always strap children under age five into approved child-safety seats. In Arizona, children must wear seat belts regardless of where they're seated. In Arizona, you may turn right at a red light after stopping if there's no oncoming traffic. When in doubt, wait for the green.

Information **Arizona Department of Public Safety** (☎602/223–2000, 602/223–2163 Highway Patrol ⊕www.azdps.gov). **Arizona Department of Transportation** (☎511 Arizona road information from within Arizona, 888/411–7623 Arizona road information from outside state ⊕www.az511.com).

GASOLINE
Gas stations, many of them open 24 hours, are widely available in larger towns and cities and along interstates. However, you'll encounter some mighty lonely and long stretches of highway in certain remote sections of Arizona; in these areas, it's not uncommon to travel 50 or 60 mi between service stations. It's prudent to play it safe when exploring the far-flung corners of the state and keep your tank at least half full. Gas prices in Arizona are about 10% to 15% higher than the national average.

PARKING
Parking is plentiful and either free or very inexpensive in most Arizona towns, even Phoenix and Tucson. During very busy times, however, such as holidays, parking in popular places like Sedona, Flagstaff, and Bisbee can prove a little challenging.

ROAD CONDITIONS
The highways in Arizona are well maintained, but there are some natural conditions to keep in mind.

Desert heat. Vehicles and passengers should be well equipped for searing summer heat in the low desert. If you're planning to drive through the desert, make sure you are well stocked with radiator coolant, and carry plenty of water, a good spare tire, a jack, a cell phone, and emergency supplies. If you get stranded, stay with your vehicle and wait for help to arrive.

Dust storms. These usually occur from May to mid-September, causing extremely low visibility. Dust storms are more common on the highways and interstates that traverse the open desert (I–10 between Phoenix and Tucson, I–10 between Benson and the New Mexico state line, and I–8 between Casa Grande and Yuma). If you're on the highway, pull as far off the road as possible, turn on your headlights to avoid being hit, and wait for the storm to subside.

Flash floods. Warnings about flash floods should not be taken lightly. Sudden downpours send torrents of water racing into low-lying areas so dry that they are unable to absorb such a huge quantity of water quickly. The result can be powerful walls of water suddenly descending upon these low-lying areas, devastating anything in their paths. If you see rain clouds or thunderstorms coming, stay away from dry riverbeds (also called arroyos or washes). If you find yourself in one, get out quickly. If you're with a car in a long gully, leave your car and climb out of the gully. You simply won't be able to outdrive a speeding wave. The idea is to get to higher ground immediately when it rains. Major highways are mostly flood-proof, but some smaller roads dip through washes; most roads that traverse these low-lying areas will have flood warning signs, which should be seriously heeded during rainstorms. Washes filled with water should not be crossed until you can

Distances

FROM	TO	DISTANCE
Phoenix	Tucson	115 mi
Phoenix	Sedona	115 mi
Phoenix	Grand Canyon	250 mi
Phoenix	Canyon de Chelly	380 mi
Phoenix	Show Low	170 mi
Tucson	Bisbee	100 mi
Tucson	Yuma	240 mi
Sedona	Grand Canyon	115 mi

see the bottom. By all means, don't camp in these areas at any time, interesting as they may seem.

Fragile desert life. The dry and easily desecrated desert floor takes centuries to overcome human damage. Consequently, it's illegal for four-wheel-drive and all-terrain vehicles and motorcycles to travel off established roadways.

ROADSIDE EMERGENCIES
In the event of a roadside emergency, call 911. Depending on the location, either the state police or the county sheriff's department will respond. Call the city or village police department if you encounter trouble within the limits of a municipality. Indian reservations have tribal police headquarters, and rangers assist travelers within U.S. Forest Service boundaries.

▌ BY TRAIN

Amtrak's *Southwest Chief* operates daily between Los Angeles and Chicago, stopping in Kingman, Flagstaff, and Winslow. The *Sunset Limited* travels three times each week between Los Angeles and Orlando, with stops at Yuma, Tucson, and Benson. There's a connecting bus (a 2½-hour trip) between Flagstaff and Phoenix.

Information Amtrak (☎800/872–7245 ⊕www.amtrak.com).

ON THE GROUND

■ COMMUNICATIONS

INTERNET

As in all major U.S. cities, high-speed and Wi-Fi connections are ubiquitous at hotels throughout Phoenix, Tucson, Flagstaff, Prescott, and virtually every decent-size city in the state (although sometimes there's a fee of anywhere from $5 to $15 per day). There are also connections at cafés, restaurants, and other businesses. In more remote areas, you'll still likely find ways to get online.

Contacts Cybercafes (⊕www.cybercafes. com) lists over 4,000 Internet cafés worldwide.

■ EATING OUT

Two distinct cultures—Native American and Sonoran—have had the greatest influence on native Arizona cuisine. Chiles, beans, corn, tortillas, and squash are common ingredients for those restaurants that specialize in regional cuisine (cactus is just as tasty but less common). Mom-and-pop *taquerias* are abundant, especially in the southern part of the state. In Phoenix, Tucson, Sedona, and increasingly Flagstaff, Bisbee, Prescott, and some smaller but sophisticated parts of the state, you'll find hip, intriguing restaurants specializing in American and Southwestern cuisine, as well as some excellent restaurants specializing in such ethnic cuisines as Thai, Chinese, Japanese, and the like.

RESERVATIONS & DRESS

Regardless of where you are, it's a good idea to make a reservation if you can. In some places (Hong Kong, for example), it's expected. We only mention them specifically when reservations are essential (there's no other way you'll ever get a table) or when they are not accepted. For popular restaurants, book as far ahead as you can (often 30 days), and reconfirm as soon as you arrive. (Large parties should always call ahead to check the res-ervations policy.) We mention dress only when men are required to wear a jacket or a jacket and tie.

Online reservation services make it easy to book a table before you even leave home. OpenTable covers most states, including 20 major cities, and has limited listings in Canada, Mexico, the United Kingdom, and elsewhere. DinnerBroker has restaurants throughout the United States as well as a few in Canada.

Contacts OpenTable (⊕www.opentable.com). **DinnerBroker** (⊕www.dinnerbroker.com).

WINES, BEER & SPIRITS

Although Arizona is not typically associated with viticulture, the region southeast of Tucson, stretching to the Mexico border, has several microclimates ideal for wine growing. The iron- and calcium-rich soil is similar to that of the Burgundy region in France and, combined with the temperate weather and lower-key atmosphere, has enticed several independent and family-run wineries to open in the past few decades in the Elgin, Sonoita, and Nogales areas. Microbreweries have sprung up throughout the state in recent years, with a number of good ones in Phoenix, Tucson, and Flagstaff.

In Arizona, you must be 21 to buy any alcohol. Bars and liquor stores are open daily, including Sunday, but must stop selling alcohol at 2 AM. In many municipalities, including Phoenix and Flagstaff, smoking is prohibited in restaurants and bars. You'll find beer, wine, and alcohol at most supermarkets. Possession and consumption of alcoholic beverages is illegal on Indian reservations.

Contacts Arizona Wine Growers Association (⊕www.arizonawine.org). **Callaghan Vineyards** (☎520/455–5322 ⊕www.callaghanvineyards. com). **Sonoita Vineyards** (☎520/455–5893 ⊕www.sonoitavineyards.com). **The Village of Elgin Winery** (☎520/455–9309 ⊕www. elginwines.com).

FOR INTERNATIONAL TRAVELERS

CURRENCY

The dollar is the basic unit of U.S. currency. It has 100 cents. Coins are the penny (1¢); the nickel (5¢), dime (10¢), quarter (25¢), half-dollar (50¢), and the very rare golden $1 coin and even rarer silver $1. Bills are denominated $1, $5, $10, $20, $50, and $100, all mostly green and identical in size; designs and background tints vary. You may come across a $2 bill, but the chances are slim.

CUSTOMS

Information **U.S. Customs and Border Protection** (⊕ www.cbp.gov).

DRIVING

Driving in the United States is on the right. Speed limits are posted in miles per hour (usually between 55 mph and 70 mph). Watch for lower limits in small towns and on back roads (usually 30 mph to 40 mph). Most states require front-seat passengers to wear seat belts; many states require children to sit in the back seat and to wear seat belts. In major cities rush hour is between 7 and 10 AM; afternoon rush hour is between 4 and 7 PM. To encourage carpooling, some freeways have special lanes, ordinarily marked with a diamond, for high-occupancy vehicles (HOV)—cars carrying two people or more.

Highways are well paved. Interstates—limited-access, multilane highways designated with an "I–" before the number—are fastest. Interstates with three-digit numbers circle urban areas, which may also have other limited-access expressways, freeways, and parkways. Tolls may be levied on limited-access highways. U.S. and state highways aren't necessarily limited-access, but may have several lanes.

ELECTRICITY

The U.S. standard is AC, 110 volts/60 cycles. Plugs have two flat pins set parallel to each other.

EMBASSIES

Contacts **Australia** (☎ 202/797–3000 ⊕ www.austemb.org).

Canada (☎ 202/682–1740 ⊕ www.canadianembassy.org). **United Kingdom** (☎ 202/588–7800 ⊕ www.britainusa.com).

EMERGENCIES

For police, fire, or ambulance, dial 911 (0 in rural areas).

HOLIDAYS

New Year's Day (Jan. 1); Martin Luther King Day (3rd Mon. in Jan.); Presidents' Day (3rd Mon. in Feb.); Memorial Day (last Mon. in May); Independence Day (July 4); Labor Day (1st Mon. in Sept.); Columbus Day (2nd Mon. in Oct.); Thanksgiving Day (4th Thurs. in Nov.); Christmas Eve and Christmas Day (Dec. 24 and 25); and New Year's Eve (Dec. 31).

MAIL

You can buy stamps and aerograms and send letters and parcels in post offices. Stamp-dispensing machines can occasionally be found in airports, bus and train stations, office buildings, drugstores, and convenience stores. U.S. mailboxes are stout, dark blue steel bins; pickup schedules are posted inside the bin (pull down the handle to see them). Parcels weighing more than a pound must be mailed at a post office or at a private mailing center.

Within the United States a first-class letter weighing 1 ounce or less costs 41¢.

To receive mail on the road, have it sent c/o General Delivery at your destination's main post office (use the correct five-digit ZIP code). You must pick up mail in person within 30 days, with a driver's license or passport for identification.

Contacts **DHL** (☎ 800/225–5345 ⊕ www.dhl.com). **Federal Express** (☎ 800/463–3339 ⊕ www.fedex.com). **Mail Boxes, Etc./ The UPS Store** (☎ 800/789–4623 ⊕ www.mbe.com). **United States Postal Service** (⊕ www.usps.com).

PASSPORTS & VISAS

Visitor visas aren't necessary for citizens of Australia, Canada, the United Kingdom, or most citizens of European Union countries coming for tourism and staying for fewer than 90 days. If you require a visa, the cost is $100, and waiting time can be substantial, depending on where you live. Apply for a visa at the U.S. consulate in your place of residence; check the U.S. State Department's special Visa Web site for further information.

Visa Information Destination USA (⊕ *www.unitedstatesvisas.gov*).

PHONES

Numbers consist of a three-digit area code and a seven-digit local number. Within many local calling areas you dial only the seven digits; in others you dial "1" first and all 10 digits—just as you would for calls between area-code regions. The same is true for calls to numbers prefixed by "800," "888," "866," and "877"—all toll-free. For calls to numbers prefixed by "900" you must pay—usually dearly.

In New York City, there are three area codes: "212," "646," and "917." Although it's not long distance, "1" plus the area code is necessary to call here.

For international calls, dial "011" followed by the country code and the local number. For help, dial "0" and ask for an overseas operator. Most phone books list country codes and U.S. area codes. The country code for Australia is 61, for New Zealand 64, for the United Kingdom 44. Calling Canada is the same as calling within the United States, whose country code, by the way, is 1.

For operator assistance, dial "0." For directory assistance, call 555–1212 or occasionally 411 (free at many public phones). You can reverse long-distance charges by calling "collect"; dial "0" instead of "1" before the 10-digit number.

Instructions are generally posted on pay phones. Usually you insert coins in a slot (usually 25¢–50¢ for local calls) and wait for a steady tone before dialing. On long-distance calls the operator tells you how much to insert; prepaid phone cards, widely available in various denominations, can be used from any phone. Follow the directions to activate the card (there's usually an access number, then an activation code), then dial your number.

CELL PHONES

The United States has several GSM (Global System for Mobile Communications) networks, so multiband mobiles from most countries (except for Japan) work here. Unfortunately, it's almost impossible to buy a pay-as-you-go mobile SIM card in the U.S.—which allows you to avoid roaming charges—without also buying a phone. That said, cell phones with pay-as-you-go plans are available for well under $100. The cheapest ones with decent national coverage are the GoPhone from Cingular and Virgin Mobile, which only offers pay-as-you-go service.

Contacts Cingular (☎ *888/333–6651* ⊕ *www.cingular.com*). **Virgin Mobile** (☎ *No phone* ⊕ *www.virginmobileusa.com*).

HEALTH

ANIMAL BITES

Wherever you're walking in desert areas, particularly between April and October, keep a lookout for rattlesnakes. You're likely not to have any problems if you maintain distance from snakes that you see—they can strike only half of their length, so a 6-foot clearance should allow you to remain unharmed, especially if you don't provoke them. If you are bitten by a rattler, don't panic. Get to a hospital within two to three hours of the bite. Try to keep the area that has been bitten below heart level, and stay calm, as increased heart rate can spread venom more quickly. Keep in mind that 30% to 40% of bites are dry bites, where the snake uses no venom (still, get thee to a hospital). Avoid night hikes without rangers, when snakes are on the prowl and less visible.

Scorpions and Gila monsters are really less of a concern, since they strike only when provoked. To avoid scorpion encounters, look before touching: never place your hands where you can't see, such as under rocks and in holes. Likewise, if you move a rock to sit down, make sure that scorpions haven't been exposed. Campers should shake out shoes in the morning, since scorpions like warm, moist places. If you're bitten, see a ranger about symptoms that may develop. Chances are good that you won't need to go to a hospital. Children are a different case, however: scorpion stings can be fatal for them. Always try to keep an eye on what they may be getting their hands into to avoid the scorpion's sting. Gila monsters are relatively rare and bites are even rarer, but bear in mind that the reptiles are most active between April and June, when they do most of their hunting. Should a member of your party be bitten, it is most important to release the Gila monster's jaws as soon as possible to minimize the amount of venom released. This can usually be achieved with a stick, an open flame, or immersion of the animal in water.

DEHYDRATION

This underestimated danger can be very serious, especially considering that one of the first major symptoms is the inability to swallow. It may be the easiest hazard to avoid, however: simply drink every 10–15 minutes, up to a gallon of water per day in summer. Always carry a water bottle, and replenish frequently, whether hiking, walking in the city, or at an outdoor sports or arts event.

HYPOTHERMIA

Temperatures in Arizona can vary widely from day to night—as much as 40°F. Be sure to bring enough warm clothing for hiking and camping, along with wet-weather gear. It's always a good idea to pack an extra set of clothes in a large, waterproof plastic bag that would stay dry in any situation. Exposure to the degree that body temperature dips below 95°F produces the following symptoms: chills, tiredness, then uncontrollable shivering and irrational behavior, with the victim not always recognizing that he or she is cold. If someone in your party is suffering from any of this, wrap him or her in blankets and/or a warm sleeping bag immediately and try to keep him or her awake. The fastest way to raise body temperature is through skin-to-skin contact in a sleeping bag. Drinking warm liquids also helps.

SUN EXPOSURE

Wear a hat and sunglasses and put on sunblock to protect against the burning Arizona sun. And watch out for heatstroke. Symptoms include headache, dizziness, and fatigue, which can turn into convulsions and unconsciousness and can lead to death. If someone in your party develops any of these conditions, have one person seek emergency help while others move the victim into the shade and wrap him or her in wet clothing (is a stream nearby?) to cool him or her down.

▌ HOURS OF OPERATION

Most museums in Arizona's larger cities are open daily. A few are closed on Monday, and hours may vary between May and September (off-season in the major tourist centers of Phoenix and Tucson). Call ahead when planning a visit to lesser-known museums or attractions, whose hours may vary considerably. Major attractions are open daily.

Most retail stores are open 10 AM to 6 PM, although stores in malls tend to stay open until 9 PM. Those in the less-populated areas are likely to have shorter hours and may be closed on Sunday. Shopping centers are also often open Sunday from noon to 5 or later.

▌ MONEY

ITEM	AVERAGE COST
Cup of Coffee	$2.50
Glass of Wine	$5
Glass of Beer	$3.50
Sandwich	$5
One-Mile Taxi Ride in Phoenix	$5
Museum Admission	$8

Prices throughout this guide are given for adults. Substantially reduced fees are almost always available for children, students, and senior citizens.

CREDIT CARDS

Throughout this guide, the following abbreviations are used: **AE**, American Express; **D**, Discover; **DC**, Diners Club; **MC**, MasterCard; and **V**, Visa.

It's a good idea to inform your credit-card company before you travel, especially if you're going abroad and don't travel internationally very often. Otherwise, the credit-card company might put a hold on your card owing to unusual activity—not a good thing halfway through your trip. Record all your credit-card numbers—as well as the phone numbers to call if your cards are lost or stolen—in a safe place, so you're prepared should something go wrong. Both MasterCard and Visa have general numbers you can call (collect if you're abroad) if your card is lost, but you're better off calling the number of your issuing bank, since MasterCard and Visa usually just transfer you to your bank; your bank's number is usually printed on your card.

Reporting Lost Cards American Express (☎800/992–3404 in the U.S. or 336/393–1111 collect from abroad ⊕www.americanexpress.com). **Diners Club** (☎800/234–6377 in the U.S. or 303/799–1504 collect from abroad ⊕www.dinersclub.com). **Discover** (☎800/347–2683 in the U.S. or 801/902–3100 collect from abroad ⊕www.discovercard.com). **MasterCard** (☎800/622–7747 in the U.S. or 636/722–7111 collect from abroad ⊕www.mastercard.com). **Visa** (☎800/847–2911 in the U.S. or 410/581–9994 collect from abroad ⊕www.visa.com).

TRAVELER'S CHECKS & CARDS

ATM machines in Arizona are ubiquitous, and it's the rare business that does not accept credit cards, so it's hard to think of a good reason to bother with traveler's checks. If you do plan on using them, ask before checking into a hotel room or sitting down to a meal to make sure the property accepts them, as not all Arizona businesses do.

American Express now offers a stored-value card called a Travelers Cheque Card, which you can use wherever American Express credit cards are accepted, including ATMs. The card can carry a minimum of $300 and a maximum of $2,700, and it's a very safe way to carry your funds. Although you can get replacement funds in 24 hours if your card is lost or stolen, it doesn't really strike us as a very good deal. In addition to a high initial cost ($14.95 to set up the card, plus $5 each time you "reload"), you still have to pay a 2% fee for each purchase in a foreign currency (similar to that of any credit card). Further, each time you use the card in an ATM you pay a transaction fee of $2.50 on top of the 2% transaction fee for the conversion—add it all up and it can be considerably more than you would pay when simply using your own ATM card. Regular traveler's checks are just as secure and cost less.

Contacts **American Express** (☎888/412–6945 in the U.S., 801/945–9450 collect outside of the U.S. to add value or speak to customer service ⊕www.americanexpress.com).

▌ SAFETY

Arizona's track record in terms of crime is fairly typical of other U.S. states. In big cities, such as Phoenix and Tucson, you should take the same precautions you would anywhere—be aware of what's going on around you, stick to well-lighted areas, and quickly move away from any situation or people that might be threatening. In both of these cities, it's easy to find yourself driving into a less-than-savory neighborhood with little notice; if you feel uneasy about your surroundings, turn around and go back the way you came.

▌TIP→ Distribute your cash, credit cards, IDs, and other valuables between a deep front pocket, an inside jacket or vest pocket, and a hidden money pouch. Don't reach for the money pouch once you're in public.

▌ TAXES

Arizona state sales tax (called a transaction privilege tax), which applies to all purchases except food in grocery stores, is 5.6%. Phoenix and Tucson levy city sales taxes of 1.8% and 2%, respectively, and Flagstaff taxes purchases at a rate of 1.51%. When added to county taxes, the total sales tax in Phoenix goes up to 8.1%; in Tucson, to 7.6%; and in Flagstaff, to 7.91%. Total state taxes throughout the state range from 7.3% to 10.1%. Sales taxes do not apply on Indian reservations.

▌ TIME

Arizona is in the Mountain Time Zone but Nevada, next door, is in the Pacific Time Zone. Arizona does not use Daylight Saving Time, though, and as a result, from spring through fall, Nevada and Arizona observe the same hours. The Navajo Nation does observe Daylight Saving Time, however, so it's always the same time on Navajo territory as in Mountain Time Zone areas outside Arizona.

▌ TIPPING

The customary tip for taxi drivers is 15%–20%, with a minimum of $2. Bell-hops are usually given $2 per bag in luxury hotels, $1 per bag elsewhere. Hotel maids should be tipped $2 per day of your stay. A doorman who hails a cab can be tipped $1–$2. You should also tip your hotel concierge for services rendered; the size of the tip depends on the difficulty of your request, as well as the quality of the concierge's work. For an ordinary dinner reservation or tour arrangements, $3–$5 should do; if the concierge scores seats at a popular restaurant or show or performs unusual services (getting your laptop repaired, finding a good pet-sitter, etc.), $10 or more is appropriate.

Waiters should be tipped 15%–20%, though at higher-end restaurants, a solid 20% is more the norm. Many restaurants add a gratuity to the bill for parties of six or more. Ask what the percentage is if the menu or bill doesn't state it. Tip $1 per drink you order at the bar, though if at an upscale establishment, those $15 martinis might warrant a $2 tip.

INDEX

A

"A" Mountain (Sentinel Peak), *305*
Abyss, The, *126*
Accommodations, *447, 449–450*
Actors Theatre of Phoenix, *79*
Adventure tours, *365*
Agate Bridge, *287*
Agate House, *287, 289*
Agave, *402*
'Ahakhav Tribal Preserve, *427*
Air tours, *129, 145, 147–148, 164*
Air travel, *456–457*
airports, 456
Grand Canyon, 160
North-Central Arizona, 213
Northeast Arizona, 256
Northwest Arizona and Southeast Nevada, 436
Phoenix, Scottsdale, and Tempe, 111–112
Southern Arizona, 411
Tucson, 362–363
Airline tickets, *450*
Airport Mesa, *190*
Ajo, *405–406*
Ajo Historical Society Museum, *405*
Ajo Mountain Drive, *406*
AJ's Fine Foods (shop), *96–97*
Alan Bible Visitors Center, *434*
Alma de Sedona ⏰, *196–197*
Alpine, *281–283*
Amerind Foundation, *395–396*
Amigo Cafe ✕, *240*
Amsterdam (gay club), *84*
Andy Devine Days, *419*
Antelope Canyon, *250, 252*
Antelope Canyon tours, *250, 252*
Antiques and collectibles, shopping for, *272*
Apache Cultural Museum, *267*
Apache-Sitgreaves National Forest, *284*
Apache Trail, *106–111*
Arboretum, *107*
Archaeology tours, *278, 454–455*
Arcosanti, *105*
Arizona Biltmore ⏰, *60*
Arizona Center, *25*
Arizona Doll and Toy Museum, *27*

Arizona Historical Society's Museum, *309–310*
Arizona Inn ⏰, *339*
Arizona Mining and Mineral Museum, *27*
Arizona Opera Company, *78, 348*
Arizona Science Center, *25*
Arizona Snowbowl, *173, 175, 179*
Arizona-Sonora Desert Museum, *15, 300, 319–320*
Arizona State Fair, *23*
Arizona State Museum, *310–311*
Arizona State University, *37*
Arizona State University Art Museum, *37*
Arizona Theatre Company, *79*
Armory Park, *305*
Art galleries and museums.
  ⇨ *See* Museums and Art galleries
Art Walk, *96*
Arts and crafts, shopping for, *95–96, 235–236, 251, 320, 358*
Asarco Mineral Discovery Center, *359–360*
Astronomers Inn ⏰, *397*
ASU Karsten Golf Course, *87*
Avi Resort & Casino ✕⏰, *432*
Axis/Radius (dance club), *83*
AZ 88 ✕, *50*

B

Babbitt Brothers Building, *173, 175*
Bacavi, *236*
Backpacking, *193*
Bajada Loop Drive, *322–323, 325, 326*
Ballet Arizona, *78*
Ballooning
North-Central Arizona, 215
Phoenix, Scottsdale, and Tempe, 91
Tucson, 351
Bandera ✕, *49*
Barrio Café ✕, *46–47*
Barrio Historica, *305*
Bars and lounges
gay and lesbian, 83–84, 350
Phoenix, Scottsdale, and Tempe, 80–81
Tucson, 349–350

Baseball, *86*
Basha's Deli & Bakery, *404*
Bear Wallow Wilderness Area, *283*
Bed and breakfasts, *449*
Bell Rock, *188–189*
Benson, *396–398*
Besh-Ba-Gowah Archaeological Park, *109*
Best Western Grand Canyon Squire Inn ⏰, *157*
Betatakin, *245*
Bicycling
Eastern Arizona, 263, 269–270, 282, 289
Grand Canyon, 129–130, 140
North-Central Arizona, 178–179, 193–194
Phoenix, Scottsdale, and Tempe, 85, 115
tours, 455
Tucson, 326, 351
Bill Williams River National Wildlife Refuge, *427*
Biltmore Fashion Park, *93*
Biosphere 2 Center, *321*
Bird Cage Theater, *377*
Bird-watching
Grand Canyon, 147
North-Central Arizona, 192, 203
Northwest Arizona, 423, 427
Southern Arizona, 368, 371, 373, 394, 413
Tucson, 326, 352, 365
Bisbee, *379–383*
Bisbee Mining and Historical Museum, *381*
Bisbee Visitors Center, *380*
Bitter Springs, *246*
Black Canyon Trail, *204*
Black Mesa, *239*
Black Theater Troupe, *79*
Blue Mesa, *287*
Blue Mesa Trail, *290*
Blue Range Primitive Area, *283*
Blue Vista, *281*
Boat tours, *254–255, 413*
Boating, *14, 254, 428, 434, 435*
Bonelli House, *423*
Books, shopping for, *96, 357*
Boot Hill Graveyard, *375*
Boulder Beach, *434*
Boulder City, NV, *433*
Boulder City Chamber of Commerce, *433*

Boulder City/Hoover Dam Museum, *433*
Boulder Dam Hotel, *433*
Boulders Resort and Golden Door Spa, The ▦ , *102*
Boyce Thompson Arboretum, *107*
Boynton Canyon, *190*
Brewery Gulch (Bisbee), *381*
Briar Patch Inn ▦ , *197*
Bright Angel Lodge ▦ , *154*
Bright Angel Point, *138, 140*
Bright Angel Trail, *123, 130, 132*
Buenos Aires National Wildlife Refuge, *403*
Bullhead City, *430–433*
Bus tours, *137*
Bus travel, *457*
Eastern Arizona, *296*
Grand Canyon, *160–161*
North-Central Arizona, *213*
Northeast Arizona, *256*
Northwest Arizona and Southeast Nevada, *436*
Phoenix, Scottsdale, and Tempe, *112–113*
Southern Arizona, *411*
Tucson, *363*
Business hours, *465*
Butterfield stage stop, *393*
Butterfly Lodge Museum, *273*

C

Cabeza Prieta National Wildlife Refuge, *405*
Cacti, *300, 357*
Cactus Forest Drive, *323*
Café Poca Cosa ✕ , *329*
Café Roka ✕ , *381*
Café Sonoita ✕ , *385*
Callaghan Vineyards, *384*
Camelback Mountain and Echo Canyon Recreation Area, *89*
Cameron Trading Post ✕▦ , *15, 157, 223, 239*
Camping
Eastern Arizona, *260, 266, 297*
Grand Canyon, *151, 155–156*
North-Central Arizona, *210*
Northeast Arizona, *224, 229, 239, 244, 245*
Northwest Arizona and Southeast Nevada, *423, 428*
Southern Arizona, *386, 399, 406*
Canyon Colors B&B ✕ , *249–250*
Canyon de Chelly, *223, 226–231*

Canyon Ranch ▦ , *342*
Canyon Rose Suites ▦ , *382*
Canyon Star Restaurant and Saloon ✕ , *153*
Canyon Wren, The ▦ , *199*
Canyon X tours, *252*
Cape Royal, *123, 140*
Car rentals, *451–453*
Car travel, *457, 459–460*
Eastern Arizona, *296–297*
Grand Canyon, *161–162*
North-Central Arizona, *213–214*
Northeast Arizona, *256–257*
Northwest Arizona and Southeast Nevada, *436–437*
Phoenix, Scottsdale, and Tempe, *113–114*
Southern Arizona, *411–412*
Tucson, *363–364*
Carefree, *99, 101–103*
Carefree-Cave Creek Chamber of Commerce, *101*
Carl Hayden Visitor Center, *253*
Carolina's ✕ , *31, 55–56*
Casa Adobe Plaza (shopping center), *355*
Casa Grande Ruins National Monument, *15, 105*
Casa Malpais Archaeological Park, *278*
Casa Malpais Archaeological Park, *278*
Casa Tierra ▦ , *347*
Casinos, *82, 272, 350–351, 407, 409, 416, 432*
Catalina Foothills, *300–301, 315–318*
Cathedral Rock, *189*
Cathedral Rock Trail, *189*
Cattail Cove State Park, *428*
Cave Creek, *99, 101–103*
Cave Creek Museum, *101*
Caverns
North-Central Arizona, *175–176*
Northwest Arizona and Southeast Nevada, *424*
Southern Arizona, *368, 396, 398–399*
Tucson, *313*
Center for Creative Photography, *310, 311*
Central Navajo Fair, *221*
Chapel of the Holy Cross, *189–190*
Chelsea's Kitchen ✕ , *44*
Childsplay, *79*

Chiles rellenos, *12*
Chiricahua National Monument, *391–393*
Chiricahua Regional Museum and Research Center, *15, 394–395*
Chloride, *423–424*
Christmas Tree ✕ , *270*
Churches
North-Central Arizona, *189–190*
Tucson, *308–309*
Chuska Mountains, *228*
Claypool, *107*
Clear Creek Trail, *132*
Cliff pueblos
Betatakin, *245*
Canyon de Chelly, *226–228*
Casa Malpais Archaeological Park, *278*
Keet Seel, *245–246*
Montezuma Castle National Monument, *15, 202*
Tonto National Monument, *110*
Tuzigoot National Monument, *15, 203*
Walnut Canyon National Monument, *184*
Cliff Springs Trail, *123, 141*
Climate, *18*
Club Congress, *350*
Coal Canyon, *236*
Cobre Valley Center for the Arts, *109*
Coconino National Forest, *178, 193*
Coffeehouses, *37, 82*
Colleges and universities
Northeast Arizona, *228*
Tempe, *21, 37*
Tucson, *300, 309–312*
Colorado River Historical Museum, *15, 431*
Colossal Cave Mountain Park, *313*
Colter, Mary, *294*
Comedy clubs, *83*
Communications, *147*
Copper Queen Hotel, *381, 382*
Copper Queen Mine Underground Tour, *380*
Coronado National Memorial, *388–389*
Coronado Trail, *281*
Cottage Place ✕ , *180*
Courthouse Butte, *191*
Crack-in-Rock Ruin, *186*
Credit cards, *8, 465*
Cruisers Café 66 ✕ , *153*
Cruises, *38, 435*

Crystal Forest, *288, 289*
Crystal Palace, *379*
Currency, *462*
Customs, *462*

D

Dahl & DiLuca ✕, *195*
Dam Bar and Grille ✕, *249*
Dance
Phoenix, 78
Tucson, 348–349
De Grazia's Gallery in the
   Sun, *316*
Dead Horse Ranch State Park,
   203
Deer Valley Rock Art Center, *98*
Desert Botanical Garden, *15,
   28, 30*
Desert Caballeros Western
   Museum, *103*
Desert View, *123, 126*
Devine, Andy, *419*
Diné College, *228*
Dining, *461.* ⇨ *Also*
   Restaurants
*Eastern Arizona, 263, 268,
   270–271, 274, 279–280,
   282–283, 291, 292–293, 294*
Grand Canyon, 150–153
*North-Central Arizona, 171,
   180–181, 194–196, 204, 206,
   210–211*
*Northeast Arizona, 221, 230,
   233, 235, 238, 240,
   244–245, 246, 249, 255–256*
*Northwest Arizona and
   Southeast Nevada, 419, 425,
   428–429, 431–432*
*Phoenix, Scottsdale, and
   Tempe, 20, 23, 31, 37,
   38–59, 102, 104, 109*
*Southern Arizona, 371, 378,
   381, 384–385, 386–387, 390,
   395, 397, 401, 406, 408–409*
Tucson, 329, 332–338
Dinosaur Tracks, *238*
Discounts and deals, *449,
   451, 453*
Doney Mountain, *186*
Dude-guest ranches, *345, 450*
Duquesne House Bed &
   Breakfast/Gallery 🖾, *387*

E

Earp, Wyatt, *375*
Eastern Arizona, *10, 260–298*
camping, 260, 266, 297
*children, attractions for, 267,
   272–273, 289*

*dining, 263, 268, 270–271,
   274, 279–280, 282–283, 291,
   292–293, 294*
educational offerings, 290
emergencies, 297
flora and fauna, 285
itineraries, 262
*lodging, 263, 268–269,
   271–272, 273, 274–275, 280,
   282–283, 284, 293, 294*
*nightlife and the arts, 272, 276,
   280*
*Petrified Forest and the Painted
   Desert, 260, 284–296*
price categories, 263
shopping, 272, 281, 296
*sports and the outdoors, 263,
   267–268, 269–270, 273–274,
   279, 282, 283–284, 289–290,
   292, 297*
timing the visit, 262
transportation, 262, 296–297
*visitor information, 288–289,
   297–198*
*White Mountains, 260,
   264–284*
Echo Cliffs, *246*
Edward Nye Fish House, *307*
El Portal Sedona 🖾, *196*
El Presidio Historic District
   (Tucson), *305*
El Tiradito, *305*
El Tovar Dining Room ✕, *152*
El Tovar Hotel 🖾, *123, 134,
   154*
Elden Lookout Trail, *176*
Electricity, *462*
elements ✕, *49*
Elephant Feet, *239*
Embassies, *462*
Emergencies, *462*
Eastern Arizona, 297
Grand Canyon, 162–163
*North-Central Arizona,
   214–215*
Northeast Arizona, 257–258
*Northwest Arizona and
   Southeast Nevada, 437*
*Phoenix, Scottsdale, and
   Tempe, 115*
Southern Arizona, 412
Tucson, 364
Encanto Park, *25*
Enchantment Resort 🖾, *196*

F

Fairmont Scottsdale Princess
   🖾, *69*
FBR Open Golf Tournament, *23*

FEZ ✕, *45*
Fiesta de Saguaro, *303*
55 Main Gallery, *383*
5th Avenue (Scottsdale), *33*
Film, *290, 321*
FireSky Resort & Spa 🖾, *72*
First Mesa, *233–234*
Fish Creek Canyon, *111*
Fishing
*Eastern Arizona, 263, 267, 270,
   274, 279, 282, 283–284*
Grand Canyon, 148
*North-Central Arizona, 190,
   204*
Northeast Arizona, 255
Flagstaff, *168, 173, 175–183*
Flandrau Science Center and
   Planetarium, *310, 311–312*
Float trips, *248*
Fly Exhibition Gallery, *377*
Food, shopping for, *96–97*
Fort Apache Historical Park,
   267
Fort Apache Indian
   Reservation, *266*
Fort Bowie National Historical
   Site, *393*
Fort Huachuca Museums, *388*
Fort Lowell Park and Museum,
   313
Fort Verde State Historic Park,
   202
Fort Yuma Quechan Indian
   Museum, *407–408*
Four Corners Monument, *243*
Four Peaks Brewing Company,
   84
Four Seasons Scottsdale at
   Troon North 🖾, *69, 71*
Four-wheeling, *85, 87.*
   ⇨ *Also* Jeep tours
4th Avenue (Tucson), *310,
   312*
Fredonia, *146*
Frontier Town, *101*

G

G. F. Spangenberg Pioneer
   Gun Shop, *379*
Gammage Auditorium, *78*
Gay and lesbian bars, *83–84,
   350*
Gear, *445*
Gem and mineral shows, *303*
Ghost towns
Northwest Arizona, 416, 425
*Phoenix, Scottsdale, and
   Tempe, 106*
Giant Logs, *288, 289*

Gila County Historical Museum, *109*
Glen Canyon Dam, *218, 246–250, 252–256*
Glen Canyon National Recreation Area, *253*
Globe, *107, 109–110*
Globe Chamber of Commerce, *109*
Gold Canyon Golf Club, *88*
Gold Road Mine, *426*
Goldfield Ghost Town, *106*
Golf
  Eastern Arizona, 263, 267–268, 270, 282, 292
  North-Central Arizona, 192–193
  Northeast Arizona, 248
  Northwest Arizona and Southeast Nevada, 426
  Phoenix, Scottsdale, and Tempe, 87–89, 101
  tours, 455
  Tucson, 352–354
Goosenecks Region, UT, *244*
Goulding's Trading Post, *223, 244–245*
Governor Hunt's Tomb, *30*
Graham Inn and Adobe Village 🖪 , *197*
Grand Canyon National Park, *9, 14, 118–166*
  arts and entertainment, 137, 150
  bicycling, 129–130, 140
  camping, 151, 155–156
  children, attractions for, 137, 141–142, 146, 150, 153, 154–155, 157, 159
  crowds, 125
  dining, 150–153
  educational offerings, 136–137, 142, 145, 150
  emergencies, 162–163
  fees, 162
  festivals and seasonal events, 120, 137
  fishing, 148
  flora and fauna, 120
  free attractions, 136
  guided tours, 121, 129, 134–135, 137, 164–165
  hiking, 130, 133, 141, 164
  horseback riding, 149–150
  itineraries, 123
  jeep tours, 134–135
  lodging, 150–151, 154–160
  lost and found, 163
  mail, 163
  money matters, 162
  mule rides, 135
  North Rim and environs, 118, 138–142
  permits, 137, 163
  pets, 163
  rafting, 142, 145, 149, 165
  shopping, 137–138, 163–164
  skiing, 135, 150
  South Rim & environs, 118, 122, 126–132, 134–138
  sports and the outdoors, 129–130, 135, 140–142, 145, 147–150
  timing the visit, 120
  transportation, 121, 160–162
  visitor information, 129, 140, 165–166
  West Rim, 119, 142–145
Grand Canyon Caverns and Inn, *424*
Grand Canyon Lodge ✕🖪 , *138, 152, 156*
Grand Canyon Music Festival, *120, 137*
Grand Canyon Railway, *125, 132*
Grand Canyon Railway Hotel and Resort 🖪 , *158*
Grand Canyon West, *123*
Grand Canyon West Ranch, *424*
Grand Hotel, The 🖪 , *157–158*
Grandview Point, *123, 126*
Grandview Trail, *132*
Grapevine Canyon Ranch 🖪 , *392*
Grayhawk Country Club, *88*
Greasewood Flats (dance club), *83*
Great Arizona Puppet Theatre, *79*
Green's Peak, *277*
Greer, *273–276*
Greer Lodge Resort 🖪 , *274–275*
Grill at Hacienda del Sol, The ✕ , *336*
Guest ranches, *345*
Guided tours, *454–454*

H

Hacienda del Sol Guest Ranch Resort 🖪 , *343*
Hall of Flame, *30*
Hampton Inn of Kayenta 🖪 , *240*
Hannagan Meadow, *283–284*
Hannagan Meadow Lodge 🖪 , *284*
Hano, *234*
Harrah's ✕🖪 , *432*
Hassayampa Inn 🖪 , *211*
Hassayampa River Preserve, *103*
Hatathli Museum and Art Gallery, *228*
Havasu Canyon, *14, 123, 144–145*
Havasu Falls, *144*
Havasu National Wildlife Refuge, *427*
Havasupai Tribe, *144–145*
Hayden Peak Trail, *424*
Health concerns, *464–465*
Heard Museum, *15, 26–27*
Heard Museum North, *101*
Heard Museum Shop, *95*
Heartline Café ✕ , *195*
Helicopter tours, *145*
Helldorado Days, *371*
Heritage Square, *27*
Hermit Road (Grand Canyon), *122, 123*
Hermit Trail (Grand Canyon), *132, 134*
Hermits Rest, *123, 127*
Hermosa Inn 🖪 , *69*
Highway 67, *138*
Hiking, *14*
  Eastern Arizona, 263, 269–270, 274, 282, 283–284, 289–290, 292
  Grand Canyon, 14, 130, 132–134, 164
  North-Central Arizona, 178, 193, 210
  Northeast Arizona, 220, 227, 228–229, 243, 246, 248–249, 254
  Northwest Arizona and Southeast Nevada, 416, 424, 437–438
  Phoenix, Scottsdale, and Tempe, 89–90, 115
  Southern Arizona, 368, 413
  tours, 164, 455
  Tucson, 326–328, 345, 354
Historama, *376–377*
Historic Downtown District (Flagstaff), *173, 175*
Historic Route 66 Museum, *422*
Hohokam petroglyphs, *325*
Holbrook, *294–296*
Hole-in-the-Rock, *30*
Holidays, *462*

Homolovi Ruins State Park, *293–294*
Hoover Dam, *433–434*
Hopi ceremonies, *224, 233, 234*
Hopi Harvest Festival, *221*
Hopi House, *138*
Hopi Mesas, *218, 223, 232–239*
Hopi Museum and Cultural Center, *223, 235*
Hopi Point, *127*
Horse Shoe Bend Trail, *249*
Horseback riding
Eastern Arizona, 270, 290
Grand Canyon, 149–150
North-Central Arizona, 178, 193, 210
Northeast Arizona, 243
Northwest Arizona, 426
Phoenix, Scottsdale, and Tempe, 90, 101
Tucson, 328, 345, 354
Hostels, *450*
Hot-air ballooning. ⇨ *See* Ballooning
Hotel Congress 🏨 , *339*
Hotel Monte Vista, *173*
Hotels, *447, 449.* ⇨ *Also* Lodging
price categories, 60, 171, 221, 263, 303, 371, 419
Hotevilla, *236*
Houseboating, *14, 429, 435*
Houses, historic
Eastern Arizona, 287
Grand Canyon, 138
North-Central Arizona, 177–178
Northwest Arizona and Southeast Nevada, 423
Phoenix, Scottsdale, and Tempe, 27
Southern Arizona, 407
Tucson, 307–308
Hualapai Mountain Park, *423*
Hualapai Trail, *144*
Hualapai Tribe, *143*
Hubbell Trading Post National Historic Site, *223, 231*
Hubbell Trading Post Store, *15, 231*
Hugh Norris Trail, *325*
Huhugam Heritage Center, *30*

I

Imperial National Wildlife Refuge, *410*
Inn at 410 🏨 , *181*

Inscription Rock, *233*
Insurance, *452–453*
International Travelers, *462–463*
Island Trail, *184*
Itineraries, *16–17*

J

J. Knox Corbett House, *308*
Jacob Lake, *146*
Jade Bar, *80–81*
Jail Tree, *103*
Janos ✕ , *337*
Jasper Forest, *287, 288*
Jazz on the Rocks Festival, *199*
Jeep tours
Grand Canyon, 134–135, 164
North-Central Arizona, 170, 215
Northeast Arizona, 218, 229–230, 243, 252
Northwest Arizona and Southeast Nevada, 427
Phoenix, Scottsdale, and Tempe, 85
Southern Arizona, 381
Jerome, *205–207*
Jerome State Historic Park, *205–206*
Jewelry, shopping for, *357–359*
John Wesley Powell Memorial Museum, *247–248*
Juan Bautista de Anza National Historic Trail, *361*
JW Marriott's Camelback Inn Resort, Golf Club & Spa 🏨 , *68*

K

Kachina Point, *290*
Kaibab National Forest, *147*
Kartchner Caverns State Park, *398–399*
Katsina dolls, *231*
Kayenta, *223, 239–241*
Keams Canyon Trading Post, *15, 223, 233*
Keet Seel, *245–246*
Ken Patrick Trail, *141*
Kierland Commons, *93*
Kingman, *422–426*
Kinishba Ruins, *267*
Kitt Peak National Observatory, *404*
Kolb Studio, *126*
Kykotsmovi, *236*

L

La Casa Cordova, *307–308*
La Cocina de Eva ✕ , *292*
La Fiesta de los Vaqueros, *303*
La Grande Orange ✕ , *42, 44*
La Hacienda ✕ , *53*
La Posada Winslow 🏨 , *294*
La Roca ✕ , *401*
Lake Havasu City, *426–429*
Lake Havasu Museum of History, *427*
Lake Havasu State Park, *428*
Lake Mead, *434–435*
Lake Powell, *246–256*
Lake Powell Boulevard (Page), *247*
Lake Powell Resort ✕🏨 , *255–256*
L'Auberge ✕ , *194*
L'Auberge de Sedona 🏨 , *197–198*
Laughlin, NV, *430–433*
Lava Flow Trail, *185*
Lava River Cave, *175–176*
Lavender Jeep Tours, *381*
Lavender Pit Mine, *380*
Le Bellavia ✕ , *181*
Lees Ferry area, *146*
Lenox Crater, *185*
Licano's Mexican Food and Steakhouse ✕ , *268*
Lipan Point, *123, 127*
Little America of Flagstaff 🏨 , *181–182*
Little House Museum, *278*
Lodge at Ventana Canyon (golf course), *353*
Lodging, *447, 449–450.* ⇨ *Also* Camping; Hotels
Eastern Arizona, 263, 268–269, 271–272, 273, 274–275, 280, 282–283, 284, 293, 294
Grand Canyon, 150–151, 154–160
meal plans, 8
North-Central Arizona, 171, 181–182, 196–199, 206–207, 211
Northeast Arizona, 221, 226, 230–231, 235, 238, 240–241, 244–245, 246, 249–250, 255–256
Northwest Arizona and Southeast Nevada, 419, 425, 429, 431–433, 435
Phoenix, Scottsdale, and Tempe, 23, 59–76, 104–105, 109–110

Southern Arizona, 371,
378–379, 382, 385, 387,
390, 391–393, 395, 396,
397–398, 401–402, 403, 406,
409–410
Tucson, 303, 338–347
Loews Ventana Canyon Resort
🏨 , *342–343*
London Bridge, *426*
London Bridge Days, *419*
London Bridge Resort 🏨 , *429*
Long Logs Trail, *289*
Lon's at the Hermosa ✕ , *49*
Lookout Studio, *126*
Los Dos Molinos ✕ , *55*
Lost Dutchman Mine, *108*
Lowell Observatory, *175, 176*
Lowell Oldham Trail, *178–179*
Lutes Casino ✕ , *407*
Lux (coffeehouse), *82*
Lyman Lake State Park, *277*

M

Madera Canyon, *360*
Mail, *462*
Main Street (Bisbee), *381*
Main Street Arts District
(Scottsdale), *34*
Manning Camp, *323*
Marble Canyon, *146, 147*
Marble Canyon Lodge ✕🏨 ,
159
Margaritas, *12, 45*
Maricopa Point, *123, 127*
Marshall Way Arts District
(Scottsdale), *34*
Mary Elaine's ✕ , *51–52*
Mather Campground 🏕 ,
155–156
Mather Point, *123, 127*
McGees Beyond Native
Tradition (shop), *296*
Meal plans, *8*
Medical services. ⇨ *See*
Emergencies
Mesa Southwest Museum, *37*
Meteor Crater, *184–185*
Mexican cuisine, *300*
Mexican Hat, *244*
Mi Nidito ✕ , *338*
Miami, *107*
Microbreweries, *84*
Mill Avenue Shops, *93*
Mine Museum, *206*
Mining operations
Grand Canyon, 127
North-Central Arizona, 207
Northeast Arizona, 236

Northwest Arizona and
Southeast Nevada, 423, 426
Phoenix, Scottsdale, and
Tempe, 27
Southern Arizona, 368,
380–381, 405
Tucson, 359–360
Miraval 🏨 , *344*
Mishongnovi, *234*
Mission San Xavier del Bac,
300, 320
Mission tours, *365*
Mittens, *242–243*
Mogollon Rim, *267*
Mohave Museum of History
and Arts, *423*
Mohave Point, *128*
Money matters, *465–466*
Montana Avenue ✕ , *334–335*
Montezuma Castle National
Monument, *15, 202*
Montezuma Well, *202–203*
Monument Valley, *239–246*
Monument Valley Navajo
Tribal Park, *223, 241, 243*
Monument Valley Visitor
Center, *243*
Monuments, national. ⇨ *See*
National monuments
Mooney Falls, *144*
Moran Point, *123, 128*
Motels. ⇨ *See* Lodging
Mount Elden Trail System,
175, 176
Mount Humphreys, *14*
Mount Lemmon, *316–318*
Mount Lemmon Ski Valley, *317*
Mountain biking, *179–180,*
193–194, 263, 279
Mountain Village Holiday, *120*
Mule rides, *135*
Muleshoe Ranch Cooperative
Management Area, *394*
Museo Chicano, *27*
Museum Club, *176*
Museum of Northern Arizona,
15, 177
Museum Store, *34*
Museums and art galleries
Eastern Arizona, 267, 273, 278,
279, 281, 287, 288, 289,
292, 293, 295
Grand Canyon, 126, 138, 143,
146
North-Central Arizona, 177,
183, 200–201, 202, 205,
206, 208–209, 212
Northeast Arizona, 224–225,
226, 228, 235, 245,
247–248, 252

Northwest Arizona and
Southeast Nevada, 422, 423,
427, 431, 433
Phoenix, Scottsdale, and
Tempe, 26–27, 28, 31, 34,
35, 37–38, 95–96
Southern Arizona, 376,
377–378, 381, 383, 387–388,
394–395, 396, 405, 407–408,
410
Tucson, 15, 300, 306–307,
309–312, 313, 316, 319–320,
356–357, 360, 361, 362
Music, classical
festivals and seasonal events,
120, 137, 199
Grand Canyon, 120, 137
North-Central Arizona,
182–183, 199
Phoenix, 78
Tucson, 347–348
Music, popular
Eastern Arizona, 272
North-Central Arizona,
182–183, 207, 212
Northeast Arizona, 251
Phoenix, Scottsdale, and
Tempe, 81–82, 83
Southern Arizona, 387
Tucson, 347–348
Mystery Castle, *30*

N

National Geographic Visitor
Center Grand Canyon, *147*
National monuments
North-Central Arizona, 184,
185–186, 202, 203
Northeast Arizona, 240, 243,
245–246, 253–254
Phoenix, Scottsdale, and
Tempe, 105, 110
Southern Arizona, 388–389,
391–393, 406
National parks. ⇨ *See* Parks,
national
Native American sites
Eastern Arizona, 263, 266–267,
276, 283
Grand Canyon, 143, 144–145
North-Central Arizona, 184,
185, 186, 190, 202–203
Northeast Arizona, 222–252
Northwest Arizona and
Southeast Nevada, 427
Phoenix, Scottsdale, and
Tempe, 105, 106, 109, 110
Southern Arizona, 392, 393,
395–396

Native American
culture, 14, 15, 26–27, 31, 98,
123, 138, 143, 144–145,
218, 223, 224, 228,
232–239, 242, 243, 260,
303, 395–396, 403–405,
407–408
history tours, 455
petroglyph sites, 98, 227, 276,
277, 292, 293–294, 325
Reservation life and rules, 224
Natural history tours, 455
**Navajo Arts and Crafts
Enterprises,** 225, 226, 239
Navajo Bridge, 147
**Navajo Cultural Center of
Kayenta,** 240
Navajo Falls, 144
Navajo Museum, 224–225
**Navajo Nation Annual Tribal
Fair,** 221
**Navajo Nation Botanical and
Zoological Park,** 225
**Navajo Nation Council
Chambers,** 223–224
Navajo Nation East, 218,
222–232
Navajo Nation Visitor Center,
245
Navajo Nation West, 218,
236–239
Navajo National Monument,
223, 245–246
Navajo Point, 123, 128
Navajo Tribal Fairgrounds,
225–226
Nevada. ⇨ See Northwest
Arizona and Southeast
Nevada
**New Cornelia Open Pit Mine
Lookout Point,** 405
Newspaper Rock, 287
Nimbus Brewing Company,
350
Nogales, 399–403
North ✕, 336
North-Central Arizona, 9,
168–216
camping, 210
children, attractions for, 176,
177, 184–185, 190, 191, 209
dining, 171, 180–181,
194–196, 204, 206, 210–211
emergencies, 214–215
festivals and seasonal events,
183, 199, 212
Flagstaff, 168, 173–183
Flagstaff side trips, 184–187
guided tours, 170, 215–216
itineraries, 170

lodging, 171, 181–182,
196–199, 206–207, 211
nightlife and arts, 182–183,
199, 207, 212
price categories, 171
Sedona and Oak Creek
Canyon, 168, 187–201
shopping, 183, 200–201, 207,
212
sports and the outdoors,
178–180, 192–194, 204, 210
timing the visit, 171
transportation, 170, 213–214
Verde Valley, Jerome, and
Prescott, 160, 201–212
visitor information, 216
North Kaibab Trail, 141
North Rim Drive (Canyon de
Chelly), 228
Northeast Arizona, 9–10,
218–258
camping, 224, 229, 239, 244,
245
children, attractions for,
225–226, 238, 241–243, 248
dining, 221, 230, 233, 235,
238, 240, 244–245, 246,
249, 255–256
emergencies, 257–258
festivals and seasonal events,
221, 225–226
Glen Canyon Dam and Lake
Powell, 218, 246–250,
252–256
guided tours, 218, 229–230,
243, 248, 250, 252,
254–255, 258
Hopi Mesas, 218, 223,
232–239
itineraries, 223
lodging, 221, 226, 230–231,
235, 238, 240–241, 244–245,
246, 249–250, 255–256
Monument Valley, 239–246
Navajo Nation East, 218,
222–232
Navajo Nation West, 218,
236–239
nightlife, 250
price categories, 221
reservation rules, 224
shopping, 226, 233, 235–236,
238, 250
sports and the outdoors, 220,
228–230, 243, 248, 254–255
time zones, 221
timing the visit, 221
transportation, 220, 256–257
visitor information, 258

**Northern Arizona University
Observatory,** 175, 177
Northlight Gallery, 37
**Northwest Arizona and
Southeast Nevada,** 11,
416–438
camping, 428
children, attractions for, 424
dining, 419, 425, 428–429,
431–432
emergencies, 437
festivals and seasonal events,
419
ghost towns, 416, 425
guided tours, 426, 427, 438
itineraries, 418
lodging, 419, 425, 429,
431–433, 435
Northwest Arizona, 416,
421–429
price categories, 419
shopping, 426
Southeast Nevada, 416,
429–435
sports and the outdoors, 416,
424, 426, 427–428, 434,
435, 437–438
timing the visit, 419
transportation, 436–437
visitor information, 438

O

Oak Creek Canyon, 190–191
Oatman, 425–426
**Oatman Chamber of
Commerce,** 426
Oatman Hotel, 425–426
OK Corral (Tombstone),
376–377
OK Corral & Stable (Apache
Junction), 90
Old Courthouse Museum, 295
Old Oraibi, 236
Old Pueblo Trolley, 310, 312
Old Route 66, 422
Old Town Scottsdale, 34, 94
Old Tucson Studios, 321
O'Leary Peak, 185–186
**Organ Pipe Cactus National
Monument,** 369, 406
Orientation tours, 115–116,
365
Orpheum Theatre, 27–28
Osmer D. Heritage Inn 🏠,
293
Ostrich Festival, 23
Outdoor activities. ⇨ See
Sports and the outdoors

P

Package deals, *453–454*
Page, *247–250*
Painted Desert, *238*
Painted Desert Inn National
   Historic Site, *287*
Painted Desert Scenic Drive,
   288
Painted Desert Visitor Center,
   287, 288
Painted Nest (shop), *267*
Paisley Corner B & B ⌗ , *280*
Pancho McGillicuddy's ✕ ,
   153
Pane Bianco ✕ , *44*
Papago Café ✕ , *405*
Papago Park, *30*
Parada del Sol Parade and
   Rodeo, *23*
Parks, national
   *Glen Canyon National
      Recreation Area, 253*
   *Petrified Forest National Park,
      260, 284–296*
   *Saguaro National Park, 301,
      322–328*
   *Tumacácori National Historic
      Park, 362*
Parks, state
   Eastern Arizona, 277, 293–294
   *North-Central Arizona,
      177–178, 190–191, 192, 202,
      203, 205—206*
   Northwest Arizona, 428
   *Southern Arizona, 375–376,
      386, 398–399*
   Tucson, 361
Passports and visas, *463*
Patagonia, *385–388*
Patagonia Lake State Park,
   386
Patagonia-Sonoita Creek
   Preserve, *386*
Patagonia Visitors Center, *386*
Peppertrees B&B Inn ⌗ , *340*
Peralta Trail, *107*
Petrified Forest and the Painted
   Desert, *260, 284–296*
Petrified Forest National Park,
   260
Petroglyph Trail, *277*
Petroglyphs, *98, 227, 276,
   277, 292, 293–294, 325*
Phippen Museum of Western
   Art, *208–209*
Phoenician, The ⌗ , *69, 72*
Phoenician Golf Club, *88*
Phoenix, Scottsdale and
   Tempe, *20–116*

Apache Trail, 106–111
*Camelback Corridor, 39,
   42–43, 60, 66*
*central Phoenix, 25–28, 43–46,
   66*
Chandler, 56–58, 75–76
*children, attractions for, 25,
   26–27, 28, 30–31, 38, 67–68,
   69, 72, 73–74, 75–76, 79, 90,
   99, 103, 104, 106, 109*
climate, 18, 23
*dining, 20, 23, 31, 37, 38–59,
   102, 104, 109*
*downtown Phoenix, 25–28,
   46–47, 66–67*
emergencies, 115
festivals and seasonal events, 23
Glendale, 58–59, 76
greater Phoenix, 28, 30, 31
guided tours, 115–116
itineraries, 22
Litchfield Park, 58–59, 76
*lodging, 23, 59–76, 104–105,
   109–110*
Mesa, 56–58, 75–76
*nightlife and the arts, 77–84,
   102, 105, 110*
north Phoenix, 67–68
north central Phoenix, 47–48
Paradise Valley, 49, 68–69
price categories, 38, 60
*Scottsdale, 33–35, 49–55, 69,
   72–74, 78*
shopping, 20, 92–98, 103, 110
side trips near Phoenix, 98–105
south Phoenix, 55, 74–75
spas, 20, 70
*sports and the outdoors, 20,
   84–92, 101*
Tempe, 35–38, 56–58, 75–76, 78
transportation, 22, 111–114
visitor information, 116
west Phoenix, 58–59, 76
Phoenix Art Museum, *28*
Phoenix Museum of History, *28*
Phoenix Symphony Orchestra,
   78
Phoenix Theatre, *79*
Phoenix Zoo, *30–31*
Photography tours, *252*
Pima Air and Space Museum,
   313
Pima County Courthouse, *306*
Pima Point, *128*
Pinetop-Lakeside, *269–272*
Pioneer Living History Village,
   99
Pioneer Museum, *177*
Plane travel. ⇨ *See* Air travel

Planes of Fame Museum, *146*
Planetariums and
   observatories
   Grand Canyon, 126
   *North-Central Arizona, 175,
      176*
   Southern Arizona, 404
   Tucson, 310, 311–312
Poetry festivals, *349, 371*
Point Imperial, *123, 140*
Point Sublime, *140*
Powell Memorial, The, *126*
Prescott, *208–212*
Prescott National Forest, *204,
   207*
Price categories
   *dining, 8, 38, 221, 263, 303,
      371, 419*
   *lodging, 8, 60, 221, 263, 303,
      371, 419*
Pueblo Grande Museum and
   Cultural Park, *31*
Puerco Pueblo, *287*
Puerto Blanco Drive, *406*

R

Rafting, *14, 115, 142, 145,
   149, 165, 248, 455*
Railroads
   Grand Canyon, 125, 149
   *North-Central Arizona, 204,
      214*
Rainbow Bridge National
   Monument, *253–254*
Rainbow Forest Museum and
   Visitor Center, *287, 288,
   289*
Rainbow Rim Trail, *147*
Rainbow Trout Farm, *192*
Ramsey Canyon Inn Bed &
   Breakfast ⌗ , *390*
Ramsey Canyon Preserve, *389*
Rancho de los Caballeros ⌗ ,
   104
Rancho Pinot Grill ✕ , *51*
Randolph Park Golf Courses,
   352–353
Ranger programs, *290*
Rawhide Western Town and
   Steakhouse at the Wildhorse
   Pass, *79*
Red Hills Visitor Center, *324,
   325*
Red Rock geology, *191*
Red Rock State Park, *191–192*
Reid Park Zoo, *313–314*
Renaissance Festival, *419*
Renée Cushman Art Collection
   Museum, *279*

Reservation rules, *224*
Restaurants, *461.* ⇨ *Also*
    Dining
price categories, 8, 38, 221,
    303, 371, 419
Rex Allen Arizona Cowboy
    Museum, *394*
Rex Allen Days, *371*
Rhythm Room (blues club),
    81–82
Rim Trail, *123, 130, 184*
Rio Lago Cruises, *38*
Riordan State Historic Park,
    175, 177–178
River City Grill ✕, *408–409*
Riverside Resort ✕⌑, *432*
Road trips, *12*
Robson's Mining World, *104*
Rock Art Ranch, *293–294*
Rock climbing, *178*
Rockin' R Ranch, *79*
Rodeos, *13, 23, 212, 221,*
    225–226, 355
Rose Peak, *281*
Rose Tree Inn Museum, *376*
Rosson House, *27*
Royal Palms Resort & Spa ⌑,
    60
Ruiz's Mexican Food & Cantina
    ✕, *397*

S

Sabino Canyon, *315–316*
Safety, *466*
Saguaro East Visitor Center,
    324–325
Saguaro Harvest Celebration,
    303
Saguaro National Park, *301,*
    322–328
Saguaros, *318, 321*
Sailplaning, *91*
St. Augustine Cathedral,
    308–309
St. Peter's Dome, *277*
Sally's Mesquite Grill and BBQ
    ✕, *196*
Salt River Canyon, *260,*
    265–267
San Carlos Apache Indian
    Reservation, *266*
San Francisco Volcanic Field,
    185–187
San Juan Inn & Trading Post
    ✕⌑, *244*
San Pedro Riparian National
    Conservation Area,
    389–390

San Pedro Valley Arts and
    Historical Society Museum,
    396
Sanctuary on Camelback
    Mountain ⌑, *68–69, 70*
Sanguinetti House Museum,
    407
Santa Cruz River & River Park,
    309
Santa Fe Depot, *173*
School House Inn Bed &
    Breakfast ⌑, *382*
Schultz Creek Trail, *179*
Scottsdale, *9, 33–35, 49–55,*
    69, 72–74. ⇨ *Also*
    Phoenix, Scottsdale, and
    Tempe
Scottsdale Arts Festival, *23*
Scottsdale Center for the Arts,
    34
Scottsdale Culinary Fest, *23*
Scottsdale Fashion Square, *94*
Scottsdale Historical Museum,
    34
Scottsdale Museum of
    Contemporary Art, *34, 35*
Sea Saw ✕, *52*
Second Mesa, *234–236*
Sedona, *168, 187–201*
Sedona Golf Resort, *192–193*
Sells, *404–405*
Shady Dell Vintage Trailer
    Park ⌑, *382*
Sharlot Hall Museum, *209*
Shemer Arts Center, *31*
Sheridan House Inn ⌑, *158*
Shopping
Eastern Arizona, 272, 281, 296
Grand Canyon, 137–138,
    163–164
North-Central Arizona, 183,
    200–201, 207, 212
Northeast Arizona, 226, 233,
    235–236, 238, 250
Phoenix, Scottsdale, and
    Tempe, 92–98
Southern Arizona, 368, 379,
    383, 387–388, 402–403, 410
Tucson, 355–358
Shops at Gainey Village, The,
    94
Show Low, *267–269*
Shugrue's ✕, *428*
Shungopavi, *234*
Sichomovi, *234*
Sierra Vista, *388–390*
Signal Hill, *324, 325*
Silver Creek Golf Club, *26879*
Singing Wind Bookshop, *396*

Sipaulovi, *234–235*
Skiing
Eastern Arizona, 262, 263, 270,
    274, 279, 282, 284
Grand Canyon, 135, 150
North-Central Arizona,
    179–180
Tucson, 317
Skywalk (Grand Canyon),
    143
Slide Rock State Park,
    190–191
Slot canyons, *252*
Smoki Museum, *209*
Snoopy Rock, *191*
Snowboarding, *179–180, 279*
Snowflake-Taylor, *291–293*
Soaring, *91*
Solar Egg Frying Contest, *419*
Soleil ✕, *336*
Sonoita, *383–385*
Sonoita Creek State Natural
    Area, *386*
Sonoita Vineyards, *384*
Sonoran Desert, *318–321*
Sosa-Carillo-Fremont House,
    308
South Kaibab Trail, *134*
South Mountain Park, *31, 90*
South Rim Drive (Canyon de
    Chelly), *227––228*
Southeast Nevada. ⇨ *See*
    Northeast Arizona and
    Southeast Nevada
Southern Arizona, *10,*
    368–414
camping, 386, 399, 406
children, attractions for,
    376–377, 380, 386, 388–389,
    390, 394–395, 408
dining, 371, 378, 381,
    384–385, 386–387, 390, 395,
    397, 401, 406, 408–409
emergencies, 412
festivals and seasonal events,
    371
guided tours, 368, 413
itineraries, 371
lodging, 371, 378–379, 382,
    385, 387, 390, 391–393,
    395, 396, 397–398, 401–402,
    403, 406, 409–410
nightlife, 379, 382–383, 387
price categories, 371
shopping, 368, 379, 383,
    387–388, 402–403, 410
southeast Arizona, 372–399
southwest Arizona, 399–410

sports and the outdoors, 373, 413

timing the visit, 371

transportation, 370, 411–412

visitor information, 413–414

wineries, 384

Spas, *20, 60, 67–69, 70–71, 72, 73–74, 274–275*

Spider Rock Overlook, *227*

Sports and the outdoors. ⇨ *See* specific regions; specific sports

Sportsman's Fine Wine & Spirits, *97*

Springerville-Eagar, *278–281*

Springerville-Eagar Regional Chamber of Commerce, *277, 279*

Springerville Volcanic Field, *277*

Stagecoach rides, *374–375*

State parks. ⇨ *See* Parks, state

Steamboat Rock, *233*

Stevens Home, *308*

Stinton Museum, *292*

Stout's Cider Mill, *394*

Submarine Rock, *192*

Sugar Bowl Ice Cream Parlor, *34*

Summerhaven, *316–317*

Sun Devil Stadium, *37*

Sunrise Park Resort, *272–273*

Sunset Crater Volcano National Monument, *185*

Sunset Trail, *176, 179*

Superior, *107*

Superstition Mountain Museum, *106*

Superstition Mountains, *106*

Surgeon's House 🖼 , *206–207*

Symbols, *8*

T

T. Cook's at the Royal Palms ✕ , *42–43*

Taliesin West, *35*

Tal-Wi-Wi Lodge ✕🖼 , *282–283*

Tanque Verde Ranch 🖼 , *341*

Taxes, *466*

Taxis

North-Central Arizona, 214

Northwest Arizona and Southeast Nevada, 437

Phoenix, Scottsdale, and Tempe, 114

Southern Arizona, 412

Tucson, 364

Taylor Museum, *292*

Telephones, *463*

Tempe, *9, 35–38, 56–58, 75–76, 78.* ⇨ *Also Phoenix, Scottsdale, and Tempe*

Tempe Center for the Arts, *37–38*

Tempe Music Festival, *23*

Tempe Town Lake, *38*

Tennis, *91–92, 101*

Tepees, The, *287, 288*

Tequila, *402*

Texas Canyon, *395–396*

Theater

North-Central Arizona, 183, 212

Phoenix, Scottsdale, and Tempe, 27–28, 77–78, 79

Southern Arizona, 377

Tucson, 349

Theodore Roosevelt Lake Reservoir & Dam, *111*

Third Mesa, *236*

Thunderbird Lodge ✕🖼 , *230–231*

Time zones, *466*

Tipping, *466–467*

Titan Missile Museum, *360*

Tohono Chul Park, *320–321*

Tombstone, *374–379*

Tombstone Boarding House Bed & Breakfast 🖼 , *378–379*

Tombstone Courthouse State Historic Park, *375–376*

Tombstone Epitaph Museum, *377*

Tombstone Visitor Center, *374*

Tombstone Western Heritage Museum, *377–378*

Tombstone's Helldorado Days, *371*

Tonto National Monument, *110*

Tonto Trail, *134*

Tortilla Flat, *111*

Totem Pole, *242–243*

Tournament Players Club of Scottsdale, *89*

Tours and packages, *453–454*

Trailview Overlook, *128–129*

Train travel, *460.* ⇨ *Also* Railroads

Eastern Arizona, 297

Grand Canyon, 125, 149

North-Central Arizona, 204, 214

Northeast Arizona, 257

Northwest Arizona and Southeast Nevada, 437

Phoenix, Scottsdale, and Tempe, 114

Southern Arizona, 412

Tucson, 364

Transept Trail, *125, 141*

Travel agents, *446–447*

Traveler's checks and cards, *465–466*

Trolley tours, *215*

Troon North (golf course), *89*

Tuba City, *223, 237–238*

Tuba City Trading Post, *237–238*

Tubac, *360–361*

Tubac Presidio State Historic Park and Museum, *361*

Tubing, *92*

Tucson, *10, 300–365*

Catalina foothills (North), 300–301, 315–318, 335–337, 342–343

central and East Tucson, 300, 312–314, 333–334, 340–341

children, attractions for, 306, 309–310, 311–312, 313–314, 319–320, 321

climate, 18

dining, 300, 303, 329, 332–338

eastside, 334–335, 341–342

downtown, 300, 304–309, 329, 332, 339

emergencies, 364

festivals and seasonal events, 303

guided tours, 365

itineraries, 302, 307, 310, 325

lodging, 303, 338–347

nightlife and the arts, 347–351

northwest Tucson, the Westside and the Sonoran Desert, 301, 318–321, 337–338, 343–347

price categories, 303

Saguaro National Park, 301, 322–328

shopping, 355–358

side trips, 359–362

south Tucson, 338

sports and the outdoors, 326–328, 351–355

timing the visit, 302

transportation, 302, 362–364

University of Arizona, 300, 309–312, 332–333, 339–340

visitor information, 365

west of Tucson, 347

Tucson Annual Gem, Mineral and Fossil Showcase, *303*
Tucson Botanical Gardens, *314*
Tucson Children's Museum, *306*
Tucson Marriott University Park ⚏ , *339–340*
Tucson Museum of Art and Historic Block, *306–307*
Tucson Poetry Festival, *349*
Tumacácori National Historic Park, *362*
Tusayan, *146*
Tusayan Ruin and Museum, *123*
Tuzigoot National Monument, *15, 203*
Twin Knolls, *277*
T'z Marketplace, *97*

U

U.S. Army Intelligence Museum, *388*
U.S. 89, *147*
Ultimate Petroglyph Trail, *277*
Uncle Jim Trail, *141*
University of Arizona, *300, 309–312, 332–333*
University of Arizona Museum of Art, *310, 312*
Upper Red Rock Loop, *190*
Upper Ruins, *110*
Utah, *244*

V

Vacation packages, *453–454*
Vail Building, *175*
Valley of the Sun. ⇨ *See* Phoenix, Scottsdale, and Tempe
Velvet Elvis Pizza Co. ✕ , *386–387*
Ventana Room ✕ , *336*
Verde Canyon Railroad, *204*
Verde Valley, *202–204*
Vermilion Cliffs, *147*
Via Delosantos ✕ , *48*

Village of Elgin Winery, *384*
Vintage clothing and furniture, shopping for, *97–98*
Visas, *463*
Visitor information, *444–445*.
⇨ *Also* specific regions
Volcanic remains, *185–187, 277, 391*
Vortex tour, *187*
Vulture Mine, *104*

W

Wahweap, *253–256*
Walking tours, *230, 365*
Walnut Canyon National Monument, *14, 184*
Walpi, *234*
Waltz, Jacob "The Dutchman", *108*
Watchtower, The, *123, 126*
Water sports, *14, 416, 428, 434*
Weather, *18*
Weaver's Needle, *107*
Web sites, *444, 446, 448, 452*
Wells Fargo History Museum, *28*
West Fork Trail, *193*
Western wear, shopping for, *358*
Westin La Paloma ⚏ , *343*
Westward Look Resort ⚏ , *346*
Whiskey Row (Prescott), *210*
White House Ruin, *227*
White House Ruin Trail, *228–229*
White Mesa Natural Bridge, *239*
White Mountains, *260, 264–284*
White Stallion Ranch ⚏ , *345–346*
Wickenburg, *103–105*
Wickenburg Chamber of Commerce, *103*

Widforss Trail, *141*
Wigwam Motel ⚏ , *295*
Wilde Meyer Galleries, *95–96*
Wildlife refuges
North-Central Arizona, 203
Northwest Arizona and Southeast Nevada, 427
Phoenix, Scottsdale, and Tempe, 103
Southern Arizona, 386, 389–390, 403, 405, 410
Willcox, *393–395*
Willcox Playa, *394*
Williams, *146*
Williams Rendezvous Days, *120*
Window Rock, *223–226*
Window Rock Navajo Tribal Park, *224*
Wineries, *384*
World Championship Hoop Dance Contest, *23*
Wupatki National Monument, *186*

X

X Diamond & MLY Ranch ⚏ , *280*

Y

Yaki Point, *123, 129*
Yavapai Observation Station, *129*
Yuma, *407–410*
Yuma Convention and Visitors Bureau, *407*
Yuma Crossing State Historic Park, *408*
Yuma Territorial Prison, *408*

Z

Zona 78 ✕ , *334*
Zoos
Northeast Arizona, 225
Phoenix, 30–31
Tucson, 313–314

tostock. **Chapter 4: Northeast Arizona:** 217, *Ron Niebrugge/Alamy*. 218, *Kord.com/age fotostock*. 221, *M. Timothy O'Keefe/Alamy*. **Chapter 5: Eastern Arizona:** 259, *Carol Barrington/Aurora Photos*. 260 (top), *National Park Service*. 260 (bottom), *Doug Dolde*. 261 (both), *National Park Service*. 263, *Richard Wong/Alamy*. **Chapter 6: Tucson:** 299, *Johnny Stockshooter/age fotostock*. 300, *National Park Service*. 301, *Visual & Written SL/Alamy*. 303, *Jeff Greenberg/Alamy*. **Chapter 7: Southern Arizona:** 367, *Walter Bibikow/age fotostock*. 368 (top), *Tom Uhlman/Alamy*. 368 (bottom), *North Light Images/age fotostock*. 369, *SuperStock/age fotostock*. 371, *Peter Horree/Alamy*. **Chapter 8: Northwest Arizona & Southeast Nevada:** 415, *Bruno Perousse/age fotostock*. 416 (top), *Lee Foster/Alamy*. 416 (bottom), *David R. Frazier Photolibrary, Inc./Alamy*. 419, *David Ball/Alamy*.

ABOUT OUR WRITERS

Andrew Collins, a former Fodor's editor, updated the Northeastern Arizona and Essentials sections of this book. A part-time resident of New Mexico who spends a great deal of time traveling throughout the Southwest, he has authored more than a dozen guidebooks and is the gay travel expert for the New York Times–owned Web site, About.com. He also writes a syndicated weekly newspaper travel column and has contributed to *Travel & Leisure, New Mexico* magazine, *Sunset,* and dozens of other periodicals.

On hiatus from traveling the globe, JoBeth Jamison recently decided to spend more time trotting around her home state of Arizona. The thirty-something Flagstaff native is a graduate of the University of Arizona and now lives in Phoenix where she works for *Arizona Highways* magazine, contributes to several local and national publications, and tours as a backup singer for a rock band.

Jill Koch is a Phoenix-based freelance writer and editor. Her writing has been published in *Scottsdale* magazine and the *New York Times.*

Cara LaBrie is a Phoenix native who recently returned to Arizona after an eight-year absence. She has worked for years as a reporter and editor for newspapers across the country, including the *Arizona Republic.* Although she missed the stunning Arizona sunsets she says she didn't really appreciate the beauty of the desert until she returned. And as far as Cara is concerned, salsa isn't a condiment; it's a beverage.

Tucson and Southern Arizona updater Mara Levin divides her time among travel writing, social work, and her role as mom to two daughters. A native of California, Mara now lives in Tucson, where the grass may not be greener but the mountains, tranquility, and slower pace of desert life have their own appeal.

Carrie Miner, who currently splits her time between Arizona and Alaska, has wandered the wilds of the Southwest for more than a decade. She has written hundreds of travel articles and is a regular contributor to *Arizona Highways.*